D1507812

Public Finance and the Price System

Public Finance and the Price System

third edition

Edgar K. Browning
Texas A&M University

Jacquelene M. Browning
Texas A&M University

Macmillan Publishing Company
New York
Collier Macmillan Publishers
London

Copyright © 1987, Macmillan Publishing Company, a division of Macmillan, Inc.
Printed in the United States of America

Earlier editions copyright © 1979 and 1983 by Macmillan Publishing Company

Macmillan Publishing Company
866 Third Avenue, New York, New York 10022

Collier Macmillan Canada, Inc.

Library of Congress Cataloging-in-Publication Data

Browning, Edgar K.
  Public finance and the price system.

  Includes bibliographies and index.
    1. Expenditures, Public.   2. Public goods.
3. Finance, Public—United States.   I. Browning,
Jacquelene M.   II. Title.
HJ7461.B75   1987   336.73   86-3000
Printing: 1 2 3 4 5 6 7 8   Year: 7 8 9 0 1 2 3 4 5

ISBN 0-02-315720-8

To Our Families

Preface

I N its third edition, *Public Finance and the Price System* continues to provide a thorough treatment of major topics relating to government expenditure and tax policies. Its broad purpose is to help students develop an
understanding of the economic principles that are most useful in examining
the government's role in the economy, particularly those principles economists have found helpful in a microeconomic analysis of tax and expenditure policies. Overall, the text reflects our view that it is better to analyze
carefully and systematically major topics that illustrate principal concepts
and techniques than to cover a wide variety of topics superficially. The emphasis is analytical, with factual and institutional material introduced when
it is relevant to an understanding of the important consequences of policies.

A distinguishing feature of the book continues to be its balanced approach to the treatment of tax and expenditure policies. Most public finance
texts describe in great detail the major taxes and analyze their economic
effects but do not apply the same approach to the expenditure side of public budgets. We devote five chapters each to expenditure analysis (Chapters
4–7 and 9) and tax analysis (Chapters 10–14), showing how the same theoretical principles can be used to identify and evaluate the major consequences of both expenditure and tax programs. The enthusiastic response
to this approach, by both instructors and students, encourages us to continue to give equal emphasis to both sides of public budgets.

While the general approach to the subject remains the same as in the
previous edition, we have made a number of significant changes and additions in this edition. A major new section has been added on subsidies to
higher education, an important topic that will be of especial interest to the

primary consumers of this product. We have expanded the analysis of government deficits, and we have included both theoretical and empirical material related to why poverty has proven to be so intractable. Value-added taxation is now discussed in a new section, and new material has been incorporated in the chapters on corporation and individual income taxes to reflect recent developments in tax policy. These and other changes will be apparent to users of the previous edition.

Beyond these more obvious changes, we have made significant alterations and improvements in almost every chapter. Each chapter now concludes with end-of-chapter questions that stress both review of material covered and application of the principles to new topics. All the institutional and factual material has been updated, and almost every chapter contains new material and expositional changes for greater clarity. Although the general structure of the book remains the same as that in the previous edition, we believe these numerous small improvements will help students learn the material and better appreciate the importance of the subject matter. In addition, Joseph Sulock of the University of North Carolina at Ashville has written an Instructor's Manual to accompany the text that contains additional problems and discussion questions and a test bank of multiple-choice questions.

Although most readers of this text will be economics majors who have completed a course in intermediate microeconomic theory, it has become increasingly common for students with a more limited background in economics to take courses in public finance. To make the text accessible for these students, we have included an appendix that explains the rudiments of consumer choice theory. This is the only analytical technique used in this book that may not be covered in principles of economics courses. For those unfamiliar with consumer choice theory (or needing a quick review), the appendix should be read early in the course. With that preparation, readers with a limited background in economic theory should have no difficulty with the material.

We would like to extend our appreciation to a number of people who have helped in the preparation of the third edition. Several economists provided detailed comments and suggestions on the second edition that aided us in revising. They are Sharon Bernstein Megdal (University of Arizona), Charles R. Kroeber (North Carolina State University), Herbert J. Kiesling (Indiana University), Richard Fryman (Southern Illinois at Carbondale), and especially Joseph Sulock (The University of North Carolina at Ashville). In addition, we would like to thank our editor at Macmillan, Jack Repcheck, for his encouragement and advice and our production editor, Ron Harris, for his careful attention to detail. We are also grateful to Lee Mason and Phil Trostel for their research assistance.

EKB

JMB

Contents

chapter 9 Analyzing Income Transfer Programs   256

chapter 10 Principles of Tax Analysis   294

chapter 1
Introduction

PUBLIC finance is the study of how government policy, especially tax and expenditure policy, affects the economy and thereby the welfare of its citizens. No one can doubt that the influence of government on the operation of the economy is immense. The average U.S. household in 1986 contributed more than $14,000 of its income to governments (federal, state, and local) through a variety of taxes. In return, it received services in varying degrees from literally thousands of different expenditure programs that were financed by these taxes.

Our subject is the investigation of these expenditures and the taxes that finance them. Some of the most pressing social issues of the day fall squarely in this domain. Public finance provides the framework for the study of such diverse policies and issues as income tax reform, the deficit, social security, welfare reform, and revenue sharing. All of these issues, and many others, will be considered in later chapters. In this chapter we will first give a brief overview of the U.S. fiscal structure and then describe the analytical framework that will be used throughout the book.

Overview of Public Sector Fiscal Operations

Government expenditures and taxes are today clearly an important part of our everyday lives. The total volume of government spending provides some indication of the involvement of government in national economic affairs. As Table 1–1 shows, the combined expenditures of federal, state, and local governments were $1,401.2 billion in 1985. This sum was 39.4 percent of net national product (NNP), indicating that government policies influence the allocation of nearly two fifths of the nation's total income.

Government budgets have been growing relative to national income throughout the twentieth century. In 1902, total government expenditures were only 8.7 percent of NNP. By 1929, this ratio had reached 11 percent. In 1950, following the New Deal legislation of the 1930s and the higher level of defense spending that was maintained after World War II, government expenditures had reached 23.3 percent of NNP. Government spending

Table 1–1 *Government Expenditures, Selected Years ($ in billions)*

Year	Federal Government Expenditures	State and Local Government Expenditures	Total Government Expenditures	Expenditures as Percent of NNP
1902	$ 0.6	$ 1.1	$ 1.7	8.7%
1929	2.6	7.8	10.3	11.0
1950	40.8	22.5	61.0	23.3
1960	93.1	49.8	136.4	29.8
1970	204.3	133.5	313.4	34.6
1980	602.0	355.0	869.0	37.2
1985*	983.0	517.1	1401.2	39.4

*Preliminary estimates.
Note: Federal grants-in-aid to state and local governments are included in both federal and state and local expenditure figures. Total expenditures are adjusted to avoid this duplication.
Source: *Economic Report of the President, 1986,* Tables B-76 and B-21.

relative to NNP continued to grow over the next two decades, reaching 34.6 percent in 1970. Since 1970, government spending relative to NNP has continued to rise but at a slower rate, reaching 39.4 percent in 1985.

In addition to the overall growth in government spending, Table 1–1 also indicates the significant change in the division of spending between the federal government and state and local governments. In 1902 federal expenditures were only one third of total government spending; today the federal share of spending is nearly two thirds. The federal government has nearly become the senior partner in our federal system of government.

Table 1–2 provides a breakdown of total government expenditures by functional categories for fiscal year 1984.[1] (Several of the categories, such as public welfare and education, however, combine a large number of separate programs that serve the same general function.) Total federal, state, and local spending equaled $1,428 billion, with federal spending accounting for 65 percent of the total. At the federal level, expenditures on defense, social security, and interest payments on the national debt topped the list, totaling two thirds of federal spending. At the state–local level education was the largest single expenditure category, followed by outlays on public welfare and health care.

A more detailed analysis of many of these expenditure programs, and the political decision-making process that produces them, is provided in Chapters 2 through 9. For example, we shall consider how social security affects

[1] Note that the figures in Table 1–2 do not correspond exactly to those in Table 1–1. This is partly because Table 1–1 is on a calendar year basis and Table 1–2 is on a fiscal year basis (October 1 to September 30) and partly because of differences in accounting procedures.

Table 1–2 *Governmental Expenditures by Function for All Levels of Government, 1983–84 (amounts in billions of $)*

Function	Federal Spending / State and Local Spending / Intergovernmental Grants*	Total
Defense	248.0	$248.0
Social Security	234.5	234.5
Education*	26.4 ／ 176.1	188.6
Interest on Debt	109.2 ／ 28.7 ／ 63.8	137.9
Public welfare*	66.4 ／ 12.9	88.4
Health and Hospitals	46.3	59.3
Natural resources*	59.4 ／ 7.4 ／ 10.2	65.3
Highways*	39.5	40.3
Postal Services	26.6 ／ 2.1	26.6
Police	19.3	21.4
Other*	135.1 ／ 216.6	347.7

Total spending: $1,428.0   Total federal spending: $928.2   Total state & local spending: $600.6

*In some cases intergovernmental grants are counted as expenditures for both federal and state-local governments.
Note: Detail may not add to total because of rounding.
Source: U.S. Department of Commerce, Bureau of the Census, *Governmental Finances in 1983–84* (Oct. 1985), Tables 1, 2, and 3.

the incentives to work, retire, and save; how subsidies to higher education influence a student's choice of what college or university to attend; how insurance and government subsidies affect the market for medical care; and how welfare affects the work incentives of low-income people and why poverty has proven so difficult to eliminate.

The taxes used to finance these expenditure programs are shown in Table 1–3. In 1984, combined tax revenues at the federal, state, and local levels were $1,308 billion, with federal tax collections totaling $754 billion, or 58 percent of the total. Individual income taxes are the largest source of tax revenue. Payroll taxes, primarily social security taxes, are a close second. (In fact, most people actually pay more in social security taxes than they do in federal income taxes.) Together, individual income and payroll taxes provide nearly half of all combined tax revenues and 69 percent of federal tax revenues. The corporation income tax, once the second largest source of tax revenue for the federal government, is now a distant third.

The importance of these taxes as revenue sources varies from the federal

Table 1–3   *Government Revenue by Source and Level of Government, 1983–1984 (amounts in billions of $)*

Source	Federal Revenues	State and Local Revenues		Total
Taxes:				
Individual Income		295.9	64.6	$360.5
Payroll*		222.9	68.7	291.6
Corporation	56.9	17.0		73.9
Property		96.5		96.5
Selective Excises	38.0	38.9		76.9
General Sales		75.2		75.2
Death and Gift	6.0 / 2.2			8.2
Customs Duties	11.5			11.5
Motor Vehicles	7.4			7.4
Other	6.5 / 18.3			24.8
Charges and Miscellaneous General Revenues†	114.7	125.6		240.3

Total revenue: $1307.5   Total federal revenue: $754.0   Total state & local revenue: $652.1

*Includes all insurance trust revenues (including contributions to social security and unemployment compensation).
†Includes miscellaneous charges, assessments, interest earnings, and net revenues of public enterprises (e.g., school lunches, postal fees, fees for parks and recreation, net revenues from utilities, liquor stores).
Note: Detail may not add to total because of rounding.
Source: U.S. Department of Commerce, Bureau of the Census, *Government Finances in 1983–84* (Oct. 1985), Table 4.

to the state and local level. At lower levels of government, individual income and payroll taxes are not as important, contributing only 21 percent to total state and local revenues. Property taxes (levied mainly by local governments) and general sales taxes (levied mainly by state governments) are the two largest sources of tax revenues at the state–local level, although they do not dominate the picture as much as individual income and payroll taxes do at the federal level.

How these taxes actually affect the economy is examined in Chapters 10 through 14. For example, we shall try to determine who really bears the burden of each tax—something often quite different from who pays the taxes to the government—and how tax burdens are distributed among the population. In addition, we shall see that these taxes frequently have significant impacts beyond providing the funds that finance government expenditures.

The facts in Tables 1–1, 1–2, and 1–3 indicate much about the size, growth, and composition of government budgets, but they do not tell us much about the consequences of these governmental activities. The rest of this chapter is devoted to setting forth the broad framework of analysis that economists use to study tax and expenditure programs and much of the remainder of the text shows how this framework can be applied to help us understand the actual ways these policies affect us all.

The Nature of the Economic Effects of Policies

To begin our discussion, it will be helpful to explain three different types of effects that government tax and expenditure (or other) policies may have on the operation of the economy.[2]

Allocation

Almost all government policies have an effect on the allocation of resources. In other words, the mix of goods and services produced by the economy is altered as a result of government policy. If the government spends money to build missiles, it bids resources—manpower and capital—away from the production of other goods and services. As a result, economic resources are reallocated so that *more* missiles are produced and *fewer* other goods and services are provided. Economic resources are scarce, and using these resources to produce one type of good necessarily implies sacrificed production of other goods.

One of the most important issues in public finance is the determination of exactly how each of the vast array of government tax and expenditure policies affects the allocation of resources. What goods and services do we get more of, and at what cost in terms of smaller quantities of other goods and services? In some cases, the impact on resource allocation is fairly obvious, but in others it is not. As we will see, some government subsidies have little or no effect on resource allocation; for example, if the government provides free food to people, the recipients may simply curtail their private purchases of food, leaving total food consumption unchanged. Other policies have seemingly counterintuitive effects, such as when public housing leads to lower housing consumption for some recipients.

To understand the allocative effects of government policies, we must know how the policy operates and how the economic behavior of people is influenced by the policy. Does a welfare program undermine incentives to work? If so, the earnings of the poor will fall when they are provided assistance.

[2]Richard A. Musgrave developed the following useful classification in his *The Theory of Public Finance* (New York: McGraw-Hill, 1959), Chapter 1.

Does the provision of social security pensions lead people to save less privately for retirement? If so, the economy's rate of growth will be affected. Economic analysis does not provide unambiguous answers to all such questions concerning the allocative effects of policies, but it provides some, and it represents a general framework that is helpful in evaluating these effects.

Distribution

Over any period of time, the economic system produces a certain mix of goods and services that is consumed by its citizens. Not only is the total output of goods and services of interest but also the manner in which it is distributed among the public. Government policies often affect both the mix of goods and services and the distribution of these goods, that is, the distribution of real income. Knowing that a particular medical policy increases the amount of medical care consumed and reduces the total amount of other things consumed does not imply that each person, or income class, ends up with more medical care and less of other goods. Some may have more of both and others less of both than before. If this is so, the policy will also alter the distribution of real income by benefiting the one group at the expense of the other.

When trying to determine the distributional impact of any policy, we are attempting to answer this fundamental question: *Who is benefited and who is harmed by the policy?* Popular discussion often obscures this issue. Advocates of any policy generally stress that the "nation" will be benefited, whereas opponents argue that "we" would be better off without it. As far as we know, there has never been any policy that benefits everyone, or one that harms everyone. Most policies benefit certain persons and groups at the expense of others. In some cases, this may be intentional (e.g., redistributional welfare programs), and in other cases it may be unintended (a defense program harming "doves"). In any event, the extent to which income is redistributed, and the direction of that redistribution (whether in favor of the poor, the elderly, homeowners, etc.), is an important effect of government policies.

Economic analysis is often essential in determining how government policies affect the distribution of real income. In some cases the effects are more obvious than in others. It is fairly clear, for example, that several of the welfare programs comprising our welfare system redistribute income in favor of certain low-income groups. But who is benefited and who is harmed by social security or unemployment insurance? Who bears the true burden of the corporation income tax? What is the overall effect of all taxes and expenditures on the distribution of income? Questions such as these pertaining to the distributional effects of policies are not easy to answer, but they are clearly important issues and will be considered in later chapters.

Stabilization

The overall level of expenditures and taxes, in conjunction with monetary policy, can have important effects on the aggregate level of employment, output, and prices. Indeed, most people first study taxes and expenditures in terms of their impact on aggregate demand. Stabilizing the economy at high (and perhaps growing) levels of output and employment is today considered a major responsibility of the federal government.

In this textbook, the macroeconomic effects of the fiscal operations of government will be largely ignored. Our neglect of this set of important issues stems from the fact that most students will take a separate course in macroeconomic analysis, and any treatment given in a chapter to two would necessarily be repetitive and probably inferior to the more detailed discussions in other courses. There is, however, a more substantive reason for giving little attention to macroeconomic effects; namely, macroeconomic effects are of little importance in the analysis and evaluation of individual tax and expenditure programs. Only when all taxes and expenditures are considered in the aggregate do these effects become significant. This point will be elaborated further when the effects of expenditure policies are studied in more detail in later chapters.

Positive Analysis and Value Judgments

Most people study economics, we suspect, with the intention of learning what types of economic policies are desirable and what types are undesirable. Because most of public finance deals with public policies, it is important to understand what economic analysis can contribute to determining what is a good policy.

Logically, to decide whether a policy is good or bad involves two steps: positive analysis and a value judgment. First, it is necessary to determine what the consequences of the policy will be, that is, its effects on resource allocation and income distribution. This is the realm of *positive economic analysis,* dealing with the measurable or observable outcomes of policy. We might consider, for example, how minimum wage law affects unemployment, or whether a particular tax loophole works to the advantage of the wealthy, or how capital taxation affects interest rates. Positive analysis of policies therefore consists of propositions about the effects of policies. The distinguishing feature of positive analysis is that it deals with propositions that can be tested, with respect to both their underlying logic and empirical evidence. Positive analysis is scientific, since it draws on accepted standards of logic and evidence that are potentially capable of being used to ascertain the truth or falsity of statements.

Economic analysis therefore can assist in determining what is desirable government policy by providing a framework for positive analysis that generally yields correct propositions about the consequences of policy. Identifying the consequences of a policy, however, is not sufficient to determine that it is desirable. A second step is necessary: We must decide whether the consequences themselves are desirable. To make this evaluation, it is necessary for each person to make a subjective assessment, a *value judgment,* to determine if the consequences of a policy are desirable. By its nature, such a judgment is nonscientific, since it cannot be proven right or wrong by facts or evidence. For instance, believing that a more equal distribution of income is desirable is an example of a value judgment. People may agree that a particular government policy produces greater equality, but some may hold that this outcome is desirable and others that it is undesirable. Their value judgments differ.

Although the distinction between positive analysis and value judgments, and the role each plays in the evaluation of policies, may seem abstruse, they are nonetheless essential to clear thinking. Economic analysis cannot demonstrate that any policy is desirable (and neither, for that matter, can any other scientific branch of knowledge). Holding that something is desirable requires a nonscientific judgment of what constitutes "desirability" that cannot be supplied by a technique of analysis; only individuals can make this type of judgment. Nonetheless, economics can assist in making that judgment by helping us determine the likely consequences of policies, which is an important contribution. Many people disagree about the desirability of policies not because of differences in their values but because they have different conceptions about their effects.

Criteria for Policy Evaluation

In a general sense, we have seen that the evaluation of a public policy must be based on a value judgment about the consequences of the policy. Some types of value judgments are widely shared and frequently used in evaluations of public policies, and further discussion of these may be helpful. Although the following criteria for the evaluation of policy do embody explicit value judgments and therefore cannot be demonstrated to be "desirable," they are widely (and often unthinkingly) used so it is important to understand the strengths and weaknesses of each.

Equity

Perhaps the most widely used criterion in the discussion of policy is that of equity, or fairness. Generally, it is felt that government policies should be equitable in their effects on people. This criterion has the advantage of being accepted by virtually everyone; no one thinks unfairness in a policy is desirable. Yet the superficial consensus in favor of equitable treatment obscures a real difficulty in defining exactly what "equity" means. Although everyone approves of equity, few interpret the term in the same way.

A few examples will illustrate the difficulty of making a judgment about equity. Is minimum wage law equitable? The minimum wage results in higher wage rates for some people, unemployment for others, and higher costs for the consuming public. Are its effects on all groups fair? What about public schools? Is it equitable for families without children to pay taxes to finance public schools? Is it equitable to require people to provide for their retirement through social security rather than in other ways they might prefer? If questions like these are considered seriously, as they should be, some of the difficulties in making an equity judgment will become apparent.

Consider the following statement: "The tax-exempt status of the interest income from state and local government bonds enables the wealthy to avoid their fair share of the tax burden by receiving tax-free interest income." Is the tax exemption granted these bonds fair? Judging from the frequency of such statements, this preferential treatment is generally considered unfair. Yet the statement misconstrues the effects of this tax exemption. People who hold tax-free bonds are not the major beneficiaries of this policy. Instead, state and local governments can sell bonds bearing a lower interest rate than other borrowers can and are the major beneficiaries. For example, a tax-free bond might require an interest rate of 7 percent to compete with an 11 percent (taxable) corporate bond. Eliminating this tax exemption would mean that state and local governments would have to pay 11 percent to compete with the other bonds. Wealthy taxpayers would then pay taxes on higher interest income, but it is not clear whether their net after-tax incomes would be any lower.

Tax-exempt state and local bonds are a good example of the importance of positive analysis in making equity judgments. Most people are prone to make judgments without a careful consideration of the actual effects of economic policies. Yet the equity issue is concerned with the actual consequences of policies, and positive analysis is necessary to determine these consequences.

Probably few people have a clearly defined idea of what equity really means, and even if they do, individual interpretations will differ. Consequently, equity is a difficult criterion to use in practice, but this does not imply that it is unimportant. Although the concept of equity may be difficult to pin down precisely, there may still be wide agreement at a fairly general level. For example, few people would argue that a policy that taxes poor people to subsidize the yachting activities of wealthy individuals is equitable. Unfortunately, most real-world issues are not so clear-cut.

Among economists, the question of equity often takes on a very narrow meaning, referring to the distributional effects of a policy. If a policy results in any redistribution, the major emphasis is on whether the people bene-fited are poorer (or more deserving in some sense) than the people harmed. Economics is well designed to explore how policies affect the distribution of income, but that is probably only one dimension of the equity issue. Although economics can help to identify the consequences of policies—notably the distributional effects—each person must ultimately decide whether these consequences are equitable.

Economic efficiency

Economic efficiency, or as it is sometimes called, *Pareto optimality,* is a criterion widely used by economists in policy evaluation. Although effi-ciency is highly regarded by economists, it is not so widely used by non-economists and is, in fact, often disparaged as dealing with such materialistic issues as cost minimizing, profit maximizing, and so on. In part this rejec-tion of efficiency as a criterion reflects a misunderstanding of its meaning as used by economists. Far from being materialistically oriented, efficiency is defined in terms of the well-being of people. Roughly speaking, an effi-cient economic system is one that makes people as well off as possible, taking into account *all* the ways the economy influences their well-being. Interpreted in this way, economic efficiency is a criterion that would prob-ably command wide acceptance.

A more careful definition of efficiency can be stated: *An efficient alloca-tion of resources is one in which it is impossible, through any change in resource allocation, to make some person or persons better off without mak-ing someone else worse off.* In short, when the economy is operating effi-ciently, there is no scope for further improvements in anyone's well-being unless someone else is harmed. A corollary to this definition is that an in-efficient allocation of resources is one in which it is possible, through a change in resource allocation, to make some person or persons better off without making anyone else worse off. Inefficiency implies waste in the sense that the economy is not catering to the wants of people as well as it could.

These definitions can be clarified with the aid of a diagram. To make matters simple, assume that society consists of only two people, Samantha and Oscar, although the discussion can be generalized for any number of people. In Figure 1–1, the level of Samantha's well-being, or welfare, is mea-sured horizontally and Oscar's welfare is measured vertically. The farther to the right we go in the diagram, the better off Samantha is (the higher indif-ference curve attained), whereas the farther up in the diagram we go, the better off Oscar is.[3] Any allocation of resources corresponds to a certain level of welfare for each person and can thus be plotted in the diagram.

---

[3] In effect, the diagram tells us only how each person ranks alternative resource allocations. It does not tell us by how much better or worse Samantha or Oscar believes one allocation to be in comparison to another.

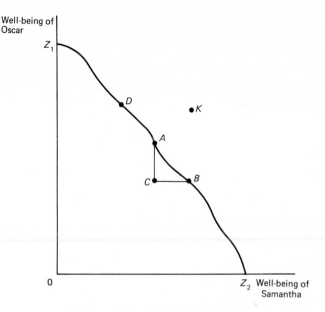

FIGURE 1–1 *Welfare frontier.*

Because of limitations in the amount of resources available to produce goods and services, there are limits to how well off Samantha and Oscar can be. These limits are shown by the *welfare frontier* (or "utility frontier") Z_1Z_2. Any point that lies outside this frontier is unattainable. The society, for example, cannot produce a mix of goods and services that would make Samantha and Oscar as well off as indicated by point K. By contrast, any point lying on or inside the frontier is attainable. That is, it is physically possible to allocate existing resources in a way to achieve any combination of welfare for Samantha and Oscar that lies inside or on the Z_1Z_2 frontier.[4]

Using this construction, we can see that *any allocation of resources that implies a point lying on the Z_1Z_2 frontier is efficient.* For example, point A represents an efficient allocation of resources because it is not possible to make Samantha better off without making Oscar worse off—because it is impossible to move outside the frontier. Note, however, that this is also true of point B; any possible move from point B makes at least one of the two worse off. Indeed, every point *on* the frontier satisfies the definition of efficiency, so there are really innumerable efficient allocations. The efficiency

[4]For a discussion that demonstrates how this utility frontier can be derived, see Francis Bator, "The Simple Analytics of Welfare Maximization," reprinted in William Breit and Harold Hochman, eds., *Readings in Microeconomics* (New York: Holt, Rinehart and Winston, 1968); and Peter Kenen, "On the Geometry of Welfare Economics," *Quarterly Journal of Economics,* 71:426 (Mar. 1957).

criterion does not allow us to claim that there is only one best state of affairs.

The different efficient points on the welfare frontier represent different distributions of welfare, or real income, between Samantha and Oscar. Thus, efficiency does not resolve the question of how real income should be distributed among people. Suppose there is only one good produced, food, and an efficient use of resources yields 100 units of food. Point A could represent the situation when Oscar has 60 units and Samantha 40 units, whereas at point B, Oscar has 40 units and Samantha 60 units. Both ways of dividing the food are efficient because there is no way to make one person better off except by giving him or her more food, and that requires taking food from the other person. The efficiency criterion provides no way of comparing points like A and B because both are efficient. Instead, an explicit value judgment is required to compare different distributions of real income.

Now consider point C. This is an inefficient point, perhaps where the economy is producing only 80 units of food. (Even in our simple one good world, this need not imply unemployment of resources; instead resources may be used unwisely and produce less output than is possible.) Point C is inefficient because it is possible to change things and benefit one person without harming the other. By moving from C to A, Oscar is made better off without harming Samantha; alternatively, moving from C to B would benefit Samantha without harming Oscar. Indeed, moves within the CAB area benefit both Samantha and Oscar. Thus, inefficiency implies that there are changes in resource allocation possible that will mutually benefit all people. Since most people would make the value judgment that changes making everyone better off are desirable, economists tend to think that efficiency is a good thing.

It should not be inferred, however, that *all* efficient points are better than *all* inefficient points. Consider a move from point D, an efficient point, to point C, an inefficient point. Admittedly, this is a change from an efficient to an inefficient allocation of resources, but the change benefits Samantha at Oscar's expense. Only if we are unconcerned about the distribution of real income, however, would we unequivocally say that point D is better than point C. Perhaps Samantha is poor and Oscar wealthy, and so the move from point D to point C is a redistribution in favor of the poor person. A person who makes the value judgment that greater equality is highly desirable might prefer point C to point D despite the fact that it is inefficient. Economists, however, would generally argue that if we intend to redistribute from Oscar to Samantha (starting at point D), it would be better to do so in a way that ended up on Z_1Z_2 in the AB range rather than at point C. A redistribution from point D to point A, for example, would benefit Samantha as much as a move from D to C would and it would leave Oscar better off. In this way efficiency considerations are relevant in situations involving redistribution. There are efficient and inefficient ways to redistribute income.

Clearly the efficiency criterion does not resolve all questions of economic policy. In particular, it is neutral with respect to distributional questions, which still require nonobjective value judgments. Furthermore, there are some practical questions about applying the criterion. For example, in the complex real world, determining exactly what policies will be most efficient is difficult, because a great deal of information (that we often do not have) is required to make that judgment. In addition, we may sometimes object to a criterion based on the assumption that the welfare of all individuals *as they themselves evaluate their well-being* is what counts. Do we want to cater to the wants of children or criminals?

Despite these obvious drawbacks, the efficiency criterion is widely used. If, in your view, a good policy is one that promotes the welfare of people as they themselves judge their welfare, then you will be led to give some weight to efficiency in evaluating policies.

Paternalism

Government policy may, in some cases, be intentionally designed to provide services that would not be selected by people if they had a choice. Instead of catering to the wants of people, the government overrides, or disregards, their wants. A policy of this type could be described as paternalistic and is ultimately based on the premise that some individuals in certain situations may not be able to make wise choices.

A few examples illustrate this criterion. A justification sometimes given for social security is that people would not independently save enough for their old age. If we assert, however, that the level of savings that some people would choose to make is "too small," then we are ignoring their expressed wants and substituting someone else's conception of the proper level of saving. Similarly, many welfare programs do not permit the poor to spend the government assistance as they wish but require that it be spent on food, housing, medical care, and so on. Children are required to attend schools until a specified age, regardless of their (or their parents') desires. And the fact that 10 percent of the public has no form of health insurance is sometimes cited as an argument for mandatory health insurance (national health insurance) for everyone. (We don't mean to imply that these policies can be supported only by paternalistic arguments, but merely to suggest how paternalistic considerations can play a role in the evaluation of policies.)

Many people support some government policies not because they think these policies give the public what it wants but because they think the government knows better what is good for the public than the public itself does. This does not imply that paternalism is in any sense bad (a value judgment)—we all approve of paternalistic policies in some cases. For example, most people agree that small children should not be permitted to purchase liquor or drugs or guns even if (and perhaps especially if) they want to. The government may be in a better position to evaluate highly specialized knowledge, such as in the area of consumer safety, and in some cases make "better" (in some sense) choices than people could on their own.

Paternalism does not, however, supply any clear basis for the evaluation of policies. Because there is no absolute standard by which people's choices can be judged, there is no limit to what could be justified on this basis. Moreover, paternalism as a criterion contains a definite antidemocratic element. If individuals are not thought competent to make decisions that mainly affect themselves (like saving for retirement), then, taking this a step further, they must be even less competent to make decisions that affect everyone in society through the voting process.

Individual freedom

Many people place a high value on individual freedom and wish to see government restrict that freedom as little as possible. Actually, the concept of freedom is difficult to pin down precisely. Individual freedom is generally taken to mean, at least in the economic sphere, that economic arrangements are voluntary. The multitude of exchanges that characterize economic organization take place through a series of mutual agreements between buyers and sellers, with the terms of trade (prices) agreed to by both parties.

Although a case can clearly be made for individual freedom, it is not clear that this criterion provides much guidance for policy issues that are dealt with in the field of public finance.[5] Whenever the government taxes people to finance public expenditures, it deprives them of the freedom to spend part of their incomes as they would have individually chosen. With subtle interpretation, however, it may be possible to argue that in certain cases some taxes or expenditures are more consistent with freedom than others are. On the expenditure side, for example, it might be argued that a welfare program of cash transfers that permits recipients to spend cash assistance as they wish is more consistent with the notion of individual freedom than is a program in which the assistance is restricted to food or housing. Even so, in the bulk of cases, it is difficult to hold that one tax is a greater infringement on freedom than another. This is not to say that individual freedom is unimportant, but only that it may not offer much specific guidance for choices among alternative tax and expenditure policies.

---

[5]For contemporary arguments emphasizing the importance of individual freedom, see Friedrich Hayek, *The Constitution of Liberty* (Chicago: University of Chicago Press, 1960); and Milton Friedman and Rose Friedman, *Free to Choose* (New York: Harcourt Brace Jovanovich, 1980).

Tradeoffs among the criteria

The four criteria discussed so far do not exhaust all the ways in which economic policies may be evaluated, but they do provide some idea of the range of effects that may be considered. Forming an overall evaluation of a policy is clearly a difficult task. Not only is it necessary to determine how well the policy satisfies each of the criteria deemed relevant, but a decision of how much weight to give each separate criterion is also necessary. Generally it will be impossible to satisfy all criteria simultaneously. For example, a policy that is considered equitable may be quite inefficient, or a policy to achieve greater efficiency may necessitate a loss of equity. Some of the criteria, in fact, are inherently contradictory. This is true of paternalism and efficiency, because efficiency involves catering to the wants of people as they themselves define those wants, whereas paternalism substitutes another judgment of what people should have. In short, a policy evaluation must reflect not only how it performs according to the separate criteria but also how the relative importance of each criterion is judged.

Economists typically emphasize two of these criteria, efficiency and equity, more than any others. In part, this simply reflects the fact that economic analysis is better suited to identifying how efficient policies are likely to be and how they affect the distribution of real income (generally felt to be relevant to making equity judgments). This emphasis also reflects the value judgment that these two broad criteria emphasize worthwhile goals. In the final analysis, however, each person must decide what criteria are important. As pointed out previously, economic analysis cannot demonstrate that policies are good or bad, but as we show in the remainder of this book, it can help in making that judgment by clarifying many of the consequences of tax and expenditure policies.

The Price System

Much economic activity is organized through private markets in which competitive forces determine prices. These market-determined prices are signals that guide resource allocation, and a system that relies on prices determined in open markets to coordinate economic activities is generally referred to as a *price system*. In studying public finance, an understanding of how the price system functions is important for two somewhat different reasons. First, relying on the price system is the major alternative to the use of government tax or expenditure policies as a means of resolving economic problems. For example, the price system offers ways for individuals to insure against medical risks and to provide for their retirement; these methods are alternatives to using government policies such as national health insurance and social security to perform these functions. Thus, in evaluating how well social security operates, it should be compared with the way the price system would perform the same function.

Second, the way in which tax and expenditure policies interact with and influence the price system has important implications for the effects of these policies. Often government policies create incentives that change the functioning of private markets. When state and local government bonds are made tax exempt, for example, the price system responds by generating a lower interest rate on these securities, which will induce heavier borrowing by state and local governments. Similarly, the provision of social security benefits may lead to less private saving for retirement, and national health insurance may result in higher prices for medical care. Therefore, to understand the full effects of tax or expenditure policies it is important to analyze how the price system will respond to them.

This is not the place to explain in detail how a price system functions, since it is assumed that the reader already has a basic understanding of microeconomic, or price, theory. It may be helpful, however, to consider briefly how a price system performs in terms of the criteria just discussed.

Economic efficiency in a price system

One of the major conclusions of modern economics is that a competitive price system tends, under certain conditions, to produce an efficient allocation of resources. Business firms in competition with one another for the patronage of consumers have incentives to provide goods in the quantities and qualities that are most preferred by consumers. The incentives provided by prices encourage resource owners to employ their resources in ways that are valued most highly by consumers. If the output of one good, beer, for example, is too high, and the output of clothing is too low, the price of beer will be too low to cover costs, and beer producers will suffer losses. Clothing producers will be making profits, and the lure of higher profits in clothing production will encourage resources to move from the beer industry to the clothing industry. In the end, the mix of clothing and beer output will reflect consumer preferences as indicated by market demands for the goods.

The way that efficient levels of output are determined in competitive markets can be explained in greater detail by examining a specific market. In Figure 1–2, the competitive demand and supply curves for beer are shown. For well-known reasons, the competitive equilibrium rate of output is 1,500 units at a price of $7 per unit where the quantity supplied and the quantity demanded are equal. Our question is whether this equilibrium level of output is the most efficient level. To explore this question, suppose instead that output is only 1,000 units. Now we wish to know if the additional, or marginal, benefits of a larger output are greater than the marginal costs of pro-

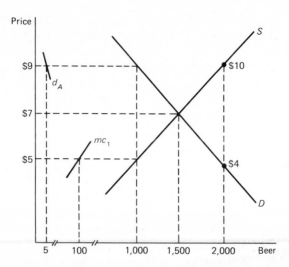

FIGURE 1–2   *Efficient output in a competitive market.*

ducing it. If so, the net benefits—the excess of benefits over costs—received by the public can be increased by producing more beer.

At an output of 1,000 units, the marginal benefit, or marginal value, of output is equal to $9 per unit. Nine dollars is a measure of how much consumers are willing to pay to get an additional unit (the 1,001st unit) of beer. This is approximately equal to the price that will prevail if 1,000 units are placed on the market, as given by the height to the market demand curve at 1,000 units of output. Note that each consumer will be willing to pay $9 (more precisely, infinitesimally less than $9) for another unit of beer; that is why we can say *the* marginal value of beer is $9 because it is the same for all beer consumers. This can be seen by noting that each consumer will consume beer up to the point where the marginal unit is worth $9. (Individual *A,* for example, with demand curve d_A, will purchase five units, at which point *A*'s marginal valuation of beer is $9.) Equivalently, recall that each consumer is in equilibrium when the marginal rate of substitution between money spent on other goods and beer is $9. The marginal rate of substitution between money and beer is a measure of the marginal benefit of more beer, that is, how much another unit is worth to the consumer.

The market demand curve is thus a measure of the good's marginal importance to consumers. Although this marginal benefit is commonly measured in dollars, this is just a means of registering the importance of beer in comparison with other goods. Saying that the marginal benefit is $9 means that consumers are willing to give up $9 worth of other goods to get another unit of beer.

Now let's consider the cost of producing more beer. The height to the competitive supply curve measures the marginal cost of beer production. At an output level of 1,000 units, the marginal cost is $5. (The marginal cost is also $5 for each firm producing beer, just as firm 1 would be operating on its marginal cost curve, mc_1, at an output rate at which marginal cost is $5.) This $5 measures the cost of the resources needed to produce one more unit of beer. To produce more beer, $5 worth of resources must be withdrawn from the production of other goods. If other markets are competitive, when $5 worth of resources is diverted to beer production, the output of other goods will fall by exactly $5. In other words, when the marginal cost of beer production is $5, this is a measure of the value of other goods that must be sacrificed to produce one more unit of beer.

Recognizing that the competitive demand and supply curves can be interpreted as measures of marginal benefits and costs makes it easy to determine the efficient rate of output. At 1,000 units of output, consumers are willing to give up $9 in other goods to get one more unit of beer; but it is only necessary to sacrifice $5 worth to produce one more unit. Additional beer production is worth more than it costs, so 1,000 is an inefficient (too low) rate of output because more beer and less of other things are preferred by consumers.

The efficient rate of output is where marginal benefit and marginal cost are equal. This occurs where output has expanded to 1,500 units, when marginal benefit and cost are equal at $7. By analogous reasoning, we can see that any output in excess of 1,500 units will be too great. At an output of 2,000, for example, the marginal cost of beer production is greater than its marginal benefit, and consumers will be better off with less beer and more of other things. Thus, because 1,500 units is the competitive equilibrium output, the competitive output with its careful balancing of benefits and costs is also the most efficient rate of output. (Note that 1,500 is the efficient output even if the beer market is not competitive; the relevant comparison is between the real schedule of marginal benefits and costs, and these remain unchanged, regardless of the market structure.)

Let's relate this discussion to our earlier discussion of efficiency using a welfare frontier (Figure 1–1). This analysis implies that a competitive price system yields an efficient resource allocation that places us at one point on the welfare frontier. Consequently, there is then no way to change a competitively determined resource allocation without harming someone. Although our discussion has emphasized only one aspect of the efficiency issue—the rate of output of a good—the results hold generally when the framework is broadened.[6]

A competitive price system generally gets high marks with respect to the criterion of economic efficiency. Nonetheless, the price system may not al-

---

[6] See Bator, op. cit.

ways function as smoothly as the preceding analysis suggests. In particular, under certain conditions a private market, even a competitive one, will not function efficiently. These conditions, which involve the presence of public goods and externalities, are considered in Chapter 2.

Equity in a price system

As previously suggested, the criterion of equity must reflect subjective and individual standards of fairness. As such, it is not possible to prove that the price system is equitable or inequitable in the same way that efficiency can be appraised. Nonetheless, a few observations should be made.

One frequent objection to the contention that a price system is efficient runs like this: How can we say that markets cater effectively to genuine needs when the children of the poor go without toys or milk, and yet the pets of the wealthy wear diamond collars? This raises a valid objection to total reliance on the price system, but it is important to see that the issue is really one of equity, not efficiency. Those with larger incomes influence resource allocation to a greater degree than those with smaller incomes. This outcome is not perverse; the market is merely responding to people's desires and other relevant circumstances, including the distribution of income. *Given* the distribution of income, a competitive price system efficiently caters to individual needs as backed up by money. One may object to the fact that some people end up with more goods and services than others do, but this is not inefficient—it simply reflects the fact that some have more income than others do. (Put somewhat differently, expressed in terms of Figure 1–1, the objection is that we are at one efficient point, *D,* but another one, *B,* would be better.)

Substantial inequality in the distribution of income can be, and frequently is, objected to on equity grounds. In general, a person's income in a competitive price system depends on how well he or she can meet the demands of consumers by supplying labor and other productive resources. Because incomes typically reflect productivities, those who are, for whatever reason, less productive will have lower incomes, and their needs will be less fully catered to by the market. Our view of what income people ethically deserve may differ from what they receive when paid on the basis of their productivity; the distribution of income generated by the price system may not necessarily conform to one's notion of equity.

Despite the evident importance of income distribution from an equity standpoint, it would probably be a mistake to view equity solely in terms of how the system distributes incomes. The process by which incomes are determined (as distinct from the end result) is also important. Is the price system a "fair game" in which people have reasonably fair opportunities to influence the size of their income? It is sometimes pointed out that a person's income is, after all, voluntarily given to the individual by the purchasers of the person's productive services, and everyone is free to compete in trying to offer more valuable services. To a large extent, the price system rewards traits such as ambition, foresight, and hard work, and that seems equitable to many people. Nonetheless, some persons are not fortunate enough to own productive resources that are highly valued by markets and will end up with low incomes in a price system. For them, the fact that the process is believed by many to be fair will be little consolation for their lack of income. Both the nature of the process and the results are relevant in making an equity judgment.

Paternalism and individual freedom in a price system

Paternalism and individual freedom can be dealt with briefly. From a paternalistic perspective, a price system may not function well. It gives people what they want and not what someone else thinks they should want. Some people may deplore the fact that the "system" allocates resources to the production of professional wrestling matches, motorcycles, cigarettes, carnival side shows, fattening foods, and video games, but these goods are produced only because some people are willing to pay for them. A person who dislikes the preferences of other people has only one avenue of influence: to try to persuade others that there are better ways to spend their money. The slow and gradual process of persuasion is a frustrating one for those who think they know (and perhaps some do) what is good for the rest of us. A paternalist will probably not consider a price system to be the best way of allocating resources in all cases.

On the other hand, a price system receives high marks for preserving individual freedom. People can choose what jobs to perform and how to dispose of their incomes, subject only to the constraint that they cannot force other people into involuntary exchanges.

What Role for Government?

If a price system is efficient, what role is there for government policy? As the preceding remarks suggest, efficiency is not the only criterion by which an economic system may be judged. A case can clearly be made for government to redistribute incomes in the interest of equity. In some instances paternalistic government policies may be warranted. In addition, a price system requires certain government actions if it is to attain an efficient allocation of resources; property rights must be defined, contracts must be enforced, and antitrust measures may be needed to ensure that markets are competitive. And still another role can be rationalized because of the existence of public goods and externalities, which is the subject of the next chapter.

Supplementary Readings

BATOR, FRANCIS M. "The Simple Analytics of Welfare Maximization." Reprinted in William Breit and Harold Hochman, eds., *Readings in Microeconomics*. New York: Holt, Rinehart and Winston, 1968.

BAUMOL, WILLIAM J. *Welfare Economics and the Theory of the State*. Cambridge, Mass.: Harvard University Press, 1965.

FRIEDMAN, MILTON, and ROSE FRIEDMAN. *Free to Choose*. New York: Harcourt Brace Jovanovich, 1980.

HAYEK, FRIEDRICH A. *The Constitution of Liberty*. Chicago: University of Chicago Press, 1960.

HEAD, JOHN G. *Public Goods and Public Welfare*. Durham, N.C.: Duke University Press, 1974, Chapter 10.

KENEN, PETER. "On the Geometry of Welfare Economics." *Quarterly Journal of Economics,* 71:426–447 (Mar. 1957).

MUSGRAVE, RICHARD. *The Theory of Public Finance*. New York: McGraw-Hill, 1959, Chapter 1.

SCHERER, FREDERIC. "General Equilibrium and Economic Efficiency." *The American Economist,* 10(1):54–70 (Spring 1966).

Review Questions and Problems

1. Choose a public policy about which you have particularly strong feelings. Sketch out your argument for or against this policy. Which parts of your argument are positive propositions and which are value judgments? Explain how a person could disagree with your conclusion but accept your value judgments.

2. Define efficiency. Explain how it differs from equity as a criterion for evaluating public policies.

3. Competitive markets are generally efficient. What would be wrong, if anything, with permitting competitive markets to develop with respect to babies? (That is, allowing childless couples to purchase unwanted babies rather than going through adoption procedures.)

4. This chapter discusses four criteria that are commonly used to evaluate public policies. What are they? For each criterion, give examples of public policies that do well and poorly in terms of that criterion.

5. Consider a public program that collects taxes from wealthy persons and gives the funds to destitute persons. Can you give any reasons for favoring this redistribution of income, other than your belief that it is fair? (You may want to review your answer after reading Chapter 8.)

6. Explain why the output of a competitive industry is efficient. Does this mean that no one would benefit if the government subsidized production so that consumers could purchase the good at a lower price? If not, what exactly does it mean?

7. Efficiency and equity are the criteria that economists usually emphasize in their analyses of public policies. Can you think of any policies in which other criteria are more important to consider than these two? Are there other criteria, in addition to the four discussed in this chapter, that you think are important to consider?

8. What is a welfare frontier? With it in mind, what does it mean to say that some policy is in the public interest?

9. Is it possible for a policy to affect the allocation of resources without changing the distribution of income? If so, give an example of such a policy; if not, explain why not.

chapter 2
Market Failure: Public Goods and Externalities

IN Chapter 1 we explained how a competitive price system tends to produce an efficient allocation of resources. The demonstration of efficiency was incomplete, however, because it depended on the implicit assumption that there were no public goods or externalities. Public goods
have peculiar characteristics that make it unlikely that private markets will
provide the efficient quantity. When this happens, *market failure* is said to
occur. The modern economic rationale for many types of government intervention is based on the inability of the price system to function efficiently
in such situations. To appreciate how government intervention may improve
on the workings of the price system, we must understand what public goods
and externalities are and how they affect the allocation of resources.

The Nature of Public Goods

The term *public good* does not necessarily refer to a good that is provided
by the government. Instead, it refers to a good (or service) that has two
characteristics, regardless of whether or not the government provides it.
These two characteristics are *nonrival consumption* and *nonexclusion*.

Nonrival consumption

*A good is nonrival in consumption when, with a given level of production,
consumption by one person need not diminish the quantity consumed by*

anyone else. In other words, a number of people may simultaneously consume the same good.[1] Some examples will clarify this concept. Consider an antimissile system that reduces the likelihood of foreign attack. Note that the protection of your property and person does not reduce the protection received by others; even if you did not exist, the level of protection available to others would be unaffected. Thus an antimissile system simultaneously protects a large number of people.

National defense—of which an antimissile system is a component—is generally considered to be one of the most clear-cut examples of a good that is nonrival in consumption. This characteristic, however, does not mean that people are necessarily benefited to the same degree. A given defense effort could afford greater protection to some geographic areas than to others. Possibly, if you live near a missile base, you might actually feel that your life and property are in greater danger because a foreign attack might concentrate on wiping out our missile systems. Similarly, if you are a pacifist, you might secure negative benefits from the defense effort. Nonetheless, an antimissile system is still a good that is nonrival in consumption because it simultaneously affects (to different degrees) a large number of people.

Once the nature of nonrival consumption is understood, it is easy to find more examples. A flood control project, for instance, is nonrival in consumption for people living in the region where the probability of flooding is reduced. The project would not benefit people living in other regions, but it is still nonrival for residents of the protected area. (As we shall see later, the geographic extent of the nonrivalry is important in considering what level of government is best equipped to deal with the good.) Weather forecasting, pollution abatement, and some public health measures that reduce the spread of disease are other examples of goods or services that are nonrival in consumption.

By contrast, most goods and services that we deal with in economics are rival in consumption. For a given level of production of hamburgers (or watches, shoes, houses, or cars), the more you consume, the less will be available for others. In these cases, consumption is rival because there is a problem in deciding how to ration output among the competing (rival) consumers. The price system resolves this problem by allocating a larger quantity to individuals who place a higher value on the good (i.e., people who are willing to pay more for it). With a good that is nonrival in consumption, there is no rationing problem. Once the good is produced, it can be made available to all consumers without reducing any individual's level of consumption.

---

[1] Nonrival consumption is sometimes referred to as *collective consumption* or *indivisibility of benefits.*

Nonexclusion

The second characteristic of a public good is nonexclusion. *Nonexclusion means that it is impossible, or prohibitively costly, to confine the benefits of the good (once produced) to selected persons.* A person will benefit from the production of the good, regardless of whether or not he or she pays for it. Although nonrivalry and nonexclusion often occur simultaneously, there is a distinction between the two concepts. Our definition of nonrivalry said that consumption by one person *need not* (not *does not*) interfere with consumption by others; this means that although all *could* consume simultaneously, it may still be possible for one person to consume the good and for others not to. There are cases in which we have potential nonrival consumption but in which it is possible to prohibit consumption by some people at a moderate cost. In these cases the goods in question are not public goods.

Television broadcasting can make the distinction between nonrivalry and nonexclusion clear. When a television program is broadcast, any number of people (in the relevant area) can receive the signal and watch it without interfering with the reception of others. Thus, a broadcast has the nonrival characteristic of a public good. It is, however, possible to exclude selected people from viewing the program. People without television sets, for example, will be unable to watch, or programs could be scrambled so that viewers could watch a program only after paying for a decoder. A television broadcast is, therefore, nonrival in consumption, but exclusion is possible at a moderate cost; such a good then does not have both necessary characteristics of a public good.

In many situations nonrivalry and nonexclusion go together; then we have a public good. National defense is a good example. How could we protect you and not your neighbor? Your neighbor might be deported and thereby excluded from securing any benefits from the defense effort. Similarly, the same means could be used to exclude potential beneficiaries of the flood control project. In both cases exclusion is possible, but it involves high costs. Whether a good is nonexclusive is ultimately a matter of degree, because in some cases the cost of exclusion is higher than in others. The relevant question is whether the cost is low enough to make exclusion feasible. In the case of national defense, most people would agree that exclusion is too costly. Thus, national defense fits our definition of a public good. In contrast, most people would probably agree that exclusion is feasible with television broadcasting, so it is not a public good.

The existence of public goods creates problems for a price system. Once a public good is produced, a number of people will automatically benefit, regardless of whether or not they pay for it (because they cannot be excluded), so it is difficult for private producers to provide the good. Unless producers can collect money for supplying the good, they will be unable to cover their costs. On the other hand, with private goods—where consumption is rival and nonpayers can be excluded—private producers have an incentive to provide the goods because they can extract payment from consumers. With private goods the price system can function effectively, but with public goods voluntary cooperation encounters a serious hindrance: the free rider problem.

Public Goods and the Free Rider Problem

A crucial question is whether voluntary cooperation through the price system will provide the appropriate quantity of a public good. To understand why voluntary cooperation often will not work, consider a community of ten people thinking of financing the construction of a dam to lessen the probability of flooding. The dam is a public good for residents of the community. Assume that the dam provides flood protection valued at $1,000 by each person and that the total cost of the dam is $5,000. If the dam is built, the benefit to each of the ten people is $1,000 so the total benefit is $10,000. Because the benefit exceeds the cost, it is in the community's interest to build the dam. Note in particular that the dam could be built if each person contributed $500, and then *everyone* would be better off (i.e., each would receive a benefit of $1,000, at a cost of $500).

Will voluntary agreement among the ten persons lead to the dam's being built? Actually it is not possible to give an unequivocal answer, but we can see the problem that could arise. Suppose one of the ten people believes that the other nine will finance the good whether or not he or she contributes anything toward the dam's construction. Due to the high cost of exclusion, if the dam is built, each resident will receive protection, regardless of whether he or she participates in its funding. But the possibility of being able to benefit from the dam without bearing any of its cost gives each resident an incentive to withhold any voluntary contribution. Each behaves as a *free rider,* attempting to avoid bearing any cost in the financing of a public good.

In this particular example it is possible that the dam would still be financed despite the free rider problem, with the remaining members of the community bearing somewhat higher costs. Whether this occurs depends on how prevalent free rider behavior is within the group. If, however, enough people in the community behaved as free riders, the dam would not be built. Although the outcome of this example is indeterminate, we can explain under what conditions the free rider problem would be most likely to create a serious misallocation of resources. Basically, it is a matter of the size of the group over which benefits are nonrival.

The larger the group, the more severe is the potential free rider problem, and hence the more likely it is that a public good could not be financed by voluntary contributions. Consider a small group of two neighbors for whom the public good is the removal of a dead tree lying precisely on the property line separating their properties. Only two people need agree on financing the tree removal, and each will recognize that without his or her participation the tree may not be removed. It is probable that both will contribute and that the tree will be removed. (There is an element of indeterminacy concerning exactly how the cost will be shared, but as long as the combined benefit of the neighbors exceeds the cost, it is likely they will bargain until agreement on financing is reached.)

The dam and tree examples differ in a significant way. With the dam, the residents in the flood-controlled area will realize that each contribution will have only a small effect on whether or not the dam is built. Even if one person contributes nothing toward the project, other people may finance the dam, and so he or she will receive the benefit at no cost. The problem is that if enough people reasoned this way and withheld their contributions, the project would not be undertaken. On the other hand, in the tree case each neighbor will realize that each contribution will have a significant impact on the outcome. Unless both contribute, the tree will probably not be removed, and so it is more likely that both will contribute.

As the group size increases, it is more likely that everyone will behave as a free rider, and the public good will not be provided. If we change the dam example slightly and assume the dam benefits 1,000 people, each by $10 (so the total benefit is the same as before), it is less likely the good will be financed than in the previous examples. In the large-group case, each person's contribution will have virtually no effect on the ultimate result. Put differently, the outcome depends mainly on what the other 999 people do, and whether any one person contributes will not affect what the others do. *Choosing not to contribute in this case is the most rational behavior.*[2] Because this is true for every person, few, if any, people will contribute, and the good will not be provided.

Therefore, when the benefits of the public good are nonrival over a large group, it is unlikely that the good will be provided (or, if provided through the contributions of a few individuals, it will not be provided in sufficient quantity). This is true even though it is in the people's interest to have the good provided, that is, even though the benefits exceed the costs. The failure of the price system—based as it is on voluntary cooperation—to function efficiently in providing public goods is a major economic justification for government intervention. In the last example, the government could levy a tax of $5 on each person and use the $5,000 in tax revenue to finance

---

[2] A formal analysis of the relationship between group size and the free rider problem can be found in James M. Buchanan, *The Demand and Supply of Public Goods* (Skokie, Ill.: Rand McNally, 1968), Chapter 5.

the dam, and each person would be better off. Each resident of the flood-controlled area would receive services from the dam worth $10, at a cost of $5 in taxes. The government expenditure of $5,000 on the dam thus would lead to a more efficient allocation of resources than would the price system.

Exactly how large the group must be before the free rider problem becomes serious is unclear because it depends on the bargaining and negotiating costs, the strategies adopted by people in these negotiations, and so on. There is little doubt that, generally, a group of 1,000 people would encounter great difficulties in reaching voluntary agreement on the financing of a public good. (Consider, however, that many small communities—but notably not large ones—manage to provide fire protection through *volunteer* fire companies.) It is in the large-group setting, such as national defense, that the strongest case for government action can be found.

There are many real-world examples that provide empirical support of the importance of free rider behavior. A particularly good example occurred in 1970, when General Motors tried to market pollution control devices for automobiles at $20 (installed) that could reduce the pollution emitted by 30 to 50 percent. Pollution abatement is a public good, at least for certain geographic areas. We may suppose that the benefits of a 30 to 50 percent reduction in pollution far outweighed a cost of $20 per car. (If this assumption is not valid, the government has made a sizable mistake, because it now requires pollution control devices on all new cars that reduce pollution by about 95 percent, at a cost of approximately $1,000 per car.) Yet GM withdrew the device from the market because of low sales. This was simply the large-group free rider problem at work. Everyone might have been better off if all drivers used the device, but it was not in the interest of any single individual to purchase it because the overall level of air quality would not be noticeably improved as a result of that solitary action.

The free rider phenomenon is not necessarily a bad thing, however. In some cases it serves a useful function. For example, the free rider problem may inhibit the formation of collusive agreements among businesses to restrict output and raise prices. The free rider problem also makes it more difficult to finance lobbies that try to persuade Congress to adopt (or reject) certain policies.[3]

Our examples of free rider behavior have dealt primarily with public goods—goods with nonrival consumption and infeasible exclusion. When a good has both characteristics in a large-group setting, the market will fail to provide the good or to provide it in sufficient quantity. If, however, a good is nonrival in consumption, but exclusion is feasible, markets can provide

---

[3]A reader who wonders how some groups containing hundreds of thousands of people have been able partially to overcome the free rider problem and finance lobbies (such as union members, doctors, and farmers) should consult Mancur Olson, Jr., *The Logic of Collective Action* (New York: Schocken Books, 1968).

the good, and there are many examples of this type of good. Movie theaters, for instance, provide a good with nonrival benefits, at least up to a group size equal to the capacity of the theater. Exclusion, however, is possible because only those who pay the cost of admission are permitted to see the movie. Thus, theaters can collect money from consumers, and this provides an inducement to incur the costs necessary to produce the good. Concerts, circuses, and sporting events, as well as schooling, are quite similar to movies in this regard. Pay television, such as HBO, for which viewers must pay for the programs they view, is also possible because the necessary metering devices are not overly costly.[4]

We have seen that the price system will not provide public goods efficiently in the large-group case. The following section shows how, in principle, the efficient level of output can be determined, as well as the difficulties encountered in attempting to put this theory into practice.

The Efficient Output of a Public Good

As with most other economic decisions, determination of the efficient output of a public good involves a comparison between the marginal benefits and marginal costs associated with different levels of output. The marginal cost of a public good reflects the cost of resources used to produce the good, just as with a private good. However, the marginal benefit of a public good differs from that of a private good because of the nonrival nature of public goods. With a private good like hamburgers, the marginal benefit of producing an additional unit is simply the value of the hamburger to the single person who consumes it. With a public good like defense, the marginal benefit of producing an additional unit is not the value that any individual alone places on it, because a large number of other people also benefit simultaneously from the same unit. Instead, we must add the marginal benefit of every person who values the additional unit of defense, and the resulting sum indicates the combined willingness of the public to pay for more defense, that is, its marginal benefit.

The way in which we derive the social marginal benefit of a public good—

[4]Although private markets can clearly provide goods where exclusion is possible at low cost, even if the benefits are nonrival, there is some disagreement over whether the private markets will operate with perfect efficiency. For an interesting discussion of this question, see Harold Demsetz, "The Private Production of Public Goods," *Journal of Law and Economics,* 13:293 (Oct. 1970); and comments on this paper by Robert B. Ekelund, Jr., Joe R. Hulett, and Earl A. Thompson in *Journal of Law and Economics,* 16:407 (Oct. 1973). See also William H. Oakland, "Public Goods, Perfect Competition, and Underproduction," *Journal of Political Economy,* 82:927 (Sept./Oct. 1974). With special reference to television, see Roger G. Noll, Merton J. Peck, and John J. McGowan, *Economic Aspects of Television Regulation* (Washington, D.C.: The Brookings Institution, 1973).

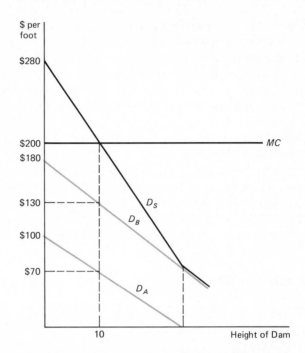

FIGURE 2–1 *Efficient output of a public good.*

in this example, a dam designed to control flooding—is illustrated in Figure 2–1, where units of the public good are measured in terms of the height of the dam. For simplicity, assume that only two people, *A* and *B,* benefit from the dam, although the analysis can be generalized for any number of people. The demand curves of the two consumers are shown as D_A and D_B. Recall that the demand price on a consumer's demand curve at any rate of output (i.e., the height to the demand curve) measures the marginal benefit for that consumer. *To determine the marginal benefit to society, we must add the demand prices of all consumers. Geometrically, this involves a vertical summation of the consumers' demand curves.* For example, in Figure 2–1 we add the marginal benefit to *A* for the first unit ($100) to the marginal benefit of *B* for the first unit ($180) and arrive at the social marginal benefit of $280 for the first unit. Proceeding in this way we can derive the social demand or marginal benefit curve, D_S, from the sum of D_A and D_B.

At any output where D_S lies above the marginal cost curve, *MC*—drawn here as horizontal at $200 for simplicity—people are willing to pay more for additional units of output than their marginal cost; thus efficiency requires an expansion of output. In Figure 2–1, at any level of output below 10, individuals *A* and *B* together are willing to pay more for another unit of output than the marginal cost of $200 (because D_S, lies above *MC*). Thus, an increase in output can be financed by individuals A and B in a way that will benefit both (with each paying somewhat less than the maximum amount he or she is willing to pay). At any output greater than 10, on the other hand, too much of the public good is being produced. That is, when the cost of the additional output is greater than the combined benefit to individuals A and B, a reduction in output can benefit both of them. Therefore, the most efficient rate of output is 10, where A's marginal benefit of $70 plus B's marginal benefit of $130 just equals the marginal cost.

The efficient output of a public good is that level of output at which D_s, *obtained by vertically summing the demand curves of all consumers, equals the marginal cost of production.* Our discussion has been in terms of finding the efficient level of output, a 10-foot dam in this example. There is no presumption that this output will be the actual, or equilibrium, output. We have already noted that voluntary cooperation in the large-group case would *not* lead to production of the efficient output. Whether the government would actually finance the efficient output depends on how political forces determine public policies, a matter to be examined in Chapter 3. Here we have simply identified the efficient level of output.

Who should pay?

In our example, a 10-foot dam is the efficient output of the public good. If this output is financed by government, however, taxes must be collected from the citizens to provide the funds. Financing the dam by a tax leads us naturally to the question of how to divide the tax burden between individuals A and B to collect the $2,000 necessary to build the dam. The key point here is that efficiency considerations alone do not permit us to say how the $2,000 tax burden *should* be divided; equity considerations are also involved in this choice.

To illustrate what is involved, let's consider alternative ways of financing the 10-foot dam. One possibility would be to charge each taxpayer an amount per unit equal to the marginal benefit the taxpayer receives from the provision of the public good. At the efficient output, A's marginal benefit is $70, and so that person's total tax liability would be $700 ($70 per unit times ten units), whereas B, whose marginal benefit is greater, would pay $1,300 in taxes. This division of the cost has the advantage of ensuring that both persons are made better off from the tax and expenditure policy. (Each person pays what the marginal, or tenth, unit is worth, but previous units are worth more than this sum.)

The way in which this specific tax combined with the provision of the dam affects the well-being of both persons is illustrated with the welfare frontier in Figure 2–2. Before the dam is provided, individuals A and B are located at the inefficient point E inside the welfare frontier. After the dam

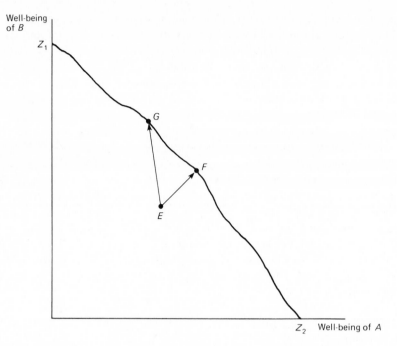

FIGURE 2–2   *Alternative ways to finance the public good.*

is built *and* the taxes paid, both persons are at point *F,* better off than before the project was undertaken. An efficient outcome, one lying on the frontier, has been achieved.

Dividing taxes according to the marginal benefits that taxpayers receive from government services accords with the *benefit theory of taxation.* This is not really a theory as much as a proposition that holds that taxes should (a value judgment) be allocated among people in this way.[5] If you believe that the beneficiaries of government expenditures should pay taxes in proportion to the benefits they receive, then this will represent an appealing solution to the question of who should pay. On the other hand, we must emphasize that economic efficiency does not require taxes to be apportioned in this manner.

Suppose instead that the $2,000 cost of the dam is financed by both individuals paying a tax of $1,000, or $100 per unit (foot) of the public good. Financing the dam in this way will make individual A worse off than if the dam were not provided at all: To individual A, the first unit is worth $100, but each additional unit is worth less. Nonetheless, the final outcome is an efficient one, unless distributing the tax burden in this way changes the

---

[5] Chapter 10 contains a further discussion of the benefit theory of taxation.

individuals' demands for the public good.[6] What would happen in this case is illustrated in Figure 2–2 by the move from point E to point G. Individual B is better off and individual A is worse off than under the alternative method of finance (point F), but we still end up on the welfare frontier. Efficiency, that is, getting to the frontier, requires that the 10-foot dam be built, but it does not resolve the question of exactly where on the frontier we should be located.

Thus, our analysis shows how to determine the efficient output for a given pattern of consumer demands; it does not, however, indicate that any particular allocation of the tax burden is preferred. This is not to say that the tax distribution is solely a question of distributional equity; there are relevant efficiency aspects to this question, but they are simply not incorporated in this analysis. For example, if individual A is heavily taxed, A might emigrate from the taxing jurisdiction. Furthermore, taxation unrelated to benefits would lead those who pay little (or no) tax to favor a larger output and those who pay heavy taxes to favor a smaller output, thereby creating conflicting pressures within the political process. These matters are discussed in later chapters.

Further considerations relating to efficiency

Government financing of a public good with taxes overcomes one aspect of the free rider problem, the tendency of people to withhold payment. It circumvents this problem by forcibly collecting the money. There is, however, another aspect of free rider behavior that government financing does not overcome: People have no incentive to reveal their demands accurately for the public good. To determine the efficient output of a public good, we must know every person's demand curve (so we can vertically add them to obtain D_S). How can we find out how much a public good, like defense, isworth to millions of people? This is probably the most difficult practical problem in implementing the analysis.

The (marginal) value of private goods to consumers is revealed in their purchasing decisions, and so market-determined prices reflect the relative values of private goods. If the government finances a public good, however, the political process does not reveal the value of that good to the taxpayer-voter with any degree of accuracy. When a person votes for candidate A rather than for candidate B, that vote reveals very little about how much incremental amounts of defense, education, or welfare are worth to that person. Nevertheless, it is conceivable that despite this problem, there is an "invisible hand" in the political process that works to promote efficiency. We will examine this question in Chapter 3.

---

[6] The efficient output is unchanged if the income effects on A's and B's demand curves are negligible, *or* if B's increase in demand (because B has $300 more income) is exactly offset by A's decrease in demand.

One other matter deserves some attention. The use of vertically added demand curves to determine efficient output is a consequence of the non-rival characteristic of a public good and is not related to whether exclusion is feasible. When exclusion is feasible, private producers face demand curves that reflect some form of vertically added individual demand curves. For example, the marginal cost of showing movies in theaters is covered by the *sum* of the admission prices paid by the viewers. (In contrast, the marginal cost of a Big Mac is covered by the price that the individual consumer pays.) When exclusion is possible, the price system can provide goods with non-rival benefits. However, is the result of private provision of such goods an efficient allocation, that is, should potential customers be excluded when it is possible?

A case can be made that consumers should not be excluded from a good with nonrival benefits even if it is possible. Once a good with nonrival benefits has been produced, an additional person can consume the good and not interfere with the consumption of others. Since excluding a person from consuming the good will harm that person without benefiting anyone else, it is often argued that such exclusion is inefficient. This has led some economists to maintain that the nonrival characteristic of certain goods alone will lead to market failure, because the use of prices by private firms will exclude some consumers.

On the other hand, the charging of prices by movie theaters, for example, does not necessarily exclude anyone. People who are willing to pay the price do consume the good. Only those who are unwilling to pay the price of admission will be excluded, and even this problem is often mitigated by using lower prices for some groups, such as children and senior citizens. There may be some inefficiency, but it must be weighed against the advantage of having production linked closely (if not perfectly) to consumer demands and having market-determined prices as a guide (possibly incomplete) to the value of the good. In any event, the degree of inefficiency in market provision will be far less for a nonrival good when exclusion is possible than when it is not. Hence, the more serious problems occur for goods with both characteristics, that is, public goods.[7]

Externalities

Sometimes in the processes of production, distribution, or consumption of certain goods, there are harmful or beneficial side effects called *externalities* that are borne by people who are not directly involved in the market exchanges. These side effects of ordinary economic activities are called *external benefits* when the effects are beneficial and *external costs* when they are

[7]See the references in footnote 4 for interesting analyses of these issues.

harmful. The term externality stems from the fact that these effects are out-side, or external to, the price system, and so their impact is not determined through mutual agreement among all those affected. A few examples will make the nature of these effects clear.

Immunization against a contagious disease is an example of a consump-tion activity involving external benefits. When a person is inoculated, that individual benefits directly, because the person's chance of contracting the disease is reduced (this benefit is *not* the external benefit). The decision to be inoculated also confers benefits indirectly on others, because they are less likely to catch the disease from the inoculated person, and this is the external benefit. The fact that other people benefit from the individual's actions, however, will not influence that person's decision as to whether being immunized is worth the cost. What the person is concerned with is the effect on his or her own health. Thus, the benefit the inoculation gen-erates for others is external to the person's decision.

Maintenance of a person's lawn or home may also produce external ben-efits for neighbors. If the neighbors' well-being is improved by living in a more attractive neighborhood, then there is an external benefit associated with home lawn maintenance. On a somewhat grander scale, education is often alleged to involve external benefits such as a reduction in juvenile delinquency, an improvement in the functioning of the political process, or greater social stability.

External costs are also quite common, and the best examples can be found in the area of pollution. Driving an automobile or operating a factory with a smoking chimney pollutes the atmosphere that other people breathe; thus the operation of a car or factory imposes costs on people not directly involved in the activity. Similarly, operating a motorcycle produces a level of noise that is often irritating to those nearby, just as the noise level of a supersonic (or subsonic) airplane may be annoying to people living near airports. Congestion is also an external cost. When a person drives during rush hour, the road becomes more congested not only for the driver, but for other commuters as well.

At a formal level, externalities and public goods are very similar. If a person is inoculated for a contagious disease, there are nonrival benefits; both that person and others benefit from the inoculation. In addition, it would be very difficult to exclude other people from benefiting from this person's inoculation. The same is true of pollution, but in this case there are nonrival costs. A large number of people are simultaneously harmed if the atmosphere is polluted, and it would be difficult to have the atmosphere (in a particular area) polluted for some and not for others.

If there is any difference between externalities and public goods, it may be the fact that external effects are the unintended side effects of activities undertaken for other purposes. For example, people do not pollute because they enjoy breathing a polluted atmosphere—they simply want to transport themselves conveniently in a car from one place to another. In addition, the distribution of the benefit, for example, from consuming a good with external benefits, is usually very skewed. We may receive some benefit from an individual's becoming better educated, but clearly the benefit that individual receives is many, many times greater. In contrast, however, those distinctions are matters of degree, and so a basic similarity between the concepts remains.[8]

Recognizing the similarity between externalities and public goods greatly facilitates appreciation of the significance of externalities. *Externalities generally lead to an inefficient allocation of resources, or market failure, just as public goods do.* Market demands and supplies will reflect only the benefits and costs of the participants in the market; the benefits and costs that fall on others will not be taken into account in determining production. For example, a person may decide against being immunized because the improvement in his or her health is not worth the cost involved. If, however, the benefits of improved health for others are added to the person's benefit, the combined benefit could exceed the cost. In this case, the person's decision not to be immunized would represent an inefficient use of resources.

External benefits

To examine the implications of externalities more fully, assume that the consumption of some product generates external benefits. The competitive supply and demand curves are shown in Figure 2–3 as S (drawn horizontally, implying a constant cost competitive industry) and D_P. D_P, however, reflects only the private demand of individuals for the product. Given these relationships, the market equilibrium occurs with an output of Q_1 and a price of $5. External benefits can be represented by the marginal external benefit curve, *MEB,* which reflects the marginal benefit to people other than the direct consumer. *MEB* is the vertically summed demands of people other than the immediate consumer of the product. The demand curves are summed vertically because of the nonrival nature of the benefits.

The competitive output, Q_1, is inefficient. At Q_1 the benefit to consumers of another unit is $5 (the height to D_P). If another unit is consumed, however, people other than the direct consumer of the product will receive a benefit valued at $2 (the height to *MEB*). Thus, the combined marginal benefit of another unit of output is $7, and this exceeds the $5 cost of producing the good. The combined, or social, marginal benefits are shown by D_S, which is derived by vertically adding (again because the benefits are nonrival) *MEB* and D_P. By comparing D_S and S at Q_1, we can see that the competitive output is too low because the marginal benefits of the greater out-

---

[8]For attempts at making a rigorous analytical distinction between externalities and public goods, see S. E. Holtermann, "Externalities and Public Goods," *Economica,* 39:78 (Feb. 1972); and Ezra J. Mishan, "The Relationship Between Joint Products, Collective Goods, and External Effects," *Journal of Political Economy,* 72:329 (May 1969).

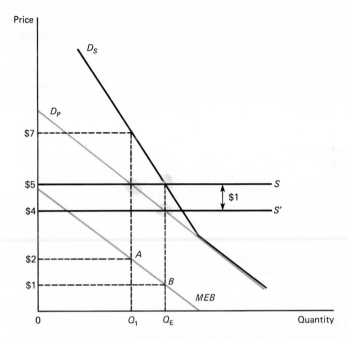

FIGURE 2–3   *External benefits in a competitive industry.*

put exceed the marginal costs. Yet there is no tendency for competitive pressures to produce a larger output because the additional benefits to the direct consumers are less than the $5 price per unit they must pay.

Figure 2–3 illustrates the general tendency for an activity to be under-produced when external benefits are involved and when production is determined in competitive markets. The competitive output is Q_1, but the efficient output is Q_E—where D_S intersects S. Government could step in with a policy designated to increase output to the efficient level, and the policy most often recommended is an excise subsidy. If the government pays firms $1 for every unit of output they sell, the supply curve confronting consumers will shift downward by $1 to S'. Although the marginal cost of production is still $5, the government is in effect bearing $1 of this cost through the subsidy, and so consumers need pay only $4. At the lower price of $4, consumers would be led to purchase Q_E units, and this is the efficient output. By using appropriate subsidies, the government can induce an expansion in output in situations in which external benefits lead competitive markets to produce too little.[9]

[9] This analysis is based on the assumption that external benefits are related to total consumption of the good, irrespective of who consumes the output. In some cases, external benefits will depend on the level of individual consumption, and it may be desirable to subsidize only those who would consume very little on their own rather than subsidize all consumers as in Figure 2–3.

The price to consumers has been lowered by \$1, exactly the amount of the marginal external benefit at the efficient level of output, Q_E. (At Q_E the marginal external benefit is given by the height to *MEB,* or \$1.) The subsidy is not equal to the marginal external benefit of \$2 at the competitive equilibrium. A \$2 per unit subsidy would confront consumers with a price of \$3, and the resulting level of consumption would exceed the efficient quantity.[10]

External costs

The analysis of external costs is symmetrical to that of external benefits. Suppose that firms in a constant cost competitive industry produce wastes as a by-product of their production and dispose of the effluents by dumping them into a nearby river. For a variety of reasons, these wastes irritate (i.e., harm) people living downstream, so the production of the industry's product involves external costs. In this case, the competitive output will be too large, because the external costs are not taken into account in the firms' production decisions.

Consider Figure 2–4. The competitive demand and supply curves are shown as D and S_P, and the equilibrium output is Q_1, with a price of \$5 per unit. The marginal damage suffered by people downstream is shown by the marginal external cost, or *MEC,* curve. The *MEC* curve is drawn upward sloping to reflect the assumption that additional amounts of pollution inflict increasing costs on people living downstream as the water becomes more polluted. (Nothing important would be changed if the marginal external costs were constant, however.) At Q_1, the marginal external cost is \$2, implying that people downstream would be \$2 better off if one unit less of the product (and the waste) were produced.

With external costs the competitive output is too large. Firms expand output as long as consumers will pay a price that covers *their* costs, but the resulting price will not cover *all* costs of production—it ignores the damage done by pollutants to people living downstream. At Q_1, firms incur costs of \$5 per unit, which is just covered by the price paid by consumers, but there is still a cost of \$2 borne by people downstream. At the competitive level of output, Q_1, the product is not worth what it costs to produce. The social marginal cost of production is \$7, but the marginal benefit to consumers is

[10]Although the subsidy depicted in Figure 2–3 attains an efficient output, it does not benefit everyone relative to the competitive equilibrium. Assuming that those who receive the external benefit bear the cost of the subsidy, the cost is \$1 times Q_E, or $\$1BQ_E0$. The benefits they receive come from the expansion in output from Q_1 to Q_E and are equal to ABQ_EQ_1, clearly below the costs. In principle, a subsidy could be designed that would benefit both consumers and externally affected parties. Check to see if you understand how a subsidy of \$1 per unit for consumption only in excess of Q_1 might achieve this.

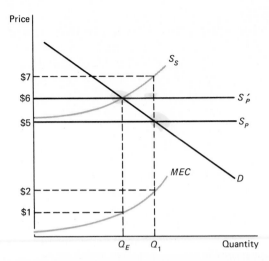

FIGURE 2-4   *External costs in a competitive industry.*

only $5. The social marginal costs of production are shown by the curve S_S, obtained by vertically adding *MEC* to the private supply curve, S_P. An efficient output occurs where S_S, which includes all production costs, intersects *D*, or at output Q_E. Competitive pressures, however, lead to an output of Q_1, larger than the efficient output.

As a corrective action, an excise tax could be used to induce firms to produce at the efficient level. A tax of $1 per unit of output would shift the supply curve up by $1 to S_P', and firms would curtail production until the consumers were willing to pay a price of $6. The result, at Q_E, is where the marginal benefit to consumers equals the social marginal cost of production. Pollution is not eliminated; instead, it is reduced to the point that a further reduction in production and pollution would cost more than it is worth.[11]

To summarize: Activities involving external benefits will be underproduced and those involving external costs will be overproduced by a competitive price system. We have seen how policies can be designed to achieve efficient outcomes, but to implement these policies it is necessary to know the size of the externalities. Unfortunately, this determination involves the same difficulties as in determining the demand for a public good.

---

[11] The analysis depicted in Figure 2–4 is fully correct only if the waste bears a fixed relationship to output and if it must be disposed of in the river. In more realistic cases, it would be desirable to use a policy that induced firms to employ production processes that generated less waste per unit of output.

Applying Externality and Public Good Analysis

Understanding how public goods and externalities lead to market failure provides important insight into the possible use of government intervention to promote greater efficiency. In such cases, there are potential mutual benefits from government action, so economists understandably attach much significance to these phenomena in their discussions of public policy. Our brief introduction to public goods and externalities, however, has ignored some relevant issues, so now let's consider some common objections, misunderstandings, and problems in applying the analysis.

Voluntary bargaining in the small group

In an important theoretical paper, Ronald Coase showed that voluntary bargaining can lead to efficient outcomes even when externalities exist.[12] Coase illustrated his analysis by considering a rancher and a farmer with adjoining properties. The rancher's cattle would occasionally stray onto the farmer's property and destroy some of his crops: an external cost associated with cattle raising. Our earlier analysis would suggest that there would be too much crop damage, but Coase argued that this might not be correct. If the rancher were legally liable for damage caused by his cattle, he would bear a cost as a result of straying cattle. In this case, the damage caused by his cattle would not then be an external cost, but a direct cost borne by the rancher (and therefore taken into consideration in his decision making), because the rancher would have to compensate the farmer for crop damage.

Coase went further and argued that even if the rancher were not liable, an efficient solution could emerge without government action. This would happen because the farmer has an incentive to offer to pay the rancher to reduce the number of cattle that stray because a reduction in crop damage will increase the farmer's profits. An agreement could therefore be struck that would reduce cattle straying to the efficient level.

Coase's ingenious analysis not only shows that voluntary bargaining can lead to efficient outcomes but also illustrates the intimate connection between external effects and property rights. As long as property rights are clearly defined and enforced, bargaining between the parties involved resolves the problem. It is irrelevant how property rights are assigned. Whether or not the rancher is liable for damage, cattle straying will be reduced. The *distributional* effects, however, depend on the exact definition of property rights. When the rancher is liable, he will compensate the farmer; alternatively, when the rancher is not liable, the farmer will pay the rancher to

---

[12] Ronald H. Coase, "The Problem of Social Cost," *Journal of Law and Economics,* 3:1 (Oct. 1960).

reduce cattle straying. In both cases, cattle straying and crop damage are reduced to the efficient level, but different people bear the cost.

Coase's analysis is applicable in many cases far removed from his agrarian example. Consider the case of the Clean Indoor Air Act, a legislative proposal debated in California in 1978. If this bill had passed (it did not), smoking would have been banned in nearly all public facilities and private businesses. The proponents of the bill stressed that it was needed to protect nonsmokers from the health hazards of cigarette smoke. If cigarette smoke does harm nonsmokers, this would appear to be an instance of external costs in which excessive smoking would take place in the absence of remedial action.

This episode invites two comments. First, an outright ban on cigarette smoking would probably be inefficient, possibly more inefficient than permitting unrestricted smoking is. Efficiency requires that we take into account the preferences of *both* smokers and nonsmokers, not just the wishes of nonsmokers. An intermediate solution, perhaps one that permits smoking at certain times or in certain places, would probably be more efficient than would an outright ban.

Second, Coase's analysis suggests that we consider a more basic question: Is government legislation required to achieve an efficient solution? The answer, perhaps surprisingly, is no. Private businesses already have incentives to take the preferences of their smoking and nonsmoking customers into account. If a business has trouble recruiting workers or loses customers when smoking is permitted, it has an incentive to consider alternatives that restrict smoking. Many businesses already do this. Some restaurants, for example, do not permit smoking or permit smoking only in certain areas. Thus, no government action is required in the case of private businesses, at least if the goal is to promote efficiency. (It should be noted, however, that some states have passed laws restricting smoking. Nonsmokers are understandably not interested in efficiency; some will support restrictions on smoking, since it benefits them, regardless of the harm done to smokers.)

Is there then ever a need to rely on government in these situations? We have already provided the answer in our discussion of the free rider problem. Private bargaining can work efficiently when small numbers are involved, as in the Coase example in which only one farmer is harmed by the straying cattle. When a factory pollutes the atmosphere breathed by thousands of people, however, private bargaining cannot be expected to lead to an efficient outcome. Our earlier conclusion of market failure is still correct, therefore, in the large-group case. Many issues of great importance, such as defense, pollution, and police protection, are large-group externalities or public goods, and the price system cannot be expected to function effectively in these areas. Coase's analysis should caution us, however, against concluding that every phenomenon that appears to be an externality requires government intervention.

Choice of a policy to deal with market failure

External effects and public goods, at least in the large-group setting, imply that voluntary behavior within a competitive price system will not result in an efficient allocation of resources. *The identification of this distortion, however, does not tell us what type of government policy is preferred.* Analysis of pollution, for example, shows that an unhampered price system will produce too much pollution, that is, that the benefits of reducing pollution exceed the costs. However, there are many different policies that could be used to reduce pollution, and one policy is unlikely to dominate all others in terms of its efficiency.

In the analysis of Figure 2–3, we saw that external benefits lead to underproduction of the good and that an excise subsidy, as a corrective measure, could be used to stimulate output to the efficient level Q_E. Other policies, however, could also lead to this efficient output. For instance, the government might simply require people to consume larger quantities (to total Q_E), much as there are now requirements concerning school attendance and vaccinations. This is also an efficient policy, but the distribution of benefits and costs differs from that of the excise subsidy. With the excise subsidy, taxpayers bear the cost of expanding consumption through taxes to finance the subsidy; consumers of the product do not. With a consumption requirement, the consumers alone pay the additional cost. In each case, an efficient allocation results, but with a different distributional impact.

Choosing among alternative policy prescriptions to deal with externalities is a problem not fully answered by externality theory, but theory does help by suggesting the nature of the corrective action required. The use of taxes (for external costs) and subsidies (for external benefits) is quite popular among economists. These policies have numerous advantages: They are flexible, because the rate of subsidy or tax can be easily adjusted depending on whether an increase or reduction in the external effect is desired; they often involve fewer administrative problems; markets can still adjust in a decentralized way to changes in supply or demand; and market prices and costs still provide information concerning the private benefits and costs. Yet no unequivocal preference for taxes and subsidies should be inferred. Each alternative policy must be examined on its own merits. Externality theory can assist by pointing in the proper direction, but it is not a detailed blueprint for action.

One further problem in designing a corrective policy lies in determining how far to pursue the corrective policy, that is, how large a tax or subsidy should be used. If we knew the exact size of the benefits and costs involved, we could easily determine the appropriate tax or subsidy, as we did in Figures 2–3 and 2–4. But the magnitude of the external effects cannot be easily (if at all) determined. The danger here is that we will go too far. In the case of external benefits, expanding output excessively can be worse

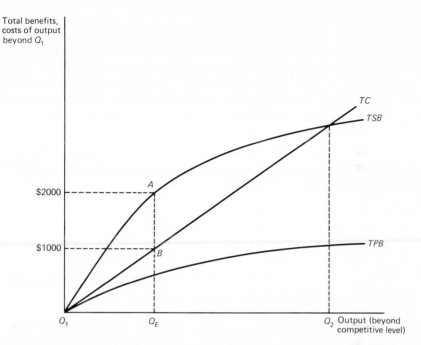

FIGURE 2–5   *Output expansion in the presence of external benefits.*

than doing nothing at all; the same is true with reducing external costs below the efficient level.

Figure 2–5 illustrates this, as well as several other points. Figure 2–5 is based on the external benefit example in Figure 2–3. In Figure 2–5, however, the horizontal axis measures *the output in excess of the competitive output, Q_1.* On the vertical axis we are measuring the total benefits and costs associated with expansion in output beyond Q_1. The *TC* and *TPB* curves show the total private costs and benefits, respectively, of additional output; they are derived from the private demand and supply curves in Figure 2–3. (The curves in Figure 2–3 show the marginal costs and benefits which are the *slopes* of the respective total curves in Figure 2-5.) The total social benefit curve, *TSB,* is the sum of the benefits to consumers *(TPB)* plus the external benefits associated with greater levels of output.

If there were no external benefits, the *TC* and *TPB* curves would reflect all the benefits and costs of the output levels beyond the competitive level. In that event, an expansion of output would be inefficient because the costs exceed the benefits. When external benefits are involved, the relevant total benefit curve, *TSB,* lies above the total cost curve over a region of output. This means that the competitive output is too low, because an expansion of output will confer benefits greater than costs.

The most efficient output occurs when total benefits exceed total costs by the greatest amount, that is, when the net gain is the largest. This occurs at Q_E, where the slopes of *TSB* and *TC* (marginal social benefit and marginal cost) are equal because this is where the vertical distance between the curves is the greatest. At Q_E, the total benefit of the additional output, AQ_E, exceeds the total cost, BQ_E, by \$1,000—the net gain. As we saw, an appropriate excise subsidy could be used to induce this expansion of output to Q_E.

If a mistake is made and the subsidy (or other policy) increases output beyond Q_2, we would be better off with no subsidy at all. Beyond Q_2 the total cost of the additional output exceeds its total benefit, even including the external benefits. This illustrates the danger of having too much of a good thing. Yet without knowing the magnitude of the external benefits, it is impossible to ascertain when we have gone too far. This is a serious problem, given the difficulty of estimating the magnitude of the external benefit, which is based on a precise knowledge of the value individuals place on the external effect.

It must be recognized that, given this and other problems, the government is unlikely to use a subsidy of exactly the proper size. Nevertheless, we should not necessarily conclude that the government should do nothing. A subsidy that achieves any output between Q_1 and Q_2 in Figure 2–5 is better than no subsidy at all. Although Q_E is the most efficient output, all the outputs in the Q_1–Q_2 range do involve some excess of benefits over costs in comparison with the competitive level of output, so some net gain is possible. Just because the optimal level of output, Q_E, may not be achieved is insufficient reason to oppose or reject a policy. As long as a program represents an improvement over the status quo, it should be considered, and perhaps eventually a more efficient policy will be found. However, the possibility that some policy might be worse than none should also be kept in mind.

Identifying the externality or public good

A first step in correctly applying externality (or public good) theory is to identify exactly what constitutes the external effect. With air pollutants emitted by automobiles, the production or use of automobiles is not an externality, it is the emission itself. Externality theory predicts that there will be too much pollution, not necessarily that there will be too many cars. An efficient policy must be designed to reduce pollution directly, not indirectly, for example, by reducing the number of automobiles or by making it harder to get a driver's license. A tax on automobiles would be inappropriate because a tax would do nothing to induce auto manufacturers to produce cars that pollute less. An automobile tax would reduce the output of all cars by increasing their cost to drivers—irrespective of whether, or how much, they pollute. If a tax is to be used, it should be levied on pollution itself. (The rate of tax should vary with the amount of damage done by pollution; for example, the pollution damage in large metropolitan areas—because there are more people to pollute and to be polluted—would be greater than the damage done in rural areas. As a consequence, the pollution tax should be higher in the larger, more densely populated areas.) Such a tax would give producers and consumers the proper incentive to reduce pollution in any way that costs less than the taxes levied.

The importance of determining exactly what constitutes the externality is frequently overlooked in policy analysis. Consider the frequent assertion that education produces external benefits—possibly in the form of a more stable society. Exactly what type of education produces these effects? Is instruction in dance, music, home economics, and physical education beneficial to anyone other than those who receive it? Yet if only certain types of education generate external benefits, then only these types should be subsidized. A policy that induces students to acquire skills they are unwilling to pay for—if these skills fail to generate external benefits—is inefficient.

Or consider the claim that education generates external benefits because it enables students to earn higher incomes and hence makes it less likely they will become criminals. Note that it is criminal activity that is the harmful effect. A subsidy to education would be inefficient because it would encourage overconsumption of education by pupils who would never become criminals. An efficient policy would be one that penalized, and thus deterred, criminal activity per se. To see the problem intuitively with this argument, note that it really claims that raising the incomes of potential criminals will reduce crime. This relationship may be correct, but it does not mean that raising the incomes of criminals is the least costly way of reducing crime. Generally, it will not be.

As a final example, consider a proposal to stop economic growth, citing such undesirable consequences as pollution and congestion. But the growth in pollution and congestion, or even their absolute levels, may be reduced without directly reducing the growth in other goods and services. A corrective policy would be more effective if designed to deal with pollution and congestion explicitly and not with economic growth.[13]

Inframarginal externalities

Inframarginal externalities are externalities with a marginal value of zero at the privately chosen equilibrium. An example of an inframarginal external benefit is shown in Figure 2–6. Individual A's demand curve is shown as

[13] There can be exceptions to the argument developed in this section, and the reader may wish to pursue the matter further. Generally, the exceptions are in cases in which it is infeasible, or administratively too costly, to deal with the externality itself, and some indirect means may be the only possibility. Such cases are probably fairly rare, and as a general rule, it appears that attempting to deal with the externality directly will be more efficient.

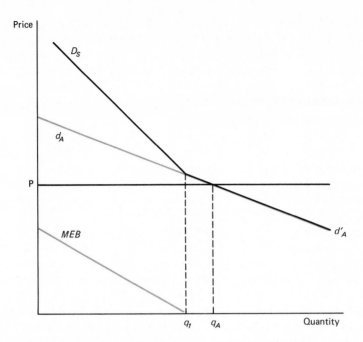

FIGURE 2–6 *Inframarginal external benefits.*

$d_A d'_A$, and it is assumed that A's consumption of the good generates marginal external benefits according to the schedule *MEB*. The marginal external benefit becomes zero at q_1; note that the point where *MEB* becomes zero is less than q_A, the level that A would choose to purchase independently. This means that the marginal value of the external benefit at the private equilibrium is zero. This type of externality is called an *inframarginal* ("inside the margin") *externality* and is noteworthy because it does *not* result in any ineffi-ciency. The social demand curve reflecting all marginal benefits is $D_S d'_A$, and at q_1 it coincides with individual A's demand curve. In other words, only A receives any benefit from consuming beyond q_1, and, because the benefit (shown by $d_A d'_A$) is less than the cost involved, it is inefficient to increase consumption beyond the level A chooses independently.

Because our primary concern is with externalities that result in inefficien-cies in resource allocation, we should make sure that the externalities we are considering have nonzero values at the private equilibrium. In other words, would a little more (or less) of the activity in question confer *more* benefits (or costs) on the externally affected parties? Frequently this distinc-tion is obscured. Consider the statement "We all benefit from living in an educated society." This statement is correct even if the external benefits are entirely inframarginal at the private equilibrium, because it can be inter-preted to refer to total external benefits rather than marginal ones. There-

fore, such a statement does not necessarily imply a misallocation of resources by the price system. The fact that we benefit from living in an educated
society is no reason for using government to encourage more education
than people would choose on their own, unless we would be even better
off in a more educated society, that is, unless the externalities associated
with increased expenditures on education are marginally relevant.[14]

Pecuniary externalities

Suppose that the demand for housing by college students increases and
drives up the price of housing for nonstudents in a college community.
Although the demand for housing by nonstudents has not increased, they
will be paying a higher price and consequently are made worse off. The
increase in demand by students harms nonstudents. Is this an external cost
we need to worry about? The answer is no. This damage to nonstudents is
transmitted through the price system (in the form of higher prices), not
outside it. It is not external to the price system. Unfortunately, this type of
effect has been given the name *pecuniary externality,* meaning that it is
monetary rather than real. All the externalities we have discussed so far are
real, or as they are sometimes called, *technological externalities.*

Pecuniary externalities are intrinsic to the workings of a price system.
Every time a price, wage rate, or interest rate changes, as thousands do
every day, some people are harmed and others are benefited. There is no
inefficiency produced by these effects; the markets are simply adjusting efficiently to changes in the underlying demand or supply conditions. The
reason there is no inefficiency involved is that the harm done to nonstudents, for example, when housing prices rise is not a *net* cost to society.
Instead it is simply a *transfer* of purchasing power from renters to owners
of rental housing. A higher price harms the buyer but benefits the seller to
the same degree, and so there is no net loss. The situation is quite different
with pollution, where the harm done to the pollutee is not offset by a gain
to the polluter. Technological externalities, or just *externalities,* as we refer
to them, reflect net costs or benefits not taken into account by the market
system. Because of this, technological externalities are a source of inefficiency, whereas pecuniary externalities are not.

Pecuniary externalities can easily be confused with the real thing. Sometimes it is argued, for example, that the vocational education of welfare
recipients is a (technological) external benefit for taxpayers: Vocational education may increase the earning capacity of welfare recipients, resulting in
a reduction in welfare payments (and a reduction in tax liabilities for taxpayers). This effect on taxpayers is a pecuniary externality, not a technolog-

---

[14]E. G. West, "The Politics of American Public School Legislation," *Journal of Law and
Economics,* 3:101–128 (Oct. 1967).

ical one, although in this case it is transmitted through a government policy rather than through the price system. The reduction in welfare payments and tax liabilities is a transfer from welfare recipients to taxpayers, with the loss to transfer recipients equal to the gain to taxpayers. Vocational education for recipients does not, of itself, lower taxes. Instead, it is the decision to reduce welfare payments that lowers taxes, and this has a purely redistributive effect.

From now on when we refer to *externalities*, we will mean the technological variety that can cause resource misallocation, not the pecuniary variety that indicates only transfers of income.

Multiple distortions

The efficiency implications we have drawn from our analysis so far are correct only when the economy is perfectly efficient except for the distortion produced by the public good or externality being examined. In other words, our conclusion that the output of a competitive industry will be too small if there are external benefits depends on the assumption that the remainder of the economy is without distortions; that is, the external benefit is the only distortion in an otherwise efficient economy. When this assumption is not correct, as is often the case, it is no longer possible to infer from the existence of externalities that there is necessarily any inefficiency. With many distortions in the economy, some may operate to offset others, and the end result is not clear.

To see this, suppose that the consumption of some industry's product yields external benefits *and* that the production of that product imposes external costs. If the external benefit is the only distortion, we can conclude that output is too low; on the other hand, the external cost by itself tends to produce too large an output. The two distortions operate in opposite directions and can cancel out, resulting in an efficient output. Similarly, a monopoly whose production involves external costs can be efficient, but a monopoly whose production involves external benefits will be more inefficient than a competitive industry with external benefits. (Can you see why?) In addition, more remote distortions in other industries can also have an effect, because all markets are interrelated.

Because there are many distortions in an economy, it is a difficult, if not impossible, task to take all of them into account, as a completely rigorous analysis should. In many cases, the quantitative significance of this problem is trivial—just because there is a monopoly in the safety pin industry, our conclusion that cars will pollute the atmosphere too much in the absence of government action is not likely to be altered. For that reason, in addition to the fact that we must first understand the implications of single distortions before we can hope to comprehend the more involved cases of interacting distortions, we will largely ignore this problem. A few important cases are, however, evaluated later.

The individual demand for public goods

How much would you be willing to pay for a 50 percent reduction in the level of nitrogen oxide in the atmosphere? How much is a base of ICBMs outside Atlanta worth to you? If you have difficulty giving fairly precise answers to these questions, then you do not have a well-defined demand for the public good or externality in question. Our analysis, however, is based on the assumption that people do have well-defined demands for such goods. Recall that the marginal external benefit and cost curves simply reflect the sum of everyone's answers to such questions. If people cannot place a precise value on these goods, then the notion of efficiency becomes fuzzy and inexact. How can we determine the efficient quantity of the good, the type of policy to pursue, or the size of the corrective action if people do not know how much the good is worth? Because of this, evaluating the efficiency of resource allocation is difficult.

This is a troublesome problem. People can also be uncertain about the value of some goods purchased in private markets (such as, perhaps, some types of medical care), but this problem is clearly more prevalent with public goods and externalities. Although economic analysis can still be used to determine some of the consequences of public policies, efficiency judgments must be made subject to a range of indeterminacy.

Public Goods and Externalities: A Summary

Understanding how public goods and externalities affect resource allocation provides significant insight into cases in which competitive markets will not function with peak efficiency. Analyzing these phenomena helps us determine what types of policies are most likely to improve resource allocation. Not surprisingly, then, economists examine the price system for these (and other) sources of inefficiency in their evaluation of public policy. When externalities and public goods are quantitatively significant, a case can be made that certain types of government intervention will generally be mutually beneficial.

Unfortunately, very little empirical evidence on the size, or even the existence, of external effects is available. (Information yielded by the burgeoning studies of pollution represents a partial exception to this and holds out promise that research in other areas will dispel some of our ignorance.) Some externalities, such as the effect of your hair style or dress on the well-being of others, are probably not important enough to bother with, particularly when we understand the difficulty of designing efficient policies. Others, such as pollution, are clearly more important. In the vast intermediate range between these extremes, there is considerable room for honest disagreement about the quantitative significance of public goods and externalities.

Supplementary Readings

BUCHANAN, JAMES M. *The Demand and Supply of Public Goods.* Skokie, Ill.: Rand McNally, 1968.

BURKHEAD, JESSE, and JERRY MINER. *Public Expenditure.* Chicago: Aldine, 1971, Chapter 4.

COASE, RONALD. "The Problem of Social Cost." *Journal of Law and Economics,* 3:1–44 (Oct. 1960).

DEMSETZ, HAROLD. "The Private Production of Public Goods." *Journal of Law and Economics,* 13(2):30–43 (Oct. 1970).

HEAD, JOHN G. *Public Goods and Public Welfare.* Durham, N.C.: Duke University Press, 1974.

McKEAN, RONALD N. *Public Spending.* New York: McGraw-Hill, 1968, Chapter 5.

MISHAN, E. J. "The Postwar Literature on Externalities: An Interpretive Essay." *Journal of Economic Literature,* 9:1–28 (Mar. 1971).

TULLOCK, GORDON. *Private Wants, Public Means.* New York: Basic Books, 1970.

Review Questions and Problems

1. Suppose there are three people in society, two "hawks" and one "dove." The dove is a pacifist and receives negative benefits from national defense; the hawks positively value national defense. Show graphically how an efficient output of defense would be determined in this case. Is there any way that the government could finance this efficient quantity that would benefit all three people?

2. A competitive market is in equilibrium. At the equilibrium output, there is a marginal external benefit of $1 per unit of output. If the government subsidizes production with a subsidy of $1 per unit, will this achieve an efficient output? Support your answer with a graph.

3. Are there any external benefits associated with students' receiving a college education? Put differently, in what way does your receiving a college education benefit other people? What type of subsidy, if any, would be appropriate for dealing with the externalities you mention? (You may want to review your answer to this question after reading Chapter 5.)

4. What are pecuniary externalities and inframarginal externalities? Give an example of each. Do they lead to inefficient allocations?

5. What is the condition for efficiency in the output of a public good? How is an efficient output identified graphically? How should the efficient output be paid for?

6. "Individuals have more of an incentive to reveal their true preferences about ice cream than about national defense." True or false. Explain.

7. What are the characteristics of a public good, and why do they imply that voluntary arrangements cannot ensure the efficient output of such a good?

8. In evaluating government activity in some area, why is it important to consider whether there are public goods or externalities involved? Can you give examples of government expenditures on goods that do not involve public goods or externalities? If so, explain why you favor or oppose these expenditures.

9. Does the free rider problem arise in connection with externalities? Explain.

10. Is the noise from crying babies an externality? How, if at all, does it differ from pollution emissions? Is it consistent to argue that the government should deal with pollution but should not regulate the noise from crying babies? Explain.

chapter 3
Public Choice

IN the last chapter we saw that externalities and public goods generally lead the price system to produce inefficient results. This conclusion implies that it is *possible* for government to intervene with a policy that will lead to a more efficient allocation of resources. The existence of market failure, however, does not mean that government intervention will always improve the situation. To determine whether government will enact and implement policies that promote efficiency or equity, we require a theory of how government functions, and this is what the theory of public choice is designed to supply.

The theory of public choice is the study of how governmental decisions are made and implemented; as such, it essentially involves an analysis of the political process. Public choice theory tries to explain what government *actually does* (or *will do* under different circumstances), as distinct from an attempt to prescribe what government *should do*. This approach is based on the premise that individuals attempt to further their own interests in their political activities just as in their economic activities. The view that people are schizophrenic—behaving in a greedy and materialistic way in their market transactions but in a public-spirited and altruistic way in the voting booth—is explicitly rejected. The same people who are our consumers and workers in economic models are also our voters and politicians when we study the political process. According to the public choice approach, the difference between political and economic behavior lies not in the differences in human motives but in the rules and institutions governing human interaction in the two spheres.

Basing the analysis of the political process on the assumption that *individual* actions are based on the attempt to achieve personally desired goals does not prejudge the collective results in the form of *governmental* actions. Competitive markets often yield socially efficient outcomes when firms, consumers, and workers try to achieve the greatest gain for themselves. Similarly, some sort of "invisible hand" may also be at work in the political realm. Indeed, it is, at least in part, the purpose of public choice theory to determine whether this is so.

One disclaimer is in order at the outset. Since public choice theory has been seriously studied only for the past three decades or so, we do not have as complete an understanding of political processes as we do of market processes. Therefore, this chapter provides no pat answers and no general model that can easily be applied in all situations. Instead, we only introduce certain topics that recent research suggests have significant implications for the functioning of the political process.

Voting and Resource Allocation

Direct majority voting

Many political decisions emerge from a process of majority voting. We begin by analyzing majority voting directly by citizens as a method of determining the total outlay to be made for the production of a public good. In reality, citizens seldom have the opportunity to determine the output of a public good directly by their votes, but it is still interesting to consider how such a process would work. Although our assumptions are unrealistic, the results of the analysis may be applicable to more realistic settings. In other words, the outcomes of citizens' first electing representatives who then vote on policies may be quite similar to the outcomes of citizens' voting directly on the policies themselves. We will consider whether this relationship holds later.

Assume for simplicity that we have a three-person community composed of individuals A, B, and C. By majority voting, these individuals must determine how much output of a public good to finance through taxes. Suppose that the citizens have decided to divide the total cost of the public good equally among themselves. If the marginal cost for each unit of the good is $30, then each citizen will pay $10 per unit of the good produced. The number of units of output to be produced (and hence each citizen's total tax liability) will be determined by majority voting.

Figure 3–1 can be used to illustrate the voting process. The demand curves of the three voters are shown as d_A, d_B, and d_C; these curves indicate the marginal benefits to each voter from different levels of output. In deciding how to vote, each voter compares the benefits he or she would receive from a change in output with the associated change in tax costs that must be borne. The tax costs are summarized in the line TP_i, indicating the *tax price* per unit of the public good for each voter. Because we are assuming that the public good costs $30 per unit and the voters will share the costs equally, the tax price per unit of output for each taxpayer is $10.[1] Total tax

---

[1] Under all real-world tax institutions, the same tax price does not confront all voters. For example, under a proportional income tax, a voter with twice the income of another would pay twice as much in taxes and hence face a tax price per unit of government output that is twice as high. Although the diagrammatic analysis becomes more complicated, the general conclusions derived in the text remain valid.

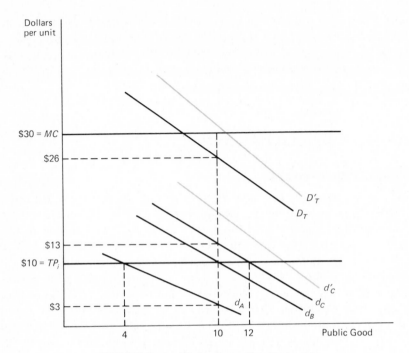

FIGURE 3–1   *Majority voting process.*

liability will depend on the number of units produced. As shown in the diagram, *A* prefers 4 units of output, *B* prefers 10 units, and *C* prefers 12 units. Majority voting will be used to determine a unique level of output.

The process of majority voting can be thought of as proceeding in this way. Beginning at a zero level of output, suppose a proposal is made to provide publicly 2 units, for example, with the costs divided as explained. Each voter compares benefits with tax costs. If the voter is better off with 2 units of the public good provided *and* paying taxes of $20, compared with no tax and none of the public good, the voter will support the proposal. If a majority of the citizens vote in favor of the proposal, it will pass. Even if a proposal for 2 units passes, however, this may not be the *equilibrium* level of output under the voting process. Other proposals to increase or reduce output can be made and voted on. *An equilibrium occurs at the level of output where any proposal either to increase or reduce output would be opposed by a majority.*

Figure 3–1 allows us to identify the equilibrium in the simple setting depicted there. If output is initially zero, all three voters will support a proposal to increase output to 2 units, because the marginal benefits of the first 2 units exceed marginal costs (the tax price) for all three voters. Similarly, a proposal to expand output to 4 units will pass unanimously. At 4 units, however, a proposal to increase output to 5 units will be favored by *B* and *C* but opposed by *A.* Because a majority prefers 5 to 4, output will be increased. The process does not stop here, however, because both *B* and *C* will vote in favor of increasing output to 10 units. Ten units of output is the equilibrium level of output, characterized by the fact that a majority of voters will oppose any change from that level. Note that a majority of voters (*A* and *B*) will oppose any increase beyond 10 units and that a different majority (*B* and *C*) will oppose any reduction below 10 units. Hence, a proposal to provide 10 units can defeat any other proposal; this is another way to describe the equilibrium under majority voting. Ten units of output will thus be provided, and each voter will be assigned a $100 total tax liability to cover the $300 cost of providing the good.

A basic implication of this analysis is that the *median* quantity preferred by voters will be selected by majority voting. Of the three preferred quantities (4, 10, and 12), 10 is the median preferred quantity, with the same number of voters favoring a larger and smaller output. This result generalizes for any number of voters.

Although this model is quite simple, it helps us understand a number of important characteristics of political decision making by majority vote. First, note that the median voter, here individual *B,* is the only voter fully satisfied with the politically determined level of output—everyone else prefers either more or less output. (Of course, in the unlikely case in which everyone had the same demand for the public good, all voters would unanimously agree.) It is *not* accurate to say that majority voting "gives the majority what it wants," because "the" majority that supports any given proposal will seldom agree among themselves.

Second, it is possible to see why so many people feel that government is not responsive to *individual* wants. By its very nature, the political process responds to an individual's wants only when they are in agreement with those of a substantial number of fellow voters; voters with preferences that are quite different from those of the bulk of voters are likely to remain dissatisfied.

Third, majority voting is likely to be unresponsive to *changes* in individual wants. Suppose individual *C*'s demand curve shifts to d_c'. Despite the fact that individual *C* wants a larger quantity of output, the equilibrium level of output remains unchanged. This characteristic is sometimes described by saying that majority voting ignores the *intensity of preferences.* All a person can do is vote yes or no, and an impassioned yes carries no more weight than a weak yes. Only if the median preferred quantity changes is the actual outcome likely to vary.

Finally, there is no inherent tendency for majority voting to produce efficient policies. Recall from Chapter 2 that the efficient level of output is the point at which the summed marginal benefits equal marginal cost. In Figure 3–1, the individual benefits for taxpayers *A, B,* and *C* at 10 units of output are $3, $10, and $13, so the combined marginal benefit is $26. ($D_T$ is the vertical summation of the three individual demand curves.) Because the marginal cost is $30, the tenth unit of output is worth less than its costs. Nonetheless, an output of 10 units is the equilibrium under majority voting. In this case, majority voting produces too large an output. The opposite is also possible. If individual C's demand were d_c' instead of d_c, the summed marginal benefits would be given by D_T', and the equilibrium level of output (still 10) would be lower than the efficient level.

Thus, there is no inherent tendency for efficient outcomes to be produced through majority voting because voting cannot reflect how strongly people feel about the various outcomes. This is not, however, a devastating criticism of majority voting. What is relevant is a comparison of majority voting with other alternatives. Majority voting may produce an outcome closer to the efficient one than, for example, the outcome produced by reliance on private markets. This is certainly likely to be the case for provision of a public good like national defense when the inefficiency of relying on private markets would be huge. However, when the inefficiency of relying on a private market is only slight, as in the case of minor externalities or monopolistic elements, the possibility that majority voting would produce greater inefficiency than leaving matters alone is also a possibility.

Logrolling

The process of majority voting will sometimes lead to the approval of policies that are actually opposed by a majority of voters. One way this can occur is through a process known as *logrolling*. Logrolling is a process of trading votes to achieve the majority necessary for approval. A simple example will indicate why it occurs.

Suppose we have three voters, A, B, and C. Only one voter, C, favors subsidizing college construction. Only one voter, B, favors subsidizing hospital construction. At first glance, it would appear that the proposals for both subsidies would fail under majority voting, because each program is opposed by two of three voters. This, however, may not be the outcome. Individuals B and C could agree to exchange votes to secure passage of their favored proposals. In other words, C could agree to vote for a hospital subsidy (which C really opposes) if B in turn will agree to support the college subsidy that C wants. Depending on how strongly each party wants a particular subsidy, the exchange of votes may be to their mutual advantage. If the exchange takes place, both subsidies will secure the needed majority, although each subsidy is really opposed by a majority of voters.

Figure 3–2 illustrates the effects of the logrolling process in more detail. Assume that the marginal cost of constructing hospitals and colleges is $30 each and that the costs are to be divided equally among the voters. The horizontal axis indicates the level of output of a composite good composed

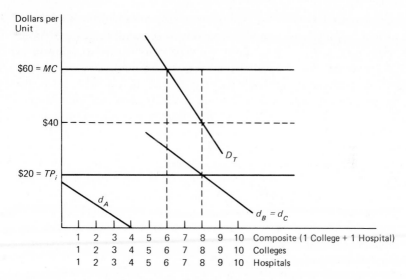

FIGURE 3–2   *Logrolling process.*

of one college plus one hospital; the marginal cost of this composite good is $60. Output is treated as a composite good because logrolling forces voters to consider several proposals simultaneously. Thus, when C votes for a college subsidy, C knows that decision also means a vote for a hospital subsidy. The relevant question concerns C's demand for both programs together. In Figure 3–2, d_C indicates C's demand for the composite good, although C may benefit from only the college subsidy, just one part of the composite good. As drawn, d_B and d_C will coincide. This occurs because the terms of trade in the logrolling agreement—here one college for one hospital—will be negotiated until both agree on what quantity of one to exchange for the other. In terms of the composite good, both B and C agree that 8 is the appropriate output, although they will have different demands for the colleges and hospitals.

The votes on college and hospital subsidies are taken separately, but B and C trade votes, and an output of 8 hospitals and 8 colleges is determined. In this case, logrolling has worked to produce a larger-than-efficient output of both goods. To see this, compare the total marginal benefits and costs at the equilibrium level of output. At an output of 8 units of the composite good, the marginal benefit to B and C is $20 each, whereas the marginal benefit to A is zero. The total marginal benefits are $40, as shown by the vertically summed demand curve D_T. Because the marginal cost is $60, 8 units of output represent too large an output.

Intuitively, the reason that logrolling produces too large an output in this case can be easily seen. Only a majority of voters is needed to achieve passage of the relevant bills. Under logrolling, the majority trade votes on terms that lead them to favor the *same* quantity of the composite good. Put differently, the majority who agree will vote to increase expenditures up to the point that *their* marginal benefits equal the marginal costs they must bear: The combined marginal benefits and marginal costs of B and C are equal at $40 in our example. (Without logrolling, only the median voter's marginal benefits and costs are equal.) There will be a minority, however, who are made worse off, that is, whose marginal benefit is less than their marginal cost, just as A's marginal benefit of zero is less than A's marginal cost of $20 in our example. Thus, the combined marginal costs of all the voters ($60) exceed the combined marginal benefits ($40). Too much is produced when the preferences of all the voters are considered.

An important question is whether logrolling always produces an overexpansion in government spending. Insofar as logrolling agreements arise in order to secure the passage of expenditure bills, the preceding analysis suggests that overexpansion is the result.[2] It is possible, however, that logrolling could block the passage of bills that would, without logrolling, pass. In that case, too low a level of spending would result. Although logrolling to expand expenditures seems more common, logrolling to reduce expenditures is a theoretical possibility.

The process of logrolling is often defended as a means of protecting minority interests. On a particular issue, a minority of voters may passionately favor a particular policy, but under majority voting without logrolling their interests will be ignored, implying a "tyranny of the majority." Logrolling, however, provides a method by which minorities can secure favorable legislation by agreeing to support other policies. Although logrolling can in this way protect minority interests, the relevant question is whether it leads to overrepresentation of minority interests. According to the preceding analysis, when logrolling occurs, it leads to inefficiency because it ignores the minority of voters who are not a party to the logrolling agreement. Too much weight may be given to minority preferences by logrolling.

A final point should be made. Logrolling among individual voters is not likely to occur when there are large numbers of voters (or when there is a secret ballot). In national elections, for example, there is little incentive for individual voters to exchange votes for senators and congressional representatives because it would have no perceptible impact on the final outcome. Logrolling is most likely to occur when a vote trade will have a significant impact on the outcomes of the votes, and that will generally be true only when a relatively small number of votes is required to achieve a majority. Decision making by representatives within legislative bodies apparently involves a small enough number of voters for logrolling to be effective, because it is quite common in such settings.

---

[2]James M. Buchanan and Gordon Tullock, *The Calculus of Consent* (Ann Arbor: University of Michigan Press, 1962).

Electing representatives

In the United States, candidates of the two major political parties run against one another for political office, and majority voting generally determines which candidate will serve.[3] Our general approach can be used to shed some light on the likely outcomes of such elections. Begin by assuming that candidates are distinguishable only in terms of a liberal-conservative spectrum. In other words, candidates will be classified according to how far left or right their policy positions are. Further assume that the voters will support the candidate whose position is closest to their own. Thus, the voter's choice is narrowed to a single issue. Although this is perhaps an oversimplified example, it serves to make some simple but important points.

The distribution of voters according to political ideology is shown by the bell-shaped curve in Figure 3–3. The line drawn at point M separates the total electorate in half; half the voters have positions to the right of this middle-of-the-road position, and the other half have positions to the left. Now consider an election between two candidates, a Republican and a Democrat. If the candidates take positions shown by R and D, who will win the election? Clearly, the Democrat will win because a majority of the voters have political beliefs closer to the Democratic candidate's than to the Republican's. A dashed line can be drawn halfway between R and D, and we will assume that all voters with beliefs to the left of the dashed line will vote for the Democrat and those to the right will vote for the Republican. Voters will then be supporting the candidate whose views are *closer* to their own position.

Faced with this likely outcome, the Republican candidate's chances of winning the election would be strengthened by shifting position to the left. By doing this, the GOP candidate can attract some votes near the middle without losing any support to the right. For example, by taking the position at R', where M is halfway between D and R', the Republican will get exactly half the votes. By staking out a position a little to the left of R', the Republican will get a majority. Of course, the Democrat can change positions too. In the limit, both candidates have an incentive to move to the middle-of-the-road position at M. The voters will be divided between the candidates, and the likely outcome will be a tie vote.

Of course, candidates do not take identical positions, and elections rarely end in ties. The analysis indicates, however, the tendency for politicians to adopt middle-of-the-road positions as they seek voter support. Because they do not have complete and accurate information about voter preferences, this is only a general tendency, but one that accords well with political realities. (As casual evidence to indicate the importance politicians place on discerning voters' preferences, recall the extensive use of polls in recent

---

[3] When more than two candidates are running, the one with the most votes (not necessarily a majority) wins. This is called *plurality voting*.

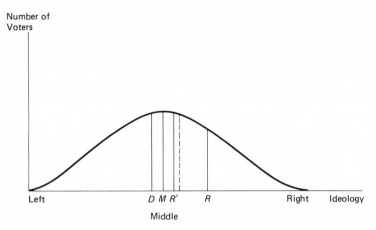

FIGURE 3–3 *Middle-of-the-road politics.*

national primaries and elections.) When a politician has the courage (?) to stake out a position far from *M,* he or she is usually defeated. This happened in the presidential election in 1964 when Senator Barry Goldwater took a position like that at *R,* offering voters "a choice, not an echo," and was soundly defeated. It happened again in 1972 when Senator George Mc-Govern took a position well to the left of *M* and suffered a similar fate. Such occurrences are relatively rare because politicians are astute enough and sufficiently interested in winning to stay fairly close to the middle.

This is simply another example of the importance of the median position in majority voting, because *M* is the median. It does, however, serve to indicate why it is generally correct for voters to feel they are not offered much choice at election time. Insofar as the lack of real choice is a result of politicians' successfully locating the median preference, this outcome is not necessarily bad. In any event, it is what should be expected from competition among politicians for votes.

In many respects, this model is an oversimplified representation of reality. When there are hundreds of policies on which politicians must take positions, it is not possible to compress all of the choices into a single left-to-right continuum. As we shall see, politicians do not always have an incentive to take the median position on every issue (even if they can locate the median).

The cyclical majority phenomenon

There are some situations in which there is no equilibrium under majority voting. No matter what policy is chosen, there is another policy that is favored by a majority. Sound impossible? Consider the situation described in

Table 3–1 Cyclical Majority Phenomenon			
Voters	A	B	C
Ranking	M	L	S
	S	M	L
	L	S	M

Table 3–1. There are three voters, *A, B,* and *C,* and there are three possible policies: a small budget *(S),* a medium budget *(M),* and a large budget *(L).* The ranking of these alternative policies for each voter is given. For example, *A*'s first choice is the medium budget, followed by the small budget, and lastly the large budget. Confronted with two alternatives, each voter will vote for the higher-ranked alternative.

If majority voting is used to select among the three alternatives, the choices must be considered on a pairwise basis. *M* can be pitted against *S,* and the winner of that vote can be pitted against *L.* In a selection between *M* and *S, M* will win, because voters *A* and *B* prefer *M* to *S.* When *M* is run against *L, L* will prevail, because *B* and *C* prefer *L* to *M.* It appears that *L* is the winner until we notice that if *L* is run against *S* (which was defeated by *M* in the first vote), then *S* will win, because *A* and *C* prefer *S* to *L.* To summarize the outcomes: *S* can defeat *L, L* can defeat *M,* and *M* can defeat *S.* There is no equilibrium because every policy can be defeated by one of the others. No matter what is chosen, something else is preferred by a majority. This is called the *cyclical majority phenomenon* because policy choices can cycle from *M* to *L* to *S* to *M* and so on indefinitely.

Understanding how this phenomenon can occur is simple, but appreciating its general significance is more difficult. To some, it has shaken their faith in democracy and majority rule; to others, it is only a theoretical curiosity of little practical relevance. What is really at issue is how often the phenomenon actually occurs in political decision making.

Clearly, there are some situations in which the cyclical majority phenomenon would not occur. In Table 3–1, if *C*'s ranking were *SML* instead of *SLM,* then *M* could defeat both *L* and *S* and represent a stable equilibrium. The cyclical majority phenomenon occurs only when the rankings of voters bear a certain relationship to one another. How likely is it that voters' rankings of alternatives will produce no stable equilibrium? If we assume that all possible combinations of rankings are equally likely, then the cyclical majority phenomenon would occur in about 11 percent of the cases. Some scholars, however, have argued that this overstates the probability of its occurrence, because the rankings that produce the cyclical outcomes are inherently unlikely. As an example, consider *C*'s ranking in Table 3–1: *SLM. C* prefers both extremes—the large and the small budget—to the intermediate position—the medium budget. Although this is conceivable, it is odd, because generally the intermediate position would be preferred to at least one of the extremes. This, for example, is true of the situation shown in Figure 3–1. For any three levels of output that are specified, no voter will prefer both the largest and the smallest output to the one in between. The rankings of voters implied by Figure 3–1 will produce a stable equilibrium: 10 units of output.

This argument implies that when voters are determining how much to spend on one particular project and when the costs are prorated in advance, a stable equilibrium is likely to result. Many political decisions, however, do not fit this description, and it is our view that the cyclical majority phenomenon is quite common in more realistic settings. Let's begin by using an example to illustrate how it might occur. Suppose the government is going to divide $1,000 among 100 voters and initially proposes to give each voter $10. Then someone proposes that the entire amount be divided among 51 voters. The second proposal would defeat the first because 51 voters, a majority, would prefer it. Next a third proposal is introduced: Give a still larger amount to two members of the original 51-member majority (to induce them to change sides) and divide the remainder among the 49 who would receive nothing under the second proposal. The third proposal would defeat the second one. In short, no matter how the $1,000 is divided among the voters, it is always possible to design another proposal that would give less to a minority and more to a majority, and that proposal would be favored by a majority. In this situation, there is no proposal that could consistently defeat all others under majority voting. This example is characteristic of real-world situations when voters select among politicians who take stands on a variety of issues. The reason is that alternative combinations of policy issues have different effects on the distribution of income (that is, on who benefits and who loses) just as in the preceding example.

For example, a politician might favor higher social security benefits, higher tariffs, and higher price supports for agricultural products. The combined impact of these three policies might redistribute income in favor of a majority, so the politician could secure majority approval. A second politician, however, might propose a policy package composed of higher food stamp subsidies, higher subsidies to college students, and even higher (than that proposed by the first politician) tariffs. The combined impact of these three policies might benefit a majority when compared with the proposals of the first politician, so the second politician could defeat the first. No matter what combination of policies is proposed, it is always possible to design another combination that would benefit a majority because it is always possible to use government policies to redistribute income in favor of a majority. When all government policies are considered as a package—which is what happens when we choose among political candidates—there is no combination of policies that represents a stable equilibrium under majority voting.

The nonexistence of a stable equilibrium does not mean that we would expect to see constant cycling among alternatives, with no decision ever being reached. Decisions are made simply because when a vote is taken on one issue, or in one election, one of the two alternatives being voted on will necessarily win (barring ties). What the absence of an equilibrium means is that the political decisions actually reached are not favored by a majority over all other alternatives.

Another possibility raised by the cyclical majority phenomenon is that a policy can be selected that will make everyone worse off. This is illustrated in Table 3–2, in which the value of each of four policies for the three voters is given. Two of the three voters (A and B) prefer policy II to policy I, two of three voters (B and C) prefer policy III to policy II, and two of the three voters (A and C) prefer policy IV to policy III. It is therefore possible that a series of majority votes will lead to the selection of policy IV, in which all three voters are worse off than with policy I.

At least two important insights can be obtained from an understanding of the cyclical majority phenomenon. First, underlying inconsistencies in government policies should be expected. Minimum wage laws that create unemployment coexist with job training programs to put the unemployed to work. Farm price supports raise the cost of food to the poor, but food stamps lower the cost. Some subsidies (such as aid to colleges) tend to benefit the relatively affluent, others benefit the poor, and still others benefit middle-income families. It is not possible to examine actual policies and infer a consistent set of "social priorities," because choices through the political process should be expected to be inconsistent. The group of voters who form an effective coalition favoring farm price supports is different from the group favoring food stamps. Because the preferences or priorities of the different groups and individuals differ, there is no reason to expect political choices to be consistent. Some political choices reflect the domi-

Table 3–2 *A Voting Sequence That Leaves All Voters Worse Off*

	Value of Policy to Each Voter		
Policy	Voter A	Voter B	Voter C
I	$1,000	$1,000	$1,000
II	1,200	1,200	400
III	600	1,300	600
IV	800	800	800

nance of the views of one group, and others reflect the dominance of a different set of values.

Second, an underlying instability in government should be expected. No matter what the government does, an astute politician can always find a new policy package that will secure majority approval. This suggests that government may provide no stable framework of laws, taxes, and expenditures within which individuals can confidently plan their lives. Frequent change can be predicted. Of course, if voters believe a stable framework is important, they may place limits on the types of policies governments can enact. Presumably, this feeling underlies the views of those who favor constitutional limitations on the power of government.

We must be cautious of attaching too much importance to the cyclical majority phenomenon. Perhaps voters' underlying preferences effectively limit the range of issues over which cycling can theoretically occur, or actual political institutions may operate to make the phenomenon occur more rarely than theoretical considerations would suggest. At this stage in the development of public choice theory, the significance of the problem is unknown.

Participants in the Political Process

Many different groups of people influence government decisions: voters, politicians, government employees, lobbies, judges, the media, intellectuals, and so on. Examining the incentives confronting some of these participants and their likely behavior can contribute to a broader understanding of the political process.

Voters

It is appropriate to begin by considering citizens in their role as voters. The voting public elects many government officials and thereby empowers them to make and enforce government policy. The voting decisions of the public therefore determine who will run the government and indirectly influence the policies enacted. Given the importance of the role played by voters, it is instructive to examine their behavior to ascertain if they have incentives to seek out and support political candidates who favor efficient and equitable government policies.

Many factors influence a person's vote: a candidate's personality; spouse; wit; honesty; and ethnic, religious, and regional background. Naturally the candidate's position on policy is also likely to be important. Other things being equal, voters will favor the candidate whose policies they believe will yield them the greatest net benefits (or smallest net costs). Voters will cast votes in an attempt to further their self-interest. This is not necessarily bad; recall that the pursuit of self-interest in a competitive price system generally tends to produce socially desirable outcomes. It is, in fact, this characteristic of voters that gives political candidates an incentive to formulate policies that benefit the public.

The basic question is whether voters will tend to favor policies that are efficient, that is, policies that have total benefits in excess of costs. In answering this question, it is helpful to distinguish between two different cases in which a policy will benefit a specific voter. In one case, a policy benefits voter A *and* involves total benefits in excess of total costs when the effects on all persons are considered. In this situation, the policy is an efficient one, and the voter will support it (and the candidate who favors it, other things being equal). In the second case, a policy benefits voter A *and* involves total costs greater than total benefits. This policy is inefficient; yet voter A will still support it because it benefits him or her.

There is no inherent tendency for voters to support efficient government policies. Even the most inefficient policies generally benefit some groups of voters (although at greater costs to the rest of the public), and those who benefit will support them. Thus, we can expect producers to support higher tariffs on competing imported products, dairy farmers to support higher milk price supports, nonsmokers to support limitations on smoking in public, the elderly to support greater social security benefits, and college students (and professors) to support higher subsidies to colleges. We do not mean to prejudge all of those policies as necessarily inefficient or inequitable, but only to suggest the importance of the pursuit of personal gain in motivating voters. People are not narrowly *self*-interested in their market behavior and then *public*-interested in the voting booth. Instead, they strive to obtain whatever goals they have through both processes. In short, voters are more interested in whether policies benefit *them* than in whether policies are efficient or equitable in some broader context.

Actually, voters are seldom given the opportunity to express a preference on a single policy. Instead, they must choose among candidates offering different bundles of policies. In this setting, voters can easily justify supporting a candidate who favors a policy greatly in their interest. A college student is likely to support a candidate who will halve college tuition. Although this clearly augments the student's wealth at the expense of the general taxpayers, the candidate also favors a multitude of other policies that benefit other groups. The student, in rationalizing his or her vote, can claim that the candidate has "something for everyone" and that the tuition subsidy indicates that the candidate has a deep concern for college students as well as other groups. Most voters no doubt believe they act "in the public interest," but people have an amazing capacity to believe (like General Motors) that what benefits them is good for the country. Sometimes it may be true, but not always.

The behavior of voters is strongly conditioned by another influence, the tendency of voters to be rationally ignorant of the consequences of their political choices. *Rational voter ignorance* is one of the most important forces operating in the political process, and it has far-reaching effects. Rational voter ignorance can best be understood as the hypothesis that voters will be relatively less informed about their political decisions than about comparable private market decisions. It does not mean that people have perfect information in the marketplace and zero information about activities in the public sector. Because acquiring information involves costs, people will seldom be perfectly informed about any choices they make.

To see why voters are rationally ignorant, let's compare the amount of information collected (and the relative costs) by a person considering the purchase of private health insurance in contrast to a voter's decision whether or not to support a national health insurance policy. To make a wise choice about private health insurance, a person would like to have a great deal of information: the types of illnesses covered by the policy, the costs of different parts of the policy, the probabilities of contracting the illnesses covered, the costs of being treated for all these illnesses, and so on. Clearly, few people will acquire all the needed information, and this behavior is rational, given the cost of acquiring information.

To evaluate national health insurance proposals, however, much more information is required. To make an informed decision, a person would need to know not only all of the above facts about alternative proposals but also how much of a tax burden the voter would bear (not an easy matter to determine), the likely impact of alternative national health insurance schemes on medical care and other prices, how the cost controls in the plan will actually affect the voter, and so on. In short, the voter needs a great deal more information to make a wise decision about the government policy, and the additional information is of a different nature, because it is more like knowledge that requires scientific research to substantiate.

The higher information cost is one reason to expect voters to be relatively uninformed in their political decision making. In addition, there is a second reason that is perhaps of even greater importance. The gain that a person can realize from acquiring political information is much less than the gain from acquiring information about goods purchased privately. Suppose a person spends several months researching national health insurance; what are the benefits? The voter can patriotically cast a better informed vote, but it is only one vote among millions, and it will have no perceptible effect on the outcome. The same national policy is almost certain to be enacted, regardless of whether any single person is well informed. Consequently, people have little incentive to obtain information about the operation of the government, the actions of politicians, or the effects of government policies. In contrast, the purchase of private goods is different. If a person becomes better informed about alternative private health policies, the consumer will receive the benefits of choosing the one better suited to his or her needs. The consumer's private choice is decisive in influencing the outcome, which contrasts sharply with his or her voting decision. In the marketplace, the benefits associated with becoming better informed are greater, the costs of information are lower, and the consumer will acquire more information.

We should stress that voter ignorance is rational. Observers often bemoan the lack of knowledge and interest on the part of voters, but no amount of cajoling is likely to effect a change. It is far more important for most people to obtain information of use in their daily lives than to engage in scientific research on social problems.

The existence of rationally ignorant voters has important repercussions for the workings of the political process, because the political process caters to voters as they actually are, not as they would be if they were fully informed. For example, rational voter ignorance accounts for the generally low level of political discourse. Political speeches (as well as newspaper editorials) often rely on slogans, oversimplifications, inadequate theories, and misleading facts. Appearances and plausibility count for more than truth. Voters lack the necessary information to evaluate the assertions made by politicians, which in turn gives politicians little incentive to achieve accuracy and balance in their views.

Although voters will generally be rationally ignorant about most government policies, some voters will be relatively more informed on certain issues. Dairy farmers are likely to know more about how milk price supports affect them than is the remainder of the public. When the consequences of a policy for some voters are desirable or disastrous and involve large benefits or costs, the affected voters are more likely to realize whether or not they will benefit. In these cases, the benefits of acquiring more information exceed the costs, and the affected groups will be better informed. Often voters will base their voting decisions on a small subset of policies that affect them strongly. It may be rational for college students to favor the candidate who wants higher tuition subsidies. The students know they will directly benefit from that policy but find it difficult to determine what the net effect of all the other policies favored by their candidate would be for their welfare. This type of reasoning often leads voters to evaluate political candidates almost wholly on the basis of a few issues that affect them directly. As we shall see, this is one reason for the prevalence of special interest legislation.

As another example, voter ignorance is the explanation for the frequently noted tendency of politicians to emphasize the obvious and short-term effects of policies while ignoring the hidden, long-term consequences. It is well known that an incumbent president is extremely concerned with the state of the economy just before the election. Reducing the unemployment rate by November may be a good strategy even if the cost is a higher rate of inflation several months later. Voters may not be aware of the long-run costs of reducing unemployment quickly, nor will they make the connection later.

An additional issue concerning voters is the decision to vote itself. Only 40 to 60 percent of potential voters actually cast ballots in national elections. In fact, it is easier to explain why people do not vote than why they do. Each individual's vote will have no perceptible effect on the outcome of an election, so there can be little benefit expected from influencing actual policy. In addition, perhaps some potential voters may feel as a bumper sticker during a recent election cynically noted, "Don't Vote: You'll Only Encourage Them!"

Politicians

Those who seek office and those who hold elected offices play a role in politics similar to the role of businesspersons in private markets. Businesspersons are the moving force in markets: They make the actual decisions concerning what to produce and in what quantities. Similarly, politicians—at least successful ones—determine what government does; their voting and logrolling activities determine the broad outlines of government policy. To stay in business, businesspersons are led to take account of consumers' interests by having to produce a product that consumers want. Likewise, politicians are led to take voters' interests into account by having to offer a policy "package" that attracts enough voters to stay in office. In both the political and the market spheres, the process used to make decisions gives us some reason to believe that the public's interest will be served.

The analogy between political and business entrepreneurs cannot be pressed too far, because there are important differences. A businessperson does not require approval of a majority of the public to operate a business; yet a politician frequently does. A businessperson cannot force any consumer to purchase a product, but a politician's programs are financed by taxes levied on many who opposed the programs. A businessperson offers wares for sale, one at a time, day after day, in competition with numerous other competitors, but a politician sells a package of hundreds of policies once every several years, and generally in competition with only one other candidate. These differences are not intended to imply that one process is any better than the other, but only that the market and political processes differ in many ways.

In trying to understand the behavior of politicians, public choice specialists have found it useful to assume that politicians behave in a way that they believe will maximize the votes they receive at the next election.[4] This is not a cynical assumption, but a realistic one. Elected officials will remain in office only if they continue to attract enough voter support. Political survival requires that politicians pay attention to the vote-gaining and vote-losing

---

[4]Alternatively, it might be assumed that they will just attempt to achieve a majority of the votes cast. In most cases, it would make little difference which assumption is made.

effects of their actions, just as business survival demands attention to the profit picture. Successful politicians—the ones who actually make government decisions—will be the ones who are best at attracting votes. Politicians may believe they are acting "in the public interest" (and indeed may be, according to their own conception of the public interest), but they would not be successful unless their actions *also* attracted votes.

The important question is: What type of government policies will result from an attempt by politicians to maximize votes? This is a complex question, and one to which public choice theory as yet provides no complete or simple answer. In trying to determine an answer, two points should be recalled. First, politicians are elected on the basis of their positions on many issues; the overall "package" offered in comparison with that of competing politicians is what counts. Politicians thus need not please the majority on each separate issue. Second, the voters are rationally ignorant of much of what politicians stand for, their past actions, and the likely consequences of their proposed policies.

The importance of these points can be illustrated by looking at some examples. Consider a politician who must take a position on the three policies listed in Table 3–3. Each program benefits only 20 percent of the voting public. Yet a politician who opposes all three policies might be defeated by another who favors them. The reason is that each group benefits by one of the policies and may secure benefits in excess of the harm done to it by the other two policies. Farmers, for example, may believe the higher taxes they would pay to finance the college and welfare subsidies will be less than the gain they would receive from higher price supports; in their view all three policies are better than none. If all three groups feel this way, they will vote for a politician favoring all three policies when the alternative is a politician opposing all three.

This example illustrates how *special interest legislation* may be passed, even though a large percentage of the public is harmed. Special interest legislation can be thought of as policies that yield large individual benefits to a small proportion of the public, coupled with small individual costs falling on a large proportion of the public. For example, a policy may grant benefits of $1,000 a year to 2 percent of the voters, at costs of $25 a year to the remaining 98 percent. A politician may win votes by favoring this policy.

Table 3–3   Implicit Logrolling

Policy	Favored by	Opposed by
Farm price supports	20%	80%
Welfare assistance	20%	80%
College tuition subsidy	20%	80%

The candidate is almost certain to gain the votes of the 2 percent who are benefited, regardless of the politician's position on other issues (at least, in comparison to an opponent who opposes this policy). Moreover, the candidate may not lose much support among the remaining 98 percent, even though this policy harms them because the damage done is small and may be offset by benefits under other policies he or she supports.

In effect, special interest legislation that enables a politician to put together an overall majority by combining numerous programs that benefit separate minorities is an example of *implicit logrolling.* As noted earlier, logrolling makes voters consider different policies simultaneously, and that is exactly what must be done when voters choose among candidates offering different policy packages. In this way, voters are led to support a politician who favors some policies they do not want to obtain the one program they do want.

Rational voter ignorance often increases the incentive of politicians to favor special interest legislation. The harm done to each member of the majority by one policy is quite small and in many cases difficult to estimate. (What annual cost do you bear from milk price supports or subsidies to airports?) Voters are often rational in not making an attempt to estimate the damage done from hundreds of policies that affect them only slightly and often indirectly. Instead, they concentrate on policies that have large and obvious effects on their own well-being, that is, on special interest legislation that benefits or harms them.

Rational voter ignorance has still other effects on the behavior of vote-maximizing politicians. Any policy has both costs and benefits, but the visibility of these effects (that is, how obvious they are to voters) varies widely from policy to policy. Some consequences of policies are more hidden and difficult than others are for the average person to perceive. For example, a policy with hidden benefits but apparent costs is unlikely to be favored by politicians, because voters underestimate the true benefits. The political process is consequently biased against policies with hidden benefits and visible costs. Conversely, it is biased toward policies with highly visible benefits and hidden costs.

Consider a policy of subsidizing medical research out of general income taxes. The benefit is an increased probability of finding a cure for some disease, but many voters who might benefit in the future if a cure is found are likely to be unaware of this benefit (some would not even be born). The tax costs, on the other hand, are quite obvious. If voters sufficiently underestimate the benefits, politicians may be led to oppose the policy even if it is efficient.

In fact, politicians may have incentives to design policies in ways that make benefits clear to those who benefit and costs difficult to perceive for those who are harmed, if it is possible. The most obvious costs are generally taxes, but even these can often be levied in a way to obscure their burden.

Taxes that are nominally paid by businesses often are actually borne by consumers or workers, but the people who bear the final burden may be unaware of it. Corporate income taxes, excise taxes, customs duties, the employer portion of social security taxes, and deficit finance are all methods of financing expenditures that depress the disposable incomes of people who are probably unaware of it. It is probably no accident that nearly 50 percent of all federal expenditures are financed by these methods.

Although it is impossible to be very precise in this matter, it seems clear that vote-maximizing politicians are sometimes led to favor genuinely efficient policies and sometimes to favor highly inefficient policies. *All other things being the same,* the greater the total benefits received by the voting public relative to the total costs of some policy, the more votes a politician can gain by supporting it. This is the positive aspect of the incentives political institutions give politicians. Other things, however, are not always the same, and politicians can sometimes gain votes by favoring policies that benefit some voters but impose greater (possibly hidden) costs on others.

Bureaus and bureaucrats

Congressional actions can be thought of as expressing a collective *demand* for public services, but there is also a need for an institution to design and implement policies. Government agencies or bureaus are generally empowered to carry out the policies enacted by Congress. Recent research has suggested that bureaus do not simply passively respond to the dictates of Congress, but, instead, take an active role in the decision-making process and exercise some degree of power in determining policy.

The term *bureaucracy* is often used to refer to any large organization, but it is necessary to recognize important differences between public and private bureaus. Private bureaus are usually part of a business organization that is operated for a profit, so the activities of private bureaus are subject to a market test: They must produce something that people are willing to purchase. Government bureaus are nonprofit organizations that do not sell their services directly to the public. In a sense, they sell their services to Congress, but they do not set a price per unit and allow Congress to determine quantity. Instead, they obtain an annual lump-sum appropriation to cover the total costs of all the services provided. In addition, public bureaus, as distinct from private bureaus, are generally monopolies. The Department of Health and Human Services, for instance, is responsible for almost all policies dealing with medical care; there are no other bureaus competing with it to obtain funds from Congress in this area.

Given these differences between public and private bureaus, we should expect that the bureaucratic supply of public services would produce different results than the private supply. To see how the results are likely to differ, let's begin by considering what goals might motivate the top-level bureaucrats. Bureaus are not allowed to operate at a profit, so we cannot assume that they try to maximize profits. Alternatively, however, bureaucrats can attempt to maximize the total size of their budgets.[5] A larger budget will generally mean higher salaries, more power, and more prestige for top-level bureaucrats. In addition, the internal advancement of personnel virtually ensures that those who reach the top will consider the activities of the bureaus highly beneficial and worthy of enlargement.

Assuming that bureaucrats attempt to maximize their budgets is not equivalent to assuming that they will be successful. (Recall that competitive firms are assumed to maximize profits; yet they end up with zero economic profits.) Congress, after all, must approve budget requests. Bureaus, however, may be in a favorable bargaining position to realize their goals. From observing congressional action over a period of years, bureaus have a fairly good idea of the maximum budgets Congress will approve. By proposing a budget of this size on a take-it-or-leave-it basis, the bureau may secure approval of a budget larger than Congress would actually prefer.

If the proposed budget is larger than Congress desires, why doesn't Congress just appropriate a smaller amount of money? The answer is that the entire legislative body does not know the actual costs associated with various programs overseen by the bureau. Legislators have to oversee thousands of different programs, and lack the time or the incentive (because their constituents are rationally ignorant) to become informed about the program costs and options in each area. Members of Congress must rely heavily on what the experts (frequently from the bureaus!) tell them about costs and benefits. In this setting, the typical congressional representative has little option but either to approve or to disapprove the bureau's proposed budget. A representative may vote to approve a budget that is larger than the one he or she would support if aware of the relevant alternatives. The all-or-nothing nature of the choice confronting members of Congress, together with lack of information, makes it possible for bureaus to secure overlarge budgets.

This analysis suggests that the interaction between Congress and government bureaus has a tendency to produce budgets that are too large. There are factors, however, that may limit this tendency. For example, Congress may take a more active and informed role in determining bureau policy, perhaps by employing its own experts (e.g., the Congressional Budget Office) to help formulate policy alternatives. In addition, the tendency toward overexpansion probably does not operate with equal force for all bureaus. If the policies being administered are sufficiently simple and easy to understand, Congress will not have to rely so much on the bureau for advice and can more effectively monitor the bureau's activities. Simplicity, then, from

---

[5]William A. Niskanen, Jr. *Bureaucracy and Representative Government* (Chicago: Aldine-Atherton, 1971).

the bureau's point of view, may have its drawbacks; bureaus may be led to make the policies so complicated that they can be understood only by the bureau's own experts.

Bureaus may also have incentive to produce a different type of service than would be provided by competitive firms under identical cost and demand conditions. C. M. Lindsay observed that the "product" of a bureau is usually a complex good with many characteristics that can be produced in different proportions.[6] For example, hospital care can be provided in lavish rooms with little attention from doctors, or with much attention from doctors in sparsely furnished rooms. Lindsay argued that some characteristics are more visible and easily monitored than others are. Just as voter ignorance may lead politicians to neglect policies with hidden benefits, ignorance on the part of politicians may lead bureaus to provide highly visible and easily measured services at the expense of other, possibly more important, services. As evidence supporting this hypothesis, Lindsay examined the operation of Veterans Administration hospitals and found that they provide small quantities of "invisible" services (e.g., the quality of service) but relatively large quantities of highly "visible" services (e.g., average lengths of stay for patients in hospitals).

To see how this concept of relative visibility may sometimes give bureaucrats perverse incentives, consider the Food and Drug Administration (FDA). Amendments in 1962 gave the FDA the authority to withhold drugs from the market until they were proven safe. A bureaucrat administering this program can impose costs on the public in two quite different ways. First, genuinely effective drugs can be withheld too long, causing suffering and death because of the unavailability of the drugs. Alternatively, dangerous drugs can be approved for sale, causing suffering and death from their use. These two errors differ greatly in their "visibility." Those who become ill or die because drugs are not marketed are unlikely to know enough to blame the FDA for the delayed introduction of the drug. If, alternatively, the FDA mistakenly approves a dangerous drug such as thalidomide, the subsequent suffering will be readily connected with its cause. Faced with these alternatives, which type of mistake would you expect the FDA to make more often? It seems likely that the FDA would be overly cautious and delay the introduction of drugs for longer periods of time than the public's interest requires, so as to avoid the possibility of the highly visible disastrous effects of approving a dangerous drug. Empirical evidence suggests that this has, in fact, been true.[7]

---

[6]Cotton M. Lindsay, "A Theory of Government Enterprise," *Journal of Political Economy*, 84:1061 (Oct. 1976).

[7]Sam Peltzman, *Regulation of Pharmaceutical Innovation* (Washington, D.C.: American Enterprise Institute, 1974).

Pressure groups and lobbies

Perhaps the most maligned villains in politics are the organized lobbies, which actively attempt to influence legislators' votes on pending legislation as well as the content of bills brought to a vote. The American Medical Association, agricultural interests, the National Rifle Association, labor unions, the Sierra Club, Common Cause, and many more groups finance lobbies that attempt to influence legislation. To many people, the successes of these organizations exemplify what is wrong with the political process.

Before considering the impact such organizations have on policy determination, we should begin by asking why lobbies exist in the first place. Groups of people often have a common interest in influencing legislation of a certain type, but that does not explain how such lobbies can be financed. A lobby that pushes for a certain type of legislation simultaneously helps all those who will benefit from the legislation; in effect, it provides a *public good* for those who favor the legislation (and a *public bad* for those who oppose it). Thus, the free rider problem will hinder the voluntary formation of lobbies. After all, each one of us has an interest in promoting (or opposing) hundreds of different policies, but we rarely donate money to support lobbies in these areas.

Compared to the hundreds of thousands of "special interests" affected by government policy, the few hundreds of active lobbies are more noticeable for their relative scarcity than anything else. The free rider problem explains why there are not more lobbies, but how can we explain the ones that do exist? One explanation is that lobbies arise when there are relatively few parties greatly affected by a particular type of policy. When small numbers are involved, the free rider problem can be overcome; this probably accounts for the way businesses in a concentrated industry are able to lobby for policies like tariffs. Alternatively, Mancur Olson developed a theory to explain the existence of lobbies in a large number of settings.[8] Often a lobby results as a by-product of an organization that is formed to further some nonpublic good type of interest. Workers often pay dues to labor unions, for example, not to obtain favorable labor legislation from lobbying efforts but, rather, in order to obtain employment (a private good). Unions can use part of the dues to finance the public good, lobbying, for its members; thus, lobbying activities are actually a by-product of union membership. Olson shows how this "by-product theory" can explain the way many important lobbies representing the interests of thousands of people obtain financial support. Nonetheless, the difficulties of overcoming the free rider problem are apparently severe enough that there are relatively few powerful lobbies.

Given the existence of lobbies, are they able to secure favorable legisla-

[8] Mancur Olson, Jr. *The Logic of Collective Action* (New York: Schocken Books, 1968).

tion? Actually, how lobbies will be able to influence legislation is not at all obvious. Politicians are interested in the vote-getting potential of their actions, and the members of unorganized groups (with no lobbies) can vote just as easily as the members of organized groups.[9] To mention an obvious example, Congress passed dozens of pieces of legislation in the 1960s benefiting the poor and elderly, but these groups were not represented by professional lobbies. This legislation was passed because members of these groups represented large voting blocs. Members of groups with lobbies also vote, but they can cast no more votes by virtue of having a lobby than they could without one. How, then, do they represent a stronger political force than an unorganized group does?

Once the prevalence of rational ignorance on the part of voters and politicians is recalled, it is possible to understand how a lobby can have an impact greater than an unorganized group of the same size. Politicians do not have full knowledge of the interests of their constituents: A lobby can inform a politician that there are x thousands of voters with a deep interest in a particular issue. Voters often do not know what politician is most likely to further their interests, but their lobby can inform them, and once informed they are more likely to vote. In a world of rational ignorance, lobbies can probably mobilize more voters and bring these votes to the attention of the relevant politicians more readily than if the group were unorganized. So lobbies may exercise some independent influence on legislative decisions.

Although lobbies can have a differential impact for these reasons, their power is probably much less than popularly supposed. We have already explained why the political process can produce special interest legislation even without lobbies. Lobbies perhaps accentuate the tendency for special interest legislation, but most of the pressure would exist even in their absence.

Public Choice Analysis: Two Examples

At present public choice theory does not provide a formal framework that can be easily applied to the analysis of concrete problems. Rather, it emphasizes a way of looking at the incentives confronting participants in the political process that can give us valuable insights into how government works. The following two examples illustrate attempts to apply this approach.

[9] Richard E. Wagner makes this point in his review of Olson's book "Pressure Groups and Political Entrepreneurs: A Review Article," *Papers on Non-Market Decision Making* (Charlottesville, Va.: Thomas Jefferson Center for Political Economy, 1966), pp. 161–170.

Governmental provision of goods and services

In some cases, governmental units provide goods or services that can also be provided by private firms. This makes it possible to evaluate the performances of these alternative methods of production. Consider the results of several studies that have attempted to make this comparison:

Richard Muth estimated that public housing projects cost about 20 percent more to produce than comparable housing built privately.[10]

In a study of garbage collection in 260 cities, E. S. Savas found that the cost of garbage collection when it was provided directly by municipal governments was about 50 percent greater than when the same service was provided by private firms contracting with cities.[11]

Roger Ahlbrandt found that the cost of providing fire-protection services in Scottsdale, Arizona, where they are provided by a private firm under contract to the community, was 47 percent less than the cost in comparable communities where the services are provided directly by the government.[12]

Sociologist James Coleman, in a controversial study for the National Center for Education Statistics, found that students in private schools performed better academically than comparable students in public schools.[13]

These studies suggest that there may be a general tendency for governmental provision to involve higher costs to provide a given level of service. From a public choice perspective, the basic questions are why this might be the case and whether anything can be done about it.

To understand why government provision of certain goods or services may involve higher than necessary costs, public choice theory suggests we consider the incentives confronting the people involved. Do providers have an incentive to produce the service at the lowest possible cost? In a private firm, if costs can be cut without sacrificing quantity or quality, profits will rise, and the prospect of higher profits gives private firms the incentive to hold costs down. In addition, if costs get out of hand, a private firm may be driven out of business by competition.

A government agency, however, is a nonprofit organization. An administrator of a government agency may not gain by reducing costs. There is no single individual (manager or owner) who receives the "profit" from a successful cost-cutting activity; instead the gain from any cost-cutting endeavor is spread widely among the general (and rationally ignorant) public. In fact,

---

[10] Richard Muth, *Public Housing* (Washington, D.C.: American Enterprise Institute), 1973.

[11] E. S. Savas, *The Organization and Efficiency of Solid Waste Collection* (Lexington, Mass.: D. C. Heath, 1977).

[12] Roger Ahlbrandt, "Efficiency in the Provision of Fire Services," *Public Choice,* 16:1 (Fall 1973).

[13] James Coleman, Thomas Hoffer, and Sally Kilgore, *Public and Private Schools,* Report to the National Center for Education Statistics, for National Center for Education Statistics, by National Opinion Research Center (Chicago: Mar. 1981), Mimeo.

government administrators may actually suffer personal losses from improving efficiency. As a businessman who was asked to manage the postal service
in 1972 noted: "Postmasters were actually paid [based] on how many employees they had, how many branch offices they had, on how many trucks.
. . . Can you imagine a greater disincentive?"[14]

In a government organization, it is difficult to give managers or employees a strong incentive to control costs, since the profit motive is absent.
Some incentives, however, may be provided by Congress or whatever legislative body oversees the organization. But at this level, too, we must consider whether members of Congress have much incentive to perform their
constitutionally mandated oversight function well. Congress passes more than
a thousand pieces of new legislation each year, and the number of existing
agencies, laws, and regulations that Congress is supposed to oversee must
run into the tens of thousands. Knowing how well existing legislation is
enforced is not a prerequisite for election to Congress (with a rationally
ignorant voting public). Members of Congress may be better able to enhance their prospects for reelection by proposing new legislation, giving
speeches, writing to constituents, and so on, than by carefully supervising
the myriad programs already in existence.[15]

When looked at from a public choice perspective, it is thus not surprising
that governmental services may sometimes be provided at unnecessarily high
costs. Whether there is any way to alleviate this problem is not clear. When
the good or service can be provided by private firms and sold to the government, we can make use of market incentives to contain costs by having
government purchase from the private sector rather than provide the good
itself. When the good or service must be provided directly by government,
however, there is no such easy solution.

The political appeal of minimum wage laws

Few government policies enjoy such widespread disapproval by economists
as the minimum wage law. Economists point out that this policy creates
unemployment, especially among the least productive, most disadvantaged
persons, and that a large part of the benefits of the policy go to families that
are quite well off (for example, many teenage members of upper-income
families work for the minimum wage). Despite its disapproval by economists, minimum wage law is firmly entrenched politically, with apparently
little prospect of being abolished. The contrast between the political popularity of the minimum wage law and its undesirable economic conse-

[14] Quoted in Charles Wolfe, Jr., "A Theory of Nonmarket Failure: Framework for Implementation Analysis," *Journal of Law and Economics* 22(1):107–140 (Apr. 1979).

[15] Some casual evidence that Congress is very lax in performing its oversight function is
given by Donald Lambro, "Congressional Oversights," *Policy Review,* 16:115–128 (Spring 1981).

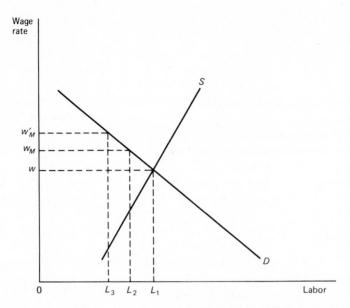

FIGURE 3–4   *A minimum wage policy.*

quences is striking and suggests that this policy may be a good one to examine from a public choice perspective. Can we determine why a minimum wage policy has such strong political support?

To begin, let's compare the numbers of people who are benefited and harmed by the policy, since the relative numbers of gainers and losers is an important political factor. In Figure 3–4, if a minimum wage of w_M is implemented, OL_2 workers will retain their jobs and receive higher pay, and L_1L_2 workers will lose their jobs. At a low minimum wage, the workers who gain outnumber the workers who lose, so a majority of the affected workers would presumably vote for the policy. As the minimum wage increases, however, the number of gainers falls and the number of losers increases. For example, at a minimum wage of w_M', OL_3 workers gain and L_1L_3 lose. At some point, a majority of workers would no longer favor increasing the minimum wage.

Although this reasoning has been offered to explain the political appeal of the minimum wage, it is incomplete because it ignores how the policy affects other people besides unskilled workers. Workers who lose their jobs are not the only people who bear a cost from the minimum wage. Economic analysis implies that the prices of goods produced using unskilled workers will rise and the prices of other inputs used in production will fall. When these costs are taken into account, it seems likely that a majority of the total population would be harmed by a minimum wage. (Fewer than 15 percent of workers are paid wages low enough to benefit directly from the present level of the minimum wage, and most other people are probably harmed by the indirect effects of the policy.)

Simply counting the numbers of gainers and losers from the policy to see which group is more numerous therefore does not adequately explain the political support that minimum wages enjoy. Suppose, however, that the upper-income groups who pay slightly higher product prices are altruistic and desire to help low-wage workers. This group may then not really lose from the policy: The benefits they perceive from helping poor workers may be greater than the costs they bear from higher prices. If this is so, a majority of the total population may actually benefit from the policy, but this argument can also be questioned. Can we really believe that the nonpoor favor a policy that harms the least productive, most disadvantaged groups of poor workers when better alternatives are available? Most economists who have studied these issues believe there are both more efficient and more equitable ways to help the poor if that is the objective. Thus, a desire to help poor workers does not by itself explain why minimum wages, rather than some other policy, would be the favored approach.

This discussion suggests that it is difficult to explain the political popularity of the minimum wage. Up to now, however, we have implicitly assumed that people understand the actual consequences of the policy. Suppose instead we consider the possibility that some voters are rationally ignorant of the effects of the minimum wage. Let's see now how the minimum wage might be perceived by different groups.

Low-wage workers who retain their jobs benefit from the policy, and they are likely to be fully aware of it. They will see their own wages going up as the minimum wage rises over time, so the connection is likely to be obvious. On the other hand, workers who cannot find employment because of the minimum wage are harmed, but it is much less clear that they will connect their inability to find work with the minimum wage. At least, we have rarely heard unemployed persons blame the minimum wage for their plight. So the group that suffers the greatest loss from the policy may not constitute a viable political force opposing the law.

Turning now to the great majority of persons who are not directly affected by the law, how will they perceive its effects? We suggest that this group contains many who are unaware of the unemployment effects of the law. In addition, typical higher-income individuals are probably unaware of the indirect cost they bear in the form of lower wage rates and/or higher product prices. If this is the case, or if they believe incorrectly that employers bear the cost of paying higher wages to the poor, they would be expected to favor minimum wages over other policies like outright transfers in which the cost they would bear (taxes) is more obvious. To many people, minimum wages probably appear to be a policy that helps the poor at no cost to themselves. If this is correct, it is not surprising that nonpoor persons support the policy.

The benefits of minimum wage laws are concentrated on workers who tend to be aware of them, whereas the costs are spread widely among people who are unaware of the extent to which they bear a cost. Seen in this way, minimum wage law is nothing more than an instance of special interest legislation, which was discussed earlier. The fact that the beneficiaries of the policy are widely regarded as poor (which is not entirely correct) and therefore deserving of assistance strengthens the appeal of the policy to those who are not directly benefited by the minimum wage.

Is Government Too Big or Too Small?

Whether the political system is biased toward producing too much or too little government intervention is a question that has attracted considerable attention over the years.[16] This is understandable because not only is it an important question on which people hold strong preconceptions but also it seems that public choice theory should logically be able to answer it. Interestingly, economists have been able to find support for quite different positions on this issue by using public choice theory. The political process is a highly complex mechanism that contains numerous conflicting forces within it, and the quantitative importance of the various forces is as yet unknown.

Anthony Downs, in a well-known article, argued that government spends too little because of rational voter ignorance.[17] He contended that voters typically underestimate the benefits of government expenditures (because they are often "remote" and "uncertain"), and consequently support smaller budgets than they would if they were fully informed. Although Downs recognized several biases in the opposite direction, he feels that they are not as powerful as is the tendency for voters to underestimate the benefits. John Kenneth Galbraith provided a complementary argument by stressing that private advertising may lead people to be more aware of the advantages of consuming private goods than of those of consuming government-provided services.[18]

Alternatively, there are several forces that probably introduce a bias toward overlarge budgets. Buchanan and Tullock argued that logrolling often produces larger-than-efficient spending programs, especially for programs that confer large benefits on a small proportion of the public but with costs spread more thinly over the remaining population.[19] The use of hidden

---

[16] See Anthony Downs, "Why the Government Budget Is Too Small in a Democracy," *World Politics* (July 1960); Buchanan and Tullock, op. cit.; R. Amacher, R. Tollison, and T. Willett, "Budget Size in a Democracy: A Review of the Arguments," *Public Finance Quarterly* (Apr. 1975).

[17] Downs, op. cit.

[18] John K. Galbraith, *The Affluent Society* (Boston: Houghton Mifflin, 1958).

[19] Buchanan and Tullock, op. cit., Chapters 9 and 10.

taxes by government may lead voters to underestimate the true burden and thus approve too much spending. Activities of government bureaus and organized lobbies may also work in this direction.

Balancing these considerations to determine their net effect is a difficult task. Our knowledge of the strength and prevalence of these forces in the political process is not yet adequate to permit a clear-cut answer to the question of whether political forces generally produce too much government. In fact, the question itself is perhaps not well put. There are thousands of different government expenditure policies, and it seems likely that some are too large and some are too small. In other words, the numerous political forces that have been discussed do not operate with equal force for each individual program. In some cases, the forces that produce too much government spending may predominate in determining one policy, whereas the reverse may be true for a different policy. Downs may be correct that for expenditures for which a large portion of the benefits are unperceived, too little will be spent. Many programs, however, do not have large hidden benefits, and some expenditure programs have large hidden costs. Although it is still interesting to consider whether, in some aggregate sense, government spends too much or too little, we should not interpret our answer to mean that all we need do is expand or contract all policies.

Significance of "Government Failure"

For many years economists have studied the functioning of private markets. Circumstances under which markets function well and under which they function poorly are fairly well understood. When markets produce inefficient results, "market failure" is said to occur. Monopolies, externalities, and public goods are now familiar examples of market failure.

Only in relatively recent years have economists (and other social scientists) begun to study how the political process *actually* functions (as distinct from how it would function in some nonexistent utopia). The result of this inquiry is the emerging theory of public choice. It has become clear that there is such a thing as "government failure," that is, government's enacting policies that produce inefficient and/or inequitable results as a result of the rational behavior of participants in the political process.

The public choice approach to the analysis of political decision making should lead to a major alteration in the way government is viewed. Thirty years ago, it was not uncommon for economists, observing that Congress had passed a housing subsidy, to make a statement like "We, the people, through our elected representatives, have decided that housing should be subsidized." As a *partial* description of the forces that shape actual government decisions, which emphasizes the positive aspects of democratic processes, this statement may be adequate. It is, however, incomplete and naive. Just as we should not think that private markets always function efficiently, it is equally incorrect to picture government as always operating to reflect accurately the public's interests.

Public choice theory, with its implication of occasional government failure, is significant for two somewhat different reasons. First, we must keep the possibility of government failure in mind when we evaluate the market and find it not functioning too well in some area. Although one frequently hears the argument "The market has failed; therefore, the government *should* intervene," this is a logical non sequitur. Both the market and the political system are processes for allocating resources and distributing incomes, and each has defects. The fact that the market is inefficient does *not* imply that government will do any better. It is always possible that government intervention will make a bad situation worse. The converse of this non sequitur is also logically invalid. In situations in which the government has performed poorly, it does not follow that the market will necessarily function better. Consider this argument: "The influence of the military-industrial complex has led to great waste in the defense budget; therefore, we should rely on the market to provide national defense." The fallacy is clear. Both types of arguments are still far too common.

In deciding whether the market or the government will produce better results, we must choose between two imperfect mechanisms. The forces that shape both market and government outcomes must be understood in order to make wise decisions. Unfortunately, public choice theory is not sufficiently developed to identify the areas in which government is likely to be relatively inefficient, but it does raise the proper questions, and future research may provide the answers.

There is a second reason why the public choice approach is important. Public choice theory emphasizes how governmental decisions depend on procedures and institutions in the political process and on the incentives created for participants in the process. These institutions and procedures are not sacrosanct; they can be changed. Reform of the governmental decision-making process may lead to better government policies being selected. Although our emphasis in this chapter has been on the way that current political institutions function, public choice theory can also be used to compare alternative methods of making and enforcing government policy.

In recent years, there have been several highly publicized reforms in the political process: Lowering of the legal voting age, easier voter registration requirements, and limits on campaign contributions are examples. As should be clear from the analysis in this chapter, these "reforms" are unlikely to have any significant impact on actual policymaking. They do not in any way modify the important factors we have identified in the political process. They are largely window dressing, exactly the types of reforms we would expect to emerge from current political processes and institutions.

What would a reform that would have major repercussions look like? Consider, for example, the following:

1. Members of Congress shall be determined by a process of random selection from among the general public.
2. Some types of legislation shall require a three-fourths majority, rather than a simple majority, to pass.
3. Decisions on major policy proposals shall be made by direct majority voting by the general public rather than by Congress.
4. Every expenditure proposal shall be linked to a (visible) tax increase so that individual voters can easily determine their share of the cost.

Clearly, these reforms would have far-reaching effects. We do not mean to imply that we think these reforms would necessarily improve the public choice process, but they illustrate substantive proposals for meaningful reform. (The reader will find it an instructive exercise to apply the approach of this chapter to determine the advantages and disadvantages of these proposals.) Even if we can identify desirable reforms, the sticky question remains: Should we expect the imperfect political process to adopt these reforms?

Supplementary Readings

BORCHERDING, THOMAS E. *Budgets and Bureaucrats: The Sources of Government Growth.* Durham, N.C.: Duke University Press, 1977.

BUCHANAN, JAMES M. *Public Finance in Democratic Process.* Chapel Hill: University of North Carolina Press, 1967.

BUCHANAN, JAMES M., and GORDON TULLOCK. *The Calculus of Consent.* Ann Arbor: University of Michigan Press, 1962.

DOWNS, ANTHONY. *An Economic Theory of Democracy.* New York: Harper & Row, 1957.

———. "Why the Government Budget Is Too Small in a Democracy." In Edmund S. Phelps, ed., *Private Wants and Public Needs,* rev. ed. New York: W. W. Norton, 1965.

EDWARDS, GEORGE C., III. *Implementing Public Policy.* Washington, D.C.: Congressional Quarterly, Inc., 1980.

McKEAN, ROLAND N. "Government and the Consumer." *Southern Economic Journal,* 39:481–489 (Apr. 1973).

MUELLER, DENNIS C. "Public Choice: A Survey." *Journal of Economic Literature* 14(2):395–433 (June 1976).

NISKANEN, WILLIAM A., JR. *Bureaucracy and Representative Government.* Chicago: Aldine, 1971.

PELTZMAN, SAM. "The Growth of Government." *Journal of Law and Economics,* 23(2):209–288 (Oct. 1980).

RIKER, WILLIAM H., and PETER C. ORDESHOOK. *An Introduction to Positive Political Theory.* Englewood Cliffs, N.J.: Prentice-Hall, 1973.

WOLFE, CHARLES JR. "A Theory of Nonmarket Failure: Framework for Implementation Analysis." *Journal of Law and Economics,* 22(1):107–140 (Apr. 1979).

YEAGER, LELAND. "Economics and Principles." *Southern Economic Journal,* 42(4):559–571 (Apr. 1976).

Review Questions and Problems

1. In a majority voting model like that illustrated in Figure 3–1, what will be the effect on the equilibrium output if a proportional tax on income is used instead of the equal-per-person tax shown in the diagram?

2. What is rational voter ignorance? Does it lead voters to prefer larger or smaller government budgets than they would if they understood completely the effects of government policies?

3. How would political outcomes differ if majority voting were used to determine the spending on each policy separately instead of having voters elect representatives who then make these decisions?

4. If majority voting is used to determine the output of a public good, will all voters be satisfied with the output selected? Will the output be efficient?

5. You are the chairperson of a three-person committee that is going to use majority voting to decide on which of three dates a test will be given. A vote will be taken on two dates, and the winner of that vote will vie with the third date to determine the final choice. If you know the preferences of the other committee members, can you influence the outcome by deciding the order of the votes? Give an example to support your answer. (*Hint:* Consider the cyclical majority phenomenon.)

6. How does the material in this chapter help you evaluate the following statement: "Private firms pollute too much because they ignore the external costs, so government must intervene to stop them."

7. How can we explain the existence of government policies that are opposed by a majority of voters?

8. "An alternative to majority voting is to require unanimous consent before a program is enacted. This would guarantee that fewer people would be harmed by the policy, whereas some people are always harmed when majority voting is used. Therefore, unanimity is a better voting rule than majority voting is." True or false? Explain.

9. One criticism of majority voting is that voters have no way of registering the intensity of their preferences. Does this mean that a minority that is passionately opposed to some policy will always lose out to a majority that is lukewarmly in favor of it?

10. "Democracy gives the majority what it wants." Discuss.

chapter 4
Principles of Expenditure Analysis

EXPENDITURE analysis involves using economic theory to determine the consequences of government expenditure programs. Unfortunately, there is no general analysis that is applicable to all expenditure programs, because these programs take many different forms. The consequences vary greatly, depending on exactly how the government spends the funds. Consequently, it is necessary to proceed case by case, although some types of programs are clearly more important than others. In this chapter we will examine some of the more significant economic effects of fairly common types of expenditure programs. Later chapters will consider specific programs in more detail.

The economic effects of expenditure programs fall primarily into two categories: allocative and distributive. *Allocative* effects refer to the way an expenditure program affects the pattern of goods and services produced by the economy. For example, does a particular subsidy lead to an increase in the output and consumption of the subsidized good? Although common folklore assumes that a subsidy increases output, some important real-world subsidies have had the opposite effect, at least for some of the people being subsidized. As we will see, subsidies to housing and education can have this effect.

The *distributive* effects of government expenditures refer to their impact on the distribution of real income, or well-being. Put most briefly, who benefits and who loses from the programs? Many government expenditures benefit some groups at the expense of others and consequently redistribute income. Such effects are obviously important but frequently are not self-evident. For example, there is reason to believe that urban renewal programs have actually harmed some low-income families. Similarly, unemployment insurance, subsidies to higher education, and agricultural subsidies have benefited middle- and upper-income families far more than low-income groups.

In this chapter we analyze some of the important effects of three basic types of expenditure programs: expenditures on nonmarketed goods, fixed quantity subsidies, and excise subsidies. In each case, our concern will be with the allocative and distributive effects of these expenditures. In the Appendix to this chapter, we describe benefit-cost analysis, a technique for systematically appraising the efficiency of government projects.

Expenditures on Nonmarketed Goods

Governments spend substantial sums of money to stimulate the production of goods and services that would not be provided by the price system (or, if provided, would be provided in negligible amounts). We call such goods *nonmarketed goods.* Examples include defense programs, foreign aid, and space exploration. Economic analysis of these expenditure programs is somewhat limited, in part because the goods often have the characteristics of a public good so consequently there is no readily available measure of the value of the good to the public. Nonetheless, a few basic points can be made.

Allocative effects

There are two ways the government can spend to stimulate output of some good that is not provided by private markets. One approach is to pay private firms to produce the good. In this case the government expenditure represents a market demand for the good that gives private firms the incentive to produce it. Another way is for the government to hire the resources (labor, capital goods, etc.) itself and oversee the production directly. There are numerous examples of both types of programs. For instance, the government purchases airplanes and rifles from private firms for use in defense activities; in providing postal services, however, the government employs resources and oversees production directly.

Whichever method is used, the allocative effect is to increase the output of the desired good. Moreover, in both cases, resources that would have been used to produce other goods in the private sector are used instead to produce goods in the public sector. Thus, we get more of one good and less of others. This tradeoff is illustrated in Figure 4–1, in which the output in the government sector is measured horizontally and the output in the private sector is measured vertically. ZZ is the production possibility frontier that shows all combinations of these goods that can be produced with available resources. Initially, suppose we are at point C, with the economy producing $0G_1$ in the public sector and $0P_1$ in the private sector. Then the government increases its production so that government sector output increases to $0G_2$, or by G_1G_2. The result is a move to point B. Note that as a consequence, the private sector output falls from $0P_1$ to $0P_2$, or by P_1P_2. The

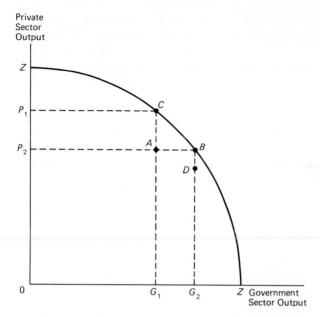

FIGURE 4–1   *Allocative effects of government provision of goods and services.*

opportunity cost associated with the increase in government output, G_1G_2, is a loss of other goods and services equal to P_1P_2. This loss reflects the fact that the resources used in the government project must be drawn from the private sector, where they would have been used to produce other goods and services.

Government expenditures that stimulate the output of some nonmarketed good therefore have an *opportunity cost* that takes the form of a reduction in other goods and services in the private sector. This is an extremely simple point but one that is frequently overlooked. Government-provided goods and services, even though they are not sold directly to the public, are not free. Yet this does not mean that they may not be worthwhile. Quite possibly the benefits accruing from the G_1G_2 increase in government sector output are greater than the costs associated with the P_1P_2 sacrifice of other goods. In Chapter 2, for example, we saw that there are cases in which the price system would not provide some goods, even though the benefits exceeded the costs. Here we are only pointing out the nature of the cost involved when the government undertakes to provide some good.

Although private sector output in the aggregate falls with an expansion of output in the public sector, this does not mean that the output of each and every good produced in the private sector will decrease. The output of some goods—those complementary to the government-provided good—could increase. If the government provides recreational areas such as national parks, then motel bookings, and camper and gasoline sales might increase because people would utilize these services while consuming the government's product. In the aggregate, however, the private sector output must fall.

Distributive effects

When the government stimulates the production of nonmarketed goods, the distribution of benefits to different individuals or groups is generally diffi-cult to determine, just as the overall benefit to the public is difficult to ascertain. This is because there are no market prices to register values that people either individually or collectively place on this type of good. Clearly, however, different people may benefit to very different degrees, just as hawks may benefit more than doves do from defense spending. Similarly, outdoor enthusiasts probably benefit more from national parks. Without consider-able information about people's preferences and the specific government-produced good in question, little can be ascertained about the distributional impact of providing the good.

Production inefficiency

Recall that the opportunity cost of increasing government output by G_1G_2 is shown as P_1P_2 in Figure 4–1. Actually, this is the *minimum* possible oppor-tunity cost associated with the production of the government good. Only if the government output is produced in the least costly way will P_1P_2 reflect the actual cost. There are many ways to combine resources to produce the additional G_1G_2 units of product, and some of them will involve a larger sacrifice than P_1P_2. In other words, if government production is inefficient, we could end up at point D in Figure 4–1 when $0G_2$ is produced. This involves a cost (sacrifice of other goods) of DB greater than is necessary to produce $0G_2$. Although D is inside the production frontier, this does not necessarily mean that resources are unemployed. If, for example, resources are misallocated so that labor resources that would be relatively more pro-ductive in producing private goods are used in the government sector, then the economy will be operating inside the frontier.

   Governmental sector output is sometimes produced inefficiently with re-sults like those depicted in Figure 4–1. In the last chapter, we cited several studies that provided evidence of this in specific cases. As we explained, the reasons that such an outcome may occur are found in the incentives con-fronting decision makers in the political process. Designing government ex-penditure programs so that the relevant decision makers have an incentive to provide services in the least costly way is not an easy task. In some cases, it may be feasible to have the government purchase the good from private firms. Because firms are profit oriented, they have an incentive to produce

in the least costly way. Even here, though, some forms of government pro-
curement, such as sealed bid contracting and cost-plus contracts, have led
to inefficiency.

It is not known exactly how important such inefficiency generally is, and
further research in this area is needed. However, the fundamental point is
that expanding government sector output involves opportunity costs in sacrificed private sector output, and sometimes this sacrifice is larger than necessary.

The role of taxes

Considering the opportunity cost of government expenditure programs naturally brings taxes to mind. Because we have discussed the opportunity cost
without any reference to taxation, a logical next question might be what
role taxes play in the analysis of government expenditures. Actually, expenditures involving the use of resources have an opportunity cost irrespective
of how they are financed. In terms of Figure 4–1, private sector output must
fall by at least P_1P_2 when the government project is undertaken. This result
holds regardless of whether the government taxes, borrows, or simply prints
money to finance the spending. Nonetheless, taxes are most often the tan-
gible embodiment of this cost, and it is convenient to think of the opportunity cost of government spending as reflected in the taxes needed to fund
the program.

The exact role of taxes in financing government expenditures is twofold.
First, the tax (or other method of finance) determines the composition of
the sacrificed output in the private sector. As mentioned earlier, P_1P_2 measures the aggregate reduction in private sector output, but whether this reduction is mainly composed of fewer cars, less food, smaller homes, or less
of some other goods depends on the exact method of funding. A tax on
cars, for example, would obviously concentrate the reduction in output more
on cars than a tax on food would. However, the overall reduction in output,
P_1P_2 (considered as an index of all private sector output), would be the
same.[1]

Second, the tax would also determine exactly who will bear the opportunity cost, P_1P_2. Although the opportunity cost for the community is P_1P_2,
different taxes will distribute this burden differently among the public. For
example, a progressive income tax would place a larger share of the cost
on high-income families than would a tax on food.

Clearly, then, the precise method of finance used has allocative effects
(what goods are sacrificed) and distributive effects (who sacrifices these

---

[1]We are ignoring here the fact that some taxes may have a larger real burden than do
others raising the same revenue because of the welfare costs of taxes. This point will be developed when we consider tax analysis in Chapter 10.

goods) of its own, in addition to the allocative and distributive effects of the government expenditure. In a complete analysis of government policies, both tax and expenditure policies must be considered simultaneously. As a practical matter, however, this is seldom feasible, because expenditure programs are not linked to specific taxes. Consequently, expenditure programs are usually analyzed separately, without regard to the precise method of finance. In doing this, however, it must be remembered that the expenditures do have opportunity costs and that these costs normally take the form of a tax that someone must pay.

A more detailed consideration of alternative taxes is postponed to later chapters.

Macroeconomic effects

So far our emphasis has been on the opportunity cost associated with a government project. The conclusion that the private sector output must fall is based on the assumption that the economy is initially operating on its production possibility frontier. In cases of involuntary unemployment of resources, the economy will be operating inside its frontier, as at point A in Figure 4–1. Starting at point A, a government expenditure program could conceivably result in a move to point B, employing previously unemployed resources to produce the G_1G_2 increase in public sector output. Note that the incremental government output does not result in a reduction in output from the private sector.

At first glance, the opportunity cost of government spending might appear to be zero when there is substantial unemployment. This is wrong, but because in one form or another it is a common error, let's consider it in some detail. The error lies in failing to understand that the notion of opportunity cost relates to alternative uses of resources. In Figure 4–1, the alternative to using the unemployed resources in the public sector is to employ them in the private sector. In other words, we could move from point A to point C. (This could perhaps be accomplished by a tax reduction, an increase in money supply, or an increase in cash transfers by government to stimulate employment in the private sector.) Point C is an alternative to point B, so the opportunity cost of using previously unemployed resources in the government sector is that they cannot be used in the private sector to increase output from $0P_2$ to $0P_1$. *The opportunity cost of increasing government output from $0G_1$ to $0G_2$ is thus correctly viewed as P_1P_2 even if resources are initially unemployed.*

A similar error occurs in the frequent discussions of government spending programs that allegedly "create jobs." Government employment of workers in public works or other programs does not "create jobs"; instead it simply induces people to work for the government rather than in the private sector. Government spending diverts workers (and other productive resources) to the government sector. Just as in the preceding case, this is true even when the workers are initially unemployed. The important question is whether the workers' services are more valuable in the government sector or elsewhere, and the concept of opportunity cost forces us to face that question.

In the past, the possible impacts of government expenditures on the overall price level (inflation) were frequently cited by presidents as a reason to veto a particular expenditure bill. This is also a source of confusion. An expenditure program is not intrinsically inflationary if taxes are used to finance the program. If taxes are not used and the government prints money to finance the program, inflation can result, but even then it is not an obvious reason to oppose the program. Inflation can be thought of as a type of tax that reduces the value of cash balances. An objection that an expenditure program is inflationary can then be seen as an objection to the particular type of tax used to finance it. Although it may be true that inflation is more harmful than other taxes are as a method of financing an expenditure program, it must be recognized that the possible inflationary impact of an expenditure program is not a valid objection to the program itself. The same program could be financed by other, noninflationary, means.

Therefore, the potential impact of government expenditures on the overall level of employment, output, or prices is largely irrelevant in an analysis of specific expenditure programs. Where these effects are important is in an examination of the combined impact of monetary policy and all taxes and expenditures on macroeconomic variables. Entire courses on these matters are taught, and our neglect of these issues does not imply that we think them unimportant. As long as there are many policy combinations compatible with full employment, however, macroeconomic considerations provide no method of analyzing and comparing the allocative and distributive consequences of different points on the production possibility frontier (i.e., of different positions of full employment). The assumption of full employment is simply a convenient way to stress the relevant alternatives.

Fixed Quantity Subsidy for Marketed Goods

Much of the recent growth in government spending has taken the form of subsidies for goods that are, or could be, provided through the market mechanism. Subsidies for education, food, child care, housing, job training, old age pensions, energy, and medical care (among others) involve subsidizing goods and services that people would have purchased anyway (but perhaps not in the same quantity). To understand the consequences of such subsidies, we must determine how people—both consumers and producers—respond to the subsidy, and this depends in part on what type of subsidy is used.

A common form of subsidy is one through which the government makes a certain quantity of a good available to a consumer at no cost, or perhaps at a cost below the market price. The essential characteristic of this particular type of subsidy is that the quantity of the good being subsidized is beyond the control of the consumer. We call this a *fixed quantity subsidy* to emphasize that the quantity being subsidized is beyond the control of the recipient; the government determines what quantity of the good is made available at the zero or subsidized price. (This is a form of "in-kind" subsidy, so called because the subsidy is linked to the consumption of a particular good.) For example, the government may provide food stamps that a consumer can use to purchase $1,500 worth of food, but if more than $1,500 worth of food is desired, the consumer must pay for the additional amount at the full market price. Here the subsidy applies only to a given quantity, $1,500 worth of food. Similarly, public schools make available a certain quantity or quality of schooling, and if more is desired, it must be paid for by the consumer. That is, if parents are not satisfied with the education provided by public schools, they can send their children to private schools at their own expense, or if parents wish to supplement their children's education (with tutoring or special classes), they may, but again they must bear the full cost. In both these examples, as well as many others that could be mentioned, the subsidy applies to a fixed quantity of the good being subsidized, with any additional quantities being purchased by consumers at the full market price. Fixed quantity subsidies can have various effects on the consumption and well-being of recipients depending on the size of the subsidy, the good being subsidized, and who pays for the subsidy. These possibilities are examined next.

Reduced private purchases

One major impact of a fixed quantity subsidy is that it causes a reduction in the out-of-pocket expenditures on the subsidized good. Such a reaction on the part of consumers is intuitively obvious, because if the government provides a good, the consumer will need to purchase less on his or her own. There are also situations in which the consumers reduce their out-of-pocket expenditures by an amount equal to the quantity provided by the government, so that their total consumption does not increase.

To illustrate the consequences of this type of subsidy more clearly, consider a consumer whose presubsidy budget line relating the subsidized good to other goods is shown by *MN* in Figure 4–2. The budget line reflects the consumer's income of $1,000 (equal to 0*M*) and the market price of food, $10 per unit (the slope of *MN*). Prior to receiving any subsidy, Percy, our consumer, is in equilibrium at point *E,* consuming 40 units of food and $600 worth of other goods and services.

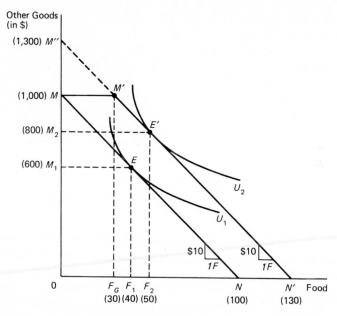

FIGURE 4–2 *Fixed quantity subsidy: reduction in private purchases.*

Now suppose the government gives Percy 30 units of food for free.[2] This means that Percy could consume at point M'—accepting the 30 units of food and spending his income of $1,000 on other goods and services. If he wants, however, Percy may also use some of his own income to purchase additional units of food at a price of $10 per unit. His entire budget line is therefore $M'N'$. The $M'N'$ segment has the same slope as the original bud- therefore $MM'N'$. The $M'N'$ segment has the same slope as the original budget line because Percy must pay the unchanged market price for each unit beyond 30. Note that if the government had given Percy a cash transfer have been $M''N'$. ($M''M$ is the dollar cost of the subsidy.) *The effect of this fixed quantity subsidy on consumption opportunities is the same as a cash transfer, except that the dotted portion of the budget line, $M'M''$, is not available to the consumer.* Actually, if Percy is able to sell some of the food provided by the government at $10 per unit, he could move along the $M'M''$ part of the budget line. It is assumed, however, that resale is not allowed.

Percy's exact response depends on how the budget line is affected, which we have just determined, and on his preferences concerning food and other

[2] It makes no difference to the analysis whether the government provides the consumer with funds that must be spent on food. This is essentially what the food stamp program does, a policy we shall examine in the next chapter.

goods, which we will now consider. If we assume that food and other goods are normal goods, then we know that after receiving the subsidy Percy will choose a point along $M'N'$ involving more consumption of both. This is illustrated by the postsubsidy equilibrium at E' on $M'N'$, with Percy consuming 50 units of food and $800 worth of other goods. Recall that at the original equilibrium, E, Percy purchased 40 units of food; after the subsidy, his consumption of food has increased by only 10 units, even though the government provides 30 units of food. Percy's *private* food purchases have fallen from 40 ($0F_1$) to 20 (F_GF_2) in response to the subsidy, but *total* consumption has risen to 50. Note also that the subsidy has allowed the consumption of other goods to increase. Before the subsidy, Percy spent $400 on food and $600 on other things; after the subsidy Percy spends $200 of his own income on food (and receives a $300 subsidy) and has $800 left for other goods and services.

A reduction in private purchases should be expected with a fixed quantity subsidy. As long as the quantity provided by government (30) is less than the consumer would purchase if given the subsidy in the form of cash (50 units would be consumed with an unrestricted cash transfer), this type of subsidy is equivalent in its effects to a cash transfer. Thus, consumption of the subsidized good increases only to the extent that the consumer would choose if given money instead of food.

Unchanged total consumption

So far our analysis of the consumer's response to a fixed quantity subsidy has neglected the taxes required to finance the subsidy. There are two possibilities to consider. First, someone other than the subsidy recipient may pay the required taxes. In that case, our previous analysis is complete, at least insofar as the effect on the recipient is concerned. Second, the recipient of the subsidy may also pay taxes to finance the subsidy, just as many families pay taxes to finance the schools their children attend. In this case, it is worthwhile to consider the combined effects of the tax and subsidy on the consumer's choice and well-being.

Figure 4–2 can be reinterpreted to handle the case in which Percy pays a tax as well as receives the subsidy, at least when it is assumed that the tax is equal to the $300 subsidy received. Although this would not normally be true for all consumers, on average the tax paid must equal the subsidy (if the program is self-supporting), so this is a convenient starting point. Suppose, then, that Percy's before-tax-and-subsidy budget line is $M''N'$, his income is $1,300, and he is in equilibrium at point E'. A tax of $300 would shift his budget line to MN. When the government returns the tax to the consumer in the form of 30 units of food, Percy's post-tax-and-subsidy budget line becomes $MM'N'$. Thus, the combined tax-expenditure policy leaves Percy's budget line completely unchanged, except for making it impossible

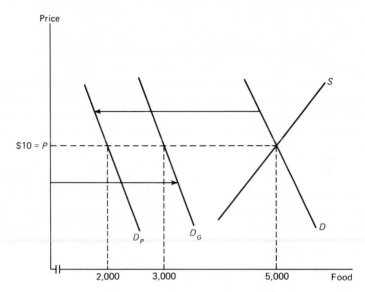

FIGURE 4–3 *Fixed quantity subsidy: unchanged total consumption.*

to consume along the original $M'M''$ portion. If Percy would not have chosen a point in this region anyway, as is true for the indifference curves shown, he ends up purchasing the same quantities of food and other goods after the tax plus subsidy as he did before.

Now let's consider how this subsidy affects the overall market for food. In Figure 4–3, the original equilibrium, with 100 consumers each consuming 50 units, is shown by the intersection of the demand and supply curves. When the government taxes the consumers and uses the revenues to purchase food for them, two things happen. First, the consumers' private demand for food falls from D to D_P, resulting from the combined effect of the tax and subsidy. Second, the government now has a demand for food, shown as D_G. As we have seen, the government demand tends to be offset by a reduction in private demand. The post-subsidy-and-tax demand is the horizontal sum of the private demand, D_P, and the government demand, D_G. Thus, the aggregate demand, D, is unchanged, and the price and output of food remain unaffected.

These conclusions suggest that many government expenditure programs may have little or no effect on the allocation of resources. Government spending may simply replace private spending. However, our analysis depended on a number of assumptions concerning the nature of the subsidy. In some cases these assumptions are not appropriate, and by modifying the analysis we can determine when and how this type of subsidy can affect resource allocation.

Overconsumption

When the consumer receives the subsidy but pays no taxes, Figure 4–2 shows how this fixed quantity subsidy can have exactly the same effects as a cash transfer of equal cost. There are times, however, when a fixed quantity subsidy will increase consumption by more than a cash transfer. This happens when the quantity provided by the government is greater than the consumer would purchase if he or she had cash rather than the in-kind subsidy. Consider Figure 4–4. MN is the presubsidy budget line with a consumer, Sybil, purchasing F_1 units of food. If the government provides F_G units of food at no cost, the budget line will shift to $MM'N'$. Given the consumer's preferences as shown by her indifference curves, her new equilibrium is at point M'. If Sybil had been given cash equal to the cost of the subsidy (MM''), her budget line would have been $M''N'$, and she would have consumed less food, F_2, at E'. In this case, the fixed quantity subsidy has

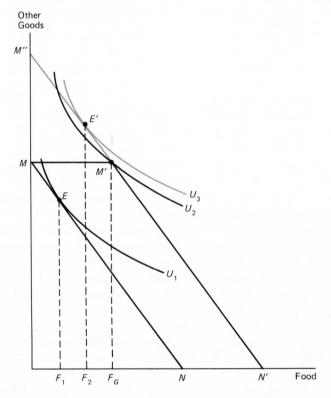

FIGURE 4–4 *Fixed quantity subsidy: overconsumption.*

increased consumption more than a cash transfer would have. Note, however, that Sybil would have been better off if given cash. That is, with a cash transfer equal to the cost of the subsidy, Sybil would be on indifference curve U_3; with the in-kind subsidy she is on U_2, a lower indifference curve.

A fixed quantity subsidy can also increase consumption when the consumer pays taxes equal to the cost of the subsidy. In this event, $M''N'$ is the before-tax-and-subsidy budget line, MN the after-tax budget line, and $MM'N'$ the after-tax-and-subsidy budget line. In this situation, Sybil's equilibrium changes from E' to M', involving a higher level of food consumption. Note, however, that although food consumption increases, Sybil is worse off; she was on a higher indifference curve at E' than at M'. This is because a government subsidy does not increase consumption possibilities when the recipient must pay the tax. Note that total expenditures on food and other goods are unchanged. The only effect of the subsidy cum tax is to alter the position along the original $M''N'$ budget line from E' to M'. Sybil could have chosen to consume more food at M' in the absence of the government policy, but according to her preferences the additional F_2F_G units of food cost more than they were worth. When the government tax-expenditure policy is in effect, it leads the consumer to consume the additional food and pay for it through taxes, and this understandably makes her worse off.

Thus, when the quantity of the subsidized good provided by the government exceeds the quantity the individual would choose to consume if he or she could spend the subsidy as desired, the subsidy is successful in stimulating consumption. This, however, occurs only when the subsidized quantity is so large that it drives private purchases to zero, leaving the government to determine the level of consumption. Such a policy makes the consumer worse off than he or she would be with no subsidy or tax (in the case in which the consumer pays taxes equal to the subsidy) or with an equal-size cash subsidy (in the case in which someone else pays the taxes).

Because the recipient is worse off with the fixed quantity subsidy than with a cash transfer, what is the justification for this type of subsidy? This is a good question. Although there are a number of possible reasons (such as the paternalistic one: "consumers don't know what's good for them"), one is of particular interest to economists. Recall that when consumption of a good involves external benefits, the private equilibrium involves too little consumption. If food consumption generates external benefits, then M' in Figure 4–4 may be a more efficient consumption pattern than E' is. Even though the immediate consumer would prefer to consume less food than at M', other people are better off when the consumer consumes at M' rather than E'. Thus, there can be some justification on efficiency grounds for overriding the consumer's preferences. In the absence of such external benefits (or other sources of market failure), however, a fixed quantity subsidy that leads to overconsumption is unequivocally inefficient.

Underconsumption

It is often taken for granted that a fixed quantity subsidy will increase consumption, but we have seen that in some cases it may lead to the same level of consumption as a cash transfer does. In addition, there are other situations in which this type of subsidy will actually reduce consumption! This paradoxical outcome can occur when it is very costly, or impossible, for the consumer to supplement the quantity of the good provided by government. Earlier we assumed that the consumer could purchase additional units of food at the market price and thereby supplement the subsidized quantity provided. For some types of goods and some types of subsidies, it is very costly to consume more than the quantity provided by the government.

An example will make this clear. Suppose the subsidized good is housing, and the government offers a family a two-bedroom apartment at no cost. The family may prefer a three-bedroom apartment and might be willing to pay the difference in cost between a two-bedroom and a three-bedroom apartment to obtain a larger apartment. The way the program is administered, however, this option is not available. The family cannot accept the government two-bedroom apartment and, by paying the cost of an extra bedroom, convert it into a three-bedroom apartment. Instead they must either accept the two-bedroom apartment or forgo the subsidy altogether and pay the entire cost of housing themselves. In this setting, it is quite possible that the family will choose the two-bedroom apartment when the government foots the bill rather than the three-bedroom apartment they would have chosen in the absence of the subsidy.

Note how the housing subsidy differs from the food subsidy considered earlier. With the food subsidy, the consumer could supplement the subsidized quantity by purchasing additional units of food at the market price. With the housing subsidy, the nature of the good provided by government makes supplementing it costly, if not impossible. Housing is typical of a good that is not highly divisible into small units; it is "lumpy," and to increase the quantity consumed usually requires moving into a larger or better housing unit. A subsidy such as described earlier provides a housing unit of a given size and is therefore difficult to supplement.

Let's see how this looks in the framework we have been using. In Figure 4–5, the presubsidy budget line relating housing and other goods is MN. (Even though housing is "lumpy," the budget line showing market options is smooth, because the family can choose more or less housing when selecting a particular housing unit to rent.) In the absence of any subsidy, H_1 units of housing are consumed. Now assume the government offers the family a smaller (or lower-quality) housing unit of H_2 units at no cost. *The budget line becomes MM'RN.* Note the difference between this and the food subsidy. With the food subsidy the budget line would be $MM'N'$, because

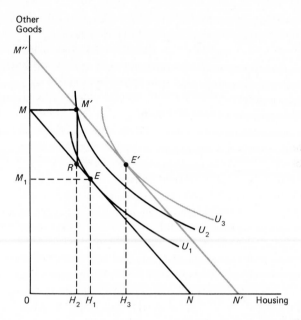

FIGURE 4–5   *Fixed quantity subsidy: underconsumption.*

the consumer could consume more of the subsidized good (to the right of M') by paying only the cost of additional units. But to consume more housing than H_2, the consumer must forgo the subsidized housing unit and bear the entire cost of the housing units along the RN portion of the original budget line. Compare, for instance, the amount of income the family has available to spend on other goods and services when they consume H_2 units of housing in contrast with H_1 units; if the family opts for the government subsidy, they have $0M$ in income, their entire income, free to spend on other goods. If, instead, the family were to consume H_1 units, they would have only $0M_1$ in income remaining.

Confronted with the $MM'RN$ budget line, the family would choose to accept the subsidized housing and consume at M', even though this involves less housing than they consumed without the subsidy. Although the family sacrifices H_1H_2 units of housing, they gain M_1M units of other goods, and the net result is that they are better off at M' than at E.

Actually, the more relevant comparison is between the consumption pattern with the subsidy (at M') and with an equal-size cash subsidy that the family can spend as they wish. Because MM'' is the cost of the housing subsidy, a cash transfer of this sum would yield the shaded $M''N'$ budget line, and the family would choose point E', with H_3 units of housing. The family would also be better off at E', on indifference curve U_3, because the extra

H_2H_3 units of housing are worth more than their cost. H_2H_3 is a measure of the underconsumption produced by the housing subsidy.[3]

It is important to recognize that this type of subsidy can lead to underconsumption for some consumers, overconsumption for other consumers, and the appropriate level of consumption for still others. The exact outcome depends on the size of the subsidy in relation to the preferences and incomes of the recipients of the subsidy. (Verify this.) In general, the subsidy is most likely to restrict consumption when the quantity being subsidized is small, when the consumer's income is high, or when the unsubsidized quantity chosen by the consumer is large. The opposite combination of circumstances is likely to lead to overconsumption.

There are a number of real-world subsidies of this sort that can lead to underconsumption. Subsidies for public schools and institutions of higher education are probably the most important examples, because schooling is a "lumpy" good just as housing is. Similarly, public housing, medical services provided by public health clinics, and Medicaid are other obvious examples. It is theoretically possible for these subsidies to lead to underconsumption, but whether they actually do is an empirical question.

Two empirical studies have investigated this question and concluded that some subsidies of this type have, in fact, operated to restrict consumption, at least for some recipients. Kraft and Olsen studied a sample of public housing tenants and estimated that 49 percent of the families were consuming less housing than if they had been given the subsidy as cash.[4] The remaining 51 percent were consuming the same amount of housing, or more than they would with cash subsidies. However, the families in this sample had higher income levels and more children than the average of all public housing tenants do, so Kraft's and Olsen's estimate cannot be generalized to all recipients of public housing.

In another study, Sam Peltzman studied the effects of state-supported colleges and universities on the consumption of higher education.[5] He found that the expenditures per student would be higher in the absence of subsidies to higher education, which supports our contention that some fixed quantity subsidies result in underconsumption. Peltzman also found that more students attended college as a result of the subsidies. Thus, some students

[3] Note that the same diagram can be used to analyze the effects of a nonredistributive housing subsidy in which the consumer pays a tax equal to the subsidy received. In this case, $M''N'$ is the before-tax budget line, and the consumer is initially at point E'. The tax shifts the line to MN, and the subsidy then produces the $MM'RN$ budget line. The net effect of the tax-plus-subsidy reduces housing consumption and makes the consumer worse off.

[4] John Kraft and Edgar Olsen, "The Distribution of Benefits from Public Housing," in F. Thomas Juster, ed., *The Distribution of Economic Well-Being*, vol. 1, *Studies in Income and Wealth* (Cambridge, Mass.: Ballinger, 1977), pp. 51–64.

[5] Sam Peltzman, "The Effect of Government Subsidies-in-Kind on Private Expenditures: The Case of Higher Education," *Journal of Political Economy*, 81:1 (Jan./Feb. 1973).

consume less schooling and others (those who would not have attended college without the subsidy) consume more as a result of state support of institutions of higher education.[6] These studies, therefore, provide some empirical support for our analysis.

Other relevant factors

We have seen that the fixed quantity type of subsidy can increase, reduce, or have no effect on the consumption of the subsidized good. The exact outcome probably varies widely from one subsidy to another and from one consumer to another. Although it is difficult to generalize, the quantitative impact of such subsidies on the allocation of resources is probably much smaller than widely believed. Before concluding, however, that they are unimportant, several factors should be mentioned that have been ignored so far.

One significant impact of subsidies like these is on the distribution of income. Frequently subsidies of the fixed quantity variety are used to redistribute income in favor of certain groups. For example, food stamps, housing subsidies, and Medicaid subsidies are concentrated exclusively on low-income households. Public schools and social security (subsidized old-age pensions) are more widely distributed, but it is important to consider the taxes used to finance the subsidies and who pays them, as well as the subsidies themselves, in determining their overall impact. In general, it is plausible to suppose that the way such subsidies operate to benefit some groups at the expense of others is more important than their impact on the aggregate level of consumption of the subsidized goods; that is, because these subsidies probably have little effect on consumption levels, their impact on the distribution of income may be of more significance.

Another interesting consequence of these subsidies is that they often cause us to lose information about the value of the subsidized goods to consumers. Earlier we noted that market prices reflect the marginal values of goods to consumers. With fixed quantity subsidies, this is sometimes not true. To see this, refer back to the equilibrium positions shown in Figure 4–4 and Figure 4–5. Note that the slope of the consumer's indifference curve at M' (which measures the marginal value to the consumer) is not equal to the slope of MN (indicating the market price ratio). In Figure 4–4 the marginal value of food is less than its market price, whereas the opposite is true in Figure 4–5. In short, with such subsidies we are often unaware of the value of the subsidized good to consumers. This poses a serious problem in designing and evaluating policies (although it provides employment for econ-

---

[6]At the risk of pointing out the obvious, it should be noted that we are discussing estimates and not facts. Effects of this type cannot be directly observed, of course, and so we must rely on empirical estimates.

omists who try to estimate values to recipients!). It is also a problem that can be avoided through the use of other types of subsidies, as we shall see.

We have also ignored the administrative costs of the subsidies, as well as the administrative (and other[7]) costs of taxes. The significance of these costs is that the amount of subsidy returned to consumers is less than the taxes paid. The importance of this factor varies widely from one subsidy to another and from one tax to another. Administrative costs are sometimes as low as 1 percent but occasionally may exceed 10 percent.

In view of these factors, and because of the importance of possible overconsumption and underconsumption, it would be premature to conclude that fixed quantity subsidies have unimportant consequences for the economic system. On the other hand, it is probably true that these subsidies are not terribly effective if their goal is to stimulate greater consumption of the subsidized goods.

Excise Subsidy

A fundamentally different form of subsidy is one in which the government pays part of the per unit price of a good but allows the quantity of the good to be determined by consumer purchases. For example, suppose the government decided to pay the consumer $5 for each unit of housing consumed. The quantity and, hence, the cost to the government depend on the level of consumer purchases and so are not fixed by the nature of the policy. Such a subsidy is called an *excise subsidy*—just the opposite of the more familiar excise tax.

Examples of excise subsidies are less common than examples of fixed quantity subsidies. Unemployment insurance is a type of excise subsidy, but with some significant differences from the "pure" type considered here. Some welfare programs operate much like excise subsidies. (These programs will be discussed in greater detail in later chapters.) But perhaps the most common examples are found in special provisions of the tax laws. These "tax subsidies" or "tax loopholes" will also be examined in later chapters. Here we will simply consider how such subsidies affect output and consumption levels.

There are two types of excise subsidies, *ad valorem excise subsidies* and *per unit excise subsidies*. With an ad valorem excise subsidy the government pays a certain percentage of the per unit cost of some good or, what amounts to the same thing, a specific percentage of the consumer's total expenditures on the good. In contrast, with a per unit excise subsidy the government pays a certain amount for each unit of the good consumed, as in the

---

[7]The principal hidden cost of taxation is a welfare cost produced by distorting resource allocation. This will be discussed in Chapter 10.

housing subsidy mentioned earlier. In this chapter, we will concentrate on per unit excise subsidies, although the allocative and distributive effects of both types of excise subsidies are nearly identical. In Chapter 11, when we analyze tax loopholes, we will consider ad valorem excise subsidies in greater depth.

Allocative effects: market perspective

Suppose we have a competitive industry for food. The supply and demand curves are shown as S and D in Figure 4–6, and the competitive equilibrium price and quantity are $10 and Q_1. For simplicity assume the industry operates at constant costs in the long run; that is, the supply curve is perfectly elastic, or horizontal, at a per unit cost of $10. The effect of dropping this assumption will be considered later.

Now assume that the government decides to expand output of this industry through an excise subsidy. The government pays the firms $5 for every unit of food sold. This is shown by a downward shift in the supply curve to S', where S' is obtained by subtracting the subsidy per unit, R, from

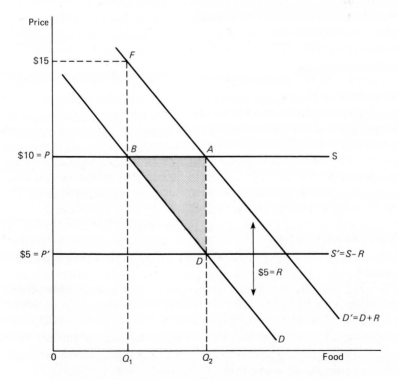

FIGURE 4–6 *Allocative effects of an excise subsidy.*

the original supply curve. The immediate or short-run effect (not shown in the diagram) would be to increase the firms' profits, giving them the incentive to expand output. As all firms increase production, the larger output can only be sold at a lower price, and a final equilibrium is established at the intersection of S' and D. The total outlay of the government is equal to $PADP'$, or the per unit subsidy times the quantity being subsidized.

The ultimate effect of this excise subsidy, even though it is paid to the firms, is to reduce the price to the consumers by $5, the amount of the per unit subsidy. As a result, consumers are confronted with a $5 per unit price, and at the lower price, consumption increases to Q_2. With an excise subsidy, consumption and output unequivocally increase as long as consumers will purchase more at a lower price. In other words, as long as the law of demand is valid (as it always is), this subsidy stimulates greater consumption.

Some care is necessary in interpreting the results of this subsidy. Although we have analyzed the subsidy by shifting the supply curve, it is clear that the subsidy does not reduce the true cost of production. It will still cost $10 per unit to produce food; the S' curve reflects the fact that the consumers need only cover half the cost, when the government subsidy covers the rest. In other words, at the final equilibrium, firms are receiving $10 per unit—$5 from the government and $5 from consumers. The price received by firms including the subsidy is given by AQ_2, or $10, in this example. The price paid by consumers is DQ_2, or $5. Thus, the subsidy per unit enters as a wedge *(AD)* separating the price received by producers from the price paid by consumers.

As an alternative, suppose the excise subsidy of $5 per unit is paid directly to the consumers. The subsidy then increases the per unit price that consumers are willing to pay to firms. At Q_1, for instance, consumers are willing to pay a maximum of BQ_1 (the height to the demand curve), or $10 per unit out of their own pockets. However, because the government will give them $5 per unit, their demand price *including the subsidy* will be $15 (at Q_1). In other words, the subsidy per unit can be added to the original demand curve to yield D', the new demand curve confronting sellers of the product. With D' and the unchanged supply curve S, equilibrium occurs at A, with output Q_2. At Q_2, producers are receiving $10 per unit—just as they did when the subsidy was paid to them. Also, consumers are paying a net price of only $5, or DQ_2; the remaining $5, AD, reflects the government subsidy.

Thus, we reach the remarkable conclusion that an excise subsidy has the same effect, regardless of whether consumers or producers are subsidized. In each case, the final equilibrium is at Q_2, with a price of $10 received by producers and a price of $5 paid by consumers. The price received by the producer and the price paid by the consumer are the same, regardless of which side of the market is nominally subsidized. It makes no difference whether we analyze the subsidy as an upward shift in the demand curve or as a downward shift in the supply curve.

The expansion of output from Q_1 to Q_2 results in overconsumption. The benefit of the additional Q_1Q_2 units to consumers is less than the cost of producing the additional output. In Figure 4–6, the benefit of increasing output from Q_1 to Q_2 is equal to BDQ_2Q_1, because the height of the demand curve gives the marginal value of each successive unit. The cost to the economy of producing this additional output is BAQ_2Q_1, or \$10 per unit times the Q_1Q_2 increase in output. The cost of expanding output from Q_1 to Q_2 exceeds the benefit by the area BAD. This is a measure of the dollar value of the *welfare cost,* or the degree of inefficiency, associated with the subsidy-induced expansion of output.[8]

What this welfare cost means is that consumers would prefer that resources used to produce the Q_1Q_2 increase in output be used elsewhere to produce other goods and services. In other words, the subsidy artificially stimulates the output of food by drawing resources from other uses where they are more valuable to consumers. The subsidy results in an output level where the marginal benefit (DQ_2) to consumers is less than the marginal cost (AQ_2) of production.

Allocative effects: individual perspective

Greater insight into the nature of the allocative effects of an excise subsidy can be gained by examining the impact on an individual consumer. In Figure 4–7, the presubsidy budget line is $MN,$ and the consumer is in equilibrium at point E. The excise subsidy lowers the price of food, so the budget line rotates and becomes flatter, as shown by MN'. Faced with the lower price, the individual's new equilibrium is at E', involving a larger consumption of food, q_2. The total cost of the subsidy is equal to $E'T$. This can best be seen by recognizing that if the consumer purchased q_2 units without the subsidy, he or she would have had only Tq_2 dollars left to spend on other goods. With the subsidy, the consumer purchases q_2 units and has $E'q_2$ dollars left to spend on other goods. So in purchasing q_2, the consumer saves the difference, $E'T$; this is the portion of the total cost of q_2 that is borne by the government.

The postsubsidy equilibrium at E' represents overconsumption: The artificially low price encourages consumers to purchase more food and less

---

[8]For those familiar with the concept of consumer surplus, this conclusion can be reached by a different route. As a result of the lower price, there is a gain in consumer surplus equal to the area $PBDP'$. This is not a net gain, because the government must raise tax revenue equal to area $PADP'$ to finance the subsidy. The difference between the gain in consumer surplus and the cost to government is the net loss, or welfare cost, of area BAD.

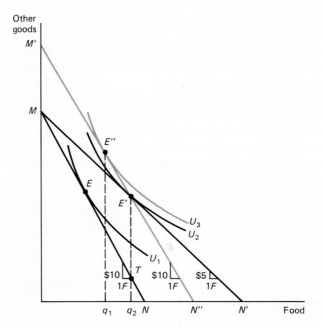

FIGURE 4–7   *Allocative effects of an excise subsidy: individual consumer.*

of other goods, and this outcome is inefficient. This inefficiency can be demonstrated by assuming that the consumer is given the subsidy in cash rather than as a subsidy that lowers the price of food. Because the cost of the excise subsidy is $E'T$, the government can give, at no additional cost, cash equal to MM' (equal to $E'T$). This cash transfer produces a parallel movement of the budget line from MN to $M'N''$, with $M'N''$ passing through point E'. This means that the consumer could still choose the consumption mix at point E' if given the subsidy in the form of cash. Given the preferences shown, however, the recipient would prefer point E'', purchasing less food and more of other goods. The consumer would therefore be better off with an unrestricted cash transfer. Compared with the cash transfer of equal cost, the excise subsidy produces a welfare cost: The consumer is on U_2 with the excise subsidy but can reach U_3 by consuming a different combination of goods of the same total cost with a cash transfer.

We have assumed that people other than the recipient of the subsidy pay the taxes to finance the subsidy. The same diagram, slightly reinterpreted, applies when the consumers must pay the taxes themselves. In Figure 4–7, we can interpret $M'N''$ as the before-tax-and-subsidy budget line, MN as the after-tax budget line, and MN' as the budget line showing the combined effect of the tax and subsidy. In this case, the net result is to increase food consumption from q_1 to q_2 and to make the consumer worse off. Overconsumption of food and a loss in welfare are, once again, the outcome. Thus, the excise subsidy produces a welfare cost by artificially stimulating food consumption in both cases. The only difference is that the welfare cost associated with the subsidy when others pay the taxes reflects the fact that the consumers would be better off consuming less food with a cash transfer. (Recall that the recipient is on a higher indifference curve with a cash transfer.) When the consumers pay the taxes themselves, the welfare cost reflects the fact that consumers would be better off consuming less food without any tax or subsidy. (That is, before the tax-and-subsidy program, the consumer was on U_3; after the program is implemented, the consumer is on U_2.) The nature of the welfare cost is the same; an artificially lower price stimulates too much consumption.

Figure 4–6 and Figure 4–7 both illustrate the welfare cost of an excise subsidy, but from different perspectives. In Figure 4–6, total overconsumption (or, equivalently, overproduction, because what is produced is consumed) equals Q_1Q_2, and area BAD is a measure of the total welfare cost. In Figure 4–7, overconsumption by an individual consumer is shown as q_1q_2, and the welfare cost is represented by the difference in well-being associated with consuming at E' rather than E''.[9]

Excise subsidies lead to a misallocation of resources. However, this conclusion is fully valid only if markets are competitive and if no externalities are present. When there are no externalities, competitive markets are efficient, and no form of subsidy can improve resource allocation. This underscores the importance economists attach to externalities. When external benefits exist, the market equilibrium is inefficient, and then some form of subsidy is capable of improving resource allocation by expanding output.

Regardless of whether externalities may be present, excise subsidies are clearly more effective than fixed quantity subsidies in increasing consumption of the subsidized good. Fixed quantity subsidies are highly uncertain, cumbersome devices, so it is not surprising that most economists regard excise subsidies as a more effective means of stimulating the production and consumption of some desired good (for whatever reason). Another advantage of excise subsidies is that the marginal value of the subsidized good to consumers is readily ascertainable. Consumers adjust their consumption to the subsidized price so that the subsidized price is equal to the marginal value of the good. Thus, in Figure 4–6, DQ_2, or $5, is the marginal value of the good to all consumers. This valuable information is often difficult to obtain when fixed quantity subsidies are used.

[9]In advanced courses in economic theory, the conditions under which these two approaches are exactly equivalent are discussed in detail.

Distributive effects

Who benefits and who loses from a subsidy depend on the exact type and size of subsidy (as well as the distribution of the tax burden). Now let's consider another dimension to the problem of determining the distributional impact: the relationship between the market structure and the incidence of the subsidy.

Economists use the term *incidence* to refer to the distributional effect of a tax, subsidy, or other policy. In the last section, the incidence of the excise subsidy fell on consumers because the price paid by consumers decreased by the full amount of the per unit subsidy. Thus, consumers benefited and sellers did not. Sometimes, however, the benefits do not accrue entirely to consumers.

Figure 4–8 illustrates the effect of an excise subsidy for a good produced by an *increasing cost* competitive industry. The only difference between Figure 4–8 and Figure 4–6 is that in Figure 4–8 the supply curve is assumed to be upward sloping, implying that per unit production costs rise as the total industry output expands. The subsidy is $5 per unit and is shown by the upward shift in demand from D to D'. The final equilibrium occurs at K, where D' and S intersect. In this case, however, the net price to consumers is $7, only $3 below the unsubsidized price. Part of the subsidy is received by sellers who now are paid $12 per unit, $2 more than before. The incidence, or benefit of the subsidy, falls on both buyers and sellers.

The extent to which buyers and sellers benefit from an excise subsidy depends on the relative elasticities of the supply and demand curves. With a perfectly elastic supply curve (shown as S_1), the benefit accrues entirely to consumers. The more inelastic the supply curve is, the smaller the price reduction for consumers and the larger the price increase for sellers will be. In fact, with a perfectly inelastic (vertical) supply curve the consumers receive no benefit, because the selling price rises by the full amount of the subsidy. The reader should also be able to work out how the incidence varies with the elasticity of demand for any given supply curve.

We have been referring to "sellers" benefiting from the subsidy, and this requires some further explanation. Recall that in equilibrium competitive firms make zero economic profits (i.e., they earn a normal return on investment but no "abnormal" profits). Businesses per se probably do not benefit from an increase in the product price induced by the subsidy because their costs of production eventually rise. As industry output expands, its demands for productive factors—labor, raw materials, and so on—increase, bidding up wage rates, prices of raw materials, and so on. Higher wage rates represent higher production costs to firms and account for the upward slope in the supply curve. These "sellers" who benefit from the higher selling price are typically owners of factors of production whose prices are bid up as total industry output expands. Thus, the benefit of the

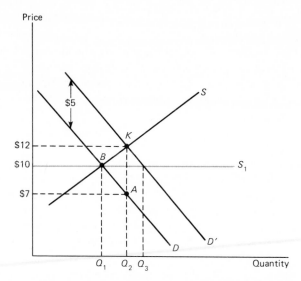

FIGURE 4–8   *Incidence of an excise subsidy for an increasing cost industry.*

subsidy on the supply side will probably be dispersed among a number of economic groups, making it unlikely that business profits will receive more than a temporary boost.

Where the benefits from a particular subsidy accrue depends on the structure and reaction of the market affected by the subsidy. Our discussion of incidence has been in the context of an excise subsidy, but the incidence of other subsidies (and taxes) can also be ascertained only by analyzing the reaction of the relevant market. For example, some of the benefits of fixed quantity subsidies can accrue to sellers of the subsidized product. If the fixed quantity subsidy does, on balance, increase consumption, this reflects an effective increase in demand. Coupled with an upward-sloping supply curve, a fixed quantity subsidy that increases demand will increase price, just like the excise subsidy in Figure 4–8. This relationship may explain some of the support by educators (such as teachers' unions and colleges and universities) for subsidies to education, or by construction unions for housing subsidies.

With a constant-cost industry, the incidence of an excise subsidy is entirely on consumers, and sellers derive no long-run benefit. Assuming a horizontal supply curve simplifies the analysis, because we need not worry about possible changes in wages and other input prices. Fortunately, research in industrial organization suggests that constant costs over the relevant range of output are quite common, so the assumption of a horizontal supply curve may be a reasonably close approximation in many cases.

Note that the welfare cost due to the excise subsidy in Figure 4–8 is shown by area *BAK.* The welfare cost due to overconsumption of Q_1Q_2 is measured by the difference in the cost associated with producing the additional output (given by the upward-sloping supply curve) and the benefits to consumers (given by the demand curve). If the supply curve were vertical, there would be no overconsumption and no welfare cost. (Verify this.)

Subsidies to a subset of consumers

So far, our formal analysis of excise subsidies has considered subsidies that apply to all consumers of some product. Actually, many subsidies are given to only some of the consumers of a particular product. This is true, for example, of food stamps, Medicaid, housing subsidies, Medicare, job training programs, and others. Our analysis can be modified to cover instances in which only a subset of all consumers is subsidized.

Suppose that only low-income consumers of food are subsidized. In Figure 4–9 we can disaggregate the total market demand, D_T, into the separate demands of low-income consumers, D_L, and high-income consumers, D_H. Given the supply and demand relationships, the initial equilibrium price and quantity are P and Q_T. At a price of P, low-income consumers purchase Q_L units and high-income consumers purchase Q_H units. Note that $Q_L + Q_H = Q_T$.

An excise subsidy given only to low-income consumers increases their

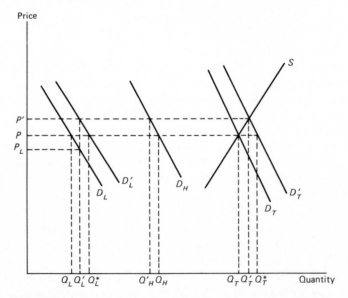

FIGURE 4–9   *Excise subsidy for low-income households.*

demand to D'_L. (A fixed quantity subsidy *could* increase demand in this way, also.) At the initial price, P, the recipients would prefer to consume Q^*_L, or $Q_L Q^*_L$ more than before. Although the demand of unsubsidized consumers is not affected,[10] total demand has increased. The new total demand curve is D'_T, obtained by summing D'_L and D_H (so $Q_L Q^*_L = Q_T Q^*_T$). Since the total market demand for the product in relation to supply is what determines the market price and total output, the market price rises to P' and quantity to Q'_T.

Higher-income consumers are harmed by the subsidy because they must pay a higher price. Because their demand is unchanged, they curtail consumption to Q'_H. Unsubsidized consumers may also bear an additional cost if they pay some or all of the taxes needed to finance the subsidy. The benefits of the subsidy accrue to the subsidized consumers, who now pay a net price of P_L and consume Q'_L. In addition, sellers benefit because the price they receive has increased from P to P'. Note, however, that we have assumed an increasing cost industry. If the supply curve were horizontal, the product price would not rise, and the entire benefit of the subsidy would accrue to low-income consumers.

This analysis suggests how the incidence of a subsidy may be spread widely and unevenly through society. And the analysis is of more than academic interest. It is precisely this combination of circumstances that, in the opinion of many economists, contributed to the surge in medical care costs (prices) following the enactment of Medicaid and Medicare in the mid-1960s. Medicare and Medicaid are subsidies that apply to the elderly and poor, so an analysis that distinguishes subsidized from unsubsidized consumers is appropriate.

Appendix to Chapter 4: Benefit-Cost Analysis

Benefit-cost analysis is a technique that can be used to evaluate government projects. The basic concept is quite simple: Identify the benefits and costs of a project and then measure them in comparable units (such as dollars). If the benefits exceed the costs, the project will lead to a more efficient resource allocation. If the costs exceed the benefits, the project will lead to a poorer allocation of resources.

Because the benefit-cost technique is a logical method to use in appraising alternatives, it is not surprising that it is occasionally used to analyze government expenditure programs. Some government agencies, notably the Bureau of Reclamation and the Army Corps of Engineers, have employed benefit-cost analysis since the 1930s to evaluate alternative potential projects. In recent years the technique has been used by other agencies and

---

[10] This assumes that the income effect of the tax on demand is small enough to be ignored.

practitioners outside government to analyze policies in such diverse areas as health, transportation, education, and social welfare programs. Such studies are sometimes available to Congress and provide information that is useful in its deliberations. Our main concern, however, will not be with how benefit-cost analysis has been employed within government but instead with the nature of the technique itself. A study of the nature and limitations of the benefit-cost approach provides further insight into the application of economics to government policy analysis.

Identifying and measuring benefits

Suppose we are trying to ascertain what benefits will result from a particular government project. Obviously, the first step is to determine the impact of the project: What goods or services will we have more of as a result of the project? Second, these effects must be expressed quantitatively; that is, the value of these effects to the public must be calculated. Usually this second step causes the greatest difficulty. An example will illustrate why.

Consider the construction of a dam to control flooding. One obvious benefit is a reduction in the probability of flood damage. How do we measure this in dollars? The generally correct theoretical answer is that the dollar value of the benefit equals the maximum amount that people would be willing to pay to secure this service. Because of the free rider problem, however, we are unable to survey the potential beneficiaries to determine this figure. Instead an alternative means of estimating the benefit must be found, and that is the difficulty. Frequently there is no way to do this accurately.

Although it may be impossible to measure the benefit with perfect accuracy, analysts have shown considerable ingenuity in devising ways to approximate the magnitudes involved. Consider how this might be done in the present case. If flooding destroys farmers' crops, then we could estimate the average annual volume of crops destroyed and multiply this amount by their market price (the value to consumers). For a variety of reasons, this approach is unlikely to yield exactly the correct answer (i.e., how much farmers would be willing to pay), but it may be a fair approximation. In any event, it is likely to be better than relying on pure guesswork.

For some projects, the valuation of benefits is easier than for others. If, for example, the output is a good or service that is already produced and sold in private markets, we can use the market price to estimate the benefit. The production of electricity by nuclear power plants falls in this category. However, in many, perhaps most, cases the output of a government expenditure project is not sold and so is not valued directly in some market. In these situations, we must devise alternative methods to estimate benefits if benefit-cost analysis is to be used.

Benefit-cost studies usually distinguish between the direct and indirect benefits of a project. In the case of the flood control project, the direct benefit might be the reduced probability of flooding. An indirect benefit might be the recreational services of the lake behind the dam (e.g., swimming, fishing, camping, boating). The value of these services is as real a benefit as flood control and should also be counted as a benefit in a benefit-cost analysis.

In principle, there is no clear-cut distinction between direct and indirect benefits. All the effects of a project that are considered desirable by those affected are benefits and should be counted as such. Admittedly, some benefits are likely to be quantitatively less important than others; the recreational value of the lake may be very small in comparison with its flood control services. In addition, some benefits are likely to be much more difficult to estimate with any accuracy than are others: How much is it worth to homeowners overlooking the lake to have a better view? What we call these indirect or intangible benefits is irrelevant as long as we generally recognize that all real benefits should, in principle, be counted. (In practice, however, many benefits may be too small or too costly to measure.)

One error frequently made in benefit-cost studies (especially in the past) was to count pecuniary externalities as benefits. Any government project is likely to affect the prices and quantities of other goods. It is important to distinguish between effects that provide clues to the net benefits and those that represent only transfers. For example, providing a recreational area may lead to higher prices for boats and fishing tackle, which benefit sellers of these items. At the same time, however, the higher prices are costs to people who purchase these items. Consequently, there are no net benefits. These effects may be treated in two ways. One is to recognize that a benefit accrues to the seller and include it along with other benefits. If this is done, the burden placed on the purchasers must also be entered as a cost. Alternatively, these effects can be disregarded altogether. In either case, the net effect is zero. The error arises when the benefit to sellers is included and not the cost to consumers, or vice versa.

Another common error is to double count benefits. An estimate of how much the view of the lake is worth to a nearby homeowner might be included as a benefit. But what about the higher property value of his home? The increased value of his home is not a separate benefit because the increase in the property value is a result of the house's commanding a better view. It might be possible to use the increment in property value as an estimate of the value of the view, but to include both is to count the same benefit twice.

The identification and measurement of the benefits of a government project constitute a difficult task, one that is likely to be even more difficult when we consider such complex areas as national defense, education, health insurance, or welfare programs. When externalities or public goods are involved, there is no accurate way to determine benefits. (This does not mean that the benefit-cost approach is faulty but only that its practical implementation is difficult.) Perhaps this explains why benefit-cost analysis has been limited to areas in which benefits are relatively easy to measure, such as in irrigation, flood control, and transportation projects. Nonetheless, as our technical ability to estimate benefits improves, benefit-cost analysis is likely to find applications in other areas.

Identifying and measuring costs

The consequences of a project that involves burdens or sacrifices for people are its costs. In the case of a dam, manpower, concrete, equipment, energy, and other productive resources must be used for its construction and maintenance. Using these resources involves an opportunity cost because productive services in other sectors of the economy must be sacrificed. The task of placing a dollar figure on these costs is generally thought to be much simpler than valuing the benefits of the project. As a first approximation, the costs are what must be paid to attract the required resources into employment on the dam. Insofar as the economy is competitive, these payments will equal the value of sacrificed output elsewhere.

When the economy is not fully competitive, however, the payments necessary to attract resources into employment on the dam may either underestimate or overestimate the true costs. For example, the wage necessary to bid a worker away from a monopoly will underestimate the costs because the monopoly pays a wage below the marginal value product of the workers. On the other hand, bidding workers away from subsidized industries requires wages above their marginal value products and overstates the costs. It will seldom be possible to identify exactly where the resources employed by the government come from, so there may be little option but to use the actual payments as an estimate of their resource cost. Because there are biases in offsetting directions, this figure may in many cases be approximately correct.

Some analysts have suggested that if the project employs previously unemployed resources, the opportunity cost of using these resources is zero. As explained earlier in this chapter, this is generally incorrect. Not only are there practical problems (the value of leisure is not zero; a worker who is unemployed when hired may not remain unemployed very long even if the project were not undertaken), but also the basic point is that unemployed resources can be reemployed in a variety of uses. Using an unemployed worker to construct a dam means that the worker cannot be used elsewhere, and that involves an opportunity cost.

Although the costs of using resources to construct and maintain the dam will normally be the most important costs associated with the project, there may be additional costs. For example, damming a river might cause environmental damage. The lake could become a breeding ground for disease-carrying insects. In addition, the dam could break and cause a flood more severe than the floods it was built to prevent. Costs such as these should also be included, although clearly it would be difficult to measure them.

The funds to finance a project are normally raised through taxation. However, the burden on taxpayers is not (with a qualification noted later) a cost in addition to the payments to productive factors. Using taxes is simply a way of distributing the burden of diverting resources to the project; it is not a separate or additional cost. The owners of the resources that are used in constructing the dam do not necessarily bear any burden, because they are paid by the government. The income they receive is a measure of the opportunity cost, but taxpayers are the ones who ultimately bear the burden.

There are, however, additional costs arising from the use of tax revenues to finance a project. To secure $100 in revenue to fund some government project, a burden greater than $100 must be placed on taxpayers. Part of this additional cost is the administrative cost of collecting taxes and the compliance costs borne by taxpayers. In addition, there is a more subtle cost that arises because taxes distort resource allocation in the economy. This cost, called an *excess burden* (or welfare cost) of taxation, will be considered in detail in later chapters. At this point, it is enough to recognize that these costs of taxation are costs associated with implementing the project; they would not arise if the project were not funded. Consequently, if a project necessitated outlays of $1 billion, for example, the actual economic costs imposed on the economy might be $1.1 billion—with the extra $0.1 billion representing the administrative, compliance, and excess burden costs of the tax. Unfortunately, most benefit-cost studies neglect these costs.

Another cost can be produced by the tax financing of a project. If the taxpayers whose incomes are reduced by the tax spend part of their incomes in ways that generate external benefits, then there will be a reduction in such external benefits as a result of the tax. In this case, collecting the tax involves another cost. (The opposite case is also possible; expenditures that generate external costs may fall.) For example, the tax may lead some families to spend less on their children's education, and if education is an external benefit, others will be harmed indirectly. This type of effect would generally be expected to be small, if not insignificant, in most practical situations. Benefit-cost analysts generally have little option but to ignore effects this remote and hard to measure.

This last point brings us to another one of the real difficulties in conducting a benefit-cost study. Benefits are generally concentrated in a certain area or sector of the economy and are often highly visible. The costs, on the other hand, are spread widely throughout the economy by taxation and may be hard to perceive. As an example, consider this list of alleged benefits from a low-income housing project: reductions in crime, juvenile delinquency, and marital instability; reductions in fire and police protection costs; improved sanitation and reduced health-related costs; reduction in traffic

congestion (dependent on location); more attractive neighborhoods and increased property values; improved access of tenants to jobs; and improved
competition in the housing market. It is easy for anyone familiar with housing projects to list these and other possible benefits—and some may conceivably be quantitatively important. However, a little thought concerning
the effects of the reduction in disposable incomes that result from the higher
taxes needed to finance the project will also produce a similarly lengthy list
of potentially harmful effects. The difference is that on a per taxpayer basis
the costs are so small and uncertain that they will be neglected, even though
in the aggregate (because there are more taxpayers than beneficiaries) they
may be significant.

In general, the more important costs are probably the use of resources
by a project and the administrative, compliance, and excess burden costs of
taxation. Other costs may be important in specific instances.

Comparing costs and benefits

Once all the costs and benefits have been identified and measured, our task
is almost over. Now we must decide if it is efficient to undertake the project.
Because benefits and costs are reckoned in dollars, the magnitudes can be
compared. (In this section, we will assume that the benefits and costs occur
in one year; the next section considers the issues involved when the effects
occur over a period of several years.) The results are generally presented
as a ratio. If benefits are estimated to be $1.5 million and the costs to be
$1.0 million, the benefit-cost ratio will be 1.5. This means that, on average,
each dollar of expenditure on the project provides services worth $1.50 to
the public.

Note that a benefit-cost study usually results in an estimate of the total
benefit and total cost of a project of a specific scale. If the benefit-cost ratio
exceeds 1, undertaking the project will lead to a more efficient allocation of
resources than doing nothing. This does not mean, however, that such a
project is the most efficient. To clarify this point further, consider Figure 4–
10. The diagram plots the total benefits and costs for varying scales of a
particular type of project. For example, the size of the dam used for flood
control might be measured on the horizontal axis.

A benefit-cost study will generally estimate the costs and benefits of a
specific project. For example, the project identified by the scale of V in the
diagram has a benefit-cost ratio of AV/BV. Because total benefits exceed total
costs, this project is more efficient than is none at all. It is not, however, the
most efficient scale. The most efficient dam size is where total benefits exceed total costs by the greatest amount, because this yields the largest possible net gain. The most efficient project is shown by point W in the diagram, where benefits exceed costs by CD, a larger amount than for any
other scale of project. This occurs where the marginal benefits of changing
the scale of the project equal the marginal costs. Although the results of a

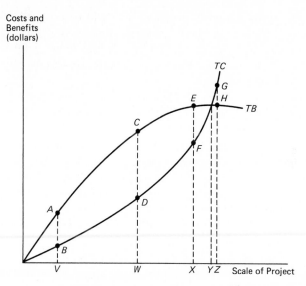

FIGURE 4–10 *Benefit-cost ratios.*

benefit-cost analysis are often summarized as a ratio of benefits to costs, the most efficient project is not the one with the largest ratio. The project of scale V, for example, has total benefits of, say, $4 million (equal to AV) and total costs of $1 million (equal to BV), for a ratio of 4/1. The project scale W, on the other hand, produces total benefits of $8 million (CW) and total costs of $4 million (DW), a ratio of only 2/1. Nonetheless, the project of scale W is more efficient because its net benefit is $4 million, compared with a net benefit of only $3 million for the project of scale V. Consequently, choosing the project with the highest benefit-cost ratio is not the appropriate strategy.

Clearly, if benefit-cost studies could be prepared costlessly, we would like to have one for each possible size of the project, for scales V, W, X, Y, Z, and all intermediate points, in Figure 4–10. With this information we could readily identify W as the most efficient project. Because of the cost and difficulty of preparing a benefit-cost study, however, we will generally have studies of only a limited range of options, frequently only one. Even in this case it can provide useful information—although there is no guarantee that a policy with benefits greater than costs is better than some alternative policies that were not analyzed.

Time and discounting

With many, perhaps most, government expenditures, the benefits received by the public are experienced at approximately the same time that the costs are incurred. This, however, is not always true. In the case of our dam for flood control, for example, during the first few years (while the dam is being constructed) there are heavy costs and no benefits. During later years, there are benefits, and much lower costs (only maintenance costs). For such projects, the time at which benefits and costs are experienced becomes an important consideration.

A benefit-cost study typically estimates the benefits and costs of a project over a number of years. We should realize, however, that a dollar in benefits received 10 years in the future is not worth as much as a dollar in benefits today. You would not be willing to pay a dollar today to receive a dollar 10 years from now because you could put the dollar in a savings account and it would grow to more than a dollar in 10 years. Thus, it is not correct to add the dollar value of benefits or costs that extend over a period of years in the future. Instead, all of the benefits and costs must be evaluated at their worth in today's dollars. To do this, benefits and costs to be experienced in the future are "discounted" using a discount (or interest) rate to arrive at a present value measure.

The very name *discounting* refers to the fact that future benefits and costs are worth less (must be discounted) today. If the discount rate is 5 percent, a dollar in benefits today is equivalent to $1.05 in benefits to be received 1 year later; that is, a person would be indifferent between receiving $1 today and $1.05 next year. Thus, the present or discounted value of $1.05 in benefits received next year is only $1 today. Putting this in a benefit-cost perspective, to consider an expenditure of $1 today, the project would have to produce a benefit of at least $1.05 a year from now (if next year's benefits were the only benefit). The present value of the benefit can be calculated from $B_1/(1+i)$, where B_1 is the benefit 1 year from now and i is the discount rate. Similarly, the present value of a dollar in benefits to be received 14 years from now is only 50 cents today: $B_{14}/(1+i)^{14}$, or $1/(1.05)^{14}$ equals $0.50.

When costs and benefits occur over a period of years, the total benefit of the project is the present value of the stream of benefits. Similarly, costs must be evaluated at their present value. Having done this, we once more arrive at a single figure for the total benefit and for the total cost, and the project can be evaluated as we did earlier.

A major issue in discounting future costs and benefits concerns what discount rate to use. The results of a benefit-cost study can depend critically on the discount rate used to calculate the present value of benefits and costs. Consider a simplified example of a government project that has costs in the first year of $1 million and no benefits until 14 years later when there are $2 million in benefits; there are no other costs or benefits. If the discount rate is 3 percent, the present value of $2 million in benefits to be received 14 years in the future is $1.32 million, and the present value of $1 million in costs incurred in this year is, of course, $1 million. The benefit-cost ratio is 1.32, and the project looks attractive. Alternatively, suppose we

use a discount rate of 6 percent; then the present value of the $2 million bene-
fit is only $0.89 million today, and the benefit-cost ratio is 0.89. If the dis-
count rate is instead 10 percent, the present value of benefits is $0.53 million,
so the present value of costs is almost double the present value of benefits.

This example illustrates that the desirability of a project can depend heavily on what discount rate is used. The higher the discount rate is, the smaller
the present value of future benefits and costs will be. (We are discounting
the future more heavily with a high discount rate.) Most government projects that yield benefits and costs over many years are similar to our example; there are high initial costs with benefits accruing later. This would be
true, for example, of many irrigation, environmental, energy, and job training policies. In cases like these, the higher the discount rate used, the less
favorable the project will appear.

What is the appropriate discount rate to use? The answer to this question
turns out to be a highly complex issue. Intuitively, it seems that the discount
rate should be related to two different variables. One is the rate at which
people are willing to sacrifice present consumption for future consumption.
If the public is willing (at the margin) to give up $1 today in return for
$1.05 a year from now, the 5 percent rate tells us how much the public
discounts future benefits. This is sometimes called *time preference rate*. On
the other hand, public investment projects use resources that can alternatively be employed in private investment projects. If private investment projects yield (at the margin) 10 percent, then diverting resources from private
investment to public projects entails an opportunity cost in the form of a
sacrificed return of 10 percent. The return on private investments is sometimes called the *opportunity cost rate*. Which of these two rates should be
used?

Frequently prices (in this case interest rates) determined in private markets can serve as a guide. If capital markets were perfectly competitive, and
there were no risk associated with investments,[11] a single interest rate would
be determined. This is illustrated in Figure 4–11, where the investment demand curve is shown as I and the saving supply curve is S. The equilibrium
rate of return (interest rate) is 6 percent. At the equilibrium level of investment, I_1, the interest rate measures both the marginal return to private investments (the height of the I curve) and the return the public requires to
sacrifice present consumption (the height of the S curve). The opportunity
cost rate and the time preference rate are equal to each other at the competitive equilibrium. If this model were an accurate description of reality,
most economists would agree that 6 percent would be the appropriate discount rate to use for discounting future benefits and costs.

---

[11]When investments differ in their degree of risk, there is a wide range of interest rates in
markets reflecting the varying risks of different projects. This is ignored in the text but is yet
another reason why it is difficult to agree on a single interest rate to use in discounting.

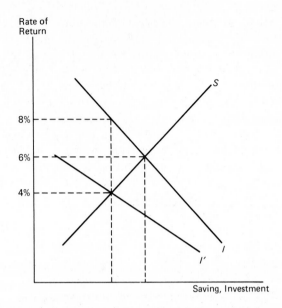

FIGURE 4–11   *Taxation and discount rates.*

For a variety of reasons, the real world differs from this model. Perhaps the most important difference is that the government taxes the return to private investments with the corporation income tax and property taxes. These taxes will be considered in detail in Chapter 13, but their relevance to the discount rate issue deserves mention here. Briefly, if a private investment yields a return of 10 percent, and the government taxes this yield, then less than 10 percent is left to be paid to investors (savers). The effect of a 50 percent tax is shown in Figure 4–11 by a pivoting downward of the *I* curve to *I'*. The *I'* curve shows the after-tax return that can be paid at each rate of investment; the *I* curve continues to show the before-tax return. The new equilibrium is at I_2. At this equilibrium, the net return to investors is 4 percent, in contrast with the before-tax return of 8 percent. Note that this means the time preference rate differs from the opportunity cost rate. The time preference rate is now 4 percent, and the opportunity cost rate 8 percent. (These figures are intended only as illustrations; actually, empirical evidence suggests that the opportunity cost rate is around 10 percent.)

We now face a dilemma because we cannot choose one discount rate that simultaneously reflects the time preference of the public and the opportunity cost of private investments. Which rate, 4 percent or 8 percent, should be used? This question has been widely debated by economists, but no one answer seems to produce a consensus. Most economists seem in limited agreement that the 4 percent rate is too low and that either the opportunity cost rate of 8 percent or some weighted average of the two rates should be used. In practice this means that many of the earlier benefit-cost studies have used discount rates that were far too low.

Our discussion thus far has not distinguished between real and nominal rates of interest, but this distinction is quite important in inflationary periods. If the future benefits and costs of a project are estimated in dollars of constant purchasing power, then it is the real rates of interest that are relevant. The numbers that we have used for illustrative purposes are closer to the level of the real rates that have prevailed in recent years. Because of inflation, nominal rates have been much higher.

Whose benefits and whose costs?

Generally, people receiving benefits from a project are not the same ones bearing the costs. The tax system usually distributes the costs widely among the public, and it would be only a coincidence if the benefits were distributed in a similar way. When this is true, exactly what meaning should be attached to the final benefit-cost ratio? To take an extreme case, suppose wealthy yacht owners receive $2 million in benefits from an irrigation project that imposes $1 million in costs on middle- and low-income families. Should this project, with a benefit-cost ratio of 2/1, be undertaken? Can we really compare the benefits and costs as evaluated by different people?

This issue has troubled many analysts. The problem is that the project has both efficiency and distributional (equity) implications, and benefit-cost analysis has evaluated only the efficiency implications. Therefore, one must avoid thinking that any project with benefits greater than costs is necessarily desirable, irrespective of its distributional implications. Value judgments must still be made concerning distributional effects of government policies.

An estimate that a project's benefits exceed its costs has a very definite meaning: It means that the beneficiaries *could* pay the entire cost and still be better off. If this were actually done, beneficiaries would be better off, and no one else would be affected—a clear efficiency gain. When other people bear some of the costs, there is still an efficiency gain, but it is coupled with a redistribution of income. Thus, benefit-cost analysis, like any other economic analysis, cannot demonstrate desirability.

Some economists have suggested that the benefit-cost technique be modified to permit an evaluation of distributional as well as efficiency effects. This could be done by using distributional weights that specify, for example, that a dollar of benefit to a wealthy person could be counted only as $0.80, whereas a dollar of benefit to a poor person should be counted as $1.20. Such a procedure is an attempt to combine efficiency and distributional effects in one measure of "desirability." This would mean that an inefficient policy could be adjudged desirable if it redistributed income to low-income persons. For example, if the government places a tax burden of $1 on a wealthy person and transfers $0.80 to a poor person ($0.20 being used up in administrative costs), the benefit-cost ratio will be $0.96/$0.80, or 1.2 (using these weights).

There are several practical and conceptual problems with this procedure. For example, there is no objective way to choose a set of distributional weights. People would disagree over what weights to use; to select one particular set of weights would require a value judgment. More importantly, many policies are available that provide alternative means of redistributing income, and these should be explicitly compared if it is decided the government should redistribute income. Using distributional weights in benefit-cost analysis could easily lead to enactment of policies that help the poor, but do so less than would an alternative policy of the same cost to other people.

For these reasons, most benefit-cost analysts have not attempted to apply distributional weights. This does not imply a judgment that distributional effects are unimportant but only that the benefit-cost analysis is more useful if it concentrates on efficiency considerations.

Benefit-cost analysis: not a panacea

Benefit-cost analysis provides a technique that is helpful in weighing the advantages and disadvantages of government policies. Our discussion has only touched on the major problems in applying this technique, notable identifying and measuring benefits and costs, and discounting to obtain present value measures. In particular, the difficulty of measuring benefits and costs has been emphasized, because this is the real problem in most attempts to grapple quantitatively with policy issues.

The remainder of this book deals with many policy issues that are, in principle, amenable to benefit-cost analysis. Unfortunately, the problems of measuring benefits and costs are extremely difficult for many of the most important government policies. No attempt is made to construct a formal benefit-cost analysis of any of the policies discussed later, but the reader should find the benefit-cost approach a helpful guide in thinking about the economic effects that will be identified.

Supplementary Readings

GRAMLICH, EDWARD M. *Benefit-Cost Analysis of Government Programs.* Englewood Cliffs, N.J.: Prentice-Hall, 1981.

HARBERGER, ARNOLD C. "On the Use of Distributional Weights in Social Cost-Benefit Analysis." *Journal of Political Economy,* 86(2):S87–120, Part 2 (Apr. 1978).

HAVEMAN, ROBERT H., AND JULIUS MARGOLIS, eds. *Public Expenditure and Policy Analysis,* 3rd ed. Boston: Houghton Mifflin, 1983.

LAYARD, RICHARD, ed. *Cost-Benefit Analysis*. Harmondsworth, Middlesex, England: Penguin Books, 1974.

McKEAN, ROLAND N. *Efficiency in Government Through Systems Analysis*. New York: John Wiley, 1958.

Review Questions and Problems

1. "Government defense expenditures created 300,000 jobs in Texas in 1985. A reduction in defense spending thus would cost Texas thousands of jobs and produce much hardship." Discuss.

2. Identify and explain why some types of government expenditures could have no effect at all on the allocation of resources. What actual government expenditures do you think are likely to be of this type and have very little effect on the composition of output?

3. What are the essential characteristics of a fixed quantity subsidy? Under what conditions would such a subsidy have no effect on a recipient's consumption pattern?

4. Explain how a fixed quantity subsidy can lead to underconsumption. Does the subsidy always have this effect, or could it lead to underconsumption for some recipients and to overconsumption for others? Support your answer with a graphical analysis.

5. Is it better for a subsidy to lead to overconsumption or to underconsumption?

6. What is an excise subsidy, and how does it differ from a fixed quantity subsidy? Can an excise subsidy ever lead to underconsumption?

7. Compare the effects of an excise subsidy and a fixed quantity subsidy (in which the consumer can supplement the quantity provided by government). Which subsidy will lead to greater consumption of the subsidized good, and which will make the consumer better off? (Be sure to compare subsidies of equal cost to the government.)

8. Senator Throckmorton, arguing for federal funds to build a dam in his district, observed: "Not only will the dam benefit the area, it will also create much needed jobs in the area. As a matter of fact, I wouldn't consider the $200 million price tag of the project as a 'cost' at all, given that we will be using unemployed workers and resources. I mean the people and resources weren't being used to do anything, right? Therefore, society doesn't give up anything to get the dam. The correct economic phrase would be the opportunity cost of the dam is zero." Evaluate the Senator's reasoning.

9. If you were to conduct a benefit-cost analysis of an excise subsidy granted to a single consumer, how would you measure the policy's benefits? How would you measure its costs? (Try to do this using a graph.) Can you say which will be larger, or will this depend on the particular good and the consumer being subsidized?

10. Why is the choice of a discount rate often important to conducting a benefit-cost analysis? Why is it difficult to determine what discount rate should be used?

chapter 5

Applied Expenditure Analysis: Food Stamps, Unemployment Insurance, and Subsidies to Higher Education

C HAPTER 4 developed the analytical framework needed to study the effects of different types of subsidies. Two categories of subsidies, fixed quantity and excise subsidies, were emphasized. In this chapter we adapt this analytical framework to examine more thoroughly three actual policies of these types: the food stamp program, unemployment insurance, and subsidies to higher education.

The Food Stamp Program

President John F. Kennedy's first executive order in January 1961 directed the secretary of agriculture to establish pilot food stamp programs for needy families. After several years' experience with the pilot programs, Congress enacted the Food Stamp Act of 1964. Begun on a small scale with total expenditures of $30.4 million in 1964, the food stamp program has registered an impressive rate of growth, increasing to $12.4 billion in 1984, as Table 5–1 shows.

Much of the expansion in the food stamp program reflects its growth

Table 5–1   *Food Stamp Program: Total Expenditures and Participation, 1964–1984*

Year	Total Federal Outlays (billions)	Participation (millions)
1964	$ .03	.4
1969	.25	2.9
1972	1.92	11.1
1974	2.86	13.5
1976	3.86	15.8
1978	5.85	16.0
1980	9.00	21.5
1984	12.40	22.0

Source: Kenneth Clarkson, *Food Stamps and Nutrition,* Table 5; *Congressional Quarterly Weekly Reports,* 1981, pp. 275–276, and Office of Management and Budget, *The Budget of the United States Government, Fiscal Year 1986.*

throughout the country: In 1964 only 43 counties and cities participated, but by 1976 approximately 3,200 counties and cities (essentially, all regions of the country) were participating in the program. In 1971 the program was amended to nationalize eligibility requirements and greatly expand benefits, which accounts for much of the spurt in outlays between 1969 and 1972. Since 1972, the growth in expenditures has been mainly the result of two factors: inflation and an increase in the number of recipients. From 1972 to 1984, real benefits per recipient showed only a slight increase, but the number of recipients doubled, and the price level more than doubled.

To become eligible to receive the food stamp subsidy, a household's net income and total assets must fall below specified amounts. These eligibility requirements are designed to restrict eligibility to families with net incomes at or below the federal poverty level. For example, to qualify for food stamp benefits in 1985, a family of four had to have a monthly net income below $880 and total assets below $1,500. Since eligibility is limited to those with low incomes, the food stamp program is essentially a welfare program.

Despite the eligibility requirements, families with incomes exceeding the poverty level may still qualify for food stamps. This can happen because eligibility depends on *net* income, or total income minus certain allowable deductions. The more important deductions are a standard deduction of $85 per month, shelter costs in excess of specified levels, and 18 percent of any earned income. As a result of these deductions, a family of four could have a total income as high as $13,848 in 1985 and still receive food stamps. In an effort to curb potential abuse of the food stamp program, Congress passed a reform measure in 1981 that limited eligibility to families with a total income below 130 percent of the poverty level. It should be emphasized, however, that even before this reform was enacted, most of the families that received food stamps had very low incomes. In 1979, for example, the average income of families on food stamps was $3,900, and fewer than 4 percent of food stamp recipients had gross incomes in excess of $10,000. The food stamp program is successful in concentrating most of its benefits on people with low income.

If households meet the eligibility requirements, they can receive food stamps. Food stamps can be thought of as checks signed by the government that can be used only to purchase food; some government publications, in fact, refer to food stamps as "food money." The amount of food stamps that a family can receive is called the *coupon allotment* and depends on the family's net income and the number of persons in the family. Larger-sized families receive a bigger coupon allotment, and families with higher incomes receive a smaller coupon allotment.

Table 5–2 shows how the coupon allotment varies with net income for four-person families. For example, a family with a zero monthly net income would receive $264 in food stamps. For each dollar of income the family earns, food stamp benefits are reduced by 30 cents. Thus, a family with an income of $100 receives $234 in food stamps, $30 less than a family with a zero net income receives. The rate at which benefits fall as income rises is called the *benefit reduction rate,* and in the food stamp program it is 30 percent. The benefit reduction rate ensures that the poorest households get the largest benefits.

The basic coupon allotment, the amount of food stamps given to a family with zero net income, is based on the "Thrifty Food Plan" of the Department of Agriculture, a low-cost plan for achieving a nutritionally adequate diet. Since 1974 the basic coupon allotments (one for each family size) have

Table 5–2   *Food Stamp Benefits, Family of Four, 1985*

Monthly Net Income	Food Stamps
$ 0	$264
100	234
200	204
300	174
400	144
500	114
600	84
700	54
800	24
880	0

been tied to a price escalator that increases the allotments to reflect changes in the prices of food items.

Economic effects of the food stamp program

In analyzing the effects of a fixed quantity subsidy like food stamps, we begin by examining how the program affects food and nonfood consumption and then consider some other effects of the program.

Consumption pattern of recipients   In terms of its effect on the consumption pattern of recipients, the food stamp program is a straightforward type of fixed quantity subsidy. The only new feature we need to consider is that the amount of food stamps varies with income, with poor families receiving more assistance.

In Chapter 4 we noted that this form of subsidy can have two different types of effects, both of which are illustrated in Figure 5–1. Throughout this analysis of the food stamp program, we will assume that at any given level of cash income, low-income families have preferences that imply they would choose to spend one third of their income on food. (Studies of household expenditure patterns find this to be a reasonable generalization.)

Given this assumption, panel [a] of Figure 5–1 shows the effects of food stamps for a family with a gross income of $500 per month. The family is assumed to have deductions of $100 per month so its net income is $400 and its coupon allotment is $144 (Table 5–2). With food measured on the horizontal axis in units that cost $1 each, the presubsidy budget line is *MN,* and food consumption is 167 units. The food stamp subsidy causes the budget line to become *MM'N'.* The budget line is kinked at *M',* indicating that the family can use food stamps to purchase 144 units of food at no cost, but the purchase of additional units of food (along *M'N'*) must be paid for by the family. The new equilibrium is at point *E'* with consumption of 215 units of food. (We know the family will choose to consume 215 units of food on *MM'N',* because if they were given $144, the cash equivalent of the coupon allotment, the family's income would be $644, and they would spend one third of it on food at point *E'* on *M"N'.*) In this case, the food stamp program has the same effect as a cash transfer.

Panel [b] of Figure 5–1 shows the results for a lower-income family with a gross income of $300 per month and $100 in deductions, which makes it eligible to receive 204 in food stamps. The budget line with food stamps is *MM'N';* the kink at point *M'* identifies the point at which food stamps finance purchases of $204 units of food. Equilibrium occurs at point *M'* where the family uses food stamps to finance all of its food consumption, leaving its entire income free to finance the purchase of other goods. Note that the family would be better off if it received $204 in cash, since that would gen-

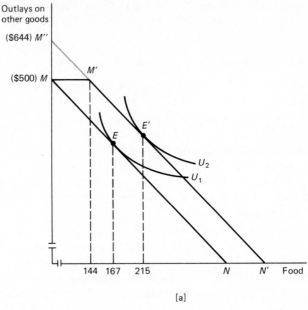

[a]

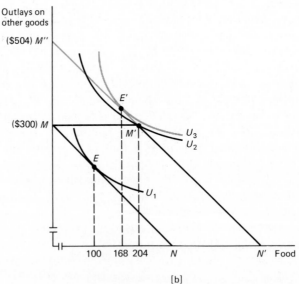

[b]

FIGURE 5–1 *Food stamps: two possible outcomes.*

erate a budget line of $M''N'$; that is, the family would reach a higher indifference curve, U_3, by spending one third of its income on food and purchasing 168 units of food at point E'.

In Figure 5–1 [b] the food stamp program produces a welfare cost by leading to overconsumption of food: The family attains indifference curve U_2 with food stamps, but it could reach U_3 at the same cost if the family were given cash instead, and it consumed less food and more of other goods. In effect, the food stamp program forces an inferior consumption pattern on the family by requiring that the subsidy be consumed as food. The welfare cost does not, however, mean that the family is worse off with food stamps than with no subsidy; the family is clearly better off at point M' than at point E. Instead, the welfare cost compares the well-being of the family under the food stamp program with an equal cost subsidy that does not distort consumption choices.

Which type of outcome, panel [a] or panel [b], is more common under the food stamp program? Although we cannot know this with any certainty, there are reasons for thinking that most recipients are in the situation shown in panel [a]. We would expect that low-income recipients are more likely to have their consumption patterns distorted, as in panel [b], because their food stamp benefits are larger relative to their incomes. But how low does income have to fall before the panel [b] outcome occurs? We can get an idea by considering the fraction of income normally devoted to food purchases. As noted earlier, family budget studies conducted before the food stamp program was introduced found that low-income families normally spent about one third of their incomes on food. If this is still true, then the program is equivalent to a cash transfer for most food stamp recipients. In 1985, the average gross income of recipients was about $5,500 a year, or around $450 per month. With deductions of $100, a family would receive $159 in food stamps but choose to spend $203 on food; the outcome would be like panel [a]. More direct evidence is afforded by the experience of Puerto Rico, which in 1982 converted its food stamp program into a program providing unrestricted cash transfers. A study of the consequences concluded that this change had no effect on the consumption patterns of recipients, supporting the view that food stamps are equivalent to cash.[1]

Families with incomes well below the average could still find themselves in the situation shown in panel [b], but it appears likely that the subsidy is equivalent to giving most food stamp recipients cash. This conclusion is significant because it means the impression most people have—that the food stamp program is distinctly different from cash welfare programs—is incorrect. Food stamps no more encourage food consumption than would cash assistance.

Regardless of whether panel [a] or panel [b] is the appropriate analysis, the food stamp program has the effect of increasing nonfood consumption as well as food consumption. This is particularly interesting, since many proponents of food stamps emphasize that the subsidy should not be used

---

[1] Robert Moffitt, "An Econometric Investigation of the Effects of Converting an In-Kind Transfer to Cash," Working Paper No. 85-23, Brown University, June 1985.

to finance consumption of "unnecessary" goods (such as liquor or cigarettes?). In practice, however, the food stamp program unavoidably leads to increased consumption of goods other than food; in fact, it is difficult to design a subsidy that will only increase consumption of the subsidized good.

Other effects   Although its impact on food consumption is perhaps the most widely emphasized effect of the food stamp program, the program does have other significant effects. The most important of these is probably the way the program affects the work incentives of the recipients. The feature in the program that bears most directly on work effort is the benefit reduction rate. With a benefit reduction rate of 30 percent, if a family reduces its earnings by $100, its food stamp benefits will go up by $30, so net income will fall by only $70. In effect, the food stamp program lowers the cost of reducing work effort. The work incentives issue is extremely important in evaluating welfare programs, but to consider it adequately it is necessary to take into account the combined effects of many separate welfare programs. Thus, we defer further consideration of this issue until Chapter 9, when we take a broader look at welfare programs.

As explained earlier, the amount of food stamps a family receives is related to net income, or total income less allowable deductions. The deductions have the obvious effect of making some families eligible for food stamps who have incomes above the poverty line. A more subtle implication of the deduction of shelter costs is that it acts as an excise subsidy to housing-related expenditures. Shelter costs (including rent, insurance, and utilities) in excess of 30 percent of income are deductible from total income in determining the net income figure on which food stamp subsidies are based. To illustrate how this acts to subsidize housing, consider a family on food stamps spending 30 percent of its income on housing. If the family increases its housing outlays by $50 per month, its "monthly net income" used to determine the food stamp subsidy will fall by $50. With a lower net income, the food stamp subsidy is larger (see Table 5–2), in this case by $15. The deduction acts to reduce the net cost of housing (in excess of 30 percent of income) by 30 percent (the benefit reduction rate) in the same way as an excise subsidy would. Thus, the food stamp program also acts to subsidize the consumption of housing of families that spend more than 30 percent of their income on shelter. As we will see in Chapter 11, this is similar to the way deductions in the federal income tax operate as implicit subsidies.

A peculiarity of the food stamp program is that eligibility depends on *monthly* net income. Consequently, a family with an *annual* income well above the eligibility limits but a low income in certain months can receive food stamps. This is the provision that allows labor union members on strike to receive benefits: in this case, the food stamp program acts to lower the costs of strikes to workers. In addition, workers who are temporarily unemployed can also frequently receive food stamps. Since going back to work entails a loss in food stamp benefits, this can encourage workers to remain unemployed longer than they otherwise would. (This is considered more fully in our discussion of unemployment insurance.) Insofar as relating benefits to monthly income is a problem, it could easily be avoided by having a year-end accounting, just as with the federal income tax, which is based on annual income but withheld on a monthly or weekly basis. Several proposals to do this have been discussed in Congress, but none has yet been enacted.

Other factors in an evaluation of food stamps

Considerations that influence congressional decisions are often different from those emphasized by economists. Food stamps are a case in point. Consider, for example, the testimony of the late Senator Hubert Humphrey in congressional hearings on food stamp reforms. Senator Humphrey summarized three arguments in favor of food stamps that are still often heard in Congress:

> The food stamp program plays a very critical role in enabling millions of low income families to have a better diet.
>
> It plays a very important role in the support of American agriculture.
>
> It also plays a very important role in keeping the economy from sliding into a deeper recession.[2]

Because these three arguments are frequently mentioned in discussions of food stamps, we shall consider each in turn.

Nutrition   Improving the nutritional adequacy of the diets of poor families is frequently stated as the primary objective of the program. With regard to the effect of food stamps on nutrition, two questions should be asked: Do food stamps improve the nutritional quality of diets? And if they do, why should this be considered desirable?

Food stamps generally lead to an increase in food consumption as measured by dollar outlays on it, but a distinction must be made between the amount of food consumed and the nutritional adequacy of the diet. Somewhat surprisingly, available evidence fails to find a significant improvement in the nutritional content of food consumed by recipients, and in some cases diets have apparently deteriorated.[3]

As we have seen, the food stamp program today is equivalent to a cash

---

[2] Statement of Senator Hubert Humphrey, *Food Stamp Hearings,* Subcommittee on Agriculture and General Legislation of the Committee on Agriculture and Forestry, U.S. Senate, *Food Stamp Reform,* Part 1 (Washington, D.C.: U.S. Government Printing Office, 1975), p. 107.

[3] Kenneth Clarkson, *Food Stamps and Nutrition* (Washington, D.C.: American Enterprise Institute, 1975).

transfer for most recipients. That means the food stamp program affects the nutritional adequacy of diets in the same way as an increase in income does. With higher incomes, families may respond by purchasing more palatable and easily prepared food, but not necessarily more nutritious food. Indeed, nutritional studies have shown that high-income families frequently have nutritionally deficient diets, and so raising a family's income is no guarantee of improving nutrition.

If improving nutrition were an overriding goal, it would be possible to restructure the program in a way that would promote it more effectively. All we would have to do is restrict the use of food stamps to food items with a highly nutritious content per dollar of cost. Instead of allowing food stamps to be used to purchase frozen TV dinners, candy, soft drinks, cakes, coffee, sugar, and so on, they could be restricted to the purchase of items like soybeans, nonfat dry milk, liver, and vitamin pills. This reform would certainly be more effective in improving nutrition, but it would also make food stamp recipients much worse off according to their own preferences.

That brings us to the second question: Even if food stamps do improve nutrition more than an outright cash transfer would, why should this be considered desirable? Viewed relative to a cash transfer, if food stamps improve nutrition, they must do so at the expense of other nonfood items considered more desirable by the recipient. In other words, recipients would be worse off under a nutrition-promoting food stamp program like the one described than they would if they could spend the funds as they wished. Claiming the nutritional improvement as an advantage of the food stamp program implicitly seems to adopt the position that we do not want the program to cater to the needs of the recipients as they themselves evaluate their needs. Although that position may be defensible, it should be clear what is really being argued.

Effect on the agricultural sector Senator Humphrey argued that food stamps "support American agriculture." In recent years, food stamps have accounted for approximately 3 percent of total food expenditures, but that does not mean that demand for food has increased by 3 percent as a result of the program. Since food stamps are like an increase in income for most recipients, food purchases by recipients will increase by less than the amount of food stamps. It is unlikely, for example, that the recipients of the $12.4 billion in food stamps in 1985 increased purchases of food by more than $4 billion, since low-income families spend about a third of their income on food, and the marginal propensity to spend on food may well be less than this average figure. In addition, the taxes needed to finance the program would probably reduce food purchases by taxpayers by at least $2 billion. Thus, the net increase in food purchases would be about $2 billion. Since total outlays in the United States on food products were about $500 billion in 1985, a $2 billion increase would imply an increase in demand of 0.4 percent resulting from the food stamp program.

No detailed study is required to see that the impact of a 0.4 percent increase in demand for food on the agricultural sector will be trivial. Less than half the retail food dollar reaches the agricultural sector; costs of retailing, transportation, and processing account for the remainder. Most, if not all, of what reaches agriculture will simply cover the costs of producing the small increment in output that results. Although the exact effects depend on the nature of the market (see Figure 4–9 in Chapter 4 for the relevant analysis), the quantitative impact is clearly very small.

Suppose, however, that food stamps really did lead to a significant increase in demand for agricultural sector products. The relevant question is whether such an impact is desirable. To the extent that the food stamp program increases the demand for food, it reduces the demand for other goods and services. Any increase in incomes, wages, or profits in agriculture is therefore accompanied by a reduction in income, wages, or profits in other parts of the economy. In short, any advantages derived by food producers reflect a redistribution of income away from other people; what farmers gain, others lose. So even if the agricultural sector does benefit, we need to determine whether this is considered desirable.

Employment and business expansion   Senator Humphrey buttressed his preceding remarks concerning the stimulative effect of food stamps by referring to a Department of Agriculture study on the impact of the program in Texas in 1972:

> The study found that $63.9 million in bonus food stamps provided in Texas that year generated $232 million in new business in Texas and appeared to generate at least $89 million in business elsewhere in the United States. In addition, the $63.9 million provided in bonus food stamps created 5031 jobs. Translated nationwide, this could mean that the food stamp program is now responsible for $27 billion in business in the United States each year and 425,000 jobs. . . . Furthermore, consider how much money we would have to spend to support those 425,000 workers and their dependents if they did not have the jobs that the food stamp program has apparently generated.[4]

Such arguments, frequently presented in Congress, represent a basic misunderstanding of the significance of the effects of the program on employment and output. The opportunity cost of the expansion of business and employment resulting from the expenditure on food stamp subsidies is a contraction of business and employment elsewhere. This expansion, if it occurs, is not a net effect because it involves drawing resources from other uses. This is easily seen when we recognize that the taxes that finance the program reduce taxpayers' demands for goods and services, reducing output and employment via multiplier effects through other markets.

At the end of his statement Senator Humphrey seemed to suggest that

---

[4]Statement of Senator Humphrey, op. cit., p. 107.

the workers were not bid away from other jobs, so the effects described represent a net increase in economic activity. This is highly unlikely; even if it were true, the implications drawn by Senator Humphrey would be wrong. As will be recalled from the previous chapter, the opportunity cost of using these resources is that they could have been employed in other jobs producing different goods and services. Had the government spent the $63.9 million on a different subsidy, or had it cut taxes, these resources would have been drawn into the production of other goods. The food stamp subsidy simply leads to a different pattern of employment and output than alternative policies. Adding up the employment and output related to food stamp subsidies ignores the fact that employment and output elsewhere could have been higher with different policies. There is, therefore, no net gain in output and employment attributable to food stamps.

Of course, we have made this last point earlier: Impacts, if any, on the level of aggregate economic activity (macroeconomic effects) are irrelevant to the analysis of specific expenditure programs. The use of arguments like the one quoted, however, is so prevalent in discussions of many expenditure programs that we thought it useful to examine this one in somewhat greater detail.

Food stamps: a summing up

Many of the arguments, like those of Senator Humphrey, that are used to defend the food stamp program are either incorrect or misleading, but that does not mean that the program is undesirable. Basically, the food stamp program is a redistributive program that provides assistance to low-income families. Since food stamps are, for most recipients, the same as cash assistance, recipients can spend the funds in the way that best serves their needs. In addition, benefits go almost entirely to families with low incomes, and the benefits are higher for families with the lowest incomes. For these reasons, many economists believe it is one of the best welfare programs in the United States.

The food stamp program is, however, one of a number of welfare programs intended to redistribute income toward low-income families. An evaluation of the entire welfare system, of which food stamps are but a part, should also consider how this combination of programs functions. We consider this broader issue more carefully in Chapters 8 and 9.

Unemployment Insurance

Government-provided unemployment insurance has been a part of American life since it was enacted into law in the Social Security Act of 1935. Systems providing unemployment compensation are operated by the states under federal guidelines. These guidelines ensure that the state systems are quite similar, although some significant differences exist.

Workers who *lose* their jobs receive financial support from the unemployment insurance system while they remain unemployed. In most states, new entrants into the labor force and persons who quit their jobs are not eligible to receive unemployment benefits. Cash benefits are provided to eligible unemployed workers, typically at a level of about 50 percent of previous wages up to some maximum amount. Some states replace as much as two thirds of an individual's previous wages, and several also use dependents' allowances, which provide an additional income supplement based on the number of family members. These benefits are normally payable up to a maximum of 26 weeks. Supplementary federal programs have in recent years generally provided additional benefits to jobless persons after they have exhausted their regular 26 weeks of benefits. In 1985, for example, an additional 8 to 14 weeks of benefits were available under the Federal Supplemental Compensation program.

Table 5–3 shows total outlays on unemployment insurance as well as related data on unemployment for recent years. Not surprisingly, total outlays under these programs are quite sensitive to the level of unemployment, tending to be larger when the unemployment rate is higher. Not all unemployed workers, however, receive benefits. To qualify for benefits, unemployed workers must have worked for at least a certain minimum time during a recent one-year period and must have lost their jobs for economic reasons (such as a plant closing). Thus, former students entering the job market for the first time are ineligible for benefits. In most years, between one half and two thirds of unemployed persons have received benefits, as indicated in Table 5–3 by the difference between the insured unemploy-

Table 5–3   *Total Expenditures on Unemployment Insurance, Related Unemployment Rates, Insured Unemployment Rates, and Average Weekly Benefit, 1960–1984*

Year	Total Outlays (billions)	Unemployment Rate	Insured Unemployment Rate	Average Weekly Benefit
1960	$ 3.0	5.5%	4.8%	$ 32.87
1965	2.4	4.5	3.0	37.19
1970	4.2	4.9	3.4	50.34
1975	16.8	8.5	6.0	70.23
1980	17.3	7.1	4.1	98.92
1984	13.1	7.4	2.8	123.47

Source: *Economic Report of the President, 1986,* Tables B-35 and B-39.

ment rate (the unemployment rate for those who receive benefits) and the total unemployment rate.

Special (earmarked) taxes are used to finance unemployment insurance. To fund the system, employers pay taxes that are based on total taxable wages paid to workers. There is some variation in the tax base and rate among states. Typically, only the first $7,000 of wages of each worker is taxable, and the tax rate averages about 3 percent. In other words, if the rate is 3 percent, an employer must pay $90 in taxes when employing a worker for $3,000. For a worker who earns $7,000 or more, the tax is $210. Even though employers are responsible for paying the taxes, workers probably bear the cost in the form of lower wages.

Although the programs are nominally financed largely by the states, there is an indirect tax advantage granted by the federal government. A tax credit is used that has the effect of allowing states to tax employers at no additional cost to the employers—if the states did not collect the tax, the federal government would. This arrangement gives the states a powerful incentive to implement an unemployment insurance program that qualifies for the tax credit, and all states have done so.

Distribution of benefits

Our discussion of food stamps observed that virtually all of the benefits go to families with low incomes. Because unemployment insurance (UI) benefits are paid to the unemployed, it is widely believed that this program also concentrates benefits on those who would have low incomes without the program. This, however, turns out not to be the case. In one of his several studies of unemployment insurance, Martin Feldstein found that in 1970 only 17 percent of total UI benefits paid went to families whose incomes were below one half the median income level. In contrast, more than half the benefits went to families with incomes (even before receiving UI benefits) that were greater than median family income. More than 15 percent of benefits went to families with incomes of more than double the median level.[5] The distribution of benefits is much the same today. The Congressional Budget Office, for instance, reports that 51 percent of UI recipients in 1983 belonged to families with incomes above $20,000.[6]

It is not really surprising that UI benefits do not disproportionally benefit low-income families, since the nature of the program guarantees this result. Since UI benefits are related to previous earnings, unemployed workers

[5]Martin Feldstein, "Unemployment Compensation: Adverse Incentives and Distributional Anomalies," *National Tax Journal,* 27(2):231 (June 1974).

[6]Congressional Budget Office, *Promoting Employment and Maintaining Incomes with Unemployment Insurance* (Washington, D.C.: U.S. Government Printing Office, March 1985) Table 1.

who had higher earnings receive higher UI benefits. In addition, most unemployment tends to be of fairly short duration (as we will see later), so a high-wage worker who is unemployed for one month will still receive UI benefits, even though his or her annual income may be quite sizable. Well-paid union members, for example, can receive benefits while temporarily laid off. In contrast, many low-income persons are ineligible for benefits for a variety of reasons. For instance, they may not have recently lost their jobs (that is, they may be retired or on welfare), they may have just entered the labor force, or they may have been unemployed so long (more than 26 weeks) that their UI benefit payments have ceased.

Unemployment insurance is therefore not a redistributive program (at least among income classes) like food stamps. Instead, unemployment insurance tends to provide temporary assistance to persons who have lost their jobs, without regard to how needy the person's family is.

Replacement rates

In analyzing unemployment insurance, a key concept is the *replacement rate,* which refers to the extent to which UI benefits replace lost earnings. For example, if a person's earnings were previously $300 per week, and his or her UI benefit is $100 per week, the replacement rate is one third. Based on a comparison of average weekly benefits (column 4 in Table 5–4) with average wages in the economy, it is frequently asserted that UI benefits replace only one third of the worker's usual pay. Consider, for example, the concern expressed on this point in a *New York Times* editorial (April 17, 1973): "The present national average benefit of roughly $55 a week is just a little over one-third of usual pay, a gap that causes unfair hardship for many."

Actually the relevant replacement rates are generally well above one third. Calculating the average replacement rate as weekly UI benefits divided by the national average weekly wage, as was done in the *New York Times* editorial, understates true replacement rates for two important reasons. First, the average benefit refers to the average wage of all covered workers whether unemployed or not. In most years, unemployed workers have previous wages that are below the national average, generally about 70 percent of the national average. Thus, if UI benefits are equal to one third of the national average, they are equal to nearly one half the average wage of unemployed persons. Second, UI benefits are not taxable for many workers. Prior to 1979, all UI benefits were nontaxable, but in that year one half of the benefits paid to upper-income families were made subject to federal income taxation. Currently, families with incomes above $18,000 must pay federal income taxes on half their UI benefits.

To see the importance of having UI benefits nontaxable, consider an example of a worker, Clancy, who earns $1,000 per month. If he is unemployed for 1 month, Clancy's disposable, or take-home, earnings will fall by less than $1,000, because of the taxes he would have paid on his gross earnings. Suppose Clancy's effective marginal tax rate is 25 percent; he might, for instance, be in a 14 percent federal income tax bracket and pay a 7 percent social security tax and a 4 percent state income tax. Then Clancy's monthly disposable earnings are only $750. UI benefits will typically replace half his gross earnings of $1,000, or $500, and this payment is not taxable. Thus, in this case, UI replaces *two thirds* of lost disposable income.

The replacement rate varies widely from one worker to another. It depends on the state of residence, type of family, and number of dependents (several states have dependents' allowances that serve to increase the replacement rate), whether the spouse is working, and other factors. There are also usually minimum and maximum UI weekly benefits. A minimum weekly benefit serves to increase the replacement rate of low-paid workers and a maximum to reduce it for high-paid workers. For example, if the minimum is $90 and a worker normally earns $150 a week, then the unemployed worker will receive 60 percent of his or her regular gross earnings; in contrast, if the maximum is $150 per week, a worker with earnings of $400 a week will receive less than half his or her regular gross earnings.

Feldstein studied the replacement rates relative to after-tax earnings for a variety of family structures in all 50 states. For workers earning less than 130 percent of the average wage in each state, he found that the replacement rate was quite high. For male earners, the replacement rates were typically above 60 percent, and for married women they were generally above 75 percent.[7] In fact, in several states the replacement rates for married women exceeded 100 percent, implying a higher net income for the family when the wife is unemployed than when she is working. Daniel Hamermesh estimated the typical replacement rate to be between 50 and 60 percent.[8] The Council of Economic Advisers puts the typical replacement rate at 70 percent for male family heads with relatively low earnings, but at 40 percent for those with high earnings.[9]

These studies estimate fairly high replacement rates for UI, but it is still likely that the true replacement rates were underestimated because they failed to include the effect of the food stamp program. In addition to receiving UI benefits, some unemployed workers become eligible to receive food stamps, and they also serve to replace lost earnings. Consider the example described earlier of a worker, whose regular pay is $1,000 a month. With a wife and two children, and assuming $100 in allowable deductions under the food stamp program, the family would be ineligible for food stamps

[7] Martin Feldstein, op. cit.

[8] Daniel Hamermesh, *Jobless Pay and the Economy* (Baltimore: Johns Hopkins University Press, 1977).

[9] Council of Economic Advisers, *Economic Report of the President, 1975* (Washington, D.C.: U.S. Government Printing Office, 1975).

while Clancy is employed (see Table 5–2). When unemployed, although his $500 in UI benefits counts as income under the food stamp program, Clancy's income is now low enough to entitle him to a food stamp subsidy of $144 per month. His net income, including the food stamp subsidy, while unemployed is thus $644 whereas his net (after-tax) pay if employed is $750. The effective replacement rate of UI and food stamps together is therefore 86 percent rather than the 67 percent calculated earlier when food stamps were ignored.

Thus, the food stamp program, as well as other welfare programs, probably increases the effective replacement rates for some workers. However, most workers receiving UI benefits do not receive aid under welfare programs. In 1983, for example, only 12 percent of UI recipients received food stamps.[10]

Duration of unemployment

The most important potential effect of UI on the allocation of resources is its impact on the unemployment rate. UI does not, of course, very often cause people to lose jobs; instead, it creates an incentive for workers, once unemployed, to extend the duration of their unemployment. The replacement rates of UI are the key to this effect. The greater the replacement rate (including food stamps), the lower the cost to the worker of extending the duration of unemployment.

When a worker is unemployed and does not receive UI benefits, the cost he or she bears is the sacrifice of net income earned if the person were employed. UI substantially reduces this cost by replacing a large fraction of lost net earnings as long as the worker is unemployed. In the example previously discussed, Clancy receives $644 in UI and food stamp benefits each month he is unemployed, or 86 percent of his previous net income. Thus, Clancy has small financial incentive to search for a new job because his net income would rise by only $106 if he found a job paying the same salary as his previous one. Indeed, if he believes he cannot find a job that pays as much, or if there are expenses associated with his work (such as transportation), his gain from finding a job will be reduced even more. It is understandable then that a worker laid off from his previous job might simply wait to be recalled, or postpone searching for a new job in order to work some around the house. Such a reaction adds to the unemployment rate.

In understanding this effect, it may help to recognize that UI is really a type of excise subsidy. UI reduces the price to the worker of a certain good—lengthening the duration of unemployment—and the law of demand reminds us that people generally consume more at a lower price. Not all

[10]Congressional Budget Office, op. cit., Table 1.

people can be expected to react to this incentive in exactly the same way, but the general direction of the effect is clear.

It can now be seen that the replacement rate is significant for two very different reasons. First, a higher replacement rate means that workers are provided greater security against the temporary loss of income because of unemployment. Second, a higher replacement rate lowers the cost to workers of remaining unemployed. The critical policy question is how to strike a balance between providing security and undermining incentives.

Although the benefits paid by UI give workers an incentive to extend spells of unemployment, there are several ways in which the UI system attempts to counter this effect. As mentioned earlier, UI benefits are normally payable for 26 weeks. Because benefits cease after that period, there is no incentive to remain unemployed indefinitely. (There is also no security provided for very long periods of unemployment.) In addition, UI benefits are generally (but not in all states) restricted to workers who have lost their jobs through no fault of their own. Workers who quit or who are discharged for misconduct are ineligible for benefits, although some states do permit such workers to collect benefits after a waiting period of 4 to 6 weeks.

In addition, unemployed workers are required to register for work at the State Employment Service and to accept a suitable job if one is offered or lose their UI benefits. These features of the program are attempts to offset the financial incentives of workers to remain unemployed, but how effective they are is uncertain. Workers are required to accept "suitable work," but what constitutes suitable work is nowhere precisely defined and is largely left to administrative discretion. In practice, suitable work is sometimes interpreted to mean a job paying the same wage rate as the one lost, with the same working conditions, and in the same location. This, of course, robs the provision of much of its force.

It is probably true therefore that these practices frequently fail to offset the financial incentive of workers to extend the duration of unemployment. No doubt, major abuses are avoided, and some workers lose UI benefits because of these practices, but it is not an easy matter to induce people to behave in a way they perceive as contrary to their best interests. Indeed, to make these provisions fully effective would probably lead to workers' having little freedom to choose among alternative jobs.

In judging the potential impact of UI on the unemployment rate, it is important to recognize some facts concerning the nature of unemployment. Many people believe unemployment consists of an unchanging pool of workers who will remain out of work unless the unemployment rate is reduced. Nothing could be farther from the truth. Actually, in most years more than 40 percent of unemployed workers are out of work for less than 5 weeks, and the median duration of unemployment seldom exceeds 7 weeks.

Table 5–4 provides some information concerning the duration of unem-

Table 5-4 Unemployment Rates and Duration of Unemployment, 1960–1984

Selected Years	Unemployment Rate	Duration of Unemployment (percent)				Average Duration in Weeks	Median Duration in Weeks
		Less than 5 Weeks	5–14	15–26	26 Weeks or More		
1960	5.5%	45	31	13	12	12.8	NA
1965	4.5	48	29	12	10	11.8	NA
1970	4.9	52	32	10	6	8.7	4.9
1975	8.5	37	31	16	15	14.1	8.4
1980	7.1	43	32	14	11	11.9	6.5
1984	7.4	39	29	13	19	18.2	7.9

Source: *Economic Report of the President, 1985*, Table B-31.

ployment in recent years. As mentioned, Table 5–4 shows that most unemployment is of short duration. If the unemployment rate is 5 percent over 1 year, this means that many more than 5 percent of members of the labor force are out of work at some time during the year, but each person is unemployed for only a relatively short period of time. Reducing the unemployment rate is largely a problem of reducing the average duration of unemployment. What appears to be a small reduction in the duration of unemployment can have a significant effect on the unemployment rate. Suppose, for example, that in 1984 when the average duration was 18.2 weeks, it would have been 15 weeks in the absence of UI. The unemployment rate would then have been 6.1 percent instead of 7.4 percent. (Obviously, we are not suggesting that this is the actual size of the impact of UI but are only trying to illustrate how a small reduction in the average duration of unemployment would affect the unemployment rate.)

In our discussion of UI so far, its macroeconomic effect on unemployment as an "automatic stabilizer" has been conspicuously absent. At the risk of belaboring what is perhaps by now obvious, let's turn to Feldstein on this point:

> it is really irrelevant to argue that the program reduces unemployment because it automatically increases government spending when unemployment rises. We have come to accept the government's general responsibility for maintaining a high level of demand through variations in spending, taxation, and monetary policy. The fiscal stimulus now provided by unemployment compensation would alternatively be provided through other government expenditure increases or tax cuts.[11]

We should note that a tax cut rather than an expenditure increase (as with UI) would increase the incentive of unemployed workers to return to work because their potential take-home (after-tax) pay would be higher.

Encouraging instability in employment

The incentive provided by UI for workers to extend the duration of unemployment is clear, but there is another way UI operates to increase unemployment. UI encourages employment in industries with high seasonal and cyclical variations in employment, that is, in short-lived jobs in which there are frequent layoffs.

In the absence of UI a firm with a very unstable employment pattern would have to pay higher wages to attract workers. The higher wages would be necessary to compensate workers for the risk that their jobs would be short-lived. With UI benefits available, however, the government compen-

---

[11] Martin S. Feldstein, "Unemployment Insurance: Time for Reform," *Harvard Business Review* (Mar./Apr. 1975).

sates workers who are employed in industries with frequent layoffs. This makes such unstable employment more attractive to workers and hence increases the supply of labor for such jobs. The result is a reduction in market wages and an increase in employment in industries in which seasonal and cyclical unemployment is high. Unstable jobs are being subsidized by the UI program, and the lower market wage rates reduce the incentive for firms to organize production to reduce the instability in employment. Thus, sectors of the economy with unusually high unemployment rates are encouraged to expand at the expense of other sectors, and the result is a higher overall unemployment rate.

Job search

Contrary to popular opinion, many economists have emphasized that the longer duration of unemployment produced by UI is not unequivocally bad. An unemployed person may devote time to "job search," that is, to looking for a new job. The longer an unemployed worker looks for a job, the more likely it is that a good job will be found. UI reduces the pressure on an unemployed worker to take just "any job" that comes along and allows the individual to search more thoroughly for a job that could make better use of the person's skills. If a greater duration of unemployment leads to a better matching of jobs and people, it may represent a productive investment.

It is important to determine whether longer spells of unemployment do lead to higher wages (implying, presumably, a better job) when workers ultimately return to work. Ehrenberg and Oaxaca found that longer periods of unemployment raise postunemployment wages. These effects, however, were statistically significant only in the cases of older males and females aged 30 to 44.[12] By contrast, Kathleen Classen found that longer durations of unemployment had no effect on postunemployment wages.[13] Thus, it is uncertain whether people find better jobs as a result of the longer duration of unemployment caused by UI.

Even if the longer spells of unemployment caused by UI do lead to higher postunemployment wages, it is not clear that this increase is efficient. There is an efficient level of job search that involves equating the marginal return from additional search to the marginal cost of continuing to look for a job. This does not generally involve waiting for the best possible job offer because there is a substantial cost—sacrificed earnings—to waiting. The prob-

[12] Ronald G. Ehrenberg and Ronald L. Oaxaca, "Impact of Unemployment Insurance on the Duration of Unemployment and Post-Unemployment Wage," Paper presented at the Meetings of the Industrial Relations Research Association, Dallas, Texas, December 30, 1975.

[13] Kathleen Classen, "The Effects of Unemployment Insurance: Evidence from Pennsylvania," The Public Research Institute of the Center for Naval Analysis, PRI 166–175, April 1975.

lem with UI is that it greatly reduces the marginal cost of looking for a job, as perceived by workers, and encourages the unemployed to wait too long to take a job. The marginal cost of looking for a job is the earnings that an unemployed worker sacrifices while searching, but as we have seen, UI makes the net sacrifice to the worker much lower by replacing a large fraction of his or her potential earnings. Workers receiving UI benefits have an incentive to hold out for a better job as long as there is almost any hope, however small, because they are sacrificing very little income by not returning to work.

An example may clarify this point. Suppose an unemployed person can return to work for $300 a week, but believes that by searching or waiting for 4 weeks a job paying $320 can be found. The marginal cost of waiting for the $320 a week job is $1,200—the worker's earnings at the $300 job for those 4 weeks. The marginal return is $20 extra per week for (we will assume) 50 weeks, or $1,000. In this case, the marginal cost is $1,200 and the marginal gain $1,000 so it is inefficient to wait for the higher-paying job. If the worker receives $150 a week in UI benefits, however, the net cost of remaining unemployed for those 4 weeks is $600, because he or she could get only $150 more per week by returning to work. The costs and gains as the unemployed person perceives them have changed; to wait for the higher-paying job would cost $600 in forgone earnings, compared with a gain of $1,000. Because the worker does not bear the entire cost of waiting with UI, he or she would then be led to wait for the better paying job even though such a decision is inefficient.

Thus, UI could be expected to lead to excessive job search. Only if people would, in the absence of UI, tend to underestimate substantially the prospects of finding a better job by additional search and thus search too little would encouraging job search be an appropriate policy. Even if this were the case, UI is not well designed to deal with the situation because it reduces not only the cost of the job search but also the cost of all other ways an unemployed person may use his or her time.

Empirical evidence

Economic theory predicts that UI tends to increase unemployment, but empirical research is necessary to determine the size of the impact. In recent years much attention has been devoted to this question. Stephen Marston, for example, compared the experiences of insured and uninsured workers and found the duration of unemployment to be between 16 and 31 percent longer for the insured. If this difference is solely attributable to UI, the unemployment rate would be 0.2 to 0.6 percentage points higher as a result of UI. (This estimate ignores the effect of UI on the unemployment rate by encouraging unstable employment.) It is not clear, however, that the differences in unemployment between insured and uninsured workers measure the impact of UI, because these groups differ greatly. For instance, the un-insured unemployed are largely new entrants in the labor force or those who quit their last job, whereas the insured are primarily those temporarily or permanently laid off from a previous job. These groups would probably have different durations of unemployment even in the absence of UI.[14]

Kathleen Classen investigated the effect of raising weekly UI benefits (i.e., raising the replacement rate) by comparing similar, insured people in the same state (Pennsylvania) before and after an increase in benefits. She found that a $15 increase in weekly benefits in 1970 increased the average dura-tion of unemployment by more than 1 week. (Note that this is not the total effect of UI on the total duration of unemployment but only the effect of a $15 increase.) As far as she could determine, there were no other changes in the economy that took place that could have led to this longer duration.[15]

Evidence from experience in other countries with UI suggests similar effects. Malkí and Spindler examined the British experience following the introduction of an extra "Earnings Related Supplement" into the UI system in Great Britain in 1966. Immediately following this increase in benefits the unemployment rate began a significant increase, rising from 1.6 percent (for males) the month before the change to 3.3 percent 5 months later. Not all of this increase is necessarily due to the Earnings Related Supplement, but Malkí and Spindler, after controlling for some other variables, estimated that the overall unemployment rate was 30 percent higher as a result of the increased benefit.[16] Similarly, Grubel, Malkí, and Sax, using time-series data for 1953 to 1972, suggested that Canada's UI system increased unemploy-ment by more than 1 percentage point.[17]

These and other studies point to a strong consensus that UI does have a significant impact on unemployment, as our theoretical analysis suggested. After surveying 14 studies, Daniel Hamermesh concluded: "There should be no doubt whatsoever that UI benefits in the U.S. do induce longer spells of unemployment."[18] Hamermesh's "best guess" of the overall impact is that UI adds 0.7 percentage points to the unemployment rate; Feldstein's "best guess" is an addition of 1.25 percentage points.

[14]Stephen T. Marston, "The Impact of Unemployment Insurance on Job Search," *Brookings Papers on Economic Activity,* ed. by Arthur Okun and George L. Perry (Washington, D.C.: Brookings, 1975). See also Feldstein's comments on Marston's paper in the same journal.

[15]Classen, op. cit.

[16]Dennis Malkí and Z. A. Spindler, "The Effect of Unemployment Compensation on the Rate of Unemployment in Great Britain," *Oxford Economic Papers,* 27(3):440 (Nov. 1975).

[17]Herbert G. Grubel, Dennis Malkí, and Shelley Sax, "Real and Insurance-induced Unem-ployment in Canada," *Canadian Journal of Economics,* 8(2):174 (May 1975).

[18]Daniel Hamermesh, "Transfers, Taxes and the NAIRU," National Bureau of Economic Re-search Working Paper No. 548, Sept. 1980, p. 15; and Hamermesh, *Jobless Pay and the Econ-omy,* op. cit.

To put them in perspective, these findings should be related to what macroeconomists call the "normal," or "full employment," unemployment rate. This concept holds that with given governmental policies and labor market institutions, there is a certain unemployment rate below which we cannot go, except for short periods of time. In the 1960s, the full employment unemployment rate was frequently held to be 4.0 percent. Solely as a result of the change in the age-sex-race composition of the labor force, this rate was estimated to be 5.5 percent by 1977.[19] If UI and food stamps add 1 percentage point to this rate, then the full employment unemployment rate would now be about 6.5 percent.

According to most macroeconomic models, attempts to use monetary and fiscal policies to push the actual unemployment rate below the full employment unemployment rate can be successful only temporarily, and then only at a cost of subsequent inflation and rising unemployment. It is noteworthy that the actual unemployment rate has been below 6.5 percent only twice since 1975 (in 1978 and 1979), and this period was followed by rising unemployment and two years of double-digit inflation. The full employment unemployment rate can be reduced, but not by macroeconomic policies. Instead, structural changes, such as the one examined next, are necessary.

Proposal for reform: loans instead of subsidies

Martin Feldstein proposed a radical reform of the UI program.[20] He suggested that the government lend unemployed workers 60 percent of their previous wage rather than giving them benefits. These loans would be repaid after the worker returned to work. Only after a worker has been unemployed for a long period, 3 to 6 months, would he or she be eligible to receive nonrepayable benefits.

A loan program to provide support for the unemployed would virtually eliminate any incentives for a worker to extend inefficiently the duration of unemployment. Each week the worker borrowed money, his or her indebtedness to the government would increase, and consequently the worker would bear the entire cost of remaining unemployed. This would be a strong incentive to avoid extending unemployment unnecessarily and also encourage the worker to search more actively for a job. On the other hand, those unemployed longer than 6 months would receive nonrepayable benefits and find unemployment subsidized thereafter.

In evaluating this proposal, it is important to recall that most unemploy-

---

⚔   [19]Belton M. Fleisher and Thomas J. Kniesner, *Labor Economics: Theory, Evidence, and Policy* (Englewood Cliffs, N.J.: Prentice-Hall, 1980), p. 408.

[20]Feldstein, "Unemployment Insurance: Time for Reform," op. cit. Actually, Feldstein's reform contains two additional proposals. The first, to make UI benefits taxable, has already been partially enacted. The second is intended to deal with what is known as "experience rating." We have ignored experience rating because it is very complex and does not materially affect the analysis in the text.

ment is short-lived (see Table 5–4). Most unemployed workers would never become eligible for nonrepayable benefits. Only those with very long spells of unemployment would receive an outright subsidy, and this group would be more likely to be the most needy among the unemployed. (To avoid possible abuses in these few cases of extended unemployment, there would probably have to be some limitation on the duration of benefits.) Therefore, Feldstein's proposal would almost completely eliminate the adverse incentives inherent in the present system.

Would the repayment of loans be a great burden on workers after they return to work? Perhaps in some individual cases, but two points should be recalled. First, under the current distribution of benefits, most of the outlays are received by middle- and upper-income families. Second, using loans rather than nonrepayable benefits would allow the government to reduce the tax used to finance UI benefits, and this would increase after-tax income and the ability of reemployed workers to repay the loan.

Actually, this proposal is a large step in the direction of eliminating UI altogether. Most unemployed persons would probably not borrow the money even if they could, but instead would finance their unemployment out of their own savings (at least, unless the government lent at below-market interest rates). In that event, workers would be using savings to "self-insure" against unemployment. Indeed, people do not need a very large nest egg to provide the same degree of insurance currently provided by UI. Recall that the average duration of unemployment seldom exceeds 12 weeks. At a replacement rate of 50 percent, UI provides on average benefits equal to 6 weeks of wages. Thus, a worker requires savings of less than one eighth of his or her annual income to provide the same average protection as afforded by UI.

Since converting UI to a loan program shifts the costs of being unemployed to the worker, why not simply eliminate UI all together? The obvious reason is that some people would be too poor to have accumulated any savings. Yet if this is the reason, the real problem is a distribution of income with too many poor families, and that could be resolved by a welfare system that raised the incomes of low-income families. Feldstein's proposal is a compromise that guarantees that those who cannot or simply do not provide for emergencies will be supported during periods of unemployment.

Subsidies to Higher Education

More than half of all high school graduates go to college, and 91 percent of them receive some form of subsidy from their state government or the federal government, or both. For many years, states have operated colleges and universities, financing them largely from tax revenues. Fifteen years ago the federal government began to subsidize higher education through a variety of programs, the most important being the Basic Educational Opportunity Grants (BEOG) and Guaranteed Student Loans. In 1984, the federal government spent about $8 billion to support higher education, with most of this assistance being direct aid to college students. Nearly 51 percent of all college students receive some form of federal aid.

Economic effects of subsidies to higher education

In 1985, the average tuition at public four-year colleges was about $1,200. This fee, however, fell far short of covering the real cost of educating the student—the actual cost averaged nearly $4,800. The difference was made up largely out of tax revenues. Thus, students attending public colleges receive a substantial subsidy from the state taxpayers, a subsidy covering nearly three fourths of the costs of the educational services they receive.

To analyze the consequences of this type of subsidy, let's begin by looking at how it affects the educational choices of a family considering sending a son or daughter to college. Suppose we simplify our analysis by assuming that "education" can be purchased in the private market at a constant price per unit. The budget line showing the private alternatives is $MALN$ in Figure 5–2[a]. (In practice, the choice is likely to be among a number of schools, with the higher-priced ones offering better—that is, more—education. Combining all the choices to form a straight line, however, seems a reasonable simplification.) Next, let the state government operate a college that provides E_G units of education. If the state-operated college can provide education at the same unit cost as the private colleges can, the cost per student would be MM_2 ($4,800, for example). At the public college, however, the students will pay a tuition of only MM_1 ($1,200), with the remaining cost, M_1M_2 ($3,600), financed by tax revenues. The budget line confronting the family then changes to $MARLN$. Point R indicates the option of attending the public college, and the RLN portion of the line shows that to get more education the student must forgo the public college subsidy and bear the entire cost of a private college. Thus, the subsidy available at public colleges is a form of fixed quantity subsidy where it is difficult for the student's family to supplement the subsidized quantity (compare the discussion of Figure 4–5).

For such families, there are a number of possible outcomes. Figure 5–2 identifies two. Figure 5–2[a] shows a family that would choose a private college providing E_1 units of education in the absence of the subsidy. But given the availability of the subsidy, the family can attain a higher indifference curve by sending its son or daughter to the public college, although that choice means consuming a lower quantity of educational services. Figure 5–2[b] illustrates a second outcome, in which the student decides not to attend any college without a subsidy; the highest indifference curve attainable is U_1 at point M, a corner equilibrium. With the subsidy, however,

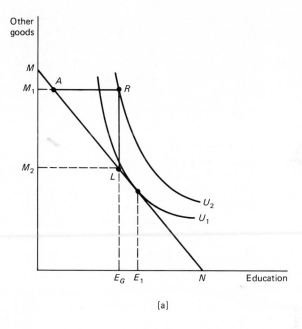

[a]

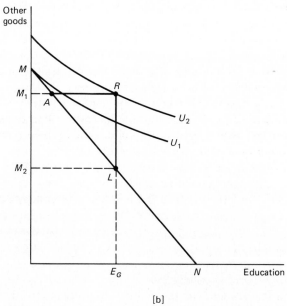

[b]

FIGURE 5–2 *Effects of state-supported higher education.*

the student will attend the public college, and the equilibrium will be at point *R*. There are also two other possibilities, not shown in the graph. First, the equilibrium could be along the *MAL* portion of the budget line without the subsidy; the subsidy produces a new equilibrium at point *R,* with the family consuming more education than they would have chosen without the subsidy. Second, the equilibrium could be along the *LN* portion of the budget line without the subsidy and remain at the same point when the subsidy is available: this outcome occurs when the family chooses a private college and forgoes the subsidy available at the public college.

In all likelihood, there are many instances of each of these four possible outcomes. On theoretical grounds, we cannot predict the relative importance of each possibility, as the actual choices made will depend on incomes, preferences, and other factors. We do know, however, that approximately 25 percent of all college students currently attend private colleges. The important question is, therefore, how the choices of the remaining 75 percent of college students attending public colleges have been affected by the existence of state-supported public colleges.

Sam Peltzman investigated this question and estimated that if public colleges were eliminated, total expenditures on higher education would fall by somewhere between zero and 25 percent. At the same time, Peltzman found that enrollment in colleges would fall by about 25 percent.[21] In other words, he concluded that there would be fewer students in college, but the students that did remain would, on the average, receive more education. This accords with our analysis, because Peltzman's findings imply that some students would choose more education without subsidies (Figure 5–2[a]) and that others would choose less or none (Figure 5–2[b]).

Initially, it may seem surprising that our system of state-supported higher education has such a small effect on the allocation of resources to higher education, but Peltzman's results are really quite plausible when we think about the extent to which public colleges reduce the cost of education. Although public colleges reduce the tuition cost to students by 75 percent, tuition is not the only cost of attending college, nor is it even the most important cost. The largest cost is the earnings that college students forgo when they attend college. The decision to attend college means sacrificing four years of earnings, and those sacrificed earnings are an opportunity cost of attending college. (Note that students' living costs while in college are not an additional cost, because such costs would be incurred whether or not the student attended college.)

The cost that a student (or his or her family) bears from attending college is largely the sum of tuition and sacrificed earnings. (There are, of course, some other costs, such as books and the subjective disutility from studying, and some offsets, such as summer earnings, that for simplicity we

---

[21] Sam Petzman, "The Effect of Government Subsidies-in-Kind of Private Expenditures: The Case of Higher Education," *Journal of Political Economy,* 81:1 (Jan./Feb. 1973).

shall ignore.) To see the practical importance of these factors, we can esti-mate sacrificed earnings by using the average earnings of male high school graduates between the ages of 18 and 24 in 1985: approximately $14,000. College students probably sacrifice about that much each year they attend college. In addition, the average cost of educational services at public col-leges is about $4,800, so the total (social) cost of a student attending college is about $18,800 per year. When students attending a public university pay a tuition of only $1,200 instead of $4,800, however, the cost falls from $18,800 to $15,200, or by 19 percent. Given this moderate reduction in the true cost, together with the restricted nature of the subsidy that leads some students to consume less education, Peltzman's results appear plausible.

Basic Educational Opportunity Grants

Now let's briefly consider the largest federal government subsidy to higher education, the Basic Educational Opportunity Grant (BEOG) program. (Guaranteed Student Loans run a close second.) Enacted in 1973, the BEOG program provides cash assistance directly to college students enrolled in public and private colleges. By 1984, total outlays exceeded $3 billion. As-sistance is related to the family's (or student's) income, with lower-income families eligible for larger grants and upper-income families ineligible for BEOG assistance.

Table 5–5 shows how the maximum grant is related to family income for a four-person family with one dependent college student. The maximum grant is related to "countable income," which is defined as gross income less certain allowable offsets and deductions. Given the typical offsets and deductions assumed in the table, families with gross incomes below $9,050 are eligible for the maximum grant of $1,750. Families with higher incomes are eligible for smaller grants, and families with incomes above $26,462 are not eligible for any assistance. Thus, the program relates the size of the grants to income in a way much like the food stamp program operates, but in this case families with much higher incomes can receive federal assis-tance.

The table shows the maximum grant that a family can receive; the actual grant is equal to one half the cost of attending college (including living expenses), up to the maximum amount of $1,750. For example, if a family with an income of $9,050 has a student in a college where the tuition is $1,000 and living expenses are $1,000, the actual grant will be one half of $2,000, or $1,000. This method of calculating the grant, together with some other technical features of the program,[22] however, has the effect of concen-trating less of the assistance on low-income families than the figures in the

---

[22]W. Lee Hansen and Robert J. Lampman, "Basic Opportunity Grants for Higher Education: Good Intentions and Mixed Results," in R. Haveman and J. Margolis, eds., *Public Expenditure and Policy Analysis,* 3rd ed. (Boston: Houghton Mifflin, 1983), pp. 493–512.

Table 5–5 *Basic Educational Opportunity Grants, 1981–82*
(Family of four with one dependent student)

Gross Income	Typical Offsets and Deductions	Countable Income	Maximum BEOG
$ 0	$ 7,700	$ 0	$1,750
7,700	9,700	0	1,750
9,050	9,700	0	1,750
14,050	11,700	2,350	1,503
19,050	11,700	7,350	978
22,462	11,700	10,762	620
24,366	11,700	12,666	420
26,462	11,700	14,762	200

Source: W. Lee Hansen and Robert J. Lampman, "Basic Opportunity Grants for Higher Education: Good Intentions and Mixed Results," in Robert H. Haveman and Julius Margolis, eds., *Public Expenditures and Policy Analysis,* 3rd ed. (Boston: Houghton Mifflin, 1983), Table 22.3.

table suggest. Students from low-income families are more likely to attend low-tuition colleges, often in their own communities where they can continue to live at home, so they often receive less than the maximum grant for which they are eligible. Students from higher-income families, however, are more likely to receive the maximum grant for which they qualify because they are likely to choose a more costly college. Consequently, a larger share of college benefits goes to families with higher incomes.

We would expect these grants to have two major effects. First, they could encourage some students to attend college who would not otherwise go. Note, however, that this program lowers the cost of college attendance by only a small amount. Drawing on our earlier example, consider a student attending a typical public college. As we saw, the sum of tuition and sacrificed earnings implies an annual net cost of about $15,200. Even for a student receiving the maximum grant of $1,750, BEOG assistance would reduce the cost of attending college by only 12 percent, and most students receive even smaller grants. Thus, we would not expect the program to have a large effect on college attendance. Evidence seems to bear this out. For example, the percentage of college-age children from families with incomes below the median who attended college in the early 1970s (before the program began) was about half the percentage for families with incomes above the median. Because the BEOG program concentrates assistance on lower-income families, if it has had an effect, we would expect to see the percentage of students from lower-income families attending college to rise relative to that from upper-income families. No such change, however, has occurred: in the late 1970s, families with above-median incomes still had twice the percentage of college-age children in college as lower-income families did. Because a major goal of the BEOG program was to increase college attendance by students from low-income families, it has apparently not achieved this objective to any significant degree.

Even if the BEOG program does not substantially affect the number of students attending college, it could have a second effect of increasing the quantity of educational services received by students who would have attended college anyway. How important this effect has been is not clear. At least for those students who would have attended a college where they would be eligible for the maximum grant allowable even without the subsidy, this effect is probably quite small. In this case the grant is equivalent to an unrestricted cash grant: the student would receive the same grant whether he or she attended the same college or a more expensive college. That is, there would be only an income effect from the grant, and given the magnitudes involved, that would be expected to have a small effect on expenditures on education.

From this analysis, publicly supported colleges and federal subsidies appear to have a rather limited effect on the amount of educational services actually produced. More students probably attend college than without these subsidies, but the increase in attendance may be rather modest. In addition, some students may actually receive less education (in the form of state-supported colleges and universities) as a result of the type of subsidy available from state governments.

Apart from these effects on the allocation of resources, the distributional effects of these subsidies are also noteworthy. There are two different ways to look at the distributional effects. One is to focus on the families that have students in college. As we mentioned, families with incomes above the median have twice as large a percentage of college-age children in college as lower-income families do, and upper-income families are also likely to send their children to more expensive schools. Although a large part of federal government subsidies probably does go to lower-income families, the federal subsidies are quite small in comparison with the support of colleges by states. Thus, the bulk of the subsidies goes to families with higher incomes.

Some economists have argued that this is not the proper way to evaluate the distributional effects of subsidies to higher education; instead, they contend that we should consider the subsidies as benefiting the students themselves (rather than their parents). From this perspective, the distributional effects of subsidies to higher education are definitely pro-rich. All college-caliber students are wealthy in terms of their lifetime earning potential. In 1983, for example, the average earnings of male college graduates over the age of 25 was $33,000, whereas the comparable figure for high school graduates was $23,000. Subsidies to higher education thus effectively benefit the brightest and most ambitious young people, and this group will, on the average, have the highest lifetime incomes even without assistance.

Who should pay for higher education?

Is there a rationale for government involvement in higher education, and if so, what is it? This is a difficult question, and there is no consensus regarding the justification for subsidies to higher education. Thinking about the issues involved is worthwhile, however, because it can provide some insight into the types of policies that are appropriate. In this section, we shall discuss three of the most common arguments supporting government subsidies to higher education.

1. *Families cannot afford to send their children to college.* College is expensive, and in recent years costs have risen slightly faster than the overall price level. Government subsidies, however, do not reduce the cost of education to society; they only reduce the cost to the recipient by shifting part of the expense to someone else. So the real issue is why people other than those who receive the educational services should bear part of the cost.

Why can't families afford to pay the full cost of college? Students who can succeed in college will, on the average, have high lifetime incomes. The fact that their current earnings are low is not relevant to their ability to pay for college. College enhances earning capacity, and the cost of college could be financed out of the higher future earnings that college makes possible. In other words, students (or their families) could borrow to finance college and repay the loan out of their future earnings. If college is really worthwhile as an investment in human capital, the higher future earnings that a college education makes possible should be more that adequate to repay the loan.

There are, however, problems with borrowing to finance college education. Although the average expected return to college education may be substantial, there is a wide variation around the average so not all students who graduate from college will realize higher lifetime earnings. This, together with the current bankruptcy laws that have enabled some students to rid themselves of their debt by declaring bankruptcy, make such student loans risky. Consequently, some economists have suggested that government facilitate educational loans, possibly by guaranteeing repayment to private lenders. Note, however, that this argument does not require that the government offer subsidized loans (as it now does) or run state-supported colleges and universities but only that the government ensure that students can borrow at market interest rates to finance their college educations. If loans are available at unsubsidized interest rates, the fact that a student's family has a low income would not affect his or her ability to attend college.

2. *We must have equal educational opportunity in higher education.* An ideal widely held in our society is that anyone capable of succeeding in college should be able to attend; that is, financial considerations should not keep talented young people from going to college. But is it necessary to subsidize college education with low-interest loans or public colleges to

realize this goal? The availability of guaranteed loans at market interest rates would provide educational opportunity without subsidizing students. Educational opportunity would seemingly be provided if any person who thinks that he or she can benefit from attending college is able to do so despite small or nonexistent current earnings.

This argument is usually raised in connection with students from low-income households where financial considerations might deter them from attending college. Even if the student's family is poor, however, loans provide a method of paying for college. The important point is that any college-caliber student, whether from a poor or a wealthy family, can expect to have income in the future that is well above the national average. To subsidize college students is to make individuals with higher expected incomes in the future even wealthier at the expense of the less fortunate.

Many believe, however, that there are reasons to offer special assistance to students from low-income families to attend college. For persons raised in an environment that does not stress the benefits of education, the availability of loans may not be enough to make college attractive. This consideration may be the basis for an argument that some type of special encouragement, perhaps a subsidy, be made available to students from disadvantaged backgrounds, but this would not seem to justify subsidies to 91 percent of college students.

3. *There are external benefits associated with higher education.* When economists evaluate the appropriateness of government action, they generally first consider whether any externalities are involved. As the analysis in Chapter 2 suggests, if the production of college-trained persons generates external benefits for other people, private markets will lead students to purchase less than the efficient quantity. In this case, a subsidy that lowers the price to students (that is, with someone else paying part of the cost) can induce students to acquire the efficient quantity of education.

What types of external benefits are associated with higher education? One common argument holds that education increases the productivity of workers, increasing national output and improving the welfare of everyone. On inspection, however, this does not describe any external benefits from education. Education generally improves students' productivity, enabling them to produce more and, therefore, increasing the national output. However, in a market system, the student is the one who receives the benefit of this higher productivity, in the form of a higher wage rate. Wages are related to productivity, and insofar as education improves productivity, it increases the wage rate that students can command in job markets.

A related argument holds that an increase in the supply of trained workers leads to lower wage rates, and lower wage rates benefit the rest of society as consumers. For instance, subsidies to education may increase the supply of engineers and lead to lower prices for engineering services. Again, however, this does not describe a true external benefit, but only a pecuniary externality. If an increase in supply leads to lower engineers' wages, this will benefit consumers, but at a cost to the engineers who were previously employed at a higher wage. This, therefore, is a transfer of real income from engineers to consumers, and not a net benefit to society.

Having considered these fallacious, externality-sounding arguments, what are the real external benefits of higher education? External benefits from education might include speaking a common language that facilitates communication with others; knowledge of laws and customs that facilitates interactions with others; acceptance of a common set of values that improves the stability of the system; and improved understanding of social processes that leads to better informed political decisions. These consequences of education can benefit people other than the student.

We should, however, realize that such general benefits from education are largely realized at lower levels of schooling. Are there really more external benefits if a high school graduate extends his or her education? Many economists feel that the answer to this question is probably no, contending that the marginal external benefits become smaller as the person becomes more educated. In other words, the primary benefit of a college education is likely to be the benefit that the student receives in the form of increased earning capacity.

Of course, certain types of higher education may generate external benefits, whereas others may not. Much of higher education today is technical training that prepares students for careers, and this type of education seems unlikely to involve external benefits. For instance, how does the general public benefit from the nearly 25 percent of college students who take their degrees in some form of business administration? Perhaps economics courses lead to better-informed citizens and ultimately to better public policies— but it is difficult to see that this has happened, even though tens of millions of people have taken basic economics.

We do not mean to deny the existence of external benefits associated with higher education. Perhaps there are some difficult-to-articulate and difficult-to-measure external benefits involved. Exactly what they are and how important they are, however, remain unclear. Moreover, we should recall from Chapter 2 that the external benefits are relevant only to the extent that there are *marginal* external benefits from obtaining more education than students would without a subsidy. If Peltzman's findings are correct, most college students would go to college even without subsidies and would, in fact, receive slightly better educations. Whatever the strength of the externality argument is in principle, existing subsidies have not significantly increased the consumption of college education, according to Peltzman. Consequently, if education produces external benefits, the current system of subsidies has been poorly designed to increase the quantity of education consumed.

Proposal for reform: vouchers

States now subsidize college students by providing funds directly to public colleges enabling them to charge tuition that is below the actual cost of educating students. There is nothing in the arguments defending subsidies for higher education, however, that requires the subsidy to take this particular form. So let's consider an alternative way of subsidizing higher education, *vouchers*. Under a voucher scheme, public colleges would no longer receive any funds directly from the government; instead they would have to charge tuitions that were sufficient to cover the cost of providing educational services to students. Students would continue to be subsidized, but now they would receive the assistance directly with a voucher, to be used at any college they choose to attend.

An example will help clarify how the voucher subsidy might be structured. Recall our earlier example in which the public college incurred costs of $4,800 per student but charged a tuition of only $1,200, with the remaining $3,600 paid by the government. With a voucher program the college would have to charge tuition of $4,800, but the students would be given a voucher by the government that could be used to cover $3,600 of the tuition cost at any college. In effect, the voucher would be much like food stamps because it could be used only to purchase the targeted good. From the student's point of view, the cost of attending the public college is unchanged. The out-of-pocket cost is still $1,200 to attend the public college, because $1,200 plus the $3,600 voucher will cover the $4,800 tuition. Now, however, the student can use the subsidy at any college or university. To attend a private college with a tuition of $6,000, for example, the out-of-pocket cost would be $2,400. In contrast, it would cost the student $6,000 to attend the private college under the current arrangement, because the implicit subsidy available at the public college could not be used to purchase educational services elsewhere.

Figure 5–3 illustrates how this program would affect the options open to the student. The original budget line is shown as *MARLN,* as explained previously. Given those options and the indifference curves shown, the student would attend the public college and be in equilibrium at point R on indifference curve U_2. The voucher changes the budget line to $MM'N'$. With the preferences shown, the student would choose a school with a higher tuition that provides E_1 units of education; equilibrium would be at point A, with the student reaching a higher indifference curve at no greater cost to the government. Of course, the actual outcome would depend on the students' preferences, and Figure 5–3 shows only one possible result. Some students, faced with the same options but having different preferences, might choose to purchase less education under the voucher arrangement. In this case, the equilibrium would be along the $M'R$ portion of the budget line. In either case, however, the student would attain a higher indifference curve.

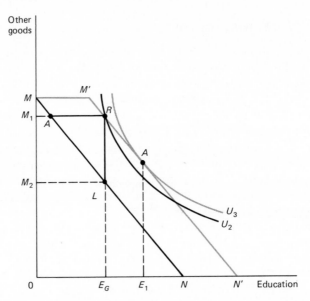

FIGURE 5–3   *Vouchers versus subsidies through state-supported colleges.*

In addition to the effects on students' options, the voucher arrangement is also likely to affect the types of education provided by colleges. Under the present arrangements, public colleges are sheltered to a large degree from competition with other (out-of-state) public and private colleges. Because students will lose the subsidy if they go elsewhere, public colleges do not have to offer an education that caters as fully to the students' interests in order to retain students. In contrast, under the voucher plan, every college would have to compete on the same basis, by offering an education that is attractive to students. Greater competition among colleges would result, advocates of vouchers believe, in a better-quality education at many colleges.

Opponents of the voucher plan argue that placing more power in the hands of students might lead to a lower quality of education. Some students might select colleges on the basis of how easy the coursework was or how attractive the social life was. We doubt that this would be a serious problem, however. Students now clamor to get into the colleges generally acknowledged to be the best and toughest, for they apparently recognize that their future prospects depend on the quality of education they receive and not just on getting a degree.

Another concern is that the voucher plan might lead to greater segregation in colleges by income, religion, or race. Quite possibly a poor family would use the $3,600 voucher to purchase an education costing $3,600 and no more, but wealthier families would supplement the voucher and send their children to more expensive schools. The voucher plan, however, can be adapted to avoid this by giving larger vouchers to poorer families. Just as poorer families receive more food stamps and more BEOG assistance, vouchers could be adjusted to offer more assistance to low-income families. In addition, the use of vouchers could be limited to schools enrolling students from all social backgrounds, or schools offering approved courses of instruction. The basic point is that the voucher approach is quite flexible and can be adapted to subsidize some kinds of students more than others or some types of education more than others.

Supplementary Readings

ALCHIAN, ARMEN A. "The Economic and Social Impact of Free Tuition." In Armen A. Alchian, *Economic Forces at Work.* Indianapolis: Liberty Press, 1977.

CLARKSON, KENNETH W. *Food Stamps and Nutrition.* Washington, D.C.: American Enterprise Institute, 1975.

———. "Welfare Benefits of the Food Stamps Program." *Southern Economic Journal,* 43 (1):864–878 (July 1976).

CONGRESSIONAL BUDGET OFFICE. *Promoting Employment and Maintaining Incomes with Unemployment Insurance.* Washington, D.C.: U.S. Government Printing Office, Mar. 1985.

FELDSTEIN, MARTIN S. "Unemployment Compensation: Adverse Incentives and Distributional Anomalies." *National Tax Journal,* 27 (2):231–244 (June 1974).

———. "Unemployment Insurance: Time for Reform." *Harvard Business Review* (Mar./Apr. 1975).

GRUBEL, HERBERT G., and MICHAEL A. WALKER, eds., *Unemployment Insurance: Global Evidence of Its Effects on Unemployment.* Vancouver, B.C.: Frazer Institute, 1979.

HAMERMESH, DANIEL. *Jobless Pay and the Economy.* Baltimore: Johns Hopkins University Press, 1977.

HANSEN, W. LEE, and ROBERT J. LAMPMAN. "Basic Opportunity Grants for Higher Education: Good Intentions and Mixed Results." In Robert H. Haveman and Julius Margolis, eds., *Public Expenditure and Policy Analysis.* 3rd ed. Boston: Houghton Mifflin, 1983.

MUNTS, RAYMOND, and IRWIN GARFINKEL. *The Work Disincentive Effects of Unemployment Insurance.* Kalamazoo, Mich.: W. E. Upjohn Institute for Employment Research, 1974.

Review Questions and Problems

1. Of the three subsidies discussed in this chapter, food stamps are a pro-poor subsidy, unemployment insurance a pro-middle-class subsidy, and support for higher education a pro-rich subsidy. Do you agree? Explain.

2. Food stamps are a type of fixed quantity subsidy. Can the food stamp subsidy lead to underconsumption? Why or why not?

3. "The average four-person family on food stamps receives about $120 in food stamps a month. You can't feed four people on $4 per day, and so food stamp benefits should be increased." Comment. (Does the average family referred to here have to finance its food purchases entirely with food stamps? See Table 5–2.)

4. Before 1979, the food stamp subsidy operated differently. Although the subsidy at each level of income was approximately the same, the family had to pay something to receive food stamps. For example, instead of receiving $150 in food stamps outright, the family had to pay $50 to receive $200 in food stamps. The food stamp subsidy costs the government $150 in both cases. This feature was called the *purchase requirement*. Explain how a family's budget line changes with this type of food stamp program.

5. Would you expect food consumption to be greater or less when the food stamp program had a purchase requirement, as explained in question 4? Do you think eliminating the purchase requirement in 1979 was a good idea?

6. If the replacement rate in the unemployment insurance program is increased, how will this change the nation's unemployment rate?

7. Could the adverse effect of unemployment insurance on unemployment be avoided if unemployed persons were given a lump-sum payment when they became unemployed, so that the subsidy would be the same, regardless of the duration of unemployment? What adverse incentives, if any, would such a UI program produce?

8. Explain Feldstein's proposal to convert UI from subsidies to loans. Who would be benefited and who would be harmed if this change in the program were made?

9. Explain why you believe government support of higher education is or is not justified. If you believe it is justified, do you think that the way that higher education is now subsidized is the best way? (In other words, what type of subsidy do you favor?)

10. Show how state-supported colleges can lead some students to consume less education than they would without this subsidy. If a voucher program were used and tuition were raised to cover the full cost of college education, how would your analysis be affected?

chapter 6
Financing Medical Care

TOTAL expenditures on medical care in the United States reached a record level of $347.1 billion in 1983; more than $1 of every $10 spent in that year was devoted to the purchase of some form of health care. Government expenditures represented 42 percent of these total expenditures. From these figures, it is clear that government now plays a large role in this important sector of the economy. In this chapter we examine the functioning of medical care markets and how they are influenced by government policy. Special attention is given to the role of insurance, both publicly and privately provided, in the health care sector.

Public and Private Expenditures on Medical Care

Expenditures on medical care have not always absorbed such a large share of national income as they do today. As Table 6–1 shows, in 1950 total medical care expenditures were only 4.5 percent of the GNP. As a result of rapidly rising private and government spending on medical care, however,

---

Table 6–1 *Expenditures on Medical Care ($ in billions)*

Fiscal Year	Total Spending	Total as a Percentage of GNP	Private Spending	Government Spending	Government as a Percentage of Total
1950	$ 12.0	4.2%	$ 9.0	$ 3.1	25.5%
1960	25.9	5.1	19.5	6.4	24.7
1965	38.9	5.6	29.4	9.5	24.5
1970	69.2	7.0	43.8	25.4	36.7
1975	124.7	8.0	72.4	52.3	42.0
1980	237.8	9.0	136.9	101.0	42.4
1983	347.1	10.5	202.9	144.2	41.5

Source: Ann Kallman Bixby, "Social Welfare Expenditures, 1963–83," *Social Security Bulletin,* 49 (2) (Feb. 1986) Table 7.

that share has more than doubled, reaching 10.5 percent in 1983. By 1983 medical care expenditures in the United States were greater—in the aggregate and on a per capita basis—than in any other country.

Both private and government expenditures on medical care have increased, but government spending has risen more rapidly. Note the particularly rapid growth in government spending since 1965, which marked the enactment of Medicare and Medicaid. By 1984 expenditures on Medicare and Medicaid alone totaled $96 billion, almost 60 percent of total government expenditures in the health care area. The remainder was devoted to a wide variety of purposes: public health, medical research, veterans' hospitals, child health programs, hospital construction, and others.

Another significant recent development in the financing of health care has been the growth of private health insurance. Table 6–2 provides a percentage breakdown of personal health expenditures by sources of funds. In 1983 private insurance covered 31.9 percent of medical expenditures, over three times as large as its share in 1950. Third-party payments, that is, insurance plus government expenditures, covered almost three fourths of medical costs in 1983. (Third-party payments are so called because they are expenses not directly incurred by either the provider or the consumer of the medical care; instead, the insurance company or the government bears the cost.) Although the public ultimately incurs the cost of third-party payments in the form of insurance premiums or taxes, the fact that the patient does not bear the costs in proportion to his or her own use of medical care

Table 6–2   *Percentage Distribution of Personal Health Care Expenditures* *

Fiscal Year	Total	Private Direct Payments	Private Insurance Benefits	Government	Third-Party Payments
1950	100%	65.5%	9.1%	22.4%	34.5%
1960	100	54.9	21.1	21.8	45.1
1965	100	51.6	24.2	22.0	48.4
1970	100	40.5	23.4	34.3	59.5
1975	100	32.5	26.7	39.5	67.5
1980	100	28.5	30.7	39.6	71.5
1983	100	27.2	31.9	39.7	72.8

*Personal health care expenditures are about 10 percent smaller than the total expenditures shown in Table 6–1 because the former do not include medical research, public health activities, and so on.

Source: 1950–1974 data, *Compendium of National Health Expenditures Data,* U.S. Department of Health, Education, and Welfare, Social Security Administration, Office of Research and Statistics Publ. No. 76-11927 (Jan. 1976), Table 2; 1980–1983 data, Robert Gibson, Katherine R. Levit, Helen Lazenby, and Daniel Waldo, "National Health Expenditures, 1983," *Health Care Financing Review* (Winter 1984), p. 15.

resources has important implications for the functioning of medical care markets, as we shall see later.

The figures in Table 6–2 give broad averages of total expenditures by people in the United States for all types of medical expenses. There is, however, a striking difference in the importance of third-party payments for different types of medical care. For example, 92 percent of hospital care costs in 1983 were borne by third parties. By contrast, 72 percent of physician services were financed in this way, but only about one third of all other medical services (dental services, drugs, eyeglasses, nursing home care, etc.) were paid for by third parties.[1] Private insurance covers only 5 percent of these latter services. The implications of third-party payments for the way these markets function will be discussed later.

Medical Care and Health

The "crisis in medical care" is a familiar topic in the news media. In describing the "crisis," it is common to contrast the rapidly rising costs of health care with the health of the American people. Although the United States spends more on health care than does any other nation, its people are far from being the healthiest in the world, at least as measured by some commonly used indices. For example, from among a group of 14 advanced economies in 1974, the United States ranked eleventh in male life expectancy, eighth in female life expectancy, and twelfth in prenatal mortality.[2]

Does this imply that our medical care system is generally inefficient? Perhaps surprisingly, it does not. A wealth of empirical evidence strongly suggests that differences in the quantity or quality of health care among developed countries are *not* significantly related to differences in health. Put another way, health levels in a country reflect a wide variety of factors; medical care is only one of these factors, and its independent contribution to the general level of health seems rather minor.[3] Thus, spending more on medical care or reorganizing the system is not likely to improve greatly the international standing of the United States.

With respect to mortality, it is easy to understand why medical care expenditures are unlikely to increase longevity. The three leading causes of death in the United States are heart disease, cancer, and accidents (mainly

---

[1] Robert M. Gibson, Katherine R. Levit, Helen Lazenby, and Daniel R. Waldo, "National Health Expenditures, 1983 *Health Care Financing Review* (Winter 1984), p. 1.

[2] A. J. Culyer, Alan Maynard and Alan Williams, "Alternative Systems of Health Care Provision: An Essay on Motes and Beams," in Mancur Olson, ed., *A New Approach to the Economics of Health Care* (Washington, D.C.: American Enterprise Institute, 1982), Table 2.

[3] This theme is stressed in Victor R. Fuchs, *Who Shall Live?* (New York: Basic Books, 1974), Chapter 2. This section draws heavily on Fuchs's interesting work.

automobile), accounting for seven of every ten deaths. More or better medical care is unlikely to prevent many of these deaths. In general, the health of a people depends heavily on other factors such as heredity, nutrition, smoking, drinking, exercise, education, environmental influences, and general "life-style." Provision of additional medical care will not alter these other influences and so cannot be expected to transform us into a healthy nation.

A striking example of the importance of nonmedical factors is provided by two adjacent states in the western United States, Utah and Nevada. These states enjoy similar levels of income and medical care, but the inhabitants of one state are apparently far healthier than those of the other. Death rates at all age levels, for males and females, are substantially higher in Nevada, typically 20 to 40 percent higher. What explains these huge differences? Although we cannot know with certainty, the answer probably lies in the fact that Utah is predominantly Mormon. Devout Mormons lead temperate lives, neither smoking nor drinking.

No intent to disparage the contributions of medical care to health and well-being should be inferred, however. Here, as elsewhere, it is important to distinguish between the *total* and the *marginal* benefits of an economic use of resources. The total contribution of medical care to health in the United States is doubtless immense, at least at the present time. (It is now generally agreed that "it was not until well into the twentieth century that the average patient had better than a 50-50 chance of being helped by the average physician."[4]) One need only imagine what would happen if we had to do without any medical care to realize its importance. All or nothing, however, is not the relevant issue. Instead, the issue is more correctly posed as a question of reorganizing the use of existing medical resources or of devoting more or fewer resources to the provision of medical care. The contention here is that such *marginal* changes are not going to produce major differences in the average level of health.

If there is a medical care "crisis," it is not demonstrated by out international standing. Our ranking internationally probably tells us more about the life-styles we have chosen (usually individually and voluntarily) than about our health care system. Nonetheless, there are important problems connected with medical care, as we will soon see.

Is Medical Care "Special"?

Just as with other goods and services, the provision of medical care requires the use of scarce resources that have alternative uses. To provide more medical care means that less of other desired goods and services can be produced. In this sense, there is an opportunity cost associated with the

[4]Ibid., p. 30.

provision of medical care, just as there is with other goods and services, and this raises the question of whether there are any special characteristics associated with medical care that require government intervention. Many economists believe that there are. Certain types of medical care have a public good or externality characteristic, implying that private provision would be inefficient. This is especially true of medical research (where production of knowledge is a public good) and the treatment of contagious disease (where there are external benefits for those not treated). A role for government in these areas can be rationalized. However, only a small share—less than 5 percent—of medical expenditures falls in these two categories.

Another more subtle type of externality is suggested by statements such as "Medical care is a right" and "No one should have to go without needed medical attention because of inability to pay." These statements imply that the general public takes an interest in the consumption of medical care by those who are ill. Insofar as this is true, there may be external benefits from consumption of general types of medical care. But for the vast bulk of the population that is nonpoor these benefits are probably inframarginal, because adequate levels of care would be purchased privately without subsidization. This argument, then, may constitute a reason for subsidizing consumption of medical care by the poor. (This argument is considered in greater detail in a later chapter because it is often also made in connection with housing, food, and education.[5])

Apart from such fairly conventional externality considerations, two other peculiarities about medical care are often stressed. First, medical expenses are irregular and unpredictable. In contrast to expenditures on goods like food and clothing, which tend to be steady and easily predicted, some types of medical expenses are incurred only in the uncertain event of illness. This particular characteristic of medical care accounts for the demand for insurance protection.

The second and probably most frequently noted characteristic of medical care is the difficulty the consumer has in evaluating the service received. In general, consumers don't know the consequences of different medical treatments, nor are they able to diagnose whether they require any treatment at all. This situation arises because knowledge is a scarce good, and it is not unique to medical care; education, legal services, and auto repairs share this characteristic. However, the lack of knowledge on the part of the consumer may be more pronounced and more important in the medical field. As a result, the consumer's demand for medical care depends in part on advice given by his or her doctor and raises the problem of whether individual demand reflects the true marginal value of the service. Although this "knowledge imperfection" is widely acknowledged, its implications for public policy are far from clear.

[5]See the discussion of cash versus in-kind transfers in Chapter 9.

Finally, we should mention two characteristics of medical care markets. First, to practice medicine one must graduate from an accredited medical school. State governments have given the American Medical Association the task of accrediting medical schools. It is widely believed that the AMA has, by limiting entry into the profession through severe accrediting requirements, operated as a monopoly and restricted the number of doctors, thereby raising their incomes.[6] Second, most hospital care is provided by nonprofit organizations, either by state and local governments or by voluntary nonprofit hospitals. Because of these two characteristics of medical care markets, it is possible that the normal competitive model may not be an adequate framework for the analysis of health care.[7] Both noncompetitive features, however, are the result of deliberate government policy; there is nothing in the nature of the market that necessitates such a lack of competition.

For all these reasons, both the positive analysis and normative evaluations of policies in the medical care field are difficult tasks.

Medical Expenses and Insurance

We live in a risky world, and one of the major risks is the probability of illness. The risk of illness carries with it risk of incurring heavy medical expenses. Most people don't like to bear risk and are willing to pay to avoid it. Insurance provides this service. By pooling the risks of many people, insurance companies are able to provide insurance on favorable terms. A simple example can be used to show why insurance markets develop.

Suppose there is one chance in a hundred of contracting an illness that costs $20,000 to treat. An insurance company sells policies agreeing to cover this expense. If it sells a large number of policies, say, 10,000, the statistical law of large numbers implies that the insurance company can be nearly certain of having to pay almost exactly 100 people (1/100 of 10,000). The number may be a few more or less than 100, but it is very unlikely to be far from 100. In effect, by pooling the risks of a large number of people, the risk borne by the insurance company is quite small. This makes it possible for the company to sell the insurance policy at a price (premium) slightly above $200 (1/100 times $20,000), which is the expected value, or average expense, incurred by the company for the people it insures. The

---

[6]While this position is held by many economists, the evidence that the AMA has acted as a monopoly is not strong. See C. M. Lindsay and Keith B. Leffler, "The Market for Medical Care," in C. M. Lindsay, ed., *New Directions in Public Health Care* (San Francisco: Institute for Contemporary Studies, 1976).

[7]An interesting attempt to analyze the behavior of hospitals is provided by M. Pauly and M. Redisch, "The Not-for-Profit Hospital As a Physicians Cooperative," *American Economic Review*, 63:87 (Mar. 1973).

price will have to be somewhat above $200 because the company must cover not only the expenses of those who become ill but also other costs (processing claims, selling costs, administrative costs, etc.).

Most people are what economists call *risk averse*. Technically, this means a person prefers to bear a given cost with certainty rather than an uncertain prospect of a greater cost with the same expected value. For example, most people would prefer to pay $200 for insurance than to remain uninsured and to take one chance in a hundred of losing $20,000. When people are risk averse they are willing to pay more, sometimes much more, than $200 for an insurance policy that covers the $20,000 medical cost if they become ill. Because businesses are able to provide this service at a cost of slightly more than $200 by pooling the risks of many people, insurance policies can be supplied at a price that consumers find attractive. Thus, markets for insurance will emerge.

It is not efficient, however, to insure against all medical expenses. To take an extreme case, suppose you know with certainty that you will have a physical checkup costing $100 next year. An insurance company would be willing to sell you a policy to cover this expense, but only at a price of $110, for example, because it has to cover its own costs in addition to the cost of your physical. You would, of course, be better off paying the $100 bill directly and saving $10. In this case, there would be no insurance protection against risk because there is no risk, and the additional $10 payment to the insurance company would provide no service.

This simple example suggests some important principles. It is generally inefficient to insure against *predictable* expenses (where the risk is small). In addition, it is generally inefficient to insure against *small* expenses because a person can provide his or her own insurance more cheaply, simply by saving a small sum. Thus, it is rational for people to bear many of the risks involved in living in an uncertain world. Insurance makes the most sense (is the most beneficial) in highly uncertain situations in which the costs may be quite large (consider life insurance, home insurance, and automobile liability insurance). This does not imply that there is one level of insurance coverage most suitable for everyone. People's abilities and willingness to bear risks vary greatly, so they prefer different types of insurance coverage.

Overinsurance

Although it makes sense for people to purchase health insurance, it is possible to have too much insurance. Indeed, many experts believe that overinsurance is a major problem in the United States. *Overinsurance* is a situation in which too large a portion of medical expenses is covered by insurance; that is, some expenses that are better left uninsured are covered. Insurance coverage of small and predictable expenses normally does not make economic sense; the cost of such coverage will exceed the benefits. Yet it is widely believed that many Americans have excessive insurance coverage. For example, group health insurance plans that cover many workers frequently cover physical checkups, routine dental work, and eyeglasses. These medical services would seem to fall in the "small and predictable" category that we argued would involve costs greater than benefits. With a nationwide average of 92 percent of hospital costs and 72 percent of physician services covered by third-party payments, it seems likely that many people have insurance coverage for small and predictable health costs.

If the costs exceed the benefits, why do people purchase such coverage? The answer, many economists believe, is to be found in the tax laws.[8] Through the use of certain tax provisions, the government has lowered the net price of insurance to the point that people find it in their interest to purchase more insurance than they would if they had to pay the full market price. For example, fringe benefits in the form of employer contributions to group health insurance plans are not subject to federal income, state income, or payroll taxes. Consider a worker in a 20 percent tax bracket. If the worker is paid $100 in cash by his or her employer, after taxes the worker will be able to purchase $80 worth of health insurance. At the same $100 cost to the employer, however, $100 in health insurance can be provided directly, and this is not taxable. Thus, the nontaxability of this fringe benefit has the effect of lowering the net price of health insurance in proportion to the employee's marginal tax bracket. In our example, by giving up $80 in after-tax pay, the worker can get $100 in health insurance by having his or her employer provide it.

In this way, the tax system subsidizes the purchase of health insurance. For many workers, it is in their interest to have insurance coverage for even small and predictable expenses, coverage they would not choose if they had to bear the full cost. Even medical expenses that are absolutely certain to be incurred may be covered because of the implicit subsidy in the tax laws. Under group health insurance, policies can pay on average $100 in medical bills at a premium cost of $111–the $11 difference covers the cost to the insurance companies of providing the insurance. In insurance terminology, the "loading rate" is 11 percent. In the absence of a subsidy, a medical expense certain to be incurred (predictable) would never be covered by insurance. It would be cheaper to pay the $100 medical bill out-of-pocket rather than purchase a $111 policy. If the tax subsidy exceeds 11 percent, however, workers can cover their normal medical bills more cheaply by having their employers provide group health insurance plans covering these expenses. For a worker in a 20 percent tax bracket, for instance, a $111

---

[8]Ronald J. Vogel, "The Tax Treatment of Health Insurance Premiums As a Cause of Over-insurance," in Mark V. Pauly, ed., *National Health Insurance,* (Washington, D.C.: American Enterprise Institute, 1980), pp. 220–249.

policy costs only $88.80 in after-tax dollars, so it is cheaper to cover the $100 medical bill with the subsidized insurance.

It was pointed out earlier (Table 6–2) that in recent years, private health insurance has come to cover a much larger share of health care costs. One of the most important reasons for this development is the tax treatment of employer-provided health insurance. The higher a person's tax bracket is, the more advantageous it is to have medical benefits paid for through employer-provided health insurance. Since the average worker's tax bracket has been rising sharply over the past several decades, it is not surprising that the percentage of payroll costs that companies devote to health insurance premiums has climbed from less than 2.3 percent in 1959 to 11 percent in 1983.[9] Much of this health insurance is probably purchased because the preferential treatment of employer-provided health insurance artificially lowers its cost. Thus the tax system is at least part of the reason that many people are overinsured. The significance of overinsurance for the operation of medical markets will be discussed later.

Underinsurance

Not all Americans are overinsured. In fact, many have expressed concern that a large number of people have too little health insurance. According to the principles of insurance discussed earlier, the most important coverage to have is against the possibility of extremely large medical costs. Many families have had their entire life savings wiped out by the need to pay medical bills to deal with serious and prolonged illnesses in the family. We would expect that such a prospect would lead people to insure themselves against extraordinary medical expenses, that is, to protect themselves against "catastrophic losses." It is possible to be both "overinsured" against small and predictable losses and "underinsured" against major losses.

Insurance coverage of major losses has been growing rapidly in recent years, but many people still have no coverage. According to one survey, 12 percent of the population under age 65 (those over 65 are normally covered by Medicare) in 1976 had no insurance at all and were ineligible for public assistance.[10] Although over 90 percent of the nonpoor are covered by some form of private health insurance, some of these are not covered against catastrophic losses.

Insurance coverage for catastrophic medical expenses is relatively inexpensive. For example, in 1979 the Equitable Life Assurance Society sold a

---

[9] Cynthia F. Gensheimer, "Reform of the Individual Income Tax: Effects on Tax Preferences for Medical Care," in Jack A. Meyer, ed., *Incentives Versus Controls in Health Policy* (Washington, D.C.: American Enterprise Institute, 1985), p. 54.

[10] Lu Ann Aday and Ronald Andersen, "Insurance Coverage and Access: Implications for Health Policy," *Health Services Research,* 13:369 (1978).

policy covering all medical expenses in excess of $3,000 a year for a 35-year-old man at an annual cost of $187. Why then doesn't virtually everyone have this form of coverage? There are several possible reasons. For example, taxpayers can deduct large medical expenses (in excess of 5 percent of their income) under the federal income tax, thereby reducing the net cost of any medical payment. Bankruptcy laws make it possible to incur a large liability but not pay it. And perhaps some people of moderate incomes don't purchase medical coverage because they believe that society will cover any large expense they cannot afford rather than letting them go without needed medical attention. Finally, some may be unaware of the risk they are running or just be willing to take the risk.

Whatever the reason, there is concern that some people have inadequate protection against major medical risks.

The Problem of Moral Hazard

Payment of medical expenses by a third party, either an insurance company or the government, encounters a problem when the size of the loss a person suffers depends partly on the individual's own behavior. Consider an insurance policy that covers all hospital expenses. When a person is hospitalized, the patient bears no financial cost if his or her stay is prolonged. In effect the insured pays a zero price for hospital care. This is likely to lead the person to overconsume hospital services: Any medical care that has any benefit, no matter how slight, would seem worthwhile if the insurance company incurs the expense. The patient's doctor is more likely to prescribe expensive tests and sophisticated treatments knowing that no financial responsibility falls on the patient. Although the value of the medical care to the patient is less than its actual cost, it seems worthwhile because the patient bears no out-of-pocket cost.

In insurance terminology, this is called the *moral hazard* problem. It really has nothing to do with morality, and to an economist it simply represents the resource misallocations caused by a particular method of finance. Figure 6–1 illustrates the moral hazard problem. The curve d_1 is a representative consumer's demand curve for a particular type of medical care if he or she becomes ill. (If the consumer does not become ill, there will be a zero demand.) At a price of $10 per unit, consumption would be 100 units, for a total cost of $1,000 in the absence of insurance. If the person is fully insured (all expenses covered), the net price of care the patient will bear at the time illness strikes is zero and consumption will be 200 units. Consumption will be greater because of the law of demand; in fact, the moral hazard problem exists because the economic behavior of people is responsive to prices. Note that there is a welfare cost because of overconsumption of medical care, which is measured by the triangle *BAD*. In effect,

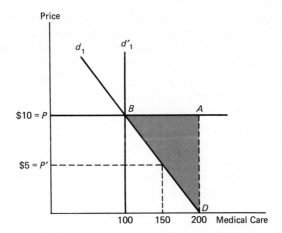

FIGURE 6-1   *Moral hazard and insurance.*

insurance that covers all costs is identical to an excise subsidy that reduces the consumer's price to zero.

In this way, insurance induces increased consumption of medical care. Because out-of-pocket cost is so modest, insured patients (or their doctors) have little incentive to economize on the use of medical resources. This effect of insurance has several important consequences for an analysis of medical care financed by insurance. First, because the effective demand of patients is increased, the price of medical care is likely to rise. Many economists believe that the rapid growth in public and private insurance (third-party payments) is directly responsible for the rapidly rising costs of health care in recent years.

Second, when the moral hazard problem exists, insurance coverage of all medical expenses, even large ones, is no longer likely to be an efficient policy. Instead the welfare gain from having insurance protection must be weighed against the welfare cost of overutilization of medical resources. Note that the induced increase in consumption increases the total cost of medical care, and hence will increase the insurance premium needed to finance the policy. In Figure 6-1, if there is a 1-in-10 chance of being ill, the premium (ignoring the loading factor caused by administrative costs) for full insurance coverage would be $200 (one tenth of the $2,000 cost of 200 units of care). Because the cost is $1,000 if uninsured, a person might prefer to remain uninsured and take a one-tenth chance of bearing a $1,000 cost rather than pay $200 for the insurance policy. Either may be efficient depending on the consumer's attitude toward risk.

The severity of the moral hazard problem depends on how sensitive consumers are to medical care prices, that is, on the price elasticities of demand. Figure 6-1 shows that if the demand curve were perfectly inelastic—

the vertical curve d_1'—consumption of medical care would not increase even at a zero price. If people's consumption of medical care is completely unresponsive to price, there is no moral hazard problem, and full insurance coverage will not distort economic choices. In general, the more elastic the demand for medical care, the more severe is the problem of moral hazard and the more inappropriate full insurance coverage is.

Much popular discussion of medical care issues implicitly assumes vertical demand curves—"needs" that do not depend on price. In life-threatening and other serious situations, price is probably not a major consideration. Most medical care is not of this sort, however, and the doctor and patient frequently have a broad range of discretion in selecting treatments. In the past several years, a considerable body of evidence has accumulated that suggests people consume more medical care at lower prices. For example, Feldstein estimated the price elasticity of demand for hospital care to be about 0.7 and Rosett's and Huang's estimates are even higher.[11] (An elasticity of 0.7 means that a 10 percent reduction in price increases quantity demanded by 7 percent.)

Demand elasticities are likely to vary for different types of medical care. For example, the demand for hospital care, especially for serious problems, is probably more inelastic than is the demand for physician services. Thus, the moral hazard problem is less for hospital care, and so insurance is more efficient in this case than for physician services. Therefore it is not surprising that insurance coverage for hospital care is much more complete (92 percent of expenses paid by third parties) than for physician services (72 percent paid by third parties). Whether this represents the appropriate degree of coverage is another matter.

Coping with the moral hazard problem

There are several ways the moral hazard problem can be dealt with. Because moral hazard implies inefficiency associated with overconsumption, it is in the interest of insurance companies (as well as insured parties) to devise ways to avoid the problem. One way to deal with the moral hazard problem is to make a fixed payment to the insured party in the event of a specified illness. For example, the insured party might be given $1,000 as a lump-sum payment; this completely avoids the incentive to overconsume because the insurance benefit is fixed and does not depend on the quantity of medical care purchased. (This is, in fact, the way home fire insurance policies are written. The insurance benefit does not cover *all* costs incurred

---

[11] Martin S. Feldstein, "Hospital Cost Inflation: A Study in Nonprofit Price Dynamics," *American Economic Review*, 61:853–872 (Dec. 1971); and R. Rosett and L. Huang, "The Effects of Health Insurance on the Demand for Medical Care," *Journal of Political Economy*, 81 (2):281 (Mar./Apr. 1973).

in purchasing a new house to replace a burned one but is fixed in amount.) In the medical care field, this approach is sometimes difficult. For adequate protection, it would be necessary to specify a different payment for each illness, but because there are many possible complications and severities of illness within each category, this would be a complex and costly way of writing insurance. Nonetheless, some policies do place upper limits on the liability of the insurance companies, and that tends to place an upper limit on the moral hazard problem.

A second approach is to require the insured person to pay part of the costs. The patient might be required to pay half the cost, for example. In Figure 6–1, the price would then be *P'*, or $5, and overconsumption would be reduced. The share of the cost borne by the insured person is called the *coinsurance rate,* a device that is widely used in insurance programs. It has the advantage of reducing the welfare cost of overconsumption but the disadvantage of requiring the insured party to bear some of the risk of illness. Focusing on where to set the coinsurance rate is a good way to understand the tradeoff between providing insurance protection and weakening the economic incentives necessary for efficient utilization of health care resources.

A third approach is the use of *deductibles.* Using a deductible means that a patient must pay, for example, the first $200 of hospital costs, and then the insurance company will cover all additional costs (full insurance), if any, or some fraction of these costs (using coinsurance rates). A deductible gives insured patients an incentive to be economical in the event of minor medical problems; it avoids, for example, the incentive for a person to enter a hospital for a brief treatment that could be just as easily provided at home or in a doctor's office. In addition, insurance itself is generally not efficient in the case of small expenses, as explained earlier, so deductibles are generally appropriate in any insurance policy.

Much of the discussion of how to structure a government policy of health insurance such as Medicare and Medicaid centers on the size of the deductibles and the level of the coinsurance rates. It is generally accepted that both features have a place in any program of health insurance, but their exact specification remains controversial. The basic issue should by now be clear: how to provide adequate insurance protection and preserve incentives at the same time.

Government-Subsidized Health Insurance

Medicare and Medicaid are the two largest government programs that finance medical care. Combined government outlays totaled $96 billion in 1984, with Medicare outlays of $57.5 billion and Medicaid outlays of $38.5 billion. Both programs are of fairly recent origin, enacted as Title 18 (Medicare) and Title 19 (Medicaid) of the 1965 amendments to the Social Security Act. Medicare is a program of medical assistance for the elderly, and Medicaid provides medical assistance to the poor. Approximately one fifth of the U.S. population (50 million people) is covered by one or both of these programs.

Medicare is a federally financed program with uniform benefit levels nationwide. It is actually composed of two separate programs. Part A is a program of mandatory hospitalization insurance that is provided to all the elderly (with minor exceptions) and is financed as a part of the social security system by a 2.9 percent payroll tax. Part B is called Supplemental Medical Insurance and covers physicians and other related services. Participation in Part B of Medicare is voluntary, but because of the subsidy involved, 96 percent of the elderly participate. Part B is financed one fourth by a monthly premium paid by participants ($15.50 a month in 1985) and three fourths by contributions from general federal tax revenues.

Medicare can best be thought of as government provision of a specified degree of insurance protection to the elderly. Part A uses a deductible ($400 in 1985) and then covers all hospital expenses up to 60 days. It uses a modest coinsurance payment for hospital stays from 61 to 90 days, but because a very small percentage of patients stay in the hospital longer than 60 days, the incentive effects of this coinsurance payment are not significant. Part B uses a $75 a year deductible and then pays 80 percent of the cost of all other services (a 20 percent coinsurance rate).

Medicaid is a joint federal-state program, with the federal government paying from 50 percent (for high-income states) to 77 percent (for low-income states) of the costs. Medicaid is operated largely by states under federal guidelines. To receive federal subsidies, states must provide Medicaid services to all persons receiving public assistance; states may also choose to cover other low-income people who are considered "medically indigent." In addition, the range of medical assistance provided to recipients varies from state to state. All states are required to cover hospital services, physician services, and nursing home services. Other types of medical care may be provided at the option of the states. With few exceptions, Medicaid covers all the costs of covered medical care services provided to eligible persons.

In recent years, Medicaid has become the largest government welfare program, at least if we interpret "welfare program" to mean a program that provides benefits almost exclusively to low-income persons. Total Medicaid outlays are about triple those of the food stamp program. Not all poor persons are eligible to receive Medicaid, however. Eligibility is generally restricted to those with low incomes who are also aged, blind, or disabled or who are members of families with dependent children. Single persons and families without dependent children are frequently ineligible for Medicaid even if they are poor.

Price, output, and usage

Medical care prices have risen rapidly over the past three decades, and economists believe a major reason is the growth in third-party payments by both public and private insurance, especially when the insurance covers a large share of the costs. Let's focus initially on the publicly provided insurance, namely, the Medicare and Medicaid programs. Figure 6–2 will help us analyze the effects to be expected of these programs.

In the absence of Medicare and Medicaid, the demand for medical care by potential recipients is shown as D_P, and the demand by all others is D_N. Total demand, D_T, is the horizontal sum of these curves, and the intersection of D_T and the supply curve determines price and output, P and M_T. Consumption levels of the two groups are M_P and M_N. As we have indicated, Medicare and Medicaid cover virtually all costs of medical care for recipients. In Figure 6–2 these policies have the effect of shifting the demand curve of recipients to the vertical curve D'_P, indicating that subsidized groups would choose to consume M'_P whatever the market price, because the government pays it, and their net price is zero. Thus, there is a large increase in effective demand by subsidized parties, and this, coupled with an unchanged demand by the other group, causes the total demand curve to shift to D'_T. With an upward-sloping supply curve, price increases to P' and total quantity to M'_T. As a result, consumption by the unsubsidized group falls to M'_N, and consumption by the subsidized group rises to M'_P.

Although this is a highly simplified exposition of a major cause of increasing health care costs, it explains, at least in part, why medical care prices rose by 29 percent between 1966 (when Medicare and Medicaid began) and 1970, while the overall consumer price index rose by only 20

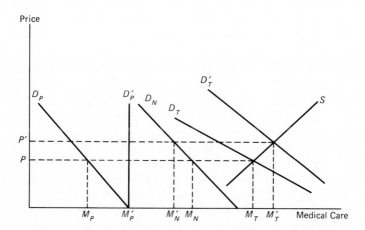

FIGURE 6–2 *Economic effects of Medicare and Medicaid.*

percent. Nonetheless, this explanation is incomplete because medical care costs were rising more rapidly than was the average of all goods and services even before 1965. For example, for the period from 1950 to 1965 the overall price level rose by 31 percent; at the same time, medical care costs increased by 67 percent.

Since medical care prices were rising much faster than other prices were even before Medicare and Medicaid were introduced in the late 1960s, other factors must have been responsible for rising medical care costs. Most health economists believe the explanation of this longer-term trend in prices lies in the increasing reliance on private insurance as well as increasing government subsidies. As explained earlier, the tax laws encourage use of private insurance even to the extent of fully covering small and predictable costs. Private insurance, especially when it covers all or most medical expenses— as the tax subsidy encourages—has the same demand-increasing effect as government subsidies do. Thus, a fuller analysis of the medical care scene using Figure 6–2 would also have D_N shifting outward as a result of subsidized private insurance.

More insight into the causes of medical care price increases is afforded by considering different types of medical care. Not all types of medical services have experienced similar increases. For example, since 1950 the cost of physician services has increased only slightly more than the consumer price index has, and no more rapidly than the price of other services generally. Drug prices have actually increased less than the average increase in all prices. In contrast, the average cost per patient day of hospital care increased from $16 in 1950 to $369 in 1983, a whopping 2,206 percent increase! The problem (if it is a problem) of rising medical care costs is almost exclusively one of rising hospital costs. Recall that hospital services are the most extensively supported by third-party payments, with patients bearing, on the average, only 10 percent of hospital costs directly. It seems likely that the rapidly increasing role of third-party payments for hospital care has been a major cause of hospital cost inflation.

Hospital administrators are quick to point out that these facts overstate the price increases for hospital care because they make no adjustment for quality changes. The quality of hospital care has improved markedly since 1950, so patients today are getting a better product for a higher price. To a large extent, this is true. Economists have contended, however, that hospitals are led to provide a more expensive product as a direct result of increased demand encouraged by public policy. In 1950 patients paid directly for over half of the cost of hospital care received; today patients pay only 10 percent of hospital costs. Because net out-of-pocket expenses are so low, doctors and patients choose more expensive and sophisticated hospital care. As long as the higher costs are paid by someone, hospitals will gladly provide higher-quality care. (Their response in upgrading the quality of care may be even greater than in other markets because most hospitals are nonprofit.)

An example will show clearly why such a heavy subsidy is likely to lead to better-quality, more expensive products. Suppose the government pays 90 percent of the cost of the automobiles consumers purchase. It is possible that some consumers would respond by purchasing more of the Chevrolets, Fords, or Hondas they use now. But another plausible response would be to move up to a better-quality car, to purchase a Cadillac or Lincoln Continental instead of a Chevy or Ford, or a Mercedes or BMW instead of a Honda. We suspect that most people would purchase not only more cars but also more expensive cars. (We know we would!) Statistics would then show a sharp rise in automobile costs because the higher-quality cars cost much more.

Something like this probably has happened in the field of hospital costs. It is a source of concern because many experts believe that consumers would not want more expensive hospital care if they had to pay for it: To most people, the higher quality of "Cadillac" care is not worth the extra cost. Patients and doctors choose this high-quality care now only because its direct cost at the time of treatment is so low, even though the actual marginal benefit of the more expensive care is below the marginal cost of providing it. This, of course, is simply a statement of the welfare cost resulting from overconsumption—but here the emphasis is on the quality dimension rather than on the more familiar quantity dimension.

Our analysis of the impact of Medicare and Medicaid on resource allocation in Figure 6–2 predicts that at the lowered price, subsidized parties would increase consumption of medical care, and this is largely borne out by the facts. Indeed, in the early 1970s, the poor were consuming more medical care (according to some measures) than were middle- and upper-income groups. For example, the poor have more doctor visits and hospital admissions than do other income groups, and health expenditures (from all sources) per person are greater for low-income groups.[12] The opposite was true before Medicaid and Medicare. (The change has not been great, however. Doctor visits per poor person increased from 4.3 per year in 1964 to 5.6 in 1973; for the nonpoor the increase was from 4.6 to 4.9.) These facts do not necessarily imply, however, excessive consumption by the poor. It should be noted that the poor typically have more health problems than do people in other income groups.

Cost controls

One important consequence of full insurance coverage for medical care prices is not made clear in Figure 6–2. In that diagram, it is implied that the price would settle at P'. With a subsidy that covers *all* (as distinguished

---

[12] See *National Health Insurance Proposals,* Legislative Analysis No. 19 (Washington, D.C.: American Enterprise Institute, 1974).

from only part of) medical care costs, however, there is no economic pressure to keep the price of medical care for subsidized parties from rising even higher. If a doctor were to charge $500, or even $5,000, for a physical checkup, a subsidized patient would not care because he or she would bear *no* cost. In this respect, a 100 percent subsidy is quite different from one that covers only part of the cost. When just part of the cost is covered, the patient still has some incentive to shop around for economical prices, and such behavior would keep the prices for subsidized patients from departing significantly from the market prices paid by unsubsidized patients. If the subsidy covers all of the costs, however, there will be no market pressure to keep prices for subsidized patients from rising above market clearing levels.

Medicare and Medicaid, as well as private health insurance stimulated by the tax laws, have greatly increased the demand for medical care. At the same time, they have tended to employ open-ended reimbursement systems that allowed doctors and hospitals to charge higher-than-market prices for medical care and often to receive payment. Until recently, health care providers have had few incentives to keep costs down. In addition, patients have had little incentive to seek out less expensive types of medical care, because the entire costs were borne by third parties. The understandable result of this type of system was enormous upward pressure on medical care costs. In an effort to hold down its budgetary costs, the government has experimented with a number of administrative devices to control costs, including price controls, reimbursements limited to "reasonable and customary" fees, revenue caps, fixed budgets, and capital expansion controls for hospitals.

It is the economic incentives created by existing government policies that may make such cost controls an attractive-sounding proposition. Providing full insurance coverage, in which patients pay a zero price, removes the normal incentive that market participants have to keep costs down. Rather than modifying the government policies responsible for the problems, however, most attention in the 1970s was directed toward formulating types of cost control policies to hold costs down directly. Overall, this approach did not work. Zeckhauser and Zook summarized the experience this way: "Recent government efforts to control health care costs through direct regulation have met with little success. Medical costs remain high and are increasing, despite the institution of a complicated, economically inefficient, and hard-to-manage collection of regulatory programs."[13]

Recent years have seen continued experimentation with policies designed to suppress the cost-increasing effects of government health care subsidies. Before 1983, Medicare reimbursed hospitals for their "reasonable costs" of providing care to covered patients, but in 1983 Medicare converted

---

[13] Richard Zeckhauser and Christopher Zook, "Failures to Control Health Costs: Departures from First Principles," in Mancur Olson, ed., op. cit., p. 87.

to a *prospective* payment system. Under the new system, hospitals are paid fixed, predetermined rates rather than being reimbursed for whatever costs they incur. The rates are set for each of 467 different diagnoses, with each rate intended to reflect communitywide averages for the treatment in question.

By fixing the prices in this way, the government hopes to give hospitals incentives to keep costs from rising too rapidly. The new prospective payment system, however, shares many problems with other attempts to use price controls. Exactly how to classify all illnesses into 467 categories and how to set the 467 separate rates and change the rates over time are enormously complicated tasks. If the rates are set at levels other than market-clearing levels, surpluses or shortages are likely to be created. Moreover, particularly efficient hospitals cannot attract patients by charging rates below the proscribed ones (since the patients don't pay these rates; third parties do), and so they may compete on the basis of quality by offering higher-quality, and thus more costly, care. For this reason, the system contains some incentives to raise costs to the levels of the predetermined rates.

Another innovation in 1985 was designed to encourage people covered by Medicare to take advantage of health maintenance organizations (HMOs). Health maintenance organizations are prepaid medical plans, in which patients pay a fixed annual amount in return for all needed medical care from the HMO at no further cost. Before 1985, Medicare would not make the up-front payments required to join HMOs, because the government's policy was to reimburse patients only for treatments already received. Now, however, subject to certain restrictions, Medicare beneficiaries can use HMOs if they wish. Since there is some evidence that HMOs are more efficient providers of care, this is a desirable step.

These and other recent changes in the way government pays medical care providers have led some observers to refer to a "virtual revolution" in the health care system. There are, in fact, some signs of improved efficiency and a slowing down of medical care cost increases. For example, in 1984, health care outlays were a slightly smaller percentage of the GNP than in the previous year—10.6 percent compared with 10.8 percent—the first drop in many years.

Rather than giving consumers an incentive to moderate their demand by reducing the subsidy (increasing the price), cost controls are an attempt to suppress the demand directly. It is too early to tell whether the new types of cost controls will be any more effective than the earlier ones were or to anticipate all of the difficulties and side effects that they may produce. If controls actually hold down health care costs, however, this means that the subsidized parties will not receive as much medical care, or as good-quality care, as they would like to receive at the zero price they pay. And if the price is not permitted to rise, some other mechanism must be substituted to restrict access to medical resources.

Other effects of Medicare and Medicaid

One can view Medicare and Medicaid as the provision of health insurance coverage to eligible households. Viewed in this way, both policies are examples of fixed quantity subsidies that were considered earlier. The insurance protection provided is fixed in amount; the recipient does not have the choice of either less or more coverage than the government provides. (The amount of medical care that can be consumed by a sick person is variable, but this variability is distinct from the fixed insurance coverage provided.) A relevant question is whether the amount and type of insurance protection provided are appropriate for the needs of the recipients.

Because the "optimal" amount of insurance depends on individual circumstances and preferences, there is no single answer to this question that would be correct for all recipients. Nonetheless, several studies have estimated that on the average, the insurance protection is greater than the recipients would prefer. Timothy Smeeding estimated a welfare cost of 32 percent for Medicare and Medicaid; Eugene Smolensky and colleagues estimated the welfare cost to be generally lower at 15 to 26 percent.[14] These figures mean that if recipients were given cash instead of insurance policies, they would choose to purchase less insurance and more of other goods and services, and would be significantly better off with this different consumption pattern. The exact figures should perhaps not be taken too seriously, but these findings suggest that the poor and elderly may be overinsured as a result of Medicare and Medicaid.

The administration of Medicaid provides a very interesting set of economic incentives for some low-income families. Generally, eligibility is restricted to families with incomes below a certain level. For example, the income limit might be $8,000, and all families below that level might receive insurance protection with an actuarial value of $2,000. Thus, a family with a cash income of $7,900 would receive $2,000 in insurance at no cost, but another family with an income of $8,100 would receive no subsidy at all. There is an obvious inequity associated with the abrupt termination of all benefits at the $8,000 level (in Chapter 9 we will see that this is called the "notch" problem that must be dealt with in the design of welfare programs), and it also strongly affects incentives. Families that would normally have earnings above the $8,000 level have the incentive to reduce their work effort to become eligible for the $2,000 subsidy; they can actually increase

---

[14]Timothy Smeeding, "Measuring the Economic Welfare of Low-Income Households, and the Antipoverty Effectiveness of Cash and Non-cash Transfer Programs," Ph.D. dissertation, University of Wisconsin, Madison, 1975; and Eugene Smolensky, Leanna Stiefel, Maria Schmundt, and Robert Plotnik, "Adding In-Kind Transfers to the Personal Income and Outlay Account: Implications for the Size Distribution of Income," Discussion Paper No. 199-74, University of Wisconsin (Madison: Institute for Research on Poverty, 1974).

their total real income by reducing their earnings. Similarly, families with incomes already below $8,000 have an incentive not to increase their incomes above that level because they would lose Medicaid benefits. Consequently, there are strong work disincentive effects built into the Medicaid program. This type of disincentive does not exist in Medicare because the subsidy is provided to the elderly regardless of income.

One other matter deserves mention because it has received so much public attention: the prevalence of fraud in Medicare and Medicaid. Allegations of widespread fraud have led to several congressional hearings devoted exclusively to the subject. Documented cases include laboratories billing for tests that doctors do not request, doctors receiving illicit payments or kickbacks from laboratories in return for sending all Medicaid work to them, pharmacies billing for brand-name drugs but giving the patient generic drugs, and laboratories billing for manual performance of a test (which is more expensive) when semi-automated tests are actually performed.

Why is there so much fraud in these programs? It should be clear that there will be some fraud in any program involving billions of dollars. Perhaps a better way to phrase the question is, Why is there more fraud in Medicare and Medicaid than in the social security retirement program, a program that involves twice as much government spending? It seems likely that the structure of Medicare and Medicaid is largely to blame, rather than poor administration. Large monetary gains can be obtained when the government nominally covers all the costs of some economic activity. Patients do not monitor or police the activity when they have no financial stake involved. (In fact, patients frequently do not even see the bills submitted on their behalf to the government.) The laws are, of necessity, often vague; how is it possible to determine what bill, or what type of medical care, is "reasonable" or "customary"? As it turns out, very little fraud has been proven, because there is often no clear distinction between fraud and simple "abuse."

There has been remarkably little study of the relationship among program structure, the incentive for fraudulent behavior, and difficulties of detection and administration. Experience under Medicare and Medicaid suggests that some relationship probably does exist.

Proposals for Reform: National Health Insurance

Much of the debate concerning the ills of the medical care system has centered on variations on a single policy option—national health insurance, or NHI. During the 1970s the enactment of some form of NHI was widely regarded as inevitable, even imminent. With the election of Ronald Reagan as president in 1980, and the emergence of federal budget deficits as a persistent problem, proposals for NHI have been removed from consideration, at least for the present. The possibility of NHI is still very much alive, however, and is considered whenever major reforms in the medical care system are discussed. Therefore, it is worthwhile to consider the likely effects of enacting an NHI program.

Actually there is a wide array of approaches commonly referred to as national health insurance. Most of these approaches, however, fit into one of two general categories: comprehensive national health insurance and catastrophic national health insurance. We shall consider each of these in turn.

Comprehensive national health insurance

The comprehensive approach to NHI essentially involves extending Medicare and Medicaid to cover the entire population. In other words, the government would finance all kinds of medical services for everyone from tax revenues. Not only would hospital care and physician services be covered but also dental services, eyeglasses, and prescription drugs—which is why the program is called comprehensive. There would be no limit on the benefits and no cost sharing by the patient. In effect, the federal government would become the primary and perhaps the sole purchaser of health care. Senator Edward Kennedy is perhaps the leading proponent of this form of NHI.

In 1982 the net budgetary cost (outlays in excess of those already undertaken for Medicare, Medicaid, and so on) would be, as a rough approximation, $180 billion.[15] This sum would be financed out of increased federal taxes. Although our main interest is not in taxes at this point, we should note briefly the distributional effect of NHI combined with the necessary financing. On balance, the program would involve a large redistribution in favor of individuals with low and middle incomes. This redistribution would occur because families with low incomes would receive the same benefits but pay much less in taxes—regardless of what mix of taxes is used—than would higher-income families.

The most obvious effect of this type of NHI would probably be a major increase in the demand for medical care, because the direct cost to patients would fall to zero. The impact would probably be greatest for those types of medical care that are not now so heavily subsidized: physician fees, dental services, and so on. (Recall that third-party payments already account for 92 percent of outlays on hospital care, so effects on this market may not be as pronounced.) Prices would rise, as would the quantity and quality of care in these areas. The response would probably be similar to the effects pro-

---

[15]This figure can be calculated by subtracting the amount of government spending from total spending on medical care in Table 6–1, since this form of NHI implies the government will finance all medical costs. This is only approximate, however, because it ignores how NHI will affect the price and quantity of medical resources. If price and/or quantity rise, as we would expect, government costs would be higher.

duced by increasing subsidization of hospital care over the past several decades. Total cost—price times quantity—would rise, so the estimated budgetary cost would probably be conservative.

The analysis in the preceding paragraph, however, ignores one element found in most comprehensive NHI proposals: cost controls. As explained earlier, any subsidy paying the full costs of some activity must of necessity be accompanied by a regulatory mechanism to limit price and quantity. Senator Kennedy's proposal, for example, envisions rather detailed supervision of the medical care system by regulatory agencies. Doctors would be reimbursed according to a schedule of fees, or they would elect to be reimbursed on a per capita basis according to the number of patients they treat. Hospitals would receive a fixed budget each year. The overall division of the total medical care budget among physicians, hospitals, dentists, and so on would also be determined by some agency.

How this regulatory mechanism would actually operate is the greatest uncertainty encountered in an attempt to analyze comprehensive NHI proposals. Quite possibly the cost controls would be so strictly applied that price and quantity would not be permitted to rise in response to the increase in effective demand. Shortages would then result.

On the other hand, the controls might be completely ineffective, and costs could rise without limit. Based on experience with cost controls in existing programs, the actual result is likely to fall between these extremes; costs would rise substantially, but not by so much as they would if people could consume all the medical care they wished at a zero price.

There are still many unsettling questions concerning how this regulatory mechanism would function. For example:

1. Because there would certainly be major shortages (people would want more and better medical care at a zero price than would be supplied), how would the available quantities be rationed among the public? Would longer waiting times provide the rationing function now performed by prices? In England, with its National Health Service providing "free" hospital care, there were over 750,000 people waiting to enter hospitals in 1979, with waiting times sometimes exceeding 3 years.[16]

2. In a similar vein, how would patients be allocated among hospitals, doctors, and dentists? There are good doctors, average doctors, and poor doctors; the same can be said of all other aspects of health care. At a zero price everyone would want the "best" care provided by the "best" practitioners, but it would be physically impossible for all patients to have the "best." Would doctors be able to accept or reject patients, or would patients be assigned to doctors, as students are now assigned to public schools?

3. What criteria would be used to determine what fees and prices would

[16]John C. Goodman, "N.H.S.: An Ill for All Cures," *Policy Review,* 14:117(Fall 1980).

be permitted? Under Medicare and Medicaid, a large uncontrolled market in medical care provides some guidance as to what are "reasonable" fees and prices, but no private market would exist to generate this information under the comprehensive NHI. (This may not be exactly true: Some people might be so dissatisfied with the "free" medical care that they would forgo the public subsidy and purchase care privately, just as some families send their children to private schools today.)

4. What incentives would doctors and hospitals have to provide good quality care? If doctors were reimbursed according to how many patients they treated, wouldn't they have an incentive to treat as many patients as they could, even if each received only superficial treatment? (This seems to have happened in some cases under Medicaid.) What incentives would hospitals have not to devote their entire (government-funded) fixed budgets to research instead of providing medical care for patients?

These questions suggest a few of the problems that a regulatory mechanism would have to confront and resolve. Unfortunately, all of the proposals for NHI containing cost controls are imprecise concerning exactly how they would operate. Yet clearly the answers to such "nuts and bolts" questions are of major importance in our analysis of comprehensive NHI. Direct controls may keep health costs down, but they also are likely to produce a major misallocation of medical resources.

The important point here is that the choice between comprehensive NHI and a system in which the patient bears part of the cost is not really a choice between free and unfree care. Rather, the choice is between a bureaucratic mechanism to ration care and allocate scarce medical resources and a price system to perform these functions. In either case, the patients will ultimately bear the costs, either in the form of prices (or insurance premiums) or in the form of taxes.

Recognizing the difficulties created when the government finances all medical care costs, few economists favor a comprehensive NHI plan. Instead, those who support an expansion of the government's role in this area wish to have patients continue to bear part of the costs of the care they receive. (In other words, a coinsurance rate or rates would be used.) Using coinsurance rates avoids the most extreme of the problems suggested in the preceding discussion, but if the coinsurance rate were set relatively low, health costs would certainly rise.

The emphasis on the cost of health care (which depends on changes in price and quantity) is intentional. Limiting the rise in health care costs seems to be the only goal that advocates of NHI all share, probably because it is a cost that seems of paramount concern to the public. Increasing effective demand (which all comprehensive NHI proposals would do) is a strange way to hold costs down, but it is conceivable that the regulatory mechanisms could offset the policy-induced increase in demand.

Catastrophic national health insurance

"Catastrophic NHI" is the name applied to government-financed insurance protection against major medical expenses. In effect, a large deductible is employed, and the government would finance medical expenses only in excess of the deductible. If the deductible is set at $3,000 per year, then families with expenses below $3,000 would bear the entire cost (either directly or through private health insurance). When expenses exceed $3,000, the government would finance the excess. With expenses of $5,000, for example, the government would pay $2,000 of the total bill. The deductible in effect places an upper limit on the out-of-pocket medical expenses incurred by any family.

Within the general framework of NHI restricted to catastrophic coverage, a wide variety of specific approaches is still possible. In particular, the deductible could be varied with family income. A $3,000 medical expense is not a financial catastrophe for a family with an income of $50,000, but it is for a family with an income of $5,000. Recognizing this, most proponents of catastrophic NHI specify the deductible as some percentage of total income. If the deductible were set at 10 percent of family income, a family with an income of $5,000 would have to pay at most $500 for medical care, but for a family with an income of $25,000, the sum would be $2,500.

The appeal of catastrophic NHI stems from an understanding of the economic principles of insurance. As explained earlier, insurance is most advantageous when it covers large and unpredictable expenses. This is the type of medical expense that would be emphasized by a catastrophic NHI plan. Moreover, because there are certain biases against private purchase of catastrophic protection in the present system, a role for government may be justified.

The provision of catastrophic NHI would not directly resolve the problem of too much private insurance coverage of small and predictable expenses. Quite possibly, once the risks of major expense are covered, people would not find it worthwhile to continue to insure against moderate and predictable expenses. The tax policies that encourage this type of coverage, however, would continue to exist. Most supporters of catastrophic NHI also favor an end to tax subsidies for private health insurance as well as the preferential treatment given to Blue Cross. If these actions are taken, the introduction of catastrophic NHI would probably lead to a reversal in the type of insurance protection most Americans have. In addition, it is frequently recommended that Medicaid and Medicare be terminated, because the poor and elderly would be covered by the catastrophic NHI plan.

The federal budgetary cost of catastrophic NHI is relatively modest. Although the exact figure depends on the specifics of the plan adopted, the gross budgetary cost of providing a plan with a 10 percent deductible for all those not now covered by Medicaid and Medicare would probably be in the neighborhood of $25 billion. This relatively low figure reflects the fact that only a small proportion of families has expenses exceeding 10 percent of income, and for these families only the expenditures in excess of 10 percent of income would be federally financed. If Medicare and Medicaid were abolished, the net budgetary cost would be less.

Three major advantages are claimed for catastrophic NHI. First, it ensures that everyone will have the most important type of insurance protection. Government aid will be concentrated on those who would be most heavily burdened by medical expenses; no one would be impoverished as a result of medical bills. Second, it will encourage more efficient use of medical resources. This advantage depends critically on the prediction that people will cease to insure against modest medical bills, an outcome that may depend on changes in other policies, as already noted. If that prediction is valid, then market incentives will be restored as doctors and patients take better account of the costs of alternative treatments. Medical care practices will be determined by comparing the expected benefits of more expensive care with the actual resource costs of providing that care, instead of largely ignoring costs, as is frequently the case under present financing arrangements. Note, however, that this argument is valid only for families spending less than the deductible amount on medical care. For families who spend more that the deductible, the perceived marginal cost of more or better medical care will be zero, because the government pays the bill, and this creates disincentives in these situations—presumably, however, in the small minority of all cases.

The third major advantage claimed for catastrophic NHI is that it would moderate and possibly reverse the inflation in medical care prices. This follows directly from the preceding analysis; removal of the subsidies favoring coverage of small and predictable expenses would reduce effective market demand. Hospital care would be the most strongly affected type of medical care because it is now the most heavily subsidized; other types of medical care would be affected to a much smaller degree.

Probably the major problem with catastrophic NHI concerns incentive effects for the families with expenditures above the deductible. Because the government would pay all the bills above this amount, a regulatory mechanism would be needed to control costs. Although the problems would be much less severe than with comprehensive NHI, some more or less arbitrary political controls would still be necessary as a substitute for market incentives. Supporters of catastrophic NHI have suggested a number of ways to ease this problem, but it cannot be avoided altogether. For example, raising the deductible amount to 20 percent of annual income would greatly reduce the number of people affected by the plan, but it would also reduce the insurance protection provided and increase the risk people would have to bear. Alternatively, coinsurance rates could be used. The NHI plan could have the family pay the full cost of medical care equal to 5 percent of income and then have the government pay half the cost between 5 and 15 percent of income; thereafter, the government would pay all costs. This arrangement would still place an upper limit on medical expenses equal to 10 percent of income but would limit the extreme disincentive problem to an even smaller minority of families who spend more than 15 percent of their incomes on medical care. Whatever procedure is used, there is clearly a difficult tradeoff between preserving incentives and providing protection against medical risks.

Proponents of comprehensive NHI emphasize one major objection to catastrophic NHI: Because the bulk of medical care would still be privately financed, monetary considerations might still deter people from receiving needed medical care. Financial considerations, they argue, should not be a barrier to medical care. This objection raises the question of what is meant by "needed" medical care. The quantity and quality of care that is "needed" are not objectively fixed—the demand curve still slopes downward, implying that the quantity people want to consume depends on its relative cost. If market prices lead some people to consume less medical care than others think they should, then the actual problem may be a lack of income rather than an inappropriate barrier to care. This line of argument may suggest that the poor deserve special help (possibly through cash transfers so they can afford more medical care), but it does not seem to provide a case for comprehensive NHI for the nonpoor.

The more fundamental point is that the choice between comprehensive and catastrophic NHI plans is not a choice between a system without and a system with barriers to the consumption of medical care. Both plans incorporate "barriers" to ensure that people will get less care than they would like at a zero price. With comprehensive NHI, the barriers could take the form of bureaucratic rules, quantity and quality limits, and waiting time. With catastrophic NHI, the barrier to the use of medical resources (at least up to the deductible amount) is the price, the same barrier that exists for most other goods and services. Basically, the choice between the two approaches to NHI turns on whether one wishes to use a price system or a bureaucratic mechanism to allocate the bulk of medical resources and ration care among competing consumers.

Supplementary Readings

DAVIS, KAREN. *National Health Insurance: Benefits, Costs and Consequences.* Washington, D.C.: The Brookings Institution, 1975.

FELDSTEIN, MARTIN S. "A New Approach to National Health Insurance." *Public Interest,* 23:93–105 (Spring 1971).

FUCHS, VICTOR. *Who Shall Live?* New York: Basic Books, 1974.

LINDSAY, C. M. *National Health Issues: The British Experience.* Roche Laboratories, 1980.

———— ed. *New Directions in Public Health Care.* San Francisco: Institute for Contemporary Studies, 1976.

MARMOR, T. "Rethinking National Health Insurance." *Public Interest,* 46:73–95 (Winter 1977).

MEYER, JACK A., and ROSEMARY G. KERN. "The Changing Structure of the Health Care System." In P. Cagan, ed., *Essays in Contemporary Economic Problems.* Washington, D.C.: American Enterprise Institute, 1986.

OLSON, MANCUR, ed. *A New Approach to the Economics of Health Care.* Washington, D.C.: American Enterprise Institute, 1982.

PAULY, MARK V. "Taxation, Health Insurance, and Market Failure in the Medical Economy." *Journal of Economic Literature,* 24: 629–675 (June 1986).

Review Questions and Problems

1. What reasons are there, if any, why medical care should be subsidized?

2. Why is it usually economically inefficient to insure against *predictable* and/or *small* medical expenses?

3. How does the tax system encourage people to insure themselves against small and predictable medical expenses, even when it is inefficient to do so?

4. What are third-party payments? Why have they grown, and how do they affect the operation of medical markets?

5. How does Part B of Medicare affect the budget line of an elderly person in regard to insurance coverage of physicians' services and all other goods? Could this subsidy lead to overinsurance? If so, show the results in your graph.

6. Recent years have seen the extensive use of various types of cost controls to deal with rising medical care costs. Could changes in the tax laws and a greater use of deductibles and coinsurance rates have accomplished the same thing? Which alternative is preferable?

7. Consider two ways to reduce the tax subsidy to medical insurance. First, employer contributions up to a maximum of $500 per worker are nontaxable; anything above $500 is taxed under the income tax. Second, only employer contributions in excess of $300 are nontaxable; the first $300 is fully taxable. Assume that these two alternatives cost the government the same. Which one will reduce the extent of overinsurance more?

8. Suppose the government knows the number of kidney dialysis machines people use per year in the United States and the number of days people stay in a hospital per year. Let's assume the government decides to provide "free" kidney dialysis machines for those who need them and "free" hospital care for anyone who stays in a hospital. The government would, of course, try to estimate the cost of providing each service "free." Is the government more likely to underestimate the cost of providing free kidney dialysis machines or free hospital care? Why?

9. If comprehensive national health insurance were introduced and financed by a flat rate tax on wage earnings, what groups would likely be benefited and what groups harmed? In particular, how would it affect the groups now covered by Medicare and Medicaid?

10. Medicare and Medicaid are much like comprehensive national health insurance for the elderly and poor. Had the catastrophic approach to health insurance been used instead, how would the effects of these programs have differed? Which approach is preferable? Can you give a public choice explanation of why the comprehensive rather than the catastrophic approach was selected?

chapter 7
Social Security

THE set of programs popularly known as "social security" actually has a far more imposing official designation: Old Age, Survivors, Disability, and Health Insurance, or OASDHI for short. Enacted as part of the Social Security Act of 1935, social security was originally designed to provide only old age or retirement benefits; it was known as OAI then. Survivors benefits were added in 1939, and the system became OASI. In 1954 disability benefits were included, and the system was thus OASDI until 1965, when Medicare was enacted and it evolved into OASDHI. Today social security is perhaps the most important, and certainly the largest, domestic expenditure policy in the United States.

Table 7–1 summarizes information relating to the growth in social security since 1945. Total expenditures have risen from $0.3 billion in 1945 to $238.7 billion in 1984. Because the rate of growth in expenditures was more than double the rate of growth in the nation's output, social security outlays have grown rapidly relative to net national product (NNP). Whereas social security outlays were a scant 0.1 percent of the NNP in 1945, they had grown to 7.3 percent by 1984. Three factors largely account for this growth. First, an increased proportion of the elderly has become eligible to receive benefits. In 1945, only 8 percent of those over 65 received benefits, but today more than 94 percent receive benefits. (Most of those who do not receive benefits under social security today receive benefits under other federal retirement programs or welfare programs.) Second, a larger proportion of the population is now elderly. In 1945, only 8 percent of the population was aged 65 or older; today the proportion is 12 percent. Third, the level of real benefits per retired person has risen. This third factor has been especially important since 1970, as we shall see later.

Social security outlays are financed by an earmarked tax on earnings. (An earmarked tax is one whose revenues must be used to finance a specific program, in this case social security.) Workers in jobs covered by social security (almost all jobs today) pay a flat rate tax on earnings up to a maximum amount. In 1986, for example, the tax was 14.3 percent of the first $42,000 in earnings. Thus, the tax liability for a worker with $20,000 in earnings was $2,860, whereas for one earning the maximum taxable earnings of

Table 7-1   *OASDHI System, Selected Data*

Year	Spending on OASDHI (in billions)	Spending as Percentage of NNP	Maximum Taxable Earnings	Payroll Tax Rate	Percentage of People 65 or over Receiving Social Security
1945	$ 0.3	0.1	$ 3,000	2.0	8
1950	1.0	0.4	3,000	3.0	17
1955	5.0	1.4	4,200	4.0	40
1960	11.4	2.5	4,800	6.0	62
1965	18.5	2.9	4,800	7.25	74
1970	39.2 (32.1)	4.3 (3.5)	7,800	9.6	84
1975	82.9 (67.3)	6.0 (4.8)	14,100	11.7	91
1980	154.2 (120.5)	6.6 (5.2)	25,900	12.26	91
1984	238.7 (175.7)	7.3 (5.4)	37,800	14.0	94

Note: Figures include cash payments plus Medicare. Figures in parentheses exclude Medicare payment.
Source: *Social Security Bulletin* (Nov. 1985) and *Economic Report of the President, 1986*, Table B-19.

$42,000, it was $6,006. Those earning above $42,000 also had tax liabilities of $6,006 because only the first $42,000 is subject to tax. Actually, the social security tax is composed of two equal levies (of 7.15 percent in 1986) each on the employer and employee. There is little doubt, however, that the economic effects would be the same as if a tax of 14.3 percent were paid entirely by the worker. (We will come back to the question of the incidence of the tax in Chapter 13.)

Social security is still primarily a system providing retired persons with benefits both in cash (in the form of pensions or annuities) and in kind (Medicare). To receive social security benefits, a retired person must have worked in a covered job and paid social security taxes for a sufficient number of years to establish eligibility. The exact size of the benefits received depends on the taxes paid, in addition to other factors. As a result of legislation enacted in 1972, retirement benefits are automatically adjusted upward with increases in the consumer price index.[1] Benefits can be increased still further by congressional action, but no additional legislation is required to ensure that benefits keep pace with inflation.

Other details concerning the working of social security will become clear as we proceed with the analysis. Although our emphasis will be on the

---

[1] Although Congress intended benefits to rise in proportion to prices, the 1972 legislation contained a mistake that resulted in double counting of price increases. This problem, referred to as *double-indexing inflation*, meant that benefits rose faster than prices until 1977 when the problem was corrected.

provision of retirement benefits, we should also note that the program includes disability and survivors benefits. The analysis can easily be extended to include these programs.

Pay-as-You-Go Financing

It is important to understand that social security does not operate like private insurance. When a person pays premiums to a private insurance company to purchase an annuity, the premiums are invested and build up a fund that will be adequate to finance the annuity, or pension. When a person pays social security taxes, however, the taxes are not invested on the worker's behalf; no fund accrues. Instead, the taxes are immediately paid out as benefits to people who are currently retired. Today's social security taxes pay for today's social security benefits. This is called *pay-as-you-go financing* to distinguish it from the procedures employed by private companies. Alternatively, social security is sometimes referred to as an *unfunded* system to emphasize the absence of a retirement fund.

The Social Security Administration does, however, have a trust fund. In 1983 this fund contained about $27 billion in government bonds. Thus, in 1983 the fund was only large enough to finance benefits about 2 months.[2] Only if people continue paying taxes into the system can benefits to the retired continue to be paid out, at least beyond the 2 months that can be financed from the trust fund. The trust fund is therefore of negligible importance in the financing of the program. The fund does, however, serve a function, namely, to act as a contingency reserve that can be drawn on if for some reason current taxes fall temporarily below current benefit levels.

Recognition that the trust fund is inadequate to finance future benefits has led many people to conclude that the system is "bankrupt." It is true that social security would be considered insolvent if judged according to the same standard applied to private insurance companies. A private insurance company must have a reserve fund sufficient to finance its obligations even if it never sells another insurance policy. If the social security system required a fund capable of meeting its already accumulated obligations, that fund would have to be about *$4 trillion.* Judged by private insurance standards, the social security system is bankrupt because its fund is only $27 billion instead of $4,000 billion.

Fortunately, it is not necessary to judge social security by private insurance standards. A *governmental* system of providing retirement benefits does not require a large fund to finance future benefits; these benefits can be financed out of future taxes. Pay-as-you-go financing is a viable method for

---

[2] These figures refer to the OASI trust fund. There are separate trust funds for disability insurance and Medicare. These other funds are also small in relation to annual outlays.

the government to use to provide retirement benefits. Workers currently in the labor force can expect to receive pensions when they retire because the government is able to tax the working generation at that time to finance these pensions. Social security is simply a different method of providing for retirement, and this does not imply that it is an inferior method.

How a pay-as-you-go system operates

Social security is different in a number of respects from private insurance, and so let us consider what the economic effects of these differences are. To understand its consequences, it is necessary to understand how the system functions over time. A simple arithmetic example will be helpful. Assume that the adult population consists of only three people, one young, one middle-aged, and one retired. There is zero population growth, and each person has a 3-year life span: young in the first year, middle-aged in the second, and retired in the third. The retired person dies at the end of each year and is replaced by a new young person the following year. Each year the young and middle-aged persons have equal earnings, and these earnings grow over time at the rate of 100 percent per year (in other words, the growth rate of the economy is 100 percent annually). These assumptions are obviously unrealistic but are made to simplify the computations and to allow us to highlight some basic relationships in the simplest possible way.

Table 7–2 shows an economy growing over time according to our assumptions. Individuals are denoted by the letters *A, B, C,* and so on. In year 1, individuals *C* and *B* are young and middle-aged, respectively, and have incomes of $250 each. In the same year, individual *A* is retired and has zero current income. In the following year, *C* becomes middle-aged, *B* retires, and a new young person, *D,* joins the labor force. *C* and *D* have incomes of $500 in year 2, double the per worker incomes of the previous year. We can follow an individual through his or her lifetime by looking along a diagonal: *C* is young in year 1, middle-aged in year 2, and retired in year 3.

Table 7–2 *Pay-as-You-Go Financing of Social Security*

Year: Tax Rate:	1 0	2 10%	3 10%	4 10%	5 10%
Young	*C*250 (0)	*D*500 (−50)	*E*1000 (−100)	*F*2000 (−200)	*G*4000 (−400)
Middle-aged	*B*250 (0)	*C*500 (−50)	*D*1000 (−100)	*E*2000 (−200)	*F*4000 (−400)
Retired	*A*(0)	*B*(+100)	*C*(+200)	*D*(+400)	*E*(+800)

Now let's introduce a system of pay-as-you-go social security in year 2. A tax of 10 percent is levied on the incomes of the young and middle-aged workers each year, and the proceeds are transferred to the retired person. The tax payments and retirement benefits are shown by the figures in parentheses. Thus, C and D pay taxes of $50 each in year 2, and B receives $100. With the same tax rate in subsequent years, the total tax revenue and retirement benefits will grow with the economy over time.

Now let's see how people fare under this system. Initially, consider individual D, because D is the first person to spend an entire lifetime under the system. D pays taxes of $50 and $100 in years 2 and 3 and receives retirement benefits of $400 in year 4. D's retirement benefits are substantially larger than the taxes paid. This is also true for later generations, such as E, F, and G, who also receive retirement benefits exceeding previous taxes paid. This would be true too if they saved privately, because they would earn interest on their savings. The relevant question is how large the rate of return is under social security. In other words, for individual D, what rate of interest would produce a $400 sum if $50 were invested for two years and $100 for one year? The answer is 100 percent: $50 invested at 100 percent for two years will grow to $200, and $100 invested for one year will also grow to $200, for a total of $400. Thus, individual D is effectively receiving an annual rate of return of 100 percent under social security. This is also true of E, F, G, and later individuals, as long as income continues to grow at 100 percent per year and the tax rate remains 10 percent.

It is no accident that the rate of return on taxes paid is equal to the rate of growth in national income. An important implication of pay-as-you-go social security is that it can provide pensions that represent a rate of return on taxes paid equal to the rate of growth of the tax base—in this case, national income. In a sense, social security allows people to "share in the growth of the economy." Of course, in reality income grows less than 100 percent per year. Taking a long-term perspective, the U.S. economy has grown at an average *real* (adjusted for inflation) rate of about 3 percent per year over the past 60 years. This growth has resulted from an increase in output per person of about 2 percent and a growth in population of about 1 percent per year. (In a more elaborate model, the rate of return under social security depends on the sum of the rates of growth of income per worker and the number of workers, a sum that gives the total rate of growth of national income.)

Present trends suggest a slowdown in economic growth due in part to slower (and perhaps nonexistent) population growth in the future. An annual real growth rate of 2 percent per year may be a reasonable prediction of the long-term prospect. Thus, persons retiring in future years may expect to receive social security benefits that represent a 2 percent rate of return on taxes paid. (Some qualifications are noted below.)

Two types of redistribution

Social security is a method of providing retirement benefits to the population. If each person's pension were strictly related to the taxes he or she paid earlier in life, the system would not tend to redistribute income among people. But as it actually operates, social security redistributes income in two different ways.

The first type of redistribution is called *intragenerational* redistribution, which refers to a redistribution among members of a given generation. For example, suppose, referring to Table 7–2, there are two people in each age group. The two Ds both can receive benefits of $400 in year 4; alternatively, the government could provide a benefit of $500 to one D and $300 to the other D. This would effectively redistribute $100 from one D to the other. Members of the same generation can therefore receive different rates of return on taxes paid, some above and some below the average rate of return. As explained in more detail later, the social security system contains several features that produce intragenerational redistribution.

The second type of redistribution is called *intergenerational* redistribution and refers to the ways some generations of retirees receive higher benefits in relation to taxes paid than other generations. Table 7–2 shows that individual D and all subsequent generations would receive a rate of return on their taxes equal to the rate of growth. Now, however, consider individuals B and C, who did not pay the 10 percent tax over their entire working lives. Individual C received a pension in year 3 after paying taxes for only one year, and individual B received a pension without ever paying taxes. The rate of return that individuals B and C received on their tax payments is far greater than the rate of growth of the economy.

Generations that retire in the early years of a pay-as-you-go social security program receive much better returns than later generations do. In the start-up phase of social security, retired persons pay taxes for only part of their working lives and fare extremely well. The same is also true for people who work and pay taxes during years when the tax rate is low and who then retire and receive benefits based on a higher tax rate enacted later on. Table 7–1 shows how low the tax rate was until recent years. People who retired in 1984 spent a majority of their working years in the work force when the payroll tax rate was 6 percent or lower and yet are entitled to receive benefits financed by the 14.1 percent tax rate in effect in 1985.

Both types of redistribution are illustrated by the data in Table 7–3. This table gives estimates of projected social security benefits expressed as an annual real rate of return on the projected taxes paid for several demographic categories and income levels. In effect, the estimates are like the real interest rates that different groups can expect to receive on their social security taxes. For example, a married couple, composed of a high-earning

Table 7–3 *Projected Real Rates of Return by Household Type and by Age Cohort*

Demographic Status	Earnings Profile	Year in Which Head of Household Becomes 65					
		1970	1980	1990	2000	2010	2020
Single Males	Low	7.5%	5.3%	3.2%	2.4%	2.2%	2.1%
	Median	6.3	4.5	2.4	1.6	1.3	1.3
	High	5.4	4.0	2.3	1.4	.9	.7
Single Women	Low	10.7	7.7	5.9	5.0	4.5	4.4
	Median	9.1	6.6	4.6	3.8	3.4	3.3
	High	6.7	5.1	3.5	2.6	2.1	1.8
Married Couples	Low/Zero	9.7	7.4	5.3	4.3	4.1	4.0
	Median/Zero	8.5	6.7	4.5	3.6	3.3	3.2
	High/Zero	7.5	6.0	4.4	3.5	2.9	2.6
Married Couples	Low/Low	8.8	6.4	4.4	3.5	3.3	3.2
	Median/Low	7.7	6.0	3.9	3.1	2.7	2.6
	High/Median	6.7	5.1	3.4	2.6	2.2	1.9

Source: Michael D. Hurd and John B. Shoven, "The Distributional Impact of Social Security," NBER Working Paper No. 1155, June 1983, Table 11.

male (earning at the taxable earnings ceiling each year) and a median-earning female, who retired in 1980 is estimated to receive retirement benefits that represent a real rate of return on their lifetime taxes of 6.0 percent.

The *inter*generational redistribution of social security is illustrated in the table by the decline in the rate of return at later years for each household category. All households retiring in 1970 receive high rates of return, but the rates are much lower for those retiring in later years. For example, a high-earning single male retiring in 1970 has a rate of return of 5.4 percent, but the return declines steadily until it reaches a rate of 0.7 percent for individuals retiring in 2020. Comparisons between earlier and later years in the table illustrate the important difference between the way the system affects people who retired in the start-up phase of the system and those who will retire later.

The *intra*generational redistribution of social security is shown in the table by the differences in the rates of return for different household types retiring in the same year. In 1980, for example, a married couple with a low/zero earnings profile received a 7.4 percent rate of return, whereas a high earnings profile single male received only 4.0 percent. In general, married couples fared better than single persons did, and low-income households fared better than high-income households did. These differences reflect the way social security benefits are calculated, which will be discussed in more detail later in the chapter.

Two important qualifications to the estimates in Table 7–3 should be mentioned. First, the projected benefits and taxes are based on the social security law as it existed in 1980, but scheduled taxes in 1980 were not sufficient to pay for the scheduled benefits, especially for the later years covered by the table. In 1983 Congress made major changes in the system, intended to balance benefits and taxes, and these reforms will significantly reduce the rate of return for individuals retiring after the year 2000. Thus, the expected rates of return for the later years are even lower than those shown in the table and are probably negative for some of the household groups.

Second, the rates of return in the table compare the social security pensions only with the lifetime taxes paid. This procedure ignores the possible adverse effects of the system on labor supply and saving, which would make the system less attractive on balance than the rates of return suggest. These effects will be discussed later in the chapter.

Is social security a good deal?

Perhaps the most basic question to ask about social security is whether it is a more attractive way of providing retirement benefits than the alternative methods available. Could we do better providing for retirement by saving privately? In answering this question, it is essential to distinguish between the start-up phase of the system and all subsequent years. Workers who retired in the early years of the start-up phase received extremely favorable returns—generally much more than they could have gotten by saving privately. Younger workers and all future generations, however, will not do as well.

As a long-term permanent mechanism, social security can offer retirees, after the start-up phase, an annual rate of return, on the average, equal to the real rate of economic growth (which we take to be about 2 percent). Could people earn more than 2 percent by saving privately? Between 1927 and 1976, real rates of return on long-term government bonds averaged 1 percent, while common stocks averaged a yield of 6.6 percent.[3] Corporate bonds and home ownership have yielded only slightly more than 2 percent. Although real yields on these investments have been higher in recent years, these comparisons suggest that a real return of 2 percent from social security over the long run is not really too bad.

[3] Robert Kaplin, "A Comparison of Rates of Return to Social Security Retirees Under Wage and Price Indexing," in Colin Campbell, ed., *Financing Social Security* (Washington, D.C.: American Enterprise Institute, 1979), Table 4.

However, it may not be appropriate to compare these market yields with the implicit return under social security. These market rates of return are lower than the real rate of return to capital investment because the government taxes the return to capital investment heavily. (See Chapter 14.) A more appropriate comparison of the relative rates of return is the before-tax return to capital investment relative to the rate of return provided by social security. The before-tax return is a measure of how much private saving that is channeled into capital investment contributes to future output—it is a measure of the real productivity of private saving. Even though an individual does not realize the before-tax return, the society does. Estimation of the before-tax return to capital investment suggests that it has averaged about 10 percent in the postwar period.[4]

Thus, private saving for retirement yields a real annual return of 10 percent, whereas social security yields 2 percent. The significance of this difference in returns can be appreciated from the following example. Suppose a person saves $2,000 a year for 41 years at a 2 percent interest rate. At the end of that time, the accumulated sum would be $124,740. However, $2,000 a year for 41 years at 10 percent grows to $1,072,390. The sum available for retirement is more than 8 times as great at 10 percent than it is at 2 percent—such is the power of compound interest over long periods. Young workers and future generations could do much better providing for their retirement by investing in real capital than by relying on social security. Not surprisingly then, this difference in yields has led several economists to urge that we rely less on social security and more on real capital accumulation to provide retirement benefits.

Social Security, Retirement, and Work Incentives

Social security can have important effects on the labor supply decisions of the elderly. If the provision of retirement benefits creates work disincentives that lead older people to retire earlier or work less, the elderly will have lower earnings. Thus, granting the elderly retirement benefits will not raise their money incomes by as much as it would without a work disincentive effect.

Social security affects the labor supply of the elderly in two distinct ways.

---

[4]See Martin Feldstein, James Poterba, and Louis Dicks-Mireaux, "The Effective Tax Rate and the Pretax Rate of Return," National Bureau of Economic Research, Working Paper No. 740, Sept. 1981; Alicia Munnell, *The Future of Social Security* (Washington, D.C.: The Brookings Institution, 1977), p. 128; and Michael Boskin, "Taxation, Saving, and the Rate of Interest," *Journal of Political Economy,* 86 (2) Part 2:S 3 (Apr. 1978).

One way is through the *earnings test,* which applies until retirees reach the age of 70. Retirement benefits are not automatically received when a person reaches age 65 or 62 (reduced benefits are available for workers retiring at age 62). Under the earnings test, a person's pension is reduced if earnings exceed a certain amount ($7,200 a year in 1985). For each dollar of earnings above $7,200 the pension is reduced by 50 cents. If, for example, a person would receive a $5,000 pension if fully retired, this means that the retiree would receive no pension if his or her earnings exceeded $17,200 a year. In effect, the earnings test is like a 50 percent tax rate on earnings above $7,200, up to the point where the pension is exhausted. In addition, social security taxes must be paid on earnings, and perhaps other taxes as well. As a result, workers over 65 have a reduced financial incentive to earn above $7,200—unless they are able to earn more than the cutoff point ($17,200 in the preceding example). If part-time employment is not readily available, some workers must stop working in order to receive their social security pension.

A second way in which social security can encourage earlier retirement is by providing a pension that is large relative to the taxes paid. As we saw, in the start-up phase of the program, pensions are several times larger than the taxes paid plus a reasonable interest rate. In effect, this large unpaid-for net benefit produces an income effect: It increases the lifetime income of early retirees and enables them to afford an earlier retirement than they otherwise would have chosen. This, of course, is only relevant for workers who retire in the start-up phase and can be expected to diminish in importance in the coming years.

Taken together, these two effects can be expected to lead to earlier retirement, especially for generations retiring in the start-up phase. The evidence tends to support this expectation. Labor force participation among men over 65 fell from 47.8 percent in 1947 (when only about 12 percent of the elderly received social security benefits) to 17.4 percent in 1983, a reduction of 64 percent. In addition, the retirement rate for males aged 60 to 64 doubled from 15 percent to 30 percent between 1960 and 1978 following legislation permitting social security benefits to be paid (at reduced levels) beginning at age 62.

The fact that people have retired earlier since the introduction of social security, however, does not mean social security caused it to happen. There had been a trend toward earlier retirement for many years before social security, reflecting growth in real incomes and the ability to afford earlier retirement. In 1900, for example, about 60 percent of men over 65 were in the labor force, and the decline to 47.8 percent in 1947 cannot be attributed in any significant degree to social security. The trend toward earlier retirement has, however, accelerated since 1947, suggesting that social security did play a role. In addition, a number of statistical studies have concluded that a significant part of the reduction in labor supply by the elderly since 1947 is directly attributable to social security.[5]

Of the two ways by which social security encourages earlier retirement, it is not clear which is more important. Earlier studies tended to emphasize the earnings test, but a paper by Anthony Pellechio suggested that the income effect—the increase in the lifetime income received by people in the start-up phase—may be more important.[6] If this hypothesis is correct, we should see the trend toward earlier retirement cease and perhaps reverse itself as the temporary windfall gains of the start-up phase become increasingly less important over the next decade or two. Most experts on social security, however, continue to believe that the earnings test has significantly affected the labor supply of the elderly.

The earnings test, which restricts benefits to those who partially or completely withdraw from the labor force, has been one of the most unpopular features of the social security system. Today its rationale is explicitly redistributive.[7] With a given amount of revenue available for social security payments, a reduction in benefits for higher-income wage earners makes it possible to settle larger benefits on those without earnings—many of whom are poor. If the earnings test were eliminated, about $6 billion in additional benefits would have to be paid to those over 65 still working. Such a change would necessitate an equivalent reduction of $6 billion for those not working or for those working and earning under $7,200.

Social Security and Saving

In the absence of social security, people have strong incentives to save part of their incomes during their working lives to provide financial support for themselves during retirement. Social security, by promising pensions to retired workers, alleviates the need to save privately and may therefore lead to a reduction in saving. Consider a person who would normally set aside 10 percent of his or her income for retirement purposes. If the social se-

---

[5] See Colin Campbell and Rosemary Campbell, "Conflicting Views on the Effect of Old-Age and Survivor Insurance on Retirement," *Economic Inquiry,* 14(3):369 (Sept. 1974); Michael Boskin, "Social Security and Retirement Decision," *Economic Inquiry,* 17 (Jan. 1977); Michael Boskin and Michael Hurd, "The Effect of Social Security on Early Retirement," *Journal of Public Economics* (Dec. 1978); and Louis Esposito and Michael Packard, "Social Security and the Labor Supply of Aged Men: Evidence from the U.S. Time Series," Working Paper No. 21, Social Security Administration, Dec. 1980.

[6] Anthony Pellechio, "Social Security and the Decision to Retire," unpublished paper, 1981.

[7] When originally enacted in the depression of the 1930s, the rationale for the earnings test was to encourage older workers to leave their jobs and make room for younger workers. This rationale commits the "lump of labor" fallacy that holds there are a fixed number of jobs, so to have more jobs for younger workers requires older workers to quit their jobs.

curity tax rate is 10 percent, and if he or she believes the pension promised by the system is comparable to what his or her private savings would produce, then that person will stop saving altogether. Social security pensions would simply replace privately provided support for retirement.

Figure 7–1 shows the impact of social security on private saving in a more rigorous fashion. Assume that Caroline has a total income of OM over her working life. If she consumed her entire income, her consumption before retirement would be OM, and she would have no resources available to finance her consumption during her retirement. By consuming less than her total income before retirement, that is, by saving, Caroline can accumulate resources for consumption after retirement. The budget line MN shows the combinations of before- and after-retirement consumption attainable; its slope reflects the interest return received on saving. With preferences shown by indifference curve U_1, Caroline would choose OC_1 consumption before retirement and OC_2 consumption after retirement. By saving MC_1 of her before-retirement income, Caroline can finance consumption of OC_2 during retirement.

Now consider how social security will affect this individual. The social security tax of MM' will produce an after-tax budget line of $M'N'$. In return for paying the tax, Caroline is also promised a pension: We will assume the government pension is OC_G, or the same after-retirement consumption that Caroline would receive if she had saved MM' privately. As a result, her after-tax-and-pension budget line is $M'SN$. Caroline remains in equilibrium at point E but reduces private saving to $M'C_1$. In other words, her saving has

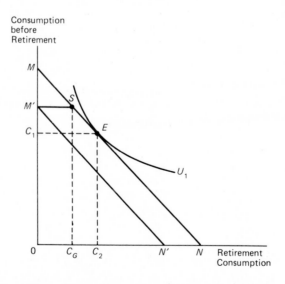

FIGURE 7–1 *Effect of social security on saving: individual taxpayer.*

fallen by the amount of the social security tax. (Note that it is not the tax alone that reduces her saving, but the tax combined with the promise of a future pension from the government.)

It might be thought that total saving is unchanged. After all, isn't the government now saving MM' for this individual? The answer to this question is no. Recall that social security is financed on a pay-as-you-go basis, and so current taxes are not invested but instead finance current benefits. Thus, the reduction in Caroline's saving is not offset by any increase in saving by government, and the result is a net reduction in total saving. We will consider the consequences of a reduction in saving in the next section, but it should be added now that Figure 7–1 is an incomplete analysis because it fails to show all of the effects of a net reduction in saving. All it illustrates is the incentive a person has to curtail his or her own saving when the government promises to provide retirement benefits.

Possible offsets to reduced saving

There are some other factors, however, that suggest social security may not cause saving to fall by as much as the preceding analysis indicates. One of these is the effect of social security on retirement; by inducing the elderly to retire earlier, the system produces a separate force tending to increase saving. An extreme example will illustrate this clearly. Suppose social security forced you to retire at age 40 on a very meager pension—because it would have to be paid for perhaps 35 years. In this case, you would have only about 20 years to accumulate sufficient assets to provide for a lengthy period of retirement. Consequently, you would increase your saving dramatically during your working years, much more so than if you did not plan to retire until age 65. Although this is an extreme example, it clarifies how lengthening the period of retirement (fewer working years to provide for longer retirement) tends to increase saving.

As we saw in the previous section, social security has had the effect of encouraging earlier retirement for some of the elderly. The size of this offsetting effect on saving, however, is almost certain to be quite small. Recall that labor force participation among men over 65 fell from 47.8 percent in 1947 to 17.4 percent in 1983. If half of this decline is a result of social security, then the system has led to earlier retirement for 15 percent of the elderly. It is only for this 15 percent that the offsetting effect on saving previously described is relevant. Even for this group, there is no reason to suspect that the positive effect on saving of induced early retirement will offset the negative effect associated with the provision of retirement benefits. Moreover, if the earlier retirement is the result of the temporary windfall gains of the start-up phase, this effect will become increasingly unimportant in future years. Therefore, the positive stimulus to saving due to induced earlier retirement will clearly be minor in comparison with the negative effect, so the net result is now, or soon will be, a substantial fall in saving.

A second factor that mitigates the depressing effect of social security on saving is the fact that in its absence some people would save less than the social security tax. If a person normally saved 5 percent of income for retirement, and the tax is 10 percent, then saving will not fall by the amount of the tax. Saving will fall to zero, but that reduction is equal to half the tax liability. For people who would save very little in the first place, saving would fall by less than tax liabilities. This is likely to be true for those with low incomes (and perhaps for those who optimistically expect to be supported by relatives when retired). Many people, however, would probably save more than the social security tax in its absence. Supportive evidence lies in the fact that large numbers of people continue to save even after paying social security taxes.

A third factor suggesting that saving will not fall so sharply is the possibility that voluntary transfers of funds between the young and the old may change in response to social security. Suppose, for example, that the social security benefits to the elderly are not used for consumption but instead are set aside and left as bequests to their descendants, who in turn leave it to their descendants, and so on. In that event, social security would reduce saving by the young but increase saving by the elderly, possibly producing no net change in total saving.[8] If it is correct, this analysis implies that the retirees in the start-up phase do not really benefit: The elderly just increase bequests to offset what they perceive as harm done to their descendants by social security taxes. In this view, social security could be eliminated overnight without harming the elderly. Judging from the reactions of the elderly to proposals to cut their social security benefits even slightly, this is not the case. The importance of this possibility therefore seems dubious.

Evidence of the effect of social security on saving

On balance the analysis seems to suggest that social security will substantially reduce saving, but what does the evidence indicate? If you have followed the analysis closely, you may be surprised to learn that saving as a percentage of national income has shown only a slight decline since World War II. This, however, does not mean that social security has not strongly depressed saving. The relevant question is what the saving rate would have been without social security. If the saving rate would have increased in the postwar period without social security, then social security has significantly depressed saving by keeping the rate from rising. This is what some economists believe has happened.

[8] Robert Barro, "Are Government Bonds Net Worth?," *Journal of Political Economy,* 82:1095 (Nov./Dec. 1974).

There are several reasons why the saving rate would have been expected to rise in the postwar period. Not only was the retirement age falling, but also life expectancy was rising. There were also fewer working years in which to save for retirement because people were staying in school until a later age. With a trend toward longer retirement and fewer working years, saving for retirement would automatically have risen. In addition, rising real incomes over the period should have reinforced this tendency. Therefore, the small reduction in the rate of saving since 1945 may mean that social security has strongly reduced saving in a situation in which otherwise there would have been a rising trend.

A number of sophisticated econometric studies in recent years have attempted to measure the effect of social security on saving. Martin Feldstein, in his seminal work in 1974, estimated that personal saving was 50 percent lower in 1971 than it would have been without social security.[9] In another study, Feldstein presented evidence that countries with larger social security systems tended to have lower private saving rates, other things being equal.[10] Most other studies, however, have concluded that the magnitude of the effect is smaller than Feldstein's estimates, and some have even concluded that social security has had no effect on saving.[11] At the present time, there is no consensus that social security has had a large negative effect on saving; there is also no consensus that it has not. The issue remains controversial. Given the apparent strength of the theoretical argument, however, it is difficult to believe that saving has not been negatively affected by social security to a significant degree.

Effects of Reduced Saving

It may not be clear why we have devoted so much attention to the way social security affects saving. If, however, social security does reduce saving, the consequences are of tremendous importance for an evaluation of the system.

[9] Martin Feldstein, "Social Security, Induced Retirement and Aggregate Capital Accumulation," *Journal of Political Economy,* 92(5):905 (Sept./Oct. 1974).

[10] Martin Feldstein, "Social Security and Private Savings: International Evidence in an Extended Life Cycle Model," in M. Feldstein and R. Inman, eds., *The Economics of Public Services,* an International Economic Association Conference Volume (New York: Halsted Press, 1977).

[11] See Alicia Munnell, "The Impact of Social Security on Personal Savings," *National Tax Journal,* 27(4):553 (Dec. 1974); Robert Barro, *The Impact of Social Security on Private Saving* (Washington, D.C.: American Enterprise Institute, 1977); Michael Darby, *The Effects of Social Security on Income and the Capital Stock* (Washington, D.C.: American Enterprise Institute, 1979); Louis Esposito, "The Effect of Social Security on Saving: Review of Studies Using U.S. Time-Series Date," *Social Security Bulletin* (May 1978); Selig Lesnoy and Dean Leimer, "Social Security and Private Saving: New Time Series Evidence," *Journal of Political Economy,* 90(3):606 (June 1982); and Martin Feldstein, "Social Security and Private Saving: A Reply," *Journal of Political Economy* 90(3):630 (June 1982).

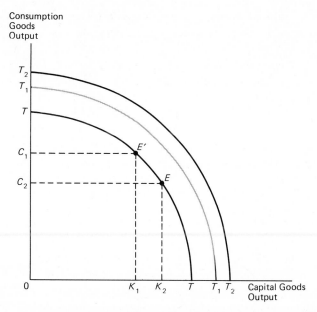

FIGURE 7–2 *Effects of reduced saving.*

The act of saving, that is, consuming less than one's income, represents a reduction in the demand for consumer goods. When the funds that would have financed current consumption are put in a bank or used to purchase bonds or stocks, they eventually provide financing for borrowers to purchase capital goods such as factories, machines, computers, and so on. Savings ultimately tend to be channeled into productive investment in real capital goods. As a result, saving tends to increase society's stock of productive capital, and this, in turn, increases the future productive capacity of the economy. The rate of saving is consequently one important determinant of the growth in real income over time.

Figure 7–2 illustrates the effect of saving on the growth rate of the economy. In year 1 the production frontier relating capital goods and consumer goods outputs is shown as TT. Suppose that the economy operates at point E, with OK_2 production of capital goods and OC_2 production of consumer goods. Because of this level of production of capital goods in year 1, the society will have a larger stock of productive capital the following year.[12] With a larger stock of capital, the productive capacity of the economy is greater, and production can take place on the new production frontier T_2T_2

---

[12] Actually, some currently produced capital goods will simply replace that part of the capital stock that wears out during the year and so will not lead to a higher capital stock in the following year. Gross investment must exceed depreciation if the capital stock is to grow over time.

in year 2. Consuming less in year 1 enables society to have higher real incomes and consumption in later years by augmenting the stock of productive capital. The real before-tax rate of return on capital investment measures the quantitative tradeoff involved. If that rate is 10 percent, saving $1 today means that we could consume $1.10 a year later (or $0.10 every subsequent year) because real output is augmented to that degree.

Now consider the effect of social security. If social security is introduced in year 1, it will tend to reduce the aggregate saving in the economy. The economy operates at E' rather than E with a higher consumption of consumer goods and a smaller output of capital goods. (Taxpayers do not generally increase their consumption, of course; they reduce saving in response to the system. However, the retirement benefits financed by the taxes raise the consumption of retired persons, so total consumption rises.) A smaller output of capital goods in year 1 means the society has a smaller capital stock in year 2. Thus, the productive capacity of the economy is lower in year 2 than it would have been, and the production frontier is T_1T_1 rather than T_2T_2. Social security, by reducing the rate of capital accumulation, results in a slower rate of growth in the output of the economy. Increased current consumption tends to have a cost in the form of reduced real incomes in the future.

The effect of reduced saving is cumulative over a period of years, and the result of any one year's reduction will be quite small. The reason is that any single year's saving represents only a small increment to the accumulated capital stock of the economy. For example, the capital stock of the United States in 1985 may be valued at roughly $7,000 billion ($7 trillion); yet net saving in a single year may be only $300 billion. If social security reduced saving from $300 billion to $250 billion, the capital stock a year later would be $7,250 billion instead of $7,300 billion—a reduction of less than 1 percent. However, social security reduces saving each year, and the cumulative effect could become very large after a number of years. Indeed, Feldstein's estimates, although admittedly rough, indicate that the capital stock in 1985 would have been about $10,000 billion if social security had never been introduced. As a result, Feldstein estimated that real GNP is today 10 to 20 percent below where it would have been if social security had not reduced the nation's rate of saving.

We have been considering the effect of reduced saving on aggregate output; now let's see how it affects individuals under the social security system. Consider Table 7–4a. This table illustrates consumption and saving behavior in the absence of social security. Thus, individuals save 10 percent of their incomes during their working years and consume the accumulated sums when they retire. (It is assumed that the annual interest return on private saving is 100 percent, equal to the rate of growth of the economy.) Thus, individual C saves $25 and $50 in years 1 and 2 (and consumes $225 and $450 in these years) and consumes the accumulated sum of $200 in year 3.

In this way, Table 7–4a shows what the lifetime consumption patterns of people would be without social security.

The introduction of social security reduces the rate of growth in incomes. Suppose the system begins in year 2, with individuals C and D paying taxes of $50 each to finance a retirement benefit of $100 for individual B. Social security does not reduce incomes in year 2, but the following year the capital stock is lower than it would have been, and the incomes of D and E are $950 rather than $1,000, a reduction of 5 percent. A tax of 10 percent then finances a transfer of $190 to individual C. The reduced saving in year 3 results in the capital stock in year 4 falling farther behind what it would have been, and total incomes are $1,800 rather than $2,000, a reduction of 10 percent. In this way, social security gradually causes incomes to fall below the level they would have attained if saving had not fallen.

Now consider how individual D fares under social security. D's consumption in years 2, 3, and 4 is $450, $855, and $360. Compare this with what D's consumption would have been without social security (from Table 7–4a)—$450, $900, and $400—D's lifetime consumption is lower under social security. For individual E, consumption is $855, $1,620, and $700 with social security, but $900, $1,800, and $800 without. Because social security causes real national income to grow less slowly, the lifetime incomes of people are lower under this system. If Feldstein is correct, young people beginning to

Table 7–4   *Distributional Effects of Reduced Saving*

a. Without Social Security

Year	1	2	3	4	5
Young	C250	D500	E1000	F2000	G4000
	(−25)	(−50)	(−100)	(−200)	(−400)
Middle-aged	B250	C500	D1000	E2000	F4000
	(−25)	(−50)	(−100)	(−200)	(−400)
Retired	A(+50)	B(+100)	C(+200)	D(+400)	E(+800)

b. With Social Security

Year Tax Rate	2 10%	3 10%	4 10%	5 10%
Young	D500	E950	F1800	G3500
	(−50)	(−95)	(−180)	(−350)
Middle-aged	C500	D950	E1800	F3500
	(−50)	(−95)	(−180)	(−350)
Retired	B(+100)	C(+190)	D(+360)	E(+700)

work now will have, roughly speaking, 10 to 20 percent less income every year of their lives.[13]

Note, however, that many people retiring during the start-up phase will still benefit from social security even if it reduces saving and the rate of growth in real income. As shown in Table 7–4b, for example, individuals B and C clearly gain. They receive retirement benefits without suffering a reduction in income before retirement. Because the effect of reduced saving on output and on real incomes is small at first and gradually grows, the negative impact on preretirement income will be more than offset by the windfall gains of early retirees. Workers who retire later are not so fortunate and will have lower lifetime consumption. When the negative effects will begin to prevail is not clear, since it depends on the unknown magnitude of the saving effect and its impact on real incomes. If the saving effect is as large as Feldstein believes it to be, quite possibly all those who have benefitted from the system are already retired or deceased, and everyone working now and in the future will have lower lifetime standards of living.

Equity-Related Issues

Individual equity versus social adequacy

The terms *individual equity* and *social adequacy* recur frequently in official discussions of social security. Individual equity refers to the degree to which an individual's benefits are related to taxes paid. If the retirement benefits were strictly proportional to taxes paid so that a person who had paid twice the taxes of someone else would receive twice the benefits, then the system would embody individual equity. Social adequacy, on the other hand, refers to the welfare objective of ensuring adequate benefits, regardless of the taxes paid.

These two objectives are competing goals that cannot be fully realized simultaneously. If benefits were strictly related to taxes paid, low-income families who paid low taxes would receive very small benefits—a violation of social adequacy. On the other hand, if everyone received a sizable benefit, regardless of the taxes paid, then the goal of individual equity would be sacrificed.

The present structure of the social security system represents a compromise between these two conflicting objectives. Retirement benefits are related to previous earnings (and hence to taxes paid), but the relationship is not proportional. To illustrate the relationship, let's consider how benefits are calculated for a single worker retiring at age 65 in 1986. The first step

---

[13]A reduction in saving will tend to increase the interest rate and reduce wage rates (because there is less capital per worker). Thus, there may also be some redistribution of the smaller total output from workers to investors.

in calculating the benefits is determining the average monthly taxable earnings over a period of years (30 years in 1986, but scheduled to reach 35 years for those retiring in 1991 and later). To figure the average monthly earnings, the worker's earnings in each year are indexed by the average annual covered wages in the economy in that year. For example, suppose the worker's earnings at age 40 (in 1961) were $5,000 but that the average covered wages in the economy had tripled (owing to increases in real wages and inflation) by 1986. When the worker's benefits are calculated at age 65, his or her earnings at age 40 are counted as $15,000, triple the nominal wages actually earned at age 40. This "wage indexing" of earnings effectively counts wages at younger ages relative to economywide wages and thereby protects workers from inflation eroding their average earnings and hence benefits.

Once the worker's average (indexed) monthly earnings have been determined, the initial monthly retirement benefit is calculated using the benefit formula. In 1986, this formula figures the monthly benefit as 90 percent of the first $297 in average monthly earnings, plus 32 percent of any monthly earnings between $297 and $1,790, plus 15 percent of any monthly earnings in excess of $1,790. For example, with average monthly earnings of $2,000, the monthly benefit would be 0.9 ($297) + 0.32 ($1,790 − $297 + 0.15 ($2,000 − $1,790), or $777. (The formula determines the first-year retirement benefits. Thereafter, the benefit is automatically increased by the rate of increase in the consumer price index, thereby preserving the real value of benefits in later years.) The "bend points" in the formula, at $297 and $1,790, are indexed to the average covered earnings and so will increase automatically as average wages in the economy rise. The marginal replacement rates, the 0.9, 0.32, and 0.15 ratios, however, are not scheduled to change in the future.

Figure 7–3 illustrates the benefit formula with the schedule O*ABC,* which identifies the monthly benefit at each level of average indexed monthly earnings. The slope of O*ABC* along the O*A* segment is 0.9, along the *AB* segment, 0.32, and along the *BC* segment, 0.15. Note that this benefit formula makes benefits a larger proportion of previous earnings for low-wage workers than for high-wage workers. For example, workers with average monthly earnings of $297 receive benefits that are 90 percent of their average monthly earnings, whereas workers with average monthly earnings of $3,500 (the maximum ultimately possible, because this is the ceiling amount of taxable earnings, or $42,000 a year in 1986[14]) receive benefits of less than a third of their average monthly earnings.

[14]No one retiring in 1986 could have average indexed monthly earnings as high as $3,500, however. This is because the ceiling on taxable earnings went up faster than average covered earnings did before the ceiling itself was indexed in 1977, and many of the years when the ceiling was lower had to be counted by those retiring in 1986. The approximate maximum average indexed monthly earnings for anyone retiring in 1986 was $2,000. This will increase gradually over time until it reaches $3,500, if the indexed ceiling is not raised further.

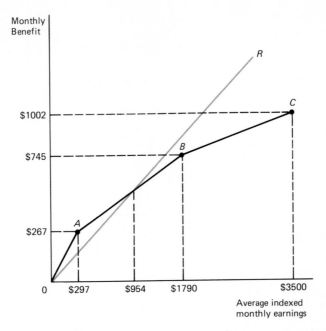

FIGURE 7–3 *The social security benefit formula for single workers, 1986.*

   In effect, the benefit formula redistributes income among the retired population from individuals who had high earnings to people who had low earnings. This is an attempt to achieve social adequacy and represents an intragenerational redistribution of income. This redistribution is why low-wage workers receive a higher rate of return on their taxes paid than do high-wage workers, as shown previously in Table 7–3. Individual equity, on the other hand, would call for workers to receive benefits proportionate to their average monthly earnings. If this were done, the benefit formula would be the straight line O*R* in Figure 7–3, with a slope of approximately 0.5. With the O*R* schedule, all workers retiring in a given year would receive the same rate of return on their taxes paid, but with the O*ABC* schedule, workers with average monthly earnings below approximately $954 receive a higher-than-average rate of return, whereas workers with higher earnings receive a lower-than-average rate of return.

   How to draw a balance between individual equity and social adequacy is unclear. One recent change, however, has weakened the case for trying to achieve social adequacy through the social security system. In 1974 the federal government began a program called Supplemental Security Income, or SSI. This is a welfare program that provides cash assistance to the elderly (as well as the blind and disabled) who have little income or assets. In effect, SSI guarantees a minimum income, with the level of support approximately equal to the poverty line for a married couple. SSI therefore serves the welfare function of providing income support for the elderly poor. With this program in place, there is less reason for social security to be concerned with social adequacy. Indeed, SSI has weakened the ability of social security to help the aged poor. Under SSI, if an elderly poor person receives a dollar more from social security, his or her assistance payment under SSI falls by a dollar. Raising social security benefits for those also covered by SSI therefore does not help them at all.

Single- and two-earner families

Under the present law, retirement benefits for married couples are calculated in one of two ways. First, the husband and the wife each can receive the benefits they are separately entitled to using the benefit formula for single workers we discussed earlier. Second, the couple can choose the "dependent spouse" option, in which the couple's benefits are equal to 150 percent of the retirement benefit due one of them according to the single-worker benefit formula. Note that this second option means that a couple with only one working spouse can receive 150 percent of the benefits of a single person with the same earnings. In other words, a working wife can receive benefits based on her own earnings or benefits equal to 50 percent of her husband's retirement benefits, or vice versa, with the choice usually determined by which alternative leads to greater combined retirement benefits for the couple.

This treatment often results in a working wife's finding that the family's total retirement benefits are no higher than had she never worked and paid taxes at all. For a wife with low earnings relative to her husband's, the total retirement benefits will be greater if she takes a benefit equal to 50 percent of her husband's benefit rather than the benefit she is entitled to based on her own earning record. Note that she would receive this 50 percent benefit even if she had not worked, and so the social security taxes she paid did not increase the family's total retirement benefits. Many working wives view this as unfairly discriminating in favor of nonworking wives. (We are referring to work in the paid labor force; obviously, wives not in the labor force provide valuable services at home.)

Another consequence of this treatment is that retirement benefits can differ between two-person families with the *same* total earnings. In 1986 a family retiring in which only one spouse worked, with average indexed monthly earnings of $1,000, could receive monthly retirement benefits of $738–$492 based on the working spouse's earnings and 50 percent of that sum in the form of a dependent-spouse benefit. However, a family with the same combined average indexed monthly earnings, but with 75 percent received by the wife and 25 percent received by the husband, would have smaller monthly retirement benefits, regardless of how they calculated them. If the benefits were figured separately, they would receive $637 ($412 + $225); if the dependent spouse option were used, the benefits would be $618 ($412 plus 50 percent of $412). So two couples with the same combined earnings would receive different retirement benefits. Outcomes like this are fairly common under the social security system. Again, they reflect a compromise between social adequacy and individual equity. Two-person families need more income than one-person families do, and so the goal of social adequacy suggests that they be given larger retirement benefits unrelated to their taxes paid. This, however, immediately produces situations like those just discussed that are widely viewed as violating standards of individual equity.

These provisions in social security are another instance of intragenerational redistribution. Single-earner families benefit at the expense of two-earner families and single individuals. When social security began, the favored single-earner families were quite common. In 1940 in only 3 of 20 households did both the husband and the wife work; in 1985, however, in over one half of households both the husband and wife worked. The increased prevalence of two-earner families has strengthened the support for reform to end this inequitable (in the sense of individual equity) treatment. Any move to increase benefits to two-earner families would, however, mean a relative decrease in benefits for single-earner families, thereby sacrificing social adequacy.

The general level of retirement benefits

Are social security benefits too high? This question is difficult because its answer depends on what the system's objective is thought to be. To those who prefer to provide privately for their own retirement, almost any level of social security benefits will seem too high. But to those who view social security as part of the welfare system and want social security by itself to provide adequate standards of living for all the elderly, almost any level of benefits will seem too low. Nonetheless, there are some points regarding the general level of benefits that should be made, especially since there are serious questions about our ability to continue financing benefits at their current levels (as we will discuss in the next section).

One measure of the adequacy of social security benefits is suggested by their replacement rates. The replacement rate is the ratio of the benefit amount payable to a worker in the first year of retirement to his or her earnings in the year before retirement. (Recall that benefits are indexed to the consumer price index in subsequent years.) Table 7–5 shows the replacement rates for selected recent years at different levels of earnings for single workers. Two points should be observed. First, in every year the replacement rate is greater for low-wage workers, reflecting the tilt in the benefit formula favoring low-wage workers. Second, the level of replace-

Table 7–5 *Replacement Rates Under Social Security (selected years)*

Year	Low-Earnings Individual	Average-Earnings Individual	Maximum-Earnings Individual
1954	51.9%	29.3%	28.3%
1960	51.8	32.8	29.8
1969	47.1	30.8	24.7
1975	59.7	40.7	28.8
1980	64.2	47.1	29.9

Source: Robert J. Myers, "Summary of the Provisions of the Old-Age, Survivors, and Disability Insurance System, the Hospital Insurance System, and the Supplementary Medical Insurance System," Social Security Administration, July 1981, Table 7.

ment rates rose sharply between 1969 and 1980. (They have not changed much since 1980.) Although there was little change from 1954 to 1969, between 1969 and 1980 the replacement rate rose by 36 percent for a low-wage worker, by 53 percent for an average-wage worker, and by 21 percent for a maximum-wage (at the ceiling on taxable earnings) worker.[15]

The recent rise in replacement rates was the result of deliberate congressional decisions to increase benefits, as well as a congressional error. The deliberate decisions were to raise benefits by 15 percent in 1970, 10 percent in 1971, and 20 percent in 1972. These increases were far in excess of the 5 percent inflation rate during these years so the real benefits that retirees received rose. The error resulted from the congressional attempt in 1972 to index benefits to inflation; at that time benefits were not automatically indexed as they are now. However, the indexing provision Congress enacted in 1972 double-counted inflation and increased benefits faster than the price level. This mistake was corrected in 1977 (when the current benefit formula was enacted), but during the intervening years, the real benefit levels increased and were then locked in at the higher levels they attained in 1977.

In judging the adequacy of these benefit levels, it should be kept in mind that the elderly's standards of living are generally much higher than suggested by these replacement rates alone. There are several reasons for this. First, the figures in Table 7–5 do not include Medicare benefits (enacted in 1965), which are now one third as large as the cash benefits, on the average. Second, the replacement rates for married couples are higher than those for single workers; they would be 50 percent higher, for example, if one

[15]Don't make the error of equating the replacement rate with the extent to which a person benefits from the system. The replacement rate relates benefits to earnings, not to taxes paid. People retiring in 1954 had paid taxes of only 2 and 3 percent for only 17 years. In fact retirees in 1981 who had worked since 1937 had paid an average tax rate of only 6 percent, although workers paying for their benefits were then paying a rate of 13.4 percent. The windfall gains to retirees in the start-up phase are not indicated by the level of replacement rates.

spouse did not work. Third, social security benefits are nontaxable for most retired persons. Replacement rates relative to after-tax earnings would therefore be higher than those shown in the table. Fourth, almost three out of four elderly households own their own homes (half with no mortgage at all) and therefore have lower housing expenses than do younger households. Fifth, retired persons do not have work-related expenses, expenses that have been estimated to be between 6 and 13 percent of earnings for workers.

When these factors are taken into account, many retired households apparently have standards of living as high as they enjoyed before retirement. Even though elderly households have lower average incomes than younger households do, there are also fewer persons in each household. By the mid-1980s, in fact, the income per person for elderly households was higher than for younger households. And this comparison does not take into account several of the preceding factors. Although many of the elderly are still poor, the poverty rate among the elderly is now lower than among younger persons, and as a group the elderly are not poor. Social security is at least partly responsible for the recent improvement in the standard of living of the elderly.

These facts do not by themselves, however, help us much in determining whether social security benefits are too high. Making that determination involves evaluating the effects of changing the level of benefits in light of the desired objectives. Even if we were to decide that benefits are too high, we must understand that reducing benefits quickly would be difficult, if not impossible. Many retired persons have withdrawn from the labor force expecting to continue receiving their benefits at their current levels, as promised under the current law. Thus, reducing the benefits for those already retired, at least if the reductions were substantial, could impose substantial hardships and would certainly be viewed by many as unfair. If social security benefits are to be reduced, then, they should be lowered gradually by decreasing benefits for new retirees in some future year so that workers can effectively plan now for their retirements.

Apart from questions of the adequacy of retirement benefits, benefits at their current levels heighten concerns about how the system affects incentives to save. Are low- and average-income households likely to save much to supplement social security benefits that already provide for a standard of living that is, for many, comparable to their preretirement years?

Demographic Trends and the Future

Among younger Americans, there is widespread skepticism concerning the future of the social security system. According to a *Washington Post*–ABC News poll in 1982, 56 percent of those aged 31 to 44 believed that the system would not even exist when they retired, and among those aged 18 to 30, 74 percent believed that they would never get any retirement benefits from social security.[16] Most experts believe such pessimism is unwarranted, but there is still reason to be concerned about the system's long-term prospects.

An important factor affecting the viability of a pay-as-you-go system of social security is the population's age distribution. The smaller the number of people working, relative to the number of people who have retired, the higher the tax burden will be per worker in order to finance a given level of retirement benefits. The ratio of workers to retirees is largely determined by two demographic factors, the longevity of elderly persons and the birthrate. Recent trends in these factors suggest that the number of workers per retiree will fall sharply in the first half of the twenty-first century, and this decline is likely to cause serious financing problems for the system.

The longevity of retirees has an obvious effect on social security: The longer retirees live, the higher the tax rate that will be needed to finance a given level of annual benefits. In 1940, the remaining life expectancy at age 65 was 11.9 years for males and 13.4 years for females. The corresponding figures in 1982 were 14.3 years for males and 18.7 years for females, improvements of 20 and 40 percent, respectively. If longevity continues to improve, as expected, the number of elderly persons will rise compared with the number of working-age persons, requiring higher tax rates to finance the system.

The pattern of birthrates over time is of perhaps even greater importance to the ratio of workers to retirees. The total fertility rate (the average number of babies born to each woman during her lifetime) is a convenient measure of the birthrate. Following a downward trend begun a century and a half ago, the fertility rate stood at 2.42 in 1945; then it started to rise as a result of the postwar "baby boom," reaching a peak of 3.77 in 1957. Since 1957 the fertility rate has declined more or less steadily, to 1.86 in 1982. (A fertility rate of 2.1 is required for zero population growth, ignoring immigration.) We thus have had a baby boom followed by a "baby bust," a bad combination from the perspective of social security financing. When the baby boom generation retires, the number of retirees will grow rapidly, and they will have to be supported by taxes on the relatively small baby-bust generation.

Prospects for the social security system in the next century depend heavily on demographic developments in the future as well as the economic performance of the economy. Obviously, future events cannot be predicted with great accuracy. It is possible, however, to make forecasts based on assumptions regarding demographic and economic factors, and that is what

[16]Barry Sussman, "Figuring Out Young Voters' Landmark Decision to Back Reagan," *Washington Post National Weekly,* Nov. 19, 1984, p. 37.

the board of trustees of OASDI does each year. Their 1984 *Annual Report* contains projections based on three sets of alternative assumptions about demographic changes and economic growth. Alternative I is the "optimistic" one (from the standpoint of social security financing) and assumes a prompt reversal in the downward trend in the fertility rate, with the fertility rate rising to 2.30 by the year 2010 and then stabilizing. Strong economic growth is also assumed in this alternative. Alternative II-B is based on intermediate economic and demographic assumptions. It also assumes an upturn in the fertility rate, but only to 2.0, and moderate economic growth. Alternative III is the pessimistic forecast, assuming that the fertility rate will continue to decline, to 1.60, and that economic growth will be weak.[17]

Although the consequences for the social security system depend on both demographic and economic assumptions, the demographic factors are the more important, because they largely determine the number of workers per retiree in each year. To illustrate what the various alternatives imply, let us begin with the current ratio of workers to retirees: there are now 3.3 workers paying social security taxes to finance benefits for each retiree. Under Alternative I, this ratio will fall to 2.5 in the year 2030, but it will fall to 2.1 and 1.6 under Alternatives II-B and III, respectively. Thus, the number of workers supporting each retiree is predicted to fall under all three alternatives, but with larger declines for the more pessimistic demographic assumptions. These changes thus have important implications for the future financing of social security.

Table 7–6 gives the projected payroll tax rates required to finance future benefits as determined under present law for each of the three alternatives. The figures give the tax rates that would be required in each year to finance the benefits in that year, with the Medicare (hospital insurance) tax rate shown separately (in parentheses) from the OASDI tax rate. Thus, the combined payroll tax rate is the sum of the two figures; for example, it would be 14.5 percent in 1990 under Alternative II-B.

Table 7–6 shows clearly why there continues to be concern over the future of social security. From its 1986 level of 14.3 percent, the combined payroll tax rate must increase significantly in order to finance benefits in the next century. Note that the required rates rise only gradually until about 2020, which is approximately the time when the baby boom generation will begin to retire. Under the intermediate set of assumptions, Alternative II-B, the required tax rate reaches 23.7 percent in 2030, 66 percent above its 1986 level. Under the pessimistic Alternative III assumptions, the required tax rate is projected to exceed 40 percent in 2060.

---

[17] For a more detailed discussion of the economic and demographic assumptions underlying these alternatives, see the *1984 Annual Report of the Board of Trustees of the Federal Old Age and Survivors Insurance Trust Funds* (Washington, D.C.: U.S. Government Printing Office, 1984), pp. 32–36.

Table 7–6   *Projected Tax Rates Required to Finance Future OASDI (HI) Benefits, Various Demographic and Economic Assumptions (in percent)*

Year	Alternative I	Alternative II-B	Alternative III	Scheduled Tax Rates Under Current Law
1985	11.2 (2.8)	11.3 (2.8)	11.5 (2.8)	11.4 (2.7)
1990	10.0 (3.2)	11.0 (3.5)	11.6 (3.7)	12.4 (2.9)
2000	8.6 (4.0)	10.1 (4.7)	11.4 (5.3)	12.4 (2.9)
2010	8.4 (4.6)	10.4 (5.7)	12.4 (6.8)	12.4 (2.9)
2020	10.2 (5.5)	12.9 (7.0)	16.0 (8.7)	12.4 (2.9)
2030	11.3 (6.6)	15.0 (8.7)	20.0 (11.6)	12.4 (2.9)
2040	10.7 (6.6)	15.2 (9.4)	22.2 (13.7)	12.4 (2.9)
2050	10.3 (6.4)	15.3 (9.5)	24.5 (15.2)	12.4 (2.9)
2060	10.1 (6.3)	15.5 (9.6)	26.1 (16.2)	12.4 (2.9)

Note: The 1984 *Annual Report* gives projected HI tax rates only for Alternative II-B. The estimates for Alternatives I and III are based on the assumption that the HI rate is the same percentage of the OASDI rate as it is for II-B.

Source: *1984 Annual Report of the Board of Trustees of the Federal Old-Age and Survivors Insurance and Disability Insurance Trust Funds* (Washington, D.C.: U.S. Government Printing Office, 1984), Tables 30 and F3.

How serious is the future financing problem?

Following several years of active public debate over the future of social security, Congress enacted the Social Security Act Amendments of 1983. These changes in the law were intended to put the system on a sound basis well into the next century. Many changes were made in the law, but two were of great importance for the future of social security: the decision to raise the retirement age to 67 beginning in 2000, and the decision to tax part of social security benefits, beginning in 1984.

Under the 1983 amendments, the age at which full retirement benefits are available will gradually rise from 65 to 66 between 2000 and 2009 and then to 67 between 2017 and 2027. This will reduce the number of retirees receiving benefits and therefore reduce the required tax rates necessary to finance benefits. In effect, an increase in the retirement age is much the same as a reduction in benefits, because retirees would receive the same annual benefits but for fewer years. However, it may be an appropriate way to reduce benefits, given our now greater longevity. Even with a retirement age of 67, people retiring in the next century could expect to receive social security benefits for a longer period of time than persons retiring at age 65 now.

Before the 1983 amendments, social security benefits were not taxed under the federal individual income tax. Under the 1983 law, up to one half of social security benefits are taxable for individuals with incomes above $25,000 and for couples with incomes above $32,000. The revenues raised from the taxation of social security benefits are channeled back directly into the social security system, so the net effect is exactly the same as a cut in benefit levels for retired households that have other large sources of retirement income. Only 8 percent of retired households had incomes high enough to be affected by this law in 1984, but that fraction will increase over time because the threshold income levels of $25,000 and $32,000 are not indexed to inflation.

These changes, along with several others, have improved the long-term financial balance in the social security system. This may appear surprising, because the estimates in Table 7–6 already incorporate the effects of the 1983 changes in the law. However, according to the board of trustees, the system will be in balance over the next 75 years (up to 2060) under Alternative II-B assumptions. What is supposed to happen can be seen by comparing the projected tax rates necessary in each year (at least for OASDI alone) under II-B with the actual tax rates that are already scheduled for each year, as shown in the last column of Table 7–6. According to these estimates, the actual tax rate will exceed the tax rate necessary to balance the system up to about 2020, and the excess tax revenues will be used to build up the trust fund. Then after 2020 the system is projected to run an annual deficit, and the accumulated trust fund will be used to make up the shortfall, until the trust fund is depleted around 2060. Over the period as a whole, taxes are projected to be adequate to finance OASDI with no increase in tax rates beyond those already scheduled.

There are, however, still reasons for concern about the future of social security. First, the preceding scenario holds only for OASDI benefits and does not include Medicare. As Table 7–6 indicates, the required tax rates projected for Medicare exceed the scheduled tax rates, and the 1983 amendments did nothing about the Medicare portion of social security. Overall, payroll tax rates will still have to be increased substantially unless Medicare benefits are cut sharply. Second, the projected long-term financial balance assumes that the government will actually implement the changes enacted in the 1983 amendments. Under the projections (for II-B) the social security system is forecast to accumulate an enormous reserve in the trust fund, reaching about 6 years' worth of benefits by 2015. Can we realistically expect the government to cut benefits (by increasing the retirement age) at exactly the time that the social security system is running large annual surpluses and has accumulated a massive trust fund? Many observers believe it more likely that the government will spend the funds rather than accumulate a reserve to help pay benefits in later years.

Third, the intermediate II-B assumptions may prove too optimistic. It is worth noting that in the 1970s, the actual demographic and economic events were consistently worse than ever the most pessimistic assumptions (Alternative III assumptions) used in preceding years by the board of trustees. Finally, it should be noted that, even if things turn out as projected under the II-B assumptions, at the end of the period, in 2060, the system will be operating with a large annual deficit with no trust fund left to help finance it, and so the problem will have to be confronted then.

For all these reasons, it seems likely that there will be serious financing difficulties facing social security in the next century. Although the 1983 amendments have improved the outlook, they have probably not done enough. Considering OASDI and Medicare together, it is probable that either workers will be subject to much higher tax rates or retired persons will receive substantially lower benefits, or some combination of the two. This tradeoff once again raises the question of whether Congress raised benefit levels during the 1970s to higher levels than can or should be sustained over the long run.

Social Security and Public Choice

Social security has always enjoyed broad public support. Even in recent years when concerns over the ability of the system to pay all of its future benefit obligations have grown, there has been little support for changing the system in any significant way. Social security seems to have great political appeal, and this presents us with a puzzle. We have seen that as a permanent institution for providing retirement benefits, social security offers an annual return of perhaps 2 percent, although the rate of return to private investment is much higher. What accounts for the political support of a retirement system that yields such a lower rate of return? The answer probably largely lies in the peculiar distributional effects of a pay-as-you-go system.

Consider how the introduction of a pay-as-you-go social security system affects the well-being of different age groups. Retired persons will benefit, since they will receive pensions without paying taxes. Persons near retirement will also secure large gains, since they pay taxes for only a few years. (Consider individuals B and C in Table 7–2.) In its start-up phase, social security will be a good bargain for middle-aged and older persons, and they would be expected to support it politically. Only very young workers and future generations (who do not vote) receive the low 2 percent rate of return. In general, starting the system or expanding its size will be more attractive the older a person is at the time the change occurs. If the tax rate is increased today, only the very young and subsequent generations will have to pay the higher rate over their entire lifetimes to get the larger pensions. In contrast, a person aged 55 will pay the higher tax rate for only 10 years before receiving the larger pension yielded by the higher tax rate. From his or her perspective, the larger retirement benefit may be well worth paying higher taxes for 10 years. This explains why older age groups support a pay-as-you-go system.

After the start-up phase, subsequent generations receive only the rate of economic growth as a rate of return under social security. As younger workers grow older, won't they reject the system? It is important to see why they are unlikely to do so. The low 2 percent return you may receive over your lifetime is an average rate of return. However, it is the marginal return from changing the size of the social security system that is the dominant consideration, and this increases as a worker becomes older. A person who is young today will be better off if the social security system is expanded when he or she is retired and worse off if it is contracted. Similarly, when a young person today reaches age 55, continuing the system for the remainder of his or her lifetime will then be more attractive than doing away with it—the retirement benefits relative to the remaining 10 years of taxes will be large. As people become older, they will increasingly favor continuing or expanding the system. At each point in time, the older portion of the population will favor pay-as-you-go social security, and so there is no reason to expect political support for the system to diminish over time.

For this reason, society may find itself locked into a pay-as-you-go social security system. Even if every young person today and all future generations would be better off providing for retirement privately, political support from the older members of the population in every future year may perpetuate the system.

Proposal for Reform: Privatize Social Security

In the early 1980s, social security experts emphasized that the system faced two different financing problems. One was a short-term problem reflected in the fact that current expenditures were exceeding current taxes and depleting the already small trust fund. This problem was the result of unusually low growth rates of real earnings (and hence lower tax revenues) in recent years and would require only modest adjustments to resolve. The 1983 amendments have apparently dealt with this problem. The other potentially more serious problem is a long-term one, traceable to the demographic factors we have discussed, and may necessitate more fundamental changes in the system. Since the long-term problem raises the more basic issues related to the nature and future direction of the system, we shall consider a proposal designed to cope with it.

Private provision for retirement

Whenever fundamental reforms of social security are seriously considered, the possibility of eliminating the system altogether and letting people provide for their retirement privately is certain to come up. Although the prospects for such a reform are remote, we should consider it carefully because it forces us to try to understand the rationale for the social security system.

The present social security system contains two potentially separate features: the requirement that people set aside a certain fraction of earnings each year for retirement and the requirement that these sums be channeled through a pay-as-you-go system. Arguing that people should be required to save for retirement is not enough to justify social security, since the government could still force people to save but allow them to choose the form of assets to hold. Both features must be defended to justify social security.

Why should people be required to save for their retirement? Two reasons are most frequently mentioned. The first is paternalistic: People may underestimate retirement needs when they are young, and by the time they are approaching retirement age, it is too late for them to remedy the situation. The second is based on the possibility that some people will not save and will go on welfare when they are older, placing an extra cost on workers who do save. In this view, people should be forced to provide for their own retirement needs so that they do not impose the burden of their support on others.

Both these arguments are logically sound, but their relevance depends on how many people would, in fact, fail to make provision for retirement if they were not forced to. Unfortunately, there is little evidence on this point one way or another. (The fact that many retired persons today have no means of support except social security does not mean that they would not have saved in its absence. The expectation of social security benefits may be why they did not save.) What if people do not save? Will they have to be supported by someone else at age 65? Usually there is the option of continuing to work. Only for those who reach age 65 without savings and who are at the same time unable to work would it be necessary to provide welfare. The number of people in this category may be quite small, in which case a welfare program for the elderly who are unable to work and who have no savings might be less costly than a social security system for everyone.

If, however, the argument for requiring people to save is accepted, the next step in defending social security is to justify its pay-as-you-go format. Here the critical question seems to be whether pay-as-you-go financing provides a better return than private saving. Over the long run, the scales tip decisively in favor of private saving. The 10 percent rate of return to private capital accumulation far exceeds the expected 2 percent rate of economic growth associated with social security. We must not forget, however, that people retiring in the start-up phase of social security receive much more than a 2 percent return. Early retirees—those retiring in the 1950s, 1960s, and 1970s—received windfall gains that exceeded what they could have earned by saving privately. Under pay-as-you-go financing, early retirees benefit, whereas later generations lose. This suggests a possible defense of social security if a redistribution in favor of early retirees is considered desirable.

Sometimes it is argued that early retirees are likely to be poorer than future generations, so that such a redistribution favors those with lower incomes. But the largest windfall gains went to those who were not particulary poor: Recall that higher benefits went to those with higher earnings.

These brief remarks only touch on the major issues, but they do suggest why some people find the rationale for social security to be far from conclusive. As an alternative, let's consider private provision for retirement. The first point to note is that social security would have to be phased out very gradually, for the same reason we noted in connection with our discussion of the level of benefits. If people no longer had to pay social security taxes, retirement benefits to those who were already retired could no longer be paid. An abrupt termination of benefits would be unfair to workers who had already retired as well as to individuals approaching retirement who had made plans based on the expectation of social security benefits.

Milton Friedman proposed a gradual transition to a private voluntary system that would work in this way.[18] Retirement benefits already accumulated would be paid, but there would be no further accumulation of benefits in the future. People already retired would continue to receive their existing pensions (including cost-of-living adjustments). People near retirement would receive a sizable pension because they had already accumulated benefits implicitly owed them as a result of paying taxes over many years. Their pension, however, would be smaller than if the social security system continued on its present course. At the other extreme, young people just entering the labor force would receive no retirement benefits under social security because they would not have accumulated benefits as a result of paying taxes. Thus, there would be a gradual reduction in the level of retirement benefits, and after 50 or 60 years social security benefits would have fallen to zero. Note what this implies for taxes. Social security taxes would also gradually fall, but very slowly at first. Because retirement benefits to those already retired would be fixed, the required taxes would fall only slowly as retired persons died and were replaced by new retirees receiving lower benefits. The taxes paid after the adoption of Friedman's proposal, however, would *not* entitle one to added benefits on retirement; only the taxes paid before that time would be accompanied by promises of future benefits.

Such a gradual phasing out of social security is feasible, but would it be beneficial? Phasing out social security should increase private saving as younger workers save more for retirement, and that implies greater output and real income in subsequent years. Future generations would be better off as they receive the high rate of return on real capital accumulation rather than the 2 percent return on social security. Workers who are young when

---

[18] Milton Friedman, "Second Lecture," in Wilbur J. Cohen and Milton Friedman, *Social Security: Universal or Selective?* (Washington, D.C.: American Enterprise Institute, 1972) pp. 44–49.

the reform is implemented will also probably benefit, but to a lesser degree. Although they will pay (declining) social security taxes over their working lives, the increasing capital stock will gradually raise their before-tax incomes. Middle-aged workers are the ones who are most obviously harmed. They will continue to pay fairly high social security taxes until they reach retirement age, but their social security pensions will not reflect these taxes (only past taxes). Although there is also an offsetting feature from the greater capital accumulation leading to higher before-tax incomes, this offset will be small for those near the end of their working lives because it occurs only gradually over time. They are too old to receive much benefit from slowly rising before-tax incomes.

Thus, phasing out social security and relying on private provision for retirement would tend to harm middle-aged groups and benefit the young and future generations. Basically, it would just reverse the process of introducing pay-as-you-go social security, which, as we saw, benefits those relatively old at that time and harm the young and future generations. Whether this reform is desirable is debatable. Because of the political factors discussed earlier, however, such a reform seems unlikely to be adopted.

Supplementary Readings

AARON, HENRY J. *Economic Effects of Social Security.* Washington, D.C.: The Brookings Institution, 1982.

AUERBACH, ALAN J., and LAWRENCE J. KOTLIKOFF. "Simulating Alternative Social Security Responses to the Demographic Transition." *National Tax Journal,* 38:158–168 (June 1985).

BOSKIN, MICHAEL J., ed. *The Crisis in Social Security: Problems and Prospects.* San Francisco: Institute for Contemporary Studies, 1977.

BUCHANAN, JAMES M. "Social Insurance in a Growing Economy: A Proposal for Radical Reform." *National Tax Journal,* 19:386–395 (Dec. 1968).

CAMPBELL, COLIN, ed. *Controlling the Cost of Social Security.* Washington, D.C.: American Enterprise Institute, 1982.

———. *Financing Social Security.* Washington, D.C.: American Enterprise Institute, 1978.

COHEN, WILBUR J., and MILTON FRIEDMAN. *Social Security: Universal or Selective?* Washington, D.C.: American Enterprise Institute, 1972.

FELDSTEIN, MARTIN S. "Social Security, Induced Retirement and Aggregate Capital Accumulation." *Journal of Political Economy,* 82(5):905–926 (Sept./Oct. 1974).

———. "Toward a Reform of Social Security." *Public Interest,* 40:75–95 (Summer 1975).

FERRARA, PETER J. *Social Security.* Washington, D.C.: Cato Institute, 1985.

———. *Social Security: The Inherent Contradiction.* San Francisco: Cato Institute, 1980.

LESNOY, SELIG D., and DEAN R. LEIMER. "Social Security and Private Saving: Theory and Historical Evidence." *Social Security Bulletin,* 48(1):14–30 (Jan. 1985).

MUNNELL, ALICIA H. *The Future of Social Security*. Washington, D.C.: The Brookings Institution, 1977.

ROBERTSON, A. HAEWORTH. *The Coming Revolution in Social Security*. McLean, Va.: Security Press, 1981.

Review Questions and Problems

1. How does an unfunded, or pay-as-you-go, social security system differ from a funded system?

2. In what two ways does the social security program redistribute income? Who are the main beneficiaries of each type of redistribution? Who is harmed by each type of redistribution?

3. Viewed as a method of providing for retirement, does social security offer an attractive rate of return?

4. How social security affects saving is a controversial issue. What are the various reasons why it might or might not affect saving? How do you think it affects saving? Defend your answer.

5. If social security does adversely affect saving, this effect will be important to determining who benefits and who is harmed by the system. Explain why.

6. One proposal for reforming social security is to have all retirees receive the same retirement benefits, instead of having the benefits depend on past earnings. What advantages and disadvantages would this reform have?

7. A common proposal for changing social security is to permit people who provide for their own retirement through private saving to resign from the system (and not pay social security taxes or receive social security benefits). Why not let all workers choose between staying in or resigning from the system?

8. The board of trustees estimated that the social security system is in balance over the next 75 years. What does this mean, and what are the reasons for thinking there will be serious financing problems in the first part of the next century?

9. Suppose around the year 2020 it becomes apparent that over the next decade or two, revenues will fall far short of the benefits promised under social security. What do you think *should* be done at that time? From a public choice perspective, recalling the changing age distribution of the population, what do you think *will* be done?

10. Does the political process produce too large a social insurance system? If so, what reforms would lead to a better political outcome?

chapter 8

Government and the Distribution of Income

MOST government policies affect the distribution of income in some way. Some policies, such as food stamps, are decidedly pro-poor in their distributional impact, but others, such as unemployment insurance and social security, spread benefits more widely and unevenly across income classes. Still others, such as agricultural subsidies and certain tax "loopholes," favor upper-income groups. Given the diversity of separate effects, perhaps it is not surprising that some people believe that government is pro-poor on balance, others believe it is pro-middle class, and still others believe it is pro-wealthy. To resolve this issue, it is important to take a broad perspective and evaluate the combined effect that all tax and expenditure policies have on the distribution of income, and that is the major objective of this chapter. We begin, however, by first considering the arguments for and against the use of government policy to redistribute income.

Arguments Favoring Redistribution by Government

Equity

Probably the most frequently encountered rationale for government redistribution is the belief that great inequalities in income are ethically unacceptable. Why should some people have incomes exceeding $100,000, and others struggle to exist on $5,000? Compassion for those with low incomes seems to suggest that a redistribution in favor of the poor would be a fairer way to divide the total income "pie." Within this context, the equity argument is simply a value judgment that greater equality is a "good" thing. It is, however, a value judgment that many people make without hesitation.

As a value judgment, it is not susceptible to proof or disproof; it simply expresses a person's feelings. If the government takes $1,000 from a wealthy man and gives it to a poor man, one person is benefited and the other person is harmed. (Some qualifications are considered later.) There is no objective way to compare the harm done to one person with the benefit received by the other, and we can express only a subjective opinion that the result is desirable or undesirable.

At a fairly general level, there is wide agreement that the goal of equity is served by having government programs to assist individuals with low incomes. There is much less agreement when we turn to more specific questions, like exactly how much assistance to grant to which groups, who is to bear the cost, and what policies should we use to effect the redistribution. People's conception of equity and the importance they attach to it differ widely, so that a general concern for equity does not provide much guidance in evaluating specific policies.

Public good element in redistribution

Raising the incomes of the poor by making transfers to them may have the characteristics of a public good. If many of the nonpoor feel (for whatever reason) that higher incomes for the poor are desirable, then the income level of the poor is a good that simultaneously affects the well-being of many nonpoor persons. It is quite similar to national defense, because actions that raise the incomes of the poor benefit not only the poor but also some (or all) of the nonpoor. If the nonpoor have a sufficiently large demand for helping the poor, a redistribution of income from the nonpoor to the poor will benefit both groups. Under these circumstances, there is an efficiency case to be made for government redistribution.

If the nonpoor want to help the poor, however, why not make transfers individually on a voluntary basis rather than have the government perform this function? Where is the case for redistribution by government? The answer, of course, is the free rider problem. Too small a volume of voluntary transfers—just as with national defense—would be supported by private contributions. Suppose, for example, that each of 10 million nonpoor would be willing to pay $1,000 if the combined incomes of the poor were increased by $5 billion. No nonpoor person would voluntarily make a transfer, because a $1,000 transfer by itself would not make a dent in the extent of poverty—just as one car equipped with pollution controls would not perceptibly clean up the atmosphere. Yet all the nonpoor would be better off if the government levied a tax of $500 on each and transferred the revenue ($5 billion) to the poor; each of the nonpoor would obtain an outcome worth $1,000 at a cost of $500. As this example suggests, there can be benefits to both the nonpoor and the poor from redistribution by government.

Figure 8–1 illustrates the gain to the nonpoor. Consider a distribution of income in which initially the nonpoor have $200 billion and the poor have

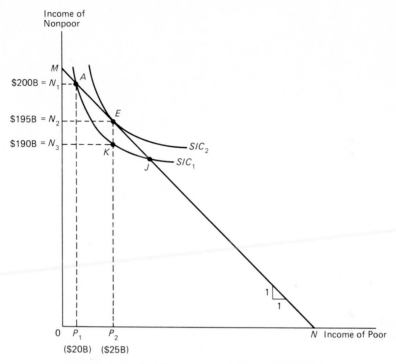

FIGURE 8–1   *Public aspects of redistribution.*

$20 billion; this is shown by point *A.* The line *MN* shows all the ways the total $220 billion in income can be divided between the two groups.[1] *SIC₁* is a social indifference curve for the nonpoor; the slope shows how much of their incomes they are willing to give up to achieve a higher income for the poor. (This is a social indifference curve for a public good, and so its slope reflects the *sum* of the *MRS*s of all the nonpoor.) The slope of *SIC₁* between points *A* and *K* shows that the nonpoor are willing to pay $10 billion to raise the income of the poor by $5 billion. Thus, a transfer of $5 billion will benefit the nonpoor: They can attain point *E* on *SIC₂* by giving up $5 billion of their income and "purchasing" $5 billion more income for the poor. Although the indifference curve for the poor is not drawn in (the *SIC* curves show the welfare effect for the nonpoor only), they will also obviously benefit from having $5 billion more income.

---

[1] For simplicity, we draw *MN* here as a straight line, implying that total income is the same regardless of how it is distributed. As we will see in the next chapter, however, redistributive programs may have adverse effects on productive incentives, thereby reducing total income.

This analysis suggests that some redistribution may be mutually benefi-cial to all groups in society, but it does *not* determine what the "best" dis-tribution of income is. Point *E* in Figure 8–1 shows the distribution pre-ferred by the nonpoor only; the poor will clearly prefer a distribution farther down the *EN* segment of the line. A further redistribution (beyond point *E*) will benefit the poor and harm the nonpoor. An efficiency criterion cannot judge the merit of this further redistribution; more redistribution is akin to a movement along a welfare frontier where one person or group benefits at the expense of another.

This entire analysis is based on the assumption that the nonpoor are willing to give up some income in order to increase the incomes of the poor. It is likely that many people share this type of feeling.[2] The relevant question is how much it is worth to the nonpoor as a group to help the poor. Because "helping the poor" is a public good for those who share this feeling, the problems of determining the demand curve for a public good make it difficult to answer this question precisely. It seems fairly clear, how-ever, that in the United States we have moved well into the *EN* portion of the constraint in Figure 8–1. (This is likely because people unanimously favor a move to point *E,* but the political process will expand policies be-yond the level where unanimous agreement is achieved.)

Insurance

Redistribution of income to lower-income groups may provide some other benefits to those who pay taxes to finance this redistribution. Even if taxpay-ers do not care about the poor per se, it may still be in their interest to support a system of transfers. There are several possible reasons for this. One is that the people who are currently nonpoor bear a risk that they could become poor in the future. Bad health, accidents, or technological progress that wipes out the demand for a particular skill can impoverish anyone. A system of government redistribution to the poor acts as a type of insurance, or "safety net," for the nonpoor; if misfortune strikes, they will be eligible for financial assistance. Insurance protection is a benefit to the nonpoor even if they never receive benefits, just as health insurance is worthwhile even if you never become ill. What type of redistributional pro-grams would be supported by this consideration, however, is not entirely clear.

---

[2]The equity argument for redistribution may be closely related to this public goods argu-ment. If the view that equity requires a redistribution from the nonpoor to the poor is shared by many of the nonpoor, and the nonpoor are willing to pay to achieve greater equity, then the common goal of more equity is a public good.

A similar benefit for the nonpoor occurs if redistribution leads to a reduction in crime, riots, or social unrest. This consideration was stressed during the wave of riots that occurred during the late 1960s. Redistribution may be a way of buying off potential criminals and thereby purchasing security. It is not clear how quantitatively important this type of effect is. Crime has increased dramatically in recent decades at the same time that the volume of redistribution has risen enormously (not that causation should be inferred). Many scholars, notably de Tocqueville, have observed that the closer we move to equality, the more remaining inequalities are resented. If so, redistribution may not lead to a more stable society. In addition, it should be noted that there are other ways besides redistribution to deter criminal activity, and there is no reason to think that redistribution is the least costly way of dealing with crime.

Political power

"One man, one vote" is a phrase sometimes used to describe the ideal that all people have equal political influence in a democracy. Yet it is widely felt that money can sometimes buy political favors that a mere vote cannot. Concentration of income or wealth in the hands of a few may confer political as well as economic power. Consequently, it is sometimes suggested that government should tax the wealthy heavily to deprive them of the means to acquire undue political influence. Note that this argument, in contrast to the preceding ones, emphasizes reducing incomes from the top for its own sake rather than raising incomes at the bottom of the income distribution.

As applied to wealthy individuals and families, this argument is weak for two reasons. First, the problem identified is a weakness inherent in our political system. Redesigning political institutions in a way to guard against excessive influence would be simpler than implementing an equitable and efficient tax-and-transfer scheme to accomplish the same goal. Second, the argument ignores the free rider problem. There are many wealthy persons, thousands, or hundreds of thousands, depending on the definition. Government actions that benefit the wealthy (such as reducing the progressivity in the income tax) are like public goods for all wealthy individuals. It is, therefore, rarely in the interest of any one wealthy person to contribute money, time, and so on, in an attempt to influence legislation that will benefit many other wealthy persons as well. This is one of the cases where the free rider phenomenon is a desirable influence.

Actually, the danger that money will buy political influence is more acute with labor unions and large businesses. These organizations already represent large groups of people, and the free rider phenomenon is not so much of a problem. It should be clear, however, that this issue is not closely related to questions concerning the distribution of income.

Arguments Opposing Redistribution by Government

Equity

Just as there are equity factors that favor government redistribution, there are also equity considerations that oppose it. Principal among these is the view that a person has the right to keep the income he or she earns. This is a value judgment and reflects the view that a competitive price system distributes rewards in a fair manner. If the system is competitive, resource prices will reflect the contribution these resources make to production; that is, prices equal marginal value products. Thus, a person's income equals the contribution each individual and his or her resources make to the "total income pie." If it is considered fair for a person to take out of the "total income pie" an amount equal to what he or she adds to it, then the distribution of income generated by a competitive price system would be equitable and any government redistribution would be inequitable.

Very few people subscribe to this value judgment without reservations because marginal value productivity and moral deservingness are not the same thing in the views of most people. A person with a skill or talent that is scarce relative to demand can receive a high income, irrespective of the individual's moral worth. Conversely, a person without—for whatever reason—resources valued highly in markets will have a low income. Markets place monetary values on productive services, not on the people who perform them. Thus, the distribution of income generated by the market need not be regarded as fair unless one's sole criterion of fairness is payment according to marginal productivity.

It would probably be going too far to completely reject the market-determined distribution of income as having no connection with most people's conception of equity. After all, the market does tend to reward ambition, hard work, foresight, and perseverance and to penalize (or reward less) laziness, ineptitude, or dishonesty. This is perhaps the reason why the market system of rewards is not totally rejected.

Incentives and economic efficiency

Most government programs that redistribute income tend to undermine economic incentives and misallocate resources. They are not, in other words, pure distortionless transfers but involve some "leakages" that reduce the total size of the income pie. We have already seen examples of the welfare costs produced by redistributive expenditure policies in earlier discussions. The welfare costs mean that the average real income of persons is reduced by efforts to achieve more equality in the distribution of income.

An extreme example will illustrate the problem. Suppose the government mandates complete equality of incomes. Every person's (or family's) income will be equal to the average, regardless of actual productive efforts. A guarantee of an income that cannot be increased or reduced by one's own actions provides no financial incentive to work, save, or bear risks. Who would work if working did not yield a higher income than not working? If no one worked, total national income would fall, and average income would fall with it. Incomes would be equal, but the absolute level of income would be very low. Most, if not all, people would be worse off than with unequal but higher average incomes.

This is an extreme example, but it serves to point out the conflict between equality and efficiency in stark terms. Recognizing the consequences of complete equality, very few people advocate it as an ideal. It is still possible, however, to move part way toward greater equality without the disastrous effects hinted at earlier.

Economists tend to emphasize the efficiency implications of redistributive schemes. Pointing out that there is an efficiency loss from redistribution does not, it must be stressed, imply that the redistribution is undesirable. Efficiency is just one criterion to use in evaluating policy, and a moderate loss in efficiency may be a price worth paying for greater equality. Economics can be of assistance in evaluating redistributive policies by suggesting the likely size of the resulting welfare costs.

Political aspects

Deciding that the market distribution of income is not ideal is not equivalent to deciding that the government should redistribute income. The political process that will determine government policy is itself an imperfect mechanism, and there is no guarantee that the policies finally implemented will bear much resemblance to the "ideal." In the context of our discussions of expenditure programs, we pointed out a few of the features in these policies that are widely recognized as inequities. Such results are to be expected; the relevant question is whether an imperfect political mechanism will be better than an imperfect market, not whether there is some conceivable distribution of income that would be better than that generated by the price system.

Resolving distributional issues also places a great strain on a democratic political process because such issues are inherently divisive. For many of the services provided by government, people have a common or similar interest in seeing that they are performed well. Although not everyone will agree on the exact content of the defense budget, everyone agrees on the need for a major commitment of resources and on the goal of achieving national security. Such a limited degree of agreement is absent when redistribution is openly contemplated. Redistributive schemes inevitably benefit one group of people at the expense of another; there is no common interest because the interests of the groups are diametrically opposed. (This need not be true for a small redistribution of income if redistribution itself is a public good.) It should be no surprise if the uneasy political compromises that result are less than satisfactory for all groups concerned.

Weighing the Pros and Cons

Economics cannot demonstrate that one distribution of income is "better" than another. Indeed, the concept of an "optimal" or "best" distribution of income must be firmly rejected. Different distributions of income involve gains in well-being for some at the expense of others; to judge such changes requires relying in part on value judgments that cannot be objectively demonstrated to be true or false. This does not imply that economics cannot aid people in making better informed decisions in this matter. Many factual and analytical questions can at least in part be resolved through the use of economics.

In view of the many factors to be considered, it is difficult for an individual to arrive at a well-reasoned and consistent view of what his or her values suggest is appropriate redistributive policy by government. In weighing the benefits and costs of redistribution, one piece of advice can be offered: Remember to evaluate these benefits and costs at the margin. The marginal benefit you perceive from the government's redistributing the first $1 billion to the poor is likely to be quite large: It could literally be a life-or-death matter. The marginal benefit of increasing the volume of redistribution from $50 billion to $51 billion will probably be much smaller. The opposite is true for the marginal costs. At low levels of redistribution, the marginal costs due to efficiency losses or inequities in government programs are likely to be small. The marginal costs of moving to complete equality will rise at increasing rates. Thus, marginal benefits fall and marginal costs rise with increased amounts of redistribution.

No suggestion is being made, however, that there is an objectively best amount of redistribution where marginal benefits and costs are equal. We are only considering what is a logical framework for an individual to utilize: The marginal benefits and costs are those factors that, according to your values, are advantages and disadvantages. Other people's values will differ. Still, recognizing the importance of thinking in terms of marginal changes will forestall much unproductive speculation about whether the arguments for government redistribution are better or worse than the arguments against it. The relative importance of the arguments depends on how much redistribution is being contemplated. If the government were not now redistributing any income to the poor, we suspect that virtually everyone would agree that some redistribution is desirable; marginal benefits are undoubtedly greater than marginal costs at low levels of redistribution. With the government already redistributing many billions of dollars annually, however, there would likely be much less agreement that a further increase is desirable.

This brings us to the question of how government is currently affecting the distribution of income. How unequally are incomes distributed, and how does government policy affect the degree of inequality? The remainder of this chapter is devoted to this surprisingly complex question.

Government Expenditure Policies Affecting Income Distribution

Almost all government policies have some effect on the distribution of real income, because some people are benefited and others are harmed by virtually all government actions. Our attention is here restricted to government expenditure programs that provide cash or goods and services directly to people, since this type of policy has the most easily measured effect on income distribution.

Table 8–1 lists the most important government income transfer programs and gives total expenditures for four recent years. The programs are divided into two categories, social insurance and welfare programs.

Social insurance programs base benefits on past contributions and/or some identifiable problem such as unemployment. Thus, people do not have to be poor to receive benefits from the social insurance programs, and a large part of the benefits do not go to the poor. Nonetheless, as we saw in our discussion of social security and unemployment insurance, those programs do have features that differentially benefit those with lower incomes. Welfare programs, on the other hand, tend to concentrate benefits almost exclusively on those with low incomes, since inadequate economic means is the principal criterion for eligibility.

In 1984, total expenditures on these income transfer programs were $375 billion, or 12 percent of net national product (NNP). Income transfer expenditures have grown rapidly in recent years, rising from $29.4 billion in 1965 to $375 billion in 1984. Since these figures are not adjusted for inflation, it is more meaningful to consider the share of NNP devoted to these programs. Here, too, we can see substantial growth, with more than twice as high a proportion of NNP devoted to income transfers in 1984 than in 1965: 12.0 percent as compared with 4.9 percent. The social insurance programs more than doubled as a share of NNP over this period, rising from 4.0 to 9.0 percent, and welfare programs more than tripled as a share of NNP, rising from 0.9 percent to 2.9 percent.

Table 8–1 also subdivides the programs into those providing cash and those providing in-kind transfers. Recall that in-kind transfers are subsidies to the consumption of specific goods and services, such as food stamps and Medicaid. One of the most significant changes in transfer programs in re-

Table 8–1   *Expenditures on Major Income Transfer Programs, Selected Years (in billions of $)*

	Expenditures			
	1984	*1980*	*1973*	*1965*
Social Insurance				
Cash Benefits:				
Social Security (OASDHI)	$178.2	$117.1	$48.3	$16.5
Unemployment Insurance	18.4	18.0	5.4	2.5
Veteran's Benefits	25.6	21.2	12.0	4.1
Railroad Retirement	3.7	4.7	2.4	1.1
In-Kind Benefits:				
Medicare	57.5	35.0	9.5	NE
Subtotal	283.4	196.0	77.6	24.2
% of NNP	9.0	8.7	6.8	4.0
Welfare				
Cash Benefits:				
Aid to Families with Dependent Children (AFDC)	17.7	14.0	7.0	1.7
Supplemental Security Income (SSI)[1]	8.5	6.4	3.3	2.7
Earned Income Tax Credit	1.2	1.3	NE	NE
In-Kind Benefits:				
Medicaid[2]	38.5	25.2	9.1	0.5
Food Stamps	12.4	9.1	2.5	0.0
Housing Assistance	11.3	5.3	1.6	0.3
Energy and Emergency Assistance	2.0	1.5	NE	NE
Subtotal	91.6	62.8	23.5	5.2
% of NNP	2.9	2.8	2.1	0.9
Total Expenditures	375.0	258.8	101.1	29.4
Total Expenditures as % of NNP	12.0	11.5	8.9	4.9

NE = Nonexistent.
[1] Aid to the Blind, Aid to the Permanently and Totally Disabled, and Old Age Assistance in 1965 and 1973. SSI was implemented in 1974.
[2] Medical Aid to the Aged in 1965.
Source: Office of Management and Budget, *The Budget of the United States Government and Appendix,* Fiscal Years 1975, 1982, and 1986; 1965 data from Robert D. Plotnick and Felicity Skidmore, *Progress Against Poverty* (New York: Academic Press, 1975).

cent years has been the growth in the importance of in-kind transfers. In 1965, less than $1 billion was spent on programs providing in-kind benefits; that is, less than 3 percent of total income transfer expenditures was on in-kind programs in that year. In 1984, however, outlays on these programs were $121.7 billion, or nearly one third of total income transfer expenditures. The change is even more dramatic in the welfare category. In-kind welfare benefits were 16 percent of total welfare spending in 1965, but 70 percent in 1984. Welfare assistance was mostly in the form of cash in 1965, but today the bulk of welfare spending takes the form of subsidies to the consumption of particular goods and services.

The changes in income transfer expenditures between 1980 and 1984 should also be noted. Ronald Reagan was elected president in 1980, and in 1981 he is credited with persuading Congress to enact a number of budget cuts in social programs. These cuts were often referred to in terms like "slashing welfare spending to the bone." The actual consequences, however, were not so dramatic. In fact, both social insurance and welfare spending rose between 1980 and 1984, whether measured in dollars of constant purchasing power or as a share of NNP. Although some programs have declined in importance relative to NNP (such as AFDC and SSI), others (such as Medicaid and housing assistance) have increased in importance. What is true is that overall spending on income transfer programs rose much more slowly between 1980 and 1984 compared with its extremely rapid growth in the preceding 15 years. After a decade and a half of explosive growth, income transfer expenditures have in recent years approximately stabilized relative to NNP.

A more comprehensive view of the way government affects the incomes of people by providing cash or services can be obtained by focusing on what the Social Security Administration calls "social welfare expenditures." Social welfare programs include not only the programs identified in Table 8–1 but also outlays on education, public employee retirement programs, job training programs, school lunches, and a number of other smaller programs. In 1983, total social welfare expenditures by federal, state, and local governments were $641.7 billion. (Education alone accounts for half the difference between social welfare expenditures and expenditures on the income transfer programs of Table 8–1.) This comes to an expenditure of about $2,700 per person in the United States, or nearly $11,000 for a family of four.

Table 8–2 traces the growth of social welfare expenditures since 1947. In the 36-year period from 1947 to 1983, social welfare expenditures grew from $17.3 billion to $641.7 billion. Inflation is partly responsible for this growth, since prices more than quadrupled over the period, but expressed in real terms, social welfare expenditures increased by a factor of 8. Relative to NNP, social welfare expenditures rose from 8.3 percent in 1947 to 22.6 percent in 1983. Much of this growth has occurred since 1965.

This massive increase in social welfare spending reflects two basic changes in government budgets. First, government spending has become increasingly important relative to net national product. Total government expenditures were only 20.4 percent of NNP in 1947 but rose to 39.6 percent by

Table 8–2   *Social Welfare Expenditures, Selected Years, 1947–1983* *

	1983	1975	1966	1959	1947
Total social welfare	$641.7	$290.1	$88.0	$49.8	$17.3
From federal funds	398.6	167.4	45.6	23.5	9.8
From state and local funds	243.1	122.7	42.4	26.3	7.5
Total social welfare as percentage of NNP	22.6%	21.8%	13.5%	11.3%	8.3%
Total government spending as percentage of NNP	39.6%	37.1%	31.3%	31.0%	20.4%

*Outlays in billions of dollars; fiscal years.
Sources: Ann Kallman Bixby, "Social Welfare Expenditures, 1963–83," *Social Security Bulletin,* 49 (2) (Washington, D.C.: U.S. Government Printing Office, Feb. 1986), Table 2; other government documents.

1983. A second basic change is that a larger part of the growing government budgets—federal, state, and local—is being devoted to social welfare spending. This is particularly true for the federal government. Only 26.6 percent of total federal spending was devoted to the social welfare category in 1947, compared with nearly 50 percent in 1983.

These figures indicate that governments (federal, state, and local) commit a large volume of resources to provide income assistance to people and that the share of national income devoted to this purpose has increased greatly in recent years. Not all of these outlays are redistributive in nature, but a sizable portion is. Now let's consider how this increase in social welfare spending has affected the extent of inequality and the distribution of income.

The Distribution of Money Income

The most widely used estimates of the distribution of income in the United States are those published annually by the Bureau of the Census. Table 8–3 shows the Census Bureau's estimates of the percentage distribution of families by money income class for selected postwar years. Incomes are expressed in 1983 dollars to remove the effects of inflation. As can be seen, even though more than 70 percent of all families had incomes between $10,000 and $50,000 in 1983, 5.7 percent of all families had incomes below $5,000. At the other extreme, 12.6 percent of families had incomes above $50,000. Considerable inequality characterizes the distribution of money income.

In interpreting these numbers several points should be noted. First, the distribution reported in Table 8–3 is composed only of multiperson fami-

Table 8–3   *Percentage Distribution of Families by Money Income Levels,*
Constant 1983 Dollars, 1947–1983

Income Class	1983	1980	1970	1960	1947
Under $5,000	5.7%	5.1%	4.4%	8.7%	13.0%
$5,000 to $9,999	10.2	9.6	9.1	12.8	20.3
$10,000 to $24,999	34.9	34.5	35.9	48.4	
$25,000 to $49,999	36.5	38.6	40.7	30.1	66.6
Over $50,000	12.6	12.2	9.9		
Median Income (1983 dollars)	$24,580	$25,418	$25,317	$18,907	$13,519

Source: U.S. Department of Commerce, Bureau of the Census, *Money Incomes of House-holds, Families, and Persons in the United States, 1983* (Washington, D.C.: U.S. Government Printing Office, 1985), Table 15.

lies—single-person households are not included. Second, this is a distribution of all *money* income. It includes not only wage and salary income, dividends, and interest, but also government cash transfer payments such as social security, unemployment insurance, and others. Thus, the figures already reflect the impact of substantial welfare expenditures; yet 5.7 percent of all families had incomes below $5,000 even after the receipt of all cash transfer outlays. Third, the figures give incomes before payment of direct personal taxes such as income and social security payroll taxes.

Although a sizable number of families had low incomes in 1983, the number was dramatically smaller than it was in earlier years. In 1947, one family in eight had an income below $5,000 (in 1983 dollars). Since 1947 there has been a major decrease in the percentage of families with incomes below $5,000 and an equally impressive increase in the percentage with high incomes. Median family income nearly doubled over this period, rising from $13,519 in 1947 to $24,580 in 1983. Economic growth was the major factor responsible for the rising level of real incomes that benefited the poor and nonpoor alike. (Government cash transfers also probably played a role in improvements at the bottom of the income distribution, but their impact was not great.) Since 1970, however, the growth in real incomes has come to a halt, with the median income in 1983 being actually slightly lower than in 1970. (Preliminary estimates for 1984 indicate a rise in median income in 1983 dollars to $25,391, almost exactly the same as in 1970.)

A different way of presenting this information, which tends to emphasize the relative distribution of income, is shown in Table 8–4. This table is constructed by grouping families according to whether they fall in the lowest 20 percent of the income distribution, the second 20 percent, and so on. Then the total income of all families in each fifth, or quintile, is expressed

Table 8–4 *Percentage Income Shares for Families, Selected Years*

Year	Lowest Quintile	Second Quintile	Third Quintile	Fourth Quintile	Highest Quintile
1929	3.5%	9.0%	13.8%	19.3%	54.4%
1947	5.0	11.9	17.0	23.1	43.0
1960	4.8	12.2	17.8	24.0	41.3
1970	5.4	12.2	17.6	23.8	40.9
1980	5.1	11.6	17.5	24.3	41.6
1984	4.7	11.0	17.0	24.4	42.9
1979*	3.8	9.7	16.4	24.8	45.3

*The distribution of families and unrelated individuals combined.
Source: 1929 data from Herman Miller, *Income Distribution in the United States,* Bureau of the Census, 1966, p. 21; 1947, 1960, 1970, and 1979 data from U.S. Department of Commerce, Bureau of the Census, *Money Income and Poverty Status of Families and Persons in the United States: 1979,* Table 14; 1980 and 1984 data from *Money Income and Poverty Status of Families and Persons in the United States: 1984, Advance Report,* Table 4.

as a percentage of the total income of all families. Thus, in 1984 the lowest quintile had a combined money income of 4.7 percent of total money income for the entire population. This means that the average money income of families in the lowest quintile was 23.5 percent of the average income of all families. (If 20 percent of all families—a quintile—have 20 percent of all income, this implies that those families have an average income equal to the average income of all families. For the lowest quintile, a percentage of 4.7 percent means that they have 4.7/20, or 23.5 percent of the average.) The top quintile had an average of slightly more than twice the average of all families, or 42.9/20, and the average income of families in the top quintile was 9.1 times (42.9/4.7) the average income of families in the bottom quintile.

Two characteristics of these numbers stand out. First, for each year they indicate substantial inequality in the distribution of income. This is to be expected because this table simply portrays the same data that underlie Table 8–3, but in a different form. Second, and more interestingly, there seems to have been remarkably little change in the relative distribution of income over the entire postwar years. In 1984, each quintile's share differed by less than one percentage point from its share in 1947, except for the fourth quintile where the difference was 1.3 percentage points. Note in particular that the share of the lowest quintile actually declined slightly, from 5.0 to 4.7 percent. Thus, although absolute incomes have risen for poor and nonpoor alike, the relative positions of the various quintiles have scarcely changed.

The 1979 row of Table 8–4 gives the income shares for families and unrelated individuals. In other words, single persons are treated as family units and combined with multiperson families. Because unrelated individuals have lower incomes than families do, this combined distribution displays greater inequality, with a top to bottom quintile ratio of 12:1, compared with the 9:1 ratio for families alone. This distribution has also shown little change since 1947.

The lack of improvement in the relative position of the lowest quintile is a finding that has bothered and surprised many people. It is curious, because low-income families are thought to be the major beneficiaries of the massive growth in social welfare expenditures. Because social welfare expenditures as a percentage of national income have more than doubled since 1947, it is reasonable to expect a significant change in the distribution of income. Why there has been no significant change is a puzzle to be considered shortly.

How many are poor?

One other set of statistics that is of interest in connection with the income distribution issue is the government's count of persons living in poverty. The government defines—admittedly somewhat arbitrarily—poverty level incomes for families with different characteristics. There are, in fact, 124 poverty levels that vary with the size of family, age of family head, and farm or nonfarm place of residence. For example, the poverty level for a nonfarm family of four, headed by a male, was $10,609 in 1984. Families with incomes below their respective poverty lines are officially designated as poor. The poverty lines are adjusted upward each year to reflect increases in the cost of living.

Table 8–5 provides some information about persons with incomes below their respective poverty lines in several recent years. The total number of poor persons declined from 39.5 million in 1959 to 33.7 million in 1984. Since the population grew over this period, the reduction is greater when

---

Table 8–5 *Persons Below the Poverty Level, Selected Years (in thousands)*

	1984	1980	1974	1966	1959
Number	33,700	29,272	23,370	28,510	39,490
Percent of population	14.4%	13.0%	11.2%	14.7%	22.4%
65 years and over	3,330	3,871	3,085	5,114	5,481
Under 65 years					
Family with female head	14,439	12,341	9,674	7,846	8,359
Family with male head	15,931	13,060	10,611	15,580	25,650

Source: U.S. Department of Commerce, Bureau of Census, *Money Income and Poverty Status of Families and Persons in the United States: 1984, Advance Report,* Table 15.

expressed as the percentage of people who were poor, falling from 22.4 percent to 14.4 percent. Poverty did not fall at a steady rate over this period, however. Most of the decline took place between 1959 and 1966. After 1966, the poverty rate decreased slightly, standing at 11 to 12 percent through most of the 1970s. In 1978, the poverty rate was 11.4 percent; then it rose every year until 1983, when it reached 15.3 percent; in 1984 it fell back to 14.4 percent. So by the end of the 1966–1984 period, the poverty rate was nearly as high as it had been in 1966.

What is striking about these figures is the contrast between the trends in the poverty rate and government welfare spending. Between 1959 and 1966, social welfare spending as a percentage of NNP rose only slightly (Table 8–2), but poverty declined sharply. Since 1966, however, social welfare spending has grown substantially, with spending on welfare programs, narrowly defined, approximately tripling by 1984 (Table 8–1), yet poverty did not fall appreciably during this period. The decline in poverty in the 1959–1966 period can be attributed largely to economic growth that produced higher real-wage rates and earnings. In the later period from 1966 to 1984, economic growth was much slower, but the rise in welfare spending beginning in 1966 should have had a significant impact on the poverty rate. Why such a large increase in government welfare spending apparently had such a small effect on the amount of poverty is a paradox we shall consider further in the next section.

It should be noted that in every year more persons would have been in poverty without existing government transfer programs. In 1984, for example, approximately 48 million people had market incomes that placed them below their respective poverty lines.[3] Since the official poverty count for 1984 was 33.7 million, this implies that approximately a third of those with below-poverty level market incomes were pushed above their poverty lines by government transfers. Table 8–5 includes only those people who remained poor even after the receipt of government cash transfers.

Measuring Inequality

For many years, the Census Bureau's figures on income distribution and poverty have provided the factual basis for most discussions of the degree of income inequality. Critics of the welfare state point to the lack of change in the percentage shares and poverty figures as evidence of the failure of government policies. Defenders of the welfare state use the same figures to argue that we need further expansion in welfare programs. In recent years,

---

[3] Calculated from Table 4 of U.S. Department of Commerce, Bureau of the Census, *Estimates of Poverty Including the Value of Noncash Benefits: 1984* (Washington, D.C.: U.S. Government Printing Office, Aug. 1985).

however, it has become increasingly evident that the Census Bureau's figures are seriously flawed as measures of the degree of inequality in relative
standards of living. In this section we shall take a closer look at the degree
of inequality in the distribution of income.

Taxes and in-kind transfers

The definition of income that underlies the Census estimates is basically a
measure of before-tax money income. But since standards of living depend
on after-tax incomes, personal taxes—principally income and social security
payroll taxes—should be deducted from the Census income figures. In addition, since the Census figures include only *money* incomes, all types of
income *in-kind* are excluded. Thus, government transfers like Medicare,
Medicaid, housing subsidies, and food stamps are not counted as income.
This omission has become more serious given the rapid growth of in-kind
transfers in recent years (see Table 8–1) and helps explain why the growth
in social welfare expenditures has had so little measured effect on the distribution of income. Half of all social welfare expenditures pay for in-kind
benefits, which are not counted as income by the Census Bureau.

To see how the omission of taxes and in-kind transfers affects the measured distribution of income, consider Table 8–6, which provides detailed
estimates on the quintile distribution of income among households (families and unrelated individuals) in 1976 and relies on a more comprehensive
definition of income than the Census Bureau uses. Unfortunately, data limitations prevented including all in-kind benefits provided by government,
but Medicare, Medicaid, housing subsidies, food stamps, and child nutrition
subsidies are included. (Educational subsidies are the major in-kind item

---

Table 8–6   *Distribution of Household Income, 1976 ($ in billions)*

						Percentage Shares	
Income Class	*Market Earnings*	*Cash Transfers*	*In-Kind Transfers*	*Taxes*	*Net Income*	*Market Earnings*	*Net Income*
Lowest Quintile	$ 5.7	$60.4	$21.6	$ 3.2	$ 84.4	0.4%	7.8%
Second Quintile	99.0	38.9	10.2	28.0	120.1	7.4	11.0
Third Quintile	209.4	23.2	4.2	59.2	176.8	15.6	16.2
Fourth Quintile	321.8	17.1	2.3	96.2	245.1	24.0	22.5
Highest Quintile	704.8	19.8	2.5	264.6	462.4	52.6	42.5

Note: Households ranked on the basis of before-transfer, before-tax incomes (market earnings).
Source: Edgar K. Browning and William R. Johnson, "Taxes, Transfers, and Income Inequality," in
Gary M. Walton, ed., *Regulatory Change in an Atmosphere of Crisis* (New York: Academic Press,
1979), Table 7-4.

omitted.) Since in-kind programs tend to concentrate benefits on lower-income households, their inclusion makes the final distribution more equal; similarly, subtracting taxes tends to equalize incomes, because higher-income households pay proportionately more in taxes.

Table 8–6 provides convincing evidence that the overall effect of government taxes and transfers is to redistribute income in favor of low-income families. The lowest quintile received a total of $82 billion in cash and in-kind transfers but paid only $3.2 billion in taxes, for a net redistribution in its favor of $78.8 billion. The bottom two quintiles together received $99.9 billion more in transfers than they paid in taxes. By contrast, the top quintile received transfers equal to $22.3 billion but paid taxes of $264.6 billion.[4] Unfortunately, comparable data more recent than 1976 are not available, but the general pattern of taxes and transfers has not changed much since then—although all the absolute dollar figures for the current year would be larger than the 1976 figures.

The extent to which government tax and transfer policies produce a more equal distribution of income may be overstated in tabulations like Table 8–6 for several reasons. For example, in the table the lowest quintile has a share of only 0.4 percent of total market earnings. This figure may be low in part because these households receive so much government assistance that they respond by earning less on their own. Thus, the distribution of income before taxes and transfers may be more unequal than it would be if government programs did not exist. In addition, the lifetime redistributive effect of social security is probably overstated. As shown in Table 8–6, most elderly persons receiving social security and Medicare are in the lower quintiles, whereas workers are predominantly in the upper quintiles. Thus, in any given year, the social security transfers go to people in the lower quintiles, and the social security taxes are paid by individuals in the upper quintiles, giving the impression of a sizable redistribution. If a longer-run point of view were taken, some of the social security benefits would not represent net transfers but would instead reflect a return on past taxes paid.

A more subtle point concerning the measurement of income distribution is illustrated by Table 8–7. This table gives the *same* data on household incomes as Table 8–6 does but ranks households in the income distribution differently. In Table 8–6, households are ranked on the basis of their market earnings before receiving transfers, so the households in the lowest quintiles are those with the lowest earnings. In Table 8–7, households are ranked on the basis of their incomes *after* receiving transfers, so those who are poorest when transfers are included are grouped in the lowest quintile. This

---

[4]Table 8–6 allocates all taxes to households, but it does not allocate all benefits from expenditure programs, since it includes only the major transfer programs and not education, national defense, or the like. Thus, the average net transfer across all households in the table is negative.

Table 8–7 *Distribution of Household Income, 1976 ($ in billions)*

| | | | | | | Percentage Shares | |
| | Market | Cash | In-Kind | | Net | Market | Net |
Income Class	Earnings	Transfers	Transfers	Taxes	Income	Earnings	Income
Lowest Quintile	$ 35.7	$31.8	$10.2	$ 10.1	$ 67.7	2.6%	6.2%
Second Quintile	114.8	36.0	12.5	31.9	131.5	8.4	12.0
Third Quintile	210.2	27.9	7.9	60.6	185.3	15.5	16.9
Fourth Quintile	317.9	26.3	4.7	95.8	253.0	23.4	23.0
Highest Quintile	681.7	32.1	4.2	255.9	462.2	50.1	42.0

Note: Households ranked on the basis of after-transfer, before-tax incomes.
Source: Unpublished estimates made by William R. Johnson using the data described in Edgar K. Browning and William R. Johnson, *The Distribution of the Tax Burden* (Washington, D.C.: American Enterprise Institute, 1979).

apparently innocuous difference actually changes the figures materially. In Table 8–7, the net transfer to the lowest quintile is shown as $31.9 billion, compared with $78.8 billion in Table 8–6. The final shares of income after taxes and transfers also differ: 6.2 percent for the lowest quintile in Table 8–7 compared with 7.8 percent for the lowest quintile in the previous table.

An example may help explain why these differences occur. Consider two households, one an elderly couple whose only income is a social security pension of $6,000, and the other a younger couple whose only income is earnings of $4,000. Ranked by market earnings (as in Table 8–6), the aged couple is in the lowest quintile with zero earnings, whereas the younger couple is in the second quintile. On this ranking, the social security transfer shows up as a net transfer to the lowest quintile. However, when ranked by after-transfer income (as in Table 8–7), the younger couple drops to the lowest quintile, and the elderly couple moves to the second quintile. Under this ranking. earnings are higher for the bottom quintile ($4,000 instead of zero), and transfers are lower (zero instead of $6,000). This is the type of shifting in the positions of households in the income distribution that produces the differences in the tables.

What does this reranking mean in terms of how we should interpret the data? In effect, government transfers to some households are large enough to move them well up in the after-transfer distribution, leaving the impression in Table 8–7 that fewer transfers go to lower-income families. (The Census Bureau tabulation is more like Table 8–7, since it ranks households on the basis of income after cash transfers.) This ranking tends to obscure the extent to which those with low market earnings receive transfers. On the other hand, Table 8–7 is probably a better indication of the actual distribution of after-tax-and-transfer income (disposable income), since it places those households that have the lowest incomes after receiving transfers at the bottom of the ranking.

Whichever ranking procedure is used (Table 8–6 or Table 8–7), the distribution of income after taxes and all transfers (including in-kind transfers) is clearly more equal than the Census Bureau's figures suggest. Table 8–6 and Table 8–7 are based on families *and* unrelated individuals, so that the results should be compared with Census figures such as those in the last row of Table 8–4. In the Census Bureau's estimates for families and unrelated individuals, the ratio of top quintile income to bottom quintile income is about 12 to 1. In Table 8–7, that ratio is less than 7 to 1 after taxes and in-kind transfers are included.

Other factors affecting income distribution

If families were alike in all relevant respects except income, the degree of inequality could be reasonably measured by data such as those in Tables 8–6 and 8–7. There are, however, systematic differences in the characteristics of families at different income levels that should also be taken into account. Table 8–8 compares several characteristics of families with relatively high and low incomes in 1983. Low-income families have a smaller number of family members, with nearly 50 percent being two-person families compared with 30 percent for the high-income category. The age of the family head also varies systematically with income: At low-income levels, a large proportion are either young or old, while at high-income levels, almost all families are headed by someone in his or her peak earning years. High-income families also have more earners and are better educated than low-income families.

These differences are perhaps not surprising. They suggest that high-income families commonly are well educated and middle-aged, with both the husband and wife working; in contrast; low-income families are frequently retired or young, with few earners and not as well educated. These differences, however, do raise the issue of comparability. Can we say, for example, that a retired couple with a pension of $10,000 really is only one third as well off as is a middle-aged family of four with both parents employed and with total earnings of $30,000? This is exactly the type of comparison that is implicit when income distribution data of the sort described earlier are used.

To illustrate the importance of one of these characteristics, age, consider how a typical person's earnings, income, and consumption tend to vary over his or her lifetime in Figure 8–2. Typically, earnings rise up to middle age and then remain constant or decline slightly until they fall to zero at retirement. Income (which includes the interest return on accumulated assets) rises, peaks at a higher level, then falls sharply at retirement, and declines

Table 8–8   *Characteristics of High- and Low-Income Families, 1983*

Characteristic	Money Income Before Taxes	
	$5,000–$7,499 (percent)	$60,000–$74,999 (percent)
Family Size		
Two members	49.1%	29.5%
Three members	20.0	22.3
Four or more members	30.9	48.2
Single-Parent Family	45.9	4.1
Age of Family Head		
Under 25	10.1	0.3
25–64	64.8	92.5
65 and over	25.1	7.2
Number of Earners		
None	44.2	2.7
One	39.6	15.9
Two	15.0	45.3
Three or more	1.2	36.1
Education of Family Head		
Elementary school or less	35.1	3.0
Four or more years of college	3.6	53.1

Source: U.S. Department of Commerce, Bureau of the Census, *Households, Families and Persons in the United States: 1983,* Tables 23, 25, 26, 29, and 32.

during retirement, as the assets previously accumulated are consumed. Consumption generally does not vary as much over the life cycle.

Figure 8–2 is a fairly typical pattern, and it has a pronounced effect on the degree of income inequality, as conventionally measured. To see this, suppose that all people were identical in the sense of having the *same* lifetime profile shown in the diagram. In any one year, however, their ages will differ and so, therefore, will their incomes. In statistical summaries, middle-aged persons would be in the top quintile and have about twice the income of the young and retired persons in the lowest quintile. (Average income of middle-aged families is twice as great as the average for those under 24 or over 65.) The statistics would display considerable inequality in annual income, despite the fact that all people have identical lifetime profiles.

Because of differences in age and the other characteristics mentioned, it is unlikely that data such as those discussed earlier convey a very accurate impression of the degree of economic inequality. It is, however, far easier to point out these problems than to overcome them. One approach that may reflect the overall degree of inequality more accurately is to look at the

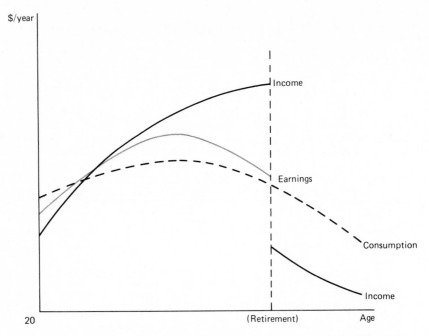

FIGURE 8–2   *Income, earnings, and consumption over the life cycle.*

distribution of income for a subset of families that is identical in terms of age and family size. We do this in Table 8–9 by considering the distribution of income among three-person families with the family head aged 35 to 44 in 1976. This exercise is not intended just to show that inequality is less among middle-aged families. Instead, it is intended as a clue to the degree of inequality in society at large when we remove the independent influences of age and family size on incomes. In comparison with earlier tables, this distribution displays less inequality in the distribution of income among households. The ratio of net income for the top quintile to net income for the bottom quintile is 4 to 1, a far cry from the 12 to 1 ratio in the unadjusted Census Bureau figures of Table 8–4.

There are several reasons why the degree of economic inequality is probably even less than suggested by Table 8–9. Because the data measure incomes in only one year, families with abnormally low incomes tend to be overrepresented at the bottom. Taking a longer-run view, a 3- or 5-year average, for example, would imply less inequality. Public education subsidies are not included, and they would equalize the distribution further. Finally, no adjustment is made for differences in hours of work, or its converse, leisure consumption. In Table 8–9, the average annual hours of work for a family in the lowest quintile is 1,328, whereas it is 3,104 for the top

Table 8–9 *Distribution of Household Income Among Three-Person Households, Aged 35–44, 1976 ($ in billions)*

| | | | | | | Percentage Shares | |
Income Class	Market Earnings	Cash Transfers	In-Kind Transfers	Taxes	Net Income	Market Earnings	Net Income
Lowest Quintile	$ 2.3	$0.78	$0.49	$0.54	$ 3.02	5.3%	9.2%
Second Quintile	5.4	0.46	0.11	1.43	4.56	12.6	13.8
Third Quintile	7.7	0.32	0.04	2.20	5.92	18.1	17.9
Fourth Quintile	9.9	0.57	0.04	2.95	7.56	23.0	22.9
Highest Quintile	17.6	0.43	0.02	6.06	11.99	41.0	36.3

Note: Households ranked on the basis of after-transfer, before-tax incomes.
Source: Unpublished estimates made by William R. Johnson using the data described in Edgar K. Browning and William R. Johnson, *The Distribution of the Tax Burden* (Washington, D.C.: American Enterprise Institute, 1979).

quintile. Net income per hour of work is, in fact, about the same for the bottom four quintiles ($5.78, $5.77, $5.68, and $6.66) and rises only to $9.82 for the top quintile. Per hour of work, families in the top quintile received (after taxes and transfers) less than twice as much as families in the lowest quintile did.

Another intriguing bit of evidence related to the difference between the income distribution measured using annual data and the income distribution estimated by using longer-run data is provided by a recent study of taxation in Canada. The Canadian study used annual data in an elaborate model to simulate the lifetime incomes of a representative sample of 500 households. Comparisons of the income distributions based on annual and lifetime incomes are given in Table 8–10, for both before-tax and after-tax measures of income. Note first that the annual distributions for Canada are quite similar to the Census Bureau's distributions for the United States. The income distributions based on estimated lifetime incomes, however, display much less inequality. Based on after-tax lifetime incomes, the share of the lowest quintile is 11.6 percent, 56 percent of the average lifetime income for all households. Moreover, the top quintile received less than three times the income of the bottom quintile, whereas on the basis of annual data the ratio is 9 to 1.

From this discussion, it should be apparent that we do not know, with any great accuracy, what the "true" distribution of income looks like. We lack the data to develop precise estimates of annual or lifetime incomes, and it is not clear conceptually how to adjust for differences in family size, leisure, education, and so on. Nonetheless, the available evidence does suggest that economic inequality is much less pronounced than the Census

Table 8–10   *Annual Versus Lifetime Income Distribution in Canada*

Income Class	Before-tax		After-tax	
	Annual	*Lifetime*	*Annual*	*Lifetime*
Lowest Quintile	4.1%	10.4%	4.6%	11.6%
Second Quintile	11.2	15.6	12.4	16.5
Third Quintile	16.7	18.8	17.9	19.3
Fourth Quintile	22.5	22.7	23.6	22.4
Highest Quintile	45.5	32.4	41.5	30.2

Source: James Davies, France St.-Hilaire, and John Whalley, "Some Calculations of Lifetime Tax Incidence," *American Economic Review,* 74 (Sept. 1984). Calculated from Tables 1 and 2.

Bureau's commonly used estimates based on annual data and before-tax cash incomes imply.

Why Hasn't the Poverty Rate Fallen?

Now let's turn to the question of why the poverty rate has not fallen significantly since 1966, even though social welfare spending has increased greatly. First we should note some important economic and demographic factors that are related to the extent of poverty. One important economic factor has been the so-called productivity growth slowdown. After many decades of nearly uninterrupted growth in the level of real wage rates, this growth has nearly ceased in recent years. In fact, average real hourly earnings in 1984 were approximately the same as those in 1969. This slowdown in the growth of real wages means that in recent years economic growth has not significantly increased the real wages of low-income workers—a factor that in the past raised some workers above the fixed (in real terms) poverty lines.

There have been two other important demographic developments that have had an impact on the poverty rate. First, the percentage of the adult population that is either young or old has been rising. In 1965, 23 percent of the population was in either the 16 to 24 age group or 65 or older; by 1984 this ratio had risen to 28 percent, a 20 percent increase. Recall that incomes tend to be low for the young and old and that poverty rates (before transfers) tend to be high for these groups. Second, there has been a major increase in the number of female-headed families, partly because of higher divorce rates and partly because of increases in illegitimacy rates. This demographic group also tends to have high poverty rates. Thus, groups that have a higher incidence of poverty have grown in numbers in recent years.

These economic and demographic changes suggest that the poverty rate would probably have risen significantly if the government had not increased welfare assistance (relative to NNP) over the 1966–1984 period. Thus, the fact that the poverty rate has not risen can be attributed, at least in part, to the increase in welfare spending.

There is more to this story, however. For at least two reasons, the official poverty rate has come to overstate the number of people living in poverty over the 1966–1984 period. The first reason pertains to the way the poverty lines are adjusted upward to take inflation into account. Adjustments in the poverty line are based on the consumer price index (CPI). During the periods of high inflation in the 1970s, however, the CPI overstated the rate of inflation because of the way it counted the cost of home ownership. Since the poverty lines were tied to the CPI, the official poverty levels were raised faster than they should have been. This mismeasurement problem with the CPI was recognized in the early 1970s, but it was not corrected until 1983 when the official CPI began to treat housing more appropriately. The net effect of this mistake, however, was to increase the official poverty line in terms of real income.

If the poverty lines had been adjusted upward in earlier years using a price index calculated as the CPI now is, the poverty lines in 1984 would have been 10 percent lower than the official poverty lines. John Weicher estimated that there would have been one eighth fewer poor persons if these adjusted poverty lines had been used.[5] Thus, the poverty rate in 1984 would have been 12.6 percent instead of the official 14.4 percent.

The second reason that the official poverty rate overstates the extent of poverty is even more serious: in-kind transfers are not counted as income in determining poverty status. Just counting money incomes means that the billions of dollars spent on Medicare, Medicaid, food stamps, and so on will not reduce the number of poor persons, as officially defined. Recall from our earlier discussion that in-kind transfers have been the fastest-growing welfare expenditure. Since in-kind assistance is not counted as income for the poor, it is understandable that the official poverty rate has not fallen appreciably.

It seems clear that in-kind transfers should be counted as income in determining whether a family is poor. If a $1,000 cash transfer to a poor person—who proceeds to spend it on food, housing, and medical care—reduces poverty, then so does $1,000 worth of these goods provided outright or at subsidized prices. When the poverty lines were first formulated in 1964, in-kind transfers were almost nonexistent (see Table 8–1), and the

---

[5]John C. Weicher, "Mismeasuring Poverty and Progress," paper presented at Public Policy Week 1985, American Enterprise Institute for Public Policy Research, Dec. 1985. It should also be noted that this same problem has affected outlays under other government policies whose benefits are indexed to the CPI, notably social security.

official poverty lines were based on the expectation that money income would be used to finance consumption.[6] Since that time, various consumption needs have increasingly been met by in-kind transfers. This change makes it important to alter the official definition of poverty—either by reducing the poverty lines for money income (less cash is needed when the government provides food, medical care, and so on) or by counting in-kind benefits—in order to obtain a more accurate measure of the number of people living in poverty.

Some feeling for the magnitude of the consequences of not counting in-kind transfers can be obtained by comparing the official income deficit, or "poverty gap," with outlays on in-kind transfers. The poverty gap refers to how much the combined money incomes of those officially counted as poor fall short of their combined poverty lines. In 1984, the poverty gap was $45.2 billion. By contrast, government expenditures on in-kind transfers were $121.7 billion (Table 8–1). If 40 percent of these in-kind transfers had gone to the poor, then the average income of officially poor families would have been above the average poverty line.

Although the official definition of poverty is still based on cash incomes, several studies, including some at the Census Bureau itself, have attempted to estimate the number of poor persons when in-kind transfers are counted as income. The results have suggested that the poverty rate would be somewhere between 33 percent and 70 percent lower than when only cash incomes are counted.[7] In addition, these studies suggest that the poverty rate would have declined since 1966 if in-kind transfers were counted, reflecting the increasing size of this form of welfare assistance.

Considering these two factors together, by using Weicher's estimate for 1984 and assuming that in-kind transfers produce a further 50 percent reduction, yields a poverty rate of 6.3 percent for 1984. This is well below half the official figure of 14.4 percent and also well below the rate in 1966 (when these adjustments were largely unnecessary). Thus, both the persistence of poverty and its overall magnitude have been exaggerated by the official measures. The increase in welfare expenditures has resulted in a reduction in poverty, but the official statistics fail to record this achievement.

---

[6]This does not apply to public schools. In 1964 schooling was supplied by government, and the poverty lines took its availability for granted. Thus, the value of publicly provided schooling should not be counted in determining poverty.

[7]U.S. Department of Commerce, Bureau of the Census, Timothy M. Smeeding, *Alternative Methods for Valuing Selected In-Kind Transfer Benefits and Measuring Their Effect on Poverty* (Washington, D.C.: U.S. Government Printing Office, Mar. 1982); Timothy Smeeding, "The Anti-Poverty Effectiveness of In-Kind Transfers," *Journal of Human Resources*, 12(3) (Summer 1977); Morton Paglin, *Poverty and Transfers In-Kind* (Stanford, Calif.: Hoover Institution, 1980); G. William Hoagland, "The Effectiveness of Current Transfer Programs in Reducing Poverty," in Paul M. Sommers, ed., *Welfare Reform in America*, 1982.

Half-full or Half-empty?

A major conclusion of this analysis is that economic inequality is a good deal less pronounced than is suggested by the widely used estimates of the distribution of money income. But this does not necessarily mean that economic inequality is not a problem. Although people may agree that tabulations like Tables 8–9 or 8–10 indicate the degree of true inequality, some may view the remaining inequalities as intolerable, whereas others may consider them acceptable. This is much like a disagreement over whether a bottle of water is best described as half-full or half-empty: It depends on how you look at it. In other words, value judgments about the proper degree of economic inequality are involved. Even though this issue cannot be scientifically resolved, some points may help put it in better perspective.

One way is to look at the data from a historical perspective to determine whether there has been a trend toward more or less inequality over time. Data problems make it difficult to make very long-run comparisons, but Table 8–4 does show a substantial movement toward equality between 1929 and 1947: The ratio of top-quintile income to bottom-quintile income decreased from 15.5 to 1 to 8.5 to 1. This change is not attributable in any significant degree to government tax and transfer policies, which were still modest in 1947. It is not clear why this change occurred, but apparently something associated with the Depression and World War II produced a large change in the income distribution.

Since 1947, the Census Bureau's data have displayed no trend toward greater equality. This, however, is misleading for some of the reasons discussed earlier. When adjustments for in-kind transfers, taxes, and demographic factors are made, we find that the trend toward greater equality continued into the postwar period. Because of data and methodological problems, there is disagreement over whether the trend has been modest or substantial, but most agree that there has been movement toward equality. In contrast with the change between 1929 and 1947, the more recent changes have largely been the result of an expansion of government transfers and taxes.

A second perspective is provided by considering the mobility of families within the overall income distribution. It is possible for the income distribution, in the sense of the annual quintile shares, to remain unchanged year after year and yet for families to move around within that distribution over their lifetimes. How much people shift positions over time is important for evaluating the equity of the income distribution. Consider two economies that have exactly the same quintile income shares year after year. In one economy, the people in the bottom quintile remain there year after year, and likewise at the top: People are locked into their income positions. In the second economy, people move up and down within the distribution

Table 8–11 *Movements of Families Within the Income Distribution, 1971–1978 (percentages)*

Income Quintile, 1971	Income Quintiles, 1978				
	Lowest	*Second*	*Third*	*Fourth*	*Highest*
Lowest	55.5%	22.0%	9.5%	7.0%	6.0%
Second	21.5	34.5	21.5	13.5	9.0
Third	13.5	23.5	30.5	18.5	14.0
Fourth	6.0	15.0	25.5	31.5	22.0
Highest	3.5	4.5	14.0	29.5	48.5

Source: Mark Lilla, "Why the Income Distribution Is So Misleading," *Public Interest* (Fall 1984), Table II. Calculated from PSID sample.

over time; no one is rich or poor for very long, yet because people are changing places, the quintile shares do not change. Even though the annual income distributions for these two hypothetical economies can be identical, equality in any meaningful sense is clearly greater in the economy with greater mobility.

Our knowledge of the extent of income mobility has been greatly enhanced by an ongoing study, the Panel Study on Income Dynamics (PSID) at the University of Michigan, which has conducted yearly interviews since 1968 with the heads of a representative sample of 5,000 American families.[8] (The same families are interviewed year after year in order to track any changes in their economic status.) Among the study's findings has been the extent to which families move into and out of poverty.

Although the number of poor was relatively stable between 1969 and 1978, *only slightly more than half the people living in poverty in one year were found to be poor the next year.* Only slightly more than one third of those counted as poor in each year were poor for eight or more years of the ten-year period. Apparently, much poverty is short term and temporary, and persistent poverty is only a small portion of the total poverty count.

Considering the entire income distribution the PSID found great movements of families even over the relatively short period between 1971 and 1978. Table 8–11 summarizes the results by showing where the families who occupied each quintile in 1971 were in 1978. For example, the last row indicates that only 48.5 percent of the families who were in the highest quintile in 1971 were still there in 1978, and 3.5 percent of them had ac-

[8] Greg J. Duncan et al., *Years of Poverty, Years of Plenty: The Changing Fortunes of American Workers and Families* (Ann Arbor: Institute for Social Research, University of Michigan, 1984).

Table 8–12 _Income Distribution in an Experimental Economy_

| | | | Percentage Shares | |
Group	Sex	Lowest/Highest Incomes	Lowest 20%	Highest 20%
I	M	$ 720/$3,347	9.5	33.1
II	M	1,114/ 5,397	9.8	35.8
III	F	282/ 3,747	6.4	42.9
I & II	M	720/ 5,397	8.8	38.5
I, II, III	M&F	282/ 5,397	6.6	37.2

Source: Raymond C. Battalio, John H. Kagel, and Morgan Reynolds, "Income Distributions in Two Experimental Economies," _Journal of Political Economy,_ 85:1259 (Dec. 1977), Table 1. Copyright © 1977 by the University of Chicago.

tually fallen to the lowest quintile. From the first row we see that 44.5 percent of the families who were in the lowest quintile in 1971 were no longer there in 1978, and 6 percent had actually moved to the highest quintile. Mobility is even greater in the middle quintiles. Changes of these magnitudes over a seven-year period are surprising.[9]

One final bit of intriguing evidence regarding income distribution was generated by a Canadian experimental study intended, in part, to consider the effects of marijuana consumption. As part of the study, three groups of voluntary subjects were kept in a controlled environment in which they could earn money by weaving woolen belts. They were paid $2.50 for each belt they made and were free to work as long or as little as they wished. Careful records of what each subject did were maintained. When the subjects' earnings over the three-month duration of the experiment were tabulated as quintile shares, the results shown in Table 8–12 were obtained. The first three rows give the results for each group, two male and one female, and the last two rows combine the groups.

The remarkable thing about the experimental results is that in this controlled situation in which the only variables were willingness to work and skill at making belts, the income distribution is not greatly different from the actual distributions of national income. This is all the more surprising since the subjects were quite similar: All were 20 to 28 years old and at least high school graduates. This seems to imply that individual choices of how

[9] It should be noted that the issue of mobility is closely related to the difference between annual and lifetime income distributions. If there were no mobility over time, annual incomes and lifetime incomes would essentially be identical. In effect, this mobility is the reason why lifetime incomes are more equally distributed than annual incomes are, as the estimates in Table 8–10 suggest.

much to work and differences in productivity may be responsible for much of the differences we observe in real-world incomes.

This evidence may help put into perspective the questions of whether incomes are still too unequal and whether government should make a greater effort to alter the distribution of income even further. One final distinction relating to the issues should perhaps be mentioned. In deciding whether we want more equality, we should consider whether our primary goal is to help the impoverished or whether our goal goes beyond that and encompasses a desire to reduce income inequality among the remainder of the nonpoor population. Most Americans express support for government efforts to help the truly needy and yet oppose massive redistribution to equalize incomes.[10] There is no inconsistency in this position: Helping those unable to support themselves adequately is different from taxing your better-off neighbor to improve your already-nonpoor position.

Supplementary Readings

BLINDER, ALAN. "The Level and Distribution of Economic Well-Being," in Martin Feldstein, ed., *The American Economy in Transition.* Chicago: University of Chicago Press, 1980.

BREIT, WILLIAM. "Income Redistribution and Efficiency Norms," in H. M. Hochman and G. E. Peterson, eds., *Redistribution Through Public Choice.* New York: Columbia University Press, 1974.

DANZIGER, SHELDON, ROBERT HAVEMAN, and ROBERT PLOTNICK. "How Income Transfers Affect Work, Savings and the Income Distribution." *Journal of Economic Literature,* 19(3):975–1028 (Sept. 1981).

LILLA, MARK, "Why the Income Distribution Is So Misleading." *Public Interest* (Fall 1984).

MURRAY, CHARLES. *Losing Ground: American Social Policy, 1950–1980.* New York: Basic Books, 1984.

OKUN, ARTHUR. *Equality and Efficiency: The Big Trade-off.* Washington, D.C.: The Brookings Institution, 1975.

SMOLENSKY, EUGENE, and MORGAN REYNOLDS. *Public Expenditures, Taxes and the Distribution of Income.* New York: Academic Press, 1977.

TOBIN, JAMES. "On Limiting the Domain of Inequality." *Journal of Law and Economics,* 13(2):263–278 (Oct. 1970).

Review Questions and Problems

1. Is there one distribution of income that is the most efficient?

2. Explain the public good argument for redistribution. Does this argument offer any reason to favor government redistribution over private charity?

[10]Jennifer L. Hochschild, "Why the Dog Doesn't Bark: Income, Attitudes, and the Redistribution of Wealth," *Polity* (Summer 1979).

3. Travis thinks a competitive economy produces a "poor" distribution of income. Yet Travis does not favor any type of government transfer programs. Is Travis being inconsistent? Explain.

4. The United States is a welfare state. True or false? Explain.

5. What are the major in-kind transfer programs, and how much have they grown since the mid-1960s? Why is it important to take account of this growth when evaluating economic inequality and poverty?

6. Interpreted as a measure of economic inequality, what are the major defects in the widely used Census Bureau figures (as in Tables 8–3 and 8–4)?

7. What factors are relevant to determining whether there is too much inequality in the United States?

8. How would you expect the social security system to affect the Census Bureau's estimates of the income distribution? In other words, does it lead to a more or less equal distribution of money income? Why might this be misleading?

9. The official poverty rate was nearly the same in 1984 as in 1966. Does this demonstrate the failure of our welfare programs?

10. Rank the following households according to which has the higher real standard of living over whatever time period you consider relevant:
  a. A single graduate student majoring in engineering (and getting straight A's). Current money income $5,000, in the form of a fellowship.
  b. A middle-aged married couple, both working full time, with two children in college. Current money income $45,000.
  c. A young married couple, with one preschool-aged child, only the husband working. Current money income $20,000.
  d. An elderly retired couple who own their own home, receive $7,000 in real interest income (from $150,000 in financial assets) and $5,000 in social security benefits, for a total money income of $12,000.

chapter 9
Analyzing Income Transfer Programs

IN the last chapter, we emphasized certain factual dimensions that are relevant to the impact of redistributive tax and transfer policies. In this chapter, the emphasis shifts to the way economic theory can be used to evaluate the effects of various income transfer programs. Neither economics nor economists can objectively demonstrate that one type of income transfer policy is best or how much redistribution is desirable, because such conclusions must reflect in part value judgments concerning the effects of those policies. Economics can, however, determine some of the effects that most people would consider relevant to an evaluation of redistributive plans. For example, economic theory can be used to investigate how various income transfer programs will affect the work incentives of recipients; this is a question of considerable importance that is covered in detail in this chapter.

We begin with a discussion of a transfer program known as the negative income tax (NIT). At this time, the United States does not have a comprehensive NIT program. Nonetheless, the NIT program is probably the most important type of transfer program and one that should be understood fully, because several existing programs essentially operate like an NIT and because most welfare reform proposals build on certain features of the NIT. After a discussion of the NIT, we turn to an analysis of several other programs and issues, including the tradeoff between equality and efficiency.

The Negative Income Tax

The negative income tax, also known as a *guaranteed annual income,* is a program of cash transfers to families, with the size of the transfer depending on the family's income and size. The distinguishing characteristic of this program is that for families of a given size, the transfer is larger, the lower their income. The poorer the family is—at least in terms of its money income—the more assistance it will receive. Table 9–1 illustrates how a hy-

Table 9–1 *Hypothetical Negative Income Tax*

Pretransfer Income	Transfer	Total Disposable Income
$ 0	$5,000	$ 5,000
1,000	4,500	5,500
2,000	4,000	6,000
3,000	3,500	6,500
4,000	3,000	7,000
5,000	2,500	7,500
6,000	2,000	8,000
7,000	1,500	8,500
8,000	1,000	9,000
9,000	500	9,500
10,000	0	10,000

pothetical NIT transfer would vary with income for a four-person family. In this example, if a family's income (pretransfer income) is zero, the transfer will be $5,000. At higher income levels, the transfer is smaller, ultimately reaching zero at $10,000.

For families of a given size, an NIT can be concisely described by its three policy variables. First is the *income guarantee,* which is the transfer received by a family with no income of its own—$5,000 in Table 9–1. The *marginal tax rate* is the second policy variable. The marginal tax rate indicates how much the transfer payment declines as pretransfer income rises; because it identifies the rate at which benefits are reduced, it is sometimes called the *benefit reduction rate.* In our example the marginal tax rate is 50 percent because the transfer falls by $0.50 for each $1 that pretransfer income increases. The third policy variable is called the *breakeven income* and is the level of income at which the transfer falls to zero—$10,000 in Table 9–1.

An NIT can also be illustrated graphically. In Figure 9–1, which shows several alternative plans, pretransfer income is measured horizontally, and disposable income (pretransfer income plus the transfer) is measured vertically. The 45-degree line indicates the equality between pretransfer and disposable income in the absence of the NIT (and other transfers or taxes). It has a slope of unity, implying that an additional $1,000 in pretransfer income adds exactly $1,000 to disposable income. The line *RB* illustrates the relationship between pretransfer income and disposable income for the NIT just described. The transfer is the vertical distance between *RB* and the 45-degree line. The distance *OR* ($5,000) is the income guarantee and *BL* ($10,000) is the breakeven income. The slope of *RB* shows that disposable income rises by only $500 for each $1,000 in pretransfer income under this

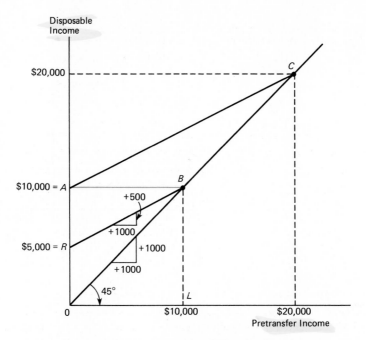

FIGURE 9–1   *Hypothetical NIT plans.*

NIT (because the transfer falls by $500). The marginal tax rate is equal to 1 minus the slope of the transfer schedule *RB*. The other NIT plans shown in Figure 9–1 are considered in the following section.

The transfer received at any income level below the breakeven income can be calculated from the following equation:

$$T = r(B - Y_i) \tag{1}$$

where T is the transfer payment, r is the marginal tax rate, B is the break-even income, and Y_i is the family's pretransfer income. If r is 50 percent, then we can say that the NIT fills 50 percent of the gap between the family's income and the breakeven income. The transfer would be equal to half the "poverty gap" if the breakeven income were set at the poverty line.

The conflict among competing goals

The three policy variables of the NIT are not independent of one another. If the income guarantee is set at $5,000 and the transfer falls by $0.50 for each $1 of pretransfer income (a marginal tax rate of 50 percent), then the transfer will fall to zero at $10,000. Thus, the breakeven income is already determined when the income guarantee and the marginal tax rate are set. Put concisely, *the income guarantee equals the marginal tax rate times the breakeven income;* in our example, $5,000 = 0.5 \times $10,000. This relationship is also apparent from equation (1), because if we set pretransfer income (Y_i) equal to zero, the transfer (the income guarantee) will be equal to rB. Therefore, specifying any two of the policy variables implicitly determines the third.

The relationship among the policy variables poses a difficult policy choice. First, consider the significance of each policy variable. The income guarantee will represent the total disposable incomes of families with no other income, so it is important that the guarantee be high enough to permit an adequate standard of living. A low marginal tax rate is desirable to preserve work incentives because a high rate means that disposable incomes will rise only slightly when earnings increase, which would give recipients little incentive to increase their earnings. (More on marginal tax rates and work incentives is presented later.) A low breakeven income appears desirable because it restricts transfers to those with low incomes and, at the same time, keeps the costs manageable (because those above the breakeven income must bear the cost of financing the NIT).

It seems desirable, then, to have a high income guarantee, a low marginal tax rate, and a low breakeven income. Because of the relationship among these policy variables, however, this is impossible: A "low" marginal tax rate multiplied by a "low" breakeven income cannot equal a "high" income guarantee. The difficult tradeoff among policy variables can be clarified by reference to Figure 9–1. Suppose the poverty line is $10,000 and the income guarantee is set at this level (0A) to ensure that no family is in poverty. If the breakeven income is also kept relatively low at $10,000, the entire transfer schedule will be AB. This implies, however, a marginal tax rate of 100 percent, because disposable income does not rise as pretransfer income increases between zero and $10,000. This plan would leave no financial incentive for low-income families to work because a family would have the same disposable income when it earned nothing as when it earned $10,000.

How can we avoid destroying the incentives that families have to support themselves? To make earning an income worthwhile, the marginal tax rate must be lowered to well below 100 percent. There are two distinctly different ways to do this, and each way has drawbacks. One method is to maintain the income guarantee at $10,000 and lower the marginal tax rate, but this implies a higher breakeven income. For example, if the tax rate were lowered to 50 percent, the breakeven income would have to be $20,000, and the entire relationship would be shown by line AC. This program would not completely destroy work incentives, but it would weaken the incentives of a much larger number of people—all those with incomes below $20,000— and many (in the $10,000 to $20,000 range) would then be subject to a marginal tax rate under an NIT that excluded them before. Perhaps more important, it would be exorbitantly costly, because it would involve transfers to about 35 percent of the American people!

A second way to lower the marginal tax rate is to hold the breakeven level of income at $10,000 and lower the income guarantee. With a 50 percent tax rate, an income guarantee of $5,000 is implied, and we are back with the schedule shown as *RB*. This method of reducing the tax rate would substantially improve the financial rewards from working for low-income families (as compared with the *AB* schedule, which removes all incentives), and it would reduce the cost of the program. However, these effects come at a cost: The level of assistance for low-income groups is reduced, and the income guarantee is now only half the poverty line.

There are harsh choices that must be made in setting the policy variables of an NIT. A high guarantee and a high tax rate (implying a low breakeven income) restrict transfers to those with low incomes but weaken incentives. A high income guarantee and a low tax rate (implying a high breakeven income) produce a large number of transfer recipients and impose a high cost that must be borne by those taxpayers remaining above the breakeven income. A high tax rate must be applied to the remaining taxpayers to finance such an NIT, and this would weaken their work incentives. Alternatively, a low income guarantee and a low or moderate tax (say, 50 percent) keep costs down and maintain work incentives, but the level of assistance will be modest.

The NIT and actual welfare programs

It is important to understand that many of the most important existing welfare programs are simply variations on the basic NIT theme. The food stamp program, for example, is nothing more than an NIT in which the subsidy is in the form of food coupons rather than cash. Refer back to Table 5–2 and note that the food stamp subsidy declines as the monthly income of the recipient rises. Such an inverse relationship between the transfer and income is the defining characteristic of the NIT. In the case of the food stamp program, the implicit marginal tax rate on net income is 30 percent.

Other welfare programs are also NITs in disguise. Aid to Families with Dependent Children (AFDC) is a program of cash assistance paid to female-headed households with children. Because the transfer is smaller when the family's income is higher, it is essentially an NIT restricted to a particular demographic group within the population. The nominal marginal tax rate has varied between 67 and 100 percent, but administrative practices often operate to make the effective rate somewhat lower. Supplemental Security Income is another NIT that is restricted to a particular demographic group, primarily the aged poor, but also the blind and disabled. Its marginal tax rate is 50 percent. Some housing subsidies, such as public housing, are also similar to the NIT combined with a restriction on housing consumption.

Even social security bears some resemblance to the NIT. Although the basic pension is not related solely to low income, the earnings test will reduce the pension if earnings exceed a certain amount, producing a marginal tax rate of 50 percent on earnings.

Therefore, studying an NIT is not merely an academic exercise; it helps us understand the workings of several existing welfare programs. For example, the food stamp program involves the same tradeoff among policy goals that was previously discussed. In one form or another, all actual and proposed welfare programs entail this same type of tradeoff. Careful attention is thus given to the NIT not only because in its "pure" form (benefits in cash available to all low-income families) it is a reform proposal that has been widely debated but also because in its several variations it is already an integral part of the U.S. welfare system.

Closing the poverty gap with the NIT

The eradication of poverty became a national goal in the 1960s, and at the time, there was much optimism concerning our ability to accomplish that goal. The Council of Economic Advisers expressed a common view in the 1964 *Economic Report of the President:*

> Conquest of poverty is well within our power. About $11 billion a year would bring all poor families up to the $3000 income level we have taken to be the minimum for a decent life. The majority of the nation could simply tax themselves enough to provide the necessary income supplements to their less fortunate citizens. The burden—one fifth of the annual defense budget, less than 2 percent of GNP—would certainly not be intolerable.

The $11 billion figure mentioned here refers to the size of the poverty gap; as explained in the last chapter, the poverty gap refers to how much the combined incomes of the poor fall short of their combined poverty lines. Expressed in 1984 dollars, the 1964 poverty gap would have been $36.8 billion. The actual poverty gap in 1984, with in-kind transfers counted as income using the Census Bureau's estimates, was $26.8 billion. Thus, in twenty years the real poverty gap had been cut by less than a third—from $36.8 billion to $26.8 billion. The increase in spending on welfare programs that produced this reduction, however, was much greater. Between 1965 and 1984, spending on welfare programs, narrowly defined, rose from $17.1 billion (in 1984 dollars) to $91.6 billion, or by $74.5 billion (Table 8–1). Apparently, an increase of $74.5 billion in welfare spending purchased only a $10 billion reduction in the aggregate poverty gap.

Why has it been so costly to reduce the poverty gap? There are a number of reasons. First, the population has grown and with it the size of the before-transfer poverty gap. Second, some of the welfare programs may not target their assistance on the neediest families. Third, as pointed out in the last chapter, demographic changes have increased the share of the population that would be poor without assistance. In addition to these reasons, however, there is another important factor that is related to the conflict among the competing goals of an NIT. (Although the expanded welfare spending between 1964 and 1984 did not explicitly take the form of an NIT, overall the welfare system is enough like an NIT that we can understand what is involved by treating the additional welfare spending as if it were an NIT.)

Figure 9–2 illustrates the relationships involved. The 45-degree line once again indicates the equality between pretransfer and disposable income. Note first that we cannot determine the size of the poverty gap from the graph: How large the poverty gap is depends on how many people are at each level of income, which is not shown. However, if we make the simplifying assumption that the population is uniformly distributed along the horizontal axis, that is, that the same number of people are at each pretransfer income level, then the areas in the graph are proportionate to the poverty gaps represented. For example, in the absence of any transfer programs, area *OAB* represents the poverty gap, and if we use a transfer schedule that cuts that area in half, the poverty gap will be cut in half under this simplifying assumption. Making this assumption will facilitate our discussion without distorting our conclusions in any significant way.

Now consider the 1964 poverty gap discussed by the Council of Economic Advisers. The Council seemed to suggest that by spending $11 billion ($36.8 billion in 1984 dollars) we could eliminate this poverty gap entirely. We already know why this is not correct: If each person is brought up exactly to his or her poverty line, we will be using an NIT with a 100 percent

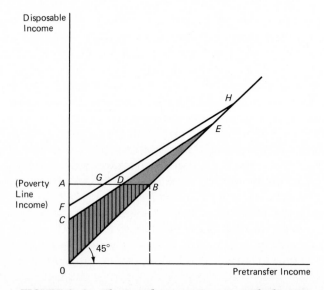

FIGURE 9–2   *Closing the poverty gap with the NIT.*

marginal tax rate, schedule *AB* in Figure 9–2. A 100 percent marginal tax rate would cause a major reduction in earnings by the recipients, so the spending required to raise each person to the poverty line would be much greater than $11 billion under this program. (The poverty gap is calculated by subtracting each person's income from the poverty line; when that income itself falls because recipients work less, the required spending rises.) Moreover, for other reasons, it is probably unwise to destroy all incentives to earn.

Therefore, actual policies generally use marginal tax rates lower than 100 percent. Suppose the NIT used is shown by schedule *CDE* in Figure 9–2. Let's compare the spending with the reduction in the poverty gap. As a first approximation, total spending is proportional to area *OCE,* but note that the poverty gap has been reduced by only part of this, that is, by *OCDB.* (The poverty gap has fallen from *OAB* to *CAD,* or by *OCDB.*) Part of the spending does not go to reduce the poverty gap. The spending shown as area *DBE* raises incomes above the poverty line, and this has no impact on the poverty gap, since the poverty gap measures only the shortfall of income from the poverty line.

For the schedule *CDE,* each dollar spent reduces the poverty gap by only *OCDB/OCE* (the reduction in the poverty gap divided by total spending), which is less than one. Even this, however, overstates the effectiveness of spending to reduce the poverty gap, because the disincentive effect of the policy is ignored. The extent to which recipients earn less will automatically increase the spending under schedule *CDE* (lower-income persons receive larger transfers) and increase the remaining poverty gap above *CAD* (since there will be more people with low incomes).

This analysis makes it clear why reducing the poverty gap by *X* dollars requires transfer spending to be much greater than *X* dollars. Not only is it necessary to make transfers to some people above the poverty line, but the disincentive effect of the policy also tends to increase the before-transfer poverty gap.

There is another important point that can be illustrated with Figure 9–2: the closer we come to eliminating the poverty gap, the more expensive it becomes to close the gap that remains. Ignoring the disincentive effect, we have seen that it cost *OCE* to reduce the poverty gap by *OCDB* using schedule *CDE.* The average cost per dollar reduction in the poverty gap is thus *OCE/OCDB.* The marginal cost of a further reduction, however, will be larger than this amount. Suppose we use transfer schedule *FGH* to further reduce the poverty gap by *CFGD.* The additional cost of this further reduction, again ignoring the disincentive effects, is *CFHE.* The marginal cost of this reduction in the poverty gap is therefore *CFHE/CFGD,* which, as can be seen, is much higher than the average cost of the initial reduction.

In 1984, the remaining poverty gap was $26.8 billion (in 1984 dollars). What the preceding discussion shows is that the cost of eliminating the remaining poverty gap is likely to be several times greater than $26.8 billion. Exactly how much greater is not known, since that depends on the magnitudes of the disincentive effects and the specific policies that are used. We do know now, however, that eliminating the poverty gap is much more difficult than the Council of Economic Advisers believed in 1964.

The NIT and Work Incentives

Much attention has been given to the question of how an NIT affects the work incentives of transfer recipients. In principle, any transfer program will affect work effort in two ways, first, through the "income effect" and, second, through the "substitution effect." By providing a transfer to families, the NIT makes them better off and more able to afford to work less. Having a higher real income, the recipient will increase his or her consumption of normal goods, including leisure or time spent not working. (Recall that an increase in leisure is the same as a reduction in work effort.) This is the income effect of the NIT, and it is related to the size of the transfer payment: The larger the transfer, the greater is the income effect favoring less work.

The NIT affects work incentives another way by reducing the net wage rate of recipients. Reducing the transfer received when a person earns more income has the effect of lowering the recipient's net hourly compensation for work. For example, if a person is employed at $4 per hour and works an additional hour, the extra $4 in earnings will reduce the NIT transfer by $2 (assuming a 50 percent marginal tax rate), so the net increase in income is only $2 for an extra hour's work. The net wage rate is cut in half by this NIT, so a person sacrifices less disposable income by working less. Thus, the relative price of consuming leisure—the sacrificed net income—has fallen from $4 per hour to $2 per hour, and this lower relative price encourages greater consumption of leisure (less work). This is the substitution effect of the NIT, and its magnitude is related to the marginal tax rate of the program. The higher the marginal tax rate, the lower is the net wage and the greater the incentive will be to substitute leisure for money earnings, because leisure will cost less in sacrificed money income.

Since both its income and substitution effects operate to reduce work effort, on balance the NIT can be expected to lead to a reduction in work effort. Some consequences of this diminished incentive to work are illustrated in Figure 9–3. An individual's budget line relating money income and leisure in the absence of the NIT is shown as YN, which has a slope of $4 per hour, the market wage rate of the individual. In the absence of any subsidy, equilibrium occurs at point E, with a money income of $0Y_1$ and leisure of $0L_1$ (so work effort is NL_1).

Introduction of the NIT shifts the budget line from YN to YRM. The break-even income, OB, is $10,000, and the income guarantee, MN, is $5,000. The

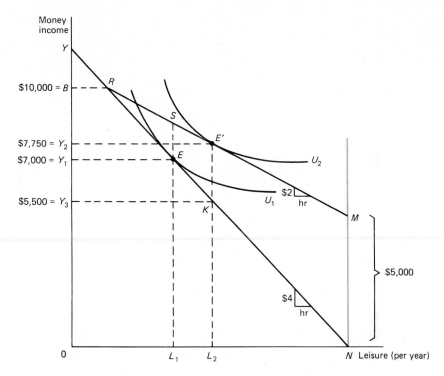

FIGURE 9–3 *Effect of an NIT on work effort.*

vertical distance between the subsidized portion of the budget line, *RM,* and the unsubsidized budget line equals the transfer. The transfer is larger when the individual works and earns less: It equals *MN* with zero work effort, *E'K* if work effort is *NL₂*, and *SE* if work effort is *NL₁*. The slope of the budget line has become flatter, $2 per hour, rather than the previous $4 per hour, reflecting the 50 percent marginal tax rate that cuts the net rate of pay in half. Note that the rotation of the budget line at point *R* lowers the price of leisure: Less money income must be sacrificed when more leisure time is consumed.

Confronted with the *YRM* budget line, the individual's new equilibrium position occurs at point *E',* with total money income of *OY₂* (or $7,750, equal to the sum of earnings of $5,500 and the transfer of $2,250), and leisure of *OL₂*. The reduction in work effort from *NL₁* to *NL₂* shows the total effect of the NIT on work effort—the combined influence of the income effect and the substitution effect. (These effects are discussed separately later.)

Figure 9–3 also illustrates several other significant points. First, note that the cost of the program depends on the work response of the recipient. Had the individual continued to work *NL₁*, the transfer would have been *SE,*

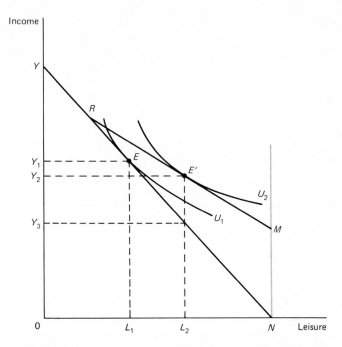

FIGURE 9–4   *An NIT may reduce total money income.*

or $1,500, but because of the reduction in earnings from $7,000 to $5,500, the transfer rises to $2,250. Second, the incomes of recipients do not rise by the amount of the transfer: In this example, the recipient's income increases from $7,000 to only $7,750, although the transfer is $2,250. Third, if the transfer is given in kind, the money incomes of recipients—which is all the Census Bureau normally counts—actually falls. In Figure 9–3, if the $2,250 transfer takes the form of food stamps and housing assistance, the individual's money income will fall from $7,000 to $5,500. This means that it is possible for an in-kind transfer actually to increase the number of persons counted as poor at the same time that it raises their standards of living.

Even when given as cash, the NIT transfer can lead to a reduction in the recipient's total money income if the reduction in work effort is large enough. Figure 9–4, which illustrates this possibility, shows that total money income falls from OY_1 to OY_2 because the reduction in earnings, Y_1Y_3, is greater than the transfer received, Y_2Y_3. Even so, the recipient ends up with a higher real income (on a higher indifference curve) as a result of the transfer. Most scholars believe that work effort will rarely fall enough to reduce total money income, but it is a theoretical possibility.

Evidence on work incentives

Economic theory predicts that there will be some reduction in work incentives from an NIT, but it does not allow us to predict its size. A growing number of empirical studies have been designed to estimate its quantitative impact and its relationship to the policy variables. The empirical evidence is of two types: (1) studies of the reactions of low-income families to existing welfare programs similar in nature to the NIT and (2) studies of the results of experimental NIT programs funded by the government.

In reviewing the nonexperimental evidence, Irwin Garfinkel concluded that the evidence supports the view that work effort will fall under an NIT. However, there is no consensus about the size of the reduction. For an NIT with a moderate income guarantee and a 50 percent marginal tax rate, the estimated reduction in work effort ranges from 3 percent to 40 percent for prime-aged married men (the group in which the disincentive problem is expected to be the smallest).[1] Estimated reductions for other demographic groups are generally somewhat larger.

Perhaps the most fascinating evidence on work incentives is based on the results of actual experiments in which random samples of low-income families were granted NIT transfers for several years and their work responses were recorded. The first of four experiments, carried out in New Jersey and Pennsylvania, was completed in 1972, whereas the last, and largest, experiment was carried out in Seattle and Denver and ended in 1978. The experiments utilized a variety of NIT plans, but on the average the income guarantee was set at the poverty level, and the marginal tax rate was set at 50 percent.

These experiments have not, however, resolved the question of just how large the labor supply effects of an NIT would be. Responses in the four experiments varied somewhat, and there are statistical problems in evaluating the results. For husbands, labor supply reductions (in hours of work) ranged between 1 and 8 percent; for wives, labor supply varied from an increase of 1 percent to a reduction of 55 percent; and for female family heads, the reductions varied from 12 to 26 percent.[2]

Among these experiments, attention has centered on the Seattle-Denver sites because this experiment involved more participants than the other three programs combined and because some participants were enrolled in a 5-year program, in contrast with the 3-year duration for the other experiments. For the Seattle-Denver experiment as a whole, Robins and West es-

[1] Irwin Garfinkel, "Income Transfer Programs and Work Effort: A Review," *Studies in Public Welfare,* U.S. Congress, Joint Economic Committee. Subcommittee on Fiscal Policy, Paper No. 13, 93rd Congress, 2nd Session (Washington, D.C.: U.S. Government Printing Office, Feb. 1974), pp. 11–32.

[2] Robert Moffit, "The Labor-Supply Effects of an NIT: The Findings of the Income Maintenance Experiments," unpublished paper, Rutgers University, Mar. 1980.

timated labor supply reductions of 7, 25, and 15 percent for husbands, wives, and female family heads, respectively.[3] For participants in the 5-year experiment, however, the response in the third year involved reductions of 13 percent, 21 percent, and 23 percent for husbands, wives, and female family heads, respectively. These results suggest that a permanent program might produce larger labor supply responses than the 3-year experiments implied.

As this brief review of the evidence makes clear, we are not yet in a position to make definitive statements about the actual size of the work disincentive effects of NIT programs.

The welfare cost of the NIT

By artificially lowering the net wage rates of the transfer recipients, the NIT will distort decisions on work effort. Consider the example of an NIT recipient, Cleo, who can earn $4 an hour but whose net wage rate is $2 under the NIT. Cleo will give up leisure (supply labor) as long as she considers an extra $2 in income worth more than the sacrificed value of an hour of leisure time. At the equilibrium level of work effort under the NIT, leisure would have a value of $2 per hour, and Cleo would be willing to work an additional hour if she received anything more than $2 in compensation.[4] Because her market wage rate is $4, her employer would be willing to pay $4 for additional hours of work. The marginal benefit from additional work—$4 per hour—is greater than the marginal cost—$2 worth of leisure given up—so there are efficiency gains from working longer hours. Yet under the NIT Cleo will not work longer hours because her *net* wage rate is $2 per hour because of the reduction in the transfer payment that occurs when she earns the additional $4. Cleo will be led to work too little because the marginal *private* benefit from working that she receives—$2 per hour—is less than the marginal *social* benefit of her labor services—$4 per hour.

Because the marginal tax rate makes market and net wage rates diverge, the NIT produces a welfare cost. This is illustrated in Figure 9–5, in which the equilibrium under the NIT occurs at E' on the subsidized budget line *YRM.* To see the loss in potential welfare, imagine that the government gives Cleo an unrestricted, or lump-sum, cash transfer instead of the NIT transfer. Because the cost of the NIT is $E'K$, a lump-sum transfer of equal cost will produce the budget line Y_2N_2 parallel to the original *YN* budget line, implying that the transfer is not reduced when more is earned; hence the net

---

[3] Phillip K. Robins and Richard W. West, "Program Participation and Labor Supply Response," *Journal of Human Resources,* 15:499–523 (Fall 1980). The entire issue of the journal is devoted to analysis of the Seattle-Denver experiment.

[4] In other words, in equilibrium the marginal rate of subsitution between income and leisure is equal to the net wage rate. This is shown by the tangency in Figure 9–2 between the recipient's indifference curve and budget line.

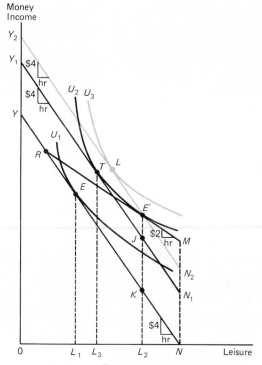

FIGURE 9–5 *Welfare cost of an NIT.*

wage rate is unaffected by the lump-sum transfer. This budget line permits Cleo to reach a higher indifference curve, U_3, at point L. Thus, Cleo can be made better off at no additional cost to the taxpayers.

Alternatively, a smaller lump-sum transfer can make the recipient equally well off as under the NIT. With a lump-sum transfer of YY_1 (producing the budget line Y_1N_1), Cleo can reach U_2 at point T, the same level of welfare as under the NIT. Note that the cost of this lump-sum transfer is only JK, or $E'J$ less than the NIT. *$E'J$ is a measure of the welfare cost of the NIT:* It shows that the NIT costs $E'J$ more than is necessary to permit the recipient to attain the level of welfare indicated by U_2.

We have seen that the recipient can be made better off with a lump-sum transfer than with an NIT of the same cost or (what amounts to the same thing) equally well off at a lower cost. This happens because the NIT lowers the net wage and encourages the recipient to consume too much leisure (work too little). This distortion of the NIT is caused by the marginal tax rate that induces the recipient to substitute leisure for money income.

Figure 9–5 can also be used to show the income and substitution effects of the NIT. The income effect is the increase in leisure from $0L_1$ to $0L_3$ that results from giving the recipient enough income to attain U_2, but without affecting the net wage rate received. The substitution effect is the increase in leisure from $0L_3$ to $0L_2$ that results from the lower net wage rate when the recipient is kept on the same indifference curve, U_2. The welfare cost of the NIT is due to the substitution effect alone: $0L_2$–$0L_3$ measures the over-consumption of leisure. The income effect of the transfer is not a distortion; it is simply the increase in consumption of leisure—and other normal goods—that results from a pure, nondistorting change in the income distribution. Economists emphasize the importance of the size of the marginal tax rate of the NIT because it lowers the net wage rate and causes the uneconomic substitution of leisure for money income.

If the welfare cost of the NIT (and other transfer programs as well) can be avoided by using lump-sum transfers, why don't economists favor such transfers? That is a reasonable question, and the answer involves under-standing the nature of a lump-sum transfer more precisely. A lump-sum transfer is one in which the amount transferred does not depend on in-come, consumption, work effort, education, family size, or any other eco-nomic characteristics under the control of the recipient. It is simply fixed in amount, totally independent of any individual's actions. By its very nature, it is impossible to restrict a lump-sum transfer to those with low incomes because, by definition, it is unrelated to any of the characteristics associated with being poor. If given only to people with low incomes, it would not be a lump-sum transfer because it would give incentive to others to reduce their incomes to become eligible for the transfer and would thereby create a distortion. Thus, in the interest of *equitably* relating assistance to need, we may choose to use transfers related to income despite the efficiency cost.

For this reason, lump-sum transfers and taxes are not generally con-sidered practical policy tools. Nonetheless, they serve a highly useful role in analysis as a conceptual benchmark against which to view the allocative effects of real-world taxes and transfers. They provide a means of under-standing how other policies may distort the allocation of resources and the factors that determine the size of these distortions. In the present context, even though the NIT produces a welfare cost, that cost may be smaller than those of alternative practical policies. This is precisely what many econo-mists believe.

The cumulative marginal tax rate problem

The key to many of the effects of the NIT, especially those relating to pro-ductive incentives, is the marginal tax rate of the program. More precisely, *what matters is the effective, or combined, marginal tax rate that results from all transfer and tax programs that affect a household*. As we have seen, the United States already has several welfare programs similar to the NIT, and so many low-income households receive benefits from more than

Table 9–2   *Estimated Marginal Tax Rates, 1976 (percentages)*

Income Decile	MTR of Transfer System	MTR of Tax System	Effective MTR
1 & 2	37.1%	14.9%	52.0%
3	36.3	26.2	56.5
4	27.1	27.2	54.3
5	15.4	30.3	45.7
6	10.4	31.3	41.7
7	4.5	33.0	37.5
8	0.7	35.5	36.2
9	0.6	40.8	41.4
10	0.0	45.8	45.8

Source: Edgar K. Browning and William R. Johnson, "Taxation and the Cost of National Health Insurance," in Mark Pauly, ed., *National Health Insurance* (Washington, D.C.: American Enterprise Institute, 1980), Table 4.

one program and also pay one or more taxes. The result is often a high effective marginal tax rate, even though the tax rate of each program separately may be modest.

Consider a family that receives only food stamps, with its marginal tax rate of 30 percent. This family is also subject to the social security payroll tax of about 14 percent on its earnings. Thus, an additional $100 in income reduces the food stamp subsidy by $30 and increases the social security tax by $14. Disposable income rises by on $56 when $100 more is earned, so the combined marginal tax rate is 44 percent.[5] In addition, state and local income and sales taxes may also be applicable, and these are likely to raise the effective rate above 45 percent.

When a family receives benefits from more than one program, the situation is aggravated. If the family just described receives a housing subsidy where benefits fall by $25 for each $100 of earnings, then its effective marginal tax rate will be about 70 percent. A family receiving aid under the AFDC program, as well as food stamps and housing assistance, is faced with a tax rate of 80 percent or more.

Table 9–2 presents estimates of the effective marginal tax rates by deciles of households (each decile contains 10 percent of all households) that resulted from the combined impact of transfer and tax policies in 1976. For the reasons just mentioned, the marginal tax rates placed on low-income households by current programs are already quite high: The bottom 40 percent of households confront marginal tax rates in excess of 50 percent. Most

[5] Actually, the effective marginal tax rate is not exactly equal to the sum of the separate rates because the income base is defined differently under the separate programs.

of this 50+ percent rate is the result of transfer programs that reduce benefits as income rises. At higher income levels, transfers are predictably less important, and taxes become more important in determining the effective marginal tax rates. These estimates are averages for all households in each income class. For low-income households in particular, there is a wide variation among households, since some low-income households receive no welfare benefits, whereas others receive assistance from several different programs.

Although the coverage of the present welfare system is uneven and overlapping, Table 9–2 suggests that the United States already has, on the average, a sizable NIT program in practice if not in name. Thus, our emphasis on the NIT is not misplaced, even if the United States never adopts an outright, comprehensive NIT program. The best way to obtain an overview of how the current welfare system operates is to recognize that, taken together, the various existing welfare programs function much like an NIT.

Wage Rate Subsidy

Can income be redistributed to low-income families without undermining their incentives to work? One approach that may accomplish this is to subsidize wage rates, using a wage rate subsidy, or WRS. The WRS transfers income by increasing the net wage rates received by workers. Table 9–3 illustrates how this program would work. The transfers take the form of supplements to the hourly wage rates, with larger supplements received by workers with lower wage rates. If, for example, a worker is paid $1.50 an hour by his or her employer, the government adds a subsidy of $1.75 per hour, bringing the net wage up to $3.25. At higher market wage rates the

Table 9–3 *Hypothetical Wage Rate Subsidy*

Market Wage Rate	Subsidy	Net Wage Rate
$1.50	$1.75	$3.25
2.00	1.50	3.50
2.50	1.25	3.75
3.00	1.00	4.00
3.50	0.75	4.25
4.00	0.50	4.50
4.50	0.25	4.75
5.00	0	5.00

subsidy per hour is reduced, but not by the full amount of the increment in the market wage. This approach ensures that workers with higher market wage rates also receive higher net wage rates, which in turn gives the recipients an incentive to increase their market wage rates.

Under a WRS, recipients can receive larger total transfers by working longer hours. There is no incentive for them to stop working altogether because the transfer is zero when hours worked are zero. It does not necessarily follow, however, that recipients will work longer hours than if they receive no transfer. The WRS increases the recipient's net wage rate, but whether a higher wage rate leads to more or less work effort depends on whether the recipient's labor supply curve is upward sloping or backward bending. The net effect on work effort is indeterminate, because the income effect of the subsidy favors less work effort but the substitution effect encourages more work.

Although a WRS may either increase or reduce work effort when compared with no transfer at all, the more relevant question is how it affects work incentives when compared with alternative transfer programs such as the NIT. In comparison with the NIT and similar programs, the WRS promotes greater work effort. Because both transfers have income effects that favor less work effort, the difference between the programs lies in their substitution effects. Because the substitution effect of the NIT's lower net wage rate favors less work and the substitution effect of the WRS's higher net wage favors more work, the net effect of the wage rate subsidy is to lead to greater work effort than the NIT does.

This means that for a given cost to taxpayers, a WRS will lead to a higher money income for recipients than will an NIT, because total transfers are the same but earnings will be higher under the wage subsidy program. This does not imply, however, that recipients will be better off under the WRS. Although they will have more money income, they will be working longer hours (consuming less leisure), so the net effect on welfare is uncertain. Whether the taxpayers who would finance the WRS would prefer the work incentive effects of the WRS depends on whether they are more interested in raising the money incomes of the poor or their leisure. Judging from most discussions of poverty—always expressed as a lack of money income alone—and the importance attached to the work incentives question, the general public would probably prefer a welfare program that encourages more work effort.

Other factors, however, should be considered in evaluating the WRS. One important problem is that unlike the NIT, the WRS will not always concentrate transfers on the poorest families. People with low wage rates receive large subsidies, but low wage rates do not necessarily imply low family incomes. If a husband works full time at a wage of $5.00 an hour and his wife works at $3.00 an hour, their combined salaries would be $16,000 a year—far above the poverty line. Yet the wife would receive $2,000 a year from the plan described in Table 9–3 (2,000 hours at a subsidy of $1 an hour). Similarly, younger people working part time at low wages would be subsidized, regardless of the incomes of their parents. In fact, among workers receiving wage rates close to the minimum wage, fully half belong to families with incomes in the upper half of the income distribution. Thus, it would be difficult for a WRS to confine benefits to those with low family incomes. For this reason, the distributional effects of a WRS are not as favorable as those of some alternative programs.

Another problem concerns the administration of a wage rate subsidy. Because the total transfer that a person receives depends on both the wage rate and the hours worked, accurate information on these variables is needed. For many, this information would be difficult to obtain. Waiters, or self-employed persons such as the operators of small farms, are typical of people who do not work at a fixed hourly wage rate. In addition, how could we deal with two neighbors who swap chores and pay each other $0.25 an hour?

Perhaps the most important problem with the WRS is its inability to provide for people who are unable to work. There is no income guarantee in the program; yet clearly some provision must be made for those who cannot work or perhaps can work only part time. This suggests the necessity of a companion program to deal with these cases. If people could easily be categorized as "able to work" and "unable to work," there would be no problem. The WRS could be used for those "able to work" and an NIT or something similar for those "unable to work." Unfortunately, people are not so easily categorized, and there would be numerous in-between cases. Consequently, there would be some difficult problems in coordinating a companion program with a wage rate subsidy.

Although a wage rate subsidy would be more favorable to work incentives than an NIT, it seems inferior in a number of other respects. Obviously, it is not easy to formulate a welfare program with no defects!

Public Employment Programs

In recent years there has been some interest in using some form of public sector employment program in combination with cash and/or in-kind assistance as a strategy for welfare reform. (President Jimmy Carter's 1977 proposal for welfare reform placed great emphasis on a public jobs program.) The rationale for this approach is based on the premise that it is possible to classify all needy families into two groups: Those who cannot (or should not be expected to) work and those who are able to work but cannot earn an adequate income. For those who are unable to work, a cash assistance program with a high income guarantee *and a high marginal tax rate* could be used without reducing work incentives for those able to work (because they would be ineligible for the cash assistance program). For those who can work and are unable to find suitable employment in the private sector, a government job at a fixed wage rate would be provided. Thus, those who are needy but are able to work would be required to do so. At first glance, this dual program approach holds out the promise of avoiding the difficult tradeoff involved when a single cash assistance program must be designed to apply to all low-income groups.

Let's consider a hypothetical public employment program that is typical of recent proposals. Each eligible family is to be guaranteed *one* public sector job. To be eligible, the family's other income (exclusive of wages on the guaranteed job) must fall below its poverty line (or other specified income level). The wage rate for the guaranteed job would be $4.50 per hour for 40 hours per week, or $9,000 per year for full-time employment. Other poor families would be ineligible for the jobs program because they would not be expected to work, such as the elderly or female-headed families with children. These groups would be eligible for cash assistance, as they are now.

A basic problem with a program of this nature is the need to classify individuals and families into three mutually exclusive groups: Those eligible for cash assistance (who need not work); those eligible for a public sector job (who must work); and those ineligible for either welfare program. Can families be classified in these three groups fairly? It is difficult to see how a classification scheme that permits only three alternatives can be fair. There is enormous variation among people in terms of family size, age, other sources of income, health, productivity, work-leisure preferences, and so on. Can having the same job guarantee for all those considered eligible possibly be fair?

Consider a few examples. Is it fair for a family with one child to have the same job guarantee as a family with five children? Is it fair to exclude childless couples? Is it fair that an elderly couple over 65 can receive cash assistance without working and a poor couple aged 60 is ineligible for any assistance at all? Is it fair that a family whose other income falls $1 short of its poverty line receives the same job guarantee (so its total income will be far above the poverty line) as a family with no income at all?

These examples are not meant to suggest that such problems could not be satisfactorily resolved, but they are indicative of the range of issues that must be faced in implementing such a program. The basic issue here is whether the distribution of benefits under a program of guaranteed public jobs can meet minimum standards of equity. Actually, in practice it would be impossible to ascertain the distribution of benefits. For a participant in the program, it is necessary to distinguish between the part of the worker's total pay that is payment for services rendered and the part that is welfare assistance. For example, a person's productivity in whatever public job is assigned may justify a salary of $6,000 a year, but the participant will receive $9,000. In this case, $3,000 of the total pay should be viewed as a welfare grant and the remaining $6,000 as unsubsidized earnings.

Clearly, people of widely differing productivities will be participating in a public jobs program. The labor services of some will be worth $4,000, some $6,000, and others $8,000; yet all will receive $9,000 a year for full-time work. This means that the welfare component of the recipient's pay is reduced by a dollar for every dollar increase in productivity. For those who participate and work full time, the jobs program is akin to an NIT with an income guarantee of $9,000 and a marginal tax rate of 100 percent, reducing the benefits (the welfare component of the pay) by a dollar for each dollar increase in real earnings. If this type of subsidy were paid explicitly, it would be viewed by most people as highly inequitable.

Turning now from the issue of equity to the issue of incentives, it is frequently held that a public employment program avoids the work disincentive effects associated with a program of cash transfers. In a trivial sense this is true: A person can receive the welfare component of his or her public sector pay only by working and so gains nothing by refusing to work. The incentives issue in welfare reform, however, is far more involved, and a jobs program produces a number of undesirable incentive effects of its own. Let us consider four.

First, the program has a strong work disincentive if it is available only to families whose other income falls below some fixed level. Consider a family of three in which the husband earns $9,000 and the wife $5,000. Because their $14,000 joint income is above their $7,000 poverty line, they are currently ineligible for a public job. If, however, the husband works less and earns only $6,999, and the wife quits her job, their total income will fall below their poverty line, and they will become eligible for a public sector job. If the wife takes the guaranteed job, the family's total income will be $15,999, a considerable increase from the initial $14,000. In this case, the husband has a strong incentive not to earn over $7,000 so that his wife will be eligible for the public sector job. (This example also shows how many people who are not needy can receive benefits under a public employment program.)

Second, there is little incentive for workers to put forth their best efforts. If jobs are guaranteed at a fixed rate of pay, why should workers strive to do a good job? They will get paid even if they slack off. Would it be politically possible to discharge poor but unproductive or uncooperative workers from their "guaranteed" jobs?

Third, administrators in the public jobs program are likely to assign workers to the wrong jobs. Workers should be assigned the tasks for which they are relatively the most productive if the total output of the public jobs program is to be as large as possible. Administrators have little incentive to do this, and political pressures ("No one should have to do menial or dead-end work") make efficient assignment of jobs within the program unlikely.

Fourth, the program may induce many workers to seek jobs in the public sector although they are more productive in the private sector. A person who can earn $8,000 in a private job has an incentive to take a public sector job paying $9,000, even if his or her productivity in the public job is only $4,000. In this case, there would be a net loss in total output of $4,000: $8,000 in sacrificed private sector output with only a $4,000 increase in public sector output. Only if the labor services of all participating workers were more valuable in public sector jobs than in private jobs could this loss be avoided, and this is certain to be untrue (especially in view of the disincentives mentioned previously).

Now consider the cost to taxpayers of providing assistance to low-income families by financing public jobs. Consider Egbert, a worker whose annual labor services are worth $6,000 in either a private or a public job. Egbert would then prefer to work in the public sector at a salary of $9,000, $3,000 of which is a welfare subsidy and the remaining $6,000 a payment for labor services. What is the cost to taxpayers of increasing Egbert's income by $3,000 above his earnings in the absence of the program? The cost to taxpayers of financing the $9,000 job is greater than $9,000 because of administrative and overhead costs. It is not clear how large a cost this would be, but a figure of 15 percent of the wage cost would probably not be too large to assume. (President Carter's proposal allowed for a cost of nearly 30 percent of the wage cost.) If this is the case, the administrative cost of a $9,000 job is $1,350, so the burden on taxpayers will be $10,350. Moreover, the administrative cost should be compared with the welfare assistance component of the $9,000. In our example, Egbert's actual welfare assistance is $3,000, and to provide that aid necessitates an administrative cost of $1,350, or more than 40 percent of the aid transferred. If these figures are representative, they suggest that the administrative cost of supplying welfare assistance through a jobs program is quite high. (It has been estimated that cash assistance programs can generally be administered at a cost of less than 5 percent of the welfare assistance that reaches the recipients.)

It seems clear that a public employment program would be quite inequitable and inefficient when considered as a welfare program. The jobs approach involves using one type of policy that has impacts on the attainment of three different government goals: (1) welfare assistance to the poor, (2) an efficient allocation of resources between the public and private sectors, and (3) a high level of aggregate employment. Jumbling these functions together produces unavoidable conflicts. For example, suppose that it is desired to reduce employment in the public sector (for efficiency reasons) and at the same time to increase welfare assistance. Under a jobs approach, this cannot be accomplished: Reducing public sector employment requires lowering the guaranteed public sector wage, but that in turn would reduce welfare assistance. In contrast, using a cash assistance program and continuing to pay public employees in accordance with their productivities avoid this type of dilemma.

Despite the defects of a public employment program, it does eliminate the possibility of gross malingering. That, in addition to the fact that its harmful effects—its inefficiencies and inequities—are well hidden, difficult to explain, and hard to document, may help explain its political appeal. Moreover, a well-designed program might avoid some of the difficulties mentioned.

Cash Versus In-Kind Transfers

A basic question in the design of a system to redistribute income is whether the transfers should be in cash that can be spent as the recipient wishes or in the form of a subsidy to particular goods and services. As emphasized in the last chapter, subsidies of particular goods and services—in-kind transfers—have grown significantly in recent years. Today, there are large subsidies to education (and job training), medical care, food, and housing. Other goods consumed by low-income households receiving somewhat smaller subsidies are child care centers, legal aid, transportation, and energy. Given the magnitude of in-kind programs, it is important to consider whether there is a more convincing rationale for this type of program than for a program of cash transfers.

Traditionally, economists have argued that cash transfers are preferable because the recipients will be better off if they can spend the subsidy as they wish.[6] We have already explained why recipients would prefer a cash transfer in connection with food stamps, but the same principles apply to other in-kind transfers as well. Proponents of in-kind transfers, therefore, must argue that there are other factors besides the well-being of recipients that need to be taken into account.

Two general arguments have been offered in support of in-kind programs. One is paternalistic and holds that if given cash, the poor would spend too much of it on nonessential goods like liquor and cigarettes and too little on medical care, food, housing, or education. This argument rejects the well-being of recipients, as judged by the recipients themselves, as a criterion for evaluating transfer policies. A second argument is based on the belief that consumption of particular goods by the poor generates external benefits for the taxpayers: "Taxpayers don't want to give the poor money; they want to give them housing (or medical care, education, etc.)." Although intangible, such a preference by taxpayers means they derive benefits from expanded consumption of particular goods by the poor. As we saw earlier, when external benefits accompany the consumption of particu-

---

[6]This argument does not mean that cash transfers like the NIT have no welfare cost. However, it is generally believed that the welfare cost of an NIT—which distorts labor supply but not the consumption mix—will be smaller than that of an in-kind transfer, which generally distorts labor supply as well as the consumption mix.

CASH VERSUS IN-KIND TRANSFERS

lar goods, the result is inefficiency in the form of underconsumption of that good (and overconsumption of other goods). A cash transfer would not achieve an efficient allocation because the recipient would consume a quantity where the individual's marginal benefit would equal the price. Efficiency would require the recipient to consume at a level where the individual's marginal benefit plus the marginal external benefit of other people would equal the price of the product. An in-kind transfer is potentially more efficient than a cash transfer in this setting because it can be designed to lead to greater consumption than the recipient would choose if he or she were free to spend the transfer independently.

Both of these arguments have in common the contention that the poor spend too little of their incomes on some goods and (therefore) too much on other goods. Proponents of these positions, however, have failed to present any evidence concerning what is considered the appropriate level of consumption of various goods or whether actual in-kind programs work to achieve desired consumption levels. Consequently, a careful appraisal of these arguments is difficult. Nonetheless, data concerning consumption patterns by income level cast some doubt on the significance of these views. Table 9–4 shows how families at different income levels spent their incomes in 1960. For our purpose, 1960 is a good year to use because in-kind programs were not prevalent then, and the expenditure patterns may be taken to reflect the actual preferences of families.

Note that families with incomes below $3,000 (about 20 percent of all families in 1960) devoted 72 percent of their budgets to food, housing, and

Table 9–4 *Percentage Distribution of Family Expenditures by Income Class, 1960*

| Category | Money Income Class | | |
	Under $3,000	$5,000 to $7,499	$15,000 and over
Food	29.4%	24.7%	20.1%
Housing*	34.4	29.1	29.1
Transportation	8.6	16.0	14.9
Medical Care	8.5	6.6	6.1
Clothing	7.1	9.9	12.2
Recreation	2.3	3.8	4.7
Tobacco	2.1	2.0	1.1
Alcohol	1.0	1.5	1.9
Other	6.6	6.4	9.9

*Includes shelter and other home-related expenses.
Source: *Consumer Expenditures and Income: Survey Guidelines,* Bureau of Labor Statistics Bulletin 1684 (1971), pp. 104–105, Table B-17.

medical care. If clothing and transportation are included, the percentage rises to 88 percent. These figures lend little support to the contention that low-income families indulge in frivolous consumption. In fact, higher-income groups devote smaller percentages to food, housing, and medical care—60.4 percent in the middle-income range and 55.3 percent at the highest income level. Middle- and high-income groups spend a larger portion of their budgets on alcohol, tobacco, and recreation than the lower-income group does.

These figures do not, however, necessarily dispose of the arguments for in-kind transfers. They do suggest that the poor would not in any flagrant way "waste" the taxpayers' money if they were given cash. It may be that popular support for in-kind programs reflects an inappropriate generalization based on a few notorious and atypical cases in which cash transfers were used in ways that offended the average taxpayer.

There are still other factors to consider. Although the externality and paternalistic arguments imply that *some* type of in-kind transfer may lead to a better consumption pattern for the poor than a cash transfer would, they do not imply that *any* in-kind transfer is better. For example, the evidence that education and housing subsidies have reduced consumption of the subsidized goods for some recipients raises questions about the effectiveness of actual programs. In addition, administrative costs are generally higher for in-kind programs. Administrative costs for the food stamp and public housing programs have been estimated at 11 and 7 percent, respectively, in comparison with an estimated administrative cost for an NIT of about 5 percent. If these figures are representative of cash and in-kind programs, they mean that cash transfers can provide 2 to 6 percent more resources to the recipients at no additional cost to taxpayers. Once this difference in administrative costs is recognized, there is no longer any theoretical presumption that an in-kind transfer can be more efficient than a cash transfer, even granting that external benefits exist. Instead it becomes an empirical question of whether the efficiency gain from a better consumption pattern, if any, is larger than the higher administrative costs involved.

Perhaps the most important problem with arguments for in-kind programs is that they must be invoked to defend subsidies for a large number of different goods. Recall that arguments for in-kind transfers hold that poor people would spend too little on some goods and too much on others if given cash. Because the poor spend 88 percent on necessities anyway, there is little scope for significantly increasing this share by using several in-kind programs. At best, the effect of in-kind programs (in comparison to cash transfers) is to increase the portion of any given budget that is devoted to selected goods, such as food, housing, and medical care, and to reduce the portion devoted to other goods. When most of the budget is already spent on the selected goods, there is little room for increasing the share of these goods in the budget, and the maximum potential advantage of subsidizing selected goods is small. Since most of a cash transfer would be spent on necessities anyway, why use several in-kind programs that would probably have a combined effect that differs very little from a cash transfer that lets the recipient spend the transfer as he or she wishes? Thus, arguments for in-kind transfers are not so convincing when they are used to defend in-kind transfers for several goods that would normally occupy a major share of recipients' budgets.

Redistribution: How It Affects Marginal Tax Rates

As we have seen, most existing welfare programs relate the size of the transfer to the recipient's level of income, just like the NIT. Reducing the transfer as income rises ensures that the largest transfers go to the neediest families, but at the same time this relationship results in marginal tax rates on the recipients—and these marginal tax rates are largely responsible for the adverse incentive effects of the programs. In most cases, redistributing income through tax and transfer policies results in marginal tax rates for both transfer recipients and taxpayers who finance the transfers. What is far from obvious, however, is how sensitive the level of marginal tax rates is to the amount of redistribution. As it turns out, *redistributive programs require greater increases in the marginal tax rates needed to finance them than other expenditure programs do.* For example, by raising everyone's marginal tax rate by one percentage point, it would be possible to spend 1 percent more of national income on national defense. By contrast, to redistribute 1 percent more of national income to low-income families requires the marginal tax rates of all households to be increased by an average of approximately 4 percentage points.

The relationship between redistribution and marginal tax rates can best be illustrated with an example. Let's assume for simplicity that transfers take the form of equal cash grants to all members of society and are financed by a flat rate tax on income. In Table 9–5, it is assumed that society is composed of five households, A through E, with earnings among households varying from $10,000 to $50,000 by increments of $10,000. Next suppose that a tax of 20 percent is levied on income and that there is no effect on work incentives; that is, earnings remain unchanged. The combined income of the 5 households is $150,000, so the 20 percent tax yields $30,000 which finances a transfer of $6,000 to each of the five households. The results of the tax-plus-transfer on each household are shown in rows 2 through 5 in the table. Note that the *net* effect is a redistribution of $6,000 from households D and E to households A and B. Only 4 percent of total income ($6,000 out of $150,000) is redistributed by this policy; yet the marginal tax rate for all households is 20 percent.

Although this example is based on a particular type of redistributive pol-

Table 9–5 *Hypothetical Tax-Transfer Policy*

Households	A	B	C	D	E
Earnings	$10,000	$20,000	$30,000	$40,000	$50,000
20 percent tax	−2,000	−4,000	−6,000	−8,000	−10,000
Transfer	+6,000	+6,000	+6,000	+6,000	+6,000
Net income	14,000	22,000	30,000	38,000	46,000
Change in income	+4,000	+2,000	0	−2,000	−4,000
	+6,000			−6,000	

icy, the implication that marginal tax rates must rise by a multiple (here 5) of the percentage of national income that is redistributed is generally true for virtually all actual and potential transfer programs. Note that it would make no difference if the government collected and dispersed only the net change in each household's income. For example, if the first $30,000 in income is exempted from taxation and a 20 percent tax is applied to income above $30,000, household D would pay $2,000 and household E would pay $4,000, and they would still be subject to a 20 percent marginal tax rate. If we also adjust transfers so that a larger transfer goes to the household with the lowest income, granting transfers of $4,000 to A and $2,000 to B implies that the transfers are reduced 20 cents per dollar of income (the implicit 20 percent marginal tax rate of the transfer program). Thus, all households would still be subject to a marginal tax rate of 20 percent in this case, although the government would be collecting and spending only 4 percent of total income.

There is simply no feasible way to avoid sharply increased marginal tax rates when redistributing moderate additional amounts of national income. Although it would be possible to redistribute $6,000 in our example in such a way that *some* households would have marginal tax rates lower than 20 percent, *other* households would necessarily be subject to higher rates. For example, suppose only the first $20,000 is exempted from taxation. Then $6,000 can be collected from households C, D, and E (who have a combined income in excess of $20,000 of $60,000) with a marginal tax rate of only 10 percent. Transferring the $6,000 to household A, however, implies marginal tax rates on income below $20,000 of 60 percent. (Since the transfer must be reduced to zero when income reaches $20,000, it must fall by 60 cents for each additional dollar of earnings from $10,000 to $20,000.) Unfortunately, there is no way to avoid having someone's marginal tax rate rise sharply. For convenience, it is simplest to describe the situation by the increment in rates that results when everyone is subject to the same rate— here, marginal tax rates go up five points for each percent of national income redistributed.

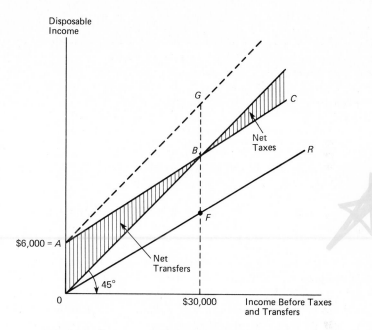

FIGURE 9–6 *Hypothetical tax-transfer program.*

The tax-and-transfer policies of Table 9–5 are illustrated graphically in Figure 9–6, in which the 45-degree line shows the equality between earnings and disposable income in the absence of any tax or transfer. A 20 percent tax rate on income is shown by line *OR* where the amount of tax at each income level is measured by the vertical distance between *OR* and the 45-degree line. The tax finances a transfer of $6,000 at each income level, and the transfers are shown by the dashed line that lies parallel to the 45-degree line and $6,000 above it. The net effect on income at each level is the difference between the transfer received and the tax paid, as shown by the line *ABC*. At incomes below $30,000, transfers exceed taxes; at income above $30,000, taxes are larger, so there is a net redistribution of income to households with earnings below $30,000. Figure 9–6 shows that in effect, this method of redistribution is equivalent to an NIT with an income guarantee of $6,000, a marginal tax rate of 20 percent, and a breakeven income of $30,000.

Although the specific numbers in this instance are intended for illustrative purposes, the actual relationship between the share of national income redistributed and the necessary marginal tax rates is similar to this example. Given the distribution of income in the United States, a redistribution of 1 percent of national income requires marginal tax rates to rise by about 4 percentage points if it is accomplished using a flat rate tax and equal transfers. This means that increasing the percentage share of income going to the lowest quintile of households by just 1 percent—a seemingly small increase—would require marginal tax rates to rise sharply for all households from their already high levels shown in Table 9–2. In fact, the required increase would be greater than four percentage points because when 1 percent of income is redistributed, only part of this amount can feasibly be transferred to the lowest quintile. (Recall that household B in our example received a third of the sum redistributed.) It would probably be necessary to redistribute a minimum of 2 percent of national income to the lowest two or three quintiles in order to raise the share of the lowest quintile by 1 percent, and that means everyone's marginal tax rates would have to rise by 8 percentage points.

The arithmetic underlying redistribution demonstrates how difficult it is to increase the share of income going to the lowest quintile significantly. Many people think that it must be simple to augment the small percentage share of income received by the lowest quintile (in the Census Bureau's tabulations) by two or three points. The harsh reality, however, is that the policies required to accomplish this would increase marginal tax rates by 15 to 20 points or more, resulting in marginal tax rates of over 60 percent for most households (as Table 9–2 indicates). To the extent that higher rates reduce incentives to earn—a matter we shall consider further in the next section—the actual gain for low-income households would be even smaller.

The cost of an income guarantee

We can arrive at the same general conclusion by approaching the problem from a different direction. Let's focus on the marginal tax rates necessary to establish a given effective income guarantee, or *floor*, for all people. Using the example involving equal transfers for all households again, the size of the transfer then effectively becomes a guaranteed income because it is the total income received by a household with no earnings of its own. Suppose we wish to have an income guarantee equal to one half the average household income: What marginal tax rate is required? Since each household will receive a transfer equal to half the average household income, total outlays on transfers will equal half of total household income. Thus, tax revenue must equal half of total household income so the required tax rate is 50 percent. In general, the necessary tax rate is equal to the income guarantee divided by average income when using a tax-transfer system in which the marginal tax rate is the same for all households. So to have an income floor of 50 percent of average income requires a tax rate of 50 percent. (Note that the guarantee of $3,000 in Table 9–6 is 20 percent of average income of $15,000 and requires a tax rate of 20 percent.)

Once we recognize that the government also requires tax revenues for nonredistributive purposes, the marginal tax rate necessary to establish an income floor at half the average income can be seen to be even higher. Suppose, not unrealistically, that 20 percent of national income is required to finance defense, schools, police, payments on the national debt, roads, and so on and that these outlays necessitate a tax rate of 20 percent. To have an income floor of 50 percent of the average would require an additional 50 percent marginal tax rate and, therefore, an effective marginal tax rate on all households of 70 percent.

These arithmetical relationships, simple as they are, are extremely important to understanding how limited our ability is to achieve a substantially more equal distribution of income through redistribution. Yet most people discussing these matters seem completely unaware of how difficult it would be for tax and transfer policies to alter materially the distribution of income further. For example, a common suggestion of scholars is that an income floor of half the average or median income level be established or that the official poverty line be set at half the medium-income level and then poverty eliminated. Such ideas are always proposed as if they would be easy to accomplish; yet our discussion shows that transfer and tax programs that established an income floor of half the average would require marginal tax rates on all households to be increased by perhaps 20 percentages points, a 50 percent increase for the average household.

The Equality-Efficiency Tradeoff

The sensitivity of the level of marginal tax rates to the amount of redistribution would be no obstacle to income redistribution except that economic incentives are affected by the level of marginal tax rates. Increasingly higher marginal tax rates are likely to diminish the quantities of labor and capital supplied, so redistributing additional income will reduce society's total income. This relationship does not mean that redistribution is undesirable, but it does imply that greater equality may be achieved only at the cost of a lower average income. Put differently, raising the income of low-income households will result in larger reductions in the incomes of upper-income households. The magnitude of this tradeoff between equality and efficiency is of obvious importance in determining the appropriate amount of government redistribution.

The size of the tradeoff between equality and efficiency depends on a number of factors, such as the current level of marginal tax rates, how responsive people's work and saving decisions are to tax and transfer programs, and the exact type of policies used to redistribute income. Since we cannot measure some of these factors with much precision, we cannot estimate the tradeoff exactly. Nonetheless, it is possible to use plausible values for the various important factors and to show how they interact to determine the cost of raising the income of low-income households.

Table 9–6 *The Marginal Cost of Redistributing Income*

Households	A	B	C	D	E	Total
(1) Initial Earnings	$10,000	$20,000	$30,000	$40,000	$50,000	$150,000
(2) Change in Earnings	−60	−50	−100	−150	−200	−250	−750
(3) Net Change in Tax Revenue	80	160	240	320	400	1200
(4) Transfer	240	240	240	240	240	1200
(5) Net Transfer	160	80	0	−80	−160	0
(6) Change in Disposable Income	+110	−20	−150	−280	−410	−750

Let's reconsider our five-household society from Table 9–5. Each household initially has the earnings shown in the first row of Table 9–6. To estimate the size of the tradeoff, we now make three assumptions. First, each household is initially confronting a marginal tax rate of 40 percent as a result of existing tax and transfer policies. (Note that this is plausible in view of the estimates in Table 9–2.) Second, we are going to increase the amount of redistribution by adding a 1 percent tax on labor incomes and using the additional revenue to finance equal-per-household transfers. As we have seen, this tax-transfer scheme will redistribute income from upper- to lower-income households. In effect, we are examining the effect of a small expansion in the amount of redistribution from its current level. Thus, the *marginal* tradeoff is what we will estimate; this estimate is the relevant measure for evaluating whether to increase or reduce the amount of redistribution.

Third, we assume that each household's labor supply elasticity with respect to the net wage rate is 0.3. This value determines how much labor supply, and hence earnings, will decline as the marginal tax rate rises.[7] The labor supply elasticity is therefore critical to determining the size of the tradeoff. Recall that an elasticity of 0.3 means that a 10 percent reduction in the net wage rate will reduce labor supply by 3 percent. This 0.3 figure was selected to reflect the available empirical evidence in the economics literature. It should be emphasized, however, that there is no consensus that the exact value is 0.3—some studies have estimated higher and others have estimated lower values.

Based on these assumptions, we can trace the consequences of our hypothetical redistributive policy. When the marginal tax rate rises from 40 to

[7] Our example has earnings depend only on the marginal tax rate, but economic theory implies that the average tax rate (determined by the size of the net tax or transfer) also matters. Marginal tax rates govern substitution effects, whereas average tax rates govern income effects. For the transfer recipient, both effects operate in the same direction, but for the taxpayer they operate in opposing directions. We neglect this complication here, but in later chapters we examine in greater detail the way taxes affect taxpayers.

41 percent, the net wage rate falls from 60 to 59 percent of its before-tax value, a reduction of 1.67 percent. With a labor supply elasticity of 0.3, labor supply and earnings will fall by 0.5 percent (0.3 times 1.67 percent). The implied reductions in earnings are shown in the second row of Table 9–6.

The additional tax revenue collected from each household is shown in the third row of Table 9–6 (rounded to the nearest $10). Note that the additional revenue is substantially less than 1 percent of earnings; that is, when total earnings fall by $750, the government loses $300 in revenue it collected under its initial 40 percent tax rate.[8] This relationship shows why the initial level of marginal tax rates is important: The higher the rates are, the greater the revenue loss from any reduction in earnings will be, and therefore the less net additional revenue will be available to finance more transfers.

The additional $1,200 in tax revenue finances transfers of $240 per household, as shown in row (4). Row (5) shows the net transfer, that is, the difference between the transfer received and the additional tax revenue collected. Taking taxes and transfers into account, the policy redistributes $240 from households D and E to households A and B. (Note that $240 is about one sixth of 1 percent of total income but that marginal tax rates had to rise by one full percentage point to accomplish that redistribution. When disincentive effects are taken into account, marginal tax rates must rise even more for each 1 percent of income redistributed.) The net transfer does not measure how much each household's income has been changed by the policy, however, because we also have to consider the reduction in earnings. The change in disposable income is given by the sum of the net transfer, row (5), and the change in earnings, row (2). The final effect on each household's disposable income is shown in row (6).

Overall, the redistributive policy has raised the disposable income of household A by $110 and reduced the disposable incomes of the other four households by a total of $860. In other words, the marginal cost of raising the income of the poorest household by $1 is about $8 to the other four households; this is our measure of the size of the tradeoff. Repeating a point made earlier, this calculation does not tell us whether the additional redistribution is desirable; it only identifies some of the relevant effects that should be weighed in making that judgment.

Although this is only a hypothetical example, what is striking is that it shows how a moderate disincentive effect can mean a surprisingly high marginal cost associated with reducing income inequality. The main reason that

---

[8] The change in earnings can be calculated by first computing 1 percent of the initial earnings of each household; this is how much tax revenue would rise if earnings did not decline. From this we must subtract the revenue loss when earnings do decline, and this loss is equal to 41 percent of row (2). The figures are rounded in the table to keep the arithmetic simple; the actual additional revenue is slightly less than shown there.

the cost of redistributing additional income is so high has already been suggested by our earlier discussion. Marginal tax rates must rise sharply compared with the amount of income actually redistributed, and the disincentive effect is related to the rise in marginal tax rates. In addition, the effects are even larger when we start from a position where marginal tax rates are already fairly high.

In interpreting this result, three points should be kept in mind. First, this is a measure of the marginal tradeoff. It indicates the cost of a little more or a little less redistribution but does not imply that if we did away with all welfare programs, the nonpoor would gain $8 for each $1 reduction in the disposable income of the poor. Second, we have measured the tradeoff in terms of money incomes alone. If we included the value of additional leisure time, since both the poor and nonpoor work less in our example, the tradeoff would be less severe. Finally, we have investigated the tradeoff for a particular type of tax-transfer policy. A different policy could require a very different tradeoff. It should be noted, however, that the distributional effects of our hypothetical policy are quite similar to the overall distributional impact of all taxes and transfers in the U.S. system. Thus, this policy may approximate the effect of an across-the-board expansion or contraction in existing programs.

Proposal for Reform: The NIT

Over the past decade, a number of economists of widely differing political persuasions have advocated an NIT as a replacement for most, if not all, federal welfare programs. At issue is whether a single transfer program with uniform nationwide standards would be more equitable and efficient than the current system, which is composed of several separate—but overlapping and interacting—programs. (Actually, there are at least 168 federal expenditure programs that aid the poor, but most of these involve outlays of only a few million dollars.) Given the complexity of the existing system and the numerous factors that are relevant, arriving at a balanced judgment is difficult. Nonetheless, the major advantages and disadvantages of an NIT are fairly clear.

At the outset it should be emphasized that we are considering an NIT of total cost equal to the programs it replaces. Thus, there would be no increase in the cost to taxpayers. The volume of redistribution is considered fixed, so we can focus on different ways of effecting this redistribution. As previously noted, adding an NIT to the present system to increase substantially the amount of redistribution would be difficult. Here we are concerned with welfare *reform,* not with an *expansion* in the system.

The principal advantages of an NIT as a replacement for existing welfare programs include the following:

1. Assistance would be in the form of cash; as shown earlier, recipients

would generally be better off according to their own preferences if they could spend the transfers as they saw fit. This advantage supposes that the NIT would replace the in-kind transfer programs now in use. Although recognizing that several arguments favor in-kind transfers, proponents of the NIT find them generally unconvincing.

2. Administrative and compliance costs of an NIT would be lower. Although there is little firm evidence on this point, it seems generally agreed that the cost of administering a single, fairly simple program would be lower per dollar of transfer than for the present system which is composed of many potentially overlapping programs. In addition, costs borne by recipients in the form of filling out forms, establishing and maintaining eligibility, and so on would probably be lower under the NIT. Lower administrative and compliance costs mean that more resources can be made available to the poor at no extra cost to taxpayers.

3. Assistance would be objectively and uniformly related to need. Under the present system, there are wide differences in the level of assistance given to families with the same incomes. These differences reflect in part the fact that current programs grant assistance primarily to the poor who are elderly, in female-headed families, unemployed, and so on. What this means, for example, is that a poor person aged 65 can receive assistance under Supplemental Security Income, but an equally poor elderly person aged 64 may receive no assistance. Proponents of the NIT view disparities of this sort as inequitable; these disparities would be avoided by an NIT because a low income—for whatever reason—would entitle an individual to assistance. Families of the same size and income would receive equal transfers.

4. The NIT would concentrate transfers on those with low incomes. Recall that under the present system many programs confer a large share of their benefits on the nonpoor. Unemployment insurance, in which over 80 percent of the benefits go to families in the upper four fifths of the income distribution, is an example. Under an NIT, larger transfers would go to those with lower incomes. Although some of the transfers under the NIT would probably go to the nonpoor, depending on where the breakeven income is set, these transfers would be small compared to those received by lower-income families.

5. The NIT would be easier to understand than the present system. Not only would it be simpler to determine how much is being transferred and who is benefiting from it (which is quite difficult to determine with current programs), but the various tradeoffs among the policy goals would also become more apparent. Existing programs require tradeoffs of much the same type as the NIT, but this is often not understood because of the number of interacting programs involved. It is clear that neither the public nor Congress comprehends the present system sufficiently well to make informed decisions about changes in or additions to the system.

A clear example of the type of problem created by the lack of simplicity in the current system of overlapping programs occurred in 1970 when the House of Representatives actually passed a type of NIT, President Richard Nixon's Family Assistance Plan (FAP), which would have resulted in marginal tax rates exceeding 100 percent for millions of low-income people.[9] (The FAP later failed in the Senate.) The reason for this unintended outcome was that the FAP, with its own 50 percent marginal tax rate, was simply added to the existing programs. But the important point is that the complexity of the present system makes it difficult to understand the tradeoffs that must be made and the interaction of overlapping programs. Although it is necessary to make difficult decisions in setting the policy variables of the NIT, the relationships are easy to understand, and it is to be hoped that the unavoidably hard choices that must be made will be based on an informed consideration of the factors involved.

Note that many of the advantages claimed for the NIT simply reflect perceived disadvantages of the present system. Proponents of the NIT view current programs as constituting a "welfare mess," with severe inequities in the distribution of transfers among the poor, avoidable distortions in consumption patterns, high administrative costs, and a complexity that makes rational decision making impossible. Although the NIT is not presented as a panacea, it is viewed as an improvement over the status quo.

There are, at the same time, a number of disadvantages to substituting an NIT for existing programs. These disadvantages should be reviewed.

1. Money income is not always an accurate indication of need. We have already emphasized the inadequacies of annual income as a good measure of a family's standard of living. Because transfers under the NIT would be based on money incomes, they would not necessarily be related to "need." For example, a family may have a child who requires expensive medical treatment and is poorer in a meaningful sense (unless they have insurance) than another family with an equal money income. Of course, an NIT could allow medical expenses to be deducted, but the more special circumstances it tries to take into account, the more complex it becomes. In any event, the relevant question is whether standards under existing programs constitute a better definition of need than would the income measure employed by an NIT—not whether the NIT's measure is imperfect. Opinions on this point differ.

2. Work incentives would be impaired by the NIT. This contention is far from obvious because we are using the NIT as a replacement for existing programs that already imply high effective marginal tax rates. On the average, marginal tax rates need not rise under the NIT when it replaces other programs. What would happen is that marginal rates would rise for some

---

[9] Milton Friedman, "Welfare: Back to the Drawing Board," reprinted from *Newsweek* in Milton Friedman, *An Economist's Protest* (Glen Ridge, N.J.: Thomas Horton, 1972), pp. 136–138.

low-income families and fall for others. Those families currently facing very high rates would generally have a lower rate under the NIT, whereas the opposite would be true of families with unusually low rates now. Whether the net effect would be a reduction in work effort is therefore unclear, but it obviously could be.

3. The NIT would treat the symptoms but not the causes of poverty. It would give money to the poor, but do nothing to help them become more self-supporting. This argument is usually advanced by those who advocate job training and educational subsidies to increase the earning capacity of the poor. The NIT would do nothing directly to increase earning capacity, but it would provide the means to finance job training if the recipient chose to use the subsidy in that way. It can be argued, however, that this is not enough. Unfortunately, evidence from the several manpower training and compensatory education programs that have been tried in the past leaves considerable doubt about the effectiveness of such policies.

4. Many poor families would find their benefit levels reduced under an NIT. No one likes the thought of reducing assistance to needy families, but some low-income families would clearly be worse off under an NIT. Families receiving unusually large benefits under the present system would have lower benefits under the NIT, just as those with unusually low benefits now would receive larger benefits. The average benefit level would go up somewhat because of the saving in administrative costs, but some would still be worse off. The real question is whether existing differences in benefit levels for families with equal incomes are equitable or inequitable. If these differences are inequitable, some people are getting too much and others too little now, and a move to the NIT would seem fair. In other words, would the distribution of benefits under the NIT formula be more or less fair than under the present system? The answer probably depends on whether the income definition of the NIT corresponds to one's view of need, as mentioned earlier.

5. It is sometimes argued that the taxpayers would not support so large a volume of redistribution under the NIT as they now do under present programs. Taxpayers, it is argued, are willing to pay taxes if the funds are used to subsidize obviously needy groups (the elderly poor, female-headed households) or support consumption of necessities (food, housing, medical care). They might not, however, be willing to bear so large a tax burden when cash transfers are made to everyone with low incomes. This argument is difficult to evaluate because we do not understand precisely how the political process functions. Some have expressed the opposite concern: that by making the redistribution open and aboveboard, political pressures would push up the benefit levels of an NIT. After all, recipients vote, too. It is certainly possible that the politically determined volume of redistribution could differ under an NIT, so this is a legitimate concern in evaluating the proposal.

Replacing the current system with an NIT therefore raises a number of issues. Although we, along with many other economists, find considerable merit in the proposal, it is important to consider both its advantages and disadvantages.

Supplementary Readings

AARON, HENRY J. *Why Is Welfare So Hard to Reform?* Washington, D.C.: The Brookings Institution, 1973.

BROWNING, EDGAR K. *Redistribution and the Welfare System*. Washington, D.C.: American Enterprise Institute, 1975.

CAMPBELL, COLIN, ed. *Income Redistribution*. Washington, D.C.: American Enterprise Institute, 1977.

CONGRESSIONAL BUDGET OFFICE. *Welfare Reform: Issues, Objectives and Approaches*. Washington, D.C.: U.S. Government Printing Office, 1977.

DANZIGER, SHELDON, and PETER GOTTSCHALK. "On Losing Ground." *Challenge* (May/June 1985).

———, ROBERT HAVEMAN, and ROBERT PLOTNICK. "How Income Transfers Affect Work, Savings, and the Income Distribution." *Journal of Economic Literature*, 19(3):975–1028 (Sept. 1981).

MURRAY, CHARLES. *Losing Ground: American Social Policy, 1950–1980*. New York: Basic Books, 1984.

OKUN, ARTHUR. *Equality and Efficiency: The Big Trade-off*. Washington, D.C.: The Brookings Institution, 1975.

Review Questions and Problems

1. Tom favors an NIT with a 50 percent MTR. Dick believes no family should receive any cash if their income is above $12,000. Harry feels no family's income should fall below $6,000. Can these goals be achieved simultaneously? Explain.

2. If a negative income tax causes a recipient to reduce her earnings so much that her disposable income does not change, the welfare cost of the NIT will be equal to the total amount spent: It will be entirely wasted. True or false? Explain.

3. Suppose we now have an NIT with an income guarantee of $5,000, a marginal tax rate of 50 percent, and a breakeven income of $10,000. Then the policy is changed so that the income guarantee remains $5,000, but the marginal tax rate is reduced to one third. How will this affect the work incentives of low-income households? (*Note:* Consider separately how it affects families with earnings below $10,000 and those with earnings between $10,000 and $15,000.)

4. "The poverty gap is now less than 1 percent of GNP. Thus, if the government increased its welfare spending by only this small amount, we could eliminate poverty in our society." Discuss.

5. Use indifference curve analysis to compare how an NIT and a WRS affect the labor supply, disposable income, and well-being of a worker. Be sure that the NIT and WRS that you compare cost the government the same.

6. "We can avoid the work disincentive problems of transfer programs just by requiring welfare recipients to work in public employment programs." Discuss.

7. "If we were to give welfare recipients cash instead of Medicaid benefits, they might choose not to purchase any health insurance. If they then became ill, society would not let them die; society would certainly see that they received medical attention. Thus, we would end up providing both cash and in-kind benefits. It would be better just to provide Medicaid benefits outright." Evaluate this argument for in-kind rather than cash transfers.

8. In what way, if at all, does economic analysis help you evaluate the desirability of the government's taking $10 billion from the nonpoor and giving it to the poor?

9. Table 9–6 illustrates the calculation of the tradeoff for certain assumptions. How would the result differ if the initial marginal tax rate were 50 percent rather than 40 percent? How would the result differ if the labor supply elasticity were 0.5 rather than 0.3? Calculate the tradeoff for each of these cases.

10. Why is the way that transfer programs affect the work incentives of recipients important to evaluating these programs? In other words, why should we be concerned about the magnitude of disincentive effects?

chapter 10
Principles of Tax Analysis

TO a large extent, the analysis of taxes parallels the analysis of expenditures. Our major concerns remain how the policy affects the pattern of output of goods and services (allocative effects) and who bears the cost (distributional effects). As with expenditures, the exact consequences depend on the particular tax employed, but some general principles are helpful to keep in mind.

Tax Incidence

The questions "Who pays the tax?" and "Who bears the burden of the tax?" can have different answers. Determining who pays the tax is a simple matter of tax liability as defined by the tax statutes. Locating the economic units responsible for writing the checks covering the tax is not of much interest to economists because these units may not be the ones that actually bear the burden of the tax. Everyone knows this and believes, for example, that the federal excise tax on liquor, although paid by liquor producers, is actually passed on to consumers in the form of higher prices. *Tax incidence theory is concerned with determining who bears the real burden of taxation.* More generally, the incidence of a tax refers to its effects on the distribution of income.

All taxes ultimately result in a reduction in the real disposable incomes of some people. To refer to "business" or "property" bearing the burden of a tax is potentially misleading because businesses and property are owned by individuals, and it is these individuals who *may* suffer reductions in their real incomes as a result of business and property taxes. (Whether or not these individuals actually *do* bear the burden of these taxes is a question of locating the actual incidence of the taxes.) Do not be misled, therefore, by references to "businesses paying their fair share" of taxes because businesses per se do not bear the burden of any tax. It makes more sense to ask whether business *owners* bear a fair share of the tax burden.

Before proceeding we should consider the meaning of incidence more carefully; it is not as unambiguous a concept as might be thought at first glance. Possible ambiguity results from the necessity of accounting for what the government does with the tax revenues raised. The consequences of any tax obviously depend to some degree on how the government uses the revenue, because the government may tax individuals and then use the revenue to provide goods and services that benefit those who originally paid the taxes. Two different concepts of incidence are widely used by economists; these concepts differ in what is assumed to happen to the tax revenue.

Balanced-budget incidence

Balanced-budget incidence refers to the distributional effects of a tax combined with the expenditure program it finances. In other words, it considers how the opportunity cost of a given spending policy is distributed among the public by the tax. Figure 10–1 illustrates this concept of incidence. ZZ is the production possibility frontier relating the outputs of food and clothing, assumed for simplicity to be the only two goods produced by the private sector. Initially, equilibrium is at point E, with outputs of food and clothing equal to F_1 and C_1.

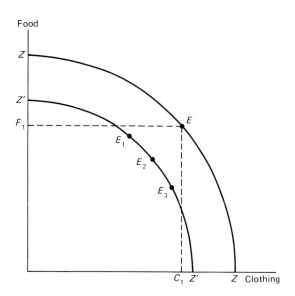

FIGURE 10–1   *Nature of tax incidence.*

Now let the government undertake an expenditure program to provide a public good. Because productive resources must be employed to produce the public good, a smaller quantity of resources will be available to produce food and clothing. The resources remaining in the private sector can produce the output combinations shown by $Z'Z'$. Suppose an excise tax on clothing is used to finance the expenditure, and the final equilibrium on $Z'Z'$ occurs at point E_1.

The balanced-budget incidence of the tax-and-expenditure program compares the distribution of private income (here just food and clothing) at points E and E_1. Of course, Figure 10–1 does not show how the lower private income of the community at E_1 is divided among persons: We must go beyond the aggregate effects shown in the diagram to determine this. When we do so, however, we will be comparing the distributions of income implied by points E and E_1.

Balanced-budget incidence seems to be what most people think of as the incidence of taxation: It tells us how the cost of spending programs is divided among the population. It has the defect, however, of making the incidence of a tax depend on how the revenue is spent.[1] In other words, there is no such thing as *the* balanced-budget incidence of a particular tax because the final effects depend on how the revenue is spent. In addition, it is usually impossible to say that a particular tax finances a particular spending program when the government utilizes many different taxes. For example, what expenditure does the federal excise tax on liquor finance? It is not possible to say, because the revenue goes into a general fund along with the revenue from dozens of other taxes, and thousands of spending programs are financed out of the general fund.

Despite these difficulties in applying balanced-budget incidence, this concept is useful in many contexts. It has the advantage of reminding us that taxes are the way we pay for government expenditures, and a comprehensive view of tax incidence often requires that both policies be considered together.

Differential incidence

The concept of *differential incidence* assumes that government expenditures are held constant and then compares the distributional effect of substituting one tax for another. In other words, differential incidence compares alternative ways to finance a given government expenditure. Figure 10–1 can also be used to illustrate differential incidence. As we saw, point E_1 shows the equilibrium with an excise tax on clothing used to finance the

---

[1] A change in the expenditure program financed by the tax will normally have an effect on consumer demand. Thus, the point on $Z'Z'$ that will be an equilibrium under a given excise tax on clothing will depend in part on how the revenues are spent.

expenditure on the public good. If an income tax were used instead of the excise tax, equilibrium might be at E_2. The differential incidence of the income tax relative to the excise tax involves a comparison of the distributions of disposable income implied by the alternative equilibria at points E_1 and E_2. The alternative method of financing could include more than two taxes; for example, E_3 might be the equilibrium under an excise tax on food.

Differential incidence avoids the necessity of considering the effects of expenditure programs by assuming that expenditures remain unchanged as one tax is substituted for another. It is still not an entirely unambiguous concept because the differential incidence of a tax depends on what other tax it is compared to. There is no such thing as "the" differential incidence of an excise tax, because the effects differ depending on whether it is compared to an income tax or a property tax. Generally, when this concept is employed, some tax is selected as a benchmark against which all other taxes are compared. A proportional tax on income is frequently used as the reference point.

Differential incidence and balanced-budget incidence are the two major concepts of incidence used by economists. Although neither concept is entirely unambiguous and without problems, they force us to be careful in defining clearly what is meant by the burden of a tax. Which concept to use depends largely on the purpose of the study. For example, if you are concerned with tax reform or with determining the "best" (according to some criteria) method of financing an expenditure, then the use of differential incidence is dictated by the subject of the investigation. On the other hand, if you are concerned with the impact of government on the distribution of income, balanced-budget incidence is the natural selection.

Incidence of Excise Taxes

A good way to begin to study tax incidence is to examine the effects of excise taxes. Although excise taxes are only moderately important as sources of revenue (in 1984 only $49 billion out of a total of $666 billion in federal revenue came from excise taxes), they permit many important principles of tax incidence to be illustrated. The incidence of the personal income tax and the corporate income tax, two more important sources of tax revenues, are examined in later chapters.

Let's consider the effect of a per unit excise tax on margarine. Assuming that the margarine industry is a constant cost competitive industry, the pre-tax equilibrium is shown in Figure 10–2 by the intersection of the supply and demand curves at a price and quantity of P_1 and Q_1. An excise tax of $0.30 per pound of margarine is levied on all firms in the industry. This means that the minimum price at which firms will supply any given quantity

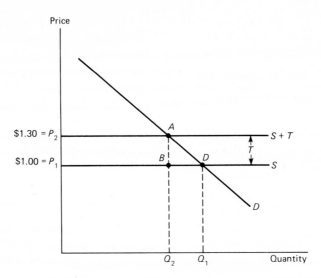

FIGURE 10–2   *Incidence of an excise tax.*

of margarine to consumers will be $0.30 higher than before. Thus, the supply curve confronting consumers shifts vertically upward by $0.30 to $S+T$, and a new equilibrium is established at a price of $1.30 and quantity of Q_2.

With a constant-cost industry, the price to consumers ultimately rises by the amount of the tax per unit. In this case, the tax is said to be *shifted forward* to consumers because they bear the burden of the tax in the form of a higher price. In the final equilibrium, firms are receiving $1.30 per unit from consumers, but since the firms must remit $0.30 of this to the government, their net, or after-tax, price is $1, the same as it was before the tax. Consequently, factors of production engaged in producing margarine bear no tax burden.[2] Total tax revenue received by government is shown by the rectangle P_2ABP_1.

The term *shifting* refers to the process by which markets adjust to a tax. This is the process that may permit the incidence of the tax to differ from the point of legal liability. In the present example, firms are legally liable for the tax, but the actual burden has been shifted to consumers through a higher price. *Unless a tax leads to a change in some market price or prices (including input prices), it cannot be shifted.* If the tax is not shifted, the economic units that are legally liable for the tax will also bear the incidence

---

[2] Here we are considering the long-run effects of the tax. In the short run, an excise tax may lead to a temporary reduction in the net price received by producers even in an industry in which the long-run supply curve is horizontal.

of the tax. Thus, determining the incidence of a tax is really a question of ascertaining if and how market prices change in response to the tax.

Shifting a tax is not a conscious process that occurs just because the firms wish to avoid the tax. Firms as well as all other taxpayers would like to avoid the burden of taxation, but whether or not they can depends on the nature of the market as well as the type of tax. Consider an excise tax levied on only one firm in a competitive industry. If this one firm raises the price, its consumers will purchase from other untaxed firms, and so the taxed firm must leave its price unchanged. Although the taxed firm would like to shift the tax to someone else, it cannot. The situation is entirely different when all firms are taxed, as in Figure 10–2. Therefore, shifting does not occur just because someone wants to avoid a tax; instead, the extent to which it occurs depends on the nature of the tax and the market to which it applies.

The analysis depicted in Figure 10–2 is not a complete analysis of the reaction of the economy to the tax. It is a partial equilibrium analysis that emphasizes the effects in the market directly affected by the tax and ignores secondary effects that may occur in other markets. Because markets are interdependent, other markets will be affected. For example, a tax that raises the price of margarine will increase the demand for butter (because butter and margarine are substitutes), and this may also increase the price of butter. Secondary effects such as this are also relevant in determining the incidence (distributional effects) of the margarine tax but are generally ignored because they are thought to be of much less importance than the direct effects in the market where the tax is levied. Incidentally, a higher price of butter is not a *net* cost to the public because the higher price paid by consumers benefits the producers: It is a redistribution of income from butter consumers to butter producers. By contrast, the higher price paid by margarine consumers because of the tax does *not* benefit producers, so in this case the higher price does reflect a net cost on the public.

We have referred to the incidence of the tax on margarine as falling on margarine consumers, but which concept of incidence is being used here? Actually, the partial equilibrium analysis of an excise tax can be made consistent with either balanced-budget or differential incidence if appropriate assumptions are made. To interpret the analysis as balanced-budget incidence, it is necessary to assume that the revenue is not spent in a way that affects the supply or demand curves of margarine. To interpret the analysis as differential incidence, it is necessary to assume that the reduction in the other tax that the margarine tax replaces has no effect on the supply or demand for margarine. In making either of these assumptions, we are clearly ignoring some conceivable secondary effects, but that is inevitable if we are to make the problem manageable. As a first approximation, then, the analysis of Figure 10–2 is probably accurate enough for most purposes.

Incidence and elasticities of supply and demand

Our conclusion that an excise tax leads to an increase in price equal to the tax per unit is valid when the industry is a *constant cost* competitive industry. In general, the extent to which an excise tax leads to a higher price depends on the price elasticities of supply and demand, that is, on how responsive consumption and production are to a change in price. As we shall see, an excise tax may not always be passed on to consumers in the form of a higher price.

In Figure 10–3(a) we show the supply and demand curves for an increasing cost (upward-sloping supply curve) industry, with an initial equilibrium at P_1 and Q_1. A per unit excise tax of $0.30 shifts the supply curve to $S+T$, but in this case as firms cut back output, their reduced demand for productive resources leads to lower input prices. Thus, unit costs of production

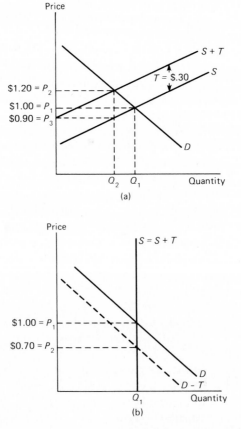

(a)

(b)

FIGURE 10–3   *Incidence of an excise tax with different supply elasticities.*

fall as output is reduced, and the price does not have to rise by the full amount of the tax to cover the now lower unit costs of production. The final equilibrium is at Q_2, with a price to consumers of $1.20, but with an after-tax price of $0.90 to producers. The final consumer price is higher than production cost by $0.30, the amount of the per unit tax, but production costs have fallen from the original equilibrium. In this case, the tax is said to be partially shifted forward to consumers (their price is $0.20 higher) and partially shifted backward to producers (their price is $0.10 lower). Both consumers and producers bear a burden from the excise tax when the supply curve is upward sloping.

When we refer to producers as bearing part of the burden of an excise tax in this case, we are using the term *producers* as a shorthand for "owners of some or all inputs used in producing the good." In fact, without knowing more about supply conditions, it is impossible to determine which input owners are burdened. For example, workers in the industry, investors in the firms, or suppliers of raw materials could be the groups that bear the burden of the tax. Which group or groups are affected depend on the elasticities of supply of the inputs to the industry.

Figure 10–3(b) shows what happens if the industry supply curve is perfectly inelastic, that is, vertical. Under this condition, firms will not reduce output if taxed. The same level of output placed on the market will fetch the same price, so the price to consumers does not rise. Producers simply accept the reduced after-tax price and continue producing at the same level of output. Formally, this is shown by the fact that a vertical upward shift in a vertical curve does not alter the supply curve ($S = S + T$ in the diagram), so the market price remains unchanged at P_1. This result can perhaps be seen more easily by imagining that the tax is paid by consumers—which does not affect the final incidence but in this case makes the geometry easier to follow. An excise tax of $0.30 on consumers shifts the demand curve downward to $D - T$, where the $D - T$ curve indicates the after-tax price that consumers are willing to pay for the product. As far as the firms are concerned, demand has simply fallen, but with a vertical supply curve a reduced demand leads to a lower price and no change in output. An excise tax on a good with a vertical supply curve therefore is borne entirely by producers.

This analysis suggests an important general principle: The more inelastic the supply curve (with a *given* demand curve) is, the greater will be the share of the tax that will be borne by producers of the good. This is a significant proposition, and it explains why economists believe that taxes on wages and salaries tend to be borne largely by workers (because labor supply is very inelastic), whereas taxes on particular products are often shifted forward to consumers (because product supply curves are generally highly elastic). A similar analysis will show that the incidence can also depend on the elasticity of demand: The more inelastic the demand curve (with a given supply curve) is, the greater will be the share of the tax that will be borne by consumers of the good. Taking these two principles together allows us to state that the incidence depends on the relative elasticities (or slopes)[3] of the demand and supply curves.

Significance of tax incidence

Determination of the incidence of taxation is important for a very simple reason: We want to know whether a tax leads to a just division of the cost of government expenditures. To determine whether the tax burden is shared fairly, we need to know the real burden placed on various economic groups by the tax; that is the subject of incidence analysis.

Economics cannot ascertain whether a tax is fair, because "fairness" must reflect a value judgment about the incidence of the tax. Economics can, however, help us make more informed value judgments by determining the actual incidence of taxes. On the other hand, many economists have attempted to formulate and refine the value judgments that are widely used to evaluate the fairness of the incidence of taxes. Our discussion of incidence would be incomplete without at least a brief mention of the criteria commonly used to evaluate the incidence of taxes.

Taxation according to benefit received   Because the government expenditures financed by taxes provide benefits to people, the magnitude of these benefits could be used to determine the size of the tax burden various people should bear. To say that taxes should be levied in accordance with benefits received is to make a value judgment explicitly about the proper division of the tax burden.[4] The great advantage of the benefit principle is that it emphasizes the essential two-sidedness of government tax-expenditure decisions. If people do not receive benefits commensurate with their tax burden, then perhaps the expenditure should not be undertaken at all.

Even if we make this value judgment (and clearly not everyone would), its practical application in many cases is virtually impossible. As we have emphasized, there is usually no way of determining the benefits to specific people from expenditures on public goods such as national defense. In addition, applying this principle would be in some instances self-defeating.

---

[3] Formally, the division of the burden between consumers and producers depends on the ratio of the slopes of the demand and supply curves, but this is exactly equal to the ratio of the elasticities of the curves. See John F. Walker, "Do Economists Ever Agree? The Case of the Teaching of Excise Tax Shifting and Incidence." *National Tax Journal,* 27:351–356 (June 1974).

[4] The "benefit principle" holds that people should be taxed according to the *marginal* benefits they receive from government spending. Taxation according to *total* benefits means that taxpayers would receive *no* net benefit as a result of government spending and taxation. The discussion on pp. 30–33 of Figure 2–1 indicates how the taxes financing a public good should be divided among taxpayers according to the benefit principle.

For example, if some people are taxed to provide funds to redistribute to other people, we cannot then tax the recipients according to the benefits they receive, for that would completely negate the effects of the redistribution.

Despite these practical problems in applying the benefit principle universally, there are cases in which people seem to approve of its selective application. Highway finance through taxes on gasoline is a case in point. Because the benefits from public provision of highways are probably correlated fairly well with gasoline use, a tax on gasoline places a tax burden on those who benefit from expenditures on highways. Another example is the payroll tax that finances social security benefits. Although taxes are not proportionate to retirement benefits received, there is some connection, as we saw in Chapter 7. Some believe that public support for social security is based in part on the perception that it is fair to base people's benefits on the taxes they pay, in effect suggesting that many feel that taxation according to the benefits received is equitable.

Taxation according to ability to pay   A second principle of fairness in taxation ignores the benefits from government spending altogether and considers how tax burdens should be allocated independently of who benefits from spending the revenues. This principle holds that taxes should be levied in accordance with the taxpayer's ability to pay, and it is often considered by many to be the basic criterion of justice in taxation. It suggests that those who have an equal ability to pay should bear the same tax burden and those who have a greater ability should bear a heavier tax burden.

Although "ability to pay" provides a convenient slogan, to implement it we must be more precise about its meaning. Under what conditions do two taxpayers have an equal ability to pay? In practice, many economists have assumed that income is the best measure of ability to pay. (As we will see, however, the definition of income is not exactly uncontroversial.) If this assumption is granted, then an equal tax burden for those equally able to pay (sometimes called *horizontal equity*) means that those with the same income should bear the same tax. By making these value judgments, we arrive at a criterion that can actually be applied as a benchmark to judge a tax. Note that an excise tax (constant-cost case) would fail the test of horizontal equity except in the unlikely event that all those with the same income purchased the same quantity of the taxed good.

What constitutes *vertical equity*—the treatment of those with different abilities to pay—is even more controversial. Although it is generally agreed that those with higher incomes have a greater ability to pay and should therefore bear a heavier tax burden, the principle does not tell us how much heavier the tax burden should be. (For example, if we decide to use an income tax to finance government expenditures, should a proportional or a progressive tax be used? In both cases, taxpayers at higher income levels would pay a larger tax than would taxpayers with lower incomes, but with a progressive rate the higher-income individuals would pay relatively as well as absolutely more.)

Note that the ability to pay principle is simply an attempt to make an explicit value judgment about the distributional effects of taxes. Insofar as our concern is with the distribution of income, however, we should not forget that expenditure policies also have a major impact on the distribution. It is not clear whether it is appropriate to make judgments about the equity of a tax, regardless of the pattern of benefits from spending the revenue. For example, could we say that a tax is unfair if it takes $1,000 from a poor person, while at the same time the person receives a $1,500 transfer from the government?

Partial Versus General Equilibrium Analysis

We employed partial equilibrium analysis in our examination of the incidence of an excise tax. Partial equilibrium analysis refers to the study of a specific market, such as the market for the output of some industry. It examines the direct effects of the tax within this market and tends to ignore the secondary effects occurring in other markets. For example, we saw that the output of the taxed industry tends to fall. This means that productive resources leave the taxed industry and find employment in other industries, thereby increasing output and possibly depressing prices in other sectors. This secondary effect on other industries is ignored in a partial equilibrium analysis, which concentrates only on the taxed industry. Why do we employ an analysis that ignores some effects? Basically, it is because economists believe these secondary effects are usually sufficiently small, uncertain, and spread over so many other industries that we may legitimately ignore them and concentrate on the taxed industry in which the effects are likely to be the most significant. More importantly, the secondary effects are unlikely to have a feedback effect on the taxed industry that would upset our conclusions concerning that market.

Partial equilibrium analysis provides an appropriate framework for the analysis of many problems, but there are some cases in which its application is inappropriate. For a policy that directly affects one industry or market, partial equilibrium analysis gives reasonably accurate results, but for a policy that directly affects many or all markets, it can be misleading. Let's consider one example to see why. A general sales tax is a tax on the sale of all goods and services in the economy; that is, it is an excise tax applied to all goods.[5] It is tempting to generalize on the basis of the results of our earlier

---

[5] To qualify as a general sales tax, the tax must be the same percentage of the market price for all goods and services.

partial equilibrium analysis of one excise tax in order to deduce the effects of a general sales tax. If we did this, we might conclude that a general sales tax tends to raise all product prices and is therefore borne by consumers. This, however, is unlikely to be so. Our earlier analysis of an excise tax in effect assumed that other industries were not taxed; when other industries are taxed—as with a general sales tax—the effect in any given market can be quite different, as we shall see next.

Incidence of a general sales tax

Let's examine the effect of a general sales tax within a broader framework that can take into account what happens in several industries. We will assume that the economy produces two products, X and Y. An excise tax is applied to both products, so the sales of both goods, X and Y, are taxed. To analyze the effects of such a tax, we will use balanced-budget incidence. To be specific about how the revenue is spent, we assume that the government simply returns the revenue to people in the form of unrestricted cash transfers. This simplifying assumption makes it plausible to suppose that the demand curves for X and Y are not affected by the tax, because the public has the same total purchasing power after the tax-plus-transfer as before. All productive resources will continue to be employed in the production of X and Y; no public good is being financed by the sales tax.

The initial (before tax and transfer) supply and demand curves in the two markets for X and Y are shown as S_Y, D_Y, S_X, and D_X in Figure 10–4. Initially, equilibria in the two markets are at outputs of Y_1 and X_1, with prices of P_Y and P_X. To examine the effects of the general sales tax, we proceed by assuming that the tax is applied in two steps: First, an excise tax is applied to X, and then one is applied to Y. A tax per unit of X equal to T_X shifts the supply curve of X up to $S_X + T_X$ in Figure 10–4(b), and so the quantity of X falls from X_1 to X_2. The tax on industry X also has an effect on industry Y because as X restricts its employment of productive resources, these resources seek employment in industry Y and therefore increase the supply of resources to industry Y. This adjustment leads to lower wage rates, land rents, and so on in industry Y. Thus, costs of production fall in Y, which is reflected by the shift in the supply of Y to S_Y' in Figure 10–4(a). Consequently, output is higher and price is lower in Y, with the opposite true in the taxed industry.

In a partial equilibrium analysis, the effects shown in Figure 10–4(a) for industry Y are generally ignored. When there are many nontaxed industries, as when we examine an excise tax only on margarine, these effects will be quite small, and it is reasonable to neglect them. But when all industries are taxed, as they will be with a general sales tax, we must not ignore the interdependence among industries.

At this point the economy has adjusted to a tax on X. Now if we add a

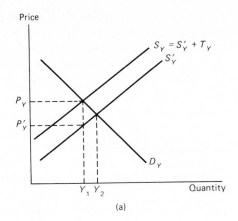

(a)

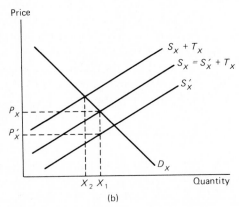

(b)

FIGURE 10-4   *Incidence of a general sales tax.*

tax on Y, both products will be taxed, and we will have a general sales tax. A tax of T_Y on Y shifts the supply curve of Y from S_Y' to $S_Y' + T_Y$, with $S_Y' + T_Y$ coinciding with the initial supply curve, S_Y.[6] Output falls from Y_2 to Y_1, and price rises to P_Y. The opposite occurs in industry X: The increase in the supply of productive resources to X resulting from reduced employment in Y shifts the supply curve (net of tax on X) from S_X to S_X', and the supply curve, including the tax on X, becomes $S_X' + T_X$. Output therefore increases from X_2 to X_1, and price falls to P_X.

Consider carefully the final equilibrium under the general sales tax. Note that the price and output of both goods are the same as before the tax! The sales tax has not led to higher product prices. (Thus, we would be seriously

---

[6]Of course, S_y and $S_y' + T_y$ coincide only if the tax on Y is the same percentage of the final market price as the tax on X.

misled if we generalized on the basis of our analysis of a single excise tax when the price of the taxed product does rise.) If consumers do not bear the burden of the tax, however, then who does? Consider Figure 10–4 again. Although consumers pay P_Y and P_X, firms receive net (after-tax) prices of P_Y' and P_X'. Consequently, firms have lower revenues to pay factors of production. The prices received by factors of production (wage rates and so on) are lower, so factor incomes are lower. The incidence of the general sales tax lies with owners of productive resources who receive less compensation for supplying services. (Although labor and capital incomes are lower, people can still purchase the same quantities of X and Y because we have assumed that the government returns the tax revenue to the public as cash transfers.)

There is still another way to approach the analysis of a general sales tax. Assume that the tax is initially applied to all industries. The immediate effect is to reduce the funds that firms have to pay for productive resources, so the demands for labor, land, and so on fall. Because all industries are taxed, productive resources cannot avoid the consequent fall in resource prices by moving to another industry. Hence, rather than be unemployed, resources are employed at lower factor prices. This perhaps overly concise analysis leads to the same result, but we prefer the preceding two-step analysis because it illustrates more clearly what happens in each industry separately and why partial equilibrium analysis in the general sales tax case leads to the wrong conclusion.

In this analysis we have implicitly assumed that the same quantities of productive resources will be placed on the market at the lower resource prices. In other words, we are assuming that the aggregate supply curves of labor, land, and capital to the economy are perfectly vertical. Economists believe that this is often a plausible assumption, at least as a first approximation. The possible effects of taxes on the overall supply of resources will be examined in later chapters.

The two-sector diagram in Figure 10–4 is not really a full-fledged general equilibrium model. (*General equilibrium analysis* refers to an analysis that takes full account of all the interdependencies among markets.) It does, however, include more relationships among markets than does the usual single-market approach. Basically, it is designed to illustrate the nature and importance of the broader framework that must be used in the analysis of certain problems.

It is not possible to lay down an ironclad rule concerning when it is appropriate to use partial and when to use general equilibrium analysis. Ideally, we would like to be able to trace out all the effects in any analysis, but no general equilibrium model has been developed that is capable of accomplishing such a gargantuan task. Instead, we try to use the simple partial approach when it seems plausible that the secondary effects are not likely to upset our conclusions. As we have just seen, however, there are some taxes for which a broader framework is necessary. Corporate income taxes, social security payroll taxes, and personal income taxes are other taxes that affect many parts of the economy simultaneously, and so the single industry approach is likely to be misleading.

Equivalence of Major Broad-Based Taxes

There are four taxes that have a tax base that is essentially equal to national income:

1. General sales tax: A tax levied on the sale of all final goods and services in the economy.
2. Individual income tax: A tax levied on all personal income in the form of wages and salaries, interest, dividends, royalties, rents, and any other payments for the services of productive resources.
3. Value-added tax: A tax levied on firms according to the value added by each firm. Value added is simply the firm's gross receipts minus the cost of intermediate goods that have already been taxed at an earlier stage of production.
4. Expenditure tax: A tax levied on the total outlays of households on goods and services.

These taxes are "broad-based" taxes because the tax base includes all of national income. Income and sales taxes are well known in the United States, and value-added taxes are used in a number of European countries. Expenditure taxes are very rare.

Now we can state a proposition that at first glance is remarkable: All four of these taxes have identical economic effects. This is a proposition concerning the differential incidence of these taxes and means that substituting a general sales tax, for example, for an income tax leaves the real disposable incomes of all people unchanged. After our analysis of a general sales tax, this can be understood easily. Recall that a sales tax tends to reduce wage rates and other resource prices. If an income tax were substituted for a sales tax, the wage rates paid by firms to workers would be higher, but the workers would have to pay part of their wages to the government. The workers' *net* wage rates would thus be reduced by either an income tax or a sales tax, and similarly for other resource prices.

Actually, this proposition of equivalence is simply an application of the result obtained earlier in our discussion of excise subsidies, but now this result is applied to the tax side of the policy: It makes no difference on which side of the market (buyers or sellers) the subsidy (or tax) is levied. The tax base of all four of these broad-based taxes is national income, but each tax is levied at a different point in the circular flow of income. Figure

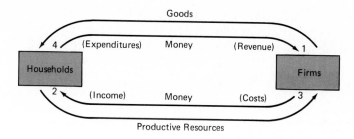

FIGURE 10–5 *Equivalence of major broad-based taxes.*

10–5 illustrates this point with the familiar circular flow diagram for a simple economy composed of households and firms. At point 1, national income is measured by the total sales of goods and services; a general sales tax is imposed at this point. At point 2 national income is measured as the sum of wages, rents, interest, and other factor payments; an income tax is imposed here. At point 3 national income is measured as the sum of value added by all firms; a value-added tax is levied on this sum. At point 4, national income is measured as the total expenditures of households on goods and services; an expenditure tax is levied on this base. Thus, all four of these tax bases are equal to national income, but the taxes are collected at different points in the circular flow.

These taxes can be shown to be *perfectly* equivalent to one another *only under certain strong assumptions.* For example, the tax base must be defined in a consistent way. Clearly, an income tax with numerous "loopholes"—deductions or exclusions—will not be equivalent to a general sales tax that strikes all goods and services. In addition, the equivalence holds only for taxes levied at a flat rate on each tax base. A progressive income tax using graduated rates will not be equivalent to a sales tax using a uniform rate.

In view of these and other possible qualifications, it is clear that real-world versions of these taxes will not be exactly identical. Nonetheless, recognizing their general similarity is quite helpful, as it allows us to see, for example, that there is likely to be little, if any, difference between a sales tax and a value-added tax in terms of their economic effects.

The Welfare Cost of Taxation

All methods of financing government expenditures, including taxation, place a burden on people, because they are part of the process that diverts control over resources to the government. In some cases, however, a tax will produce a burden that is larger than necessary to raise a given amount of tax revenue. This additional burden occurs because the tax leads to a mis-allocation of the resources that remain in the private sector. This welfare cost of taxation is also frequently referred to as the *excess burden* of taxation, to emphasize that it is a cost in addition to the direct burden as measured by the tax revenue raised.

It is important to distinguish clearly between the welfare cost of a tax and its direct cost as reflected in the withdrawal of resources from the private sector. This distinction can be seen most clearly with an example. Suppose an excise tax is levied on vacuum cleaners, but the tax is set at such a high level that the output of vacuum cleaners falls to zero. In this case there is no direct cost due to the tax because no tax revenue is collected (and thus no resources are diverted to the public sector), but there is clearly a burden resulting from the tax. Resources are misallocated: Too few vacuum cleaners are produced and too much of other goods. We know that consumers would prefer to have more (than zero) vacuum cleaners and less of other goods because they chose that pattern of production through their purchases in the absence of the tax. Thus, consumers are worse off (they bear a burden) with the resource allocation produced by the tax. Note that this welfare cost exists even though there is no tax revenue (no direct cost) so the two types of burdens are conceptually quite different.

When an excise tax is levied at a rate that yields some positive amount of tax revenue, there is *both* a direct cost and a welfare cost. We can examine this case with the aid of Figure 10–6, in which it is assumed that the vacuum cleaner industry is a constant cost competitive industry. An excise tax of $25 per vacuum cleaner raises the supply curve to $S+T$, so output

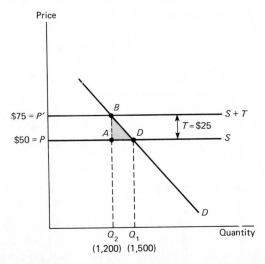

FIGURE 10–6 *Welfare cost of an excise tax: constant-cost industry.*

falls from Q_1 to Q_2 and price rises from P to P'. Tax revenue—the direct cost of the tax—is equal to $PP'BA$. Note that the price to consumers ($75) is now above the true marginal cost of production ($50); this difference is the source of the misallocation of resources that causes the welfare cost. *The tax has driven a wedge between the price that guides consumer decisions and the price (net of tax) that guides producer decisions.*

The welfare cost is reflected in a misallocation of resources involving too low an output of vacuum cleaners and too large an output of other goods. The reduction in the output of vacuum cleaners from Q_1 to Q_2 means that consumers sacrifice cleaners that are worth more than the cost of producing them. The reduction in vacuum cleaner consumption means a loss of benefits equal to BDQ_1Q_2—the sum of the marginal value of units from Q_1 to Q_2. This area BDQ_1Q_2 is *not* the welfare cost because it is not a *net* loss in welfare. The resources that were producing the Q_1–Q_2 units can be used to produce more of other goods. Thus, the tax restricts production of the taxed good and diverts resources to other uses, so that we get more of other goods. The value of the other goods produced, however, is less than the loss in value caused by the smaller output of the taxed good. The resources that produced the Q_1–Q_2 units have a market cost of ADQ_1Q_2, which is a measure of how much these resources are worth in the production of other goods. Thus, consumers sacrifice BDQ_1Q_2 in benefits because of restricted production of vacuum cleaners but gain ADQ_1Q_2 as a result of stimulated production of other goods. The loss exceeds the gain by the area *BAD: This triangular area is a measure of the net loss or welfare cost caused by the misallocation produced by the excise tax.* It is simply the difference between the demand curve (giving marginal value) and the supply curve (giving marginal cost) over the range of the output restriction that results from the tax.

Welfare cost: an alternative perspective

An excise tax leads to an inefficient restriction in output of the taxed good. This distortion in resource allocation is, as we have mentioned, a cost in addition to the direct cost as measured by the tax revenue. The nature of this welfare cost can be further clarified by considering the effect on a single consumer's welfare. In Figure 10–7, MN is the initial budget line, with vacuum cleaner consumption measured horizontally and consumption of other goods measured vertically. Before the tax, the consumer was in equilibrium at point E. An excise tax raises the price of vacuum cleaners and pivots the budget line to MN'. The consumer's most preferred point on MN' is at point E_1, consuming q_2 units of the taxed good. Total tax revenue is equal to E_1R.

To identify the welfare cost caused by this tax, we must show how the *same* tax revenue could be raised by another type of tax and yet leave the consumer better off. To do this, we assume that the tax revenue is raised

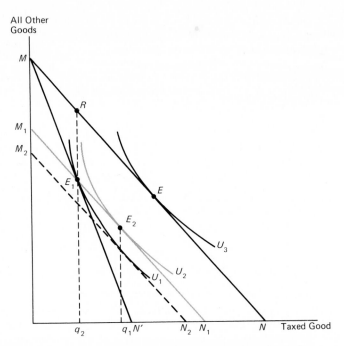

FIGURE 10–7   *Welfare cost of an excise tax: individual perspective.*

with a *lump-sum tax*. A lump-sum tax is a tax with a total tax liability that is fixed and independent of the taxpayer's consumption pattern, income, or wealth. For example, the taxpayer might be assigned a tax of $1,000 that must be paid—it cannot be avoided by not earning income, not consuming vacuum cleaners, and so on. Governments typically do not use lump-sum taxes, and they are used in our analysis only as a benchmark against which to compare the other taxes. Lump-sum taxes are a particularly good benchmark because they have no welfare cost: They do not interfere with the operation of any market by driving a wedge between prices on the two sides of the market.

A lump-sum tax that raises the same revenue as the excise tax (equal to E_1R) would shift the original budget line, *MN*, parallel and downward to M_1N_1. It would reduce the income of the consumer by MM_1 (equal to E_1R) but not affect the relative prices of goods. Confronted with the M_1N_1 budget line, the consumer would be in equilibrium at point E_2, consuming more vacuum cleaners and less of other goods. Note in particular that the consumer would be better off (on a higher indifference curve) with the lump-sum tax, even though the tax revenue is the same as with the excise tax. The same amount of revenue raised by the excise tax could therefore be obtained without affecting the consumer's well-being as much. The extra loss in welfare (the difference between U_2 and U_1) caused by the excise tax is the welfare cost.

The size of the welfare cost in dollars can also be shown in this diagram. A lump-sum tax that produces the same level of welfare as the excise tax for the consumer is shown by the budget line M_2N_2 (tangent to U_1). This tax yields MM_2 in revenue, and MM_2 is a measure of the total (direct plus welfare) cost of the excise tax. Because the direct cost (tax revenue) of the excise tax is only MM_1, the difference, M_1M_2, is the welfare cost of the excise tax. In more advanced courses, the conditions under which M_1M_2 in Figure 10–7 (summed over all consumers) is equal to the area BAD in Figure 10–6 are spelled out. For our purposes, it is sufficient to note that both diagrams show the same distorting effect of the tax, but from different points of view. The q_1q_2 restriction in consumption shown in Figure 10–7 corresponds to the Q_1Q_2 restriction shown in Figure 10–6.[7]

Welfare cost: increasing cost industry

So far, our analysis has been confined to an excise tax levied on a constant cost competitive industry. The welfare cost for an increasing cost competitive industry is shown as the area BAD in Figure 10–8. It is still measured by the area between the original demand and supply curves over the output restriction. Note in particular that the welfare cost is not equal to the area BAC—a fairly common error.

An excise tax therefore produces a hidden cost in the form of a misallocation of resources that remain (after the tax) in the private sector. The total sacrifice borne by people is greater than would be anticipated by considering only the tax revenue. This is also true of all other real-world taxes. Note, however, that this analysis says nothing about whether the expenditures financed are worthwhile. The expenditures may provide benefits that are greater than the sum of the direct and welfare costs of the taxes. We are now restricting our attention to the tax side of the budget in an attempt to understand the nature of the costs of taxation.

One significant qualification to the analysis should be mentioned: It was implicitly assumed that the taxed market was efficient in the absence of the tax. When this is not true, the analysis becomes more complex. For exam-

---

[7]The careful reader will note that the q_1q_2 reduction in consumption in Figure 10–7 is not the difference in consumption before the tax and after the tax. It is instead the difference in consumption under the excise tax and under an equal yield tax that does not distort the consumer's decisions. For Figure 10–6 to be perfectly consistent with this, the demand curve must be constructed on the assumption that consumers continue to pay the same total tax burden at all points on the demand curve. Such a demand curve is called a *compensated* demand curve and is the relevant one in estimating welfare costs. In most cases, this complication is a theoretical subtlety that has little practical significance; in the case of an income tax, however, it is of some importance, as seen in the next chapter.

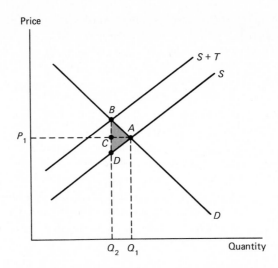

FIGURE 10–8 *Welfare cost of an excise tax: increasing cost industry.*

ple, an excise tax levied on a good whose production generated external costs might not produce a welfare cost. In fact, in this setting, as we saw in Chapter 2, a tax might actually improve resource allocation. On the other hand, an excise tax on a monopoly would be doubly inefficient because it would restrict production of a good that is already being produced in too small a quantity.

Other sources of welfare cost

Economists usually emphasize the distortions in resource allocation that taxes produce by driving a wedge between buying and selling prices in one or more markets. There are, however, other types of welfare costs that can be important on occasion.

Administrative costs Government administrative costs are a type of welfare cost because these costs reduce the *usable* revenue received by government. If the government collects $100 billion in revenue, but $1 billion must be spent in keeping records, auditing, printing and mailing forms, and so on, then the government will have only $99 billion to spend. Thus it will cost the public $100 billion (plus the other welfare costs) to provide $99 billion in revenue that can be used to finance desired expenditures. The size of the administrative costs will vary from one tax to another. For all federal taxes taken together, the administrative cost of the Internal Revenue Service typically runs at only 0.5 percent of tax revenues.

Compliance costs   Administrative costs recorded by the government do not include all collection costs because individual taxpayers bear significant costs in complying with tax laws. Compliance costs include the time used in reading, understanding, and filling out tax forms; using tax lawyers and accountants; keeping records in order to fill out (and possibly defend) the tax forms; mailing the completed returns; and using the banking system to transfer funds. Complying with the tax laws can be quite costly. For example, a recent study estimated that taxpayers devoted about 2,000 billion hours to filing tax returns in 1982.[8] Even though this cost is not recorded as a monetary outlay, it makes the burden on the public greater than the revenue received by government. Valuing this time cost using market wage rates, Slemrod and Sorum estimated that the compliance cost was between 5 and 7 percent of the revenue collected from income taxes. This evidence suggests that compliance costs are substantially larger than the administrative costs recorded by the government.

The Magnitude of Welfare Costs

We have discussed the nature of the welfare cost produced by the "tax wedge." It is also important to understand under what conditions this welfare cost will be high. In other words, what determines the size of the welfare cost? Two important determinants are considered here.

Price elasticities of supply and demand

In Figure 10–9, the original demand and supply curves are D and S. As we have seen, a tax of \$25 per unit produces a welfare cost that can be measured by the triangular area BAD. Now suppose we keep the tax per unit fixed and see what happens to the welfare cost if the price elasticity of demand for the taxed good is greater. A more elastic demand curve—which implies the same before-tax price and quantity—is shown by D'. With this demand curve, the tax would reduce output to Q_3, and the welfare cost would be equal to area KLD. Note that KLD is larger than BAD. Both triangles have the same height ($KL = BA = $ tax per unit), but the base of KLD (LD) is greater than the base of BAD (AD). (Recall that the formula for the area of a triangle is one half the base times the height.)

This illustrates an important proposition: *The more elastic the demand curve for the taxed good is, the greater will be the welfare cost of a given per unit tax.* In other words, taxing goods in inelastic demand will produce a smaller welfare cost. An inelastic demand means that consumption is *less responsive* to the higher price, so the reduction in output produced by the

---

[8]Joel Slemrod and Nikki Sorum, "The Compliance Cost of the U.S. Individual Income Tax System," *National Tax Journal* 38:461–474 (Dec. 1984).

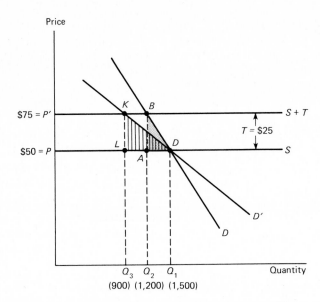

FIGURE 10–9   *Effect of demand elasticity on welfare cost.*

tax will be smaller. Thus, resource allocation is less distorted because it depends to a smaller degree on relative prices in this case.

Other things being equal, then, taxes on goods with inelastic demand are to be perferred. Unfortunately, other things are not always equal. Goods with inelastic demands are often "necessities" that are consumed heavily by low-income households. Cigarettes, for example, are in inelastic demand, but a tax on cigarettes would place a relatively heavier burden on low-income smokers compared with high-income smokers. In short, we must be concerned with the distributional effects (incidence) of taxes as well as their welfare costs, and this frequently involves unpleasant tradeoffs.

On the supply side, a similar analysis can be employed to show that the welfare cost of a given per unit tax will be smaller the more inelastic is the supply curve of the taxed good. (The reader may wish to verify this.) Thus, goods in inelastic demand or supply are good bases for taxes. Because labor supply (in the aggregate) is thought to be very inelastically supplied, a tax on labor income would produce a relatively small welfare cost. Indeed, the belief that the supply of productive resources (land, labor, and capital) is relatively inelastic is in part the basis for support among economists for broad-based taxes such as income taxes. Because the demand and/or supply elasticities of specific goods are generally high relative to the elasticity of labor supply, for example, economists believe that taxes on labor income will produce smaller welfare costs than excise taxes.

The tax rate

By now it is probably obvious that the welfare cost will be greater the larger
the tax per unit (with given demand and supply curves). The exact relationship between the tax rate and the size of the welfare cost is, however, not
obvious and requires careful consideration.

In Figure 10–10, the welfare cost of a $25 per unit tax is equal to area
BAD. Now consider a larger tax per unit of $50. This tax shifts the supply
curve to $S+T_2$, and equilibrium is established at Q_3 and P_3. The welfare cost
is equal to area *KLD*. Triangle *KLD* can be decomposed into four triangles
of equal size: *KRB, RBL, LBA,* and *BAD*. Thus, the welfare cost of the $50 per
unit tax is four times as great as the welfare cost of the $25 tax per unit.
Doubling the tax per unit *quadruples* the welfare cost.

The reason why the welfare cost increases faster than the tax rate can be
understood by considering what happens as the tax is gradually increased.
Raising the tax curtails consumption that is increasingly worth more than its
cost. The additional (marginal) welfare cost is equal to the excess of the
marginal value of curtailed consumption over its marginal cost. For example, if the tax is $25 per unit and is increased slightly, the 1,200th unit will
not be produced (consumed). This unit has a marginal value of $75 and a
marginal cost of $50, so forgoing this unit of output causes a *net* loss of $25.
If the tax is $50 per unit, a small increase will lead to the 900th unit's not
being produced, and that unit is worth $50 more than its cost. In other

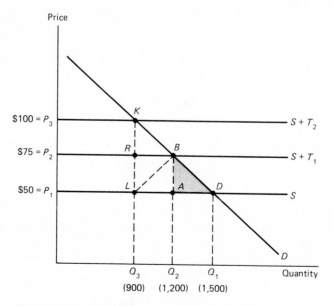

FIGURE 10–10   *Effect of tax rates on welfare cost.*

words, as the tax is increased, the additional consumption that is choked off has a higher and higher net benefit (excess of demand over supply price). The marginal damage done by the tax increases with the tax rate, which implies that the total welfare cost increases more than in proportion to the tax per unit.

One implication of this conclusion is that a number of low-rate taxes can produce the same revenue at a lower welfare cost than one tax levied at a higher rate. Instead of doubling one tax rate (and quadrupling the welfare cost), we can use a second tax and raise the additional tax revenue by only approximately doubling the welfare cost. As we tax more goods at low rates, we begin to approach a broad-based tax like a general sales or income tax. Thus, this analysis also suggests that broad-based taxes are likely to have a smaller distorting effect than will a high tax rate levied on a few goods.

Estimation of the welfare cost of taxation

Our analysis of the determinants of the magnitude of the welfare cost of an excise tax can be summarized by deriving a general formula for estimating the welfare cost. Referring back to Figure 10–10, the welfare cost of the $25 excise tax is given by the triangular area *BAD*. The height of the triangle *(BA)* equals the tax per unit, and the base *(AD)* equals the quantity reduction. Thus, the welfare cost can be expressed as

$$W = \tfrac{1}{2}T\Delta Q \tag{1}$$

where W is the total welfare cost (area *BAD*), T is the tax per unit, and ΔQ is the reduction in quantity caused by the tax. The quantity reduction depends on the elasticity of demand, and we can express the ΔQ term in terms of the demand elasticity. Recall that the price elasticity of demand is defined by

$$\eta = \frac{\Delta Q/Q}{\Delta P/P} \tag{2}$$

By solving equation (2) for ΔQ, we get

$$\Delta Q = \frac{\eta(\Delta P)Q}{P} \tag{3}$$

which shows how the change in quantity depends on the elasticity of demand and the change in price. For an excise tax on a constant cost competitive industry, the change in price caused by the tax (ΔP) is equal to the tax per unit *(T)*, and so the right side of equation (3) can be rewritten as $\eta TQ/P$. Substituting this for ΔQ in equation (1), we get

$$W = \tfrac{1}{2}\left(\frac{\eta T^2 Q}{P}\right) \tag{4}$$

This formula shows that the welfare cost varies in proportion to the elasticity of demand and with the square of the tax per unit, conclusions we have already explained. Equation (4) has been derived for a per unit excise tax; actually, most excise taxes are *ad valorem,* levied as a certain percent of market price rather than as a fixed sum per unit of output. Equation (4) can easily be modified to yield the formula for an ad valorem tax. The tax rate of an ad valorem tax *(t)* is equal to the tax per unit *(T)* divided by the price, or $t = T/P$. Thus, we can substitute tP for T in equation (4) to obtain

$$W = \tfrac{1}{2}\eta t^2 PQ \tag{5}$$

Equation (5) is the most commonly used formula for estimating the welfare cost of an excise tax. As we now understand, the welfare cost depends on the demand elasticity, the tax rate, and the total expenditures on the taxed good *(PQ)*. Variations of this formula have been used to estimate the welfare costs of monopolies, tariffs, and other taxes: It is quite a general formula and well worth understanding thoroughly.

The derivation of equation (5) was based on the assumption that the taxed good was produced under constant-cost conditions. For an increasing-cost industry—one with an upward-sloping supply curve—the formula is slightly different because the welfare cost depends on both supply and demand elasticities. The formula is[9]

$$W = \tfrac{1}{2}\left(\frac{\eta\epsilon}{\eta+\epsilon}\right)t^2 PQ \tag{6}$$

where ϵ is the price elasticity of supply. Equation (5) is the one most frequently used because constant costs are thought to be a reasonable approximation in many cases.

Now let's apply equation (5) to a few hypothetical examples to get a feeling for the likely quantitative significance of the welfare cost of an excise tax. Suppose an ad valorem excise tax of 20 percent were applied to a good with total expenditures *(PQ)* of $1 billion and a demand curve of unitary elasticity. By applying equation (5), $W = \tfrac{1}{2}(1)(0.2)^2 \times \$1$ billion, or $20 million. Because the tax revenue would be $200 million, the welfare cost in this example would be 10 percent of the tax revenue. For a tax rate of 40 percent, the welfare cost would be $80 million, equal to 20 percent of the tax revenue. Whether or not these welfare costs are considered large depends on one's viewpoint, but they are far from insignificant. (Recall too that the formula does not measure the welfare costs due to administrative and compliance costs.)

[9] For a derivation of this formula, see David N. Hyman, *The Economics of Governmental Activity* (New York: Holt, Rinehart and Winston, 1973), pp. 169–171. Note that as ϵ becomes larger and approaches infinity, then $\left(\dfrac{\eta\epsilon}{\eta+\epsilon}\right)$ approaches η as a limit. Thus, for high elasticities of supply, equation (6) approaches equation (5) as a limit.

Incidentally, equation (5), or equation (6) if appropriate, can be used to estimate the welfare cost caused by externalities. In this case, the term t in the formula is interpreted to be the marginal external effect at the market equilibrium as a percent of market price. For example, suppose the marginal external benefit is 10 percent of the market price of some good. If total expenditures on the good are $1 billion and the demand elasticity[10] is 1, then $W = \frac{1}{2}(1) \times (0.1)^2 \times \$1$ billion, or $5 million. The welfare cost is only 0.5 percent of the $1 billion size of the market. This suggests that small external effects are probably not worth trying to correct by government policy. (This is especially true when we recall how difficult it is to design an appropriate corrective policy.) On the other hand, large external benefits will have large welfare costs because the welfare cost here also varies with the square of the marginal external benefit.

Importance of the Welfare Cost of Taxation

The welfare cost of taxation is significant for the analysis of two quite different problems. First, it is useful in comparing taxes with one another to determine what tax or taxes can raise a given revenue at the smallest welfare cost. Although all real-world taxes produce welfare costs, the distortions produced by different taxes are likely to vary considerably. For example, both theory and evidence suggest that an income tax produces a smaller welfare cost than does an excise tax yielding the same revenue.[11] Unless distributional considerations suggest otherwise, this analysis implies that an income tax is better than an excise tax.

The welfare cost of taxes is significant for another, probably more important reason. *It is necessary to consider the welfare cost of taxation as part of the cost involved in carrying out government expenditures.* If the government spends $1 billion on some project, the cost to the public is the direct cost of sacrificing $1 billion in tax revenue *plus* any welfare costs resulting from the taxation. If the welfare cost is $200 million, then the total cost borne by the public will be $1.2 billion when the government spends the $1 billion. Unless the government expenditure of $1 billion produces benefits greater than $1.2 billion, the expenditure policy will be inefficient.

In our earlier discussions of government expenditures, the welfare cost of taxation was ignored. Figure 10–11 illustrates how to incorporate the welfare cost of taxation into an analysis of government spending. Government spending is measured on the horizontal axis, and the marginal bene-

---

[10] The demand elasticity relevant for this computation is the elasticity of the social demand curve including the external benefits, not the consumers' private demand curve.

[11] Arnold C. Harberger, "Taxation, Resource Allocation, and Welfare," in his *Taxation and Welfare* (Boston: Little, Brown, 1974).

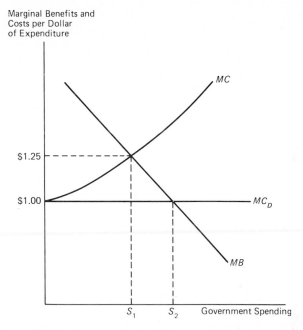

FIGURE 10–11 *Efficient level of government expenditures financed with distorting taxes.*

fits and costs per dollar of expenditure are measured on the vertical axis. The marginal cost of spending is the direct cost ($1 in tax revenue per $1 of expenditure) *plus* the marginal welfare cost of raising revenue. If taxes that produced no welfare costs (i.e., a lump-sum tax) were used, the marginal cost of spending $1 would be $1, and MC_D would be the relevant curve. In this case, the efficient rate of government spending would be S_2, where the government spends up to the point where the marginal benefit equals $1.

When the government uses taxes producing welfare costs, the marginal cost of spending $1 is greater than $1. This is shown by the *MC* curve, where the difference between *MC* and MC_D equals the *marginal* welfare cost of taxation. The *MC* curve slopes upward because the marginal welfare cost of taxation rises with the level of taxation. Recall that the total welfare cost of taxation varies with the square of the tax rate. Thus, each successive increase in the rate (and hence revenue) costs more than the one before, so the *MC* curve slopes upward.

With the upward-sloping *MC* curve, the most efficient level of government spending is at S_1. At this rate of spending, marginal benefits of $1.25 are equal to marginal costs ($1 in direct costs plus $0.25 in marginal welfare cost). Even though there are spending projects available that would produce

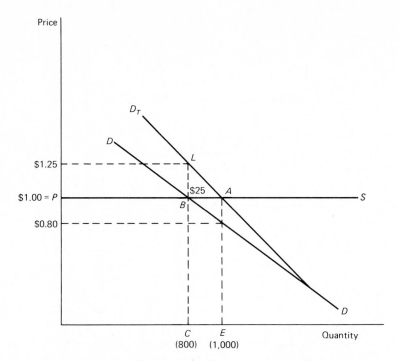

FIGURE 10–12   *Efficient subsidy with external benefits.*

benefits of more than $1 for each $1 spent—as shown over the S_1S_2 range—these projects should not be undertaken. *Note that this means it is not efficient for the government to correct all inefficiencies in resource allocation.* The fact that marginal benefits of spending in the S_1S_2 range exceed the direct costs implies that some inefficiency in resource allocation will remain. However, spending to correct these inefficiencies would produce an even greater inefficiency through the greater welfare cost of the taxes needed to finance the spending.

An example indicates how potentially important this point is. Figure 10–12 shows a competitive industry in which production (or consumption) of the product generates external benefits. *DD* is the private demand curve of the consumers, and the market equilibrium occurs at a price of $1 and an output of 800 units. D_TD shows the social demand curve obtained by adding the marginal external benefit curve (not shown separately) to the private demand curve. Its intersection with the supply curve indicates that the efficient rate of output is 1,000. The welfare cost associated with the competitive underproduction of the good is measured by the area *BAL*. In this example, the welfare cost is $25, or about 3 percent of total expenditures on the good. This welfare cost of $25 is also the *maximum potential welfare gain* possible from increasing output to the efficient level with, for example, a subsidy.

We emphasize that this is only a *potential* gain, which can be realized only if the sole costs of increasing output to 1,000 are the costs of the resources required to produce the additional units of output, as given by the area *BCEA* in the diagram. Any other costs will make the *actual* gain less than $25. Suppose, for example, that an excise subsidy of 20 cents per unit is used to lower the price to consumers to $0.80 in order to induce them to purchase 1,000 units. This subsidy involves a total outlay of $200, and raising this amount of revenue results in additional costs in the form of marginal welfare costs of taxation (taken to include administrative and compliance costs). In addition, there will be administrative and compliance costs associated with the subsidy itself. If the sum of these costs exceeds 12.5 percent of the total cost of the subsidy, or $25, then this subsidy will actually produce a less efficient outcome than would the original market equilibrium. It would then be better not to introduce the subsidy at all.

Note that we are considering a fairly substantial misallocation caused by the externality: The efficient output is fully 25 percent above the market equilibrium output. Nonetheless, a subsidy is likely to make matters worse when all the costs involved are taken into account. This suggests that market misallocations must be quite severe before we can realistically expect an improvement through the use of government spending. Small inefficiencies in the market allocation of resources are best left alone—it would cost more than it is worth to try to correct them.

In short, when the government uses taxes that produce welfare costs, government expenditures must produce substantially larger benefits than would be generated if the taxpayers spent the same sums as they wanted. Otherwise, the expenditures will reduce welfare. In evaluating expenditure programs, it is therefore important to consider the marginal welfare costs of taxation.

Supplementary Readings

BARZEL, YORAM. "An Alternative Approach to the Theory of Taxation." *Journal of Political Economy,* 84(6):1177–1198 (Dec. 1976).

BLUM, WALTER J., and HARRY J. KALVEN, JR. *The Uneasy Case for Progressive Taxation.* Chicago: University of Chicago Press, 1953.

BREAK, GEORGE F. "The Incidence and Economic Effects of Taxation." In Alan S. Blinder et al., eds., *The Economics of Public Finance.* Washington, D.C.: The Brookings Institution, 1974.

MIESZKOWSKI, PETER. "Tax Incidence Theory: The Effects of Taxes on the Distribution of Income." *Journal of Economic Literature,* 7(4):1103–1124 (Dec. 1969).

MUSGRAVE, RICHARD. *The Theory of Public Finance.* New York: McGraw-Hill, 1959.

Review Questions and Problems

1. "Those who pay the tax may not be the ones who bear the tax burden." Explain what this means, and give an example of a tax where such a distinction is important.

2. "In the presence of excise taxes, the price received by producers will differ from the price paid by consumers, and both these prices may differ from what the price would be in the absence of the tax." Give an example to illustrate the point made in this statement, and explain how the relationships among these three prices are used to ascertain the incidence of the tax.

3. In applied tax incidence analysis, economists often assume that excise taxes are borne entirely by consumers. Under what conditions is this assumption appropriate?

4. Suppose the demand curve for a product is perfectly horizontal and that an excise tax of $1 per unit is levied on suppliers. Use supply and demand curves to illustrate who pays the tax.

5. Explain why it is not inconsistent to hold that excise taxes are shifted forward to consumers in the form of higher prices, but to argue that a general sales tax does not lead to higher product prices but instead to lower input prices.

6. The real burden of a tax is the sum of the revenue it raises plus the welfare cost it creates. True or false? Explain.

7. Why does an excise tax produce a welfare cost? Describe this welfare cost. Would there be a welfare cost if the excise tax were placed on an industry with external costs?

8. The excise tax on cigarettes is generally thought to produce a smaller welfare cost (per dollar of revenue) than does the excise tax on wine. Why? Does this imply that the excise tax on cigarettes is a better tax than the excise tax on wine? Why or why not?

9. Why is it important to recognize the welfare cost of taxation when analyzing a government expenditure policy? What role does the welfare cost play in the analysis?

10. A product has a demand curve given by $Q = 2500 - 50P$, and it is produced by a constant cost competitive industry with a supply curve horizontal at a price of $10. Construct a table that shows the tax revenue and total welfare cost with an excise tax of $1 per unit, $2 per unit, and so on up to $10 per unit. What is the average welfare cost per dollar of tax revenue for each tax? What is the marginal welfare cost (the additional welfare cost per dollar of additional revenue) at each tax rate? Do your results conform to the relationships shown in Figure 10–11?

chapter 11
The Federal Individual Income Tax

When most people think of taxes, they think first of the federal individual income tax—*the* income tax. This reaction is not surprising, since in terms of the revenue it raises the individual income tax is the most important tax in the United States. Revenues from this tax totaled $335 billion in 1985 and accounted for nearly half of total federal tax revenues. Put on a more personal level, the average taxpayer paid about $4,000 in federal income taxes in 1985.

Although criticized on several counts, the individual income tax is still considered to be potentially the fairest and most efficient revenue source of the federal government. For this reason, as well as its size, we shall consider this tax in some detail.

What Is Income?

The popularity of the income tax as a revenue source stems from the wide agreement that income is the best measure of a person's ability to pay taxes. The credibility of income as a measure of taxpaying capacity depends critically on the way it is defined. Any definition of *income* is of necessity somewhat arbitrary, but the definition most widely accepted by economists is the following: *Income is the monetary value of consumption plus any change in real net worth over a period of time* (usually taken to be a year).[1]

As a general matter, income can be defined in terms of where it comes from (on the *sources* side of the budget) or where it goes (on the *uses* side of the budget). The formal definition just given is in terms of the uses of income; that is, income is either consumed or saved (thereby affecting net worth). In terms of the sources side of the budget, anything that permits

---

[1] An early case for the use of this general definition was made by Henry Simons, *Personal Income Taxation* (Chicago: University of Chicago Press, 1938).

consumption or adds to net worth would be considered income. This would include wages and salaries, dividends, interest, government transfers, rents, royalties, and gifts (among other things), since all of these either finance consumption or are saved. Hence, the economic definition accords with common usage of the term. Further examination of this definition will show, however, that other, less obvious, items are considered income by economists.

Although income, according to our definition, is measured in monetary units, it need not be received as cash. Fringe benefits provided by an employer, such as free lunches, health insurance, or contributions to pensions, are income, just as are wages paid in cash. Fringe benefits are an example of income in kind rather than cash. Government in-kind transfers (as well as cash transfers) also count as income because the source of income is irrelevant.

There are other important types of income in kind. A person who owns a home consumes housing services, and the monetary value of these housing services should be treated as income. Similarly, goods and services that are produced and consumed within the home also qualify as income. Food preparation, growing of foods at home, housecleaning, and childrearing provided by the husband or wife all constitute services that have a monetary value to the family and hence are income. Even leisure can be considered a consumer good and thus part of income.

The second dimension of our definition of income concerns changes in the value of capital assets. If the value of an individual's home rises from $80,000 to $88,000 over a year, the $8,000 increase in value (or capital gain) is income because it represents an increase in net worth. Two points should, however, be noted. First, only the real increase in the value of the home constitutes income: If the price level rises by 10 percent because of inflation over the year, and at the same time the dollar value of the home rises by 10 percent from $80,000 to $88,000, this nominal gain is not income, since it does not augment the homeowner's ability to consume. Second, the house need not be sold for this appreciation in value to be considered income. Thus, our definition counts income as it *accrues,* not when it is realized through a market sale.

The definition of income is explored further later in the chapter. Before proceeding, however, it should be stressed that the definition discussed here is not the one embodied in current tax laws. Instead, we have developed a broad and comprehensive concept of income that can be used as a benchmark against which the actual definition of taxable income in the tax laws can be compared. There are two reasons why a broad concept of income is important. One is to ensure that the tax is equitable. Income, broadly defined, is a comprehensive measure of the resources available to pay taxes; it is also a primary determinant of an individual's standard of living. Unless income is broadly defined, people who receive income in nontaxable forms will pay lower taxes, and that would be unfair.

A second reason to use a broad measure of income is to promote economic efficiency. If certain types of income are not taxed, people will have an incentive to convert their income into these nontaxable forms, and such a reallocation of resources, induced by tax considerations, would be inefficient. As explained in the last chapter, a broad-based tax leaves few avenues that allow tax liabilities to be reduced by rearranging the use of resources, and therefore the welfare cost of the tax is likely to be small.

Although equity and efficiency criteria seem to favor a broad definition of income, other factors should be considered. In particular, in some cases it is administratively difficult to tax some forms of income. This is especially true when the goods or services consumed are not purchased in the market and therefore have no easily measured monetary value. Consider the value of the services of a stay-at-home spouse: How much are they worth? Although these services have a monetary value, it would be difficult and costly, if not impossible, for the tax collector to measure their value accurately. In such cases, the cost of measurement and the inequities and inefficiencies resulting from incorrect measurement make the exclusion of some items from the tax base the wisest course of action. Thus, our comprehensive definition of income is not intended to be an assessment formula but instead a guiding principle to be considered along with other factors.

Definition of Taxable Income in Practice

The Internal Revenue Code does not explicitly define income; instead, it enumerates items to be included in, and excluded from, the tax base. Altogether the tax laws and regulations, and interpretations based on them, total more than 40,000 pages. It would clearly not be possible, or worthwhile, to describe the tax provisions in detail. In fact, since reforms of the income tax laws are frequently made—seven major reforms were made between 1969 and 1985—any detailed discussion of the tax laws would probably become dated fairly quickly. However, some enduring features of these laws are worth focusing on.

As a result of the numerous provisions in the tax laws, the income that is actually subject to tax—taxable income—is far smaller than the comprehensive measure of income described in the last section. The most comprehensive measure of income available from the National Income and Product Accounts is "personal income." Although personal income is less comprehensive than our definition, it provides some idea of the potential tax base available if income were defined in a comprehensive manner. In 1984, aggregate personal income was $3,112 billion. In the same year, however, taxable income under the income tax was only $1,715 billion, or 55 percent as large as personal income. Actually, because of the use of a "zero bracket amount," the amount of income subject to positive tax rates is about $200 billion less than the Treasury Department's measure of taxable income. *As a consequence, less than half of personal income is subject to tax under the federal income tax laws.*

The difference between taxable and personal income represents the net effect of multitudes of special provisions in the tax laws that specifically exclude some items from taxation. These provisions, which are sometimes called tax preferences and sometimes tax loopholes (depending on whether or not you approve of them), fall into several general categories, which will be discussed next.

Exclusions

Certain types of income are excluded from the tax base and need not be reported as income on the taxpayer's federal tax return. The most important exclusion is government transfers. With minor exceptions, government cash and in-kind transfers are not subject to income taxation. Other items that fall in this category include interest income on state and local bonds; the first $100 of dividend income ($200 for married couples filing a joint return); most types of fringe benefits of employment (most importantly, employer contributions for health insurance and retirement plans); and imputed rents on owner-occupied housing. How large these exclusions are in the aggregate is not known with great accuracy, but these items probably contributed more than $500 billion in nontaxable income in 1984.

Exemptions

The broadest measure of income entered on tax returns is called *adjusted gross income* (or AGI), which is basically income less exclusions. In 1984, the aggregate AGI was $2,158 billion. Several adjustments to AGI are made before taxable income is determined. One of the most important adjustments is the personal exemption. Taxpayers are allowed a personal exemption for the taxpayer, spouse, and each dependent. The personal exemption is a fixed sum that is subtracted from AGI. In 1984, the personal exemption was $1,000 for each person in the family. Thus, a family of four is allowed to subtract $4,000 in personal exemptions from its AGI. Further exemptions are allowed for each taxpayer or spouse who is 65 or older, or blind. In 1984, aggregate personal exemptions removed about $225 billion from the potential tax base.

Deductions

One other major adjustment is made in determining taxable income: The taxpayer either may itemize certain expenditures and deduct them from AGI or may subtract from AGI a fixed sum, formerly known as the *standard deduction* and now known as the *zero bracket amount*.

Which alternative the taxpayer chooses depends on which option provides the larger tax saving. The standard deduction, which is in the form of the "zero bracket amount," was $3,400 for a married couple filing a joint return in 1984. Thus, if a taxpayer gets a larger total deduction without itemizing ($3,400), he or she will take the standard deduction; if the taxpayer's total itemized deductions exceed $3,400, itemizing is better. In general, this means that only higher-income families itemize deductions. In 1984, about 38 percent of taxpayers chose to itemize deductions. The most important allowable deductions are interest paid on loans ($155 billion in 1984); state and local taxes paid ($116 billion); charitable contributions ($42 billion); and allowable medical and dental costs ($21 billion).

Subtracting personal exemptions and deductions from AGI yields taxable income. The relevant schedule of tax rates (more on this in the next section) is applied to taxable income to determine the amount of tax liability. There are, however, two other special features of the tax law that also deserve brief mention.

Tax credits

Tax credits are a relatively new device that permits some specified amount to be deducted directly from the amount of tax paid. For example, there is a 30 percent tax credit for child and day care expenses (decreasing to 20 percent for those earning over $28,000) in connection with the taxpayer's employment. If the taxpayer has $1,500 in child care expenses, then $450 (30 percent of $1,500) can be subtracted directly from taxes due. A variation of the tax credit, the earned income tax credit, is available for low-income families with dependent children. The earned income tax credit is equal to 10 percent of earnings up to $5,000 and then declines until it reaches zero at $10,000 or above. If the earned income tax credit exceeds the amount of income tax due, the government will pay the taxpayer the difference. There are only a few tax credits now in the law, and so quantitatively they are much less important than exclusions, deductions, and exemptions.

Capital gains

When assets are sold or exchanged for a sum larger than the taxpayer paid for them, the excess is called a *capital gain*. For example, if shares of corporate stock are purchased for $10,000 and later sold for $15,000, the capital gain will be $5,000. Capital gains on assets held less than 6 months are counted fully as income, but long-term capital gains—on assets held longer than 6 months—receive a different treatment. Only 40 percent of long-term capital gains are counted as income and subject to tax. This effectively puts an upper limit of 20 percent on the rate that is applied to long-term capital gains. In 1984, total long-term capital gains reported on tax returns equaled $53 billion. Note that capital gains are taxable only when the gain is realized through a sale—if a home or corporate stock is not sold in the tax year, the appreciation in value is not subject to tax.

Tax Rates and Tax Revenues

Any tax can be described by defining the tax base (taxable income in the case of the federal income tax) and the tax rate, or structure of rates, that is levied on the base. Before describing the rate structure of the federal income tax, it is important to identify the different types of rate structures that may be used. There are three major alternatives: *proportional, progressive, and regressive.* The distinction among these rate structures relates to how the average tax rate (total tax liability divided by the tax base) varies with the tax base. If the average tax rate is the same at all levels of the tax base, the tax is proportional; if the average tax rate rises with the tax base, the tax is progressive; and if the average tax rate falls as the tax base increases, the tax is regressive.

Table 11–1 shows examples of each type of rate structure. The proportional tax is levied at a flat rate of 10 percent on taxable income. The average tax rate is 10 percent at all income levels. The marginal tax rate—the rate applicable to additional taxable income—is also constant at 10 percent. Under the progressive tax, tax liability is a higher percentage of taxable income at higher income levels. Note this implies that the marginal tax rate is above the average at each income level (beyond the minimum level). When taxable income rises from $2,000 to $3,000, or by $1,000, the tax goes up by $250, so the marginal rate is 25 percent over this range—greater than the average rate. To achieve a rising average tax rate—a progressive tax—it is an arithmetical necessity for the marginal rate to be above the average

Table 11–1 *Tax Rate Structure*

		Taxable Income					
	$0		$1,000		$2,000		$3,000
1. Proportional tax	$0		$100		$200		$300
Average tax rate	—		10%		10%		10%
Marginal tax rate		10%		10%		10%	
2. Progressive tax	$0		$ 50		$150		$400
Average tax rate	—		5%		7.5%		13.3%
Marginal tax rate		5%		10%		25%	
3. Regressive tax	$0		$150		$200		$250
Average tax rate	—		15%		10%		8.3%
Marginal tax rate		15%		5%		5%	

rate. Under the regressive tax, tax liability is a lower percentage of taxable income at higher income levels. A falling average tax rate implies that the marginal rate at each income level is below the average rate.

Some additional points concerning this classification of tax rate structures should be mentioned. First, note that the absolute size of the tax liability is larger at higher income levels under all three taxes. At least this is true of the hypothetical examples in Table 11–1; it is possible for a regressive tax to impose a higher absolute tax liability at lower income levels, although no real-world taxes do this. Thus, it is somewhat misleading to view a regressive tax as one in which "the poor pay more" despite the common use of this description. The poor would pay a higher *percentage* of their income as taxes than would the nonpoor under a regressive tax, but generally not higher *absolute* taxes than those with higher incomes.

Second, the rate structure influences the distribution of after-tax income in a particular way. The more progressive the rate structure is, the more equal will be the distribution of after-tax income. (A possible exception arises when the incentive effect of the tax changes the before-tax distribution of income. For the moment, this will be ignored.) Under a proportional tax, if taxpayer A has twice the taxable income of taxpayer B before the tax, taxpayer A will have twice the disposable income of taxpayer B after the tax. In this sense, a proportional tax leaves the relative distribution of income unchanged. In contrast, with a progressive tax, taxpayer A will have less than twice the after-tax income of taxpayer B. Therefore, a progressive tax makes the relative after-tax distribution more equal. The opposite happens under a regressive tax because taxpayer A will end up with more than twice the income of taxpayer B.

Third, and perhaps most important, the technical distinction between rate structures is defined in terms of the average tax rate and the tax base. A flat rate tax of 30 percent on the price of cigarettes is a proportional tax, as is a 4 percent sales tax or a 2 percent tax on property values. In this technical sense, there are no regressive taxes in the United States: All taxes are either proportional or progressive with respect to their own tax bases.

These terms, however, have come to be used in a different, but not necessarily incorrect, way to refer to tax burdens in relation to income—regardless of the legal bases. For example, if the tax burden of a consumer under an excise tax is considered relative to the individual's income (rather than to the person's purchases of the taxed product), then a tax that is proportional with respect to its own base might be either regressive or progressive with respect to income. Consider the excise tax on cigarettes. Cigarette expenditures are a higher fraction of the incomes of low-income families, so an excise tax proportional to cigarette consumption will be regressive relative to income.

There is no reason why the terms *progressive, proportional,* and *regressive* should not be used in this way; indeed, most economists, as well as other interested persons, typically use this designation so perhaps this is the strongest indirect evidence that income is considered a good tax base. If people did not feel that income was the most appropriate tax base, why compare tax burdens under nonincome taxes with income? If income is considered the best possible tax base, however, why bother to use any other tax? If we wish to have tax burdens bear a definite relationship to income, there is only one way to accomplish this with certainty, and that is by taxing income explicitly rather than indirectly through the use of excise, sales, and other taxes.

Rate structure of the federal individual income tax

Having identified the various types of possible tax rate structures, let's look at the actual rate structure of the federal individual income tax. Table 11–2 shows the rate structure for married taxpayers filing joint returns in 1986. (There are different rate schedules for single taxpayers, unmarried heads of households, and married taxpayers filing separate returns.) The rates are expressed as marginal rates applying to different taxable income brackets.

From this schedule, it can be seen that taxpayers with taxable incomes up to $3,670 paid no income tax. ($3,670 is referred to as the *zero bracket*

Table 11–2   *Rate Structure of the Federal Income Tax, 1986*

Taxable Income	Marginal Tax Rate	Tax at Midbracket	Average Tax Rate (tax as percentage of taxable income at midbracket)
$0–3,670	0%	$ 0	0%
3,670–5,930	11	124	2.6
5,930–8,200	12	385	5.4
8,200–12,840	14	844	8.0
12,840–17,260	16	1,523	10.1
17,260–21,800	18	2,285	11.7
21,800–26,540	22	3,214	13.3
26,540–32,260	25	4,451	15.2
32,260–37,980	28	5,967	17.0
37,980–49,420	33	8,656	19.8
49,420–64,740	38	13,454	23.6
64,740–92,360	42	22,165	28.2
92,360–118,040	45	33,743	32.1
118,040–175,230	49	53,533	36.5
175,230 and above	50		

Source: *The Administration's 1985 Tax Proposals* (Washington, D.C.: American Enterprise Institute, 1985), Table A1 and calculations by the authors.

amount; formerly, it was called the *standard deduction.*) People with taxable incomes pay taxes that are calculated as follows. If taxable income is $4,000, the 11 percent marginal rate will apply only to income in excess of $3,670, or to $330. Thus, the tax will be $36.30. If taxable income is $7,000, falling in the third bracket, the tax will be equal to 11 percent of the second bracket amount, $2,260 ($5,930 minus $3,670), or $248.60, *plus* 12 percent of the next $1,070 (the amount of taxable income falling in the third bracket, $7,000 minus $5,930), or $128.40. Thus, the total tax will be $377. Obviously, for taxpayers in higher brackets, this calculation can be quite tedious, but the Internal Revenue Service simplifies matters by providing detailed tables that show the tax due at all income levels except the relatively high ones.

As indicated in the table, the marginal tax rates ranged from 11 percent in the lowest bracket to 50 percent on all taxable income in excess of $175,230. Consequently, the average tax rate rises with taxable income, at least beyond the zero bracket amount, so that the tax is progressive relative to taxable income. The marginal tax rate at each income level exceeds the average tax rate, again beyond the zero bracket amount.

Before 1985, the bracket amounts did not change from year to year unless there was a deliberate change in the tax law. However, in 1985, the bracket amounts (as well as the personal exemption) were indexed for the first time, as a result of provisions in the Economic Recovery Tax Act of 1981. With indexing, the bracket amounts rise from one year to the next by the same percentage as the increase in the overall price level. For example, if prices rise by 10 percent over the relevant year, the $21,800 to $26,540 bracket will become the $23,980 to $29,190 bracket in the following year. That bracket will still be subject to a 22 percent marginal rate, however; the rates are not automatically adjusted.

Indexing has the effect of imposing the same *real* tax burden on taxpayers with the same *real* incomes year after year, regardless of how their nominal incomes have been affected by inflation. Before indexing, the tax code was subject to what is called *bracket creep;* that is, inflation pushed taxpayers into higher rate brackets and increased their real tax burden even if their real incomes did not rise at all. This was a major problem in the 1970s when rapid inflation resulted in millions of taxpayers' finding themselves in higher tax brackets and paying a larger share of their incomes in taxes. If the tax law is not changed further, the indexing provisions in current law will "inflation-proof" the tax in the future.

Note that in Table 11–2 the average and marginal rates are given as they apply to *taxable income.* As explained in the last section, taxable income is much smaller than the comprehensive measure of income we defined earlier. Thus, if tax burdens were given as a percentage of a more inclusive measure of income, the average rates would be lower. For example, in 1986 a family of four with an AGI of $9,575 actually paid no income tax: Its average tax rate relative to its total income was zero because of the combined effect of the personal exemptions, the earned income tax credit, and the zero bracket amount. To put this in perspective, total federal income taxes are only about 10 percent of personal income in the United States, despite the use of tax rates ranging from 11 to 50 percent. The reason is the existence of many exclusions, deductions, and exemptions that make total taxable income roughly half as large as total personal income.

Where the revenue comes from

In 1983, 96 million individual federal income tax returns were filed, resulting in total tax revenues of $276.1 billion. Table 11–3 provides more detailed information on how income taxes were distributed among various adjusted gross income classes in that year. Of the 96 million tax returns, more than 80 percent reported AGIs between $5,000 and $75,000. At the extremes, 15.5 percent had AGIs under $5,000 and 1.6 percent had AGIs of more than $75,000.

The last two columns in Table 11–3 give taxes as a percentage of AGI and taxable income for each AGI class. In both cases, the average tax rates rise steadily with AGI, reflecting the progressivity of the income tax. At low AGI levels, the tax is a relatively small percentage of either taxable income or AGI. This is because personal exemptions and the zero bracket amount exempt most of the income of low-income families from taxation. As we move to higher AGI classes, a larger percentage of each taxpayer's AGI is subject to tax, and at higher marginal rates. Thus, the average tax rates rise as AGI increases from a rate of 1.1 percent of AGI for those in the under-$5,000 class to a rate of 35 percent of AGI (or 43.5 percent of taxable income) for taxpayers with AGI of more than $150,000.

Considering how average tax rates vary by income level conveys some feeling for how the income tax burden is distributed among the population. Another perspective is provided by looking at the share of total taxes paid by selected income classes. For example, Table 11–3 indicates that the 58.1 percent of taxpayers with AGIs under $20,000 paid only 12 percent of total income taxes. At the other extreme, only 1.6 percent of taxpayers reported AGIs above $75,000, but this small group paid more than 25 percent of total income taxes. The top 10.9 percent of taxpayers, those with AGIs above $40,000, paid fully 52 percent of the tax. For many years, the top 10 percent of taxpayers have contributed around half of all federal income taxes.

Table 11–3 suggests that high-income taxpayers pay a substantially larger share of their incomes in taxes than other groups do and, in fact, provide most of the revenue. This evidence contrasts sharply with apparently widely held perceptions that wealthy persons avoid paying their "fair share" of taxes through the use of tax loopholes. For example, according to a poll by the Roper Organization, the prevailing view is that more than half of the

Table 11–3   *Distribution of the Tax Burden, 1983*

AGI Class	Percentage of All Returns	AGI (in billions)	Taxable Income (in billions)	Taxes (in billions)	Taxes as % of AGI	Taxable Income
$0–4,999	15.5%	$ 43.0	$ 24.1	$ 0.5	1.1%	2.0%
4,999–10,999	21.2	156.8	111.6	7.8	5.0	7.0
11,000–19,999	21.4	291.8	231.4	25.7	8.8	11.1
20,000–24,999	11.5	235.8	191.6	25.8	10.9	13.5
25,000–39,999	19.1	561.7	452.4	72.2	12.9	16.0
40,000–74,999	9.3	440.9	348.5	73.4	16.6	21.1
75,000–149,999	1.3	126.4	98.2	29.9	23.7	30.4
150,000 and over	0.3	116.2	93.6	40.7	35.0	43.5
All returns	100.0	1,972.0	1,551.3	276.1	14.0	17.8

Note: Details may not add to total because of rounding.
Source: "Selected Statistical Series," *Statistics of Income Bulletin,* 4:3 (Winter 1984–1985), Table 3.

very wealthy pay no income tax at all. The Roper poll also found that 76 percent of the public felt that high-income families paid too little in income taxes.[2] In view of the data in Table 11–3, such findings suggest widespread misunderstanding of how income tax burdens are actually distributed. There is, however, another possibility. Recall that AGI itself is not a comprehensive measure of income, so the tax rates in the table do not show tax burdens relative to true incomes. Thus, if high-income taxpayers have true incomes larger than their AGIs, then the tax rates in Table 11–3 will overstate their true burden.

To determine how tax burdens are related to a more comprehensive measure of income than AGI, we use the results of a study by Joseph Minarik.[3] To measure taxpayers' incomes more accurately, Minarik broadened the definition of income to include many types of income that are excluded from AGI under the tax laws. Using 1977 data, Minarik added the following to each taxpayer's AGI: the one half of long-term capital gains that were excluded in 1977; other excluded capital gains; excluded dividends; interest on state and local securities; life insurance interest; imputed rent of homes; employee fringe benefits; and government transfer payments. The result was

[2] The Roper Organization Inc., *The American Public and the Income Tax System,* vol. I: *Summary Report,* July 1978, pp. 42, 45.

[3] Joseph Minarik, "The Yield of a Comprehensive Income Tax," Table A–1, in Joseph Pechman, ed., *Comprehensive Income Taxation* (Washington, D.C.: The Brookings Institution, 1977).

Table 11–4 *Taxes Relative to Comprehensive Income, 1977*

AGI Class	Comprehensive Income (CI) (in billions)	Taxable Income (TI) (in billions)	TI/CI	Tax (in billions)	Tax/CI
$0–5,000	$ 124.2	$ 16.3	13.1%	$ 0.7	0.5%
5,000–10,000	183.8	97.5	53.0	8.4	4.6
10,000–20,000	453.9	304.7	67.1	39.8	8.8
20,000–30,000	345.4	241.6	69.9	40.8	11.8
30,000–50,000	204.4	144.1	70.5	31.5	15.4
50,000–100,000	86.9	61.5	70.8	19.4	22.3
100,000 and over	58.2	40.1	68.9	19.1	32.8
All Returns	$1,456.8	$905.9	62.1%	$159.8	10.9%

Source: Comprehensive income calculated using ratios given in Joseph Minarik, "The Yield of a Comprehensive Income Tax," Table A-1, in Joseph Pechman, ed., *Comprehensive Income Taxation* (Washington, D.C.: The Brookings Institution, 1977); other data from U.S. Treasury, Internal Revenue Service, *Statistics of Income—1977 Individual Income Tax Returns* (Washington, D.C.: U.S. Government Printing Office, 1980), Table 1.1.

a measure of "comprehensive income" that was 27 percent larger than AGI on average.

Table 11–4 builds on Minarik's results for 1977 to show how tax burdens were related to his measure of comprehensive income. Note first that taxable income as a percentage of comprehensive income (TI/CI) is lower for low AGI classes than for higher AGI classes. In fact, only 13.1 percent of comprehensive income is subject to tax in the lowest AGI class. (The main reason is that government transfers are not counted in AGI but are included in comprehensive income.) *Taken in their entirety, the various exclusions, deductions, and exemptions shield a larger portion of income from taxation for low- and middle-income taxpayers than for high-income taxpayers.*[4] As a result, the tax system is still quite progressive when taxes are compared with comprehensive income. Average tax rates rise from 0.5 percent for the lowest AGI class to 32.8 percent for the highest. The median federal taxpayer, whose AGI fell in the lower range of the $10,000 to $20,000 AGI class, paid less than 8.8 percent of comprehensive income in taxes, below the national average rate of 10.9 percent and far below the 32.8 percent rate paid by taxpayers with AGIs above $100,000.

Thus, the available evidence suggests that special tax provisions do not

[4] The figures in Table 11–4 actually understate the extent to which this is true because the zero bracket amount is counted as taxable income, whereas it is, in fact, nontaxable income. Since the zero bracket amount is a larger fraction of low than high incomes, it increases the share of low incomes that are not taxed by more than that for high incomes.

enable the wealthy to avoid paying income taxes. This is not the same as concluding that the distribution of tax burdens is fair; it is still possible to make the value judgment that the wealthy should pay even more in taxes. Nor is it the same as concluding that every high-income taxpayer pays a sizable income tax. In fact, each year a number of wealthy persons pay no federal income tax at all. In 1982, of the 169,367 tax returns with AGIs above $200,000, 262, less than 0.2 percent, were nontaxable. In most of these cases, the nontaxability reflects innocuous and legitimate considerations. For example, 153 of the 262 nontaxable returns were nontaxable because the taxpayers paid taxes to other countries (because their incomes were earned there) and could therefore make use of the foreign tax credit.[5] The foreign tax credit is a provision designed to avoid double taxation of the same income. Tables 11–3 and 11–4 include both nontaxable and taxable returns in each AGI class and, therefore, give the average position of all persons in each income class.

Evolution of the income tax structure

There have been numerous changes in the federal income tax over the last several decades. Some of these changes have reflected deliberate changes in the tax laws, but others, like the effects of bracket creep, have occurred as a result of interactions between the tax code and economic conditions. In this section we shall summarize briefly what these changes have meant for the average and marginal tax rates at different levels of income.

Table 11–5 gives estimates of the average and marginal tax rates for hypothetical four-person, husband-wife families at different relative positions in the income distribution. Income levels are specified as multiples of the median family income in each year, and the families are assumed to claim deductions equal to the average deduction at their income level. Average tax rates are given as a percentage of AGI.

Let's consider average tax rates first. By looking across each row, we see that average tax rates rise with income in every year, reflecting the progressivity of the tax. Now, however, we want to focus on the changes in the tax rates over time. Table 11–5 shows a fairly steady increase in average tax rates at all income levels between 1960 and 1980. At the median-income level, the increase was from 8.6 percent to 11.6 percent, an increase of 35 percent. The increases were even greater at higher income levels: at three and five times the median-income level, the tax rates increased by 50 percent over this period. Thus, the tax became more progressive, since tax rates were increased more for upper-income families.

[5] See Section 5, "High Income Returns: Taxable and Nontaxable," U.S. Treasury, Internal Revenue Service, *Statistics of Income—1982* (Washington, D.C.: U.S. Government Printing Office, 1984).

Table 11–5 *Average and Marginal Individual Income Tax Rates, 1960–1984*

Year	Multiple of the Median Income				
	0.25	0.5	1	3	5
Average Tax Rates					
1960	0%	1.7%	8.6%	16.2%	21.5%
1970	0	6.0	10.1	18.3	25.0
1975	−10.0	2.7	9.6	20.2	28.1
1980	−8.6	5.4	11.6	24.7	32.4
1984	−5.0	6.0	10.3	20.5	26.1
Marginal Tax Rates					
1960	0%	20.0%	20.0%	30.0%	38.0%
1970	0	16.8	19.5	32.8	49.2
1975	−10.0	16.0	22.0	42.0	53.0
1980	0	16.0	24.0	49.0	59.0
1984	12.5	14.0	22.0	42.0	49.0

Note: The negative rates for the lowest-income families reflect the impact of the refundable earned income tax credit.
Source: Joseph J. Minarik, *Making Tax Choices* (Washington, D.C.: Urban Institute, 1985), Tables 3 and 4.

Congress did not, however, legislate higher tax rates during the 1960–1980 period. In fact, there were several cuts in tax rates. Despite this, tax burdens increased at most income levels. The reason was bracket creep: inflation was pushing taxpayers into higher rate brackets faster than Congress cut the rates.

Between 1980 and 1984, average tax rates fell at most income levels. The changes reflect the Reagan tax cut (the Economic Recovery Tax Act of 1981) which cut all marginal tax rates by approximately 23 percent. This cut in rates was gradually phased in between 1981 and 1984. Note, however, that tax rates did not fall by 23 percent; rather, average tax rates fell by approximately half that amount. Once again, the reason was bracket creep. Inflation during this period continued to push taxpayers into higher brackets at the same time the rates themselves were coming down, and the net effect was that bracket creep offset about half the tax cut. (Recall that indexation did not begin until 1985.) For low-income taxpayers, their tax rates actually rose somewhat, since inflation continued to erode the real value of personal exemptions and the zero bracket amount over this period and so thrust more low-income families into positive tax brackets.

In 1984, average tax rates stood approximately at the levels they had attained in the mid-1970s, when they were higher than at any previous time in the postwar period. Thus, despite the Reagan tax cuts of 1981–1984, the tax rates are still quite high by historical standards.

The bottom part of Table 11–5 shows how marginal tax rates changed over the 1960–1984 period. The pattern is similar to that of average tax rates. Marginal rates rose sharply between 1960 and 1980, especially for upper-income taxpayers, and then declined somewhat between 1980 and 1984. In 1984, marginal tax rates were also at about the same levels they were in the mid-1970s and so were still quite high relative to those in previous years. Note that at most income levels, marginal tax rates were approximately twice the corresponding average tax rates. This difference is significant because the adverse incentive effects of income taxation are related to the level of marginal tax rates.

Proportional Income Taxation

Incidence

As our discussion of tax incidence in Chapter 10 indicated, the person responsible for paying a tax may not be the economic unit that actually bears the burden. In our discussion of tax liabilities among income classes, however, we implicitly assumed that the size of tax payments measured the size of the tax burdens. Now we need to examine whether a person who pays $5,000, for example, in federal income taxes actually bears a tax burden of precisely that size.

If the income tax changes before-tax incomes—for example, by causing a reduction in labor supply, which, in turn, increases wage rates—then a person's tax liability will tend to overstate his or her actual tax burden because part of the total burden is shifted to others in the form of a higher wage rate. Clearly it is *possible* for an income tax to be shifted in this way, but the relevant question is whether it *actually* is. To begin our examination of this question, we analyze the incidence of a proportional tax on labor income and defer consideration of the more relevant case of progressive taxation until the next section. Although the income tax applies to other types of income as well as labor income, wage and salary income accounts for 85 percent of AGI so an emphasis on labor supply effects is not misplaced. A proportional tax on labor income (e.g., wages and salaries), wherever earned, is a broad-based tax that cannot be avoided by workers' moving from one industry to another. In contrast, recall the method of shifting in response to an excise tax on one industry—in which productive resources move to untaxed industries. With an income tax, workers can reduce their tax liabilities only by reducing the quantity of labor supplied, that is, by working and earning less. Leisure is not taxed, only money income is, so workers might be led to consume more leisure and less money income in response to a tax on money income.

Consider a flat 40 percent tax on labor income. As a first approximation, this reduces a worker's net rate of pay by 40 percent. If the worker's market wage rate is $10 per hour, a 40 percent tax means that the individual's net, or take-home, wage rate will be $6, because the government receives $4 of every $10 earned. The primary question is whether a lower net rate of pay will lead workers to reduce the quantity of labor services supplied. According to economic theory, the answer is unclear. A reduction in the net wage rate influences labor supply decisions in two opposing ways. One is through the income effect: Workers are made poorer and thus will tend to work more to partially offset the income loss due to the tax. The other influence is the substitution effect: The net rate of pay is lower, so consuming leisure (working less) involves a smaller sacrifice in income. *The income effect of an income tax thus favors more work, whereas the substitution effect favors less work;* hence, the net effect is uncertain.

The net effect of a change in effective wage rates on the quantity of labor supplied is reflected in the slope of the labor supply curve. If the income effect of a lower wage rate exactly offsets the substitution effect, the labor supply curve will be vertical. In this case, a proportional income tax does not change the quantity of labor supplied and therefore has no effect on market wage rates. The income tax will not be shifted, and the final incidence will fall on workers whose take-home pay falls by exactly the amount of the tax.

Figure 11–1 illustrates this case. D_L is the market demand for labor services: It shows the maximum wage rate that employers are willing to pay for alternative quantities of labor. S_L is the supply curve, drawn as vertical under the assumption that income and substitution effects exactly offset one another in the aggregate. Before the tax, $10 is the market wage rate. A proportional tax of 40 percent can be analyzed in one of two equivalent ways: an upward shift in the supply curve or a downward shift in the demand curve. With a vertical supply curve, it is simpler to view the tax as shifting the demand curve. Thus, D_L' shows the maximum net (after-tax) rate of pay associated with alternative quantities of labor. The net rate of pay is 40 percent (rather than a fixed amount) lower than the market wage rate at each quantity, so D_L' is determined by pivoting the original demand curve downward rather than by a parallel shift. The new equilibrium under the income tax occurs where S_L intersects D_L', because workers make labor supply decisions in response to their net rates of pay. With the vertical supply curve, the quantity of labor is unchanged, and the effect of the tax is to reduce the net rate of pay from $10 to $6. Employers, of course, are still paying $10 ($4 of which goes to the government), so their productive activities are not influenced by the tax. *When the supply curve is vertical, the*

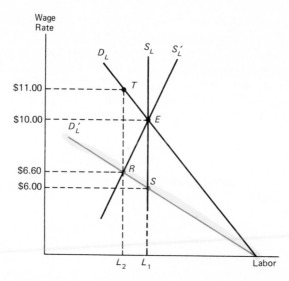

FIGURE 11–1   *Proportional tax on labor income.*

incidence of a proportional tax on labor income falls on workers who bear the full burden of the tax in the form of lower net rates of pay.

If the supply curve is upward sloping, which will be true if substitution effects outweigh income effects, market wage rates will rise and workers will not bear the full burden of the tax. In Figure 11–1, if the supply curve is instead the upward-sloping S_L' curve, equilibrium under the tax will occur at point *R*. In this case, at the lower net rate of pay, $6.60, workers have reduced their labor supplied, so with labor scarcer, it commands a higher market wage rate, $11. The wage rate actually received by workers has fallen from $10 to $6.60, or by $3.40, but the tax per unit of labor is $4.40. With an upward-sloping supply curve, the incidence of the tax lies only partially with workers because their net rate of pay does not fall by the full amount of the tax. Unless labor supply is quite elastic, however (that is, unless the quantity of labor falls sharply with a change in net pay), the major part of the tax is still borne by workers.

Economists generally believe that the quantity of labor supplied is fairly insensitive to moderate changes in net wage rates. Empirical evidence (to be considered later) as well as common sense suggests that this is plausible. Many factors other than the monetary return influence work effort decisions (such as prestige, a desire to get away from home, to avoid boredom, or to associate with congenial co-workers), and it may be that the independent effect of the wage rate is relatively modest. If this is true, then the assumption of a vertical supply curve is reasonably plausible, and the incidence of

a proportional income tax falls on the workers. This is an important conclusion, and it strengthens the case for using an income tax, because it means
that the true burden of the tax can be divided among people according to
a reasonable, comprehensive measure of their taxpaying capacity, namely,
their income. On the other hand, if an income tax is shifted capriciously
through the economic system, it would be difficult to use it and achieve an
equitable distribution of the true tax burden by this means.

Welfare cost

Now let's consider the welfare cost, or excess burden, of a proportional tax
on labor income. It is sometimes argued that an income tax will have no
welfare cost if it leads to no change in the quantity of labor supplied. This
is untrue. As indicated earlier, an unchanged quantity of labor reflects two
opposing influences of equal size: an income effect that stimulates more
work effort and a substitution effect that stimulates less. Any tax will have
an income effect because it reduces after-tax income; this is not an excess
burden, however, but rather an unavoidable effect of the tax. It is the substitution effect of the tax that is responsible for the excess burden, and this
exists even if the net effect of the income and substitution effects together
is zero.

Figure 11–2 illustrates this point. The budget line relating money income
and leisure before the tax is YN, and a worker, Rufus, is initially in equilibrium at point E, working NL_1 hours and earning EL_1. A proportional tax
lowers the net wage rate, confronting Rufus with the $Y'N$ budget line. Assuming that Rufus prefers to work the same number of hours, his new equilibrium is at point E_1; he is still working NL_1 hours, but with a lower after-
tax income of E_1L_1 and tax liability of EE_1. The move from point E to point
E_1 reflects the combined effect of the income and substitution effects of the
tax.

To show the welfare cost, assume that a lump-sum tax is used instead to
raise the same amount of revenue. A lump-sum tax equal to EE_1 dollars
shifts the budget line downward to KK', parallel to the original budget line
but lying below it at all points by the amount EE_1. The KK' budget line
passes through point E_1, but it is steeper than the $Y'N$ budget line produced
by the income tax because the net rate of pay (at the margin) is not reduced
by a lump-sum tax. With the KK' budget line Rufus's preferred point is E_2
where KK' is tangent to indifference curve U_2. At point E_2 Rufus is working
more and is better off despite paying the same tax ($ME_2 = EE_1$) as under the
income tax. Thus, it is possible to raise the same revenue as the income tax
without harming Rufus so much; the income tax has a larger burden (an
excess burden) than necessary to generate any given amount of revenue.
The size of the welfare cost is measured by the difference in welfare under

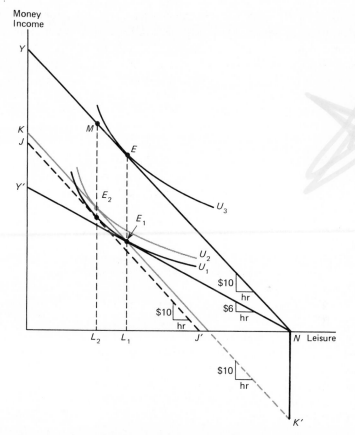

FIGURE 11–2 *Welfare cost of a tax on labor income.*

the income tax (U_1) and under an equal-yield nondistorting tax (U_2), equal to *KJ* measured in dollars.

An income tax distorts labor supply decisions by leading taxpayers to work less (NL_1 rather than NL_2) than is economically efficient. Even though work effort may be the same before and after the tax (comparing points *E* and E_1), the relevant comparison is between work effort under the income tax and under an equal-yield nondistorting tax such as a lump-sum tax. Work effort and welfare will always be greater under a lump-sum tax, and this is an indication of how the income tax stifles productive labor effort.

The reason why an income tax produces a welfare cost is that work effort decisions are guided by the after-tax return to working, whereas the actual productivity of working is indicated by the higher before-tax return. If a person's market wage rate is $10 an hour, this is a measure of the value of the workers' labor services. With a 40 percent tax, the taxpayer will work up to the point where $6 just compensates for giving up the last hour of leisure (at point E_1 in Figure 11–2). The marginal cost of working an additional hour is then $6 (the value of the leisure sacrificed), and the marginal social benefit is $10. Even though the marginal social benefit of greater work effort exceeds marginal cost, the worker will not work longer hours because, as a result of the tax, the individual receives only $6 for his or her efforts, not a wage equal to the $10 marginal social benefit. Thus, taxpayers are led to undersupply labor services by an income tax because of the "tax wedge" that separates market and net wage rates. (Compare this analysis with our discussion of the welfare cost of the NIT: Note that both a positive and a negative income tax produce the same type of welfare cost.)

Progressive Income Taxation

The qualitative analysis of a progressive tax on labor income is quite similar to that of a proportional tax. In both cases, the tax reduces the net rate of pay to workers and so may influence the quantity of labor supplied. Just as with a proportional tax, a progressive tax has opposing income and substitution effects; so the net effect is uncertain on theoretical grounds. If a progressive tax does not lead to a change in the quantity of labor supplied, then market wage rates will be unaffected, and the incidence of the tax will be borne by workers, just as with the proportional tax.

In considering a progressive tax, however, it is important to understand the roles played by the marginal and average tax rates. Under a proportional tax, the marginal and average rates are equal, and, furthermore, they are equal for all taxpayers. Under a progressive tax, the marginal tax rate exceeds the average tax rate, and the rates vary from one taxpayer to another (because they vary with income). This is significant because *the size of the income effect depends on the average tax rate, whereas the size of the substitution effect depends on the marginal tax rate.*

The average tax rate of any type of income tax for a taxpayer indicates how large a share of income is sacrificed to the tax collector. The greater is the share of income paid in taxes, the larger the incentive will be to work more to recoup some of the loss. Hence the income effect favoring more work is related to how much tax is paid, and this depends on the average tax rate. The marginal tax rate determines the reward associated with changes in work effort and is therefore related to the substitution effect. Welfare costs reflect substitution effects and so are dependent on the marginal rate of tax.

Table 11–6 will clarify these remarks. Assume we have a taxpayer with an income of $10,000 and we want to compare three alternative ways of raising $2,000 in tax revenue. One way is to use a proportional tax of 20

Table 11–6   *Taxpayer with $10,000 Income*

Tax Structure	Tax	Average Tax Rate	Marginal Tax Rate	Sacrificed Disposable Income If $1,000 Less Is Earned
1. Proportional: 20% on all income	$2,000	20%	20%	$800
2. Progressive: exempt $5,000; 40% tax on income above $5,000	$2,000	20%	40%	$600
3. Progressive: exempt $7,500; 80% tax on income above $7,500	$2,000	20%	80%	$200

percent. A second way is to use a progressive tax that exempts the first $5,000 in income and taxes income in excess of that amount ($5,000 for a taxpayer with a total income of $10,000) at a rate of 40 percent. A third way is to use a progressive tax that exempts the first $7,500 in income and taxes income above that amount ($2,500 for our taxpayer) at a rate of 80 percent.

A taxpayer with $10,000 in income will pay $2,000 in taxes under all three taxes. This loss in income implies an income effect to work more, with the size of the effect roughly equal for all three taxes because they have the same average tax rate. The substitution effects will differ greatly among these taxes, however. The marginal tax rate determines how any change in earnings affects disposable income. Under the proportional tax, if the taxpayer earns $1,000 less, disposable income will fall by $800 (taxes fall by $200). Because disposable income would have fallen by $1,000 with the same reduction in earnings in the absence of the tax, the tax lowers the cost of reducing earnings (working less) by $200, from $1,000 to $800. It thus becomes less expensive to consume leisure rather than work; this is the reason for the substitution effect favoring less work. Note, however, that the relative cost of earning less is even lower under the progressive tax alternatives. With the most progressive tax, the taxpayer sacrifices only $200 by earning $1,000 less, because the *marginal* rate of tax is 80 percent. It is clear that the taxpayer will be more likely to work less under the progressive taxes because the net rate of pay for work at the margin (in the neighborhood of $10,000) is lower, so the incentive to substitute leisure for money income is greater.

These remarks do not prove that people will work less under a progressive tax, because there is still an income effect favorable to work effort. Instead, we are only pointing out the respective roles of the average and marginal tax rates. The size of the marginal tax rate governs the strength of the incentive to work less (as well as the other adverse incentive effects of the tax to be considered later). Because the marginal tax rates are above the average tax rates for a progressive tax, adverse incentive effects due to the substitution effects of the tax are likely to be of greater significance. Still, in comparision with a no-tax situation, the income effect on work effort might be (and probably is for many taxpayers) large enough to produce no change in work effort.

Comparison of progressive and proportional taxes

In general, it is not possible on theoretical grounds to predict how work effort will be affected by a progressive tax relative to no tax at all. Although it is true that the higher marginal tax rates are relative to average rates, the more likely work effort is to fall, we cannot be certain of the net effect of opposing income and substitution effects. Somewhat more can be said, however, when we compare a progressive tax with an equal-yield proportional tax.

Figure 11-3 illustrates this analysis. The budget line under a progressive tax is shown as the truncated line Y_1BN. The tax illustrated exempts a small amount of income (along BN) and then taxes increments in income above that level at successively higher marginal rates. The budget line becomes flatter as the taxpayer works more, indicating that disposable money income rises by successively smaller amounts as the taxpayer works (and earns) more and moves into successively higher marginal rate brackets. Equilibrium under the progressive tax occurs at point E_1, where U_1 is tangent to Y_1BN. Tax liability equals ME_1, the difference between gross earnings and after-tax disposable income. For reference purposes, line KK' shows the budget line produced by an equal-yield lump-sum tax. The taxpayer would be in equilibrium at point E_3, working more and on a higher indifference curve under the lump-sum tax. The fact that the taxpayer is better off under the lump-sum tax illustrates the welfare cost of the progressive tax, which is qualitatively similar to a proportional tax.

A proportional tax that raises the same revenue is shown by the budget line Y_2N. Confronted with Y_2N, the taxpayer is in equilibrium at point E_2, where U_2 is tangent to Y_2N. Note that point E_2 also lies on KK', indicating that the tax revenue is the same as under the progressive tax. (Tax revenue under the proportional tax equals RE_2, which is equal to ME_1.) The only difficulty in making this comparison is that one must imagine varying the tax rate under the proportional tax (pivoting Y_2N about point N) until an equal tax yield equilibrium is found. A little experimentation will confirm that there must be such an equilibrium somewhere between E_1 and E_3 on KK'. Exactly where this occurs does not matter for the qualitative conclusions.

An equal-yield proportional tax leads to more work effort and a higher level of welfare than a progressive tax does. Greater welfare under the proportional tax means that it has a smaller (but not zero) welfare cost than

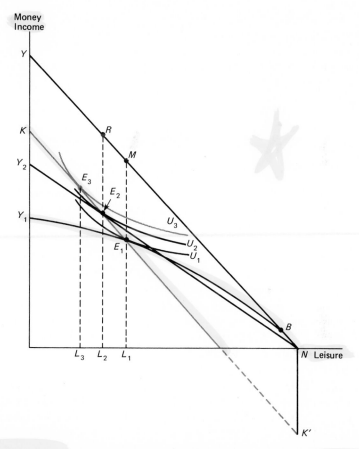

FIGURE 11–3 *Comparison of proportional and progressive taxes on labor income.*

the progressive tax does. Although the diagram may seem complicated, the reason for these findings is simple. Because both taxes are designed to yield the same revenue, the income effects are approximately the same. Marginal tax rates are higher under the progressive tax, however, so the incentive to work less is greater. The higher the marginal tax rate is for any given amount of revenue, the greater will be the labor supply distortion. (In fact, the reason a lump-sum tax has no welfare cost is that its marginal tax rate is zero—tax liability does not increase if a person earns more.)

The conclusion that work effort is greater under a proportional tax of equal yield cannot be fully generalized for a group of taxpayers with different incomes. Figure 11–3 shows that one taxpayer *who pays the same tax under the two alternatives* will work more under a proportional tax. If a flat rate tax on all taxpayers is used instead of a progressive tax, some taxpayers will pay larger taxes under the proportional tax, and others will pay smaller taxes. (Refer to Table 11–1.) For example, higher-income taxpayers pay larger taxes under a progressive tax, so substituting a proportional tax will lower their marginal and average tax rates. A lower marginal tax rate produces an incentive to work more, but a lower average tax rate produces an incentive to work less so the net effect on this income group is uncertain. For some groups of taxpayers, therefore, we cannot state definitely that total work effort will be greater under a proportional tax. Only for taxpayers who have lower marginal and the same or higher average tax rates under a proportional tax can we be reasonably sure that work effort will be greater than under a progressive tax. It may be greater for other taxpayers (if the substitution effect is larger than the income effect), but we cannot demonstrate that on theoretical grounds.

Empirical evidence

So far, we have seen that an income tax may either increase or reduce the quantity of labor supplied, compared with a hypothetical situation with no tax. Empirical evidence is needed to determine the direction and magnitude of the effect. Unfortunately, this turns out to be a difficult problem to grapple with empirically. Basically, this is because the income tax is of universal coverage, so there is no group of workers whose behavior can be interpreted as reflecting what work effort would be in the absence of the tax. Furthermore, variations in labor supply can take a variety of forms, some of which are very difficult to measure: longer vacations, earlier retirement, less overtime, less labor force participation by married women, or less intense work while on the job. Despite these difficulties, there are some studies that consider the labor supply effects of income taxes.

The earliest empirical work dealing explicitly with income taxes was based on surveys of workers who were questioned concerning the determinants of their work effort. Generally, these surveys concentrated on high-income workers (such as lawyers, accountants, and business executives) who were in high marginal tax brackets.[6] Without exception, these studies concluded that income taxes had little effect on work effort. A majority of people interviewed in these surveys typically reported that taxes had no effect on their

---

[6]George Break, "Income Taxes, Wage Rates, and the Incentive to Supply Labor Services," *National Tax Journal,* 6:333 (Dec. 1953); T. H. Sanders, *Effects of Taxation on Executives* (Boston: Graduate School of Business Administration, Harvard University, 1951); R. Barlow, H. E. Brazer, and J. N. Morgan, *Economic Behavior of the Affluent* (Washington, D.C.: The Brookings Institution, 1966); and Daniel M. Holland, "The Effects of Taxation on Effort: Some Results for Business Executives," *1969 Proceedings of the National Tax Association* (Columbus, Ohio: National Tax Association, 1970), pp. 428–516.

work effort, 10 to 20 percent reported they worked less, and a somewhat larger percentage reported they worked more.

Survey methods in economics are, however, generally felt to be unreliable, and more recent research has been based on econometric methods. Much of this empirical research, done by labor economists, has involved estimating labor supply elasticities for various subgroups within the population.[7] A common finding has been that married men are relatively unresponsive to variations in net wage rates, with a labor supply elasticity estimated as close to zero. On the other hand, females—especially married females—are quite responsive to changes in net wage rates, with labor supply elasticities sometimes estimated as high as 1.0. A survey of the econometric research by the Congressional Budget Office concluded that the labor supply elasticity of the population as a whole (a weighted average of the population subgroups) lies in the 0.1 to 0.3 range.[8] More recently, Don Fullerton surveyed the evidence and concluded that 0.15 is a reasonable value for the aggregate labor supply elasticity.[9]

To see what such elasticities imply for the effect of income taxes let's suppose for simplicity that taxes on labor income (taking income and payroll taxes together) are levied at a flat rate of 40 percent. A labor supply elasticity of 0.15 implies that these taxes would reduce the quantity of labor supplied by 6 percent. A progressive income tax would cause a somewhat larger reduction. A study by Jerry Hausman focused directly on the labor supply effects of income taxes;[10] Hausman concluded that taxes on labor income reduce the labor supply of husbands by about 8 percent and of wives by about 30 percent. To date, Hausman's findings represent the largest estimated effects of income taxes on labor supply.

As this discussion suggests, there is no consensus on how large an effect income taxes have on labor supply. Fifteen years ago, the prevailing view was that the effects were small or nonexistent, but more recent work has come to conclude that there is a significant negative effect. However, it still seems safe to conclude that the aggregate labor supply curve is quite (though not perfectly) inelastic, so the incidence on income taxes is largely borne by the workers themselves.

[7] Glen G. Cain and Harold W. Watts, eds., *Income Maintenance and Labor Supply* (Chicago: Rand McNally, 1973), contains several studies dealing with the responsiveness of labor supply to marginal tax rates in taxes and transfer programs. In particular, see their article, "Towards a Summary and Synthesis of the Evidence."

[8] Congressional Budget Office, *An Analysis of the Roth-Kemp Tax Cut Proposal,* Oct. 1978.

[9] Don Fullerton, "On the Possibility of an Inverse Relationship Between Tax Rates and Government Revenues," *Journal of Public Economics,* 19:3–22 (Oct. 1983).

[10] Jerry A. Hausman, "Labor Supply," in Henry J. Aaron and Joseph A. Pechman, eds., *How Taxes Affect Economic Behavior* (Washington, D.C.: The Brookings Institution, 1981), pp. 27–72.

Tax Preferences

Up to this point our theoretical analysis has assumed that all types of income (except leisure) were subject to tax and that a person's tax liability did not depend on how his or her income was spent. The federal income tax, however, contains numerous exclusions and deductions, and these provisions in the tax law—tax preferences, or tax loopholes—have economic effects of their own. As we will show, in fact, these tax provisions have much the same economic effects as excise subsidies.

For simplicity, assume that we have a proportional income tax levied at a rate of 50 percent. If there are no exclusions, exemptions, or deductions, our taxpayer, Rufus, with a total income of $10,000 will pay $5,000 in taxes. Now suppose expenditures on good X can be deducted from total income; the 50 percent rate applies to taxable income, which is now defined as total income less expenditures on good X. If Rufus spends nothing on good X, his taxable income will be $10,000 and his tax will be $5,000, so he will have $5,000 remaining after taxes to spend on other goods (besides X). If, on the other hand, he spends $1,000 on good X, his taxable income will be $9,000, and his tax liability only $4,500. Spending $1,000 on good X reduces his taxes by $500, so the net cost to Rufus of consuming $1,000 of good X is only $500 (i.e., the cost of X minus the tax saving). *For every $1 spent on the deductible item, taxable income falls by $1, so taxes fall by $1 times the (marginal) tax rate*—in this case, 50 percent. This lowers the net cost of consuming the deductible item, just as an excise subsidy does.

To develop this analysis more fully, consider Figure 11–4. The before-tax budget line relating consumption of good X and other goods is MN. It has a slope of $1, assuming the market price of X is $1 per unit. A 50 percent proportional income tax with *no* deductions shifts the budget line to M_1N_1, parallel to MN but $5,000 below it. (This parallel shift does not mean that the income tax is a lump-sum tax. Rather, we are taking work effort and, hence, before-tax income as given and examining the effects on consumption of various goods with after-tax income. An income tax does not affect the relative costs of consuming different goods, so the M_1N_1 budget line is parallel to MN.) When no deduction is permitted, Rufus must give up $1 in other goods to consume a unit of X, and the slope of M_1N_1 is $1. His equilibrium is at point E, consuming X_1 units of X.

If expenditures on good X are deductible, Rufus's budget line will become M_1N. Because tax liability falls by $0.50 for each unit of X consumed, the net cost of consuming X falls from $1 to $0.50, and the slope of M_1N is $0.50. The tax liability now depends on how much X is consumed. If no X is consumed, Rufus will be at point M_1, consuming $5,000 worth of other goods and paying taxes of $5,000 (equal to MM_1). At the other extreme, Rufus can consume 10,000 units of X and pay no taxes; he will then be at

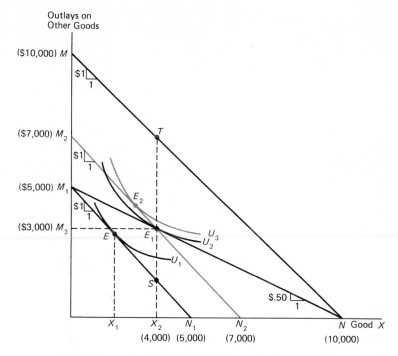

FIGURE 11–4   *Economic effects of tax loopholes.*

point N. In general, the tax liability equals the vertical distance between MN and M_1N. Confronted with a lower net price for X, Rufus increases his consumption. Equilibrium occurs at point E_1, where M_1N is tangent to indifference curve U_2. At this point, Rufus is consuming 4,000 units of X and \$3,000 of other goods. His tax liability is \$3,000, equal to TE_1 in the diagram. His taxes are therefore \$2,000 lower than if the deduction had not been allowed. This tax savings is equal to E_1S because in the absence of the deduction his taxes would have been TS ($=MM_1$, or \$5,000); with the deduction they are only TE_1.

Note that the effect of the deduction is the same as when the government uses no deduction and grants an excise subsidy to good X. If the deduction were not permitted, the government would have \$5,000 in revenue and Rufus would be confronted by the budget line M_1N_1. If the government then pays half the unit cost X, Rufus would face the M_1N budget line, and the cost of the subsidy would be \$2,000 (E_1S.) Rufus would end up at the same point (E_1), and the government would still have \$3,000 to finance other expenditures. *It makes no difference whether the government permits the deduction, or does not permit it and uses part of the greater tax revenue to subsidize consumption of good* X. This is why the tax savings, E_1S, due to the deduction is sometimes called a *"tax expenditure"* by economists: The deduction has the same effect on resource allocation as would an outright excise subsidy of the same magnitude. The only difference between subsidizing explicitly and subsidizing indirectly with a deduction is in the size of the government budget. With the deduction, the tax revenue is $3,000, whereas with an explicit subsidy it is $5,000 ($2,000 of which is spent subsidizing good X).

In recent, years, the Congressional Budget Office has been required to produce a "tax expenditure budget" that estimates the revenue loss (comparable to E_1S in Figure 11–4, summed over all taxpayers) caused by tax preferences. All together, there are more than 100 tax preferences that have been examined in this way. Table 11–7 provides estimates of the revenue losses in 1986 attributable to some of the more important tax preferences.

These estimates show clearly that the tax preferences in the tax code amount to quite substantial, hidden subsides for certain types of activities. Indeed, some activities are more heavily subsidized through the tax code than through outright spending. For instance, home ownership is encouraged by the deductibility of mortgage interest and property taxes on owner-occupied housing: The combined revenue loss is greater than $40 billion. This is several times larger than the expenditures on housing programs (see Table 8–1). Of course, the tax expenditure primarily encourages housing outlays by middle- and upper-income families (the ones who itemize deductions), whereas outlays on housing programs primarily benefit low-income families.

A major purpose of the tax expenditure budget is to draw attention to the extent to which the tax code affects resource allocation and the distri-

---

Table 11–7   *Selected Tax Expenditures, Fiscal Year 1986 (billions of dollars)*

Exclusion of employers' contributions to medical insurance premiums	$27.7
Exclusion of pension contributions and earnings	83.7
Exclusion of social security benefits	25.8
Partial exclusion of capital gains	16.4
Deductibility of mortgage interest	32.8
Deductibility of state and local taxes	41.7
Deductibility of charitable contributions	12.3
Credit for child care expenses	2.5

Note: The estimates are projections based on 1983 data.
Source: Congressional Budget Office, *Tax Expenditures: Current Issues and Five-Year Budget Projections for Fiscal Years 1984–1988* (Washington, D.C.: U.S. Government Printing Office, 1983), pp. 48–58.

bution of income through its favorable treatment of certain items. Many economists believe we should apply the same criteria to the evaluation of these indirect subsidies that we do to the outright expenditures of government.

The welfare cost of tax preferences

Because the government permits expenditures on certain goods to be deductible, taxpayers have an incentive to devote more of their incomes to purchasing these goods because the tax deductibility lowers their net prices to taxpayers. The same general analysis applies when some types of income are excluded from the tax base. Because fringe benefits of employment are excluded, workers have an incentive to have employers provide health and life insurance (among other items) for them because it is untaxed. If an employer gives a worker $1,000 in health insurance, it is not taxed; however, if the $1,000 is paid in cash, taxes must be paid. If the worker's marginal rate is 30 percent, he or she will be able to purchase only $700 in health insurance; however, at the same cost to the employer, $1,000 can be provided as a fringe benefit. This is one reason for the rapid growth in fringe benefits in the last several decades.

Returning to Figure 11–4, when the deduction is used, tax revenue is equal to $3,000, or 50 percent times taxable income of $6,000 ($10,000 minus the $4,000 expenditure on X). This same revenue could be raised by taxing *total* income, $10,000, at a rate of only 30 percent. This is what much of the tax reform debate is all about: *Is it better to use lower rates on a more comprehensively defined tax base or to use higher rates on a smaller tax base?* Figure 11–4 can help us understand one factor relevant to making that choice. A tax rate of 30 percent on total income would produce an after-tax budget line M_2N_2, lying $3,000 below the before-tax budget line. This budget line passes through point E_1, the equilibrium when the deduction is allowed, because TE_1 equals $3,000. Although the same tax revenue is raised, Rufus is better off under this tax without the deduction: He is in equilibrium on indifference curve U_3 at point E_2. Rufus is better off with a more comprehensive tax base and a lower tax rate. The reason is that the tax deduction distorts the taxpayer's choices by artifically lowering the price of X and leads to overconsumption of X. The broad-based income tax does not distort choices among different ways of spending income and is therefore more efficient.[11]

What we have just illustrated is the welfare cost of the resource misallocation that results from tax preferences: The same tax revenue could be raised using a tax without preferences, which would place a smaller real

---

[11]This conclusion does depend on the assumption that work effort will be the same whether or not a loophole is used, which is plausible in most cases.

burden on the taxpayer. A recent study estimated the total welfare cost for all tax preferences in 1974 to be $8 billion—which was about 7 percent as large as federal income tax revenue was in that year.[12] With the increases in marginal tax rates since 1974, the distorting effects of tax preferences would be higher today. Note that this loss is in addition to the loss caused by the effects on labor supply. (Recall that in Figure 11–4 we assumed that labor supply was fixed.)

In addition to distorting the way taxpayers receive or spend their incomes, tax preferences may be responsible for other types of welfare costs. A multitude of special tax provisions adds greatly to the complexity of the tax law. This probably increases the administrative costs for the Internal Revenue Service. Even more important, complexity imposes compliance costs on taxpayers. A majority of taxpayers now seek professional assistance in preparing tax returns. Among taxpayers with only an elementary school education, over 90 percent required professional assistance; by contrast, over half of college-educated taxpayers did their own returns. In 1982 the professional tax service industry grossed about $3 billion. Moreover, this figure does not count the value of the time spent by taxpayers who do their own returns. According to one recent estimate, taxpayers' compliance costs were between $17 and $27 billion in 1982, or from 5 to 7 percent of tax revenue.[13] Not all of this cost is exclusively the result of the complexity produced by tax preferences, but a significant portion probably is.

Efficiency considerations therefore seem to suggest that it would be better to eliminate tax preferences (use a more comprehensive definition of income) and use lower tax rates on a larger tax base. Before accepting this conclusion, however, let's look at some of the arguments for keeping tax preferences.

Rationales for tax preferences

There are some logically valid arguments for using special tax provisions in the income tax. The most important relate to equity, externalities, and administrative costs, which we consider in turn.

Equity   Tax preferences can have implications for both horizontal equity and vertical equity. Let's consider vertical equity first. Recall that *vertical equity* means taxing people with different taxpaying abilities differently. Be-

---

[12]Jacquelene M. Browning, "Estimating the Welfare Cost of Tax Preferences," *Public Finance Quarterly,* 7:199–219 (Apr. 1979). To show the welfare cost in dollars in Figure 11–4, draw a budget line parallel to *MN* and just tangent to U_2. The distance between the vertical intercept of this budget line and point M_2 gives the welfare cost.

[13]Joel Slemrod and Nikki Sorum, "The Compliance Cost of the U.S. Individual Income Tax System," *National Tax Journal* 38:461–474 (Dec. 1984).

cause there are so many different special tax provisions, it is easy to single out particular preferences that benefit special groups. For example, excluding cash and in-kind transfers from taxation benefits the poor; the standard deduction (zero bracket amount) benefits the middle class; and the treatment of capital gains benefits the wealthy.[14] When all departures from a comprehensive definition of income are considered, however, the evidence shows that a larger share of real income is taxed at higher income levels—though there is not much difference between middle- and high-income levels in this regard (see Table 11–4). This finding implies that low-income taxpayers benefit from special provisions somewhat more than other income classes do.

Tax preferences can be used to increase or reduce the real tax burden across income classes. The same results can be achieved, however, by varying the tax *rates* that apply to different incomes, thereby avoiding the inefficiencies associated with tax preferences. For this reason, vertical equity considerations do not seem to provide a strong case for tax preferences.

Horizontal equity means taxing people equally who have equal taxpaying capacity. If income (comprehensively defined) is used as the tax base, then it should be a reasonable index of the taxpayers' ability to pay taxes. Is it possible that we can achieve a better measure of taxpaying capacity by departing from a broad definition of income?

To see why this may be so, consider medical expenses. It is widely felt that medical expenses should be deductible from total income in the interests of equity, and the present tax law permits this to some degree. The relationship between horizontal equity and the deductibility of medical expenses can be illustrated by comparing two families' ability to pay, who have equal incomes but different medical expenses. Family A has a total income of $10,000 and $2,000 in medical expenses. If no deduction is allowed, family A will be taxed the same amount (other things being equal) as family B will, with an income of $10,000 and no medical expenses. If the deduction is allowed, family A will have a taxable income of only $8,000, and it would then pay the same taxes as family C will with an $8,000 income and no medical expenses. The question is this: Should families A and B be considered to have equal taxpaying capacities (as when no deduction is allowed), or should families A and C be considered equal (as when the deduction is allowed)?

To answer this question, it is necessary to make a value judgement. Many believe that it is more equitable to permit the deduction, arguing that medical expenses are a burden on people and do not constitute any taxpaying capacity. This view is strongest when it is applied to catastrophic medical expenses and becomes less plausible when it is extended to certain types of medical care that are voluntarily chosen and are in part consumption

---

[14]Philip Stern, *The Rape of the Taxpayer* (New York: Random House, 1973).

items. For example, a person can deduct the cost of installing air conditioning if a doctor will certify that it is necessary to relieve allergy symptoms. In this case, there are nonmedical benefits not only for the allergy sufferer but for other family members as well. Should the cost of the air conditioning be fully deductible, partially deductible, or not deductible?

Whether, on balance, the existing special tax provisions lead to a more equitable measure of taxpaying capacity is debatable. As the medical expenses example may suggest, it is clearly possible to make a value judgment that horizontal equity is improved by certain tax preferences. Few important tax preferences, however, have been seriously defended on this basis. Most tax experts seem to believe that equity considerations strengthen the case for using a broad measure of income as the tax base.

Externalities   In our discussion of the welfare cost of tax preferences, it was implicitly assumed that only the taxpayer secured benefits from consuming the tax-subsidized good. If, however, external benefits are associated with consumption of some good, the private equilibrium level of consumption is too low, and it is possible for a subsidy to improve resource allocation. Thus, tax preferences—which are akin to indirect excise subsidies—could lead to a more efficient pattern of resource allocation if they are targeted on goods with significant external benefits.

Two questions should be raised concerning the externality argument for tax preferences. First, do the activities that are now encouraged by the tax laws really have important external benefits? In all probability, some—like charitable contributions—probably do, whereas others—like home ownership—do not. There is little evidence on this matter one way or the other.

Second, even if we grant that there are external benefits, is the particular type of subsidy implied by a tax preference capable of leading to a more efficient resource allocation? As we saw in Chapter 2, an incorrectly designed subsidy can make matters worse even in the presence of external benefits. In general, a per unit subsidy equal to the size of the marginal external benefit at the efficient quantity (see Figure 2–3) is required to attain the efficient level of consumption. But the subsidy implicit in tax preferences is linked to the taxpayer's marginal tax rate: A tax preference lowers the price by a percentage equal to the marginal tax rate. Only by coincidence will the marginal tax rate be the correct rate at which to subsidize externality-generating activities.

A related problem arises from the graduated rate structure of the income tax. Taxpayers are in different marginal tax brackets, so the implicit subsidy rate of a loophole varies among taxpayers. Thus, the net cost of giving a dollar to charity is $0.50 for a taxpayer in a 50 percent marginal tax bracket and $0.80 for someone in a 20 percent bracket. If there are external benefits, such a subsidy would be efficient only if the marginal external benefit were $0.50 per dollar for the taxpayer in the 50 percent marginal tax bracket, $0.20 per dollar for one in the 20 percent bracket, and so on. This is unlikely to be the case: Why is $1 given to charity more valuable to society when donated by someone in a 50 percent bracket than when given by someone in a 20 percent bracket? In general, the externality argument for a subsidy calls for the same rate of subsidy for all consumers, and loopholes violate this condition. (There are exceptions to the rule that the rate of subsidy must be the same for all individuals, but they generally involve subsidies to poor persons and appear to have little relevance for tax loopholes.)

On balance, these remarks suggest a certain weakness in the externality argument for tax loopholes. When external benefits exist, an outright subsidy is probably more capable of improving resource allocation than a tax loophole is.

Administrative costs   Some types of income are excluded because it is argued that including them would be too costly on practical grounds. Income must be valued in money terms to be taxed, and it is difficult to place a monetary value on some types of income. A clear example is provided by household services (such as food preparation, child care, and housekeeping) provided by the taxpayer. These services are income, but what is their monetary value?

The issues here are, in principle, clear-cut. If any type of income is not taxed, there will be equity and efficiency costs. But the process of placing a money value on some types of income also has a cost that must be weighed against the equity and efficiency gains of taxing all income equally. In addition, the difficulty of placing an accurate money value on items such as household services can also lead to inequities. These factors must be weighed against one another in each separate case. The types of income to which this rationale for exclusion from the tax base has been applied include unrealized capital gains, household services, imputed rent on owner-occupied housing, and some in-kind transfers. Experts differ on the validity of this argument in specific cases; many feel that imputed rents, in-kind transfers, and some types of unrealized capital gains could be included at moderate cost. Whatever the merits of this argument in specific cases, it is valid in principle, and it warns against trying to apply the theoretical definition of income as the sole criterion in defining the tax base. Some types of income are too costly to tax.

Other Effects of Income Taxation

Saving

The rate of return to private saving is part of income and is also taxed subject to some important qualifications noted later. Income taxation may reduce saving by lowering the return a person can realize by saving. For example, suppose the interest rate is 8 percent; in the absence of the income tax a person can, by saving $1 now, consume $1.08 a year from now. If this $0.08 in interest income is subject to tax at a marginal rate of 25 percent, $0.02 in taxes must be paid, leaving only $1.06 to be consumed. In other words, income taxation at a marginal rate of 25 percent reduces the return to saving from 8 percent to 6 percent. This makes present consumption less expensive compared with future consumption: Without the tax, consuming $1 now means sacrificing $1.08 in consumption a year later (or $2 in consumption 9 years later), whereas with the tax, only $1.06 is sacrificed next year to consume $1 now. Confronted with a lower net return to saving, the taxpayer has a greater incentive to consume rather than save.

One important form of saving that is frequently overlooked should be mentioned, investment in human capital. People can save and increase their future income by undertaking training or schooling in a way that increases their productivity. Spending $40,000 to attend college[15] might result in earnings of $6,000 more per year thereafter. This increment in earnings, however, is also subject to tax. If the marginal tax rate is 25 percent, the effect of increasing gross earnings by $6,000 will be to increase disposable income by only $4,500. The incentive a person has to augment earning capacity is therefore diminished in the same way as is the incentive to save in other ways.

What complicates the analysis of the effect of the income tax on saving is the existence of several provisions in the tax law that treat saving preferentially. For instance, employers' contributions to pension plans (subject to ceiling amounts) and the interest income earned each year from these plans are excluded from taxation. Similarly, in 1981 in an effort to encourage saving, Congress enacted a new tax preference that permits workers to make a tax-deductible contribution of up to $2,000 each year to individual retirement accounts (IRAs). Because of such provisions, the law effectively taxes some forms of saving and not others, or taxes them at different rates. As a consequence, determining the net effect of taxes on the incentive to save is difficult. Because of the limitations that apply to the tax preferences intended to encourage saving, however, Galper and Steuerle argued that the overall effect is to discourage saving.[16]

Even if the overall level of saving is not affected, it is clear that the tax affects the allocation of capital. For example, mortgage interest payments are deductible, and the imputed income of owner-occupied housing is not taxed. These provisions give taxpayers the incentive to accumulate their savings in the form of homes, rather than as investments that finance industrial plants and equipment.

---

[15]Earnings that are sacrificed while attending college should also be considered as part of the cost of increasing productivity through schooling.

[16]Harvey Galper and Eugene Steuerle, "Tax Incentives for Savings," *The Brookings Review,* Winter 1983, pp. 116–23.

Several other taxes, such as the corporation income tax and property taxes, also affect the level and form of saving and capital accumulation. After discussing these taxes in the next two chapters, we shall consider the way the tax system as a whole affects saving and capital accumulation in Chapter 14.

Inflation and mismeasurement of capital income

Inflation potentially has two important consequences for the way our income tax laws operate. First, inflation will cause bracket creep unless the rate brackets and exemptions are properly indexed. Indexation became a part of the tax law in 1985, and so inflation-produced bracket creep is a thing of the past, unless the law is again changed. Inflation, however, has another important effect on the operation of the income tax: Inflation causes capital income to be measured incorrectly.

The tax system bases taxes on nominal capital income rather than real capital income, and these two magnitudes differ significantly in inflationary periods. As an example, suppose you purchase a $10,000 corporate bond that yields a 10 percent interest return. The $1,000 in annual income is the nominal capital income on your investment. If there is a 10 percent inflation rate, however, your real capital income will be zero, since the $1,000 interest payment just offsets the loss in purchasing power of the $10,000 bond. Although your real capital income is zero, you will be taxed on the $1,000 in nominal interest income. Similarly, if you purchase corporate stock for $10,000 and sell it for $20,000 10 years later after the price level has doubled, your real capital gain will be zero, but your tax will be based on the $10,000 nominal capital gain.

What this mismeasurement of capital income means is that the rate of taxation on real capital income is largely determined by the rate of inflation. Table 11–8 illustrates this point by considering the case of a taxpayer who invests $10,000 in a bond. We assume that the interest rate on the bond (column 2) is always two points greater than the inflation rate (column 1),

Table 11–8 *Inflation and Tax Burden on Interest Income:*
40% Rate Bracket

Inflation Rate (1)	Nominal Interest Rate (2)	Interest Income on $10,000 (3)	Real Income Before Tax (4)	Income Tax (5)	Average Tax Rate on Real Interest Income (6)
0%	2%	$ 200	$200	$ 80	40%
4	6	600	200	240	120
8	10	1,000	200	400	200
12	14	1,400	200	560	280

so the real rate of interest is always 2 percent. This means that real capital income (column 4) is always $200 but that nominal capital income (column 3) is greater than $200 whenever inflation exceeds zero percent. The income tax on the capital income for a 40 percent bracket taxpayer is shown in column (5): The income tax is 40 percent of nominal capital income. The last column shows how the effective tax rate on real capital income varies with the rate of inflation. Even at low rates of inflation, taxes on real capital income may exceed 100 percent.

By taxing nominal capital income instead of real capital income, the income tax law levies extremely severe tax rates on capital income whenever the inflation rate is high. In effect, the interaction of inflation and the income tax sharply lowers the net (after-tax) real return to saving, diminishing the incentive of taxpayers to save. In addition to the potential significance of this for capital accumulation, it is also relevant from an equity standpoint. Those who receive capital income pay higher taxes than do those with equal real incomes derived from other sources. Since high-income taxpayers receive a larger share of their income in the form of capital income, their real tax burdens are increased during inflationary periods by more than other income classes.[17]

The marriage tax

Married couples and single taxpayers use different tax rate schedules to calculate their taxes. Since the marginal rates rise more rapidly with income on the single taxpayer's schedule, a single person will pay a larger tax than a married couple with the same combined income will, sometimes as much as 20 percent more. Single people often feel, understandably, that this is unfair. Another charge of unfairness is that two single people may find their tax liability considerably larger if they marry. This is the so-called marriage tax and has led to such bizarre outcomes as couples divorcing on December 31 (so they can file as single taxpayers for that tax year) and then remarrying on January 1.

Table 11–9 shows how the tax system affects tax liabilities according to the combined incomes of husbands and wives, based on the tax law in 1983.[18] (The figures in the table give the *change* in combined tax liability for the two persons, not the total amount of tax.) As Table 11–9 shows, some couples will pay more in taxes if they are married, but others will pay

---

[17]According to Tables 11–3 and 11–4, this means that average tax rates, especially for upper-income families, tend to be understated. The income figures given there include nominal capital income and therefore overstate the real incomes of taxpayers.

[18]The figures in Table 11–9 already take into account the deduction allowed for married working couples. Couples may deduct 10 percent of the income of one spouse, up to a ceiling amount of $3,000.

Table 11–9   *How Marriage Affects Tax Liabilities*

Husband's Income	Wife's Income				
	$0–5,000	*$5–10,000*	*$10–20,000*	*$20–30,000*	*$30,000+*
$0–10,000	$ −22	$ 169	$ −89	$−471	$−871
10–20,000	−298	255	331	598	702
20–30,000	−754	139	474	1,050	1,690
30–40,000	−1,270	−8	627	1,460	2,300
40–50,000	−1,730	7	1,120	2,550	2,650
50,000+	−3,240	−1,250	209	1,300	2,980

Source: Daniel Feenberg, "The Tax Treatment of Married Couples Under the 1981 Tax Law," *National Bureau of Economic Research Working Paper No. 872,* Apr. 1982, p. 14.

less. The outcome depends on the sizes of their respective incomes. If one person has a high income and the other a low income, marriage will reduce their combined tax liabilities. (This situation is illustrated by the first column and first row in the table.) On the other hand, if two people have fairly similar incomes, marriage will increase their tax liability, and even more so if their incomes are fairly high. This is the "marriage tax" outcome.

With the rapid growth of two-earner families, the number of families subject to the marriage tax has increased greatly, and charges of unfairness have become common. Avoiding outcomes that will appear unfair to some parties, however, is extremely difficult. For example, the marriage tax could be avoided by not allowing joint returns, thereby requiring all persons to file single returns. Then two single persons who marry will continue to file two returns, and their combined tax liability will be unaffected.[19]

Sounds simple, doesn't it? But this change would produce a tax that differently affects two families with the same total incomes. For instance, if couples must file separately, a couple with incomes of $50,000 and zero will pay more in taxes than will a couple with incomes of $25,000 and $25,000. This follows from the progressivity of the rate schedule. Eliminating one apparent source of inequity simply produces another.

With a progressive tax, it is impossible to design a tax system that both equally taxes families with the same income and avoids the marriage tax. We saw that we could easily change the tax so that it is "marriage neutral," but this immediately produced a situation in which families with the same incomes paid different taxes.

[19] This ignores the possibility that the income of one person could be claimed as income on the other person's tax form. Transfers of income from the higher- to the lower-income spouse would reduce the couple's total tax liability under a progressive rate schedule.

The only way to design a tax that treats equally families with the same incomes and avoids the marriage penalty is to use a proportional tax (sometimes called a *flat rate tax*). Under a proportional tax, tax liability is not affected by being divided between two or more people, and families and individuals with the same incomes would pay the same tax. As long as the tax is a progressive one, however, conflicts among these equity objectives are unavoidable, and any compromise that is achieved, such as the current tax, will still appear unfair to some people.

Proposal for Reform: A Flat Rate Tax

Let's examine a proposal to substitute a flat rate, or proportional, tax on a broad measure of income for the current graduated (progressive) income tax that reaches less than half of total income. If personal income, as defined in the National Income and Product Accounts, is used as the tax base, a flat rate tax of 11 percent would raise the same revenue that the 1985 tax structure raised with tax rates ranging from 11 to 50 percent on the narrower base of "taxable income." We do not mean necessarily to advocate personal income as the tax base; the important point is that it is feasible to define income broadly enough so that a surprisingly low tax rate is capable of raising the same revenue as the present tax. For example, if AGI were the tax base, a tax rate of 14 percent would suffice (see Table 11–3).

Advantages of a flat rate tax

A flat rate tax avoids many of the perceived defects of the present graduated tax. For example, the present tax uses high marginal rates on a narrow tax base. This type of tax undermines economic productivity in two ways. First, it seems likely that total output will be lower than efficient because of the way high marginal tax rates reduce the incentive to supply labor and capital. A flat rate tax would not avoid this cost altogether, but a lower marginal rate would probably reduce the magnitude of the disincentive effects significantly. Second, high tax rates on a narrow base reduce productivity by inducing taxpayers to channel part of their incomes into nontaxed forms. This is the welfare cost resulting from tax preferences, and a flat rate tax on a broad measure of income would also diminish this problem. (It would probably be impossible in practice to define income so broadly as to completely eliminate this distortion, however.)

In addition to these efficiency advantages, it is claimed that a flat rate tax is simpler. Much of the complexity of the present tax is the result of the numerous special provisions and its graduated rate structure. In principle, most taxpayers could comply with a flat rate tax of 11 percent, for example, by filling in a tax return composed of a single page: Enter all income and multiply by 0.11. Thus, compliance costs borne by taxpayers should be lower under a flat rate tax.

Using a broad base with a flat rate tax would also mean that horizontal equity could be achieved more easily. Currently, taxpayers with the same real incomes bear different tax burdens because of special provisions that some taxpayers can utilize more fully than others.

A flat rate tax also performs better in an inflationary environment. Because there is only one rate bracket, inflation does not push taxpayers into higher brackets. A proportional tax does not require an indexing provision to guard against bracket creep. Note, however, that a flat rate tax does not solve the problem of mismeasurement of capital income; that would require capital income to be defined in real terms in the tax laws.

Finally, there may be an advantage to a flat rate tax from a public choice standpoint. One classical indictment of a graduated tax rate is that it is politically irresponsible because "a majority is allowed to set the rates that fall exclusively on the minority." Although the possibility of such an abuse of majority rule arises in other connections, "progression poses difficult problems of equity among taxpayers which need not otherwise arise, so it places strains on the majority rule principle which perhaps need not otherwise arise."[20] Since a flat rate tax represents, in effect, a rule that determines not only how the present tax burden is to be distributed but also how any future increases or decreases are to be allocated, the constant political bickering over how to reform the tax and redistribute its burden may be reduced.

In short, proponents claim that, compared to the present income tax, a flat rate tax on a broad base will be simpler, more efficient, more equitable, more inflationproof, and a politically more responsible formula for apportioning tax burdens.

Disadvantages of a flat rate tax

The flat rate tax proposal really combines two potentially separate major tax changes: the elimination of tax preferences (use of a broad base) and taxation of that base at a single flat rate. Thus, the proposal can be criticized on one or both grounds.

In our earlier discussion of tax preferences, we pointed out that certain tax preferences may be defended for equity, externality, or administrative cost reasons, but it is not clear how many of these preferences can be defended in this way. Moreover, if special concessions are granted to certain types and uses of income, even if for legitimate reasons, it may be politically difficult to avoid the spread of tax preferences to any items that are important enough to command a political constituency. For this reason, the real choice we face may be between a broad income measure with no tax preferences and a measure riddled with loopholes, like the existing tax system.

[20]Walter J. Blum and Harry J. Kalven, Jr., *The Uneasy Case for Progressive Taxation* (Chicago: University of Chicago Press, 1953), pp. 19, 21.

Given those alternatives, the broad income definition—even if it falls short of perfection—may be the preferable option. Most of the objections to a flat rate tax, however, are not over the proposal to use a more comprehensive definition of income; instead the controversy centers around the redistributive effects of using a flat rate tax.

Substituting a flat rate tax for the present progressive tax will alter the distribution of the tax burden; it will increase tax burdens on low- and middle-income taxpayers and reduce tax burdens on upper-income taxpayers. For example, under the present tax, taxpayers (families of four) with AGIs of about $9,000 or less pay no income taxes; with a 14 percent flat rate applied to AGI, the tax liability on a $9,000 income would be $1,280. At a $30,000 income (AGI) level, tax liability would rise from about $3,100 to $4,200, or by $1,100. A flat rate tax would therefore redistribute income away from low- and middle-income classes.

Whether this change is considered undesirable is largely a matter of whether the income tax is viewed as a redistributive mechanism. In this regard, it should be recalled that government transfer programs are our primary redistributive policies. Even if a flat rate tax is used, the poorest quintile of households would continue to receive three times as much in transfers as they pay in all (federal, state, and local) taxes combined. The net income position of low-income households is largely determined by transfers, and only transfers are capable of actually increasing their net incomes. A case can be made that transfer programs should be the primary redistributive mechanism since they can target benefits more equitably on needier families instead of manipulating the tax rate structure to serve that goal. It is not necessary for every policy to redistribute income since transfers can be adjusted so that the net effect of the system as a whole is to help the poor.

Nonetheless, the distributional consequences of a flat rate tax are likely to be viewed as its major, if not its only, drawback. To some extent, the efficiency gains of the tax will reduce the harm associated with larger tax liabilities for low- and middle-income taxpayers, but it is doubtful that they would offset the additional tax burden completely. As we have seen before, value judgments are necessary to decide whether this proposal for reform is, on balance, worthwhile.

Supplementary Readings

BLUM, WALTER J., and HARRY J. KALVEN, JR. *The Uneasy Case for Progressive Taxation.* Chicago: University of Chicago Press, 1953.

BROWNING, EDGAR K., and JACQUELENE M. BROWNING. "Why Not a True Flat Rate Tax?" *Cato Journal,* 5:629–650 (Fall 1985).

BROWNING, JACQUELENE M. "Estimating the Welfare Cost of Tax Preferences." *Public Finance Quarterly,* 7(2):199–219 (Apr. 1979).

CONGRESSIONAL BUDGET OFFICE. *Revising the Individual Income Tax.* Washington, D.C.: U.S. Government Printing Office, July 1983.

FREEMAN, ROGER A. *Tax Loopholes: The Legend and the Reality.* Washington, D.C.: American Enterprise Institute and the Hoover Institution, 1973.

GOODE, RICHARD. *The Individual Income Tax.* Washington, D.C.: The Brookings Institution, 1976.

MINARIK, JOSEPH J. *Making Tax Choices.* Washington, D.C.: Urban Institute, 1985.

SIMONS, HENRY. *Personal Income Taxation.* Chicago: University of Chicago Press, 1938.

U.S. TREASURY. *Blueprints for Basic Tax Reform.* Washington, D.C.: U.S. Government Printing Office, Jan. 17, 1977.

Review Questions and Problems

1. Define *marginal tax rate* and *average tax rate*. Then give an example of an income tax that would result in an average tax rate of 20 percent and a marginal tax rate of 40 percent for a person with income of $20,000. Can the tax be changed so that the average rate falls while the marginal rate increases? If so, give an example.

2. What are the most important differences between the way economists define income and the way the tax code defines income?

3. Describe briefly how the income tax burden is distributed among different income classes. Explain what characteristics of the income tax are responsible for producing this distribution.

4. Explain under what conditions a tax on labor income will be shifted. If it is shifted, who bears the shifted portion of the burden?

5. How does a tax on labor income produce a welfare cost? Use a graph to illustrate the nature of this welfare cost.

6. "It is possible that the benefits a person receives when the government spends tax revenues are larger than the cost the person bears in paying the tax. In this case, the person is benefited by the tax, and there is no welfare cost." True or false? Explain.

7. What are the economic advantages of using a more comprehensive measure of income for tax purposes? In other words, why do many economists favor closing tax "loopholes"?

8. How can the elimination of a tax preference item actually benefit a taxpayer who uses that tax preference? In view of this, why are taxpayers so reluctant to give up their tax preferences?

9. Homeownership receives preferential treatment under the income tax in the form of the deductibility of mortgage interest, the exclusion of imputed income from owner-occupied housing, and the deductibility of property taxes on owner-occupied housing. Defend or attack this preferential treatment, pointing out its implications for efficiency and equity.

10. Define "bracket creep." Construct an example to show how it can produce a larger real tax burden for a taxpayer whose real income has not changed. How does indexation avoid this outcome?

chapter 12
The Corporation Income Tax

A PPROXIMATELY 3 million incorporated businesses filed federal corporation income tax returns in 1985 and paid in total over $67 billion in
taxes. In terms of federal tax revenue, the corporation income tax is the
third largest federal tax, following the individual income tax and the social
security payroll tax. Before 1968, the corporate income tax was the second
largest federal revenue source, but in that year the rapidly growing social
security tax surpassed it in yield. In addition to the federal government,
most states use corporation income taxes, although at substantially lower
rates than the federal tax. In 1984 corporate tax receipts by subnational
levels of government were less than $19 billion.

Tax Base, Rates, and Revenues

Corporation income taxes are generally described as taxes on the profits of
incorporated businesses. In the sense that accountants use the term *profits,*
this is correct, but the tax base is not pure profit, at least not as the term is
used by economists. In the federal tax statutes, the tax base is defined as
the total receipts of the corporation minus certain allowable expenses, or
revenues minus costs, for short. Not all economic costs, however, are treated
as deductible in the tax law. Although wage and salary outlays, depreciation
on capital invested, and interest paid on loans are counted as costs, a normal return for invested capital is not included as a cost. This means that the
tax base is really equal to the normal return to capital invested plus any
economic profits.

An example will clarify this important point. Consider a corporation with
$1 million invested in plant and equipment. In one year, its sales revenues
equal $2 million, and it pays out $1.9 million in wages. Its taxable net income under the corporation income tax is $100,000, but this is not eco-
nomic profit. If the going interest rate is 10 percent, the $1 million invested

in this corporation could have been loaned out and earned $100,000 elsewhere. Thus, the $100,000 realized on the investment in the corporation has an opportunity cost—sacrificed earnings if the capital had been invested elsewhere—of $100,000. In this case, the $100,000 "profit" of the corporation is really only the normal return to capital invested; yet that return is subject to the corporation income tax. To avoid confusion, we refer to the tax base of the corporation income tax as the net income of equity capital rather than as "profits."

More detail on the source of corporate income tax payments is provided in Table 12–1, which shows that most corporations are relatively small. More than 2.4 million of the 2.9 million corporations in 1982 had total assets below $500,000, and these businesses paid $3.0 billion in taxes, or only 6 percent of total corporate income taxes. At the other extreme, 20,000 corporations (less than 1 percent of all corporations) had assets above $25 million and contributed $34 billion in taxes (two thirds of total revenue). In fact, the largest 3,000 corporations—0.1 percent of all corporations—paid almost half of all corporate income taxes. Consequently, in terms of revenue, the corporation income tax is primarily a tax on several thousand large corporations.

The tax rate structure of the federal corporation income tax is slightly progressive. The first $25,000 in net income is taxed at 15 percent; the next $25,000 at 18 percent; the next, at 30 percent; the next, at 40 percent; and all income in excess of $100,000 is subject to a rate of 46 percent. Over 90 percent of total tax revenue, however, is collected from corporations with net income above $100,000. For all practical purposes, most corporate net

Table 12–1 *Corporation Income Tax Returns, 1982*

Size of Total Assets ($1,000)	Number of Returns (thousands)	Net Income in Class ($ billions)	Tax ($ billions)
Under $100	1,647	$ 5.9	$ 1.3
100–250	535	5.2	0.8
250–500	301	5.3	0.9
500–1,000	197	6.3	1.3
1,000–10,000	207	23.4	7.9
10,000–25,000	18	10.2	3.9
25,000–100,000	14	15.8	6.1
100,000–250,000	3	11.1	4.0
Over 250,000	3	122.1	24.1
Total	2,926	$205.2	50.3

Note: Tax column gives tax less foreign tax credit and investment tax credit.
Source: U.S. Treasury, Statistics of Income, *Corporation Income Tax Returns, 1982* (Washington, D.C.: U.S. Government Printing Office, 1985), Table 4.

income is subject to the 46 percent marginal rate. Therefore, in our analysis of the tax, we use the simplifying assumption that the corporation income tax is a proportional tax, an assumption that is not far off the mark for the corporations paying the bulk of the corporation income tax.

Incidence

One of the most difficult and controversial issues in tax analysis is to determine who bears the burden of the corporation income tax. Because the tax applies to all corporations and not just to one industry, a general equilibrium analysis must be used to examine its incidence. That is difficult enough, but matters are complicated further by the fact that industries within the corporate sector are of various degrees of competitiveness. In our analysis, it is assumed that the corporate sector, taken as a whole, is generally competitive enough for the competitive model to yield reasonably accurate results. Not all analysts agree with this assumption, but unfortunately there is no general equilibrium model of an imperfectly competitive economy to provide an alternative basis for the analysis.

The corporation income tax is applied to the net income of capital invested in the corporate sector of the economy. There is also a noncorporate sector of the economy that employs capital. Although corporations are perhaps the most highly visible employers of capital, actually the noncorporate sector employs half of all real capital. The noncorporate sector includes most of the agricultural and real estate industries, owner-occupied housing, and a smattering of firms in other industries. Capital invested in this sector is not subject to the corporation income tax.

In competitive markets, the net returns to capital invested in different uses will tend to be equal. Investors will invest capital where it yields the greatest return; if the return is higher in some uses, investors will shift capital to (increase investment in) those uses, thus driving down the rate of return until it is equal to the return in alternative uses. The tendency for capital to be allocated in such a way that the net return is equalized in all sectors is the basic equilibrating force of the economy adjusting to a tax on the return to capital in the corporate sector.

In the absence of the corporate tax, suppose that the rate of return on capital is 8 percent in both the corporate and noncorporate sectors. Now assume that a 50 percent tax is levied on net income (the return to capital) in the corporate sector. The immediate or short-run effect is to tax away half the return of investors in the corporate sector, leaving them a net yield of only 4 percent on their investment. This will not be a final equilibrium, however, because the net (after-tax) return on capital is now 4 percent in the corporate sector and still 8 percent in the noncorporate sector. Therefore, investors have an incentive to shift capital into the noncorporate sector, where it will earn a higher net return. As investors reduce the supply of capital to the corporate sector, its gross return there rises, while increasing the supply to the noncorporate sector drives down the return there. This process continues until the net return is the same in both sectors. Assume that this equilibrium occurs when the net return is 6 percent in both sectors.

Note carefully what this equilibrium implies. Because of a reduction in capital employed in the corporate sector, its gross (before-tax) return is now 12 percent, which yields a net return of 6 percent after the corporate income tax. Because the return was previously 8 percent, investors in the corporate sector are receiving a return 25 percent below their earlier return. *This is also true for investors in the untaxed noncorporate sector;* their return is now 6 percent compared with 8 percent before the tax, even though the tax does not apply to noncorporate investments. In this way, the corporate tax places a burden on *all* owners of capital, regardless of whether their capital is employed in the corporate sector. The net return to all investors has fallen from 8 percent to 6 percent.

We have traced the effects of the corporation income tax on owners of capital, but other persons will also be affected. Because corporations must pay a higher gross return on capital as a result of the tax, the prices of products produced by corporations will rise, and their consumption will fall. The opposite occurs in the noncorporate sector; output will rise and price will fall as capital in this sector becomes less expensive. Does this mean that consumers bear a burden because of higher prices of corporate sector products? Not necessarily. Corporate prices are higher, but noncorporate prices are lower, and there is no reason for the overall or average price of goods and services to be affected. Only consumers who spend a greater-than-average percentage of their incomes on corporate products (where prices have risen) will be worse off. On average, consumers are not burdened.

This analysis is a good illustration of a general equilibrium analysis of tax incidence. In a general equilibrium approach, we emphasize not only what happens in the taxed sector but also the repercussions in the nontaxed sector. In addition, attention is given to how the tax affects individuals through changes in input prices (the return on capital in this case) and through changes in output prices that occur in all sectors of the economy. In the case of the corporation income tax, the analysis suggests that owners of capital, wherever their capital is employed, bear a burden as a result of the tax.

Diagrammatic analysis

A diagrammatic presentation of this analysis as it pertains to capital markets should prove helpful. Figure 12–1 shows the effects of different allocations of a given quantity of capital between the corporate and noncorporate sec-

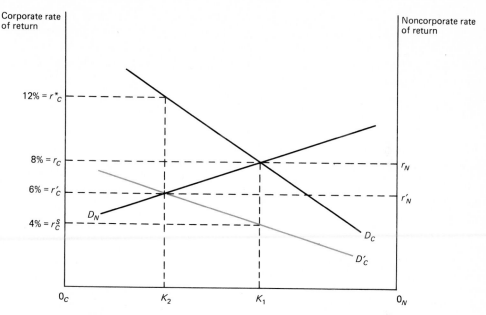

Corporate rate of return

Noncorporate rate of return

$12\% = r_C^*$

$8\% = r_C$

$6\% = r_C'$

$4\% = r_C^S$

r_N

r_N'

D_N

D_C

D_C'

0_C

K_2

K_1

0_N

FIGURE 12–1   *Incidence of the corporation income tax.*

tors on the rate of return in the two sectors. The curve D_C indicates the productivity of capital employed in the corporate sector, expressed as a rate of return. For example, if $O_C K_2$ is employed, the return will be 12 percent, whereas a larger quantity of capital, $O_C K_1$, yields a return of 8 percent. The curve D_N shows the productivity of capital in the noncorporate sector, but it is drawn relative to the origin at O_N. Thus, if $O_N K_1$ is employed in the noncorporate sector, the return is 8 percent, whereas if more is employed, $O_N K_2$, the return is 6 percent. (The curve D_N is just a reversed demand curve drawn so that the origin lies at the right.)

The horizontal dimension of this boxlike diagram, $O_C O_N$, measures the total amount of capital to be allocated between the two sectors. Any point on the horizontal axis indicates the distribution of capital between the sectors. Thus, point K_1 means that there is $O_C K_1$ capital in the corporate sector and the remainder, $O_N K_1$, is in the noncorporate sector. A movement to K_2 means that $O_C K_2$ is now employed in the corporate sector and $O_N K_2$ is in the noncorporate sector. Hence a movement from K_1 to K_2 means that there is $K_1 K_2$ less capital in the corporate sector and $K_1 K_2$ more capital in the noncorporate sector; $K_1 K_2$ capital has moved from the corporate to the non-corporate sector.

Before proceeding with the analysis, it may be worthwhile to explain more fully what is meant by capital "moving" from one sector to another. Capital refers, of course, to productive resources such as factories, machinery, and trucks. But how can factories and equipment designed to produce automobiles, for example, in the corporate sector "move" to the agricultural industries in the noncorporate sector and produce food? In general, they seldom can move in this sense, but that creates no problem for the analysis. Over a period of time the same result—more capital in agriculture and less in automobiles—can occur. Factories and equipment in the automotive industry can be allowed to wear out while new investment expands the capital stock in agriculture. Thus, the passage of time allows the capital stock to be reallocated *in effect* by channeling more new investment toward the sector with the higher net return and less toward the sector with the lower net return. Although we continue to refer to capital moving from one sector to another, it should be understood that this is a shorthand expression for the process described above.

Returning now to Figure 12–1, in the absence of the corporation income tax, the equilibrium allocation of capital is at K_1, where D_C and D_N intersect, with $O_C K_1$ in the corporate sector and $O_N K_1$ in the noncorporate sector. With this allocation, the returns to capital in the two sectors, r_C and r_N, are both equal to 8 percent. When the corporate tax is imposed at a rate of 50 percent, the net return to capital in the corporate sector is reduced by half; the new schedule showing the net (after-tax) return is D_C'. In the short run, before enough time has elapsed for capital to "move," the owners of capital in the corporate sector bear the full burden of the tax and receive an after-tax return of r_C^s, or 4 percent. The allocation at K_1, however, is not a long-run equilibrium because the capital in the untaxed noncorporate sector is earning a higher net return of 8 percent. The owners of capital will move it from the corporate to the noncorporate sector until the net returns are equalized. The net returns are equal where D_C' and D_N intersect, with $O_C K_2$ capital in the corporate sector and $O_N K_2$ in the noncorporate sector. Note, however, that this implies that the before-tax rates of return are not equal. Capital investment is yielding a return of 12 percent before taxes in the corporate sector, whereas the before-tax return in the noncorporate sector is 6 percent.

Thus, the corporation income tax produces a reallocation of $K_1 K_2$ capital from the corporate sector to the noncorporate sector as investors seek a higher return in the untaxed sector. The final equilibrium is where the net return to all owners of capital is at 6 percent, down from its original 8 percent level. All owners of capital suffer a loss of 25 percent of their pretax capital income, regardless of whether or not they are stockholders in corporations.

The preceding analysis is based on the assumption that capital income in the noncorporate sector is untaxed. Actually, income in the noncorporate sector may be subject to tax under the federal individual income tax and property taxes levied by local governments. The effective rate of tax on capital income in the corporate sector, however, is much higher because of the corporation income tax, and differences in tax rates between sectors are all that is necessary for the preceding analysis to hold. Because capital income in the corporate sector is more heavily taxed than in the noncorporate sector, there is an incentive for the reallocation of capital previously described to occur.

To say that all owners of capital bear a burden from the corporation income tax does not necessarily imply that they bear the entire burden (equal to tax revenue raised). The final incidence depends on whether the total *gross* return to capital (the return to capital income in both sectors) is altered by the reallocation of capital produced by the tax. If the total gross return is unchanged, then capital owners will bear the entire burden. For example, if before-tax capital income is $160 billion (8 percent times $O_C O_N$) and gross (before-tax) capital income after the tax (12 percent times $O_C K_2$ plus 6 percent times $O_N K_2$) is still $160 billion, the after-tax capital income will be less than $160 billion by the amount of the tax [$(r_C^* - r_C')$ times $O_C K_2$]. Capital owners then bear the entire burden of the tax. Whether or not this is exactly true depends on a number of underlying elasticities in production and consumption. After examining a number of plausible relationships, Arnold Harberger (on whose seminal work this analysis is based)[1] concluded that in all likelihood, owners of capital bear approximately the entire burden of the tax.

What does it mean to accept Harberger's conclusion that owners of capital bear the full burden of the corporation income tax? If Harberger is correct, then the incidence of the tax is equivalent to a proportional tax (of 25 percent in the preceding example) on capital income wherever capital is employed. In interpreting this, it is important to realize that the noncorporate sector actually contains about half the capital in the United States: The major uses of capital in the noncorporate sector are in agriculture and homeownership. Homes represent a way to invest in capital, and it is the major form of capital ownership for millions of families. (The capital income from homeownership is partly in the form of housing services directly consumed, a form of in-kind capital income.) Thus, people who purchase their own homes will realize a lower return because of the corporation income tax. The same is true for savers, who will earn a lower rate of interest on their savings accounts. Stockholders of corporations also bear a burden. In this connection, it should be noted that the millions of workers who own stock indirectly in the form of pension funds are also affected. (In 1980,

---

[1] Arnold C. Harberger, "The Incidence of the Corporation Income Tax," *Journal of Political Economy,* 70:215 (June 1962), reprinted in his *Taxation and Welfare* (Boston: Little, Brown, 1974), pp. 135–162. For a simplified exposition of the general equilibrium model used by Harberger, and its applications to a variety of taxes, see Charles E. McLure, Jr., and Wayne R. Thirsk, "A Simplified Exposition of the Harberger Model, I: Tax Incidence," *National Tax Journal,* 28:1(Mar. 1975).

about 35 percent of all corporate stock was owned by pension funds.) In short, the burden of the corporation income tax is spread widely through the population, even though most of the people who bear this burden are unaware of it.

Other factors affecting incidence

The Harberger model is probably the most widely accepted view of the effects of the corporation income tax, but not all economists accept this analysis as a correct or complete analysis of the tax. One frequently criticized feature of the analysis is Harberger's assumption that the corporate sector can be treated as competitive. Not all corporations operate in highly competitive industries; some corporations have some degree of monopolistic market power. In a noncompetitive market, the incidence of the tax could be different than Harberger's competitive model would predict.

Generally speaking, economists who believe that the corporate sector is characterized mainly by monopoly or oligopoly hold that the corporation income tax is really like an excise tax on corporate sector products. Whether that is correct is far from obvious. Harberger, in his original paper, modified the basic analysis to examine a particular type of monopoly pricing on the part of all corporations. He assumed that corporations set a price that was based on a fixed markup over average cost. Even in this model, however, Harberger found that the incidence of the tax was essentially the same as in the basic competitive model.[2] Anderson and Ballentine extended Harberger's approach further by assuming that all corporations were profit-maximizing monopolies. The incidence results in their model are still almost identical to incidence estimates obtained under competitive assumptions.[3] Thus, although a nagging suspicion may remain that the results will differ in real-world markets, there is some basis for believing that Harberger's basic results may hold even in noncompetitive settings.

A second factor neglected in this analysis was the possibility that the rate of capital accumulation could be affected if the amount of saving changes as a result of the corporation income tax. It is important to note that the analysis of Figure 12–1 focuses on the way the corporate tax affects the allocation of a *given and unchanged amount of capital* between sectors. But one effect of the tax is to depress the rate of return that people receive on their capital investments. If people save less at a lower rate of return, then the total amount of capital will fall or grow more slowly over time with the tax than

---

[2] Harberger, op. cit.

[3] Robert Anderson and J. Gregory Ballentine, "The Incidence and Excess Burden of a Profits Tax Under Imperfect Competition," *Public Finance/Finances Publiques* 31 (2):157–176 (1976).

in its absence. The analysis presented earlier is fully correct only if the rate of saving is unaffected by the corporation income tax.

If the corporation income tax does depress saving (and hence accumulation of real capital), the burden of the tax will be spread even more broadly over the population. A reduction in the amount of capital means that the amount of capital per worker falls so that the marginal productivity of labor and thus wage rates fall (or, perhaps more realistically, grow more slowly over time). Consequently, some of the burden is shifted from capital owners (less capital means a higher rate of return) to workers in the form of lower wages. We shall continue to ignore this possibility here but consider it further in Chapter 14.

Another complicating factor in the analysis of the corporation income tax stems from differences in the tax treatment of investments financed by equity and those financed by debt. If a corporation finances an investment with equity funds (supplied by the owners, or shareholders, either through purchases of new shares of stock or through investment of retained earnings), the return on that investment is subject to the corporate income tax. On the other hand, if the corporation borrows to finance the investment, the interest payments on its debt are considered a cost of operation under the corporation income tax and are therefore deductible. When investments are equity financed, a normal return on capital is not allowed as a cost but is fully subject to the tax. With debt financing, a normal return (as approximated by the interest rate that is paid) is deductible, and the tax applies only to any return in excess of that level.

As a consequence, the corporation income tax leads corporations to favor debt over equity finance. By using debt to finance new investments, corporations reduce their corporate tax liabilities. Thus, the effective tax rate on capital invested in the corporation depends on how it is financed, and as a consequence, the effective tax rate on corporate net income can be below the statutory rates. The significance of this point, however, is a matter of some dispute. In reviewing the literature on this topic, J. Gregory Ballentine concluded that the incidence of the tax is not greatly affected by the favorable treatment given debt finance.[4]

For these reasons, the question of the incidence of the corporation income tax remains a somewhat controversial issue. Accepting for the present, however, the conclusion of our earlier analysis that the tax places a burden on people in proportion to their income from capital, let's consider what this means for the distribution of the tax burden. A proportionate tax on income from capital is not the same as a proportionate tax on total income. Typically, families with higher incomes receive a larger share of their in-

---

[4] J. Gregory Ballentine, *Equity, Efficiency, and the U.S. Corporation Income Tax* (Washington, D.C.: American Enterprise Institute, 1980), Chapter 4.

Table 12–2 *Corporate Tax Burdens by Income Class, 1976*	
Income Decile	*Tax As a Percent of Household Income*
1	2.4%
2	1.9
3	2.0
4	1.9
5	1.8
6	1.7
7	1.7
8	1.8
9	2.4
10	6.8
Total	3.6%

Source: Edgar K. Browning and William R. Johnson, *The Distribution of the Tax Burden* (Washington, D.C.: American Enterprise Institute, 1979), Table 14.

comes in the form of capital income. Thus, the burden of the corporation income tax will be a larger fraction of total household income for families in upper-income classes.

Table 12–2 presents estimates of the corporate tax burden as a percent of household income for income deciles in 1976. (Each decile contains 10 percent of all households, with households ranked in order of their before-tax incomes.) Average tax rates vary between 1.7 and 2.4 percent of the first nine deciles and rise sharply to 6.8 percent for the highest decile. For practical purposes the corporation income tax is approximately proportional over the first nine deciles but becomes progressive at the tenth decile. Since the effective tax rate applied to corporate net income has fallen since 1976, the actual rates would be lower than in the table, but the general pattern across income classes would be the same.

A major reason for considering the incidence of any tax is to determine whether the distribution of the tax burden among taxpaying units is fair. Making that determination requires value judgments, which are more likely to differ when vertical equity, or the treatment of people at different income levels, is considered. In terms of horizontal equity, however, if we accept the value judgment that families with the same total incomes *from whatever source derived* should bear the same tax burdens, then the corporate tax is clearly an inequitable source of revenue. In comparing two families with the same total income, the family receiving a larger share of its income in the form of capital income will bear a heavier tax burden.

Welfare Cost

In addition to the direct burden of the corporation income tax, it distorts resource allocation in several important ways. First, it leads to a misallocation of a given stock of capital among competing uses in the economy. Second, it leads to a capital stock that is too small. Since other taxes also interact with the corporate tax to affect the size of the total capital stock, a discussion of this second type of misallocation is deferred to Chapter 14. Third, it biases investment decisions within the corporate sector. This point will be explained later in this chapter. Here we shall discuss only the way the corporate tax distorts the allocation of capital between the corporate and noncorporate sectors of the economy.

Consider Figure 12–2. In the last section, we saw that the equilibrium under the corporation income tax occurred where the net returns to capital in the corporate and noncorporate sectors were equal. This is shown at K_2 with $O_C K_2$ in the corporate sector, and $O_N K_2$ in the noncorporate sector. At this allocation, the gross return to capital differs between the two sectors; it is 12 percent in the corporate sector and 6 percent in the noncorporate sector. Capital is misallocated between the two sectors because it is more productive in the corporate sector than it is in the noncorporate sector.

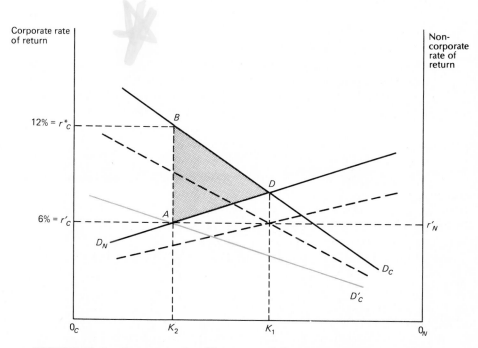

FIGURE 12–2   *One type of welfare cost of the corporation income tax.*

Although investors will be guided by the net returns, the gross returns, or true physical productivities, are what are relevant for efficiency considerations. With the allocation at K_2, there are investment projects with yields just below 12 percent in the corporate sector that will not be undertaken because investors are interested in the after-tax yields. The after-tax yield on an investment paying a gross return of 11.9 percent will be only 5.95 percent, less than the return realized in the noncorporate sector. Thus, a reallocation of capital from the noncorporate sector to the corporate sector will increase the real return on the total capital stock, but the corporate tax will inhibit that reallocation. The result is a welfare cost.

Efficiency requires that the gross yields in the two sectors be equal, and this condition occurs at K_1. The corporate tax produces underinvestment of K_1K_2 in the corporate sector (and overinvestment of K_1K_2 in the noncorporate sector). By reducing capital from K_1 to K_2 in the corporate sector, projects yielding from 8 to 12 percent (along D_C from point D to point B) are sacrificed, and projects yielding from 8 percent to 6 percent in the noncorporate sector (along D_N from point D to point A) are undertaken. The net loss from this reallocation of K_1K_2 between the sectors is the difference between the returns on these projects in the two sectors. This is shown by area BAD, the loss involved in investing K_1K_2 less in the corporate sector (area DBK_2K_1) minus the gain from investing this capital in the noncorporate sector instead (area DAK_2K_1).

Several economists have developed estimates of the size of the welfare cost as a result of the sectoral misallocation of capital produced by the corporation income tax. Harberger was the first. Using data from the mid-1950s, Harberger estimated the welfare cost to be about 0.5 percent of gross national product (GNP).[5] John Shoven used a disaggregated model (more than two sectors), corrected a numerical error in Harberger's calculations, and still found a welfare loss of about 0.5 percent of GNP.[6] To put these estimates in perspective, they represent a loss equal to approximately 12 percent of tax revenues.

In addition, it should be recalled that there is also a welfare cost caused by the depressing effect of the tax on saving and capital accumulation. Estimates of this resource misallocation vary widely, and since several taxes interact to affect saving and capital accumulation, it is difficult to identify a certain portion of this welfare cost as being exclusively the result of the corporate tax. However, there is some suspicion that this welfare loss is significant, perhaps larger than the welfare cost associated with the misal-

---

[5] Arnold C. Harberger, "Efficiency Effects of Taxes on Income from Capital," in Marian Krzyzaniak, ed., *Effects of Corporation Income Tax* (Detroit: Wayne State University Press, 1966), pp. 110–117.

[6] John B. Shoven, "The Incidence and Efficiency Effects of Taxes on Income from Capital," *Journal of Political Economy,* 84:1261–1283 (Dec. 1976).

location of resources between the corporate and noncorporate sectors illustrated in Figure 12–2. Ballentine, for instance, suggests that the combined welfare cost of both types is at least one third as large as the tax revenue generated by the corporation income tax.[7] If Ballentine is correct, this would probably make the corporation income tax the most inefficient method of raising tax revenues in the U.S. tax system.

Because of the general perception that the corporation income tax is quite inefficient, many economists have recommended fundamental reforms. One suggested change is capable of reducing, if not eliminating, the inefficiency caused by the sectoral misallocation of capital. Recall that capital is misallocated between the corporate and noncorporate sectors because its return is taxed at different rates in the two sectors. If capital income were taxed at the same rate, regardless of the sector in which the capital is employed, the misallocation could be avoided.

This point is also illustrated in Figure 12–2. Suppose that capital income in both sectors is taxed at a rate of 25 percent, instead of taxing only the corporate sector at a rate of 50 percent. Under this tax, the demand curves identifying the net returns in the two sectors would be shown as the dashed lines in the diagram. With a tax rate of 25 percent of capital income wherever earned, the equilibrium allocation would be at K_1, and capital would be efficiently allocated between the two sectors. With capital taxed equally, no incentive exists for capital to move from one sector to the other. Note that the owners of capital would be no worse off than under the corporation income tax; they would still receive a net return of 6 percent.[8] Resources, however, would be allocated more efficiently between the corporate and noncorporate sectors.

Issues in Tax Base Determination

Thus far, we have given little attention to the tax base of the corporation income tax. In general, special tax preferences or loopholes are not as numerous for the corporate tax as they are for the individual income tax. Nonetheless, some special features of the corporate income tax have important implications and require further discussion.

Depreciation

Probably the most important topic related to the definition of taxable net income for corporations concerns the treatment of depreciation allowances.

---

[7] Ballentine, op. cit., Chapter 5.

[8] This is true once capital is allocated so that the net return is equal everywhere, that is, in the long run. In the short run, capital would temporarily be earning more in the corporate sector and less in the noncorporate sector.

"Depreciation" refers to the fact that capital equipment frequently lasts a number of years but tends to wear out gradually over its life span. For tax purposes, the cost of the capital equipment is a legitimate expense which (along with other costs) must be subtracted from revenues in determining net income. Since the equipment contributes to production over a period of years, however, there is a problem in determining how much of the total equipment cost to consider a cost of production each year.

In principle, the apportionment of the cost of real capital assets over the service life of assets should reflect the rate at which they actually wear out. For example, if a piece of equipment costs $100 in year 1 but is worth only $90 a year later, the firm should be able to count $10 as a cost of production in year 1. Over the life of the equipment, the firm should be able to deduct the entire cost of the equipment and pay tax on only the net return to the investment. However, for practical reasons it would be impossible for the tax authorities to determine the true rate of depreciation and apply this principle precisely to all investments. It is not clear how the rate at which equipment wears out can be measured or, when the equipment is acquired, how many years it will last.

The tax treatment of depreciation is important because it influences the effective tax rate that is applied to net income. *If assets can be depreciated faster than they actually wear out, then the effective tax rate will be reduced below the statutory level.* To illustrate, suppose a corporation purchases equipment with a cost of $100. If the corporation can depreciate the equipment in one year and subtract the entire cost that year (*very* rapid depreciation), its net income subject to tax will fall by $100 and its taxes (assuming a 46 percent rate) will fall by $46. If, alternatively, the asset cannot be counted as a cost until ten years later and then deducted fully in the tenth year, the corporation will save $46 in year 10. The first method is clearly preferable, since the firm achieves the $46 tax saving in year 1 instead of year 10. The firm could then invest the tax saving in year 1 at the market interest rate, and the sum would grow to much more than $46 by year 10. Put differently, the present value of the tax saving is greater when the portion of the cost that can be written off in the early years is greater. Rapid depreciation allows the firm to postpone paying the tax, which reduces the present value of the tax to the firm. Allowing more rapid depreciation is therefore similar to reducing the effective tax rate on corporate net income.

For purposes of computing depreciation allowances, the tax laws as of 1986 classify all assets into three classes according to expected durability: a 3-year class, a 5-year class, and an 18-year class. These "tax lives" specify the number of years over which various assets may be depreciated for tax purposes. Businesses are then given three options to determine how much of the original cost may be written off in each year. The straight-line method is the simplest. Using the straight-line method means that for an asset in the 3-year class, one third of the original cost is taken as an expense in each year. The other two methods, the double-declining-balance method and the sum-of-years'-digits method, allow a larger portion of the cost to be written off in the earlier years than the straight-line method does.

These depreciation practices, originally introduced in 1981 and modified somewhat in 1982 and 1983, permit depreciation at a far more rapid rate than that at which assets typically wear out. For example, most buildings can be depreciated over an 18-year period, but buildings typically have usable lives of 30 to 50 years. Thus, the current depreciation allowances have the effect of reducing the tax paid on new investments. These depreciation allowances were introduced, in fact, to stimulate corporate investment. Economists generally have favored lower tax rates combined with true depreciation allowances (insofar as possible), rather than rapid depreciation as a way to encourage investment. Rapid depreciation has the disadvantage of tending to favor longer-lived investments and distorting the type of investments undertaken by corporations.

Rapid depreciation, however, has one advantage: liberalizing depreciation practices reduces taxes only on new investments and not on existing assets. This implies that tax revenues will fall very little at first, but new investment will be encouraged by the lower taxes that will be paid in the future on that investment. As time passes, however, an increasingly larger portion of investments will be covered by the new depreciation provisions, and tax revenue losses will therefore rise over time. In the long run, there is no advantage to liberalizing depreciation practices rather than cutting tax rates. The government was therefore following a short-run strategy (trying to stimulate investment at low initial revenue loss) by modifying depreciation practices rather than cutting tax rates.

Investment tax credit

The investment tax credit was introduced at a rate of 7 percent on new investment in 1962, temporarily suspended between 1966 and 1967, "permanently" eliminated in 1969, reintroduced in 1971, and increased to 10 percent in 1975. At its current 10 percent level, the investment tax credit permits a corporation to reduce its taxes paid by 10 percent of the cost of new qualified investments. Thus, if new equipment costs $100, there will be an immediate $10 reduction in tax liabilities, and this will effectively reduce the net cost of the equipment to $90. (The firm can still, however, claim depreciation allowances equal to 95 percent of the original cost of the equipment.) The effect is again similar to an outright tax rate reduction, but with the short-run advantage of applying only to new investments rather than to all capital inputs.

The investment tax credit applies only to investments in machinery and equipment, and not to investments in buildings and structures. Because the ITC reduces only the tax rate on certain types of investments, different investments will be taxed at different rates. In conjunction with the depreciation allowances, this produces wide variations in the tax rates that apply to various investments. We will consider the effects of this differential treatment later.

Capital gains

Corporations, like individuals, occasionally sell assets they have held for over 6 months and realize a capital gain on the transaction. These gains are fully taxable as income but are subject to a special maximum tax rate of 28 percent. The special treatment given to capital gains has led to efforts to extend this treatment to some unusual assets. Consider the following example:

In 1951 the sale of livestock used for breeding, draft, or dairy purposes and the sale of unharvested crops (sold at the same time as the land on which they were located) were singled out for capital gains treatment. Turkeys were also included in the original definition of "livestock" in the first draft of the bill. Former Minnesota Senator Edward Thye, however, felt that if turkeys received capital gains treatment, chickens should too, and he proposed an amendment to that effect. At that point, the following exchange ensued on the Senate floor:

> Senator Douglas: Would the Senator from Minnesota consider the possibility of adding ducks, angora cats, and dogs to his amendment?
> Senator Thye: There would be some justification for adding the duck, though ducks are not equal in importance to either turkeys or chickens with respect to national income. The Senator has an argument there, but when one goes too far down the ladder . . . he may get into a category which causes someone possibly to look upon the proposition as ridiculous.

Senate Finance Chairman Walter George, fearing that the Senate might indeed look ridiculous, argued "I cannot [accept] the chicken amendment . . . I cannot conceive that Congress ever had in mind [giving capital gains treatment] to assets that are purely transitory." But when another senator tried to amend the tax bill to deny capital gains treatment to all livestock, arguing that livestock was transitory, Senator George quickly backtracked, noting that it "would be a dangerous thing indeed to say that the whole [livestock capital gain] section should be impaired" by a chicken or a turkey. (The turkey amendment passed the Senate but was eliminated by a House-Senate Conference Committee; the remainder of the livestock provision passed.)[9]

---

[9] See Philip Stern, *The Rape of the Taxpayer* (New York: Random House, 1973), pp. 295–306, for a further discussion of this and other, similar examples.

As this episode illustrates, once you depart from the principle of a broad definition of income, it becomes difficult to "draw the line." Special tax provisions often beget still more special tax provisions.

Inflation and the measure of income

As we saw in the last chapter, the individual income tax does not handle inflationary situations well. The same is true of the corporation income tax. With respect to the individual tax, we identified two problems: bracket creep and mismeasurement of capital income. Since most corporate income is already subject to the highest rate bracket in that tax, bracket creep is not a major problem for the corporate tax. But the measurement of income is a problem, and with inflation, real corporate net income is not properly measured.

For the corporate tax to measure net income correctly, all components of costs and revenues must be measured in dollars of the same purchasing power. This, however, does not occur in two important instances. One is depreciation allowances, which are based on the historical cost of the asset, and its historical cost may differ greatly from its real cost when prices are rising. If certain equipment costs $100 in 1986, the firm can deduct a total of $100 as depreciation over the allowable years, even though as a result of inflation, it may cost $200 to replace the equipment. Depreciation allowances based on historical cost tend to *understate* true costs in inflationary periods and therefore *overstate* the real net income of the corporation. On this count, inflation increases the real tax burden on corporate net income.

There is, however, an offsetting effect. Corporations are permitted to deduct their nominal interest payments on borrowed funds. In inflationary times, the nominal rate exceeds the real rate of interest, so that firms are permitted to take deductions that are larger than their real borrowing costs warrant. This works to the advantage of corporations.

Considering the corporate sector as a whole, these two factors have been estimated to approximately offset each other, implying that corporation income taxes are not greatly affected by inflation. However, a significant distortion caused by inflation is still present because particular corporations are affected quite differently from the average. Firms that have not borrowed to finance investments find their real tax burdens greatly increased, whereas corporations relying heavily on borrowing find their real tax burdens reduced.

Although corporation income taxes in the aggregate are not greatly affected by inflation, the taxation of corporate income by the tax system as a whole is. Firms gain from being able to deduct nominal interest payments, but those who receive these interest payments pay taxes on the nominal rather than the real interest income and therefore lose from inflation. Feldstein and Summers showed that the higher real taxes paid by the recipients of the nominal interest income are as large as the tax saving to the corporation.[10]

Thus, in a broader sense there is no combined tax advantage from nominal interest deductibility, but the depreciation problem still remains and that unambiguously increases the real tax burden on corporate sector income.

Effects of Changes in the Tax Base

The statutory tax rates of the corporation income tax have not changed a great deal in the last several decades. As Table 12–3 shows, the top statutory tax rate fluctuated between a high of 52 percent in 1960 and a low of 46 percent in 1985. The actual consequences of the tax, however, varied greatly over this period as a result of three major factors: changes in depreciation allowances, the introduction of and changes in the investment tax credit (ITC), and the interaction of the tax code with varying inflation rates. Some of the consequences of these "hidden" influences on the corporation income tax are reflected in the estimates in Table 12–3.

In this table, the average tax rate refers to actual corporate taxes divided by an estimate of the corporate sector's net income. The average tax rate would be quite similar to the top statutory tax rate if the corporate tax were levied on real economic income. As Table 12–3 shows, the average rate was only slightly below the top statutory rate between 1960 and 1980 but has dropped sharply since then. The reduction in the average tax rate since 1980 reflects the liberalized depreciation allowances introduced in 1981 and the slowing of inflation from its rapid pace during the 1970s. By 1983, the actual tax burden had fallen to less than 25 percent of corporations' real economic income, a decline of more than 40 percent from most years before 1980.

The average tax rates in Table 12–3 measure the taxation of corporate income from all existing assets. When we are concerned with investment incentives, however, the anticipated tax that will have to be paid on new investments is what is relevant. In other words, the marginal tax rate that will apply to new investments is what is relevant to a firm's decision whether to undertake an investment. The marginal tax rate can be quite different from the average tax rate that applies to past investments.

Table 12–3 also contains estimates of the effective marginal tax rates that apply to new corporate investment in each year. Note that in 1960, the marginal tax rates applying to machinery and structures were similar, and both

---

[10]Martin S. Feldstein and Lawrence H. Summers, "Inflation and the Taxation of Capital Income in the Corporate Sector," *National Tax Journal,* 32:445–470 (Dec. 1979).

Table 12–3   *Statutory and Effective Corporate Tax Rates*

Year	Top Statutory Rate	Average Tax Rate	Effective Marginal Tax Rates		
			All Assets	General Industrial Machinery	Industrial Structures
1960	52.0%	46.3%	49.6%	50.9%	49.2%
1965	48.0	37.3	33.7	29.5	45.4
1970	49.2	44.2	50.6	55.4	53.4
1975	48.0	41.4	37.1	30.0	54.8
1980	46.0	43.8	34.8	24.4	53.3
1983	46.0	24.5	18.6	2.1	38.9
1985	46.0	NA	16.4	−4.5	39.7

Source: Congressional Budget Office, *Revising the Corporate Income Tax* (Washington, D.C.: U.S. Government Printing Office, 1985), Table 3.

were close to the average tax rate. In 1962, however, the investment tax credit was introduced. Since the ITC applied only to machinery and equipment, it produced divergent marginal tax rates on machinery and structures, as shown for 1965. (The ITC was eliminated in 1969 and reintroduced in 1971, accounting for the similar rates in 1970.) With the liberalization of both depreciation allowances and the ITC in 1981, the spread between the tax rates applying to machinery and structures widened even more. By 1985, the tax rate applying to new investments in structures was 39.7 percent at the same time that the rate applying to machinery was actually negative! This meant that the government was actually subsidizing investment in machinery.

The marginal tax rates that will apply to the income of investments in the future depend greatly on the rate of inflation. As we saw earlier, depreciation allowances are based on historical cost, and so the higher the rate of inflation is, the less the allowances will be worth and the greater the real tax rate will be. (In calculating the marginal tax rates in Table 12–3, it is assumed that future inflation rates are a function of past inflation rates.) Table 12–4 indicates the importance of this relationship, by giving effective marginal tax rates as they apply to different types of assets and showing how sensitive the tax rates are to future inflation rates. As expected, the higher the rate of inflation is, the greater the tax burden falling on new investments will be. The impact of the inflation rate is surprising, especially for the shorter-lived asset classes in which investments are subsidized at low inflation rates and taxed at high inflation rates.

Note that at each rate of inflation, assets in the machinery and equipment category (which are eligible for the ITC) are much more lightly taxed than

Table 12–4 *Inflation, the ITC, and Effective Tax Rates*

Asset Class	Depreciation Class (years)	Inflation Rate			No ITC and 6 Percent Inflation
		2	6	9	
Automobiles	3	−65.9%	−19.0%	0.5%	39.7%
Computers	5	−88.6	−12.4	11.4	51.4
Aircraft	5	−50.4	−8.5	8.4	43.0
General Industrial Equipment	5	−32.3	−6.1	6.3	35.5
Electrical Machinery	5	−31.1	−5.9	6.1	34.8
Industrial Buildings	18	33.8	41.6	45.1	41.6
Commercial Buildings	18	30.3	37.7	41.1	37.7

Source: Congressional Budget Office, *Revising the Corporate Income Tax* (Washington, D.C.: U.S. Government Printing Office, 1985), Tables 9 and 12.

buildings are. The difference in tax treatment, however, becomes greater when the inflation rate is low. At a 2 percent inflation, for example, investment in automobiles is subject to a minus 66 percent tax rate, but buildings are still taxed at a positive rate of more than 30 percent. How much of this difference in tax rates is due to the ITC is shown in the last column, which indicates what tax rates would be if the ITC were repealed and the inflation rate were 6 percent. Although there would still be differences in the tax rates applying to different assets, the differences would be much smaller than before.

Incidence and welfare cost of differential taxation of assets

One implication of the differing tax treatment of different types of assets is that corporate tax liabilities will differ widely across firms and industries. Firms that rely more heavily on equipment and machinery relative to buildings will have lower overall tax burdens. One recent study of 238 corporations over the 1981–1983 period, for example, found that 58 corporations paid no tax or received a tax refund, even though their reported earnings totaled $47.4 billion. Another 30 companies paid an average tax rate of more than 30 percent.[11]

Findings like these often are interpreted as evidence of great unfairness in the tax law. But what does this result really tell us about the incidence of the tax? More specifically, how does the differential tax treatment of differ-

[11] Robert S. McIntyre and Dean C. Tipps, *The Failure of the Corporate Tax Incentives* (Washington, D.C.: Citizens for Tax Justice, Jan. 1985).

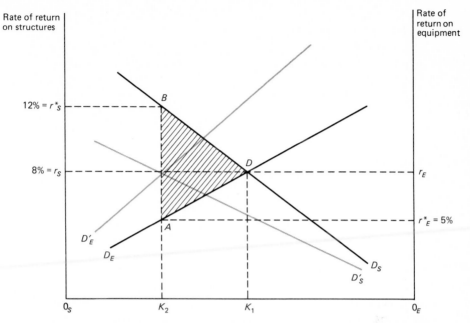

FIGURE 12–3 *Differential tax treatment of structures and equipment.*

ent assets affect the incidence of the corporation income tax? Perhaps surprisingly, it may have little effect at all. Recall the basic Harberger model, in which different tax treatments of investments in the corporate and noncorporate sectors resulted in the same tax burden for investors in both sectors. The same analysis applies here. If some types of investments are taxed lightly, resources will flow into those investments until the after-tax rate of return is the same as the return earned on other, more heavily taxed investments. Thus, in the long run, the incidence of the tax would still fall on capital owners, subject to the earlier qualifications regarding the basic Harberger model. (In the short run, however, this differential tax treatment can produce windfall gains and losses for different firms and industries, a consequence that is also relevant to an overall evaluation.)

The differential taxation of various types of investments is more important to the tax's welfare cost. Figure 12–3 shows how we can adapt our earlier analysis to examine this situation. We assume that the total amount of capital invested (shown by the distance $O_S O_E$) is unaffected but that the allocation between structures and equipment can be varied. D_S and D_E show the before-tax rates of return associated with different levels of investment in structures and equipment. In the absence of any tax, the equilibrium would be at point K_1, where D_S and D_E intersect, with $O_S K_1$ invested in structures and $O_E K_1$ invested in equipment.[12] The common rate of return on both types of investment is 8 percent.

Now consider a tax that applies a *positive* tax rate to structures and a *negative* tax rate to equipment. The net-of-tax returns are now shown by D'_S and D'_E, where D'_E lies above D_E because equipment is effectively being subsidized. Equilibrium occurs where the net rates of return are equal, as explained earlier, and as shown here by the intersection of D'_S and D'_E. Not surprisingly, investment in equipment expands (it is subsidized) at the expense of investment in structures (it is taxed). Taxing equipment and structures at different rates produces a welfare cost, as shown by the area *BAD;* equipment investment is expanded at the expense of structures, even though its real rate of return is lower.

As drawn, Figure 12–3 shows a combination of positive and negative tax rates that leaves the net rate of return unchanged at 8 percent. This illustrates how it is possible for the corporation income tax to produce no net tax revenue and yet still lead to a substantial misallocation of investment resources. Although this is more extreme than the outcome for the corporate sector as a whole, since it continues to pay substantial taxes, certain industries and firms have found themselves in this position. Thus, the diagram shows how a *reduction* in the corporate tax burden can *increase* the welfare cost if the reduction in rates widens the differences in the effective tax rates that apply to different assets. Some economists believe that the attempt to increase investment incentives by using liberalized depreciation allowances and the ITC has had this effect. In contrast, reducing statutory tax rates instead of using these special tax preferences could have improved investment incentives just as much without producing a welfare cost associated with differential taxation of different assets.

The R & D tax credit

A recent innovation in tax preferences for business is the tax credit initially granted in 1981 to spending on research and development (R & D). In the original law, this tax credit was intended in part to be experimental. Although the R & D tax credit expired on December 31, 1985, Congress seems likely to reinstate it in some form. But even if it fails to resurface, it was an interesting attempt to use the tax system to encourage an important activity.

Research and development can be thought of as a form of productive investment. As such, the immediate question is why it should be subsidized when most other investments are taxed. One reason, favored by economists, is that spending on R & D may produce external benefits. One outcome of R & D spending is the production of new knowledge, which later can be

---

[12]Note that an equal rate tax applied to structures and equipment would not affect this equilibrium. The analysis is identical to that of Figure 12–2.

used by those who did not share in the cost of producing it. That gives people an incentive to underinvest in R & D. For example, would you spend millions to develop a better mousetrap knowing that once you succeeded other firms would immediately copy your design and therefore capture part of the benefit of your investment? Although patent and copyright laws attempt to restrict the use of knowledge to those who produce it, at least for a limited time, there are serious problems in enforcing these laws.

Therefore, externality theory provides a rationale for a subsidy to this particular form of investment spending. But what form of subsidy should be used? In 1981 Congress chose a 25 percent tax credit but restricted the tax credit to *increases* in R & D spending above the average R & D spending of the preceding two or three years. This restriction was intended to keep the cost of the subsidy manageable. In 1985, total R & D spending by industry was $55 billion, and if the credit had been available for all R & D spending, it would have cost the Treasury more than $13 billion in lost tax revenues, nearly 20 percent of total corporate tax revenue in that year. The tax credit applied only to incremental spending, however, and was estimated to have cost only $1.5 billion in lost revenues. Moreover, by applying the incentive at the margin, Congress thought that a great deal of new activity might be stimulated at a relatively low cost, since the subsidy applied only to the increases in spending.

Estimates of the effect of the tax credit on R & D spending suggest that spending did increase, but by less than its proponents had hoped, probably by less than $1 billion a year. What has become clear is that the tax credit was not as well designed to provide incentives to increase R & D spending as Congress thought. There are at least three reasons for this. First, firms must have positive tax liabilities in order to benefit from the credit, since it is nonrefundable. Many firms that actively invest in R & D are young, rapidly growing enterprises, however, and these firms frequently operate in the red in the early years.[13] Second, the temporary nature of the tax credit probably limited its impact. R & D spending is essentially long term in nature, and few firms would be likely to undertake long-term commitments to research projects on the basis of a tax credit that was scheduled to expire four years after it was introduced.

The third reason is perhaps the most interesting: the particular incremental form of the tax credit often actually weakens its incentive effect in many instances. For example, suppose a firm increases its R & D spending by $100 this year and receives a $25 tax credit. The firm's higher R & D spending this year, however, will increase the base used to calculate the tax credit in

---

[13] The tax credit can be "carried forward" for up to 15 years, which means that if there is any tax liability in the following 15 years, the tax credit can be used later. However, if the firm is unable to use the credit for several years, the credit's present value will be significantly reduced, especially during inflationary periods, since the credit is not indexed.

future years. That is, the additional $100 in R & D spending this year will increase the base by $33 for each of the next three years, since the base is the average of R & D spending over the previous three years. Thus, by spending $100 more this year, the firm can lose future tax credits of 25 percent of $33 for each of the next three years, for a total loss of $25 (3 x 0.25 x $33), ignoring the discounting of future loss. Because of the way the tax credit base is calculated, the incentive to expand R & D spending is substantially diminished.

For these reasons, the R & D tax credit has not had a pronounced effect on R & D spending. This experience illustrates the difficulties of designing effective tax incentives while simultaneously trying to avoid substantial revenue losses.

Proposal for Reform: Integration of the Corporation and Individual Income Taxes

The corporation income tax turns out to be a complicated levy with a number of undesirable features. As a tax on capital income, it reduces the net (after-tax) return to saving and probably reduces saving and real capital accumulation. Since the corporation income tax applies only to capital income generated in the corporate sector, and at different rates to different assets, it is an uneven tax that distorts the allocation of capital among different assets and industries. On equity grounds, the corporation income tax violates the principle of horizontal equity, since taxpayers who receive more capital income bear a heavier tax burden. The vertical equity implications are not as clear. The corporation income tax does result in a higher tax rate for the top decile, but it also applies a sizable tax burden on low-income families with capital income. Under the individual income tax, families with less than about $9,000 in income are considered too poor to pay taxes, but if that income were capital income (such as pension income), it would be subject to a substantial tax burden from the corporation income tax before it reached the family.

For these reasons, a number of economists have for many years urged reform of the corporation income tax. One proposal is simply to eliminate the tax altogether, but that has at least one major disadvantage: Although individuals would still pay individual income taxes on corporate income paid out as dividends, they would pay no taxes on corporate income held within the corporation. Thus, retained corporate earnings would escape taxation, at least until the shareholders realized a capital gain from the sale of the stock, and then that gain would be taxed at preferential rates under the present law.

To ensure that retained corporate earnings do not escape taxation when the corporate tax is eliminated, the individual income tax must be changed.

The way generally recommended to accomplish this is to require a corporation to inform each shareholder that it has retained a certain sum of income on his or her behalf; then that sum is taxed as income under the individual income tax on an annual basis. For example, if a corporation has net income of $1,000 that it does not pay out as dividends, and there are 10 shareholders, each owning one tenth of the shares, then each shareholder would be considered to have income from the corporation equal to $100 for individual income tax purposes.

This proposal is commonly referred to as the integration of the corporate and personal income taxes. Under this integration, all corporate income (whether paid out as dividends or retained) would be taxed as ordinary income in the hands of shareholders. This reform has several advantages. Horizontal equity would be improved: Two taxpayers with the same incomes would pay the same tax even if one received only corporate source income and the other entirely labor income. Vertical equity might also be improved, but this is more a matter of viewpoint. Low-income families with zero taxable income would no longer be paying a sizable tax on their corporate source income. In general, taxes on lower- and upper-income classes would fall, but the reduction in average tax rates would be larger for those with low incomes.

The integration of the corporate and personal income taxes would also result in efficiency advantages. Integration would end the differences in the tax treatment of corporate and noncorporate income. (In fact, the proposal basically would extend the same treatment to corporate income that is now applied to unincorporated businesses.) This change would avoid the misallocation of capital between the two sectors, as illustrated in Figure 12–2. Integration would also lower the overall taxation of capital income, since it would avoid having the same income taxed at both the corporate and personal levels, which could lead to an increase in saving and capital accumulation.

Integration, however, also has some disadvantages. First, it would reduce federal tax revenue. The revenue loss must be offset in some way, and so a complete evaluation of the proposed reform should take this factor into account. Second, corporate net income would still have to be defined and measured by the tax authorities, even though it is not subject to a separate tax. Otherwise, the amount of retained earnings allocated among households to be taxed under the individual income tax would not be known. This means, however, that government would still have to specify depreciation allowances and the like. If accelerated depreciation were used, the tax system would continue to tax various classes of assets differentially.

One different sort of objection to integration holds that it permits corporations to avoid paying their "fair share" of the nation's tax burden. This objection is based on the notion that corporations have some independent taxpaying ability apart from the taxpaying ability of their workers, customers, or owners. Those favoring integration reject this view. They see the corporation income tax only as an indirect and inefficient means of taxing individual income—but with no attempt made to adjust the tax to the tax-paying capacity of the individuals who are ultimately being taxed.

Supplementary Readings

AUERBACH, ALAN J. "The New Economics of Accelerated Depreciation." National Bureau of Economic Research, Working Paper No. 848, Jan. 1982.

BALLENTINE, J. GREGORY. *Equity, Efficiency, and the U.S. Corporation Income Tax.* Washington, D.C.: American Enterprise Institute, 1980.

BREAK, GEORGE F., and JOSEPH A. PECHMAN. *Federal Tax Reform: The Impossible Dream.* Washington, D.C.: The Brookings Institution, 1975.

BROWN, KENNETH M., ed. *The R & D Tax Credit.* Washington, D.C.: American Enterprise Institute, 1984.

CONGRESSIONAL BUDGET OFFICE. *Revising the Corporate Income Tax.* Washington, D.C.: U.S. Government Printing Office, 1985.

FULLERTON, DON. "Which Effective Tax Rate?" *National Tax Journal,* 37:23–41 (Mar. 1984).

MCLURE, CHARLES E., JR. "Integration of the Income Taxes: Why and How." *Journal of Corporate Taxation,* 2(4):429 (Winter 1976).

———, and WAYNE R. THIRSK. "A Simplified Exposition of the Harberger Model, I: Tax Incidence." *National Tax Journal,* 28(1):1–28 (Mar. 1975).

Review Questions and Problems

1. The rate structure of the corporation income tax is progressive; yet when economists analyze the tax they often assume that it is proportional. Why?

2. "If the corporate sector of the U.S. economy were really competitive, firms would be earning zero profits, and the corporation income tax would generate no revenue." True or false? Explain.

3. "To corporations, the corporate tax is a cost just like any other cost, and the price of the product must rise enough to cover it. Therefore, the tax is shifted forward to consumers." Evaluate this argument.

4. Explain Harberger's analysis of the incidence of the corporation income tax. In this analysis, does the price of goods produced by corporations rise? If so, why doesn't the analysis conclude that the tax is at least partially shifted forward to consumers?

5. Harberger's analysis assumes that the nation's capital stock is not affected by the tax. Is this assumption reasonable? If not, how would you expect the capital stock to be affected, and how would this affect the analysis of the incidence of the tax?

6. If the corporate tax is borne in proportion to capital income, what does this tell us about the horizontal and vertical equity of the tax?

7. "The market adjustment to the corporate tax tends to produce equality in after-tax rates of return, implying that the before-tax rates of return diverge. Therefore, there is a misallocation of resources." Does this statement accurately describe how the tax produces a welfare cost in the way it affects the allocation of capital between the corporate and noncorporate sectors?

8. This chapter discussed two types of welfare cost produced by the corporate tax: how the tax affects the allocation of capital between the corporate and noncorporate sectors, and how it affects the allocation of capital to different types of investment within the corporate sector. Describe each of these welfare costs and the features of the tax that are responsible for them.

9. Devise a numerical example to show how it is possible for a 10 percent investment tax credit to produce negative tax rates as large as minus 50 percent, as shown in Table 12–4.

10. How would you change the tax code to stimulate R & D spending, keeping in mind that you would like to minimize the revenue loss?

chapter 13
Other Major Revenue Sources

IN this chapter we continue to apply the principles of tax analysis to several more sources of government revenue. We begin with a discussion of the second largest tax in the United States, the social security payroll tax, and then turn to sales and excise taxes and property taxation. In the last section, we analyze a policy that is rarely considered as a tax, deficit finance, and show how the general approach of tax analysis can be used to clarify the effects of this policy.

Social Security Payroll Tax

In our earlier analysis of the social security system in Chapter 7, the expenditure part of the program was emphasized. Now we take a more careful look at the tax side of the social security system. As we shall see, however, it is frequently important to consider both the taxes and the benefits they finance simultaneously. Because the social security tax is an *earmarked tax,* with revenues linked to specific expenditures, changes in the tax imply changes in the retirement program and vice versa, so a broad view incorporating both sides of the budget is often required.

The social security payroll tax applies to the wage and salary income of employees and to the earnings of self-employed persons. For employees, the social security payroll tax is composed of two equal rate levies, one paid by the employee and the other by the employer. In 1986, each rate was 7.15 percent, for a combined tax rate of 14.3 percent of employees' earnings. The tax applies to earnings up to a ceiling amount, $42,000 in 1986. Thus, a worker earning $10,000 in 1986 will pay $715 (or, more precisely, $715 will be withheld from the worker's paycheck) and the employer will also pay $715, for a total tax of $1,430. For a worker earning at the maximum level of taxable earnings, $42,000, the total tax liability is $6,006. Workers

Table 13–1 *Social Security Tax Data, Selected Years*

Year	Tax Rate	Maximum Wage Base	Maximum Tax per Earner	Maximum Tax (1985 dollars)	Tax Revenue (billions)	Social Security Taxes As a Percentage of All Federal Taxes
1950	3.0%	$ 3,000	$ 90	$ 402	$ 5.9	11.8%
1955	4.0	4,200	168	675	9.4	12.9
1960	6.0	4,800	288	1,046	17.6	18.3
1965	7.25	4,800	348	1,187	25.0	20.1
1970	9.6	7,800	749	2,075	52.9	27.0
1975	11.7	14,000	1,650	3,298	101.6	34.4
1980	12.26	25,900	3,175	4,145	186.8	33.7
1985	14.1	39,600	5,584	5,584	309.9	39.4
1986	14.3	42,000	6,006			

Sources: Department of Health and Human Services, *Social Security Bulletin* (Washington, D.C.: U.S. Government Printing Office, Dec. 1985); and *Economic Report of the President, 1986* (Washington, D.C.: U.S. Government Printing Office, 1986), Tables B-55 and B-78.

earning above $42,000 also incur a tax liability of $6,006, since the tax applies only to the first $42,000 of income earned by each worker.

Table 13–1 contains a variety of information about the evolution of the social security tax over time. After the discussion of the growth of social security benefits in Chapter 7, it comes as no surprise that the tax that finances these benefits has also grown rapidly. In 1950, total revenue was $5.9 billion, or 11.8 percent of total federal tax revenues; in 1985, revenue from the social security tax was $309.9 billion, which amounted to nearly 40 percent of total federal tax revenues. The tax liability incurred by workers earning at or above the maximum wage base increased more than thirteen-fold in real terms between 1950 and 1985. In terms of revenue, the social security tax is the second largest tax in the United States, following the federal individual income tax, and a majority of taxpayers now actually pay more in social security taxes than they do in income taxes.

Division of the tax between employer and employee

By splitting the social security payroll tax between the employer and the employee, Congress apparently intended to divide the burden of the tax between them. Whether or not this has actually been accomplished is far from clear. Most economists believe that the way the tax is divided into employer and employee portions has no effect on who actually bears its burden. The analysis supporting this view is just an extension of what was discussed in Chapter 4 in connection with an excise subsidy.

To examine the significance of the division of the tax into employer and employee portions, we compare the two extreme cases, one in which the entire tax is collected from employees and the second in which it is collected from employers. In Figure 13–1, before any tax is levied, the supply and demand curves for labor are shown as S and D, the wage rate is $10 per hour, and employment is OL_1. Now suppose a payroll tax is levied on *employers* which requires them to pay $2.00 to the government for each hour of labor employed.

To understand how to incorporate the tax into the analysis, recall that the demand curve for labor shows the maximum amount per hour that the employers will pay for each alternative quantity of labor. For example, the demand curve in Figure 13–1 means that employers will pay a maximum of $10 per hour to hire OL_1 units of labor. With the tax in place, employers will still pay no more than $10 per hour for the quantity OL_1, but since $2 must be paid to the government, this means that the amount that employers will be willing to pay workers for OL_1 units of labor will fall to $8 per hour. In the diagram, the effect of the tax is therefore shown as a vertical shift downward by $2 in the demand curve to D'. The downward shift in the demand curve means that with a $2-per-hour tax, employers will pay $2 less to workers at each level of employment. With the supply curve, S, the tax

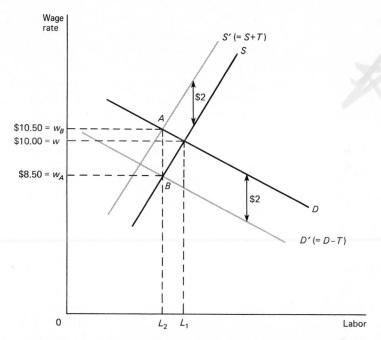

FIGURE 13–1 *Tax on employers versus tax on employees.*

thus reduces employment to OL_2, and the wage rate paid to workers falls to w_A, or \$8.50. To employers, the cost of labor *including the tax* is now \$10.50 per hour.

Alternatively, if the \$2-per-hour tax is collected from *employees* rather than employers, it will have the effect of shifting the supply curve vertically upward by \$2, or to S', without affecting the demand curve. The shift in supply reflects the fact that workers must be paid \$2 more per hour to yield the necessary after-tax wage to compensate them for supplying each alternative quantity of labor. For example, if workers must pay the \$2-per-hour tax, they will continue to supply OL_1 only if they receive a \$12 hourly wage. That is, OL_1 hours of labor will be provided only if workers receive a net (after-tax) payment of \$10 per hour. When the tax is collected from workers, the intersection of S' and D determines the new equilibrium, involving employment of OL_2 and a wage rate of \$10.50. Since workers must remit \$2.00 to the government, their take-home pay is \$8.50.

Note that the real effects of the tax are exactly the same whether the tax is collected from employers or employees. When collected from employers, employment is OL_2, firms pay a wage of \$10.50 per hour, but \$2.00 goes to the government, and workers receive the remaining \$8.50. When employees pay the tax, employment is again OL_2, and firms pay \$10.50 as before; although the workers receive $10.50, they keep only $8.50, since they must remit $2.00 to the government. In both cases, the $2-per-hour tax, the distance *AB,* reflects the difference between the gross-of-tax cost of labor to employers and the net-of-tax payment to workers.

The government therefore really has no control over who ultimately bears the cost of the tax by the way the tax is collected. The results are the same whether the employer or employee pays the tax. Although we have shown that the effects are identical for the extreme cases (when the employer *or* the employee pays the tax), it holds for the intermediate cases, too. For instance, if $1 of the tax were collected from employers and $1 from employees, firms would pay $9.50 to workers (plus $1.00 to the government for a total unit cost of labor of $10.50, as before), and workers would receive a gross wage of $9.50 and get to keep $8.50, since they would turn over $1 to the government.

Incidence

The real effects of the social security payroll tax are thus the same, regardless of how it is divided for collection purposes between employers and employees. This is not the same as saying that workers bear all the burden of the tax. Note that in our example, the $2-per-hour tax led to a $1.50 reduction in the net wage rate ($10.00 to $8.50) so in that case workers did not bear the full burden of the tax in the form of a lower wage rate.

Although the incidence of the social security tax does not depend on how it is divided between employers and employees, it does depend on the elasticities of labor supply and demand. Basically, the tax is a proportional tax on labor income, and as observed in Chapter 11, such a tax falls fully on workers when the labor supply curve is vertical. Since the social security tax applies to almost all industries and workers, it is likely that the relevant aggregate supply curve will be highly inelastic. Figure 13–2 illustrates this case. Since it makes no difference whether the tax is collected from employers or workers, we can analyze the tax by assuming it shifts the demand curve downward. In addition, we can now more realistically treat the tax as levied at a certain rate on earnings rather than (as in Figure 13–1) a fixed sum per hour of labor, so the demand curve pivots downward rather than shifting downward in a parallel fashion. With a vertical supply curve, the wage rate received by workers falls by $2—the amount of the tax—to $8. When the supply curve is vertical, the net wage rate received by workers falls by the full amount of the tax so workers bear the entire burden of the tax.

Note that the cost of labor to employers has not risen; it is still $10. Now, however, $2 goes to government and $8 to workers, rather than $10 to workers. Since costs associated with hiring labor have not risen, the prices of products are unaffected. Much popular discussion of payroll taxes, espe-

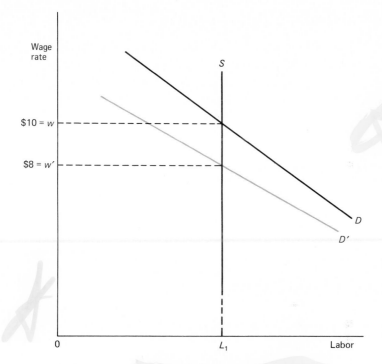

Wage
rate

$10 = w

$8 = w'

S

D

D'

0

L_1

Labor

FIGURE 13–2   *Incidence of the social security tax.*

cially the employer portion, holds that higher employer payroll taxes add
to labor costs and thus contribute to higher prices. This analysis, however,
indicates that total labor costs do not rise: When taxes go up, wage rates go
down. (Perhaps more plausibly in a dynamic setting, when employer payroll
taxes go up, wage rates do not rise over time as much as they would have
otherwise. The final result, however, is the same.)

One special feature of the social security tax differs from a proportional
tax on labor income and may have some bearing on its effect on labor
supply decisions. Under the social security tax, if a worker earns more and
incurs an additional tax liability, the tax may not be viewed as a net loss.
Because the worker's future social security pension will be larger the more
taxes paid, there is an offsetting benefit associated with paying higher taxes.
Thus, in Figure 13–2 workers may not believe that their net wage has fallen
from $10 to $8 because they will receive a pension when they retire. If this
is so, it becomes even more likely that the quantity of labor supplied remains unchanged in response to the tax. This point should not be pushed
too far, however, because the link between taxes paid by a worker and the
subsequent pension is not very strong.

In all, it seems reasonable to conclude that workers bear the full burden of both the employee and employer portions of the social security tax. This analysis has, however, ignored the expenditure side of the social security system. If saving falls in response to the provision of pensions, then the combined (balanced-budget) impact of the tax and expenditure will produce further effects. Because a reduced capital stock means less capital per worker and lower productivity per worker, the D curve in Figure 13–2 will shift downward (or rise less rapidly over time), reducing wage rates still further. The impact of the entire social security system on saving is usually ignored in an analysis of the tax, which is reasonable if the differential incidence approach is adopted. (Recall that with the differential approach we compare different taxes to finance the same expenditures, here pensions. Then the effect on the capital stock, and hence the position of D, will be the same under alternative taxes.)

If workers bear the full burden of the tax, what does this mean for the distribution of the tax burden among households? It is frequently argued that the social security tax is regressive for two reasons. First, individuals earning above the maximum wage base pay no more in taxes than do workers at the maximum wage base. (But more than 90 percent of all workers earn below the maximum wage base.) Second, the tax does not apply to capital income, which is more important to high-income households. This argument, however, is not complete, since many low-income families receive income in the form of government transfers that also escape the tax. Consider, for example, a family with earnings of $5,000 and transfers of $5,000. The family will pay a social security tax of about 14 percent on its $5,000 earnings, or $700, but this tax is only 7 percent of its total income. Because of the importance of transfers to low-income families, the social security payroll tax is actually progressive up to about the seventh decile of households ranked by income; then it becomes regressive at the top three deciles.

It can be argued that the distribution of the social security tax burden should not be evaluated in the same way other taxes are. Because each person pays social security taxes in some years and receives retirement benefits later, it may be preferable to take a lifetime perspective and consider both the taxes paid and the benefits received. We took this approach in Chapter 7, where we saw that the benefit formula and other provisions favor relatively low-wage earners; that is, low-wage earners receive a higher rate of return on their taxes than high-wage earners do. Thus, viewed from a lifetime perspective, the social security system as a whole is progressive.

Welfare cost

Since the social security payroll tax is so similar to a proportional tax on labor income, we can analyze it in the same way. Like a proportional tax, the payroll tax produces a welfare cost by distorting labor supply decisions.

Taxpayers will work less and be worse off than under an equal-yield lump-sum tax; the graphical analysis would be exactly the same as in Figure 11–2.

The analogy to the welfare cost of a proportional tax must be qualified in two respects, however. First, there is a zero welfare cost as a result of labor supply distortions for workers who earn more than the maximum wage base. The *marginal* rate of the social security tax was zero for workers earning above $42,000 in 1986, and it is the marginal tax rate that distorts labor supply decisions. Consider, for example, workers earning $50,000. Their social security tax liability will not be changed even if they earn $1,000 less, and so the tax does not give them an incentive to modify their labor supply decisions at the relevant margin. (As an exercise, modify Figure 11–2 to show that the social security tax does not produce a welfare cost for workers earning above the ceiling on taxable earnings.) Although fewer than 10 percent of all workers earn more than the maximum wage base, their total earnings are probably about 25 percent of national labor earnings so the absence of labor supply distortions for this group is far from insignificant.

A second qualification pertains to workers earning below the maximum wage base. To the extent that paying an additional dollar in social security taxes is accompanied by an increase in the pension received in retirement, the distorting effect of the tax is reduced. This occurs because workers will not view their net wage as reduced by the full amount of the tax—there is an offsetting future benefit.[1] For this factor to be relevant, however, there must be a consistent relationship between individual taxes paid and future benefits, and workers must recognize the relationship. (But as we have seen, this link is fairly weak.)

Issues in social security tax reform

Over the past decade, social security expenditures have had a tendency to exceed annual tax revenues, with the shortfall made up from shrinking trust funds. Projections suggest that the reforms introduced in 1983 may result in an annual surplus, starting around 1990. However, these projections may prove to be wrong, but even if they are correct, the system is likely to face financing problems early in the next century. So let's consider what tax changes could be made to raise additional revenues. In other words, we shall assume that a decision has been made to increase tax revenues flowing into the social security system and compare alternative ways to raise extra

---

[1] Note how this differs from the federal income tax. Under the income tax, if a worker earns more and thereby pays $100 more in taxes, this is completely a net loss to the worker because the additional tax payment brings with it no additional government benefits. Under the social security payroll tax, paying $100 more in taxes may result in a larger pension in retirement.

revenue. We shall explore this problem because it allows us to focus on some perennial issues related to changing the social security tax—not because it is of urgent importance today.

Using general tax revenue   Except for a portion of Medicare, social security benefits are financed exclusively by the social security payroll tax. One common proposal to generate more revenue without raising payroll taxes is to use general federal revenues to supplement the payroll tax. This is sometimes proposed as if "general revenues" were a free source of funds, which, of course, they are not. Basically, what this approach advocates is the use of the federal income tax instead of payroll taxes to fund the shortfalls in the social security system. Proponents of the use of general revenues emphasize that the income tax is more progressive than the payroll tax, so using general revenues would place a larger share of any additional tax burden on high-income families who are better able to afford it.

In evaluating this option, as well as others, it is important to look beyond the short-run effect of permitting existing benefit obligations to be financed without increasing payroll taxes. What happens to the future benefits? If benefits go up only for individuals who pay the additional taxes (as "individual equity" requires), that is, mainly for high-income families, then using general revenues would not in the long run increase taxes or benefits for low-income families. This is not, however, what most proponents of this approach have in mind. Instead, with this reform, they intend for benefits to still be related to taxable earnings under the social security payroll tax, but additional taxes paid under the income tax would not count toward future social security benefits. Consequently, benefits financed by general revenues would apply across the board, regardless of each individual's contribution to general revenues. And because the benefit formula is tilted in favor of workers with low earnings records, most of the benefits financed by general revenues would go to individuals with low earnings, whereas most of the taxes would be paid by workers with high incomes. In short, the proposal to use general revenues is essentially a method to make the system more redistributive.

Raising the ceiling on taxable earnings   Another method of increasing revenues is to continue to rely on the payroll tax as the sole source of revenue but to increase the maximum wage base without increasing the tax rate. For example, the ceiling might be increased from $42,000 to $60,000. (Recall that the ceiling amount is indexed to average wages in the economy and so automatically grows over time. What we are considering here is an increase beyond this automatic increase.) Because the tax rate remains the same, the tax on persons earning below $42,000 would not increase; all of the additional tax burden would be placed on workers earning over $42,000 with the largest increases falling on those earning $60,000 and above.

This proposal raises the basic issue of why there should be a ceiling on taxable earnings in the first place. After all, the ceiling is what contributes to the regressivity of the tax at high income levels. But once again, we must consider what this change would mean for future benefits. Currently a person earning $75,000 pays social security taxes only on the first $42,000, and the retirement benefit is related to the $42,000 in taxable earnings. Thus, the future retirement benefit is only a small fraction of this person's preretirement earnings, and this provides a strong incentive to save privately. If the ceiling is raised or eliminated, retirement benefits to high-income persons must be increased sharply (insofar as individual equity is preserved), reducing the incentive to save privately.

The ceiling on taxable earnings serves the function of maintaining incentive for high earners to save privately. Since those with relatively high incomes provide a large share of national saving, removing the ceiling could have a disporportionate effect on saving and capital accumulation. In addition, the ceiling also serves to avoid a distortion in the labor supply decisions of workers earning above that level.

As a practical matter, the maximum wage base is already so high (following increases enacted in 1977) that its removal would not provide much additional revenue. Total earnings in excess of the ceiling are now only about 6 percent as large as earnings already subject to tax. This means that complete elimination of the ceiling would increase social security revenues by only 6 percent.

Increasing the tax rate   A final option is to increase the tax rate but to leave the ceiling unchanged. If the tax rate is increased, an additional tax burden would be placed on all wage earners. As a percent of total income, the increase in taxes would be lower at low-income levels because of the importance of transfers. In this case, higher retirement benefits could be provided to low-income retirees without violating individual equity, because they would bear some of the additional tax burden while they are employed. Even in this case, some further redistribution in favor of low earners would occur because of the nature of the benefit formula. It would, however, be less for an increase in the tax rate than for either of the other two options, because workers with low earnings would pay a larger share of the tax increase.

Taxes on Output

Sales and excise taxes

Taxes on output are used by all levels of government, although their types differ. The federal government uses only excise taxes on particular products, with taxes on gasoline, tobacco, alcohol, and public utilities accounting for most of the revenue. In 1985, federal excise taxes generated $48 billion, or about 7 percent of total federal revenue. State governments rely more on general sales taxes, but they also often tax specific products using excise taxes. Nearly a third of state government revenues is generated by sales and excise taxes. Local governments also uses these taxes, but to a lesser extent; only about 7 percent of local revenues come from sales and excise taxes. For all state and local governments together, sales and excise taxes produced about $120 billion in revenue in 1985.

Sales and excise taxes are frequently held to be shifted to consumers in the form of higher product prices. According to this view, these taxes are borne by persons in proportion to their consumption outlays and tend to be regressive. The earlier analysis of these taxes in Chapter 10 may already have suggested that these conclusions are not fully correct. Now we take a more careful look at the incidence of sales and excise taxes.

Let's consider a general sales tax that applies to all goods and services. The economy could respond to this tax in two different ways. In one case, if the overall level of absolute prices is unaffected by the imposition of the tax, then firms, after paying the tax, will have lower revenues remaining to compensate factors of production. Wage rates and other factor prices will therefore decline. (This was the conclusion in our analysis of Figure 10–4.) A second possibility is that product prices will rise by the amount of the tax per unit and that wage rates and other factor prices will remain unchanged. Since we do not have a theory that accurately predicts what determines the absolute level of prices, this possibility cannot be ruled out.

Does it make a great deal of difference which of these alternatives is correct—whether product prices increase and factor prices remain unchanged or whether product prices remain unchanged and factor prices fall? Actually, under certain conditions, the incidence of the tax is the same, regardless of which alternative is correct. To see this, suppose that labor is the only factor of production and that workers consume their entire earnings. If prices rise and wage rates remain unchanged, the purchasing power of wage earnings will fall (real wage rates will fall), and workers will bear a burden in proportion to their earnings. Alternatively, if prices are constant and wage rates fall, the purchasing power of earnings will also decline since real wage rates have fallen, and workers again will bear a burden in proportion to their earnings. In both cases, the wage rate relative to the price of products—the real wage rate—will fall.

Thus, in this simple setting, it makes no difference whether, or by how much, the absolute prices of goods rise, since the real effects of the tax will be the same. To identify the distribution of tax burdens among persons, we could allocate the tax in proportion to either consumption or wage earnings; both would yield the same result.

However, this conclusion is not fully satisfactory for two reasons. The first involves the fact that some people receive income in a form other than factor earnings. Government transfers have become an important alternative source of income, especially for low-income households. For a recipient of a government transfer, it may well make a difference whether or not a sales tax increases prices. If the transfer payment is unchanged and the price level rises, the recipient will bear a burden under the sales tax; if the price level does not rise, there will be no burden on this transfer recipient, since the purchasing power of the transfer is unchanged. The view that sales taxes burden consumers, regardless of whether their consumption is financed by wage earnings or transfers, must be based on the assumption that sales taxes cause the price level to rise. If the price level does not rise, the consumer whose income is wholly in the form of a government transfer will bear no burden.

It is possible to argue, however, that consumption financed by government transfers bears no burden under sales taxes, regardless of what happens to the price level. If the price level does not change, then clearly transfer-financed consumption will not be affected. Now consider the second alternative, that the price level rises. If the price level increases, but the purchasing power of the transfer is maintained by government policy, then once again there will be no tax burden. For example, if the price level rises by 10 percent and a person's transfer also rises by 10 percent, then the transfer recipient will bear no tax burden. This outcome does not necessarily require continued adjustments in government transfer policy. In fact, about three fourths of all government transfers are indexed to the price level, so that the size of the transfer automatically varies with changes in the price level.

In view of this, it seems plausible to assume that the real value of transfers is constant when we analyze taxes. This has great significance for the incidence of any tax that is thought to affect consumers through changes in product prices. In the case of sales and excise taxes, it implies that the taxes are progressive rather than regressive because these taxes reduce real factor earnings but not real transfers. Since transfers are a larger proportion of total income for low-income households, the tax burden as a percentage of total income is smaller for low-income households.

A second factor, however, may be relevant, which operates to make sales and excise taxes regressive, namely, that people consume different proportions of their disposable incomes. Since sales and excise taxes apply primarily to consumer goods, people who consume a larger fraction of their incomes will bear a greater burden from increases in the prices of consumer goods, other things being the same. Moreover, when annual data are examined, we find that low-income households consume a much larger fraction of their disposable incomes than do higher-income households. This is shown in the first column of Table 13–2. Households in the lowest-income decile are estimated to consume almost 50 percent more than their disposable incomes! By contrast, households in the highest-income decile consume less than two thirds of their disposable incomes.

Table 13–2   *Sales and Excise Tax Burdens of Income Classes, Alternative Assumptions*

Income Decile	Percent of Disposable Income Consumed	Taxes Allocated in Proportion to	
		Annual Consumption	Market Earnings
1	148.5%	10.6%	2.3%
2	115.4	8.2	2.6
3	101.0	6.8	3.4
4	98.7	6.4	4.1
5	96.9	6.0	4.7
6	95.1	5.7	5.0
7	91.6	5.4	5.2
8	88.9	5.2	5.3
9	86.0	4.9	5.3
10	65.6	3.3	5.5

Source: Edgar K. Browning and William R. Johnson, *The Distribution of the Tax Burden* (Washington, D.C.: American Enterprise Institute, 1979), Table 18.

How is it possible for households to consume so much more than their disposable incomes? For prolonged periods of time it is impossible; households can, however, finance consumption from previously accumulated assets or by borrowing on a temporary basis. For instance, people who are temporarily unemployed or ill may continue to finance their previous consumption levels by using their savings until they return to work. The fact that such consumption behavior can be only temporary casts doubt on its relevance to tax incidence analysis. Many economists believe that tax burdens should be related to longer-run measures of economic status, such as lifetime incomes. Over a person's lifetime, consumption cannot exceed income. Indeed, evidence suggests that relative to lifetime income, there is very little difference in the percentage of income consumed among income classes. This means that a tax that falls on consumption will be approximately proportional to lifetime income, even though the annual data on consumption suggest that a consumption tax is quite regressive.

The last two columns in Table 13–2 illustrate the importance of these points. The second column shows the average tax rates as a percentage of income when sales and excise taxes are allocated in proportion to annual consumption. Note that the figures exhibit a pronounced regressive pattern, exactly as expected from the consumption data in the first column. For many years, this approach has been the conventional view of the incidence of taxes on output. However, it is now clear that the conclusion—that sales and excise taxes are regressive—is the result of three assumptions, each of which can be challenged. First, this approach assumes that sales and excise taxes cause the price level to rise exactly in proportion to the taxes. Second, it assumes that government transfers fall in real value when the price level rises (unindexed transfers). Third, it assumes that the annual consumption data provide meaningful indications of how the taxes affect people at different income levels.

An alternative approach to the incidence of sales and excise taxes that reaches a far different conclusion is shown by the estimates in the last column of Table 13–2. Here, the taxes are allocated in proportion to the market earnings of households in each income class. Using the second approach, sales and excise taxes are found to be progressive, because market earnings are a smaller share of total income for low-income households, which receive proportionally larger transfers. The decline in the importance of transfers as we move up the income distribution makes the tax burden progressive relative to total income. This alternative approach reflects two assumptions. First, it is assumed that real transfers are constant, that is, that transfers will be effectively indexed if prices rise. Second, it is assumed that approximately the same percentage of income is consumed at each income level, as would be the case if we measured incomes over a longer period of time than a single year. Under these assumptions, sales and excise taxes fall in proportion to market earnings and will therefore be progressive relative to total incomes.

Economists do not agree on which of these approaches is more accurate. The importance of the topic, however, extends beyond the question of the incidence of sales and excise taxes. Exactly the same issues arise in analyzing any type of tax that is felt to be partially or wholly "shifted to consumers" through higher product prices. If, as some economists believe, corporation income and property taxes are partially shifted in this way, their incidence will also depend on resolving the problems discussed here. So too does the incidence of a value-added tax, which is considered next.

The value-added tax

A value-added tax (VAT) is basically a multistage sales tax that is collected from firms at each stage in the production and distribution process. The VAT is an important revenue source in many European countries but not, at the present time, in the United States. Over the past several years, however, the VAT has received more attention as a possible addition to the federal government's tax arsenal. Some of the support for a VAT comes from people who want a new tax to help reduce federal budget deficits, whereas others would like to see the tax replace the corporation income tax or part of the social security payroll tax.

The base on which a VAT is levied is the value added by each firm, that

Table 13–3   *The Value-added Tax Base*

	Firm A (Manufacturer)	Firm B (Wholesaler)	Firm C (Retailer)	Total
	Stage of Production			
Sales	$500	$800	$1,000	$2,300
Purchases	0	500	800	1,300
Value Added	500	300	200	1,000

is, the firm's sales less its purchases of material inputs from other firms. Table 13–3 illustrates how a VAT would operate. Suppose that firm A employs only workers as inputs and manufactures a product that is sold to firm B for $500. Firm A's value added is then $500, its sales less its (zero) purchases from other firms. Firm B distributes the product to retail establishments, selling it for $800. Firm B's value added is its sales of $800 less the payment of $500 to firm A, or $300. Firm C sells the product to consumers for $1,000, and since it purchased the product for $800, its value added is $200. Under a VAT, each firm would be taxed on its value added, as shown by the last row in the table. Note that the total tax base, the sum of the value added by each firm, is $1,000 and that this is exactly the retail value of the final product. *The tax base of a VAT is the same as a retail sales tax.* If firms are permitted to deduct purchases of capital goods, the tax base essentially becomes total consumption in the economy. (Different treatments of investment goods can transform the VAT into a tax on consumption and saving, but all proposals have specified the consumption type of VAT, on which we shall focus here.)

A general sales tax on consumption goods and a VAT both have the same tax base and are therefore equivalent in most important respects. Our previous analysis of general sales taxes applies equally to the VAT. What is novel about recent discussions of the VAT in the United States is the proposal that the federal government adopt this form of tax. Forty-five state governments already use general sales taxes, but the federal government does not.

Proponents of a federal VAT cite four main advantages for this tax, as compared with alternative ways the federal government might raise revenue with its existing taxes. First, the VAT is a broad-based tax utilizing a uniform rate. Since all goods and services would be taxed at the same rate, the tax would not favor the production of some goods over others. In other words, a VAT avoids the sort of welfare cost produced by a selective excise tax on one product. Moreover, as a broad-based tax, it can raise a large amount of revenue using relatively low rates. For example, the Treasury Department estimates the potential tax base of a U.S. VAT in 1988 to be $3.1 trillion, so a 10 percent tax could potentially raise $310 billion.[2]

A second advantage lies in the administration of a VAT. It would be very difficult for firms to avoid paying a VAT tax, since the records of transactions among firms leave a clear trail for auditors. With increasing concern about cheating on income taxes and the belief that substantial amounts of income in the "underground economy" escape taxation, a tax that is relatively easy to administer and collect looks attractive. Third, supporters note that the VAT falls on consumption and not on saving. Because of the desire to encourage investment and saving, a tax that does not penalize saving compares favorably with alternatives like the individual and corporate income taxes.

A final advantage is that the public generally views sales taxes favorably. In recent years, opinion surveys have found that retail sales taxes are a significantly more popular form of taxation than the federal individual income tax is. Even low-income persons, who bear larger burdens under sales taxes than under the federal individual income tax, favor sales taxes by a margin of 1.75 to 1.[3] Whether these findings imply that the public does not understand how the income tax operates (believing, for example, that the wealthy avoid paying income taxes) is not clear. Whatever their source, these attitudes may make adding a VAT more politically feasible than raising some other tax, regardless of the objective merits of the alternatives.

The most commonly stated objection to a VAT is that it would be regressive. Our earlier analysis of the incidence of sales and excise taxes is relevant to this, since a VAT would have the same pattern of incidence. For reasons explained earlier, it is not at all certain that a VAT would be regressive; it almost certainly would not be regressive when viewed relative to lifetime income. Still, it remains true that a VAT would be less progressive than the federal individual income tax is, so it may suffer by comparison.

The perception that a VAT would be regressive, however, has often led its supporters to favor modifying its structure to make it less so. For instance, instead of applying a VAT to all goods and services, food, housing, and medical care could be exempted from the tax base. Indeed, many European countries go further and tax some goods ("luxuries") at higher rates than other goods. But the evidence suggests that trying to fine-tune the VAT tax base in this way would not significantly increase its progressivity (reduce its regressivity).[4] Using different tax rates or exempting certain goods and

---

[2]U.S. Department of the Treasury, *Tax Reform for Fairness, Simplicity, and Economic Growth* (Washington, D.C.: U.S. Government Printing Office, Nov. 1984), vol. 3, Table 7–1.

[3]Advisory Commission on Intergovernmental Relations, *Changing Public Attitudes on Governments and Taxes* (Washington, D.C.: ACIR, 1982).

[4]U.S. Department of the Treasury, *Tax Reform for Fairness, Simplicity and Economic Growth*, op. cit., Chapter 8.

services would, however, complicate the tax and increase its distorting effects through the nonuniform treatment of different goods. This leads to a
second disadvantage of the tax: it is susceptible to becoming riddled with
special tax preferences, just as the income tax has, and that lessens its attractiveness from an efficiency standpoint.

A third disadvantage may simply be the mirror image of the popularity
of retail sales taxes. It is argued that because a VAT would be concealed in
the prices of goods and services, people would bear more of a burden than
they would realize. This is basically a public choice argument, made by
those who are concerned that taxpayers will agree to more government
spending than they really want because they are unaware of how large the
costs will be. Since tax rates of more than one half-dozen European VATs
have risen to 18 percent or more, this concern may be a real one.

Property Taxation

Property taxation, as it is used in the United States, is primarily a tax used
by local governments. Property taxes are levied by almost all local governments and are their major source of revenue. In 1985, property taxes produced more than $100 billion in revenue for local governments, totaling
more than 75 percent of all local tax revenue. Because the nature of the tax
is determined independently by local governments, there is wide variation
in property tax rates and in the definition of taxable property.

In general, the property tax is levied on the assessed value of real property, including land, homes, buildings, and equipment owned by businesses,
and sometimes consumer durables such as automobiles. Although most people
encounter the tax in their role as homeowners, half of the total revenue
raised by property taxes accrues from the taxation of business property.

There have long been two conflicting views about who bears the burden
of property taxation. One view holds that the tax is eventually reflected in
higher prices of goods produced using taxed property and so would be
much like a general sales tax. The other view is that the tax is borne by
owners of property—which would make the tax more progressive. Recently,
these two views have been reconciled[5] and partially incorporated into a
third approach. The "new view" is best explained by first analyzing a uniform national property tax and then considering what difference it makes
when many local property taxes are levied at different rates.

---

[5]Peter M. Mieszkowski, "The Property Tax: An Excise or a Profits Tax?" *Journal of Public
Economics,* 1:73 (Apr. 1972).

National property tax

Property is simply another name for what economists usually refer to as capital. Property, or capital, is a durable asset that produces a flow of services (income) over a period of time. It is important to understand that taxing the value of property has the same effect as taxing the income generated by that property. Consider a piece of property with a market value of $10,000 that yields an income of $800 per year, a rate of return of 8 percent. A property tax of 2 percent on the market value would yield $200 in tax revenue per year. Similarly, a tax on the property (capital) income of 25 percent would also yield $200 per year. These two taxes have identical economic effects: A 2 percent tax on the market value of an asset that yields 8 percent takes one fourth of the return to the asset, just as does a tax of 25 percent on the income from the asset. Thus, the taxation of property and the taxation of capital incomes (as under the corporation income tax) can be analyzed in the same way.

Let's consider a national property tax levied at a rate of 2 percent on the market value of all capital. Before the tax, the rate of return to capital is 8 percent, so the property tax is equivalent to a 25 percent tax on the income from capital. To prepare for the analysis of different property taxes in different localities, we divide the nation into two geographic localities and call them X and Y. Because the property tax applies at the same rate in both localities, there is no incentive for capital owners to shift capital from one locality to another. If capital is in perfectly inelastic supply, its before-tax return will not change, and capital owners will bear the entire burden in the form of a lower after-tax return.

Figure 13–3, similar to the earlier diagram used for the corporation income tax, illustrates this analysis. Now, however, capital (property) employed in geographic locality X is measured to the right from O_X, and capital employed in locality Y to the left from O_Y, so $O_X O_Y$ is the total stock of capital. D_Y and D_X show the productivities of capital in the two localities. Before the tax is imposed, $O_X K_1$ is employed in X and $O_Y K_1$ in Y, with the rate of return equal to 8 percent in both localities. A national property tax of 2 percent is equivalent to a 25 percent tax on the return to capital in both localities, making the net return to capital 25 percent below its gross return. D_X' and D_Y' show the after-tax returns available for alternative allocations of capital. Equilibrium still occurs at K_1 because the after-tax returns are equal at 6 percent in both localities.

This analysis implies that the owners of capital bear the full burden of a national property tax; property owners receive an unchanged gross return on their capital but must pay a tax of 25 percent to the government. The prices of goods and services produced using the input, capital, are not affected. Renters pay no higher rents for apartments, whereas the owners of

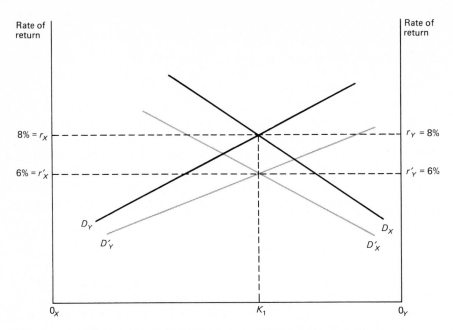

FIGURE 13–3   *Incidence of a national property tax.*

apartments receive the same gross return, and a lower net return, on their investment. Homeowners pay the same prices for homes and receive the same gross return (partly in the form of housing services directly consumed) but a lower net return because of the tax payment. (Note also that property owners have no incentive to invest less in housing and more in stocks because the net return on stocks is also lowered to 6 percent.) Only owners of capital bear a burden. The incidence will be progressive because capital income is a larger proportion of total income in higher income classes.

System of local property taxes

The United States does not have a national property tax but, instead, a multitude of local property taxes. If all localities taxed property at the same effective rate, the analysis above would still be correct. However, localities employ a wide variety of effective rates, ranging from about 1 to 5 percent, with an average around 2 percent. The analysis must therefore be modified to incorporate the diversity of effective rates, but the earlier framework can be easily adapted to accomplish this.

Suppose that locality X levies a 1 percent tax on property holders, and locality Y utilizes a 3 percent tax, or an average for the two localities of 2 percent. These taxes correspond to levies on capital income of 12.5 percent and 37.5 percent. The effects of these two taxes on the allocation of capital between the localities is easily worked out. In the short run, before the capital can move, the after-tax return to capital in Y will be reduced by more than in X. The net return available to investors is therefore higher on investments in the locality with lower taxes. In the long run, capital will move from Y to X until the net returns are equalized. In equilibrium, the net returns to capital will be the same in both localities and will be lower than the 8 percent return achieved before the taxes were levied.

Figure 13–4 illustrates this analysis. The heavier tax in Y shifts D_Y down proportionately more than the lighter tax in X affects D_X. The short-run effect would be for the net return in Y to fall to aK_1, but to fall only to bK_1 in X. Thus, capital owners can achieve a higher after-tax return in X and will move capital there. Equilibrium occurs at K_2, where K_1K_2 units of capital have moved from Y to X to produce the same net return of 6 percent in both localities. Equal after-tax returns at 6 percent mean that the before-tax returns diverge: In Y the before-tax return is 9.6 percent, whereas in X it is 6.9 percent.

In terms of their effect on capital income realized by capital owners, these two property taxes at rates of 1 and 3 percent have the same effect as does a national property tax at a rate of 2 percent. In both cases, the net return to all owners falls from 8 percent to 6 percent. In this sense, a system of hundreds of local property taxes of different rates has an effect on capital income akin to a national property tax levied at the average rate of all localities taken together. On the basis of this analysis, many economists now

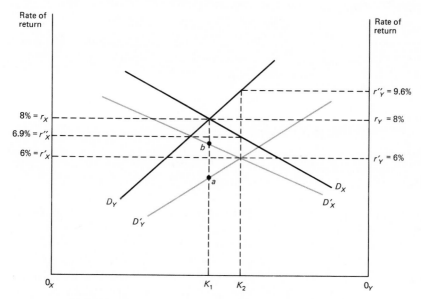

FIGURE 13–4 *Incidence of local property taxes.*

believe that owners of capital bear the burden of the *combined* effect of many different local property taxes.

There are, however, still other effects to consider. With a national property tax, there are no effects on prices of goods and services. When local governments use property taxes at different rates, some prices are affected. In locality *Y,* with the higher-than-average tax rate, the gross return necessary to attract capital has risen from 8 to 9.6 percent. This higher cost will be reflected in higher prices for goods and services produced with capital employed in that locality. Consumers and renters in locality *Y* will therefore bear some burden. The opposite occurs in locality *X.* The gross return has fallen from 8 to 6.9 percent, so lower net prices result in that locality.

With higher prices in localities with above-average tax rates and lower prices in localities with below-average tax rates, the overall price level for the entire nation is not affected. If the aggregate effect on consumers in all areas is considered, there is no net burden—some lose but others gain. Owners of capital bear the full burden of the property taxes taken all together.

This approach reconciles the apparent differences between the view that capital owners bear the burden and the view that output prices are affected. Prices are affected, but in some areas they go up and in other areas they go down. This means that our view of the effects of property taxation depends on whether we are looking at the overall effects for the nation as a whole or at the effects within a specific locality. What is the incidence of the system of property taxes as a whole? The answer is that capital owners bear the burden. Because positive and negative price effects cancel out, consumers, on the average, are not burdened by property taxes. If, by contrast, we consider the effects within a single locality, and if I am a local government official and ask who *in this locality* will be burdened if we raise property taxes here, the answer is that local consumers (who pay higher prices) will bear a large share of the burden. Although prices to consumers in other areas will go down slightly, that is not relevant when the effects within one locality are being examined, rather than those nationwide.

The welfare costs of the system of property taxes are of two types. First, the capital stock is misallocated, with too little capital in high-tax areas and too much in low-tax areas. Second, by driving down the net return on capital, saving may fall and produce too small a total capital stock.

Our brief treatment of property taxes has stressed the broad and general consequences of this tax on investment. A fuller treatment would incorporate more carefully the fact that land is a form of capital that cannot move from one region to another and the distinction between goods produced and consumed in a locality versus those produced in one locality and sold elsewhere.[6] In addition, the way property taxes are administered by local

---

[6] For a fuller discussion of these and many other issues related to property taxation, see Henry J. Aaron, *Who Pays the Property Tax?* (Washington, D.C.: The Brookings Institution, 1975).

governments is a source of concern to many people. Because property (e.g., homes or factories) is not frequently sold and therefore does not have an accurately revealed market value, administrators must rely on assessments to estimate the value of property. A frequent criticism of the tax is that some types of property are assessed at higher ratios of their true market value than are other types of property. In fact, some localities apparently intentionally assess business property at higher rates than they do homes, implying that the effective tax rate varies between the different types of properties. This type of treatment, whether intentional or not, raises further questions about equity and efficiency.

Deficit Finance

Governments do not finance all expenditures from tax revenues. An important alternative method of finance is borrowing from the public. When government spending exceeds tax revenues, the difference, called the *deficit,* can be financed by selling government debt obligations (such as government bonds and Treasury bills) and using the proceeds to pay for the excess. Financing expenditures through the issuance of government debt is engaged in primarily by the federal government because there are economic (and frequently constitutional) limits to the use of debt finance by state and local governments.[7]

Since 1960, the federal government has run a deficit in every year except two. The sizes of the deficits have grown gradually over time. In the 1960s, the deficits averaged about 1 percent of GNP (or about 5 percent of government outlays) and then rose in the 1970s, averaging about 2 percent of GNP. In the early 1980s, the size of the deficits increased rapidly, reaching $221.6 billion in 1985, or 5.4 percent of GNP in that year. Our first task is to explain how the deficit has become so large, and then we shall examine the economic effects of deficit finance.

The emergence of large federal deficits

As recently as 1981, the federal deficit was only about 2 percent of GNP, but three years later it exceeded 5 percent of GNP. Deficits of this size are unprecedented during peacetime (during World War II they were an even larger share of GNP). Moreover, projections suggest that the deficit will stay at approximately this level into the early 1990s unless major tax and/or spending changes are made. What produced these large deficits?

Table 13–4 provides some basic data that can help answer this question. The table gives federal spending and taxes as a percentage of GNP over a number of years. Let's first consider the rapid growth of the deficit between

[7] Wallace E. Oates, *Fiscal Federalism* (New York: Harcourt Brace Jovanovich, 1972).

Table 13–4   *Federal Expenditures, Receipts, and Deficits As a Percentage of GNP (by fiscal years)*

	1960	1970	1980	1985*	CBO Baseline Projections 1987	1989
Total Expenditures	18.5%	20.2%	22.4%	24.6%	24.2%	24.4%
National Defense	9.7	8.4	5.2	6.5	6.9	7.4
Net Interest	1.4	1.5	2.0	3.4	3.4	3.6
All Other	7.4	10.3	15.2	14.8	13.9	13.4
Total Receipts	18.6	19.9	20.1	19.2	19.1	19.3
Individual Income Tax	8.2	9.3	9.5	8.8	8.8	9.1
Corporate Income Tax	4.3	3.4	2.5	1.6	1.9	1.9
Social Security Taxes	2.9	4.6	6.1	6.9	6.8	7.0
Other	3.1	2.6	1.9	1.9	1.6	1.4
Deficit	−0.1	0.3	2.3	5.4	5.1	5.1

*Estimated.
Source: For 1960–1980 data: William J. Beeman, Jacob S. Drezer, and Paul N. Van de Water, "Dimensions of the Deficit Problem," in P. Cagan, ed., *Essays in Contemporary Economic Problems, 1985* (Washington, D.C.: American Enterprise Institute, 1985), Tables 2-6 and 2-9. For 1985–1989 figures: Congressional Budget Office, *The Economic Budget Outlook: An Update* (Washington, D.C.: U.S. Government Printing Office, Aug. 1985), Table II-7.

1980 and 1985. In 1980, federal spending was 22.4 percent of GNP and taxes were 20.1 percent, so the deficit was 2.3 percent of GNP. Five years later, spending had risen to 24.6 percent of GNP and taxes had fallen to 19.2 percent, producing a deficit of 5.4 percent of GNP. Thus, the short answer to the question is that government spending has risen relative to GNP, whereas tax revenues have declined.

A more careful consideration of the data yields further insight. The spending increase took place primarily in two categories of expenditures: national defense and net interest on the public debt. (*Net interest* is the annual interest cost of the outstanding government debt, which in turn reflects the sum of previous deficits and surpluses.[8]) Defense spending rose by 1.3 percent of GNP, and net interest rose by 1.4 percent; other government spending was approximately unchanged relative to national income. On the tax side, individual income and corporate taxes declined by 1.6 percent of GNP,

[8] It is important to keep in mind the difference between the outstanding public debt at a point in time (a stock concept) and the annual deficit over a year (a flow concept). If government operations begin in year 1, for example, and the government runs a deficit of $100 billion for each of the next 5 years, the deficit in the fifth year will be $100 billion, but the outstanding public debt at the end of the year will be $500 billion.

but this reduction was partially offset by an increase in social security taxes of 0.8 percent, so the overall decline in tax revenues was 0.9 percent of GNP.

To a significant extent, these recent changes reflect the policy changes under the Reagan administration, which began in 1981. Two of its goals were a buildup of defense spending and a tax cut. Despite the tax cut introduced in 1981 and the planned increases in defense spending, however, no one at the time predicted that the deficit would increase so sharply. Several unexpected changes in economic conditions over the period played a major role in increasing the deficit. First, the inflation rate, which was at double-digit levels in 1980 and 1981, declined much more rapidly than anyone thought it would. As a result, the tax cut turned out to be larger than anticipated. Recall that the tax code was not indexed for inflation until 1985. Had the inflation rate declined to only 8 percent, as expected, instead of plummeting to 4 percent, bracket creep would have offset more of the cut in tax rates than it ultimately did. Second, there was a deep recession in 1982 and 1983, which added to the deficit in those years and increased the outstanding public debt, thereby raising interest costs in later years. Third, interest rates remained at higher levels than expected, which also contributed to greater spending on net interest on the debt.

If we only look at the 1980–85 period, the large deficit in 1985 seems to result from the tax cuts and increased spending on defense and net interest. Taking a longer run view, however, provides a different perspective. As suggested in Table 13–4, federal tax revenues in 1985 were about the same percentage of GNP as they were in most years before 1980. In the late 1970s, federal taxes climbed to above 20 percent of GNP, and the tax cuts simply returned the ratio to 19 percent, where it had been in the mid-1970s and earlier. Over the long run, taxes have not declined relative to GNP.

What has changed over the long run, however, is federal government spending, growing from 18.5 percent of GNP in 1960 to 24.6 percent in 1985. Note that this increase was not caused by defense spending. Indeed, defense spending was a substantially smaller share of GNP in 1985 than in 1960. What the Reagan defense buildup did was only partially to reverse the downward trend in defense spending over the preceding two decades. Nondefense spending is the category that has grown, rising from 7.4 percent of GNP in 1969 to 14.8 percent in 1985. We have already discussed this spending increase, as this category includes social insurance and welfare spending (see Table 8–1).

What this longer run perspective suggests is that the large deficit of 1985 resulted from increases in nondefense spending, whereas tax revenues have been a constant share of GNP. Which of these perspectives better explains the deficit depends, of course, on whether you find the pattern of spending and taxing in 1980 more appropriate than the pattern in 1960, or the reverse.

Table 13–4 also contains the Congressional Budget Office's projections of expenditures, taxes, and deficits for 1987 and 1989. These projections are based on the assumption of no changes in tax or spending policies, plus a number of assumptions about future economic conditions. What they show is that the economy will not automatically grow its way out of the deficit, at least not in the near future. Unless there are expenditure reductions or tax increases, or both, the deficit is likely to remain large for several years. It should be emphasized, however, that these projections are extremely sensitive to assumptions about future economic conditions. The Congressional Budget Office assumed real economic growth of about 3.5 percent per year from 1985 to 1989. *If the growth rate were one percentage point higher per year, the deficit in 1989 would fall from 5 percent of GNP to 3 percent of GNP. Conversely, if the growth rate were one percentage point lower, the deficit could rise in 1989 to a (peacetime) record high of 7 percent of GNP.* In addition, it is quite likely that there will be changes in tax and spending policies during this period.

How large is the deficit, really?

The numbers in Table 13–4 measure the deficit as the difference between expenditures and taxes in each year, the way the deficit is officially measured. There are, however, some serious problems with this method of measuring the deficit, especially during inflationary periods. Indeed, some economists argue that the deficit, when inflation is taken into account, is substantially smaller than the official measure.[9]

To see the significance of inflation in measuring the deficit, consider the following example. Suppose that at the beginning of 1987, the public holds $1,700 billion in government debt obligations (approximately the correct figure). Then during 1987 the federal government runs a deficit of $200 billion, which it finances by borrowing from the public. Thus, at the end of 1987, the public holds $1,900 billion in government debt. The increase in the amount of government debt from one year to the next is equal to the deficit over the year.

Now, however, suppose that the price level rises by 5 percent in 1987. Thus, the $1,700 billion in debt held at the beginning of the year falls in value because of inflation; the real indebtedness of the federal government on this $1,700 billion also falls. Although the government's *nominal* indebtedness rises from $1,700 billion to $1,900 billion, its *real* indebtedness (measured in end-of-1987 dollars) increases from only $1,785 billion to $1,900 billion, or by $115 billion. The real deficit over the year is thus only $115 billion, rather than $200 billion as it is conventionally measured.

During inflationary periods, this implies that the official measure of the

[9]See, for example, Robert Eisner and Paul J. Pieper, "A New View of the Federal Debt and Budget Deficits," *The American Economic Review,* 74:11–29 (Mar. 1984).

deficit overstates the extent to which the government's real indebtedness to the public has increased. Economists contend that it is the real deficit that is responsible for whatever effects it has on the economy. Correcting the official measure of past deficits for the erosion in the real value of outstanding debt caused by inflation produces a different picture: Instead of running a deficit in most of the past twenty-five years, the government actually ran a real surplus in most of those years. But despite this correction for inflation, the government still ran large deficits in recent years; these adjustments suggest, however, that the deficit problem may not be as serious as it is often portrayed to be. Nonetheless, even with this correction, real deficits in the mid-1980s were higher than they have ever been since World War II.

Incidence of deficit finance

Although not technically a form of taxation, debt finance raises the same question: Who actually bears the burden of government programs financed by borrowing from the public? Two sharply opposing views are held on the incidence of debt finance. One holds that government borrowing, just like private borrowing, shifts the burden of paying for current expenditures into the future when the debt is repaid. The other view holds that current expenditures impose a burden on the economy at the time the spending and borrowing take place. In trying to disentangle the issues involved, it will initially be assumed that when people buy governmental bonds their purchases will be financed by a reduction in consumption spending. This means that private savings available for investment and capital formation does not fall. Although such an assumption is probably invalid, it allows us to disregard momentarily the complications that arise when future productive capacity is affected. (That aspect of debt finance is examined in the next section.)

Suppose the government sells bonds to the public and uses the proceeds to finance the construction of a dam. The argument that this operation imposes no burden in the future runs as follows: To build the dam now, concrete, manpower, energy, and so on will be used today. These resources must be withdrawn from alternative uses in the private sector, thereby reducing the output of private goods and services. Because the output of private goods falls in the present, the sacrifice involved in constructing the dam occurs in the present and is borne by the present generation.

But what happens if the debt is repaid in some future year? If the government raises taxes at some future date to purchase the bonds back from the public (retire the debt), doesn't this impose a burden? Not so, according to this argument. In the future, the taxes are collected from the same groups (the general public) that receive the proceeds. Repayment of the debt is a transfer among those living at the time, and no net burden is imposed on future generations. In particular, debt repayment does not divert resources into the public sector, so private sector output of goods and services is unaffected.[10]

A similar argument applies to taxes used to pay interest on government bonds before the principal is repaid. Citizens pay taxes to finance interest payments, but they also own the bonds and receive the interest payments. There is no net burden, just a transfer of funds among the public.

This view of debt finance, conveniently summarized in the expression "We owe it to ourselves," was almost universally held in the economics profession from the 1930s until 1958. In 1958, James Buchanan published a book that argued that the burden of debt finance was shifted to future generations.[11] No one, according to Buchanan, bears a burden at the time the expenditure financed by debt is carried out. Although it is certainly true that the resources used in the government-built dam must come from the private sector, this does not mean that any person bears a burden in the relevant sense of sacrificed utility or well-being. Citizens who give up control over resources when they purchase bonds do so *voluntarily* in return for the government's promise of interest and principal to be paid in the future. They reduce current consumption in return for bonds, which permit greater consumption later; their lifetime consumption does not fall. Accordingly, it seems correct to say that no one bears a burden at the time the government borrows the money to build the dam.

To determine who does bear a burden, it is necessary to examine what happens in the future. Suppose the debt is retired in a later year. According to the earlier view, taxpayers lose and bondholders gain, so there is no net burden. In contrast, according to Buchanan, although taxpayers lose, bondholders do not gain, so there is a net burden falling on taxpayers when the debt is retired. Bondholders do not gain because they simply exchange one asset (bonds) for another (money). This exchange represents no more of a gain for bondholders than when a person takes a $100 bill to the bank and exchanges it for five $20 bills. Taxpayers, on the other hand, lose when they pay the higher taxes to retire the debt. Consequently, there is a net burden in the future from debt finance.

A similar argument applies to taxes used to pay interest on the government debt. Bondholders do not gain, because the promised interest payment was just sufficient to induce them to purchase the bonds in the first place. (Put another way, a bondholder could have purchased a private asset

---

[10] In the discussion that follows, it is assumed that the government sells the bonds to the general public rather than to other governmental institutions. When the government sells bonds to the Federal Reserve System, the effect is to increase the money supply. This is not really borrowing, but a form of "disguised money creation."

[11] James M. Buchanan, *Public Principles of Public Debt* (Homewood, Ill.: Richard D. Irwin, 1958).

and received the same interest return as on the government bond, so there is no differential advantage to receiving interest on government bonds.) Taxpayers, however, bear a burden in paying taxes to finance interest payments. So the necessity of raising taxes to pay interest also creates a burden in time periods after the government expenditure is undertaken.

Now we come to a fairly subtle point that partially reconciles the two views. It can be most simply explained with an example. Suppose the government finances the dam by borrowing in year 1 and announces that it will levy a $100 tax per person in year 2 to purchase back the bonds. All persons in year 1 will know that their taxes will be $100 higher in year 2. They will then "feel" the burden in year 1 because they know their lifetime taxes will be higher as a result of the government borrowing in year 1. The act of government borrowing carries the obligation to levy higher taxes in the future, and if taxpayers realize this, they will know that the present value of their lifetime disposable incomes is lower. Hence they will *feel* (bear) the burden in year 1, although the actual payment is postponed until year 2.

In this example, the burden is felt by taxpayers in the present because they anticipate the higher future taxes. This suggests the element of truth in the first view described, although the arguments used to justify that view were largely irrelevant. Practically speaking, however, Buchanan's position may be more relevant. To hold that people perceive a burden when the government borrows, it is necessary to believe that citizens are well informed about current spending and tax policies—and about the future consequences of present government policy. It is plausible to suppose, however, that few people know how much government spending is financed by borrowing or what borrowing means for future tax policy, much less for their own taxes. If this is so, the general public may perceive no burden when the government deficit-finances, as Buchanan argued, and may recognize that burden only when higher taxes must actually be paid in the future. This possibility is strengthened by the fact that some people will die before the debt is retired—if it ever is—or before much interest must be paid.

There is clearly a real burden involved when the government finances expenditures by borrowing, and the real issue seems to be, at what point in time do people recognize that burden?

Impact on capital markets

We assumed above that government borrowing does not depress private investment but, instead, that people reduce consumption spending to purchase bonds. This will generally be untrue. Government must compete with other borrowers when it sells its bonds, and it is likely to bid away funds that would otherwise have financed private investment.

Figure 13–5 shows the results of this process. The S curve shows the

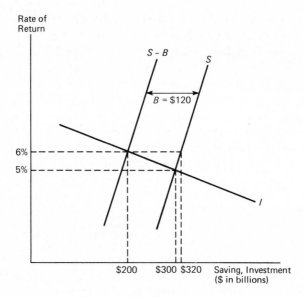

FIGURE 13–5   *Effect of debt finance on capital markets.*

amount of current income people will save at alternative rates of interest: It is drawn as very inelastic, in line with our earlier discussion. The *I* curve shows the demand for funds to invest as related to the interest rate that must be paid. In the absence of government borrowing, equilibrium occurs with $300 billion of investment and saving at a 5 percent interest rate. At any given interest rate, every $1 the government borrows means that the amount of saving that can be channeled into private investment must fall. Government borrowing reduces the effective supply of funds available for private investment. If the government borrows $120 billion, the effective supply-of-saving curve shifts to the left by $120 billion. *S−B* becomes the effective supply schedule confronting private borrowers, and the new equilibrium occurs at an interest rate of 6 percent, with $200 billion in private investment.

In this example, government borrowing bids up the interest rate to 6 percent and induces people to save $320 billion, $20 billion more than before. One hundred and twenty billion dollars of this total is used, however, to finance government expenditures, leaving only $200 billion for private investment. Government borrowing of $120 billion here leads to a reduction of $100 billion in private investment (and a $20 billion decrease in consumption). The amount by which private investment falls depends on the elasticities of the *S* and *I* curves. The more inelastic the saving schedule is, the greater will be the reduction in investment. If the saving schedule is very inelastic, as drawn in the diagram, private investment will fall by almost as much as the government borrows.

Some economists hold that the analysis depicted in Figure 13–5 is incorrect, arguing that government borrowing will not lead to a reduction in private investment.[12] They believe that when taxpayers become aware of the government borrowing, they will realize that their future taxes will be higher. So in order to pay the higher future taxes, taxpayers will save more in the present, shifting the S curve in Figure 13–5 to the right. In some cases, the saving supply curve could shift so much that the net effect would be no reduction in private investment at all. This outcome requires, among other things, a degree of foresight and rationality on the part of taxpayers that seems unrealistic. As Herbert Stein, former Chairman of the President's Council of Economic Advisers, observed: "I have never encountered anyone who says that he has raised his own saving rate because of the budget deficit."[13] Most economists seem to agree and regard the analysis of Figure 13–5 as reasonably accurate.

If debt finance does lead to a reduction in investment (rather than consumption, as earlier assumed), a different type of burden will be produced. The nation's capital stock will grow more slowly, and future productive capacity will be sacrificed. In effect, people will end up owning government bonds rather than real capital that would have augmented productivity. Aggregate output (income) will be lower in subsequent years, so people will bear a burden in the form of lower incomes in the future. The results are quite similar to those produced by the social security system when it reduces saving.

The sacrifice in future output occasioned by debt finance depends on the productivity of private investment. In Figure 13–6 the $100 billion in sacrificed investment projects would have produced returns between 5 and 6 percent, with the marginal investment sacrificed having a yield of 6 percent, equal to the interest rate paid by the government on its debt. *In reality, however, the interest rate paid by the government on its bonds is well below the real return sacrificed in the private sector.* Because of property taxes and the corporation income tax, the net return paid to owners of capital is well below its gross, or real, productivity. Government must compete only with the net return that people can obtain in private investments and can therefore divert resources away from projects with real returns substantially above the interest rate paid on government bonds.[14]

---

[12] Robert Barro, "Are Government Bonds Net Worth?" *Journal of Political Economy,* 82:1095 (Nov./Dec. 1974).

[13] Herbert Stein, "Controlling the Budget Deficit: If Not Now, When? If Not Us, Who?" *The AEI Economist,* Dec. 1983, p. 4.

[14] This is not precisely correct because the interest on government bonds is taxable under the federal individual income tax. It is not, however, subject to the corporation income tax and property taxes that fall on most capital income. For example, for corporations to pay stockholders a return of 5 percent (with the 5 percent subject to federal individual income tax), their investments must yield perhaps 10 percent before corporate and property taxes. Government bonds would have to pay only 5 percent to compete with corporate stock.

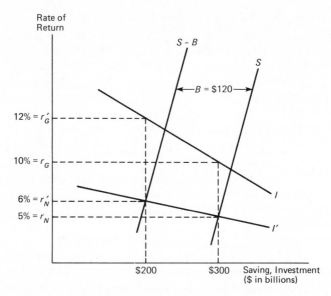

FIGURE 13–6   *Debt financing in the presence of capital taxes.*

Figure 13–6 shows the effect of government borrowing in the presence of taxes on the return to capital. The *I* curve continues to show the real return to private investment, but because some of that return accrues to government the net return is shown by *I'*. (It is assumed that the tax rate on the return to capital invested is 50 percent.) Equilibrium in the absence of government borrowing occurs at a rate of saving and investment of $300 billion, with a net return to savers of 5 percent, equal to half the before-tax return of 10 percent realized by the investment. Now when the government borrows $120 billion, investment falls by $100 billion, and the net return rises to 6 percent as before. In this case, however, investment projects yielding between 10 and 12 percent are sacrificed. Although the government pays an interest rate of 6 percent, this is sufficient to bid resources away from investment projects yielding just under 12 percent before taxes.

Because investment projects with high yields are sacrificed, debt finance is likely to impose a substantial cost in the form of reduced future productive capacity. Of course, almost all ways of financing government expenditures will cause some reduction in private investment. An income tax that raises $120 billion will reduce private investment by $12 billion if people save 10 percent of their incomes. Government borrowing, however, probably has a more concentrated impact on private capital markets than any other form of taxation.

Therefore, one cost of deficit finance is reduced private investment and the consequent sacrifice of future output. Another cost should also be remembered: when the government runs a deficit in the present, it must pay the interest on its debt obligations in the future. The increase in future government expenditures that flows from current borrowing can be financed in one of two ways. First, the government can borrow more in the future to finance the higher interest outlays. This, of course, means a further negative impact on private investment, adding to the cost we identified in Figure 13–6. Alternatively, the government can finance its higher future interest costs by raising taxes in the future. In that case, the direct burden of the higher future taxes as well as their welfare costs should be considered part of the cost of using deficit finance. Because current deficits imply higher future government expenditures in the form of interest outlays, the cost of financing these outlays in the future (however they are financed) should be seen as part of the cost of using deficit finance in the present.

Should we reduce the deficit?

Few topics have attracted more public attention in the past several years than how to reduce the federal budget deficit. It is often taken for granted that it is important to reduce it. Before examining the ways the deficit can be reduced, however, we should consider further whether deficits are "bad," especially because the alternatives, increasing taxes or reducing expenditures, are not exactly painless.

Four major disadvantages to using deficits as a way of financing government expenditures should be considered.[15] First, the cost of expenditures financed by deficits is shifted to the future, either to current taxpayers later in their lives or to future generations, or both. Since the benefits from government spending are received predominantly in the present, it can be argued that imposing the costs on people in the future is unfair. This is basically an application of the benefit theory of taxation, which holds that those who receive the benefits of government spending should bear the costs.[16]

Second, the costs of financing expenditures through deficits are thought to be quite high. These costs include the sacrificed future output resulting from reduced investment, in addition to the welfare costs of imposing higher taxes in the future to pay interest on the debt. Feldstein, for example, estimated that these costs of deficit finance are substantially larger than are the costs of using taxes to finance all expenditures.[17]

---

[15]In this discussion, we are explicitly ignoring the possible macroeconomic stabilization effects of deficits.

[16]There are cases in which imposing costs in the future may be deemed desirable. For example, when the government undertakes a capital investment whose benefits will accrue in the future, the benefit theory calls for the costs to be imposed in the future, and that result can be achieved with deficit finance.

[17]Martin Feldstein, "Debt and Taxes in the Theory of Public Finance," *NBER Working Paper No. 1433,* Aug. 1984.

Third, large deficits create political pressures that can lead to inflation. Whether deficits per se are inflationary is debatable, but they certainly can produce pressure on the Federal Reserve to try to keep interest rates low by expanding the money supply.

Fourth, the option of using deficits to finance expenditures may lead politicians to make irresponsible decisions about spending programs. Deficits are a form of "hidden taxation," with the actual costs often difficult to perceive (such as lower future incomes from reduced investment). As such, the public might support expenditures financed by deficits that they would not be willing to pay for through taxes.

Such perceived disadvantages of deficit finance have convinced many people that deficits are worse than the alternatives. But what are the alternatives? Basically, there are two: reduce government spending or increase taxes (or a combination of the two). Let's consider each briefly.

When asked how the government ought to cut the deficit, most people immediately answer that expenditures should be reduced. Cutting federal spending is a possibility, but it may not be as easy as often imagined. Table 13–5 lists federal expenditures by major categories in 1985. Let's consider how expenditures could be cut to eliminate the deficit. Since total expenditures were $959.1 billion and the deficit was $221.6 billion, we need to cut expenditures by 23 percent. How would you do this?

Table 13–5 *Major Federal Expenditures, 1985 (in billions of $)*

Category	Amount
National Defense	$253.8
Social Security and Medicare	257.4
Net Interest	130.4
Income Security	127.2
International Affairs	19.6
Natural Resources and Environment	13.0
Agriculture	20.2
Transportation	27.0
Education, Training, Employment	30.4
Health	33.9
Veterans Benefits	26.9
All Other (net)	19.3
Total Expenditures	959.1
Deficit	221.6

Source: President's Council of Economic Advisers, *Economic Report of the President* (Washington, D.C.: U.S. Government Printing Office, 1985), Table B-71.

In reality, political pressures limit what cuts can be made. Every expenditure had a constituency that will lobby to retain its benefits. Moreover, actual attempts to cut spending in recent years have had to accommodate some restrictions. The Reagan administration, for example, did not wish to cut defense spending, arguing that expenditures on defense were much lower than in the past (relative to GNP) and lower than defense spending by the Soviet Union. In addition, during the 1984 presidential campaign, Reagan pledged not to cut social security or Medicare. (As we argued in Chapter 7, even if cuts were made in these programs, they would need to be phased in gradually.) In addition, expenditures on net interest cannot be cut, because the government is legally obligated to meet its interest obligations.

Where does this leave us? In 1985, spending on defense, social security, and interest totaled $641.6 billion of a $959.1 billion budget. If we exempt defense, social security, and interest payments from the budget cuts, then only $317.5 billion of federal spending remains. So to eliminate the $221.6 billion deficit, we would have to cut all the remaining federal programs by 70 percent! Welfare programs (the income-security category) would be among the casualties. But if welfare programs were declared off limits, it would be impossible to eliminate the deficit even if we cut out all remaining government spending programs.

This brief discussion should indicate why it is difficult to eliminate the deficit exclusively through spending cuts. Unless substantial cuts are made in the major categories—defense, social security, and welfare—it is virtually impossible.

The only remaining way to eliminate the deficit is to raise taxes. Since tax revenues were $737 billion in 1985, taxes would have to be raised by 30 percent to eliminate the deficit. However, since the social security payroll tax is earmarked for social security benefits, the major feasible tax alternatives are the individual income and corporation income taxes. These taxes raised $396 billion in 1985; so to eliminate the deficit, they would have to be increased to raise 56 percent more in revenue. Most taxpayers would rebel at the idea of their tax liabilities rising by 56 percent. Indeed, it is not even clear that we could increase revenue that much from these taxes as they are currently structured. Tax rates would have to go up by more than 56 percent because the tax bases would shrink as a result of the disincentive effects of the higher rates. At some point, higher rates might lead to reduced revenues, but whether this would occur before we could get 56 percent more revenue is not clear. This difficulty of getting substantially more revenue from existing taxes is one reason that attention has been given to new tax options, like the value-added tax.

We should also recall that each dollar of additional tax revenue has an added cost, the marginal welfare cost of the tax. At current levels of tax rates, most estimates suggest that the marginal welfare cost of major taxes is in the range of 25 to 50 percent. If tax rates are increased significantly in order to reduce the deficit, the marginal welfare cost will rise (see Figure 10–11). In principle, the choice between expenditure cuts and tax increases should be based, at least in part, on a comparison of the marginal benefits from spending programs with the marginal cost of raising revenue. If the marginal welfare cost were 50 percent, for example, this would mean that efficiency would call for the elimination of any spending that produced benefits of less than $1.50 per dollar spent.

There remains the possibility of some combination of tax increases, expenditure cuts, and living with a smaller remaining deficit. In this connection, we should mention that we have been discussing the elimination of the official nominal deficit. But as we saw earlier, the real deficit is lower. With an inflation rate of 4 percent, as in recent years, an official deficit of about $70 billion would correspond to a zero real deficit. Thus, if we try to reduce only the real deficit to zero, the task need not be as difficult as the preceding discussion suggests.

At the time of this writing, Congress is deliberating over various ways to reduce the federal deficit. How the issue is resolved over the next few years should prove interesting.

Supplementary Readings

AARON, HENRY J. *Who Pays the Property Tax?* Washington, D.C.: The Brookings Institution, 1975.

BRITTAIN, JOHN. *The Payroll Tax for Social Security.* Washington, D.C.: The Brookings Institution, 1972.

BROWNING, EDGAR K., and WILLIAM R. JOHNSON. *The Distribution of the Tax Burden.* Washington, D.C.: American Enterprise Institute, 1979.

BUCHANAN, JAMES M., and RICHARD E. WAGNER. *Democracy in Deficit.* New York: Academic Press, 1977.

FERGUSON, JAMES M. *Public Debt and Future Generations.* Chapel Hill: University of North Carolina Press, 1964.

MAKIN, JOHN H. "The Effect of Government Deficits on Capital Formation." In P. Cagan, ed., *Essays on Contemporary Economic Problems, 1985.* Washington, D.C.: American Enterprise Institute, 1985, pp. 163–194.

McLURE, CHARLES E., JR. "The 'New View' of the Property Tax: A Caveat." *National Tax Journal,* 30(1):59–68 (Mar. 1977).

Review Questions and Problems

1. "The employer portion of the social security payroll tax is a cost of hiring labor, and just like any other labor cost it will ultimately be reflected in the price of the product. Thus, increasing this tax will increase prices, and consumers will bear the burden." Discuss.

2. Use a graphical analysis (like Figure 11–2) to determine how the social security payroll tax would affect the labor supply decision of a worker earning above the tax's maximum wage base.

3. It is widely held that sales and excise taxes are regressive. What is the basis for this claim? Do you think it is correct?

4. What type of welfare cost does a value-added tax have?

5. If the social security system is running an annual deficit and taxes are raised in order to close the deficit, would it be better to increase the tax rate and maintain the same maximum wage base or to increase the maximum wage base and not increase the tax rate?

6. In what way is the local property tax similar to the corporation income tax?

7. Some argue that consumers bear the burden of local property taxes, since the prices of goods produced using taxed property will rise. Others contend that the entire burden falls on capital owners. Reconcile these differing views.

8. Economists agree that if debt is used to finance a dam, the resource cost of concrete, labor, energy, and so on, occurs in the present. Nonetheless some economists would argue that a cost is imposed on future generations. Explain their argument. That is, explain how society can incur a "burden" or "cost" in periods after that in which the resources are actually used.

9. "Insofar as our current deficits are placing a burden on future generations, this is only fair. After all, future generations will be wealthier than we are (because the economy grows over time), so it is in accord with the principle of progressivity in distributing tax burdens that they bear greater costs than we do." Explain why you agree or disagree with this statement.

10. What combination of expenditure cuts and/or tax increases would you use to eliminate the deficit, assuming that it has been decided that the deficit is to be eliminated? Defend your answer.

chapter 14
The Tax System

IN the previous three chapters, we examined each of the major taxes in the U.S. tax system separately. In this chapter we consider these components of the tax system together and take a broader view of the way in which taxes affect economic activity. Most households pay, or bear, the burden of several different taxes, and in this situation it is necessary to consider the combined effect of the various taxes to analyze accurately how households will be affected. This is analogous to the analysis of income transfer programs, in which we saw the importance of taking into account the overlapping and interacting nature of many transfers.

The first section of this chapter examines the distribution of the tax burden by income class for the tax system as a whole. The next three sections are concerned mainly with the effect of taxes on resource supplies and hence on the level and rate of growth of national output. A proposal for seemingly radical change in the tax system, the taxation of consumption rather than income, is discussed in the last section.

The Distribution of the Tax Burden

How are tax burdens distributed among income classes? Is the overall tax system progressive, proportional, or regressive? Now that we have examined the incidence of each major tax separately, we are in a position to consider these important issues for the tax system as a whole. In this section, we discuss the results of a study that estimated the incidence of the tax system in 1976.[1]

There are two important steps in any tax incidence study. The first step is the estimation of the before-tax incomes of households. A comprehensive measure of income is desirable for the reasons discussed in Chapter 11. Thus, available estimates of money income, or adjusted gross income, must be augmented by adding types of income that are usually excluded from

[1] Edgar K. Browning and William R. Johnson, *The Distribution of the Tax Burden* (Washington, D.C.: American Enterprise Institute, 1979).

these statistics. The employer portion of the social security payroll tax must be added to money income received by persons, since it represents income that would have been received in the absence of the tax (that is, it is part of before-tax income). Similarly, all indirect business taxes must be added. In addition, in-kind transfers, imputed income of owner-occupied housing, and retained corporate earnings are other forms of income that should also be included. After adjustments of this type are made, we have a broad measure of before-tax income. Income estimated in this way is about 30 percent greater than the money income actually received by households. (One consequence of using this comprehensive income measure is that average tax rates tend to be lower than most households perceive them to be, since most people think of their income as money income alone.)

The second step in a tax incidence study is to assign the burden of each tax to households. To accomplish this, it is necessary to rely on tax incidence theory to provide guidelines for allocating the actual burden of each tax. For the study whose results are shown in Table 14–1, the following incidence assumptions are used: Individual income taxes are allocated to the taxpayers themselves; payroll taxes are allocated in proportion to taxable earnings; corporate income and property taxes are assumed to fall on capital income whatever its source; and sales and excise taxes are allocated in proportion to factor earnings (labor plus capital income). The theoretical analysis supporting these assumptions was explained in the previous three chapters. Note that these assumptions emerge from a competitive analysis; to the extent that noncompetitive conditions characterize some sectors of the economy, these incidence assumptions may not be completely accurate. Recall that we assumed that the total supply of labor and capital was unaffected by the taxes—an assumption that we shall consider later.

Tax burdens by income classes

Table 14–1 summarizes some of the results of a study based on the procedure described. Households were ranked on the basis of before-tax income and grouped into deciles, with each decile containing 10 percent of all households. For each decile the average rate of tax was computed for four basic groups of taxes in the U.S. tax system. (Property and corporation income taxes are combined together, since the tax burdens of both are allocated in proportion to total capital income.) The tax rates were calculated by estimating the total tax burden of all households in each decile and dividing by the total before-tax income of that decile. Thus, the tax rates do not apply to every household but instead represent an average for all households in each decile.

Looking at the last column in Table 14–1, we note that the overall tax system is estimated to be quite progressive. Taxes are 11.7 percent of total before-tax income of households in the lowest decile, and this fraction rises

Table 14–1   *Average Tax Rates by Income Decile, 1976 (percent)*

	Type of Tax				
Income Decile	*Sales and Excise*	*Payroll*	*Income*	*Property and Corporation Income*	*Combined*
1	2.3%	3.3%	0.7%	5.5%	11.7%
2	2.6	3.9	1.8	4.2	12.5
3	3.4	5.4	3.0	4.5	16.3
4	4.1	6.9	4.7	4.4	20.2
5	4.7	8.0	6.4	4.1	23.2
6	5.0	8.5	8.1	3.9	25.5
7	5.2	8.2	9.5	3.8	26.7
8	5.3	7.9	10.8	4.1	28.1
9	5.3	7.2	12.2	5.3	30.0
10	5.5	3.8	13.6	15.4	38.3
Top 1 percent	5.6	1.1	12.4	28.8	47.9
All deciles	4.9	6.2	10.0	7.9	29.1

Source: Edgar K. Browning and William R. Johnson, *The Distribution of the Tax Burden* (Washington, D.C.: American Enterprise Institute, 1979), Table 6.

steadily until it reaches 38.3 percent for the highest decile. For the wealthiest 1 percent of households, taxes absorb nearly half of their incomes.

Of the four major groups of taxes, all place a higher tax rate on the top decile than on the bottom decile. Individual income taxes (federal and state together) are the most progressive element of the tax system, with the highest ratio of tax paid by the top decile to that paid by the lowest decile. This progressivity stems from both the inherent progressivity of rates in income taxes and the fact that income in the form of government transfers, which is not taxed, constitutes a major source of income for the bottom range of the income distribution.

The social security payroll tax is the only tax for which rates decline at higher income levels. Even payroll taxes, however, are progressive up to the sixth decile, becoming regressive (relative to total income) above that level. Contrary to the accepted view that this tax is regressive throughout, the social security payroll tax does not impose a greater-than-average burden on the bottom third of the income distribution. The low rates on the low-income households reflect the small share of labor income in their total income (recall how important transfers are at low-income levels). The regressivity at upper-income levels results from the ceiling on taxable earnings and the exclusion of capital income from the tax base of the social security payroll tax.

These estimates are based on specific assumptions regarding the incidence of each type of tax. Different assumptions would create different patterns of tax burdens. For example, if sales and excise tax burdens were allocated in proportion to annual consumption outlays rather than factor earnings, these taxes would be regressive instead of progressive, and the overall tax system would be less progressive. (The estimates from Table 13–2 can be substituted for those here to show how this assumption will change the results.)

There have been a number of changes in the tax system since 1976, the year for which the estimates in Table 14–1 are based. Although total tax revenue was about the same percentage of GNP in 1985 as in 1976, the relative importance of the various taxes changed. In particular, corporation income taxes declined in importance, and social security payroll taxes increased in importance. The decline in corporate taxes tended to make the tax system less progressive, but the way in which social security taxes were increased tended to make it more progressive. (The higher tax rates of social security taxes did not change the degree of progressivity, but in 1977 Congress legislated about a 25 percent increase in the maximum wage base before indexing it, and this increased taxes primarily for upper-income households, making the tax more progressive.) Overall, we believe that the various changes have approximately offset one another, so the estimates in Table 14–1 should continue to indicate the distribution of tax burdens by income classes.

Other measures of tax burden distribution

Another way of depicting the distributional effects of the tax system is shown in Table 14–2. Here the share of the total tax burden borne by each income class is given. In other words, the table shows the fraction of total revenue from each tax that is derived from households in each decile.

For all taxes, households in the higher deciles provide a greater share of total tax revenue. With a proportional tax system, each share would be equal to the decile's share of total income. For progressive taxes, both the rates faced by higher-income households and the income to which those rates are applied are greater so that the shares of tax burden exceed the shares of income. Taking all taxes together, the top 15 percent of households provide approximately half of total tax revenue, and the top decile alone contributes 41 percent of total tax receipts. In contrast, the bottom decile pays less than 1 percent of all taxes, and the entire lower half of the income distribution pays less than 15 percent.

A final matter of interest is the way the tax system differentially treats labor income compared with income from capital. Some taxes, like the social security payroll tax, fall exclusively on labor income, whereas others, like the corporate income and property taxes, fall on capital income. The

Table 14–2   *Share of Total Tax Paid by Decile, 1976 (percent)*

Income Decile	Sales and Excise	Payroll	Income	Property and Corporation Income	Combined
			Type of Tax		
1	0.7%	0.8%	0.1%	1.0%	0.6%
2	1.6	2.0	0.6	1.7	1.4
3	3.0	3.8	1.3	2.5	2.5
4	4.7	6.3	2.7	3.2	3.9
5	6.6	9.1	4.5	3.7	5.6
6	8.6	11.6	6.9	4.3	7.5
7	10.6	13.5	9.6	5.0	9.4
8	13.1	15.7	13.3	6.5	11.9
9	16.9	18.2	19.1	10.6	16.2
10	34.2	19.0	42.0	61.5	40.9
All deciles	100.0	100.0	100.0	100.0	100.0

Source: Edgar K. Browning and William R. Johnson, *The Distribution of the Tax Burden* (Washington, D.C.: American Enterprise Institute, 1979), Table 11.

individual income tax, by contrast, places a burden on both labor and capital incomes. Table 14–3 shows the estimated average tax rates on labor and capital income. The overall average tax rate on labor income across all income classes is 26.6 percent, whereas the corresponding figure for capital income is 56.1 percent, more than twice as high. For these estimates, it was assumed that individual income taxes strike labor and capital income proportionately. Actually, as a result of the special provisions in the tax laws, individual income taxes apply more heavily to labor than to capital income. Thus, the estimates in the table probably somewhat understate the burden on labor and overstate the burden on capital income. This factor, together with changes in the tax laws since 1976, probably means that the effective tax rate on labor income by 1985 was nearly 30 percent. On the other hand, capital income became less heavily taxed, and the effective tax rate on capital income was probably not above 50 percent by 1985. In interpreting the significance of these figures, it should be mentioned that total labor income is three times as large as total capital income.

Tax rates relative to labor and capital incomes tend to be less progressive than tax rates on total income (as shown in Table 14–1). The low tax rates on the total incomes of low-income households are not the result of light taxation of their labor and capital incomes but, instead, result from such a large proportion of their total incomes taking the form of untaxed transfers.

Table 14–3   *Tax Rates on Labor and Capital Income, 1976 (percent)*

Income Decile	Average Tax Rate on Capital Income	Average Tax Rate on Labor Income
1	45.9%	19.9%
2	48.3	21.0
3	49.3	22.1
4	50.8	23.5
5	52.1	24.8
6	53.5	25.9
7	54.7	26.4
8	56.0	27.2
9	57.6	27.8
10	58.5	26.8
All deciles	56.1	26.6

Source: Edgar K. Browning and William R. Johnson, *The Distribution of the Tax Burden* (Washington, D.C.: American Enterprise Institute, 1979), Table 16.

All of the estimates in Tables 14–1 to 14–3 are of average tax rates. These are the rates that are relevant to assessing the distributional effects of taxes. Marginal tax rates, however, tend to be higher (see Table 9–3), and the marginal rates are of more importance in evaluating the way taxes affect economic behavior.

Taxation and Labor Supply

When we take a broad view of the economy and classify all productive resources as either labor or capital, it is clear that the quantities of labor and capital used in production have a pronounced effect on the level of total output. Total output, in turn, effectively equals total real income. If the tax system affects the quantities of labor or capital supplied, it affects the level of real income. Because of this, economists have always been interested in trying to determine exactly how total resource supplies are affected by taxation. In this section, our concern is with the effect of taxation on labor supply.

In 1984, 105 million persons were employed in the U.S. economy. Their combined before-tax labor income was about $2,400 billion, equal to about 70 percent of net national product (or net national income) of $3,250 billion.[2] Of this $2,400 billion in before-tax labor income, about $700 billion, or 30 percent, was paid as taxes to federal, state, and local governments. The most important of these taxes were the federal individual income tax, the social security payroll tax, state income taxes, and indirect business taxes (sales and excise taxes). To evaluate the effect of taxes on labor supply correctly, it is necessary to take into account the effect of all these taxes together.

In Chapter 11, we developed a theoretical analysis to describe the way a tax on labor income affects a person's decision regarding labor supply. As we explained, the tax becomes a wedge between the before-tax and after-tax rate of pay, and it is the after-tax rate of pay that guides labor supply decisions. The tax affects labor supply in two different ways. The income effect of the tax, which depends on the average tax rate, encourages greater work effort (labor supply), as the taxpayer attempts to recoup some of the lost income. The substitution effect of the tax, which depends on the marginal tax rate, encourages less work effort, as the taxpayer finds he or she gets to keep less of each additional dollar earned. In theory, the net effect on labor supply can go either way, depending on the relative sizes of the opposing income and substitution effects.

To go much further than this requires information on how responsive people are to tax-induced changes in their wage rates. In making this determination, the wage elasticity of labor supply is crucial. Recall that the wage elasticity of labor supply is defined as the percentage change in labor divided by the percentage change in the wage rate. Letting ϵ (epsilon) stand for the wage elasticity, we can express the relationship as

$$\epsilon = \frac{\Delta L/L}{\Delta w/w} \qquad (1)$$

Recall that taxes on labor income reduce net wage rates by a percentage equal to the *marginal* tax rate, and it is the wage rate at the margin to which the worker will adjust. So if the marginal tax rate is 40 percent, for instance, the percentage change in the wage rate, or $\Delta w/w$, equals (minus) 40 percent. Thus, if we know the labor supply elasticity and the marginal tax rate, we can calculate the percentage change in labor supply, $\Delta L/L$, from (1); that is, $\Delta L/L$ equals ϵ times $\Delta w/w$, or ϵm where m is the marginal tax rate.

The problem is that we do not know the magnitude of labor supply elasticities with any precision. Various empirical studies have yielded different estimates. Two surveys of these studies cited in Chapter 11 suggest val-

---

[2] The *Economic Report of the President, 1985* reports that total compensation of employees was $2,173 billion. To this can be added about $80 billion in total proprietors' (self-employed) income of $155 billion (part of which is really capital income). In addition, to arrive at a before-tax figure, we must add in that part of the $147 billion in sales and excise taxes that would have accrued to labor in the absence of these taxes. The result is a total before-tax labor income of about $2,400 billion.

ues of ϵ in the range of 0.1 to 0.3 and equal to 0.15. (What is relevant here is an average value of ϵ for the labor force as a whole. Some population subgroups, like married women, are believed to have higher elasticities than do other groups, like married men.) Let's take 0.15 as a reasonable compromise. In addition, suppose that the combined effect of all taxes on labor income produces a marginal tax rate of 40 percent, interpreting this as a weighted average of the different marginal tax rates that apply to different people. If these estimates are correct, then taxes can be estimated to reduce labor supply by 6 percent ($\Delta L/L = \epsilon m$, or 0.15 times 0.4); this implies a reduction in labor income of about \$150 billion in 1984 when total labor income was \$2,400 billion.

A loss of \$150 billion due to taxes on labor income sounds substantial, but this estimate, even if it is close, suffers from two defects. First, it compares the level of labor supply (labor income) under the current tax system with a world with no taxes on labor income at all. For almost any conceivable purpose, this is not a relevant comparison, since no one is suggesting that we do away with all the expenditure programs that these taxes finance. Second, even ignoring this problem, a reduction of \$150 billion in labor income is not a *net* loss to society. The reason for this loss is that people are working less, and that means they are enjoying greater amounts of leisure. To determine the net effect on well-being, we must weigh the loss in income against the gain in leisure.

These remarks lead us to consider the sense in which taxation of labor income produces a net loss, or welfare cost. We discussed this topic earlier, but we now take another look as we try to estimate the likely magnitude of the welfare cost from distortions in labor supply.

In Figure 14–1, YN illustrates a budget line for a worker, Wanda, in the absence of any taxes on labor income. With a progressive tax, which we represent for simplicity as a flat rate tax above an exempted amount of earnings, the budget line is $Y'BN$. Wanda's equilibrium is at point E_1, where U_3 is tangent to $Y'B$; note that this implies that Wanda's marginal rate of substitution between income and leisure is equal to the net marginal wage rate (the slope of $Y'B$). As we saw before, the welfare cost is identified by imagining a lump-sum tax that raises the same tax revenue. The lump-sum tax budget line is shown as HH', and Wanda moves to point E_2 and is on a higher indifference curve, although she still pays the same amount of tax. The welfare cost is indicated by the fact that Wanda can be better off (on U_2 rather than U_3) and still pay the same amount in taxes. Put the other way around, the tax places a burden on Wanda by moving her from U_1 to U_3; since it is possible to get the same revenue at a burden of only U_1 to U_2, the difference in well-being between U_2 and U_3 is an avoidable net loss—a welfare cost.

Now let's consider how to measure this welfare cost in dollars. When Wanda moves from E_1 to E_2, she increases her labor supply from NL_1 to NL_3,

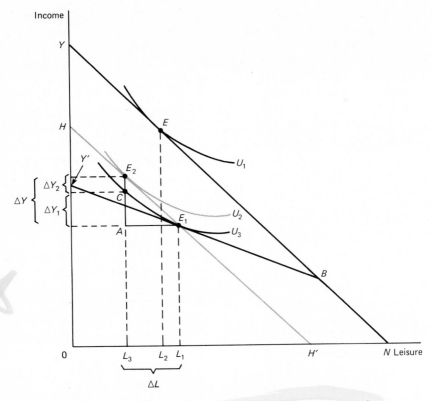

FIGURE 14–1   *The welfare cost of labor income taxation.*

or by ΔL. (ΔL is also the reduction in leisure time.) In return, Wanda's disposable income rises by AE_2, or by ΔY. This change in income, ΔY, is not a net gain, since part of it just compensates Wanda for the amount of leisure time she gave up to earn the additional income. Wanda would need to receive extra income of AC, or ΔY_1, just to stay on indifference curve U_3 to compensate her for the sacrificed leisure. But she actually receives the larger amount AE_2, or ΔY, which is larger than ΔY_1 by an amount equal to CE_2, or ΔY_2. So ΔY_2 is a measure of the net benefit to Wanda from paying a lump-sum tax rather than the income tax. Conversely, ΔY_2 is the net loss, or welfare cost, resulting from the tax.

To measure this welfare cost we need to know how much more workers will work when they can keep all *additional* earnings, that is, when they can choose a point on HH'. Recall that along HH' Wanda's tax liability is constant so working more does not increase her taxes; in effect, the marginal tax rate on additional earnings is zero. In the diagram, this additional work effort is ΔL. To estimate ΔL, we require a particular type of wage elasticity of supply that shows how work effort is affected when the *mar-*

ginal tax rate falls from its current value (along $Y'B$) to zero (along HH'), thereby raising the net marginal wage rate that Wanda gets to keep. Note that this elasticity is different from the one discussed earlier, which pertained to the movement from E to E_1. That elasticity, called an *uncompensated* elasticity, identifies the labor supply response taking into account *both* the income and substitution effects of the tax—from NL_2 to NL_1. For purposes of estimating the welfare cost, we need to use a labor supply elasticity referred to as a *compensated* elasticity that identifies the labor supply responses when tax revenue is constant. In effect, the compensated elasticity, which identifies the ΔL change in labor supply, *contains only the substitution effect,* since the taxpayer continues to pay the same amount in taxes. And, as long as leisure is a normal good, the compensated elasticity is larger than the uncompensated elasticity. This is illustrated in the diagram by the fact that work effort increases more along HH' (by ΔL) than if the worker pays no tax at all (by L_1L_2).

This is a subtle distinction, but what is really important is how much more taxpayers will work when they are confronted with a lump-sum tax that is equal in amount to the income taxes they pay.

Estimating the welfare cost

To develop a formula that can be used to estimate the welfare cost caused by distorted labor supply decisions, it is convenient to work directly with the labor supply curve. In Figure 14–2, S^* is Wanda's compensated labor supply curve, which identifies the substitution effects of tax-induced changes in the wage rate, and it is always upward sloping because as the wage rate rises, leisure becomes more expensive and less is consumed (that is, more labor is supplied). Wanda's market wage rate is w, and she is subject to a marginal tax rate of m. Thus, Wanda's net-of-tax marginal wage rate is $(1-m)w$, and at that net wage, her labor supply is L_1. This is a different way of representing the equilibrium shown at point E_1 in the previous diagram.

If a lump-sum tax is used to raise the same tax revenue, the marginal tax rate on any additional earnings will be zero, thereby raising Wanda's net wage rate from $(1-m)w$ to w. The increase in the net wage rate induces an increase in labor supply of ΔL (corresponding to ΔL in the previous diagram). Additional earnings would equal BAL_3L_1 (ΔY in the previous diagram), but in earning that income Wanda would give up leisure time worth DAL_3L_1 (ΔY_1 in the previous diagram). The difference, triangle BAD (ΔY_2 in the previous diagram), is the money measure of how much better off Wanda is with a lump-sum tax, which is the same as the welfare cost of using the income tax instead of the nondistorting lump-sum tax.

Area BAD is a triangle whose base equal to BD, or $w-(1-m)w=mw$, and a height equal to BA, or ΔL. Thus, the welfare cost, W, can be expressed as

$$W = \tfrac{1}{2}mw\Delta L \qquad\qquad (2)$$

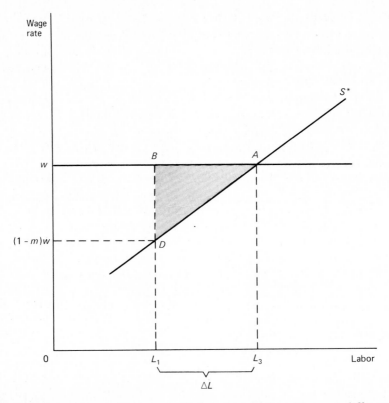

FIGURE 14–2   *The welfare cost of labor income taxation—a different perspective.*

The compensated change in the quantity of labor supplied, ΔL, can be expressed as the inverse of the slope of the supply curve, $\Delta L/\Delta w$, times the change in the marginal wage rate, wm, and so

$$W = \tfrac{1}{2}\left[\frac{\Delta L}{\Delta w}\,wm\right]wm \qquad (3)$$

If we multiply both sides by $L_1(1-m)/L_1(1-m)$, we get

$$W = \tfrac{1}{2}\left[\frac{\Delta L}{\Delta w}\,\frac{w(1-m)}{L_1}\right]\frac{m^2}{1-m}\,wL_1 \qquad (4)$$

In this expression, the term in brackets equals the elasticity of the compensated labor supply curve evaluated at the net of tax wage rate (point D in Figure 14–2). Thus, equation (4) can be rewritten more simply as

$$W = \tfrac{1}{2}\epsilon^* \frac{m^2}{1-m}\,wL_1 \qquad (5)$$

This formula is similar to the one developed in Chapter 10 for the welfare cost of excise taxes.[3] Here, we see that the welfare cost depends on the compensated labor supply elasticity ϵ^*, the marginal tax rate m, and total labor earnings (wL_1). Total labor earnings and marginal tax rates can be measured with reasonable accuracy, but we have less reliable information about the compensated labor supply elasticity, and that is the critical figure.

Ideally, to apply equation (5) we would estimate the welfare cost for each taxpayer separately and then add them up, since taxpayers face different marginal tax rates and may have different labor supply elasticities. We can, however, get a rough idea of the size of the welfare cost by using national labor earnings and average values for m and ϵ^*. In 1984, total before-tax labor earnings were about $2,400 billion. For m, we will use a value of 40 percent; since the national average tax rate on labor income is about 30 percent and federal and state income taxes apply marginal rates well above the average rates, a figure of 40 percent should not be far off the mark. For ϵ^*, we will use 0.3; since uncompensated labor supply elasticities have been estimated primarily in the range of 0.1 to 0.3 and the compensated elasticity must be larger, a value of 0.3 seems plausible.

Using these values, the welfare cost caused by labor supply distortions from all taxes falling on labor income in 1984 is

$$W = \tfrac{1}{2}(0.3)\frac{(0.4)^2}{(0.6)} \$2,400 \text{ billion} = \$96 \text{ billion}$$

An annual loss of $96 billion is far from negligible, but it should be viewed in comparison with the tax revenues raised. Since all taxes on labor income raised about $700 billion in 1984, the welfare cost is equal to 13.7 percent of tax revenues.

We should emphasize once again that we do not know the compensated labor supply elasticity with any great accuracy. When Harberger developed his original estimate of the welfare cost of the federal income tax in 1964, he used a value of 0.125.[4] More recent studies have generally concluded that people's labor supply decisions are more sensitive to taxation than was thought in 1964. By using a value of 0.3 for the compensated elasticity, we are in effect assuming that people would increase their labor supply by 20 percent $[\epsilon^*m/(1-m)]$ if they continued to pay the same tax but faced a marginal tax rate of zero rather than 40 percent. Although this seems plausible, we cannot rule out the possibility that the actual response could be somewhat greater or smaller.

---

[3] The earlier editions of this book gave a different formula, $\tfrac{1}{2}\epsilon^*m^2wL$, as originally derived by Harberger. The Harberger formula is correct if we measure the elasticity of the labor supply curve and earnings at their undistorted levels, that is, at point A in Figure 14–2. However, since our estimates of labor earnings and labor supply elasticities pertain to their actual levels with the taxes in place, equation (5) is the appropriate one to use.

[4] Arnold C. Harberger, "Taxation, Resource Allocation, and Welfare," *The Role of Direct and Indirect Taxes in the Federal Revenue System* (Princeton, N.J.: Princeton University Press for the National Bureau of Economic Research and The Brookings Institution, 1964), pp. 25–80.

So far, we have just considered the way that taxes on labor income affect the quantity of labor supplied. These taxes, however, affect economic behavior in other ways. The use of tax preferences in the income taxes, for example, can affect the form in which income is received (e.g., cash or fringe benefits) and how it is spent, as we saw in Chapter 11. Earlier, we cited a study that concluded that the welfare cost of tax preferences in the federal income tax was about 7 percent of tax revenues. If that figure is appropriate for all taxes on labor income, then the combined welfare cost of these taxes may be approximately 20 percent of tax revenues raised, or $140 billion in 1984.

It is unlikely that these welfare costs can be fully avoided; any feasible method of raising revenue is certain to distort some economic decisions. However, it may be possible to reduce the loss significantly. Suppose, for example, that we use a proportional tax on labor income of 30 percent (marginal and average rates both 30 percent) to raise the same revenue. In addition, let the tax base be defined comprehensively so that there are no special tax preferences. Then the only welfare cost would be the distortion in labor supply, and it can be estimated as

$$W = \tfrac{1}{2}(0.3)\frac{(0.3)^2}{0.7}\, \$2,400 \text{ billion} = \$46 \text{ billion}$$

This welfare cost estimate of $46 billion is $94 billion lower than our $140 billion estimate for the current system and suggests that the potential gain from tax reform is likely to be sizable. Efficiency, however, is not the only criterion; proportional taxes would place a heavier tax burden on lower-income classes and lead to a different distribution of after-tax income.

All of our estimates have been of the total welfare cost and the average welfare cost per dollar of tax revenue. As we pointed out in Chapter 10, the marginal welfare cost of taxation must also be considered in analyzing expenditure programs. The marginal welfare cost is the additional welfare cost associated with a marginal dollar of public spending, and it will be higher than the average cost because the welfare cost rises with the square of the marginal tax rate. Assuming ϵ^* is 0.3, the marginal welfare cost is probably in the range of 25 to 50 percent, depending on exactly how taxes are modified to produce additional revenue.[5] This estimate implies that any expenditure program that does not generate benefits of at least 25 to 50 percent more than direct costs is inefficient.

---

[5] Two recent studies developed estimates of marginal welfare cost that tend to fall in this range. However, it should be emphasized that the exact figure depends on several assumptions, most importantly the compensated labor supply elasticity. For certain combinations of assumptions, however, the estimated marginal welfare cost lies outside this range. See Charles Stuart, "Welfare Costs per Dollar of Additional Tax Revenue in the United States," *American Economic Review*, 74:352–362 (June 1984); and Charles L. Ballard, John B. Shoven, and John Whalley, "General Equilibrium Computations of the Marginal Welfare Costs of Taxes in the United States," *American Economic Review*, 75:128–138 (Mar. 1985).

Taxation and Capital Accumulation

By almost any measure, the performance of the U.S. economy over the past ten to fifteen years has been disappointing. Perhaps this is most clearly indicated by the rate of growth of per capita income. Between 1947 and 1973, real gross national product (GNP) per capita grew at an annual rate of 2.4 percent. Since the early 1970s, however, the rate of growth in real GNP per capita has slowed markedly, averaging only 1.2 percent per year over the 1973–1985 period. The reduction in the rate of growth of real per capita income suggests that the average standard of living has been rising only half as fast in recent years, but even this understates the deterioration in economic performance, since more people are working now than ever before. The 1970s and early 1980s saw an unprecedented expansion in the number of people working: The baby-boom generation entered the labor force, and the number of married women working rose significantly. But even with an increasing percentage of the population working, GNP per capita grew more slowly than in previous years. In fact, real GNP *per worker* scarcely grew at all from 1973 to 1985, although it had been rising at a rate of 1.9 percent per year between 1963 and 1973.

Put differently, Americans' standards of living have increased only slightly, if at all, since the early 1970s, although living standards grew steadily over previous decades. What caused this slowdown in the growth of productivity is not fully understood. No doubt some role was played by the energy price increases of 1973 and 1979, the inflation of the 1970s, and the changing demographic composition of the labor force. Attention has also focused on the rate of investment in productive capital. The amount of capital invested per worker is an important determinant of output per worker. If the stock of capital grows more slowly over time, output per worker will grow more slowly, other things being equal. And there is some evidence of a slowdown in the rate of capital accumulation in recent years.

Table 14–4 gives several alternative measures of capital formation over a period of years. The first two columns focus on the rate of net investment relative to GNP. (Recall that it is net investment, not gross investment, that adds to the nation's capital stock and therefore contributes to economic growth.) As can be seen, there was only a slight decline in this measure of capital formation. However, the last two columns suggest a far more drastic decline in the late 1970s. Here, the growth rate of capital per worker or per hour worked is measured, and sharp drops are recorded for the late 1970s. These reduced rates of growth were partly the result of a lower rate of net investment, but to an even greater degree to large increases in the labor force. Whatever the exact cause, the fact that capital per worker has been growing very slowly is a major reason that output per worker has been growing so little over the past fifteen years.

It is not entirely clear how large a contribution real investment makes to

Table 14–4 *Capital Formation in the U.S., 1951–1980*

| Year | Net Private Investment As Percent of GNP | | Growth Rate of Net Capital Stock | |
	Total Investment	Nonresidential Fixed Investment	Per Worker	Per Hour
1951–1955	7.2%	2.9%	3.1%	3.5%
1956–1960	6.1	2.6	3.5	4.1
1961–1965	6.7	2.9	2.5	2.4
1966–1970	7.1	4.0	3.9	4.9
1971–1975	6.4	3.1	2.2	2.6
1976–1980	6.0	2.9	0.4	0.9

Source: Council of Economic Advisers, *Economic Report of the President 1983* (Washington, D.C.: U.S. Government Printing Office, 1983), Table 4-1.

economic growth. Table 14–5 suggests, however, that the relationship is likely to be quite important. Several measures of investment for selected developed countries are compared with the annual growth rate in output per hour in manufacturing. Japan has the highest investment rate and also the highest growth rate of productivity, whereas the United States has the lowest investment rate and the lowest growth rate. The table thus implies a strong relationship between investment and the growth in standards of living. Although other factors also contribute to productivity growth, Table 14–5 does suggest that investment in real capital plays an important role, and other evidence supports this.

What determines the rate of net investment? Ultimately, private saving provides the funds that finance capital investment, so we must consider factors that influence the level of saving. Once again, many factors affect the level of saving and investment, and we do not know exactly how important each is. But there are a number of government policies that could affect the level of saving and investment. For example, several taxes fall on capital income which reduce the rate of return received by private savers. These taxes include individual income taxes, corporate income taxes, and property taxes. Insofar as people save less at a lower net rate of return, taxes on capital income tend to inhibit the flow of funds that finance capital investment.

We have also studied two other government policies that can affect the level of saving significantly. As was explained earlier in Chapter 7, the social security system provides retirement benefits on a pay-as-you-go basis, and that arrangement probably has reduced individual saving for retirement purposes to some degree. Social security has grown rapidly since the late

Table 14–5 *Capital Formation and Growth Rates in Selected Countries, 1971–1980*

| Country | Investment As a Percent of GDP | | | Growth Rate of Output per Hour in Manufacturing |
	Gross Investment	Gross Fixed Investment	Net Fixed Investment	
France	24.2%	22.9%	12.2%	4.8%
Germany	23.7	22.8	11.8	4.9
Italy	22.4	20.1	10.7	4.9
Japan	34.0	32.9	19.5	7.4
United Kingdom	19.2	18.7	8.1	2.9
United States	19.1	18.4	6.6	2.5

Source: Council of Economic Advisers, *Economic Report of the President 1983* (Washington, D.C.: U.S. Government Printing Office, 1983), Table 4-2.

1960s, and this factor may have played some role. In addition, deficit financing tends to absorb funds that would otherwise be channeled into private investment, as we saw in the last chapter. Thus, deficit financing and social security may be part of the explanation for the decline in investment. In addition, nongovernmental factors, such as the rapid rise in energy prices that occurred following the Arab oil embargo in 1973–1974, probably had some effect. In the remainder of this section, however, we shall focus on the way taxation of capital income affects saving, investment, and economic well-being.

Just as with taxes on labor income, it is important to recognize that a number of separate taxes fall on capital income, and it is their combined effect that is relevant. For example, suppose that a corporate investment yields $100 in income. Part of that income goes to pay property taxes, and the remainder is subject to federal and state corporation income taxes. What is left is either reinvested by the corporation or paid out as dividends. If the remaining funds are reinvested, it will lead to a capital gain on the stock held by shareholders which will be taxed under the individual income tax when realized; if they are paid as dividends, they will be immediately taxed under the individual income tax. Inflation may also interact with the tax code to increase the taxation of real capital income.

Table 14–6 presents some of the results of a study that examined how various taxes interact to determine the effective tax rate on capital income generated by investments in the corporate sector. Corporate investment is about 60 percent of total national investment, with residential investment (housing) accounting for 25 percent and noncorporate business accounting for the remaining 15 percent. Columns (1) to (7) show how much each of seven different types of taxation contributes to the total effective tax rate.

Table 14-6 *The Taxation of Corporate Capital Income*

| Year | Federal Corporate Tax (1) | State and Local Corporate Tax (2) | State and Local Property Tax (3) | Individual Income Tax | | | | Total Effective Tax Rate (8) | Before-Tax Rate of Return (9) | After-Tax Rate of Return (10) |
				Tax on Dividends (4)	Tax on Real Capital Gains (5)	Tax on Nominal Capital Gains (6)	Tax on Interest (7)			
			Contribution to Total Effective Tax Rate							
1955	45.0%	2.1%	7.7%	7.7%	1.2%	0.8%	1.0%	65.4%	13.2%	4.6%
1960	40.1	2.3	11.6	8.6	1.0	0.7	2.1	66.5	10.4	3.5
1965	31.8	2.2	9.1	6.2	1.7	0.7	1.9	53.5	14.8	6.9
1970	30.8	3.6	15.4	7.7	1.8	3.5	6.6	69.5	9.8	3.0
1975	28.3	4.6	13.9	6.4	2.6	6.6	7.8	70.3	9.1	2.7
1979	31.7	5.5	10.5	6.9	2.6	4.2	8.0	69.4	9.0	2.7

Source: Martin Feldstein, James Poterba, and Louis Dicks-Mireaux, "The Effective Tax Rate and the Pretax Rate of Return," National Bureau of Economic Research, Working Paper No. 740, Aug. 1981, Tables 2, 3, and 4.

Except for the federal corporation income tax, the separate rates are moderate, but together they produced a total effective tax rate of 69.4 percent in 1979. Over the entire 1955–1979 period, corporate investments were taxed at rates well in excess of 50 percent, with rates somewhat higher and approaching 70 percent in the 1970s.[6] The increase in the effective rate in the 1970s, was in large part the result of the interaction of inflation and the tax system. This is shown by the sharply higher rates in columns (6) and (7) beginning around 1970 when the inflation rate began its upward trend.

The last two columns in Table 14–6 indicate how taxes on capital income drive a wedge between the before-tax and after-tax real rates of return. During the 1970s, the before-tax real rate of return to corporate investment (including estimates for years not shown in the table) averaged almost 10 percent. With an effective tax rate of about 70 percent, however, the after-tax rate of return was only about 3 percent. Taxes act to reduce the net return, and it is the after-tax return that guides household decisions regarding how much to save. As explained in the last chapter, the corporate tax now imposes lower effective rates, and so it is likely that the combined effective rate is now closer to 60 percent than to 70 percent.

Figure 14–3 illustrates how the taxation of capital income can affect the level of saving and investment. The before-tax rate of return associated with each level of investment is shown by the investment demand curve, I. The saving supply curve is shown as S. In the absence of any taxes, the intersection of S and I determines the equilibrium with investment of I_1 and a rate of return of r. A tax on the rate of return at a rate of t, however, means that the after-tax, or net, rate of return associated with each level of investment is shown by the curve $I(1-t)$. Assuming a tax rate of 60 percent means that the $I(1-t)$ curve will lie 60 percent lower than the I curve does. With the S and I curves as drawn, the capital income taxes reduce the net return to savers to 4 percent and the level of saving and investment declines to I_2.

The extent to which taxes that fall on capital income reduce capital investment depends on the elasticities of the I and S schedules. Since the I schedule is generally thought to be relatively elastic, the net return will fall by almost as much as the tax. (Note that the return to savers falls from r to r_N, which is not a 60 percent drop because the before-tax return rises to r_G as the level of investment falls.) This means that the way savers respond to lower rates of return—that is, how elastic the saving supply curve is—is critical. If the saving supply curve were vertical (perfectly inelastic), there would be no reduction in the level of saving and investment in response to taxes on capital income; if instead the saving supply curve were relatively elastic, the level of saving and investment would be reduced sharply.

---

[6]The effective tax rate on capital income estimated here differs from that in Table 14–3 for two reasons. First, the study reported in Table 14–3 did not take into account the way inflation affects the tax rate, but Table 14–5 does. Second, Table 14–5 pertains only to corporate investment, whereas Table 14–3 gives an average for the economy as a whole.

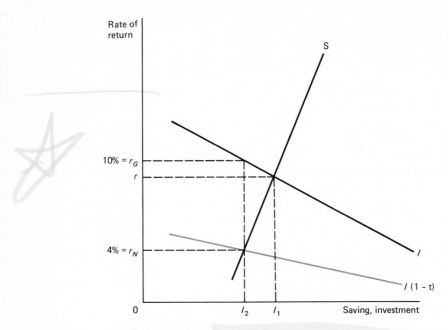

FIGURE 14–3 *Effects of capital income taxation.*

Until quite recently, it was generally believed that the supply curve of saving was quite inelastic, if not vertical. Recent empirical evidence and theoretical work, however, have suggested that this view is incorrect. On the empirical side, Boskin argued that earlier studies of the relationship between saving and interest rates did not look at the relevant after-tax rates of return. Correcting for this deficiency, he found an interest elasticity of saving of 0.4.[7] This value implies that capital income taxes reduced saving by perhaps $100 billion in 1981. On the theoretical side, Summers argued that in a multiperiod model in which households save for a number of years to provide for future retirement, theoretical considerations alone strongly suggest that a reduction in the net rate of return received by savers will reduce saving substantially.[8] Since both these findings contrast sharply with earlier research results, it is understandable that they are controversial. At the present time, the quantitative effect of capital income taxes on saving is best regarded as an open question.

[7]Michael J. Boskin, "Taxation, Saving, and the Rate of Interest," *Journal of Political Economy,* 86 (2) Part 2: S3–S28 (Apr. 1978).

[8]Lawrence H. Summers, "Capital Taxation and Accumulation in a Life Cycle Growth Model," *American Economic Review,* 71:533–544 (Sept. 1981).

Is the rate of investment too low?

In recent years, the view that the level of capital investment is too low in the United States has come to command wide respect. But what does it mean to say that investment is "too low"? Before answering this question, let's first evaluate two common arguments made in favor of increasing the rate of investment.

One frequently heard argument advocates increased capital investment as the cure for the sluggish economic growth of recent years. Although it is true that increased investment tends to increase the growth rate of real GNP, the relevant question is how much of an effect it will have on the growth rate. Since the before-tax rate of return is what measures the contribution of investment to output in subsequent years, let's use the 10 percent figure suggested by Table 14–6 to get an idea of the magnitude involved. Suppose we increase net investment by $100 billion annually, which would be a substantial increase from its 1985 level of approximately $250 billion. At a 10 percent return, $100 billion in additional capital investment this year would add $10 billion to annual output in subsequent years. Since GNP is about $4,000 billion, a $10 billion increment in output would add only 0.25 percentage points to the growth rate. In other words, the growth rate of GNP might rise from 2.5 to 2.75 percent. Although this is not negligible, it seems clear that feasible increases in investment will not transform the United States from a slowly growing to a rapidly growing economy overnight. Physical capital investment is only one of a number of factors that determine the rate of growth, and its independent role should not be exaggerated.

Another argument for increased investment stresses that business requires more capital in order to increase employment as the labor force expands rapidly. Put differently, capital investment "creates jobs." This argument is almost wholly fallacious. A given level of capital investment is consistent with any level of employment as long as wage rates can adjust. Downward-sloping labor demand curves mean that the level of employment will depend on wage rates—not that there is just one level of possible employment with a given stock of capital. As evidence, recall that the number of persons actually employed increased more rapidly in the 1970s than in any previous decade, despite an unusually low rate of investment.

In deciding whether the rate of investment is too low, economists emphasize that we should compare the costs of increasing investment with its benefits. To increase investment, people must reduce their current level of consumption; that is, they must save a larger portion of their incomes. There is no way to avoid this, and the sacrifice of current consumption is therefore the cost of increasing investment. The benefit associated with reduced current consumption is increased future consumption, since higher levels of investment now make it possible to consume more in the future because they add to the productive capacity of the economy. The magnitude of that benefit is correctly measured by the before-tax real rate of return to capital investment. If the before-tax real rate of return is 10 percent, then giving up $1 in consumption today will make it possible to consume $1.10 one year later, or $2.00 after only seven years.

The relevant question is whether people would be better off by sacrificing present consumption in return for increased future consumption. Since much saving is done to finance consumption in retirement and since 20 years is the approximate average length of time between when one starts to save for retirement and then consumes during retirement, the size of the tradeoff can be illustrated in the following way: At a 10 percent rate of interest, one dollar saved now will grow to $6.73 in 20 years so the present cost of $1 in retirement consumption is $0.15. Would people be better off saving more (consuming less) now in return for that payoff? And if they would, why aren't they saving more? The answer is that households do not get to keep the before-tax return of 10 percent; they only get to keep the lower after-tax return of 4 percent, for example. One dollar saved now at 4 percent will grow to only $2.19 in 20 years so the present price of retirement consumption is $0.46 per dollar. The tax on capital income of 60 percent triples the present price of retirement consumption, increasing it from $0.15 to $0.46 per dollar of retirement consumption. Faced with that much less favorable rate of exchange, it is understandable that saving remains low, even though the real before-tax return to saving justifies the cost of reduced present consumption.

What we have just described is the way capital income taxation can distort the choice between present and future consumption and lead to a welfare cost. Let's consider this further with the aid of Figure 14–4. Consumption of a household before retirement is measured on the vertical axis, and consumption after retirement is measured on the horizontal axis. In the absence of any taxes on capital income, MN is the budget line, with a slope of $0.15 in present consumption per dollar of retirement consumption, reflecting the 10 percent rate of return. Saving is initially MC_1. With a 60 percent tax on capital income, the budget line becomes MN', with a slope of $0.46 in present consumption per dollar of retirement consumption. Because of conflicting income and substitution effects, the effect on saving is uncertain. Let's suppose, however, that the level of saving still remains at MC_1 so the household's new equilibrium after the tax is at point E_1.

To see how the tax on capital income distorts the household's choice between present and future consumption, we perform the familiar experiment of substituting a lump-sum tax that yields the same revenue as the capital income tax. With the equal-yield lump-sum tax, the budget line is HH' and passes through point E_1. Using an equal-yield lump-sum tax means that the household can keep the full 10 percent return on any additional saving in excess of MC_1. Faced with the higher rate of return, the household

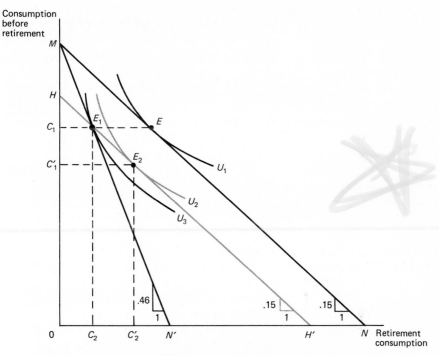

FIGURE 14–4 *The welfare cost of capital income taxation.*

chooses point E_2, saving an additional $C_1C'_1$ before retirement in return for extra consumption of $C_2C'_2$ after retirement. The household is better off under the lump-sum tax than under the capital income tax, reflecting the excess burden or welfare cost of the capital income tax.

It is in this sense that economists claim that investment (saving) is too low. The benefits to the public from the greater future consumption that additional investment makes possible ($C_2C'_2$) are greater than the sacrifice involved in reducing present consumption ($C_1C'_1$).

Trying to estimate the size of this welfare cost from capital income taxation is a tricky business, in large part because of the necessity of looking at the effects over a long period of time. However, several recent studies estimated the annual welfare cost to be in excess of $120 billion in 1985 dollars.[9] Since the total revenues from the relevant taxes are about $350 billion, a welfare cost of this size would be one third as large as tax revenues. Although this research is somewhat controversial and needs to be supported by further evidence, economists now recognize the possibility that capital income taxes can impose severe efficiency losses on the economy.

[9]Summers, op. cit.; Boskin. op. cit.; and Martin Feldstein, "The Welfare Cost of Capital Income Taxation," *Journal of Political Economy,* 86 (2) Part 2:S29–S52 (Apr. 1978).

Tax Rates, Tax Revenues, and the Laffer Curve

In the late 1970s, and particularly during the 1980 presidential campaign, the public became aware of something called *supply-side economics.* At the risk of oversimplifying, *supply-side economics emphasizes the way that government programs, especially taxes, can reduce national output (and hence national income) by reducing the incentive of people to work, save, and invest.* That is precisely the topic examined in the previous two sections. But supply-siders go on to emphasize a novel and often overlooked point: A higher tax rate will not necessarily produce more tax revenue if the base of the tax (income, or whatever) falls significantly in response to the higher rate. Moreover, a lower tax rate might actually increase revenues if enough additional productive activity were stimulated by the lower rate. To be able to lower tax rates and still get more revenue would seem to be the ideal free lunch, and some people thought that the supply-side approach might work in the United States.

To evaluate this possibility, let's examine the relationship between tax rates and tax revenues by considering a proportional income tax on earnings applied to an individual worker. Then we shall examine the implications of this analysis for the economy as a whole. We begin by assuming an income tax levied at a flat rate of 25 percent. As we have seen, the income and substitution effects of this tax are in opposite directions, so the net effect of the tax on work effort cannot be predicted on theoretical grounds. It is possible that an income tax would lead people to work more if the income effect dominated. We can, however, go a bit further with the analysis. Although an income tax levied at a low rate might increase the taxpayer's work effort, as the rate becomes increasingly higher, we will ultimately reach a point at which work effort will fall. We know, for example, that a 100 percent tax on earnings, which implies that the worker gets to keep no income, regardless of how much is earned, will lead a person to stop working altogether. Therefore, as the tax rate rises, it is more likely that the substitution effect will dominate and work effort will decline. Predictably, work effort will decline to zero by the time the rate reaches 100 percent.

Panel [a] of Figure 14–5 shows what this implies for the relationship between tax rates and tax revenue. The before-tax budget line is MN. A 25 percent income tax rotates the budget line to M_1N, and the worker chooses to work NL_1 hours. Tax revenue, the difference between before-tax earnings when work effort is NL_1 (BL_1) and after-tax earnings (AL_1), is the distance AB. If the tax rate is increased to 50 percent, the budget line will become M_2N. With the 50 percent tax on earnings, let's assume that the worker reduces his work effort moderately to NL_2 so that tax revenue is the distance CD. *Even though the worker's earnings are lower under the 50 percent tax, tax revenue is still higher (CD is greater than AB) because the doubled rate*

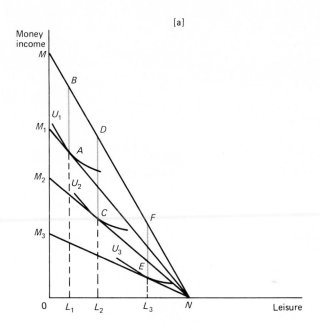

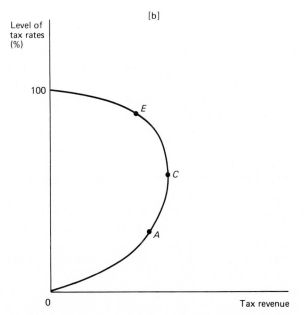

FIGURE 14–5   *Derivation of the Laffer curve.*

applied to moderately smaller earnings still yields more tax revenue. (Do not make the mistake of concluding that if a tax rate increase has disincentive effect, revenues will fall. The disincentive effect must be large relative to the rate increase if revenues are to fall.) However, when the tax rate is increased to 75 percent and the budget line becomes M_3N, work effort drops more sharply to NL_3, and tax revenue, EF, is lower than it was at the 50 percent rate. In this example, if the tax rate is initially 75 percent for the worker, a reduction in the rate will actually increase the government's tax revenue and also benefit the worker—just as the supply-siders predicted.

This suggests a general relationship: At low tax rates, an increase in the tax rate will increase tax revenues, but beyond some point a further increase in the tax rate will reduce tax revenues. This relationship is illustrated in panel [b] of Figure 14–5 where the points A, C, and E correspond to the three tax rates depicted in panel [a]. The curve in panel [b], well known among economists for many years, is now popularly known as the "Laffer curve" after contemporary economist Arthur Laffer. Rumor has it that Laffer drew the curve on a napkin for some politicians in a posh Washington restaurant sometime in the 1970s, and those politicians have never been the same again.

Where are we on the Laffer curve?

There is no doubt that a relationship of the general form shown in Figure 14–5(b) exists. The critical question is to determine where we are on the curve. If the current tax system puts us at a point like A, then higher tax rates will produce more tax revenues—despite a reduction in productive activity—and lower tax rates will mean less revenue. If we are at a point like E, however, taxes have depressed productive activity so far that a reduction in rates will spur sufficiently greater output to increase tax revenues.

In trying to determine whether a reduction in tax rates in the United States would lead to increased tax revenue, we immediately encounter a difficulty. What tax rates would be reduced? Because of the variety of different taxes and, more important, the fact that these apply at different marginal and average rates to different persons and activities, there are innumerable ways in which tax rates can be reduced. We might possibly find some activities so heavily taxed and in such elastic supply that a carefully designed rate reduction could lead to increased tax revenues, but the more important question is whether an economywide reduction in marginal and average tax rates is likely to have this result.

To investigate this question, let's consider the taxation of labor income since our knowledge of how labor supply responds to taxation, imperfect as it is, is better than our knowledge of how saving and capital accumulation respond to capital income taxes. As we explained earlier, a typical person is subject to a marginal tax rate of about 40 percent on labor earnings and an average tax rate of about 30 percent. Suppose a representative household's current earnings are $30,000, so its tax equals $9,000. Next let the marginal rate be reduced from 40 to 30 percent and the average rate to 22.5 percent (at $30,000 in earnings[10]), so that the original ratio of marginal to average tax rates is maintained. A bit of arithmetic shows that earnings would have to rise by $7,500 to $37,500 for these lower rates to generate the same revenue. (That is, 22.5 percent of $30,000 equals $6,750, and with a marginal tax rate of 30 percent, if earnings rise by $7,500, an additional $2,250 in tax revenue results, for a total of $9,000.) Thus, a 25 percent increase in earnings is necessary for revenue to remain the same, and this would require work effort to increase by at least 25 percent. Larger increases are necessary if tax revenue is to be higher at the lower rates.

Is it likely that work effort will increase by 25 percent if the marginal tax rate is reduced by 10 percentage points? For a person working a 40-hour week, this would mean an increase to 50 hours per week—and the workweek has not been at that level since early in the twentieth century. Intuitively, such a large change in hours worked would seem unlikely to follow from a 10 percentage point reduction in the marginal tax rate. We can also evaluate the possibility of such a large increase in work effort in terms of the wage elasticity of labor supply. Since reducing the marginal tax rate from 40 to 30 percent corresponds to an increase in the net marginal wage rate from 60 to 70 percent of the market wage, the implied increase in the net marginal wage rate would be 16⅔ percent. For a 16⅔ percent increase in the wage rate to increase labor supply by 25 percent, the labor supply elasticity would have to be 1.5 (25 percent divided by 16⅔ percent). As we mentioned, most evidence suggests the labor supply elasticity is in the 0.1 to 0.3 range, far below the required value. For an intermediate value, an elasticity of 0.15 would imply increased work effort of 2.5 percent, only one tenth of the 25 percent increase necessary to keep tax revenue from falling.

Reasoning along these lines has convinced most economists that the United States is not on the upper part of the Laffer curve. There are, however, two other ways that we should consider that might result in higher tax revenues without increased labor supply. One way is to induce currently untaxed economic activity in the so-called underground economy to move back into the taxed sector. To avoid taxes, some persons do not report their actual earnings. A carpenter or lawyer, for example, may be paid for a job in cash and not report the income. The gain from such activity is the tax saving; the cost is the risk of being caught and prosecuted. When tax rates are lower,

---

[10] For a progressive tax, the average tax rate is not a fixed number but depends on how much is earned. We assume that the tax structure changes so the average rate will be 22.5 percent as long as the household continues to earn $30,000.

the gain from not declaring income is reduced, which might induce some of this income to be reported rather than those individuals' running the risk of legal sanctions.

The best estimates of the size of the underground economy suggest that it is about 10 percent as large as measured GNP.[11] For the hypothetical tax reduction of 10 percent, we saw that taxable earnings would have to increase by 25 percent to keep tax revenue from falling. Allowing for a 2.5 percent increase in earnings from those already taxed, even if the entire underground economy went legal, the increase in taxable earnings would only be about 12.5 percent—still far short of the required 25 percent increase needed. And there is no reason to think that the entire underground economy would become legal when marginal tax rates fell by one fourth; at best, probably only a small fraction would.

Another potential source of additional taxable income when tax rates are lower is the reduced use of legal tax preferences. At lower rates, for example, untaxed fringe benefits become less attractive relative to taxed cash income. Consequently, workers might take a larger part of their salaries as cash, and this would increase their taxable earnings. But the total amount of excluded income under the federal income tax that would be affected by such a type of change—primarily itemized deductions in excess of the zero bracket amount plus exclusions other than government transfers—is only about 10 percent of GNP. Only a small part of this total could realistically be expected to become taxable income when the marginal rate falls by 10 percentage points, and this would not be nearly enough.

Thus, it appears unlikely that a reduction in tax rates would lead to the same or greater tax revenue through an expansion of taxable income. Taking account of the illegal underground economy and the legal use of tax preferences in addition to labor supply responses, however, does increase the probability of such an outcome, but that probability still seems low.

Where should we be on the Laffer curve?

It may be tempting to argue that the point at which tax revenues are as large as possible—point C in Figure 14–5—is somehow special. In fact, one popularizer of the Laffer curve observed "It [point C] is the point at which the electorate desires to be taxed. [At lower tax rates] the electorate desires more government goods and services and is willing—without reducing its productivity—to pay the higher rates consistent with the revenues at point [C]."[12] Indeed, point C is special, but it is distinct only because government is raising and spending too much revenue at that point.

[11] Carl P. Simon and Ann D. Witte, *Beating the System: The Underground Economy* (Boston: Auburn House, 1982).

[12] Jude Wanniski, "Taxes, Revenues, and the Laffer Curve," *The Public Interest,* 5:5 (Winter 1978).

It is impossible to determine the appropriate (efficient) level of taxing and spending without evaluating the benefits from the expenditures of tax revenues, and these benefits are not identified by the Laffer curve. As we move up the Laffer curve, however, we know that each successive equal

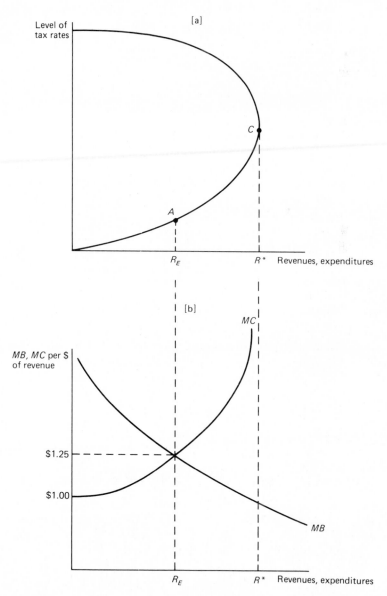

FIGURE 14–6 *The Laffer curve and efficient government taxing-spending.*

increase in tax rates imposes a larger burden (direct burden plus welfare cost) on the public than the previous increment did. At the same time, each successive equal increment in tax rates generates less revenue than the previous increment did. Thus, the marginal burden per dollar of revenue, or the ratio of additional burden to additional revenue, rises as we move up the curve, and it approaches infinity at point C, since the denominator—the increase in tax revenue—goes to zero at that point. In other words, as we near point C, an increase in tax rates raises almost no more revenue but continues to increase the burden on taxpayers. Since the marginal burden, or marginal cost, per dollar of revenue is infinite at point C, the only way that point could represent the efficient level of government spending is if the marginal benefit of government spending is also infinite—and that is impossible.

Figure 14–6 clarifies the relationship between the Laffer curve and the efficient level of government taxing-spending activity. Both the upper and lower panels measure total tax revenue—assumed equal to total government spending—on the horizontal axes. In the lower panel, the MC curve shows the marginal cost of raising tax revenue. MC is upward sloping, since the welfare cost of taxation rises with the square of the marginal tax rate, whereas tax revenue rises less than proportionally to that rate. (See also Figure 10–11.) The MC curve becomes vertical—the marginal cost becomes infinite—at R^*, which corresponds to point C on the Laffer curve in the upper panel. The marginal benefits from spending tax revenues are shown by the downward-sloping MB curve in the lower panel. Efficiency requires that taxing-spending be expanded until marginal benefit and marginal cost are equal, at R_E in Figure 14–6.

The efficient level of taxing and spending will always be somewhere on the lower part of the Laffer curve, not at point C. Actually, the Laffer curve is not useful in helping us identify the efficient level, since it does not tell us the magnitudes of either MC or MB at different rates of taxation. At least, this is true at all tax rates lower than the revenue-maximizing rate at point C. If we were at point C, or higher, we would know that tax rates were unambiguously too high.

Can targeted tax rate reductions increase revenues?

So far in our discussion of the Laffer curve, we have focused on the way that across-the-board tax rate changes may affect total tax revenues. Our conclusion was that lower general tax rates are likely to reduce total tax revenues. However, that leaves the question of whether more carefully targeted changes in tax rates might have a different effect. Can carefully targeted selective cuts in tax rates increase tax revenues? Indeed, according to evidence from the 1981 Economic Recovery Tax Act, the tax rate reductions that were phased in over the 1981–1984 period show that cutting the tax rates that apply to very high income taxpayers may actually increase the taxes they pay.

A numerical example will illustrate how. Consider a hypothetical taxpayer, Garfield, with a taxable income of $100,000, and suppose that the tax is progressive, imposing a marginal rate of 20 percent on the first $40,000 of income, 40 percent on the next $40,000, and then 60 percent on all income over $80,000. With $100,000 in taxable income, Garfield will initially be paying $36,000 in taxes ($8,000 on the first $40,000, $16,000 on the next, and $12,000 on the $20,000 over $80,000). Now suppose that the 60 percent rate is reduced to 50 percent but that the lower rates are kept constant. At the margin, this increases the after-tax return from 40 to 50 percent of the before-tax return, an increase of 25 percent. In response to this, suppose that Garfield increases his taxable income by 4 percent, to $104,000. Then his total tax liability will be the same as before the rate cut! Garfield will pay the same tax on the first $80,000 ($24,000), plus 50 percent of the next $24,000 ($12,000), or $36,000. Thus if the taxpayer responds by increasing taxable income by more than 4 percent—certainly not implausible in view of the 25 percent increase in the marginal after-tax return—more tax revenue will be collected from the lower tax rate.

The 1981–1984 tax cut did not cut just the top rates but was approximately an across-the-board cut in marginal rates. Even in this case, the incentive effect is likely to be greatest for those initially in the highest brackets. Consider a 10 percent reduction in all marginal tax rates, and compare its effect on taxpayers who are initially in the 20 percent and the 60 percent brackets. The taxpayer in the 20 percent bracket will find the after-tax rate of return increased from 80 to 82 percent of the before-tax return, an increase of only 2.5 percent. However, the taxpayer in the 60 percent bracket will· find the after-tax rate of return increased from 40 to 46 percent, or by 15 percent. Proportionate reductions in marginal tax rates are therefore likely to enhance incentives more for taxpayers with the highest rates.

Preliminary evidence from the first full year of the tax cut, 1982, when rates were cut by approximately 10 percent (not taking account of the bracket creep that offset part of this), suggested that high-income taxpayers responded to the lower rates quite strongly. For example, Gwartney found that the taxable incomes of the top 1.36 percent of federal taxpayers (roughly, those with AGIs above $80,000 in 1982) rose by 12.2 percent (in nominal terms) from 1981 to 1982, whereas the taxable incomes of all other taxpayers rose by only 5.5 percent.[13] Taxes paid by the high-income group actually increased from $58.0 billion to $60.5 billion. This was, however, a slight decline in real terms, but since it was a short-term response, the possibility

---

[13]James Gwartney, "Tax Rates, Taxable Income and the Distributional Effects of the Economic Recovery Tax Act of 1981," testimony before U.S. Congress, Joint Economic Committee, June 12, 1984.

still remains that real revenue might ultimately rise. In another study, Lindsey found that tax revenues rose in real terms for the top 0.18 percent of taxpayers (roughly, those with adjusted gross incomes above $200,000).[14] Both studies concluded that the share of total income taxes paid by higher-income taxpayers rose, suggesting that they responded more to the tax rate reductions than lower-income taxpayers did, as might be expected from our earlier discussion. Note that the tax's incentive effects not only reflect labor supply changes but also reduced use of tax preferences. Indeed, the evidence suggests that the reduced use of tax preferences may have been more responsible for the increase in taxable income than increased labor supply from upper-income taxpayers.

These recent findings, tentative though they are, suggest that further tax rate reductions targeted on the wealthy might actually raise more revenue from them. Whether that is so will certainly be the subject of further research, as more evidence from the 1981–1984 tax cut becomes available.

Proposal for Reform: A Consumption Tax

In recent years, there has been growing support among tax specialists for a seemingly radical change in the tax system. Many now advocate that taxes on income be eliminated and that a consumption tax be used instead. Support for such a reform has come from the U.S. Treasury Department itself,[15] in addition to many private economists.

Consumption taxes in the form of sales and excise taxes have been used for a long time in the United States. The personal consumption tax discussed in this section, however, differs from these taxes significantly, since it would be levied at the individual level and be based on each taxpayer's consumption. That may not seem to be a major difference, since we saw in Chapter 10 that the point of collection of a tax—whether from firms or individuals—does not affect its real economic consequences. Indeed, a personal consumption tax levied at a flat rate would have the same general effects as would a national retail sales tax, or VAT, levied on a comparable base. One advantage of a personal consumption tax, however, is that it can be levied at graduated rates, taxing those who consume more at a higher rate, for example. This means that the consumption tax can be a progressive tax, if desired—something that is difficult to achieve with sales taxes collected from business firms.

Until recently, personal consumption taxation was thought to be too dif-

---

[14]Lawrence B. Lindsey, "Taxpayer Behavior and the Distribution of the 1982 Tax Cut," National Bureau of Economic Research Working Paper No. 1760, Oct. 1985.

[15]U.S. Treasury, *Blueprints for Basic Tax Reform* (Washington, D.C.: U.S. Government Printing Office, Jan. 17, 1977).

ficult to administer. The vision of each taxpayer's having to fill out a tax return listing every consumption outlay over the year indicates what an administrative nightmare it could be. Recent research, however, has shown that it is administratively feasible, and some economists believe that a personal consumption tax would be simpler to administer than an income tax is. For example, it would not be necessary for each taxpayer to identify every consumption expense; instead, the tax base could be measured as the difference between income and the amount saved. Recall that consumption plus saving (change in net worth) equals income, and so subtracting current saving from income measures consumption. Although it would not be quite that simple in practice, we will proceed on the assumption that a personal consumption tax is administratively feasible.

Equity

One of the strong claims made on behalf of an income tax has always been that income is the best measure of a taxpayer's ability to pay taxes. Consider two taxpayers, Alma and Barney, who each have incomes of $20,000. If Alma consumes her entire income and Barney consumes half and saves half, a consumption tax would require Barney to pay lower current taxes. A proponent of the income tax would argue that Barney must be just as well off as Alma, since he had the same options as Alma; therefore Barney should pay the same tax. In this view, horizontal equity calls for the broader income base.

Proponents of consumption taxation have turned this argument upside down, claiming that the consumption tax is fair and the income tax is not. They agree that Alma and Barney are equals but stress that we must examine the taxes over a longer period than a single year. Under a consumption tax, the saver, Barney, does not avoid paying taxes by saving; he merely postpones the tax until he ultimately consumes the funds accumulated through his saving. To judge the fairness of income versus consumption taxes, we must therefore look beyond the current year.

Table 14–7 illustrates three alternatives: no tax, an income tax, and a consumption tax. We assume that Alma and Barney live for only two years; Barney saves part of year 1's income to consume in year 2; and the interest rate is 10 percent. The no-tax option shows their preferred consumption patterns over time in the absence of taxes. The consumption tax advocate would argue that these two persons have identical taxpaying capacities because both have the same opportunities to consume; the fact that Barney prefers to consume more in year 2 should not subject him to any tax penalty.

Now notice what happens under a 20 percent income tax. Both Alma and Barney pay a $4,000 tax in year 1, but Barney pays an additional tax of $160 in year 2—20 percent of the $800 in *interest income* earned on his $8,000

Table 14–7   *Income Versus Consumption Taxation*

		No Tax	
Person	*Earnings*	*Year 1 Consumption*	*Year 2 Consumption*
Alma	$20,000	$20,000	$ 0
Barney	20,000	10,000	11,000
		Income Tax	
Person	*Earnings*	*Year 1 Consumption (and tax)*	*Year 2 Consumption (and tax)*
Alma	$20,000	$16,000 ($4,000)	$ 0 ($0)
Barney	20,000	8,000 (4,000)	8,640 (160)
		Consumption Tax	
Person	*Earnings*	*Year 1 Consumption (and tax)*	*Year 2 Consumption (and tax)*
Alma	$20,000	$16,000 ($4,000)	$ 0 ($0)
Barney	20,000	8,000 (2,000)	8,800 (2,200)

saving of the year before. Although both Alma and Barney have exactly the same consumption opportunities, Barney pays a higher tax because the interest return on saving is subject to income taxation. By contrast, under a consumption tax (levied at a 25 percent rate[16]), Barney pays $2,000 in year 1 and $2,200 in year 2. In present value terms, over the two-year period, Barney pays the same amount of tax as Alma, since $2,200 paid in year 2 with an interest rate of 10 percent is equivalent to $2,000 in year 1.

A person's lifetime tax liability under a consumption tax is the same (in present value), regardless of how much is saved. Savers do not avoid the tax, they just postpone it by saving. Under income taxation, those who save a larger portion of their incomes end up paying more in lifetime taxes than do those equally situated who choose to save less. Thus, it is argued that consumption is a better base for taxation than income is, since it treats equals equally. Not all economists accept this argument, but the case is a strong one if you are willing to take a long-run view of tax equity, rather than comparing tax burdens in a single year.

One equity problem in actually adopting a personal consumption tax is

---

[16] Since consumption is a smaller tax base than income, a higher tax rate must be applied to consumption. The 25 percent consumption tax raises the same tax revenue from Alma in year 1 as the 20 percent rate applied to income does, since Alma consumes $16,000.

the transition from an existing income tax to a consumption tax. How should a newly implemented consumption tax treat those who have saved in the past and expect to consume the principal amount later with no further tax on that sum? Consider Barney's position under the income tax in Table 14–7. If a consumption tax were introduced in year 2, when Barney consumed his saving, he would have to pay a tax of much more than $160 in year 2. This only compounds the unfairness of the income tax because Barney already paid $4,000 in taxes in year 1. Since savers have already paid income taxes on the amounts they saved, taxing the same sum again when consumed would be unfair under any view of tax equity.

The case for a consumption tax is strongest when we are designing a tax system starting with a "clean slate." When an income tax is already in place, however, the transition to a consumption tax raises the difficult issue of equity for those with accumulated savings. Although some provision can be made for this, it may be difficult to do so fairly and at low administrative cost.

Efficiency

As we have seen, an income tax distorts two important types of economic decisions. First, it distorts labor supply choices. Second, it distorts the saving decision, since the after-tax return to saving is lower than the before-tax rate of return. A consumption tax also distorts labor supply choices, since people work not for wages per se but for the consumption that wages make possible. A consumption tax, however, does not distort the saving decision.

Refer back to Table 14–7 and note how the consumption tax affects Barney. Barney could have consumed $16,000 in year 1 and nothing in year 2 (as Alma did), but by reducing consumption by $8,000 in year 1, Barney is able to consume $8,800 one year later. Since the interest rate is 10 percent, this means that each dollar of reduced consumption in year 1 makes possible $1.10 of increased consumption the next year. Taxing consumption at the same rate in both years does not alter the relative price of future consumption, compared with that of present consumption. A consumption tax does not drive a wedge between market and net rates of interest as an income tax does.

We have already discussed how taxes that reduce the net return to saving produce a welfare cost by distorting the choice between present and future consumption. A consumption tax avoids this welfare cost. We cannot, however, conclude that this necessarily implies that a consumption tax is superior to an income tax. Since consumption is a smaller tax base than income is, higher tax rates must be used to raise the same revenue under a consumption tax. It is possible that this will make the labor supply distortion of the consumption tax greater than that of the income tax. This is not certain, however. The consumption tax taxes the labor used to finance current consumption more heavily than the income tax does, but it taxes the labor used to finance future consumption less heavily, since the return to saving is not taxed. Since people work to provide both current and future consumption, a consumption tax may not distort labor supply more than an income tax does.

Whether a consumption tax has a lower overall welfare cost than an income tax does depends on the relative degrees of responsiveness of labor supply and saving to taxation. If labor supply is relatively unresponsive to taxation but saving is quite sensitive, then the consumption tax is the more efficient alternative. In view of our earlier discussion, it is clear that we cannot be certain whether this is so, given the available empirical evidence. But the recent research findings of large welfare costs from the taxation of the income from saving have convinced many economists that a consumption tax is worth a try.

Supplementary Readings

AARON, HENRY J., and JOSEPH A. PECHMAN, eds. *How Taxes Affect Economic Behavior.* Washington, D.C.: The Brookings Institution, 1981.

BOSKIN, MICHAEL, J. "Efficiency Aspects of the Differential Tax Treatment of Market and Household Activity." *Journal of Public Economics,* 4:1–25 (Feb. 1975).

———. "Taxation, Savings, and the Rate of Interest." *Journal of Political Economy,* 86 (2) Part 2:S3–S28 (Apr. 1978).

BOSWORTH, BARRY P. *Tax Incentives and Economic Growth.* Washington, D.C.: The Brookings Institution, 1984.

BROWNING, EDGAR K. "The Marginal Cost of Public Funds." *Journal of Political Economy,* 84 (2):283–298 (Apr. 1976).

———, and WILLIAM R. JOHNSON. *The Distribution of the Tax Burden.* Washington, D.C.: American Enterprise Institute, 1979.

FELDSTEIN, MARTIN S. "The Welfare Cost of Capital Income Taxation." *Journal of Political Economy,* 86 (2) Part 2:S29–S52 (Apr. 1978).

———. *Capital Taxation.* Cambridge, Mass.: Harvard University Press, 1983.

MEYERS, LAURENCE H., ed. *The Supply-Side Effects of Economic Policy.* St. Louis, Mo.: Center for the Study of American Business, 1981.

MIESZKOWSKI, PETER. "The Choice of Tax Base: Consumption Versus Income Taxation." In Michael J. Boskin, ed., *Federal Tax Reform,* San Francisco: Institute for Contemporary Studies, 1978.

ROSEN, HARVEY S. "What Is Labor Supply and Do Taxes Affect It?" *American Economic Review,* 70:171–176 (May 1980).

SEIDMAN, LAWRENCE S. "The Personal Consumption Tax and Social Welfare." *Challenge,* 23:10–16 (Sept./Oct. 1980).

U.S. TREASURY. *Blueprints for Basic Tax Reform.* Washington, D.C.: U.S. Government Printing Office, Jan. 17, 1977.

Review Questions and Problems

1. For each category of tax shown in Table 14–1, explain why it has the particular pattern of incidence shown. In other words, what features of the tax, what theoretical analysis, and what characteristics of the data combine to produce these rates?

2. What tax in the U.S. tax system is the most progressive? What tax is the least progressive? In what ways do your answers depend on the theoretical analysis of the taxes' incidence?

3. One recent study estimated that the compensated labor supply elasticity (an average for all groups) of U.S. workers is approximately 0.7. Do you find this plausible? Why or why not? If correct, what does it imply about the size of the welfare cost caused by the labor supply distortions?

4. Use the formula in the text to calculate the welfare cost caused by the labor supply distortion for each of the following two workers:

a. Worker A, who earns $25,000, pays total taxes on labor income of $5,000, faces an effective marginal tax rate of 30 percent, and has a compensated labor supply elasticity of 0.3.

b. Worker B, who earns $75,000, pays total taxes on labor income of $25,000, faces an effective marginal tax rate of 50 percent, and has a compensated labor supply elasticity of 0.3.

5. Can the welfare cost of a tax caused by labor supply effects be greater than the tax revenue collected from a worker? If so, use a diagram to illustrate this result, and also illustrate it using the formula in the text.

6. "We must cut taxes on capital income in order to get the country growing again." Discuss.

7. How will the incidence of a tax on capital income be affected if the tax leads to a reduction in the level of investment? (Remember that our analysis of the corporation income tax assumed that the amount of capital was not affected by the tax.)

8. The maximum amount of revenue that can be raised is lower for a progressive tax than for a proportional tax. True or false? (Try to adapt Figure 14–5a to compare the two taxes.)

9. Why are tax rate reductions for the wealthy less likely to reduce the tax revenue collected than are tax rate reductions for middle-income taxpayers? Suppose that the tax rates could be reduced by 25 percent for those with incomes above $100,000 without any loss of revenue. Would you favor this tax cut?

10. "A tax on income is fairer than a tax on consumption because income is a broader measure of the taxpayers' ability to pay." True or false? Explain.

chapter 15
Federalism

THE United States has a federal form of government, with one central government, 50 state governments, and thousands of local governments. The existence of a multiplicity of government units raises a number of interesting questions: What is the rationale for so many different levels of government? Are some types of economic policies better carried out by local governments than by the federal government? How does the free movement of people and businesses among local government units affect their performance? These are a few of the questions that are considered in this chapter.

Overview of State and Local Expenditures and Taxes

A casual observer of contemporary affairs could easily believe that the federal government overwhelms lower levels of government in terms of its economic impact. In a sense this is probably true: The federal government spends almost 50 percent more than the combined expenditures of all state and local governments. If only domestic expenditures (thereby excluding national defense) are considered, however, state and local outlays are on a par with federal outlays. For many persons, the governmental services provided by subnational levels of government are more important to their day-to-day lives than the services provided by the federal government.

Table 15–1 shows the major expenditures of state and local governments in 1984. Taking state and local governments together, total expenditures were $567 billion, or about $2,500 per person. The general categories of education and social services–income maintenance (generally, redistributive programs) together account for almost half of this expenditure. Other major types of expenditures included transportation (mainly highways); public safety (mainly police, fire protection, and prisons); interest on debt; and government administration; but none of these categories accounted for as much as 10 percent of total outlays. When we look at state and local government expenditures separately, we see that grants to local governments and social services-income maintenance expenditures are the largest categories

Table 15–1 *State and Local Government Expenditures, Fiscal 1984 (amounts in billions of $)*

Function	Combined State and Local	State	Local
Education	$178.5	$ 44.8	$121.3
Grants to local governments	—	99.1	—
Social services and income maintenance	105.7	68.2	35.6
Transportation	41.6	21.9	19.7
Public safety	38.3	10.9	27.3
Environment and housing	39.2	7.9	31.4
Government administration	24.5	9.2	15.3
Interest on debt	24.1	11.3	12.9
Insurance trust expenditures	47.3	42.2	5.2
Utility expenditures	50.0	4.4	45.6
All other	30.1	14.2	18.9
Total expenditures	$567.0*	$334.0	$335.1

*Net of duplicative intergovernmental transactions.
Source: U.S. Department of Commerce, Bureau of the Census, *Governmental Finances in 1982–1983* (Washington, D.C.: U.S. Government Printing Office, Oct. 1984), Table 13.

for state governments, together accounting for half of all state outlays. At the local level, education is by far the single largest expenditure function.

Not all expenditures by state and local governments are financed from their own taxes. Some expenditure programs are partially or wholly financed by the federal government through grants (subsidies) given directly to lower levels of government. In 1984 the federal government made grants totaling $97 billion to state and local governments, thereby financing about 18 percent of the total expenditures of subnational governments out of federal taxes. These "intergovernmental grants" have become increasingly important in recent years, and their rationale and consequences are considered later in the chapter.

Sources of revenue for state and local governments are shown in Table 15–2. Although subnational levels of government use much the same types of taxes as the federal government does, their relative importance differs greatly. At the state level, general sales and excise taxes produce nearly half of total revenue. Individual income taxes have also become an important source of revenue in recent years and now produce one fourth of state tax revenue. By contrast, at the local level the tax picture is dominated by the property tax, which generates three fourths of local tax revenue.

Taxes actually finance only about half of all state-local expenditures. The remaining funds come from "charges and miscellaneous" and intergovern-

Table 15–2 *State and Local Government Revenue, Fiscal 1984 (amounts in billions of $)*

Type of Revenue	Combined State and Local	State	Local
Taxes:			
Individual income	$ 64.6	$ 58.9	$ 5.7
Corporation income	17.0	15.5	1.5
Property	96.5	3.9	92.6
General sales	75.2	62.6	12.6
Selective sales (excise)	38.9	33.2	5.6
Payroll	16.8	16.7	.1
Other	27.0	22.7	4.8
Total taxes	337.0	213.5	122.9
Charges and miscellaneous	218.1	102.2	115.9
Intergovernmental revenue:			
From federal government	97.1	76.1	20.9
From state government	—	—	105.8
Total revenue	$652.1*	$397.1	$366.2

*Net of duplicative intergovernmental transactions.
Source: U.S. Department of Commerce, Bureau of the Census, *Governmental Finances in 1983–1984* (Washington, D.C.: U.S. Government Printing Office, Oct. 1985), Tables 4 and 21.

mental grants. The charges and miscellaneous category includes such revenues as college tuition, parking fees, sewage fees, license fees, and receipts from the operation of state liquor stores. Intergovernmental grants are particularly important to local governments. Local governments received $127 billion from the federal and state governments as grants, and that sum actually exceeded the tax revenues raised by the local governments themselves.[1]

One important characteristic of our federal system cannot be shown in tables such as Table 15–1 and 15–2, which combine the accounts of all subnational governments. This characteristic is the great diversity of tax and expenditure policies employed by the states and localities. Not all subnational governments use the same taxes, apply them at the same rates, or spend the same amounts on the various programs; they are independent units making their own individual tax and expenditure decisions, and these decisions can and do vary considerably. Table 15–3 indicates the variation in state expenditures and taxes per capita among selected states in 1984. Taxes per person range from a low of $433 in New Hampshire to a high of

[1] For a comparison of expenditure and tax policies of the federal and state-local governments, see Tables 1–1, 1–2, and 1–3 in Chapter 1.

Table 15–3 *State Government Expenditures and Taxes, Selected States, Fiscal 1984*

State	Tax per Capita	Expenditure per Capita	Taxes As a Percentage of Personal Income of State
Alabama	$ 678	$1,301	7.4%
California	1,000	1,745	7.7
Delaware	1,162	1,976	9.3
Florida	668	940	5.9
Indiana	735	1,167	7.0
Michigan	944	1,693	8.2
Missouri	610	1,051	5.6
New Hampshire	433	1,155	3.7
New York	1,061	2,025	8.2
Texas	615	1,056	5.4
All states	$ 836	$1,492	7.2%

Source: U.S. Department of Commerce, Bureau of the Census, *State Government Finances in 1984* (Washington, D.C.: U.S. Government Printing Office, 1985), Tables 4 and 6.

$1,162 in Delaware; the national average was $836. Expenditures per capita are much higher (recall that charges and miscellaneous and federal grants also finance state expenditures), but there is still wide variation. New York leads the way with per capita expenditures of $2,025, more than double those of Florida. Some of this variation simply reflects the fact that average per capita incomes are higher in some states, so it is not surprising to find per capita expenditures and taxes higher in those states. Yet even when we consider taxes as a percentage of personal income, there is still considerable variation as shown in the last column of Table 15–3. State taxes range from 3.7 percent of personal income in New Hampshire to a high of 9.3 percent in Delaware.

Even greater differences are found among lower levels of government. Table 15–4 shows taxes and expenditures per capita for selected cities with populations of 50,000 or more in 1983. Bloomington, Indiana, and Gainesville, Florida, are apparently tax havens, with taxes per capita of $104 and $123, respectively. (These are city taxes only.) By contrast, New York City clearly deserves its reputation as a high-tax city, since its taxes per capita are $1,351.

The diversity in tax and expenditure policies among subnational governments is quite important. If all subnational governments chose identical policies, there would be little reason to have a multitude of different governments.

Table 15–4   *Taxes and Expenditures per Capita, Fiscal 1984, Selected Cities with Population 50,000 or More*

City	Tax per Capita	Expenditure per Capita
Montgomery, Alabama	$ 218	$ 326
Los Angeles, California	346	618
Hartford, Connecticut	764	1,921
Gainesville, Florida	123	500
Decatur, Illinois	164	306
Bloomington, Indiana	104	364
Boston, Massachusetts	628	1,606
Albuquerque, New Mexico	219	857
New York City, New York	1,351	2,603
Austin, Texas	262	783

Source: U.S. Department of Commerce, Bureau of the Census, *City Government Finances in 1983–1984* (Washington, D.C.: U.S. Government Printing Office, 1985), Table 6.

Economic Advantages of Subnational Governments

To some people, it is an article of faith that a local government will perform more efficiently than a state government will, and a state government more efficiently than the federal government will.[2] Other people believe the opposite. Actually, what requires emphasis is that some governmental functions are more efficiently performed by lower levels of government, whereas other functions are carried out better by the federal government. For some types of policies, local government is better, but care is needed in determining exactly what policies are more suitable for local governments.

In our earlier discussion of market failure, we defined public goods and externalities and showed the potential efficiency gains from government policies. It is now time to recognize that there are frequently geographic or spatial dimensions to the provision of public goods. Consider, for example, the public provision of a police force in Richmond, Virginia. This provides benefits to virtually all Richmond residents, but very few benefits accrue to residents of Charlottesville, Virginia, and even fewer benefits, if any, to residents of College Station, Texas. There are *nonrival* benefits from the police force in Richmond, but they do not extend over the entire U.S. population. Instead, the benefits are concentrated mainly on people living in or near Richmond and diminish rapidly as one moves farther away.

[2]This section and the following one draw heavily on Wallace E. Oates, *Fiscal Federalism* (New York: Harcourt Brace Jovanovich, 1972), Chapter 1.

Such a public good, with benefits concentrated geographically, is referred to as a local public good, as distinguished from a national public good such as national defense. Similarly, there are local externalities such as the pollution of a particular lake or stream. Note that whether a good is a "local" or "national" public good is really a matter of degree. Not all "local" public goods benefit only those who live in a specific locality (tourists and shoppers in Richmond may benefit from police protection in that city), and not all "national" public goods benefit everyone in the nation. Still, the benefits from some goods are far more limited geographically, and that is the essential point.

With respect to the provision of local public goods, it is possible for different communities to provide different levels of output. This is also true of other governmentally provided services that are not, strictly speaking, public goods at all. Because the preferences of residents are likely to vary from one community to another, a federal system of government makes it possible for consumption levels to vary with the preferences of residents. A community that wants (and is willing to pay for) a strong police force but no parks can have such a pattern of services without interfering with another community that prefers the opposite pattern of services. Thus, a federal system is capable of greater efficiency than is a system that provides the same level of government services to all citizens. In principle, a federal system of many subnational governments is able to provide a range of outputs that correspond more closely to differing preferences among communities than could a national government.

Figure 15–1 illustrates this advantage of subnational governments. Suppose there are three communities, A, B, and C, and a local public good, X. The curves A_1A_2, B_1B_2, and C_1C_2 show the distribution of quantities of X preferred by the residents of each community. If a national government were to provide a uniform level of X to all communities, it would probably supply a level near the overall median at X_B. This equilibrium would be very unsatisfactory for those residents of communities A and C whose preferences are at the A_1 and C_2 tails of their respective distributions. By contrast, if we have independent governments in the communities, three different levels of output, for example, X_A, X_B, and X_C, would be provided. Community C, whose residents have a large demand for X, would thus get a larger output than would community A, with its smaller demand. This range of outputs possible when X is provided by local governments is likely to be more efficient than is a uniform level of output supplied by a national government.

In comparing the uniform level of provision, X_B, for all communities with different levels for the three communities, note that not all persons will be better off under the latter. In particular, residents of communities A and C whose preferences place them near the A_2 and C_1 tails of their respective distributions will be worse off when X_A and X_C are provided than when X_B

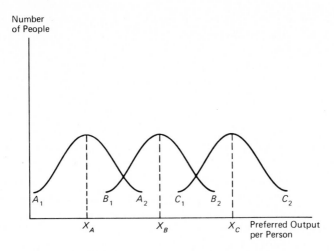

FIGURE 15–1 *Provisions of services by subnational governments.*

is. This point brings us to a second major advantage of a federal system: People are free to move from one community to another. In a federal system, it is possible for people to shop around for the community whose tax and expenditure policies are the best suited to their needs. Persons in community A who prefer X_B more than X_A (whose preferences are close to A_2) can move from community A to community B. In this way, an element of individual choice among various combinations of government policies is possible, an option that is not possible for federal policies.[3]

As a result of consumer mobility, one would ultimately expect residents of communities to have similar tastes for government policies. Some communities will emphasize good public schools and attract families with school-age children. Others will stress security and hospitals and tend to attract retired persons, and still others may emphasize low taxes (and government services) for those who prefer private goods to government services. This process of consumers' choosing places of residence in response to differences in governmental services enhances the efficiency advantages of subnational governments. Of course, this process does not guarantee that every person will obtain exactly the type of government he or she would prefer. Within each community there will still be differences of opinion. Moreover, many factors in addition to government policies influence a person's choice of a location: The availability of jobs, proximity to friends and relatives, climate, and other factors play a role in a locational decision. Nonetheless, the

---

[3] This advantage of a federal system was first stressed by Charles Tiebout in "A Pure Theory of Local Expenditure," *Journal of Political Economy,* 64:416 (Oct. 1956).

possibility of "voting by foot" clearly enhances to some degree the attractiveness of a federal system as an institutional arrangement for providing government services.

A further advantage is that local government may be more responsive to the needs of its citizens. The political process in smaller government units may be more efficient than in larger units. Logrolling and pressure groups constitute less of a problem, and voters are likely to be more knowledgeable about how their tax dollars are spent. In short, when government is "closer to the people," it may possess fewer inherent defects as a decision-making mechanism. It is not entirely obvious that this is always true, but it is widely believed to be so.

Finally, experimentation and innovation are likely to be greater in a federal system. With thousands of local governments, some are certain to be experimenting with new policies that are quite different from those used by the bulk of communities. Different approaches to police investigation, instruction in schools, and environmental policies will be tried. This process of experimentation can be beneficial even if some of the new policies prove to be failures. A successful policy innovation in one community can be adopted by other communities. If a new policy fails, other communities benefit from that knowledge too and can avoid a similar error.

It is not an easy matter, however, to determine whether a new policy is a "success" or a "failure." (Indeed, since preferences of citizens differ among communities, a policy that is successful for one community might be judged a failure by another community.) Nonetheless, a federal system provides the raw material for more direct comparisons among different policy approaches than is possible in a system in which one policy (of a particular type) applies to everyone. As an example, Campbell and Campbell compared the fiscal systems of Vermont and New Hampshire. Although taxes as a percentage of personal income are 50 percent higher in Vermont, the Campbells found no evidence that public services are any better.[4] This conclusion is understandably controversial (especially among government officials in Vermont), but the important point is that a federal system makes such comparisons possible.

In summary, a system of subnational governments possesses a number of advantages. Communities can provide different levels and combinations of services more in line with the preferences of their citizens, and citizens are free to move to communities that they feel are doing a better job. The political process may be more efficient at the subnational level. Experimentation and innovation are more likely, and direct comparisons among different approaches to economic problems are facilitated.

---

[4]Colin D. Campbell and Rosemary G. Campbell, *A Comparative Study of the Fiscal Systems of New Hampshire and Vermont, 1940–1974* (The Wheelabrator Foundation, 1976).

Economic Disadvantages of Subnational Governments

Despite its advantages, a system of subnational governments is likely to be ineffective in resolving certain policy issues. For example, if local governments are relied on to provide national public goods, the result is certain to be substantial inefficiency. Each community would be responsible for its own defense against foreign aggression, but all communities taken together would probably be underdefended. The reason is that a large part of the benefits from, for example, a missile system provided by one community accrue to residents of other communities. In determining how much to spend on missiles, each community would consider only the benefits its residents receive and ignore the benefits to nonresidents. The free rider phenomenon is relevant here, just as it is when we consider whether an individual has incentive to contribute to the financing of a good that benefits other persons in addition to himself or herself. Because each community has incentive to free ride, fewer resources would be devoted to defense than is justified by the interests of all persons in the nation considered together.

Efficient provision of a public good that benefits persons in all communities thus necessitates a central government. The key issue here is the geographic area over which persons necessarily benefit from provision of the good. Some goods, such as a sewer system or a police force, have benefits that extend over a limited area, and a city or county government can supply the good more efficiently, because most, if not all, of the benefits and costs occur within one locality. Some environmental policies may have effects over larger regions and require state governments, but defense is clearly the province of the federal government. Thus, subnational governments will not be efficient in providing all types of government services.

A second area in which subnational governments will be relatively ineffective is in redistributing income. If one community embarks on a redistributive program by taxing its higher-income residents and transferring the proceeds to its poorer residents, two things will happen eventually to hinder the goal of providing assistance to the poor. First, wealthy residents can move to another community where taxes are lower. Second, poor persons in other areas can move to the community providing higher welfare benefits. As a result, the average per capita income in the community will fall, and it will become increasingly difficult to finance high welfare benefits.

Thus, *the very consumer mobility that is beneficial when subnational governments engage in nonredistributive programs tends to limit their use of redistributive measures.* This remains true even if those with higher incomes genuinely wish to help the poor. Each wealthy individual who leaves a community has a negligible effect on the extent to which the poor are helped, and so it is in each person's interest to leave. If all wealthy persons leave, of course, there can be no redistribution. This is simply the free rider problem once again.

Any significant degree of income redistribution must be carried out by a central government. Even in this case, there are limits, because wealthy persons can always leave the country, and poorer immigrants may be permitted to enter. Mobility, however, is far more restricted between countries than between regions within a country, so a national government has greater latitude in carrying out redistributive programs. Moreover, insofar as our concern is with poor persons, regardless of where they reside within the nation, only a national program is capable of accommodating this goal by helping the poor in all regions.

This does not mean that local governments cannot adopt policies that benefit some residents at the expense of others, because they obviously do, but there are limits. In addition, the redistribution that occurs often takes a form that cannot be avoided by moving from the region. If a heavy property tax is placed on land owned by a wealthy person, the landowner cannot fully avoid the burden by selling the land; the sale price will be reduced because the buyer will pay less for heavily taxed property. The immobility of property, especially land, makes it possible for local governments to engage in some redistribution, but still only to a limited degree.

A third policy area in which subnational governments are relatively inefficient is in the pursuit of macroeconomic objectives. Although our primary concern here is not macroeconomics, it should be pointed out that subnational governments have little effect on employment and price levels within a specific region. These governments have no power to change the money supply, and any fiscal policies would be greatly diluted through the movement of persons and goods across jurisdictional boundaries.[5] The national government must assume the responsibility for macroeconomic stabilization policy.

Certain government functions can therefore best be performed by a central government. Although we have been referring to the "advantages" and "disadvantages" of subnational governments, it should be clear that it is not necessary to choose between total reliance on one form of government or another. Instead, the real issue should be to determine which functions are best carried out by local governments and which by the national government. The "optimal" system is obviously one that relies on both types of government, with each performing the functions it does best. Our discussion should provide some guidance in determining what level of govern-

---

[5]The proper division of responsibilities between national and subnational governments is stressed by Wallace E. Oates in "The Theory of Public Finance in a Federal System," *Canadian Journal of Economics,* 1:37 (Feb. 1968).

ment is best suited for the performance of different types of policies. Still, there are many "in-between" cases that do not fit neatly into the categories we have considered. Some examples are discussed later in this chapter.

Tax and Expenditure Analysis

Principles

In earlier chapters we considered general principles pertaining to the analysis of expenditure and tax programs. Many of the points made remain relevant when we turn to the consideration of the fiscal activities of subnational governments. We still wish to ascertain, for example, how policies affect the distribution of income and the allocation of resources. In the context of subnational government policies, however, the framework of analysis is more complicated. Our earlier models entirely disregarded locational aspects of government policies. For national policies, this is generally appropriate: Where a business chooses to operate or where a consumer chooses to live, work, or purchase products is generally not influenced by a national policy. Instead, emphasis is placed on the level of output, consumption, or work effort, because locational decisions are not affected. On the other hand, when local government policies are considered, locational decisions must be incorporated into the analysis. Decisions by businesses about where to operate or where to sell as well as consumers' choices of where to live and work may be affected and so need to be considered explicitly.

Local government jurisdictions are generally "open" economies in the sense that movement of persons and goods across jurisdictional boundaries is prevalent. In this sense, they are much like small countries engaging in international trade with neighboring countries. Goods produced in one locality are often sold ("exported") to persons in another locality, and residents often purchase ("import") goods produced elsewhere. The policies of local governments can often influence the flow of goods and services, as well as people and productive capital, across government boundaries.

If we could assume that people and productive resources were completely immobile among government jurisdictions, most of our earlier analysis would remain valid. For some specific problems, it may be reasonable to assume such immobility, not because people are unable to move, but because many policies have little *net* impact. To take an example, if a community raises taxes to finance better public schools, how will this affect locational decisions? If only the improved school system is considered, an incentive for families with children to move into the community has been created. At the same time, however, the higher taxes considered alone create an incentive for people to move away. With these two opposing influences, what will the net effect be? It is entirely possible that little or no net movement of people to or from the locality will occur: the *net* attractiveness of the community as a place of residence may remain unchanged. If this is the case, an analysis that ignores locational decisions will be a reasonable approach.

This highly simplified example suggests one important general principle: It is especially important to consider both sides of the budgets of local government policies in determining whether locational decisions will be affected. A balanced-budget approach to the study of local taxes and expenditures is frequently essential. It would be a mistake to conclude that a community with better public services is a more attractive place to live; it will also have higher taxes so it will be more attractive only to those who consider the better services worth the additional tax cost.

Thus, in some situations there may be little net effect on locational decisions from local government policies. The difficulty, however, is to determine in what situations this is likely to be true. Just because the government spends and taxes more, it does not follow that no business or person will be led to relocate. For some individuals, the tax increase may impose costs in excess of the benefits derived from the expenditure, and the community will become a less attractive place. This will be true, for example, for people without children when school spending increases. The opposite may be true for other persons. In other words, it is not only the total benefits and costs for the community as a whole but also the pattern of individual benefits and costs that is relevant to locational decisions.

These remarks suggest that there may be a tendency for local governments to provide benefits to individual taxpayers in proportion to taxes paid. To see why, consider what would happen to a community that provided superb schools out of property taxes levied on all families. Clearly, families without children would be paying taxes and receiving no benefits. They would leave the community, and only those who wanted and were willing to pay the required taxes would stay. Thus, the community would end up with those who felt the schools were at least worth their tax cost. Alternatively, to avoid the departure of dissatisfied taxpayers, the community could use some of the tax revenue to provide services to those without children. In either case, the end result would be that all families received benefits roughly in line with their tax costs. This conclusion reflects the difficulty that local governments have in redistributing income, that is, in using taxes from some people to provide benefits to other people. As suggested earlier, there is probably only a weak tendency of this sort, but it does perhaps have some effect on expenditure and tax patterns of subnational government units.

Locational decisions are emphasized basically because they represent the one really new element in the study of state and local government finances. Efficiency requires not only appropriate output decisions but also appropriate locational decisions—and the latter are more strongly affected by policies of subnational governments than by policies of the federal government. As an example, an excise tax at the national level only reduces output, but at the local level it can have additional effects. Consider an excise tax on liquor in one state. A consumer may stock up in a neighboring state or city where liquor is untaxed or less heavily taxed. The cost of time and transportation is then a welfare cost of the local excise tax—a distortion that is quite different from, and in addition to, that produced by a federal excise tax.

Clearly, the analysis of the expenditure and tax policies of subnational governments can be complicated. Although much of our analysis in earlier chapters remains valid, this analysis must sometimes be amended to incorporate influences on locational decisions. There are no simple rules to lead us to the correct conclusions in all cases. Perhaps the best advice is simply always to consider how locational decisions will be affected by any policy being examined.

The mobility of goods and services across governmental boundaries is also relevant, because of what it implies for price elasticities of supply and demand for various products and inputs. In general, price elasticities are likely to be higher when submarkets within particular localities are considered. For example, if the price received by producers of ball-point pens in Michigan is reduced sharply by a tax (and the price is unchanged in other states), pen producers have an incentive to leave Michigan. This suggests a high price elasticity of supply within the state. Similarly, if a retail sales tax raises consumer prices sharply in some city, sales will fall significantly as consumers shop in other communities or by mail, implying a high price elasticity of demand.

High price elasticities have important implications for the tax and expenditure policies adopted by subnational governments. Price elasticities are not, however, high for all products and inputs. For example, land cannot move (it is in perfectly inelastic supply), and structures cannot move in the short run. Thus, it is not surprising that local governments rely heavily on property taxes as a source of revenue. Similarly, Texas and Oklahoma have been able to tax oil production at high rates without fear of their tax base's migrating to another state.

The birth of an (illegal) industry[6]

Both state and local governments frequently impose excise taxes, and cigarettes are among the most important items that are most often subjected to these taxes. If all tax rates on cigarettes were the same, the effects would be the same as for a national excise tax, as analyzed in Chapter 10, except that

---

[6]This section draws on Carl P. Simon and Ann D. Witte, *Beating the System: The Underground Economy* (Boston: Auburn House, 1982), Chapter 2.

revenue would accrue to states approximately in proportion to the cigarette consumption in each state. States, however, have chosen to tax cigarettes at different rates, and the result is a substantial variation in cigarette prices from state to state.

The differences in cigarette prices among states has other consequences too; namely, to create incentives for consumers in high-tax states to take advantage of the lower prices in low-tax states. One common way for consumers to react to the cigarette tax differential is to load up on cigarettes when they travel in low-tax states. This type of activity is probably a minor problem, since few consumers regularly travel from New York (a high-tax state) to North Carolina (a low-tax state). More enterprising individuals, however, have found a way to take advantage of economies of scale in transportation and operate on a larger scale by smuggling cigarettes by the truckload. All that is necessary is to rent a truck, drive to a low-tax state, and purchase cigarettes from a legitimate cigarette wholesaler or retailer. After the individual returns to a high-tax state, the cigarettes are sold to wholesalers or retailers there. Although it is illegal, this activity can be quite profitable. For example, it is possible for the cigarette smuggler to make $5,000 per trip on the New York–North Carolina run using a 1-ton panel truck.

The incentive to engage in cigarette smuggling is related to the spread in tax rates between states. Smuggling on a large scale was not a serious problem in the 1950s when the tax rate differences were relatively small. By 1965, however, state tax rates on cigarettes varied between $0 and $0.09 a pack, and that offered an opportunity for substantial profit. Apparently, the cigarette smuggling industry began to grow rapidly in the 1960s. By 1976, the differential in tax rates had widened even more, ranging from $0.02 a pack in North Carolina to $0.21 a pack in Massachusetts and Connecticut, spurring greater growth in cigarette smuggling. It is estimated that over 2 billion packs of cigarettes were smuggled in 1975. One expert suggests that cigarette smuggling is second only to selling narcotics as a source of funds to organized crime.[7] Naturally, such estimates of the extent of illegal activity must be recognized to be subject to considerable error, but the evidence suggests that cigarette smuggling is a big business.

Although the price elasticity of demand for cigarettes is low, it is not low for sales within a single state when the price there differs greatly from that in other states. The extent of cigarette smuggling is evidence of this. Legal sales of cigarettes in high-tax states have fallen sharply, at an estimated cost in lost revenue of $391 million in 1975. Conversely, tax revenues in three (low-tax) states (Kentucky, New Hampshire, and North Carolina) have increased significantly, since the smugglers purchase most of their cigarettes there.

---

[7]Morris Weintraub, "The Bootlegging of Cigarettes Is a National Problem," *1966 Proceedings of the National Tax Association,* pp. 21–22.

Evaluation of this side effect of state tax policies is difficult, since some states gain and others lose. From a national point of view, there is a loss in state tax collections, but in part this is just a transfer of income to consumers and smugglers. To the extent that the smugglers' transportation costs are no higher than the legal transportation costs, there is no welfare cost on this score, and there could actually be a welfare gain if the effective price spread between states were narrowed as a result of the smuggling. But the enforcement costs of government and the costs that smugglers incur to avoid apprehension should not be ignored.

From the viewpoint of the individual states, however, cigarette smuggling should serve as a warning: Taxing goods that are easily transported across state boundaries at rates higher than those of other states may produce little revenue and a great deal of illegal activity.

Washington, D.C., learns a lesson

In August 1980 city officials of Washington, D.C., hard-pressed for tax revenues, levied a 6 percent excise tax on the sale of gasoline. This tax was added to an already existing $0.10-per-gallon tax. As a result of the added 6 percent levy, the price of gasoline rose by about 6 percent in Washington, making it well above the gasoline prices in the neighboring Virginia and Maryland suburbs.

Not surprisingly, except perhaps to officials in Washington, the higher price of gasoline in Washington led many motorists to fill their tanks outside the city limits. Within three months, the amount of gasoline sold in Washington had fallen by 33 percent. With a 6 percent price increase producing a 33 percent quantity reduction, the implied price elasticity of demand was about 5.5—and this was only the short-run response. (By contrast, the nationwide price elasticity of demand has been estimated to be in the 0.5 to 1.5 range.) Additional tax revenue produced by the 6 percent tax fell well below expectations. Although the 6 percent tax added to the earlier $0.10 per gallon levy represented an 80 percent increase in the tax rate, tax revenues went up only by about 20 percent because of the sharp reduction in quantity. In the longer run, it is quite possible that gasoline tax revenues might actually have declined. For this particular tax, the 6 percent rate increase was apparently enough to move the city close to the revenue-maximizing point on the Laffer curve. (Recall that with high elasticities of demand and/or supply, relatively low tax rates can place you on the upper part of the Laffer curve.)

The 6 percent gasoline tax was repealed in Washington, D.C., in December 1980. At that time Mayor Marion Barry cited "overwhelming evidence" that the tax had not worked and that it had "caused undue hardship both on the consumers of gas . . . and those who operate retail gas businesses."[8]

[8]"Barry Asks Gasoline Tax Repeal," *Washington Post,* Nov. 25, 1980, p. A1.

Special Topics in State-Local Public Finance

Tax competition

It is helpful to think of subnational governments as being in competition with one another. They provide public services to their residents in return for taxes. Because all communities do this, each community must offer its public services on terms sufficiently attractive to induce people and business to locate there. If any community provided deplorable services in return for exorbitant taxes, it would find its tax base eroding as people moved elsewhere. Each community is therefore subject to competition from other subnational governments. Just as with competition among private business firms, we would normally expect competition among governmental units to have a beneficial influence by inducing communities to provide a mix of services in line with the preferences of its citizens.

It is sometimes held, however, that one aspect of the competition among governmental units leads to inefficient results. Business investment in a community may be deterred by an excessive level of taxation; consequently, government officials are often reluctant to increase taxes for fear of driving away part of their tax base. Competition among neighboring communities may lead to holding down taxes to maintain a favorable climate for business. Many local government officials believe this "tax competition" results in suboptimal expenditures, arguing that "tax competition enters into the war between communities for new industrial and commercial activities; each competing community avoids making otherwise justified tax increases for fear of decreasing its attractiveness to new business."

This oversimplified view of tax competition ignores the expenditure side of the budget. If a tax increase is "justified," then the benefits from expanding public expenditures will exceed the costs of higher taxes. How could providing net benefits to the community make it less attractive to business? Generally, one would expect just the opposite. It is possible, however, that the tax increase exceeds the benefits that go to business; the increased expenditures may be on public schools, for example. If this is so, however, then the community is really attempting to redistribute income from business (more specifically, its owners or consumers) to other groups. As we have already seen, subnational governments are constrained in their ability to redistribute income.

If a tax increase is really worthwhile, it should be possible for the local government to raise taxes without driving business away. There are at least two ways to accomplish this. The first is to levy the taxes on the beneficiaries of the proposed expenditure policy. Taxes on business would then be increased commensurate with any benefits received. This approach may be difficult in practice if the government is legally constrained in the form of taxes it may use. For example, it may not be possible to increase property tax rates on homeowners to finance better schools without also increasing business property tax rates. In this case, the second approach may be followed: Combine the school expenditure with another policy that directly benefits business (police services, utilities, highways, and so on). Then business, paying higher taxes and receiving commensurate benefits, will not be driven from the community by the higher tax rates.

In principle, tax competition is no barrier to efficiency in local government operations. In fact, it is a spur to efficiency because it forces government officials to keep benefits in line with the taxes paid. It will inhibit localities, however, if they wish to tax some groups in order to finance benefits for other groups, a desirable limitation insofar as redistribution is intrinsically a function of the national government. It is understandable that local government officials do not like tax competition, but the public is probably better off because of the discipline it enforces.

"Impure" local public goods

When considering public services provided by subnational governments, we saw that these services are sometimes local public goods with benefits limited to a certain geographic area. A further distinction should also be made. A good can have nonrival benefits for the residents of a certain area, but the benefits per person may depend on the number of persons in the area. If so, it is called an impure local public good. A comparison between weather forecasting and police protection should clarify this distinction. A weather forecast for a particular geographic area provides nonrival benefits for residents of that area. Moreover, more people can enter the area and benefit from the forecast without reducing the benefits to the original residents. The weather forecast is a "pure" local public good.

A police force is clearly different. If more people move into the area, police services will be spread more thinly over a larger population, and so the benefits for the original residents from a given police force will decline. (It is sometimes said that this type of good is subject to "congestion costs" from an increased population.) The benefits are still nonrival for the population, but in this case the individual benefits depend on both the size of the police force and the number of people in the area. A police force is thus an "impure" local public good. It is clear that most of the services provided by local governments are more appropriately described as "impure" rather than "pure" local public goods. Fire stations, sewer services, and public schools are clearly "impure" in the sense that the larger the population is, the smaller the benefits per person will be for a given size facility.

There are important implications for the functioning of a system of subnational governments because of the prevalence of impure local public goods. Consumer mobility may be a mixed blessing in this setting. We have stressed that a person may move from community A to community B when the individual prefers the mix of public policies in the latter. The person will benefit from the move, but the original residents of commmunity *B* may suffer from the "congestion cost" that the newcomer's presence imposes. When the welfare of all concerned is considered, it is not obvious that the relocation leads to a better allocation of resources on balance.

This discussion, however, ignores one point: When a person moves into a community, the new resident will also normally pay taxes there. For example, the person's taxes may permit the police force to be expanded. If the tax payments are large enough, the expansion in the police force will be sufficient to keep benefits unchanged for the initial residents. The real question is whether the taxes that newcomers contribute to the local treasury are sufficient to cover the costs their presence imposes on the original residents. If so, consumers will take account of the true costs associated with their locational decisions, and consumer mobility will function to enhance the efficiency of a federal system.

Many of the fiscal problems of local governments result from the fact that their tax systems do not require all newcomers to pay taxes commensurate with the cost that their presence imposes on the community. This is because taxes generally are not (and perhaps cannot be) levied in proportion to benefits received. For example, a family with five school-age children may purchase a modest home in a community, thereby contributing a modest sum in property tax revenues but imposing a much larger cost on the school system. To avoid the influx of newcomers who would consume more public services than they pay for through their taxes, many communities adopt restrictions on entry into the community. These restrictions take the form of zoning ordinances, limitations on the type of home that can be built, and so on. Although these restrictions are, in principle, inferior to taxing persons in proportion to the costs they impose on the other residents, they can contribute to efficiency when such a tax system cannot be implemented. Unfortunately, these restrictive practices can also be used to serve other ends.

Benefit "spillovers"

Local government spending programs undertaken in one locality will sometimes confer benefits on residents outside its political jurisdiction. This phenomenon is called a *benefit spillover,* because some of the benefits of the local expenditure policy "spill over" onto other localities. This is actually just a form of external benefit, but the literature on federalism uses the term *spillover,* presumably to emphasize its geographic aspect.

Pollution programs adopted by one subnational government often create benefit spillovers for people residing outside the community. If actions are taken to reduce pollution in a river and the river passes through a number of communities, persons residing in communities downstream will benefit from pollution-abatement programs adopted by an upstream community. Similarly, a welfare program adopted in one region will benefit the non-poor in other regions if the nonpoor care about the degree of poverty in all regions of the country. These two examples illustrate how people living outside a community can benefit from the community's policies without bearing any cost. Consumer mobility among localities gives rise to a some-what different type of benefit spillover. A person may reside in one area but purchase goods or work in another. Thus, tourists or shoppers will benefit from the police and highway services of a town they only visit. In this case, too, nonresidents receive some benefit, at no cost, from the expenditure programs of a community.

Benefit spillovers are significant for much the same general reason as external benefits are. The political process in a community is likely to be influenced only by the benefits received by its own residents. Local voters, in determining how large an expenditure to approve, will consider only the benefits they receive and disregard the benefits accruing to outsiders. Con-sequently, when benefit spillovers are substantial, expenditures are likely to be too small, because they will reflect only the preferences of residents and not all those who benefit from the policy.

Benefit spillovers often occur because the geographic range of benefits does not precisely coincide with the political boundaries of government jurisdictions. One way to deal with them, therefore, is to define political boundaries in terms of the area over which benefits accrue. Unfortunately, this would generally require a different boundary for each of many govern-ment expenditure programs. Imagine, for example, having a regional gov-ernment to deal with pollution, a government encompassing a smaller area to provide police services, a still different one for schools, and so on. When the administrative and decision-making costs of operating so many overlap-ping governments are considered, it seems clear that this approach is far from ideal. In any event, political boundaries have been determined histor-ically and must, for most purposes, be taken as fixed.

Thus, benefit spillovers are to a degree inevitable. Because they imply some inefficiency in local expenditure decisions, this raises the question of whether the inefficiency can or should be avoided in some way. Several approaches are possible. One is to do nothing. If only a small share of benefits accrues outside the community, the magnitude of the inefficiency will be small (for the reasons discussed in connection with the measure-ment of welfare costs).[9] A second approach is to rely on voluntary negotia-tion among governmental units. Because an inefficiency implies the possi-bility of mutual benefits from coordinated action, neighboring communities often have incentives to jointly undertake programs. When the number of affected communities is small, the "Coase theorem" is relevant; local gov-

[9] See Chapter 10.

ernments themselves have incentives to bargain until an efficient outcome is achieved. Although relatively rare, such bargaining among neighboring governments does occasionally take place.

If the benefit spillovers affect residents in a large number of communities, however, bargaining will be infeasible because of the free rider problem. In that event, it is possible for a higher level of government, such as the federal government, to improve matters by providing grants directly to lower levels of government. Properly designed, these intergovernmental grants can increase expenditures in cases in which benefit spillovers are important. Intergovernmental grants are considered in greater detail later in this chapter.

Tax "exporting"

A portion of the taxes levied by a subnational government is sometimes borne by persons living outside the taxing community. In this event, taxes are said to be "exported" to outsiders. There are a number of ways in which locally levied taxes can have an incidence that places part of the tax burden on nonresidents. For example, an excise tax on a product produced in one locality but purchased by consumers in other parts of the country can achieve this result. (Care must be taken, however, not to tax the product so heavily that production will shift to another locality.) Similarly, the property tax may be applied to property owned by nonresidents that places a burden on outsiders. This is commonly the result of business property taxation.

The federal government also facilitates tax exporting through provisions in its income tax laws. For taxpayers who itemize, certain state and local taxes are deductible in computing federal income tax liability. Thus, when a locality levies a tax on its residents their federal tax payments are automatically reduced. For persons in the 40 percent federal tax bracket, for example, $1 in local taxes costs them only $0.60 because their federal tax falls by $0.40. This loss of $0.40 in available federal revenues is a burden on taxpayers throughout the country, so part of the local tax is effectively exported to federal taxpayers in general. In the same manner, the federal income tax exempts interest on the bonds issued by subnational governments. This allows local governments to issue debt at lower interest cost; local taxpayers pay smaller taxes to finance interest payments on locally issued bonds, with the federal government losing revenue, as in the previous case.

There are a number of important consequences of tax exporting. For instance, the true distribution of the burden of locally supplied government services becomes more difficult to identify. Each person is a citizen of many local and/or state government units that export some of their taxes and so will to that extent gain. At the same time each person is likely to bear some of the costs of government services supplied in other regions, because a portion of these costs is exported to him or her. The net effect of these influences on the distribution of the tax burden is quite complex and uncertain.

Tax exporting also has important allocative effects on the tax and expenditure policies of subnational governments. Each local government, for example, has incentives to rely heavily on types of taxes that are borne largely by nonresidents. Some states are quite successful at this. Take Florida, for example. As one tax expert in Florida observed: "We have done an excellent job of shifting a large portion of the tax burden to tourists—the tax system is designed to tax the service industries quite heavily."[10] More subtle effects also occur; states are encouraged to use progressive rather than proportional income taxes, for example. A progressive state income tax places a heavier nominal burden on those in higher federal tax brackets in which the net burden (after the deduction) is not as great.

Expenditure decisions of local governments are also affected. If 30 percent of local taxes are exported, every $1 in expenditures costs local residents only $0.70. The unit price of supplying government services is reduced, and the tax prices of local voters are 30 percent lower. At a lower price, voters will approve larger government expenditures. Expenditures are likely to exceed the point at which marginal benefits equal true marginal costs, because the residents of a community bear only part of the marginal cost.

The tendency to overspend produced by tax exporting may be mitigated by the presence of benefit spillovers. Benefit spillovers taken alone will lead to a suboptimal level of spending, because residents receive only a portion of the true marginal benefits. If benefits spill over to the same degree that taxes are exported, these two distortions, which operate in opposite directions, may exactly offset each other, fortuitously leading the community to make efficient expenditure decisions.[11] Such a fortunate outcome should not be generally expected, because benefit spillovers are restricted to certain policies whereas tax exporting lowers the cost to residents of all expenditure policies.

Unlike benefit spillovers—where virtually nothing is known about the empirical significance of the phenomenon—tax exporting has been the subject of some limited empirical investigation. Charles McLure examined the extent of tax exporting among states, finding that an average of 20 to 25 percent of state tax burdens were borne by nonresidents.[12] For some states,

---

[10] C. H. Donovan, "Recent Developments in Property Taxation in Florida: A Case Study," in Harry L. Johnson, ed., *State and Local Tax Problems* (Knoxville: University of Tennessee Press, 1969), p. 59.

[11] This may be true in some cases with respect to tourists. Tourists often receive government services (e.g., police and highway) when they visit an area. If they bear a tax burden just sufficient to finance the services they enjoy, there is no *net* tax exporting.

[12] Charles E. McLure, Jr., "The Interstate Exporting of State and Local Taxes: Estimates for 1962," *National Tax Journal,* 20:49 (Mar. 1967).

fully 40 percent of the tax burden was exported. Unfortunately, no study has examined the extent of tax exporting for lower levels of government.

John Bowman explored the effect of tax exporting on locally financed school expenditures.[13] He assumed that property taxes on commercial and industrial property were exported, whereas taxes on residential and farm property were not.[14] In a study of independent school districts in West Virginia, Bowman found that the degree of tax exporting was positively related to locally financed school expenditures. A 10 percent increase in the degree of tax exporting was estimated to produce a 15 percent increase in spending, suggesting a relatively high price elasticity of demand. To the extent that school districts would finance efficient levels of school expenditures if they bore all costs, this finding also implies that tax exporting leads to overly large budgets.

Despite its apparent importance, tax exporting has been given scant attention by economists. There has been little emphasis on how the inequities and inefficiencies introduced by this phenomenon could be overcome. Some partial remedies are obvious, such as eliminating the tax subsidies introduced in the federal income tax. Communities could still, however, adopt taxes that imposed some costs on nonresidents. An approach that might be worth considering is for the federal government to require subnational governments to finance all expenditures with a tax that cannot be easily shifted to nonresidents, such as a personal income tax. We leave it as an exercise for the reader to determine what disadvantages this proposal would have.

Intergovernmental Grants

Intergovernmental grants are subsidies from one governmental unit to another. Generally, these grants flow from higher to lower levels of government. In 1984, for example, the federal government made grants of $97 billion to state and local governments, and state governments made grants of $106 billion to local governments, with the bulk earmarked for education. Intergovernmental grants have grown rapidly over recent decades and are now an important source of revenue to lower levels of government, as documented by Table 15–5. Federal grants have increased from $2.5 billion in 1950 to $97 billion in 1984 and represented about one eighth of total federal expenditures in 1984. Table 15–5 also shows the extent of which lower levels of government are dependent on grants as a source of revenue. In 1984, nearly one fourth of total state revenues was in the form of federal

---

[13]John H. Bowman, "Tax Exportability, Intergovernmental Aid, and School Finance Reform," *National Tax Journal,* 27:163 (June 1974).

[14]This is unlikely to be fully true, but it can be argued that property taxes on commercial and industrial property are "hidden taxes" that residents don't realize they bear, even if they do. This would have the same political effects as exported taxes.

Table 15-5 *Intergovernmental Grants, Selected Years (amounts in billions of $)*

Year	Federal Grants to State and Local Governments	Federal Grants As a Percentage of Federal Expenditures	Federal Grants to States As a Percentage of Total State Revenues	State Grants to Local Governments*	Federal Grants to Local Governments	Grants Received by Local Governments As a Percentage of Total Local Revenue
1950	$ 2.5	5.8%	16.4%	$ 4.2	$ 0.2	27.5%
1960	7.0	7.6	19.4	9.5	0.6	27.2
1965	11.0	9.3	20.2	14.0	1.2	28.4
1970	21.9	11.1	21.6	26.9	2.6	33.1
1975	47.1	14.4	23.4	51.1	10.9	38.8
1980	83.0	13.5	22.3	81.2	21.1	39.6
1984	97.1	11.4	24.5	105.8	20.9	34.6

*State grants include substantial amounts of federal funds that are channeled through state governments to localities.

Source: Data for 1950–1975 from Wallace E. Oates, "Fiscal Structure in the Federal System," Table 10–1, in J. Richard Aronson and Eli Schwartz, eds., *Management Policies in Local Government Finance* (Washington, D.C.: International City Management Association, 1981), p. 244. Reproduced with permission of the publisher. Data for 1980 from Department of Commerce, Bureau of the Census, *Government Finances in 1979–80* (Washington, D.C.: U.S. Government Printing Office, Sept. 1981), Tables 4 and 21; data for 1984 from *Government Finances in 1983–84* (Washington, D.C.: U.S. Government Printing Office, Sept. 1985), Tables 4 and 21.

Table 15–6 *Federal Grants to State and Local Governments, Fiscal 1984*

Type of Aid	Amount ($ billions)
Conditional-Categorical Grants	
Income security	$25.7
Health	21.8
Transportation	15.0
Education, training, social services	16.7
Other	13.8
General Revenue Sharing	4.6
Total	$97.6

Source: Executive Office of the President, Office of Management and Budget, *Special Analyses, Budget of the United States Government, 1986* (Washington, D.C.: U.S. Government Printing Office, 1985), Table H-3.

grants, whereas local governments received more than one third of their revenues from federal and state governments.

Intergovernmental grants are of two basic types: conditional and unconditional. With conditional grants the granting government specifies the way in which the funds may be spent by the recipient government; they are similar to in-kind subsidies to governmental units. In contrast, unconditional grants can be spent any way the recipient government chooses.

Intergovernmental grants provide financing for a wide variety of programs. In Table 15–6, which gives a breakdown of federal grants for 1984, note that conditional grants are far larger than unconditional grants. The only major program of unconditional grants at the federal level is general revenue sharing with expenditures of $4.6 billion. Among the conditional grants, grants to finance redistributive programs, income security, and health (primarily Medicaid) account for a large portion of the total grants. Only major categories of federal grants are shown in Table 15–6; actually, there are over 500 separate federal grant-in-aid programs. Many of these are quite small, with total spending on 420 of the smaller programs amounting to only 10 percent of all federal grants.

Conditional grants

Conditional grants must be devoted to certain specified uses. These grants are of two general types, matching and nonmatching. A *nonmatching grant* is a fixed sum; in contrast, the size of the *matching grant* depends on the recipient government's own expenditures on the specified program. For example, a matching grant formula might specify that the federal government contribute 40 percent of the cost and that the state government contribute the remaining 60 percent. As can be seen, a matching grant is really a form of excise subsidy that is applied to government units rather than to individuals. Similarly, a nonmatching grant is a form of fixed quantity subsidy.

The analysis of matching and nonmatching conditional grants closely follows our earlier analysis of excise and fixed quantity subsidies. There is, however, one basic difference: The recipients of conditional grants are government units and not individuals. Thus, the response of the recipient government will reflect the workings of the political processes of the local government. Before the grant, local taxpayers had to pay $100 in taxes to receive school services costing $100 (ignoring tax exporting). With a 60–40 matching grant, local taxpayers can receive the $100 in services at a tax cost of $60, because the federal government contributes the remaining $40. Thus, the tax price of each taxpayer has fallen by 40 percent, and taxpayers will prefer a larger quantity at the lower price. Because all taxpayers will be affected in this way, it seems reasonable to suppose that the local political process will approve greater expenditures under the matching grant. In effect, the matching grant lowers the price of school services to residents of the community, and so they purchase more—but the decision to consume additional units is a political one.

For ease of exposition, it will be assumed that the choices made by the political process of a recipient government can be represented diagrammatically by a set of community indifference curves. (Although this is a heroic assumption, the conclusions of this analysis can be demonstrated using a majority voting model.[15]) These are shown in Figure 15–2 as the CIC curves. The aggregate budget line of the community is MN. In the absence of any grant, X_1 of a particular government service is supplied at a tax cost of MM_3. A matching grant applied to this government service lowers its price to the community, and the budget line shifts to MN'. At the lower price, the community chooses X_3, and the total subsidy from the federal government is $E_1 J$. A nonmatching grant of the same amount will shift the budget line to MM_1N_1. Under the nonmatching grant, the community will select a lower level of the government service, X_2. A nonmatching grant has the same income effect for the community, but it does not lower the per unit price of the service, as does the matching grant. Thus, the matching grant leads to greater output of the government service.[16]

The community is better off with the nonmatching grant—at least in this case in which the nonmatching grant is equivalent to an unconditional grant of MM_2. It should not be thought, however, that every member of the com-

---

[15] David Bradford and Wallace E. Oates, "Towards a Predictive Theory of Intergovernmental Grants," *American Economic Review*, 61:440 (May 1971).

[16] Note that this analysis is formally identical to our discussion of an excise subsidy in Chapter 4. The same qualifications and extensions discussed there apply here also.

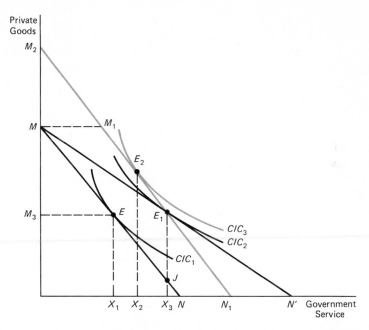

FIGURE 15–2   *Revenue-sharing comparison of matching and non-matching grants.*

munity will prefer the nonmatching grant. Taxpayers who prefer unusually large quantities of the government service will often be better off with a matching grant. In this case, the use of community indifference curves tends to obscure the distributional effects among different members of the community. Nonetheless, the matching grant results in too much output of the government service, at least if the political process functions to attain the efficient output when residents bear the entire marginal cost of supplying additional units.

Evaluation of conditional grants   A major rationale for matching grants is the presence of benefit spillovers. If benefits from a local program accrue to nonresidents, the community may spend too little on its own (ignoring tax exporting). Welfare programs provide a possible example: Assistance provided to the poor by any state may benefit the altruistic nonpoor in other states. Insofar as states are relied on to provide welfare assistance, benefit spillovers provide a rationale for matching grants. In the context of welfare programs, however, the major issue is whether the national interest is sufficiently great to warrant a uniform federal assistance program rather than relying, even partially, on state governments.

To conform to the benefit spillover rationale, federal grants should be matching grants that lower the price to the state, with the federal share being dictated by the percent of program benefits that accrue to nonresidents. For instance, if 20 percent of the benefits are received by nonresidents, lowering the price by 20 percent to the recipient government would be appropriate on efficiency grounds. Under most federal matching grants, however, the federal contribution is subject to a maximum amount, and if the recipient government spends beyond this level, it must bear the entire marginal cost. (Major exceptions to this are most grants for public welfare purposes.) The maximum amounts specified are frequently quite modest, with most states exceeding those levels. This means that grants do not lower the price to recipient governments at the margin and so do not induce them to take the spillover effects associated with the program into consideration. In terms of Figure 15–2, this type of grant produces a kinked budget line like ME_1N_1, and for governments that choose a point along the E_1N_1 portion, the grant is equivalent to an unrestricted cash grant.

An additional question is whether benefit spillovers are really large enough to justify the share of the cost borne by the federal government. Since benefit spillovers can rarely be measured accurately, we are on uncertain ground. Consider, though, that the federal share of interstate highway construction costs is 90 percent; it seems unlikely that 90 percent of the benefits of an interstate highway in a given state go to nonresidents. Moreover, with respect to sewage waste-treatment systems, it seems unlikely that nonresidents receive 75 percent of the benefits; yet that is the federal share of their construction costs. Since in most federal grant programs the federal government's share of the costs is 50 percent or more, we can question whether spillover benefits are generally important enough to justify so large a share.

For these reasons, it is difficult to justify many existing grant programs on the grounds of spillover benefits. In this sense, they are much like in-kind transfers to persons, and much of our discussion of in-kind transfers in Chapter 9 is also applicable to conditional grant programs.

General revenue sharing

After several years of debate, general revenue sharing was instituted by the federal government in 1972. In the latter part of that year, the Treasury Department mailed checks totaling about $2.5 billion to 37,000 state and local governments. (Because Indian tribes are considered governmental units, a check for $26 was sent to the Cortina Rancheria tribe, a tribe with one member.) By 1984, outlays on general revenue sharing had reached $4.6 billion.

The original conception of revenue sharing, as discussed widely in the economics profession in the 1960s, was a simple one. Revenue sharing was to be a system of unconditional grants to state and local governments, with the size of the grants related to population. As actually enacted, revenue

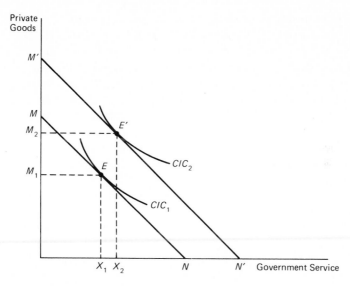

FIGURE 15–3 *Effect of unconditional revenue-sharing grant: Balanced-budget approach.*

sharing was far removed from this simple vision, but our discussion will be simplified if a hypothetical "pure" program is considered first.

In Figure 15–3, a community has a budget line relating private and local government services, as shown by MN. Equilibrium occurs at point E. An unconditional revenue-sharing grant of MM' is given to the community, and the budget line becomes $M'N'$. A new equilibrium occurs at E', with X_2 in government services and M_2 in private goods being selected. Note in particular that local taxes have been reduced from MM_1 to MM_2: The income effect of the grant encourages the community to consume more private goods by reducing local taxes.

So far, this analysis has ignored the effect of the federal taxes used to finance revenue-sharing grants. Because these taxes are collected from persons in the same communities that receive the grants, they should be incorporated into the analysis. Suppose members of this community pay federal taxes equal to the revenue-sharing grant the community receives. Then the before-federal-tax-and-grant budget line would be $M'N'$, and the community would be at point E' in the absence of the program. Federal taxes shift the after-tax budget line to MN, and the revenue-sharing grant shifts the budget line back to $M'N'$. This balanced-budget approach implies that the local community consumes the same level of private goods and government services with revenue sharing as it would without it. There is only one significant change. Before the program, local taxes were $M'M_2$, but after the program, local taxes fall to MM_2, or by $M'M$, whereas federal taxes on residents rise by $M'M$. In other words, federal taxes are substituted for local taxes. Local residents pay the same total taxes, but with revenue sharing, part of the taxes that would have been paid to the local government go to the federal government and then are returned as a revenue-sharing grant.

In contrast with this analysis, many people feel that a pure type of revenue sharing must have some effect on the level of government services; they believe that local governments will view the grant as "free" money and use it fully to expand local government spending. This is conceivable, especially because we are dealing with political processes that may not respond in the same way as an individual would. If true, however, this argument implies that local government political processes are inefficient in a strange way: Why should local residents accept a higher level of government spending than they are willing to pay for with local taxes, just because the taxes first go to Washington and then come back to the community as a grant? It must be stressed that the real opportunities open to the communities, as summarized by the $M'N'$ budget line, are not changed in any way by the program.

In practice, general revenue sharing is more complicated than a set of unconditional grants that are related only to population. The size of the grant received by each subnational government is determined by one of two formulas. (The subnational government can choose whichever formula is more favorable to it.) These formulas make the grants depend not only on population but also on the average tax rate in the state, the extent to which the state relies on personal income taxes, and average per capita income. On balance, poor states probably gain slightly, on the average, but the redistribution among states is somewhat capricious. For example, Washington, D.C. (treated as a state), and New York are the wealthiest and the third wealthiest states, respectively, but their per capita grants are, respectively, the sixth and fifth largest in the nation.

When the taxes that finance general revenue-sharing grants are taken into account, probably no more than 10 percent of the $4.6 billion represents net transfers among states. Although this is a trivial redistribution at current levels of revenue sharing, it raises the question of whether a policy that redistributes income among governmental units is desirable—a question that is also relevant when evaluating conditional grants. Is it better to redistribute income to poor *communities* or to poor *persons?* A redistribution from wealthy to poor communities is a very ineffective way to help poor persons. Not only do communities with low average incomes have some nonpoor residents who would benefit, but also communities with high average incomes have some poor residents who would be harmed. Many would argue that it makes more sense to redistribute income directly to poor persons (as with the NIT) and then leave it up to those individuals to vote for more local government services if they want to use some of their transfer in that way.

Apart from simple redistributive effects, general revenue sharing can have effects on resource allocation. In general, the revenue-sharing formulas reduce somewhat the price of government services to local residents, since a higher average tax rate entitles a state to a larger grant. The incentive to raise local taxes, however, is not generally very large; some states would receive about $5 more in grants by raising their taxes by $100. Another incentive contained in one of the two formulas encourages states to rely more heavily on state income taxes than on other forms of taxation.

Proposal for Reform: End Tax Deductibility

Federal taxpayers have been permitted to deduct state and local taxes on their federal individual income taxes since the income tax was introduced in 1913. Today this deduction represents the second largest deduction. A total of $116 billion in state and local taxes was deducted in 1984, at an estimated revenue cost to the federal government of approximately $38 billion, equal to more than 10 percent of the total federal income tax collections. As this tax preference item has grown in importance over time, more attention has been given to the possibility of eliminating it. Many private analysts have proposed its elimination, and one of the central elements in President Ronald Reagan's 1985 tax reform package was the elimination of the state and local tax deduction.

The original justification for this tax preference was that the taxes paid to state and local governments were not really income to the taxpayers, since the funds were not available to pay federal taxes. Put slightly differently, it was (and still is) argued that a taxpayer should not have to pay a tax on a tax. This argument, however, has come under increasing scrutiny. State and local taxes are the costs that taxpayers pay for receiving services from subnational governments; those who pay larger taxes typically receive more in services. Viewed in this way, state and local taxes are not significantly different from taxpayer expenditures on clothes or food, except that tax payments are determined politically rather than individually. If state and local taxes are viewed as payments for government services (which are income to the recipients whether or not they are in the form of cash), equity calls for disallowing the deduction for state and local taxes.

Of course, this argument is not conclusive, and so let's consider a specific proposal to end tax deductibility. Since eliminating deductibility would increase federal income tax revenue by 10 percent, a careful evaluation requires that we specify how this revenue would be used. For the purposes of this analysis, suppose we assume that the revenue would be used to lower the tax rates of the individual income tax. In other words, we would combine a broader tax base with lower rates so that there would be no net change in federal revenue. This could be done in many ways, but let's assume that all marginal tax rates would be reduced by 10 percent, so the rates would range from 9 to 45 percent rather than over their current range of from 10 to 50 percent.

In analyzing this proposal, we shall proceed in two steps. First, we shall tentatively assume that state and local government tax and expenditure policies are not changed and consider the effects of the change in the federal tax alone. Then we shall examine the implications of the program for the policies of subnational governments.

If the deductibility ends, federal taxpayers will pay higher taxes because of the broader tax base but lower taxes because of the lower rates. Overall, these effects will cancel out each other, but not necessarily for each taxpayer. In particular, it is important to note who uses the state and local tax deduction. In 1982, only 6 percent of taxpayers with adjusted gross incomes below $10,000 used the deduction, but 80 percent of those with incomes between $30,000 and $50,000 did, and more than 90 percent of taxpayers with AGIs above $50,000 deducted state and local taxes.[17] Thus, ending the deduction will increase taxes primarily for upper-income taxpayers, whereas the lower tax rates will reduce taxes for all taxpayers. Taking these two elements of the policy together, it is clear that upper-income taxpayers will lose more when deductibility ends than they will gain from the lower rates, and the reverse will be true at the lower income levels. Thus, the policy will increase the federal tax burden on higher-income taxpayers and reduce it for lower-income taxpayers. However, within the income classes, eliminating the state and local income tax deduction will tend to benefit those who do not itemize, at the expense of those who do.

Much discussion of this proposal tends to end at this point, but we must also consider the response of state and local governments to this change in federal tax policy. As noted earlier in this chapter, the deductibility provision in the federal tax results in subnational governments' exporting part of their taxes to the general federal taxpayer. By lowering the net cost of providing local government services to local taxpayers, deductibility probably increases the spending by state and local governments. Several empirical studies have suggested that state and local spending may be increased by as much as 10 to 20 percent because of deductibility.[18] Thus, eliminating deductibility would reduce state and local spending and also state and local taxes.

A reduction in subnational taxing and spending is relevant for both efficiency and equity. From an efficiency standpoint, if deductibility leads to overexpansion in subnational spending because the local residents do not

---

[17] Thomas R. Dye, "Impact of Federal Tax Reform on State-Local Finances," *The Cato Journal,* 5:597–608 (Fall 1985), Table 3.

[18] See Edward M. Gramlich, "The Deductibility of State and Local Taxes," *National Tax Journal,* 38:447–466 (Dec. 1985); and the other research cited there.

bear all of the costs of their local government spending programs, then eliminating deductibility will improve efficiency. From an equity standpoint, the distributional effects of contractions in subnational taxing and spending must be considered. If subnational taxpayers benefit in proportion to the subnational taxes they pay, then the contractions will not change the distribution of income. However, if state and local government policies tend to redistribute income downward, on balance, as seems likely, a contraction will redistribute income from low-income taxpayers to upper-income taxpayers. Note that this tends to offset the redistribution accomplished at the federal level.

A second possible response by state and local governments is also worth considering: the governments may make their tax systems less progressive (or more regressive). Since deductibility is utilized mainly by high-income taxpayers, state and local governments may place a larger share of their taxes on these taxpayers, knowing that they will only bear part of the cost. In short, deductibility gives subnational governments an incentive to use more progressive tax structures, and so eliminating deductibility will induce them to shift part of their tax burdens to the lower-income classes. This also tends to offset the distributional effect at the federal level.

Now let's put the two parts of the analysis together. At the federal level, eliminating deductibility tends to redistribute income in favor of the lower income classes. However, we now see that the responses of the state and local governments are likely to have the opposite effect. Overall, determining how the elimination of deductibility will affect the distribution of income among income classes is not easy. From the point of view of horizontal equity, there is likely to be a gain from using a broader federal tax base. In addition, there may be an efficiency gain from the reduced spending by state and local governments. There is little doubt, however, that taxpayers who prefer more government spending, particularly if they reside in high-tax states, will lose from the reform. Not surprisingly, Governor Mario Cuomo of New York has led the fight against this reform proposal.

Supplementary Readings

BREAK, GEORGE F. *Financing Government in a Federal System.* Washington, D.C.: The Brookings Institution, 1980.

OATES, WALLACE E. *Fiscal Federalism.* New York: Harcourt Brace Jovanovich, 1972.

———. "Fiscal Structure in the Federal System." In J. Richard Aronson and Eli Schwartz, eds. *Management Policies in Local Government Finance.* Washington, D.C.: Institute for Training in Municipal Administration, 1981.

PHARES, DONALD. *Who Pays State and Local Taxes?* Cambridge, Mass.: Oelgeschlager, Gunn and Hain, 1980.

STIGLER, GEORGE J. "The Tenable Range of Functions of Local Government." In

Edmund S. Phelps, ed. *Private Wants and Public Needs,* rev. ed. New York: W. W. Norton, 1965.

WAGNER, RICHARD E. *The Fiscal Organization of American Federalism.* Chicago: Markham, 1971.

Review Questions and Problems

1. What are the major principles that should be taken into account in deciding whether a particular government function is best handled by the federal government, state government, or local (city or county) government?

2. For each of the following types of economic activities, explain whether it should be carried out by the federal government, state government, local government, or private sector: national defense, police protection, fire protection, medical research, elementary education, college education, welfare, and highway construction.

3. How will the analysis of a general sales tax differ if it is used by a local government rather than by the federal government?

4. "Since cigarettes are in inelastic demand, a tax on cigarettes is a good tax for a state government to use." True or false? Explain.

5. Explain how tax exporting and benefit spillovers affect the spending and taxing decisions of subnational governments.

6. Suppose that a locality increases its property taxes and uses the proceeds to increase spending on public schools. What effects is this likely to have on the locational decisions of households?

7. What policies of the federal government encourage greater spending by subnational governments? What is the rationale for these policies?

8. Sometimes matching grants impose limits on the amount of the subsidy. For example, the federal government might cover half the cost of a certain policy, but only up to $10 million; beyond that, the local government must bear all of the additional cost. How does this type of matching grant affect the budget line of the recipient community?

9. How would a community composed entirely of upper-income households be affected by ending the deductibility of state and local taxes?

10. In the absence of federal tax deductibility, suppose that a local community uses the benefit theory of taxation to distribute the costs of local spending policies (see Figure 2–1 and the discussion there). Then the federal government introduces deductibility, but only a minority of local taxpayers itemize their deductions. Explain how this will affect the community's tax and spending policies, assuming that it continues to apply the benefit theory of taxation.

appendix:
Consumer Choice Theory

FOR students unfamiliar with analysis using budget lines and indifference curves, or those in need of a quick review, this appendix contains some fundamentals.[1] The treatment is brief, with emphasis on certain concepts that are relevant to the analyses developed throughout the text. Our purpose is to present a simple model of consumer behavior that permits us to determine how consumer choices among goods are affected by objective circumstances such as prices, incomes, and subsidies. The goods can be anything—beer, shoes, or public schooling. We begin by explaining the way a consumer's tastes or subjective preferences can be shown using indifference curves, and then we consider how objective conditions such as income can be represented. Next, the consumer's preferences and income are treated jointly in a single model. Finally, several implications of the model are examined.

The Consumer's Preferences

Consumers have different tastes or preferences, which will be reflected in their consumption decisions. The consumption of goods and services provides satisfaction or utility to the consumer, and the consumer will arrange his or her consumption to maximize satisfaction. To understand how the consumer determines what combination of goods will maximize his or her well-being, we begin by making the following assumptions about the consumer's preference patterns:

[1] For a more detailed and comprehensive discussion of indifference curve analysis, see an intermediate microeconomics textbook, for example, S. Charles Maurice, Owen R. Phillips, and C. E. Ferguson, *Economic Analysis* (Homewood, Ill.: Richard D. Irwin, 1986); Edwin Mansfield, *Microeconomics—Theory and Applications* (New York: W. W. Norton, 1985); and Edgar K. Browning and Jacquelene M. Browning, *Microeconomic Theory and Applications* (Boston: Little, Brown, 1986).

1. The consumer is able to rank different combinations or bundles of goods in terms of desirability. For example, suppose the consumer is confronted with three bundles of goods: one hamburger and one beer, three hamburgers and two beers, and two hamburgers and four beers. From among these groupings, the consumer is able to decide whether he or she prefers the third bundle to the second, is indifferent among them, prefers the second to the first, and so on. To say that a consumer is indifferent between two bundles of goods means that either bundle will yield the same level of utility and that the consumer has no preference for one over the other. The consumer will either prefer one bundle to another or be indifferent between them.

2. The consumer's preferences are transitive. If, for instance, there are three bundles of goods, A, B, and C, and the consumer prefers bundle A to bundle B and bundle B to bundle C, then it follows that the consumer will also prefer A to C.

3. The consumer always prefers more of a commodity to less. Referring to the hamburgers and beer in the example, the consumer would always prefer either the second or the third combination to the first, because each of these involves more of both hamburgers and beer than the first alternative does.

Having made these assumptions, we can begin to develop our model.

Indifference curves

Consumer tastes can be represented by indifference curves. To understand this concept, first consider the alternative bundles of goods listed in Table A–1. Assume that the groupings are deliberately arranged so a consumer, Kimberly, is indifferent among them. In Table A–1(a), Kim is equally satisfied with 10 units of food and 1 unit of clothing, or 7 units of food and 2 units of clothing, and so on. Similarly, each of the combinations in Table

---

Table A–1   *Preferences for Food and Clothing*

	(a)		(b)	
	Food	Clothing	Food	Clothing
A:	10	1	13	2
B:	7	2	10	3
C:	5	3	8	4
D:	4	4	7	5
E:	3	6	6	7
F:	2	9	5	10

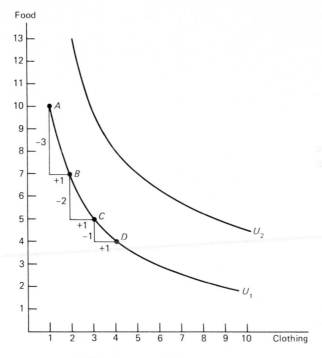

FIGURE A–1   *Indifference curves.*

A–1(b) is as desirable as any other. Note, however, in (b) that with the same quantity of clothing, more food is provided compared with (a). So, given the assumption that the consumer always prefers more to less, any combination in (b) will be preferred to any in (a).

These alternative bundles of goods can be represented as points on indifference curves. An indifference curve is a locus of points indicating different combinations of goods that yield the consumer the same level of satisfaction. In Figure A–1 an indifference curve, U_1, has been drawn to represent the alternative combinations of food and clothing detailed in Table A–1(a). Food consumed per time period is measured on the vertical axis, and clothing consumed per time period on the horizontal axis. Thus, a point such as A represents 10 units of food and 1 unit of clothing. Kim is equally well off consuming any combination of goods shown on U_1.

Indifference curves have the following characteristics:

1. Indifference curves are convex. Typically, an indifference curve is fairly steep at the top and relatively flat at the bottom. Its shape is a function of the relative importance of the two goods to the consumer. Starting at the top of an indifference curve and moving down it, the consumer gives up food for additional units of clothing. At *A,* for instance, Kim has 10 units of food and 1 unit of clothing: at *D* Kim has 4 units of food and 4 units of clothing. Recall that at either point she is equally well off.

At the top of the curve Kim has a substantial amount of food and very little clothing; to move from point *A* to point *B* (less food and more clothing), Kim would be willing to give up 3 units of food for another unit of clothing. As she moves down the curve to the right, however, the situation changes. Kim has relatively more clothing and relatively less food. To move from *C* to *D,* for instance, Kim would be willing to give up a maximum of only 1 unit of food for an extra unit of clothing. If she had more food and less clothing, as at point *A,* Kim would have traded 3 units of food for another unit of clothing, but at point *C* she would be only willing to exchange 1 unit. The rate at which the consumer is willing to trade one good for another (while maintaining the same level of utility) is called the *marginal rate of substitution.*

The marginal rate of substitution *(MRS)* is shown in the diagram by the slope of the indifference curve. At point *A,* for example, the slope is $-3F/1C,$ indicating that the *MRS* at that point is 3 units of food per unit of clothing. Note that the *MRS* is a measure of the subjective value of one good in terms of another. At point *A,* another unit of clothing is worth 3 units of food to Kim, because that is the maximum quantity of food she will give up to acquire another unit of clothing.

Assuming that indifference curves are convex is equivalent to assuming that the *MRS* will decline as we move down an indifference curve; that is, the curve will become flatter, since the slope measures the *MRS.* Basically, this is an empirical proposition regarding the nature of people's preferences. Although it may not always be true, it makes sense as a generalization. It means, for example, that Kim will give up *more* food to get another unit of clothing when she has a great deal of food and very little clothing (as at point *A*) than when she has little food and a large amount of clothing (as at point *C*). At *A,* clothing is relatively scarce, and Kim will give up 3 units of food for another unit of clothing; at *C* she has more clothing and less food, so an additional unit of clothing is less important to her, and she would give up only 1 unit of food for it.

2. Indifference curves that lie farther from the origin represent higher levels of utility or well-being than do those lying closer to the origin. So far only one indifference curve has been discussed. Actually, a complete description of a consumer's tastes would involve an infinite number of indifference curves. Consider Table A–1(b) again. Recall that with all levels of clothing consumption, more food is provided than in Table A–1(a). This combination of goods is represented by the indifference curve U_2 in Figure A–1. Curve U_2 lies farther from the origin than U_1 does and represents a higher level of utility. A utility-maximizing consumer would prefer to consume *any* combination of goods on U_2 to *any* combination

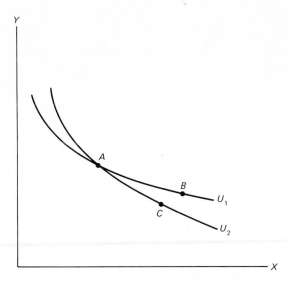

FIGURE A–2 *Intersecting indifference curves.*

on U_1. Whether the consumer is able to consume at the desired higher level is determined by his or her income and the prices of the two goods, factors that will be considered shortly.

3. Indifference curves cannot intersect. If indifference curves intersected, our assumption of transitivity would be violated. Figure A–2 is drawn *incorrectly* so that two indifference curves cross. Let's examine the implications. Indifference curves U_1 and U_2 intersect at A. On curve U_1, points A and B yield the same level of satisfaction to the consumer, because they lie on the same indifference curve. The same is true for points A and C on U_2. Therefore, C is as desirable as A, and A is as desirable as B. This seems to imply that C and B are equally desirable. Note, however, that point B is clearly preferable to C, because B contains more X and Y than point C does—and we have assumed that the consumer always prefers more to less. Point B cannot be preferred to C and have the same utility as C. Thus, intersecting indifference curves are inconsistent with our assumptions.

The Consumer's Budget

When using indifference curves to explain and predict consumer behavior, we must know more than the consumers' tastes. Because higher indifference curves correspond to higher levels of well-being, a rational utility-maximizing consumer will want to achieve the highest indifference curve *possible*. In maximizing well-being, however, the consumer is constrained by the level of money income. To want a villa on the French Riviera is not the same as being able to afford it. Even the wealthiest individuals have budget or income constraints, because their income is not infinite. In addition to money income, the consumer must consider the prices of all relevant commodities. Price changes as well as changes in the level of the consumer's income will affect consumption patterns.

The budget line

Let's begin by assuming that our consumer, Kim, has an income of $1,000 per year and that she is considering the purchase of two goods, X and Y, with the price of X, $5 per unit, and the price of Y, $10 a unit. If Kim spent her entire income on X, she could purchase 200 units ($1,000/$5); if she spent her entire income on Y, she could purchase 100 units ($1,000/$10). In Figure A–3, the straight line MN connecting 200 units of X and 100 units of Y defines Kim's *budget line*. The budget line shows all combinations of quantities of X and Y that Kim can purchase per year. Kim can buy 200 units of X, or 100 units of Y, or various combinations of X and Y (e.g., 50 units of

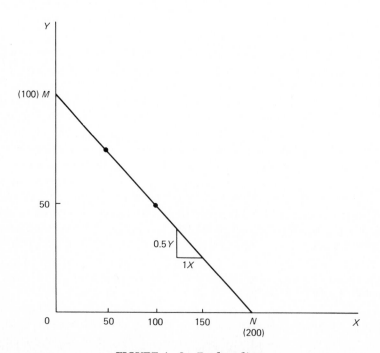

FIGURE A–3 *Budget line.*

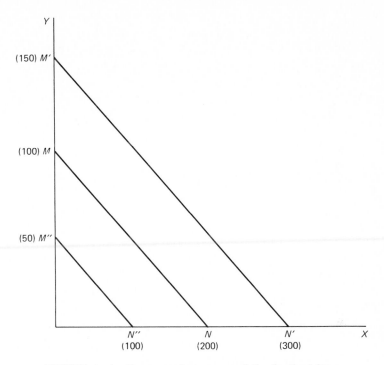

FIGURE A–4 *Income changes and the budget line.*

X and 75 units of Y, or 100 units of X and 50 units of Y) that lie on the budget line.

The slope of the budget line is equal to the negative of the price ratio, P_X/P_Y (in this example $-\$5/\$10$, or $-0.5Y/1X$). The slope at any point shows how much of one good must be given up to get an additional unit of the other. For the prices assumed, if Kim wishes to consume 1 more unit of X (at a price of $5 per unit), she will have to spent $5 less on Y (and thereby purchase a half unit less, because Y costs $10 per unit). Thus, the slope of the budget line is $0.5Y/1X$ at every point, because to purchase an additional unit of X always necessitates consuming a half unit less of Y.

The position of the budget line depends on the size of the budget. If Kim's income increases, the budget line will be farther from the origin; if her income falls, it will be closer. This is illustrated in Figure A–4. We begin again with an income of $1,000, and the prices of X and Y at $5 and $10, respectively. The budget line, identical to the one derived in the preceding discussion, is the line MN. If income increases to $1,500, a new budget line will be defined by a line connecting $300X$ and $150Y$, or $M'N'$: similarly, if income falls to $500, another budget line will be drawn joining $100X$ and $50Y$. Note that the three budget lines are parallel. This is because the prices

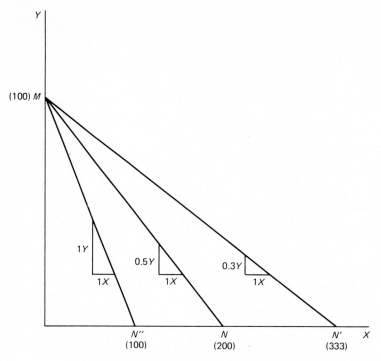

FIGURE A–5   *Price changes and the budget line.*

of X and Y have not changed, so the slopes (P_X/P_Y) of all three budget lines are the same.

In addition to changes in income, changes in the prices of goods affect the budget line. To illustrate, again assume that Kim's income is $1,000 and the price of X is $5 and the price of Y is $10. The initial budget line is shown by the line MN in Figure A–5 connecting $200X$ and $100Y$. Now assume that the price of X falls from $5 to $3 per unit. To reflect this change, the budget line rotates to MN'. Point M ($100Y$) is unchanged because the price of Y is still $10; now, however if Kim spends her entire income on X, she can purchase 333 units. The slope of the line has been affected, becoming flatter to reflect the lower price of X. (Originally, the slope was $-\frac{1}{2}$; after the price reduction, it becomes $-0.3Y/1X$.) Because the price of X is lower, Kim now has to give up only three tenths of a unit of Y (saving $3) to purchase 1 more unit of X. Alternatively, if the price of X increases to $10, the budget line will rotate toward the origin to MN'', with the steeper slope ($-1Y/1X$) reflecting a higher price for X (1 unit of Y must now be sacrificed to obtain an additional unit of X). *In this way, the slope of any budget line indicates the price of one good relative to that of the other.* At a lower price of X, the budget line is flatter, implying that X is now relatively lower priced than before—less Y has to be given up to purchase an additional unit of X.

The Consumer in Equilibrium

The budget line shows the combinations of goods from which Kim can choose, and the indifference curves show how Kim subjectively ranks all combinations of goods. It is assumed that the consumer will choose the most preferred combination of X and Y from among the combinations attainable. Consider Figure A–6. The set of indifferences curves, U_1 through U_3, reflects Kim's preferences. Curve U_3 is the most preferred among these three because it represents the highest level of utility. The budget line, MN, identifies the consumption options available to the consumer. Any point along MN (or below it[2]), such as A or B, represents a real consumption possibility. Points above the budget line, such as Z, are not feasible because Kim lacks the necessary income. Because Kim will seek the highest level of well-being possible, given her budget, equilibrium will occur at B, where the budget line and U_2 are tangent. Kim will purchase OX_1 units of X and OY_1 units of Y. Note that A is also on the budget line but that A lies on U_1; B, however, is on a higher indifference curve, U_2, so the latter is preferred. Kim's desire to maximize her well-being also rules out the possibility of an equilibrium at a point such as D; although D is within Kim's budget (in fact, Kim would not be spending all her income on X and Y), it is not the highest possible level of well-being attainable, because it lies on a lower indifference curve. Thus, the combination of X and Y represented by the tangency at B is Kim's equilibrium level of consumption.

It is important to understand the meaning of the tangency between the consumer's indifference curve and her budget line at point B. Recall that the slope of an indifference curve reflects the consumer's subjective valuation of one good in terms of the other, that is, the rate at which she is willing to substitute one good for another—the marginal rate of substitution between X and Y. At A, for example, Kim will be willing to exchange 3 units of Y for 1 more unit of X, at B, 2Y for 1X, and at C, 1 unit of Y for 1 additional unit of X. The slope of the budget line at all points is P_X/P_Y, the rate at which X and Y can be exchanged in the marketplace. Assume that the price of X is \$2 and the price of Y is \$1. This means that 2 units of

---

[2]Any point below the budget line implies that the consumer is not spending her entire income; we will assume, however, that the consumer allocates her entire income in some way between X and Y. In a more general model, saving can be incorporated into the treatment by taking the two goods to be present consumption and future consumption.

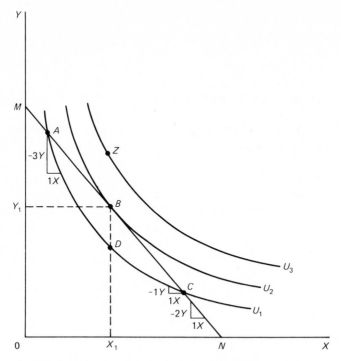

FIGURE A–6 *The equilibrium of the consumer.*

Y can be exchanged for 1 unit of X. The slope of MN is $2Y/1X$. In equilibrium, the marginal rate of substitution between X and Y for the consumer is equal to the price ratio; that is, the rate at which the consumer is subjectively willing to substitute X for Y is just equal to the rate at which market exchange can occur. At B Kim is willing to give up 2 units of Y for another unit of X; at a price of \$2 per unit for X and \$1 a unit for Y, this coincides with the market rate of exchange. Only at B, where the slopes of an indifference curve and the budget line are equal, does this balance between subjective evaluation and objective terms of trade hold.

Note that Kim *could* consume at point A on her budget line, but that she would then be on U_1, a lower indifference curve than at point B. Point A is *not* an equilibrium, because the MRS is greater than the price ratio. To see that this is so, note that at A, Kim is willing to give up 3 units of Y to get another unit of X but *has* to give up only 2 units of Y to consume 1 more X (because X costs twice as much as Y). This means that 1 more X costs less (a sacrifice of $2Y$) than Kim is willing to pay ($3Y$), so she will be better off consuming more X and less Y than at point A. This is shown, of course, by the fact that point B lies on a higher indifference curve than point A does.

Before the analysis is continued, a modification in the model will be made. So far Kim has been choosing between two goods, X and Y, typically dividing her budget between them. From now on we'll let the vertical axis measure money spent on all other goods except X for a given time period and let the horizontal axis measure the quantity of X consumed. In effect, the vertical axis measures consumption of non-X items as a group. This modification gives us more flexibility. The indifference curves can now show the tradeoffs between good X and money spent on other goods. The slope of an indifference curve will then show how many dollars' worth of other goods Kim is willing to give up to acquire 1 more unit of X. With this modification, the budget line can be constructed as follows: Assume that Kim's income is $1,000 and that the price of X is $2. In Figure A–7, OM ($1,000) is the amount of money available to spend on other goods (i.e., her entire money income) if Kim purchases zero units of X. If she spends her entire income on X, she could purchase ON units of X (500) with no money remaining to purchase other goods. By joining the two points, the budget line MN is derived. Given the preferences reflected by her indifference curves, Kim is in equilibrium at E. She consumes OX_1 (200) units of

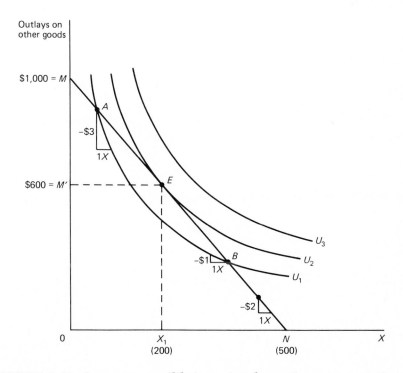

FIGURE A–7 *Consumer equilibrium—An alternative representation.*

X and has OM' ($600) in income left to spend on goods other than X. Note that Kim's total outlay on X is measured by MM', or $400.

As we did before, let's carefully interpret the tangency at E in Figure A–7 between the consumer's indifference curve U_2 and budget line. The slope of the indifference curve now represents the rate at which the consumer is willing to trade off expenditures on other goods for additional units of X; the consumer is, in effect, placing a dollar value on the benefits received from a marginal unit of X. At A, for example, Kim is willing to pay $3 for another unit of X (willing to consume $3 less of other goods to consume 1 more unit of X); at B only $1. The budget line reflects the market rate of exchange between X and other goods. Because the vertical axis now represents expenditures on other goods, it is measured in dollars, and the price of one dollar's worth of other goods is $1.

To the left of E on the budget line, the consumer places a higher dollar value on X than its market price. For instance, at A, Kim is on U_1 and is willing to pay $3 for an additional unit of X, but she has to pay only the *market price* of $2—the slope of MN. Because the benefit received from the marginal unit is greater than its cost, Kim will purchase the extra unit. Moreover, she will continue to consume additional units as long as this condition persists, that is, until point E is reached, where the additional dollar value of benefits received from consuming 1 more unit just equals its price (in this example, at E the consumer places a value of $2 on an extra unit, which equals its market price). At point E she has attained the highest indifference curve possible. Kim will not purchase any additional units (to the right of E) because the dollar value of benefits received from consuming additional units is less than its price—the marginal benefit is less than marginal cost. Thus, Kim is in equilibrium at E, where the marginal benefit of an extra unit of X is equal to its price. This means that when the consumer is in equilibrium, the market price of the good is a measure of the marginal value of the good to the consumer.

Having changed the vertical axis to money spent on other goods, we can now continue and consider how consumption levels of X are affected by changes in income and prices.

Changes in income

We noted earlier how changes in income produce parallel shifts in the budget line. Now that indifference curves have been incorporated into the analysis, changes in the consumer's level of income and the corresponding changes in the level of consumption of X can be examined. To illustrate, consider Figure A–8(a). Given the set of preferences reflected by U_1 through U_3, when the budget line is MN, X_1 units of X are consumed. When Kim's income increases to OM' and the budget line becomes $M'N'$, the consumption of X rises to X_2. And finally, when income reaches OM'' Kim purchases

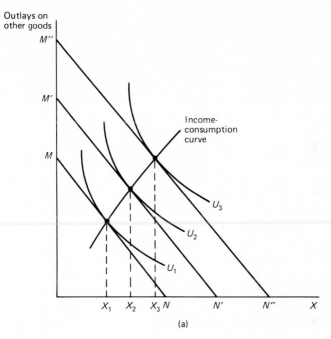

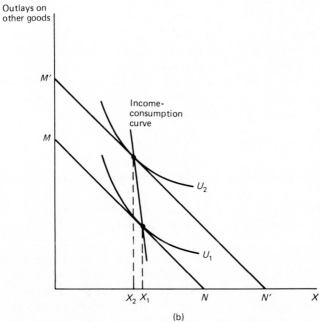

FIGURE A–8 *Income changes and consumption choices.*

X_3 units of X. At each income level, Kim chooses the most preferred combination of goods from among the combinations available. A line connecting the consumer equilibria yields the *income-consumption curve,* which identifies the various quantities of X that will be consumed at different income levels. If the curve is upward sloping to the right, X will be considered a *normal good;* that is, as income rises when prices are unchanged, the consumption of X increases.

In contrast to normal goods, there are *inferior goods.* A good is an inferior good if the quantity consumed falls when income rises. Consider Figure A–8(b). In this case, as income rises and the budget line shifts from MN to $M'N'$, the consumption of X actually declines from X_1 to X_2. The income-consumption curve slopes backward to the left. Typically most goods are normal goods, but it is possible to find examples of inferior goods. Perhaps, for example, as a person's income rises, he or she switches from hamburger to filet mignon, and so hamburger, in this particular case, would be an inferior good.

Changes in prices

So far we have considered the effects of changes in consumer income on the quantity of X consumed with prices assumed constant. Now let's hold income constant and vary the price of X and observe how the consumption of X changes. Recall that a variation in price is reflected by a change in the slope of the budget line; if the price of X falls, the budget line will become flatter, rotating to the right; if the price rises, the budget line will become steeper, rotating toward the origin. To begin, assume that the consumer's income is $100 in a given time period and the price of X is $5 per unit. In Figure A–9 (a) the budget line is MN, and given the consumer's preferences, equilibrium occurs with X_1 units of the good being consumed. Now let the price of X fall to $3.50 per unit. A new budget line, MN', results. At the lower price, X_2 is purchased, as indicated by the tangency between U_2 and MN' at X_2 units of X. Finally, let price fall again—this time to $2 a unit. The budget line rotates outward to MN'', and X_3 is purchased. Each decrease in price establishes a new budget line and a new equilibrium. The line drawn through the tangencies depicting the equilibrium points is called the *price-consumption curve.* It shows how the consumption of X varies with changes in its price.

The concept embodied in the price-consumption curve should strike a familiar note. It contains the same information as the consumer's demand curve—how the quantity consumed varies with changes in price when money income is unchanged. So we are now at the point where the demand curve can be derived from the indifference curves in Figure A–9 (a). On the axes of a demand curve diagram, price is measured vertically and quantity horizontally, and we need only to make a few modifications to translate the

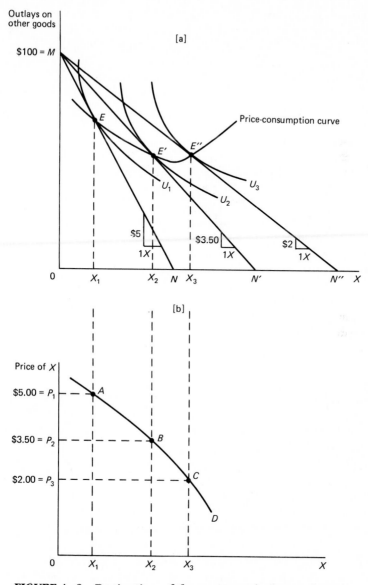

FIGURE A–9   *Derivation of the consumer's demand curve.*

information in Figure A–9(a) into a demand curve. The three alternatives prices for X, $5, $3.50 and $2, are plotted in Figure A–9(b), and the corresponding quantities of X consumed are identified. In this way, the demand curve is derived using indifference curves and budget lines.

Because the tangency between an individual's budget line and indifference curve represents the point where the marginal value of the last unit of X to the consumer is just equal to its price, and these tangencies in turn define points on the consumer's demand curve, the demand curve must contain the same information. In fact, each point on the demand curve can be interpreted as a measure of the marginal benefit associated with the consumption of the corresponding unit of X. Taking this a step further, because each quantity of X is associated with a price, the price of X can be considered a dollar measure of the marginal benefit of X to the consumer: The price reflects the *MRS* between money spent on other goods and good X. The vertical distance between the demand curve and the horizontal axis can be taken as a measure of the marginal benefit of X. For example, the distance BX_2, or \$3.50 per unit of X, is a measure of the marginal value, or benefit, of the good when X_2 is the quantity consumed. This way of measuring the marginal value of a good will be useful later in the analysis of many government tax and expenditure programs.

Substitution and income effects of price changes

When the price of a good changes, the consumer is affected in two distinct ways. One effect is called the *income effect* and the other the *substitution effect*. To illustrate, suppose the price of beef falls by half. The income effect stems from the fact that the consumer is better off as a result of the price change because his or her budget now goes farther. The consumer can buy the same amount of beef as before and still have more income left over to spend on other goods and services. The price change, in effect, raises the consumer's *real* income (in the sense of the level of well-being attainable). With a higher real income, the consumer can now afford to purchase more of all goods—including beef. So when the price of beef decreases, the consumer, as a result of the income effect, will expand his or her purchases of beef, if it is a normal good. The substitution effect results from the consumer's decision to substitute the now-cheaper good, beef, for other goods such as poultry or pork. To the consumer, beef, because of its lower price, has become a relatively more attractive buy, and so the consumer will choose to purchase more beef relative to other types of meat and poultry. The decrease in the price of beef has caused the consumer's purchases of beef to increase for two independent reasons. The income effect makes the consumer better off by increasing real income, which induces him or her to purchase larger quantities of beef. The substitution effect leads the consumer to substitute the cheaper good for now relatively more expensive ones, and in doing this the consumption of beef increases.

The total effect of a reduction in the price of X from \$5 to \$3 is shown in Figure A–10 as the increase in consumption of X from X_1 to X_2. The original budget line is shown by MN, with our consumer, Kim, in equilibrium at E purchasing X_1 units of X. The lower price of X is reflected by the

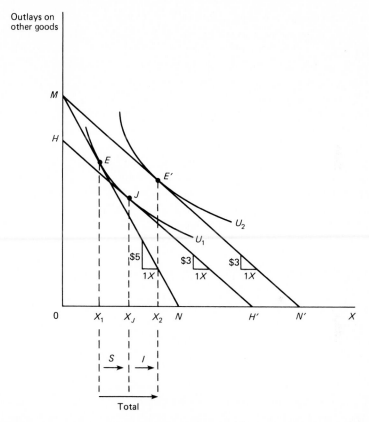

FIGURE A–10 *Income and substitution effects of a price reduction.*

new budget line *MN'*, with a slope of $3 per unit. The price decline involves a new equilibrium for Kim at *E'*, with X_2 units of *X* being purchased. The total effect of this price change, X_1X_2, as noted earlier, can be divided into an income effect and a substitution effect. When the price of a good falls, it increases Kim's real income. However, we want to ignore the income effect for the moment and instead concentrate on how much of the increase in the consumption of *X* can be attributed to the consumer's substituting *X* for other goods. To do this and identify the substitution effect, Kim's real income must be decreased by an amount sufficient to return her to her original indifference curve U_1 in Figure A–10. (This is referred to as keeping real income unchanged.) To nullify the income effect, a hypothetical budget line, *HH'*, is constructed parallel to *MN'* and tangent to U_1. The tangency occurs at *J*. The *HH'* budget line must be drawn parallel to *MN'* because we want to keep Kim on her original indifference curve with the *new* price of *X* to see how the lower price of *X*—isolated from the income effect—causes

Kim to increase her consumption of X. The substitution effect can be identified by comparing the quantity of X consumed at the initial equilibrium, E (where the slope of MN reflects the original price), with the quantity consumed at J, where the slope of HH' indicates the new lower price of X. On the horizontal axis, the quantity X_1X_J is the increase in consumption associated with the substitution effect.

Next we consider the income effect. Assume now that the budget line HH' shifts to the right to coincide with MN'. The vertical distance between HH' and MN' represents the gain in real income attributable to the decline in the price of X. This rise in income alone is responsible for an increase in the purchase of X by the amount of X_JX_2 because an increase in real income will induce Kim to expand purchases of all goods.[3] Thus, the total effect of the reduction in the price of X, X_1X_2 can be divided into a substitution effect, X_1X_J, and an income effect, X_JX_2.

An Application

To become more familiar with indifference curve theory and at the same time to lay the groundwork for some further analysis, let's examine individual labor supply decisions associated with changes in wage rates. Assume that workers can vary the amount of time they work,[4] and then consider Figure A–11. On the vertical axis, money income per week is measured, and on the horizontal axis, reading from left to right, leisure for the same time period is shown. The more hours worked, the less leisure time will be available; the more leisure consumed, the less time will be available to spend at work. Because time that is not spent working is considered leisure time, the amount of work effort supplied can be read from right to left in Figure A–11. Indifference curves can be drawn representing the preferences of a worker, Kim, for income and leisure. They have a normal shape because both money income and leisure are desirable economic goods. As Kim moves down a curve to the right, money income falls as she consumes additional amounts of leisure. The slope of a curve at any point represents the rate at which the worker is subjectively willing to give up money income for leisure. At A, for example, it would require more income to induce her to work more (consume less leisure) than it would at B.

The worker's wage rate is reflected in the slope of a budget line showing the tradeoff between money income and leisure. The flatter the budget line is, the lower the wage rate; the steeper the budget line is, the higher the

---

[3] This assumes that X and the other goods purchased by the consumer are normal goods.

[4] Although many workers work an 8-hour day, they can still vary their work effort with overtime or take a second job. In addition, workers can exercise some control over the number of hours worked by the type of job they choose.

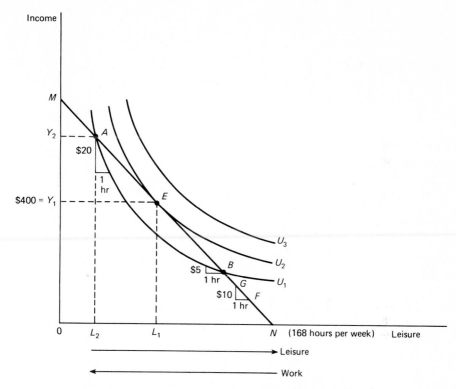

FIGURE A–11   *Income-leisure choice of the worker.*

wage rate. In Figure A–11, let the slope of *MN* reflect a wage of $10 per hour. If Kim works a 40-hour week, for example, her weekly income will be $400. Of course, how many hours Kim chooses to work at the $10 wage rate will depend on her preferences relating money income and leisure, as shown by her indifference curves. In Figure A–11, Kim's equilibrium—showing the most preferred combination of money income and leisure on her budget line—is point *E,* with weekly earnings of $400 and a labor supply of *NL₁*, or 40 hours. Note that Kim could earn more by working longer hours, at point *A,* but she would then be on a lower indifference curve. This means that Kim considers the additional earnings she could earn by working longer hours insufficient compensation for having to give up additional hours of leisure.

So far this describes a worker's equilibrium at a give wage rate. (For most consumers labor income is the main, and often sole, source of their money income—we assumed money income as given in earlier diagrams.) If the wage rate changes, the budget line will rotate around the horizontal intercept. In Figure A–12, the budget line with a $10 wage rate is shown as

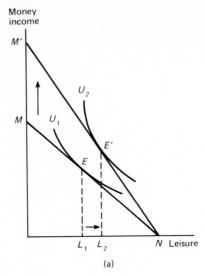

(a)

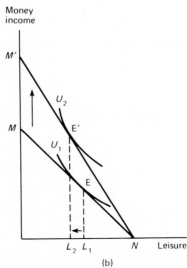

(b)

FIGURE A–12 *Effect of wage rate changes on labor supply.*

MN in both diagrams. If the wage rate rises to $15, the budget line will shift to $M'N$. The slope (equal to the wage rate) is now greater, showing that for every hour of leisure given up (for every hour worked), more money income is received than before. At any given level of work effort, total money income will be higher at a wage rate of $15 than at a wage rate of $10.

How a worker responds to changes in wage rates is an interesting question. An increase in the wage rate has two effects on labor supply decisions: an income effect and a substitution effect. The income effect is a result of the fact that the higher wage rate raises the worker's income for any amount of work effort supplied; at higher income levels, the income effect will lead the worker to consume more of all goods, including leisure. Thus, the higher income associated with higher wage rates encourages the increased consumption of leisure (or reduced work effort).

The substitution effect, on the other hand, encourages greater work effort. If the wage rate rises from $10 an hour to $15, the relative cost of consuming leisure will increase, and the quantity consumed will decline. More specifically, when the wage rate is $10 per hour, the cost of consuming an additional hour of leisure is $10 in forgone earnings; when the wage rate rises to $15, the sacrifice in earnings also increases, inducing the worker to consume less leisure and to work more.

Because the income and substitution effects work in opposing directions, it is impossible to predict whether a person will work more, less, or the same amount, in response to changes in the wage rate. If the income effect is greater than the substitution effect, then work effort will fall in response to a higher wage rate, as in Figure A–12 (a). If, on the other hand, the substitution effect predominates, then work effort will rise in response to an increase in wages; see Figure A–12 (b). If the two effects exactly offset each other, then work effort will be unchanged.

The response of labor supply to changes in wage rates is of particular interest to us in public finance because many taxes fall on labor income and consequently affect labor supply decisions.

Index